Andrew J. Keck

München   1926.

Pension Nordland

Ohmstrasse 11

EX · LIBRIS

Andrew J. Keck

1926

THE HISTORY OF MUSIC

THE ORGAN AT HAARLEM.

THE

HISTORY OF MUSIC

A HANDBOOK AND GUIDE
FOR STUDENTS

BY

WALDO SELDEN PRATT

PROFESSOR OF MUSIC AND HYMNOLOGY IN HARTFORD THEOLOGICAL SEMINARY
LECTURER ON MUSIC HISTORY AT THE INSTITUTE OF MUSICAL ART
AUTHOR OF "MUSICAL MINISTRIES IN THE CHURCH"

NEW YORK
G. SCHIRMER, INC.

Printed in the U. S. A.

PREFATORY NOTE

THE present book is the outgrowth of a fragmentary syllabus for classes that was issued in 1897. It is meant to be distinctly a book of reference for students rather than a literary or critical survey of a few salient aspects of the subject, or a specialist's report of original research. Aiming at a certain degree of encyclopædic fullness, it brings together facts and conclusions from a great variety of sources. Much labor has been expended in grouping the material in such a way as to give a systematic impression of the enormous field in view. In many cases somewhat full lists and summaries of details are given, partly to provide means for easy reference, partly to suggest how multifarious are the facts, and sometimes to indicate upon what sort of data are based the general statements that are offered. At every point an effort is made to emphasize the leading tendencies or movements of musical advance, referring to particular styles and composers as illustrations.

It was originally intended to include fairly exhaustive bibliographies, and a great amount of material was collected; but the magnitude of this branch of the subject precluded its presentation in this volume. In connection with each period in the history, however, a brief statement is made concerning the musical literature of the time, but without any attempt at completeness.

This is not in any sense a history of instruments, but some hints are given of the range and interest of the topic, both by statements in the text and by illustrations of selected specimens. The latter are drawn from the well-known collections of the Metropolitan Museum in New York and of the University of Michigan at Ann Arbor, to the custodians of which the heartiest thanks are due for multiplied courtesies.

7

In arranging the material for presentation, specially helpful suggestions have been derived from Prosniz' "Compendium der Musikgeschichte" and Riemann's "Geschichte der Musik seit Beethoven." For the statistical facts recourse has been had to a variety of authorities, chief of which is the colossal "Quellen-Lexikon der Musiker" of Eitner.

Every acknowledgment is also made of the liberality of the publishers in making the book rich and attractive, and for the invaluable assistance of the several advisers whose criticisms have been helpful in bringing the text into its final shape.

In a work of this character the number of names and dates is necessarily great, and, in spite of every effort, errors can hardly be avoided. The indication of such errors will be gratefully received.

Since this volume was originally published many persons referred to from page 500 onward have died. A list of such death-dates is appended on pages 684-5, following the Indexes.

For the help of students and classes, a small manual, "Class Notes in Music History" (36 pp.), is issued by the publishers of this work, giving condensed summaries of important topics from about 1500, with numerous references to standard general treatises and biographies.

CONTENTS

INTRODUCTION

ILLUSTRATIONS

The originals from which Figs. 1-16, 18, 20-30, 49-52, 54-57, 65-69, 77, 79-81, 88-96, 103-106, 108-109 are taken are in the Stearns Collection at the University of Michigan, Ann Arbor; and those from which Figs. 17, 19, 31, 33-34, 36-37, 40, 48, 58-64, 70-72, 75-76, 78, 82-87, 97-101, 110 are taken are in the Crosby-Brown Collection at the Metropolitan Museum of Art, New York. The remaining illustrations are from photographs or engravings variously secured.

The instruments were drawn by Charles K. Stevens, and the portraits by Otto Schneider, both of New York.

PORTRAITS

MAPS

INTRODUCTION

INTRODUCTION

THE HISTORY OF MUSIC IN GENERAL

1. The Field of the History of Music.
2. Its Value.
3. Its Natural Divisions.
4. Its Sources and Authorities.

THE HISTORY OF MUSIC

INTRODUCTION

THE HISTORY OF MUSIC IN GENERAL

1. The Field of the History of Music. — The history of music
is one department of the general history of human culture,
more particularly of the history of the fine arts as special
embodiments and instruments of that culture.   Its field is
extensive, including all ascertainable facts regarding musical
efforts wherever found, from the earliest times to the present,
and ranging from the childish attempts of the savage to the
monumental achievements of the greatest civilized artists.   Its
general object being to present these facts in their relations as
features of a development that has been governed by large
principles or tendencies, its main topics may be roughly tabulated as follows : —

(1) Rudimentary experiments by savage or uncivilized peoples in various parts of the world,

(2) The organized and reasoned systems of the dominant races and
countries of history,

(3) The growth of a positive science of composition, with the theories
and rules by which it has been governed,

(4) The evolution of those specific types or forms of composition that
have most affected progress as a whole,

(5) The origin and development of musical instruments and implements,
including notations,

(6) The advance of vocal and instrumental performance as an artistic
specialty,

(7) The lives, works and styles of composers and performers, especially
those that are typical or influential,

(8) The literary or scholarly treatment of musical subjects in books
and periodicals,

(9) The educational or commercial enterprises devoted to the maintenance or expansion of the art, including schools, societies, publishing houses, manufactories, etc.

While the ideal scope of the subject is thus wide, the field of a particular written history is at once less and more. It is less, because it is utterly impossible to compress into a single book all the facts. It is more, because the practical historian must be something of a critic as he works, selecting certain groups of facts for emphasis, classifying them under logical heads, and seeking at every point to keep what he conceives to be of special importance in the foreground.

2. Its Value. — Historical study has often been neglected by practical musicians because its literary or scholastic character seems so different from the artistic efforts upon which they are engaged. The history of music has been much overlooked by general historical students, partly because of a curious disdain of the fine arts as essential parts of culture, and partly because of the lack, until recently, of adequate handbooks. Now, however, since music-history is fully established as a branch of critical investigation, such neglect by musicians or others is inexcusable. Its obvious utilities lie in a general broadening of thought about musical art, in disclosing dominant lines of progress and effort, in exhibiting the personality and genius of creative artists and leaders, in providing rational grounds for appreciation, criticism and practical procedure, and in showing how musical life has been interlocked with literature and the other fine arts and with the advance of social life in general. For these reasons, music-history appeals not only to the musician, but to all cultivated persons.

3. Its Natural Divisions. — Music-history divides into two great sections, of which the first deals with a variety of peoples that lie outside the present circle of civilized nations and whose musical activity has not affected the latter, while the second concerns the greater historic peoples from classical times until the present. The first section is much the less important, and can be treated only in a summary, descriptive way. The second presents a clear continuity and an organic development. The natural subdivisions are as follows : —

A. Uncivilized Music

I. **Primitive** — among races that have not reached the point of artistic organization. Although music of this sort has always existed, we know it only as it has been recently examined.

II. Semi-civilized — including two distinct groups:

    (1) *Peoples now existing*, like the Chinese, Hindus, etc., whose music has a real system, but without relation to our own;

    (2) *Ancient peoples*, like the Egyptians, Assyrians and Hebrews, who seem to have been on a similar footing with the above. This group shades off into the next, though the connection is not clear.

B. Civilized Music

III. Greek and Roman — including whatever was the direct basis of the Early Christian and Mediæval development. The end of this period may be variously fixed, 300 A.D. being a convenient date. The countries affected all lie about the Mediterranean.

IV. Mediæval — with four subdivisions:

    (1) *The Plain-Song Period*, when ritual music was gradually perfected and diffused through Europe — to the 12th century;

    (2) *The Rise of True Composition*, both sacred and secular, including the first contrapuntists on the one side and the Troubadours and Minnesinger on the other;

    (3) *The Netherland Counterpoint* of the 15th century;

    (4) *The Sixteenth Century* as the culminating period of mediæval progress and the time of transition to modern styles. Most of Europe is now affected except the most northern countries.

V. Modern — including stages that may well be marked by centuries:

    (1) *The Seventeenth Century*, including the rise of the Opera and of Instrumental Music as specialties;

    (2) *The Eighteenth Century*, with (*a*) the culmination of previous progress in the first half, and (*b*) the appearance in the second of the Sonata and Symphony and the modern Orchestra, with new ideas also about the Opera and the Song;

    (3) *The Nineteenth Century* — by far the most complex and productive of all — divisible into three main periods, including (*a*) the culmination of classical methods, (*b*) the efflorescence of romantic enthusiasm, and (*c*) the recent expansion of ideas and forms in manifold further ways.

4. Its Sources and Authorities. — So far as the facts of music can be directly observed, as by watching the actual work of composers or by hearing adequate performances of representative compositions, the data of its history can be studied at first hand. But since this original investigation is possible only to a limited extent, recourse must be had to rescripts of music in written or printed form, to standard summaries in which the facts are set down and discussed, such as histories, cyclopædias, biographies and technical monographs, and to the opinions of trustworthy critics, however expressed.

The scientific cultivation of music-history and the vigorous development of its literature are of rather recent date. Some histories began to appear before 1800 and much detached work on special topics was undertaken, but all the comprehensive treatises belong to the 19th century, especially to its latter half. In fullness of research and in scholarly method of presentation many of these are fully abreast of works in other fields of historical study.

For convenience of reference, a condensed summary of the general histories and cyclopædias is here inserted.

Histories. — Without reckoning the innumerable monographs on particular periods and topics, at least 125 somewhat comprehensive Histories of Music may be named. The pioneers were, in German, *Printz* (1690); in Italian, *Bontempi* (1695); in French, the brothers *Bonnet*, using materials gathered by *Bourdelot* (1715); and in English, *Roger North* (c. 1728, but not published till 1846).

Of the older books about 30 were prior to 1850, those of the most importance being by *G. Martini*, 3 vols., 1757–81; *J. Hawkins*, 5 vols., 1776 (revised in 2 vols., 1853–75); *C. Burney*, 4 vols., 1776–89; *J. N. Forkel*, 2 vols., 1788–1801; *R. G. Kiesewetter*, 1834 (2d ed. 1846, Eng. trans. 1848); *A. L. de Lafage*, 2 vols., 1844 (unfinished).

Of the many works since 1850 some are based upon original research and aim at scientific thoroughness, while others are concise and popular. Several examples of the latter are here included : — *F. Brendel*, Gesch. d. Musik in Italien, Deutschland u. Frankreich, 2 vols., 1852 (7th ed. 1888, 636 pp.); *A. W. Ambros*, Gesch. d. Musik, 5 vols., 1862–82 (3d ed. extensively revised, 1887–93; also continuation by *Langhans*, below); *A. Reissmann*, Allgem. Gesch. d. Musik, 3 vols., 1863–5; *A. von Dommer*, Handbuch d. Musikgesch., 1867 (2d ed. 1878, 625 pp.); *F. J. Fétis*, Hist. gén. de la musique, 5 vols., 1869–75; *E. Naumann*, Die Tonkunst in d. Culturgesch., 2 vols., 1869–70; *Paul Frank*, Gesch. d. Tonkunst, 1863 (3d ed. 1878, 219 pp.); *B. Kothe*, Abriss d. Musikgesch., 1874 (7th ed. 1904, 351 pp.); *Heinrich Köstlin*, Gesch. d. Musik im Umriss, 1875 (5th ed. 1899, 636 pp.); *Robert Músiol*, Katechismus d. Musikgesch., 1877 (3d ed. 1905, 412 pp.); *Wilhelm Langhans*, Musikgesch. — 12 Vorlesungen, 1878 (2d ed. 1879, 215 pp., Eng. trans. 1886, 184 pp.); *E. Naumann*, Illustrirte Musikgesch., 2 vols., 1880–5 (Eng. trans. n.d.); *Laure Collin*, Hist. abrégée de la musique, 1881 (7th ed. 1891, 364 pp.); *W. Langhans*, Gesch. d. Musik d. 17., 18. u. 19. Jahrhunderts (continuing *Ambros*), 2 vols., 1882–6; *F. Clément*, Hist. de la musique, 1885, 819 pp.; *J. F. Rowbotham*, Hist. of Music, 3 vols., 1885–7 (abridged, 1893, 419 pp.); *W. S. Rockstro*, Gen. Hist. of Music, 1886, 535 pp.; *H. Riemann*, Katechismus d. Musikgesch., 2 parts, 1888–9 (5th ed. 1914, Eng. trans. n. d.); *J. C. Fillmore*, Lessons in Music Hist., 1888, 215 pp.; *W. S. B. Matthews*, Pop. Hist. of the Art of Music, 1889, 534 pp.; *J. E. Matthew*, Manual of Musical Hist., 1892 (2d ed. 1893, 436 pp.); *Adalbert Swoboda*, Illustrirte Musikgesch. 2 vols., 1892–4; *C. H. H. Parry*, The Art of Music, 1893 (4th ed. 1905, 342 pp.); *Alfredo Untersteiner*, Storia della musica, 1893 (2d ed. 1902, 330 pp., Eng. trans. 1902, 349 pp.); *Henri Lavoix*, Hist. de la musique, 1896, 368 pp.; *W.J. Henderson*, How Music Developed, 1899, 413 pp.; *Adolf Prosniz*, Compendium d. Musikgesch., 2 vols., 1900 (2d ed. 1901–); *M. Vogel*, Gesch. d. Musik, 1900, 218 pp.; The Oxford Hist. of Music: — *H. E. Wooldridge*, The Polyphonic Period, 2 vols., 1901–5, *C. H. H. Parry*, 17th Century, 1902, *J. A. F. Maitland*, Age of Bach and Handel, 1902, *W. H. Hadow*, Viennese Period, 1904, *Edward Dannreuther*, Romantic Period, 1905; *Hermann Ritter*, Allgem. illustrirte Encyclopädie d Musikgesch., 6 vols., 1902; *H. Riemann*, Handbuch d. Musikgesch., 2 vols., 1901–13; *Otto Keller*, Illustrirte Gesch. d. Musik, 1894 (2d ed. 1903, 2 vols.); *Karl Storck*, Gesch. d. Musik, 1904, 848 pp.; *Edward Dickinson*, Study of the Hist. of Music, 1905, 409 pp.; *W. J. Baltzell* (editor), Hist. of Music, 1905, 564 pp.; *J. K. Paine*, Hist. of Music to the Death of Schubert, 1907, 314 pp.; *C. G. Hamilton*, Outlines of Music Hist., 1909 (rev. ed. 1913, 308 pp.); *Thomas Tapper* and *Percy Goetschius*, Essentials in Music Hist., 1914, 365 pp.; *C. Villiers Stanford* and *Cecil Forsyth*, Hist. of Music, 1916, ... pp.; *Helen A.* and *Clarence Dickinson*, Excursions in Musical Hist., 1917, 209 pp.

Dictionaries. — The pioneers here were (*a*) Terms only — *Tinctoris* (1474), *Ducange* (1678), *Janowka* (1701), and *Brossard* (1703); (*b*) Biographies only — *E. L. Gerber* (1790–2); (*c*) Both terms and biographies — *J. G. Walther* (1732) and *J. J. Rousseau* (1767).

Of the many works of this class it is enough to name the larger or most recent, such as *G. Schilling*, Universallexikon d. Tonkunst, 6 vols., 1835–8 (2d ed. 1840–2); *F. J. Fétis*, Biographie universelle des musiciens, 8 vols., 1835–44 (2d ed. 1860–5, with Supplément by *Pougin*, 2 vols., 1879–81); *E. Bernsdorf*, Neues Universallexikon d. Tonkunst, 3 vols., 1856–61 (Nachtrag, 1865); *H. Mendel* and *A. Reissmann*, Musikal. Conversations-Lexikon, 12 vols., 1870–83; *O. Paul*, Handlexikon d. Tonkunst, 2 vols., 1873; *J. Stainer* and *W. A. Barrett*, Dict. of Musical Terms, 1876 (latest ed. 1898, 464 pp.); *George Grove*, Dict. of Music and Musicians, 4 vols. and Index, 1879–90 (2d ed. 5 vols. 1904–10) and American Supplement, 1920; H. Riemann, Musik-Lexikon, 1882 (8th ed., 1916, and Eng. trans. 4th ed. 1908); *J. D. Champlin* and *W. F. Apthorp*, Cyclopedia of Music and Musicians, 3 vols., 1890; *Theodore Baker*, Biographical Dict. of Musicians, 1900 (3d ed. 1919, 1094 pp.); *R. Eitner* Biographisch-bibliographisches Quellen-Lexikon, 10 vols., 1899–1904 (additions and corrections issued since 1912 as periodical).

PART I

UNCIVILIZED AND ANCIENT MUSIC

PART I

UNCIVILIZED AND ANCIENT MUSIC

CHAPTER I

PRIMITIVE OR SAVAGE MUSIC

5. In General. — Some form of music is found in every part of the uncivilized world, from the islands of the southern Pacific round to the Americas, and from the equatorial zone far toward the poles. This extensive diffusion points to a spontaneous use by all races of song, dance and instrument as means of expression, amusement and even discipline. The primary impulse to music seems to belong to mankind as a whole.

Although most savage music is crude and to us disagreeable, yet its interest for the student is considerable. By noting how it arises, how it is used, and with what it is associated, we gain insight into the essence and relations of the musical impulse. The widespread combination of song with dancing, mimicry and poetry, as well as with religious exercises, challenges attention. The painstaking care in fashioning instruments is impressive and instructive. The naïve experiments in scale-making suggest the probable sources of modern theory. The analogies between the musical efforts of primitive adults and those of civilized children have a bearing upon current pedagogy. For the critical student of either history or æsthetics, therefore, the facts of savage music are valuable.

The great difficulty of the topic lies in the variable accuracy and clearness of the first-hand reports of the facts that come from travelers, missionaries and other observers.

6. As a Social Institution. — In primitive conditions music is first of all a social diversion or play, affording an outlet for surplus animal spirit, stimulating emotional excitement, and helping to maintain muscular and nervous energy. Singing and dancing are always conspicuously social — a centre of interest for perhaps a whole village or tribe. The craving for popular activity in these ways often leads to stated gatherings of a festal character, the ceremonies usually being specifically associated with an occupation or event, as with hunting, agriculture, worship or war, or with birth, sickness or death. The psychical reactions of motions in rhythm and of tones are far more striking than among civilized peoples, and are sought both for their effect on the individual performer or percipient and for their mesmeric control of the crowd.

> The practice of music is sometimes shared by men and women alike, but sometimes, for obscure reasons, is reserved to one or the other sex exclusively. Sometimes there is a musical class or guild that superintends musical exercises and maintains traditions. Often music is held to be more or less of a superhuman mystery—a notion duly utilized by the priest and the necromancer.

Among savage peoples music seldom appears as an independent art. Its association with dancing is so close that the two are really twin activities. Rhythmic motions with some recurrent noise, like hand-clapping or the striking of sticks, pass over readily into a rude chant or singsong, perhaps aided by some instrumental accessory. Conversely, the rhythm of singing tends to induce bodily motions. Rhythm thus inevitably brings dancing and song together.

Again, since speaking and singing are both vocal processes, they tend to react upon each other. All primitive speech that is highly emotional or meant to be specially impressive is cast in forms of poetry. To conceive such utterance with reference to singing, and actually to chant it, seems instinctive. Where there is a guild of tribal minstrels, they are expected to provide odes or ballads of various sorts—heroic, martial, mythical, fanciful or humorous. In form such odes are usually rhythmic, but true recitative or cantillation is not uncommon.

> In some cases the text has an evident charm or pathos, but in others it seems devoid of sense or sentiment. Instances occur of the use of mere nonsense-jingles and of even a song-jargon, quite distinct from ordinary speech—thus testifying to an interest in the rhythmic or tonal effect apart from the thought.

Finally, since mimicry or pantomime is instinctively sought by all races, dancing and song readily assume a dramatic character, involving personification, plot and action. The story may be serious or comic, exciting or diverting, strenuous or enervating, but, whatever its character, the effect is likely to be heightened by musical or orchestral treatment. Religious exercises are frequently cast in the form of such song-pantomimes.

Indeed, it seems as if primitive religion felt itself forced to adopt musico dramatic modes of expression.

7. Its Technical Features. — All savage music is conspicuously accentual. Usually the accents fall into definite rhythms, duple varieties being commoner than triple. The basal rhythm is made emphatic by bodily motions, noises or vocal cries. The metric patterns (schemes of long and short tones) and the larger phrase-schemes are often curiously intricate, puzzling even the trained observer.

> In accompanied songs there are instances of duple patterns in the voice against triple ones in the accompaniment.

The vocal decoration of rhythms leads directly to melodic figures, though the latter doubtless also result from experiments with instruments. As a rule, a given melody contains but few distinct tones, though sometimes varied with indescribable slides or howls. One or two tone-figures are usually repeated again and again. Generally a rudimentary notion of a scale (or system of tones) is suggested, though no one type of scale is universal. Scales and the melodies made from them are more often conceived downward than upward (as is our habit). Whether a true keynote is recognized is often doubtful, the whole intonation being vague and fluctuating. The total effect is generally minor, though major intervals and groups of tones are not unusual.

> On the one hand, cases occur in which short intervals, like the semitone, are avoided, yielding melodies that imply a pentatonic system, and these are common enough to lead many to urge that the essentially primitive scale is pentatonic. But, on the other, what we call chromatic scales are also found, utilizing even smaller intervals than the semitone. Scales approximating our diatonic type are also reported, implying a fair sense of tone-relationship.
>
> Just what stimulates the invention of melodies and controls their development is uncertain. In some cases the habit of improvisation seems influential; in others, ingenuity with instruments. A form of melody, once established, is apt to be tenaciously preserved.

It has been thought that ideas of harmony or part-singing are impossible for the savage mind. But it appears that some tribes in Africa and Australia do sing in parts and even attempt concerted effects between voices and instruments. Such combinations, however, are rare and do not show any real system.

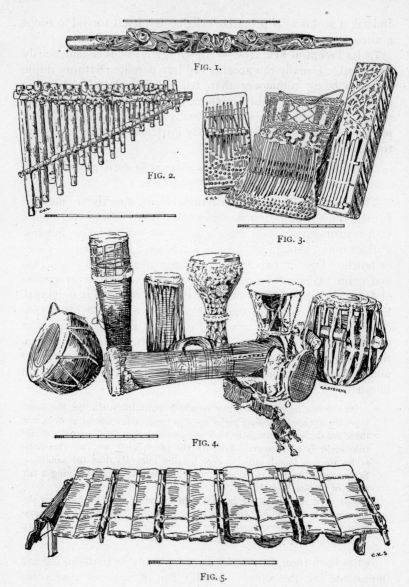

FIG. 1. — Alaskan Stone Flute — design like a totem-pole. FIG. 2. — Arab Pan's-Pipes or Syrinx. FIG. 3. — African Zanzes — iron or bamboo tongues mounted on a resonance-box, played by twanging. FIG. 4. — Miscellaneous Drums — primitive, Egyptian, Turkish, Japanese, etc., one (Thibetan) made of a skull cut in two. FIG. 5. — African Marimba or Xylophone.

8. Instruments. — This branch of the topic is made specially clear and interesting by the existence of many actual specimens in all large ethnological museums. Yet a systematic summary of the facts in any brief form is impossible, since the details vary indefinitely.

Extraordinary cleverness and genuine artistic feeling are often displayed in fashioning musical implements by peoples otherwise very rude. Great patience and dexterity are expended in working such materials as are available into the desired condition and form, and elaborate carving or tasteful coloring is often added. Well-made instruments are held to be precious, sometimes sacred.

The following summary is designed simply to give a hint of the indefinite variety of forms under three standard classes : —

Flatile or wind instruments. — The different flutes and flageolets found are innumerable. They are made from reeds, grasses, wood, bone (even human bones), clay, stone. They are blown across a mouth-hole or through a whistle-mouthpiece, and either by the mouth or by the nose. They are both single and double, or, in the case of syrinxes or Pan's-pipes, compound. Often they are fitted with from two to several finger-holes for varying the pitch, though, curiously, all these are not always habitually used. Occasionally a reservoir for the air is provided, such as a flexible bag or sack, with the pipe or pipes attached. The tones vary greatly in power and sweetness, though the tendency is toward shrill and piercing qualities.

Horns and trumpets are also common, of every shape, size and quality, made of horn, shell, ivory, bamboo, wood, metal. Generally there is little variation of pitch, though overtones are used somewhat. The tones produced are usually powerful, often harsh.

Percussive or pulsatile instruments. — Clappers of bone or wood are frequent, and various hollowed tubes and the like that can be beaten. Castanets of shell or metal are often found. Everywhere rattles and jingles abound, made of bunches of pebbles, fruit-stones or shells (occasionally of a human skull filled with loose objects). All sorts of gongs or tam-tams occur, made of wood, stone, brass, copper, iron ; these sometimes appear in sets, so that rude melodies or harmonies are possible. The varieties of drum and tambourine are endless, all characterized by a stretched head of skin over a hollow bowl or box, the latter being usually a gourd, a hollowed piece of wood (as the trunk of a tree) or a metallic vessel. They are sounded either by the hand or by sticks. Much ingenuity is sometimes shown in devising signals and intricate tattoos, and drums are often used in combination.

A specially interesting invention is the African 'marimba' or gourd-piano. This consists of a graduated series of gourds surmounted by resonant pieces of wood that can be struck by sticks, like the modern

xylophone or glass-harmonicon.   Similar forms occur in Asia and elsewhere.

Stringed instruments. — The bow being one of the first implements of
hunting and warfare, it may have been among the earliest of musical instruments.   Certain it is that rude harps shaped like a bow occur frequently among savages.   The number of strings varies from one or two
upward, though the weakness of the framework usually limits both number and tension.   Experiments are frequent with rude lyres or zithers
having strings stretched over a resonance-body, such as a flat piece of
wood or a hollow box.   These types pass over into rudimentary lutes,
having both a resonance-box and a neck to extend the strings.   Much
ingenuity is shown in making the strings out of plant-fibres, hair, other
animal tissues, metal.   Many examples are found of instruments sounded
by the friction of a bowstring, prefiguring the great family of viols.

Fig. 6. — Primitive Harps and Zithers, strung with plant–fibres, gut or
bamboo-strips, and with various devices for resonance.

Occasionally pieces of wood or metal of different sizes are so fastened to
a resonance-box that they can be sounded by snapping, as in the African
' zanze.'

Apparently the impulse to instrument-making arises largely from the desire for a sound to accentuate a dance-rhythm — clappers, whistles, twanged strings. In prehistoric remains some bone whistles occur, and everywhere pipes abound.

Hence it has been urged that flatile instruments were the earliest. Another theory is that the order of invention was drums, pipes, strings. It is better to say that instruments were first used to keep time, then to produce sustained tones, then to make melodies. The precise way in which these results were secured probably varied with the materials at hand and the ingenuity at work.

9. The Origin of Music.— After noting facts like these we naturally ask how music came into existence. It is true that external nature supplies suggestions, as in the sighing and whistling of the wind, the rippling and roar of falling water, the cries of beasts, the buzzing or calls of insects and the songs of birds; but the influence of these on primitive song is apparently slight. Herbert Spencer argued that song is primarily a form of speech, arising from the reflex action of the vocal organs under stress of emotion (as a cry follows the sensation of pain). More likely is the hypothesis that music is derived from some attempt to work off surplus energy through bodily motions, to coördinate and decorate which rhythmic sounds, vocal or mechanical, are employed, and that what was at first only an accessory to dancing was finally differentiated from it. But these speculations are not specially fruitful.

> The traditions of many races recount the impartation of instruments or of musical ideas to men by the gods. These myths are significant, not as historic statements of fact, but as testimonies to the strange potency and charm residing in musical tones.

CHAPTER II

SEMI–CIVILIZED MUSIC

10. In General. — Music enters the semi-civilized stage along with the other activities of developing society. When a people emerges from the heedless and irregular habits of savagery, its music usually attracts enough reasoning and skill to make it in some sense artistic. The advance appears in heightened dexterity with song and instruments, in more exactly defined styles of composition, and in some attempt at literature about music, including often the use of a notation. Why some peoples cross this line and others do not is an enigma. However this may be, brief reference must be made to certain past or present systems of this grade, even though our knowledge of them is imperfect and though they seem wholly unconnected with our own music.

Among existing systems, those of China, India and the Mohammedans will be emphasized, and among ancient systems, those of Mesopotamia, the Hebrews and Egypt — the latter being probably rather more than 'semi-civilized,' though decisive data are lacking.

11. China. — From Chinese literature it appears that music has had a long and honorable history in connection with Confucianism and under the patronage of the imperial court. Some of the temple music to-day is impressive, and the tone-system and many instruments are notable. Yet the status of popular music, as heard in the streets and the theatres, is notoriously low. Possibly the present is a time of degeneracy from ancient standards, or perhaps in past times suggestions of progress were so partially assimilated as not to affect general use. It seems as if music, having reached a certain point, became fixed, without the power of further advance.

Tradition ascribes the origin of music to divine inspiration, and names the Emperors Fo-Hi (c. 3000 B.C.) and Hoang-Ti (c. 2600 B.C.) as pioneers in organization. Confucius (d. 478 B.C.) and his more studious disciples seem to have favored a serious use of music and acute speculation about it. It is said that actually hundreds of treatises are extant upon the art, the contents of which are but slightly known to us. The details of music at state and religious functions are supervised by an imperial bureau, and degrees in music are given on examination. Yet the popular use of music is limited, being largely in the hands of traveling beggars (often blind).

The tone-system is theoretically complicated. Its basis is probably tetrachordal, like the Greek, but in practice it tends to a pentatonic scale, discarding semitones. But the division of the octave into twelve semitones is also known and in theory is applied somewhat intricately. The rhythms of song are emphatic and almost always duple. Some rudiments of harmony are known, but are rarely used except for tuning.

The tones of the pentatonic series may be roughly represented by our tones *f*, *g*, *a*, *c*, *d*. They bear fantastic Chinese names — 'Emperor,' 'Prime Minister,' 'Subject People,' 'State-Affairs,' 'Picture of the Universe.' For each there is a written character, so that melodies can be recorded in a letter-like notation, written vertically. Many melodies have been transcribed by foreign students. Their pentatonic basis gives them a peculiar quaintness, recalling old Scottish songs. In 1809 Weber took one of these as the theme for his overture to Schiller's *Turandot*, but such adaptations are extremely rare.

One peculiarity of Chinese speech has musical significance. The language consists almost wholly of monosyllables, each of which has different meanings according to the 'tone' or melodic inflection with which it is pronounced. It is possible that these 'tones,' which are four or five in number, have relation to song. At all events, dignified or poetic utterance tends towards chanting or cantillation.

It is interesting that in cases where European music has been introduced by missionaries it has sometimes been adopted with astonishing ease and enthusiasm, extending even to elaborate part-singing.

Chinese instruments are numerous and important. But it is uncertain which of them are indigenous and which are borrowed from other parts of Asia. Native writers say that nature provided eight sound-producing materials — skin, stone, metal, clay, wood, bamboo, silk, gourd — and classify their instruments accordingly.

Thus dressed *skin* is used in manifold tambourines and drums, with one or two heads, the sizes running up to large tuns mounted on a pedestal. *Stone* appears in plates of jade or agate, single or in graduated sets, hung by cords from a frame and sounded by a mallet or beater, producing a smooth, sonorous tone. *Metal* is wrought chiefly into bells, gongs and cymbals of many shapes and sizes (the gongs sometimes arranged in graduated sets), but also into long, slender trumpets. *Clay*

D

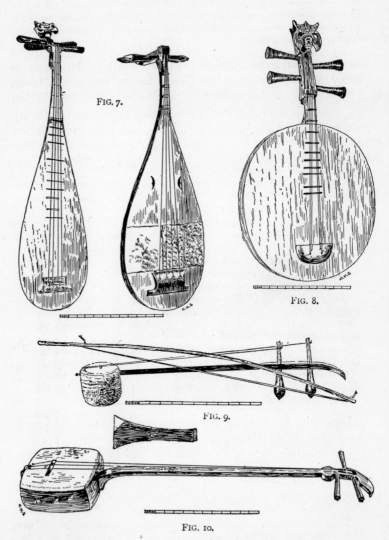

FIG. 7.

FIG. 8.

FIG. 9.

FIG. 10.

FIG. 7. — Chinese Pipas or Japanese Biwas.   FIG. 8. — Chinese Moon-Guitar or Yue-kin.   FIG. 9. — Chinese Ur-heen or Japanese Kokiu — the bowstring passes between the strings.   FIG. 10. — Japanese Samisen, played with a wooden plectrum tipped with ivory.

furnishes whistles of the ocarina type, often molded into fantastic animal shapes. *Wood*, besides forming the bodies of stringed instruments,
is made into clappers or castanets, into curious boxes that are sounded
by striking, and into coarse oboes (usually with metal bells and other fit-
tings). *Bamboo* provides the tubes of both direct and tranverse flutes,
with 6–9 finger-holes, and for syrinxes and the 'cheng' (see below). *Silk*
furnishes the strings for zithers (as the 'che,' with 25 strings, and the 'kin,'
with 7), lutes (as the 'moon-guitar,' with 4 strings, the 'pipa,' also with 4,
and the 'san-heen,' with 3), viols or fiddles (as the 'ur-heen,' with 2 strings,
and the 'hu-kin,' with 4), and bow-zithers (as the 'la-kin,' with 20 strings).
[Several other instruments are strung with wire, as the 'yang-kin' or dulcimer and the 'tseng' or bow-zither, both with 20 strings.] A *gourd* makes
the resonance-bowl of the 'cheng,' having also some 13 or more little bamboo pipes, each of which contains a minute free reed of brass.

Bell-founding is supposed to have been acquired by Europe from China,
and the 'cheng' is the prototype of several free-reed instruments in Europe
invented since 1800, including the accordion and the reed-organ.

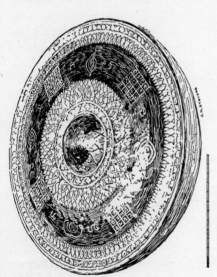

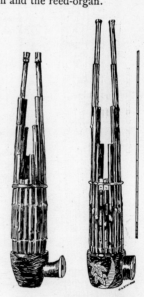

FIG. 11. — Chinese Temple Gong,　　　　FIG. 12. — Chinese Cheng
　　elaborately damascened.　　　　　　　　and Japanese Sho.

The Japanese musical system was derived from China, but
so long ago that it has now become distinct. The popular use
of singing and of instruments is here an almost universal
accomplishment of importance, but, on the other hand, the
literary treatment of the art is meagre.

For a time, from 1878, the Japanese government sought to establish American methods of singing in the public schools, and through foreign intercourse generally the national system is being much modified.

Japanese instruments are in general replicates of the Chinese, but with many variations of detail and usually with greater external beauty.

> Notable types are the 'koto,' a large zither with 6–13 silk strings, and the 'samisen,' a lute with 3 strings. The 'kokiu' corresponds to the Chinese 'ur-heen,' the 'biwa' to the 'pipa,' the 'hyokin' to the 'yang-kin,' the 'sho' to the 'cheng,' etc.

12. India. — The details of Hindu music are better known than those of Chinese. Evidently from the time of the Aryan immigrations (c. 2000 B.C.) much attention has been paid to the art. But, since India has been repeatedly invaded and even subjugated by foreign peoples, and has been for ages in close commercial relation with Western countries, no one can say what of its music is original.

> Native legends attribute the gift of music to the gods, and mythical and mystical notions are frequent in musical nomenclature and writing. References to music abound in the old literature, and musical treatises have been accumulating for centuries. Theorizing about music has run to incredible intricacies.

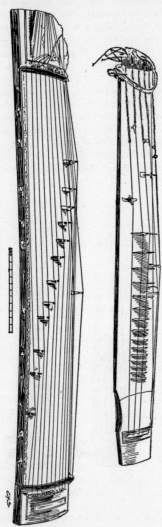

FIG. 13. — Japanese Kotos.

Music exists chiefly in the form of popular song or as an accompaniment for dancing. In religious ceremony it is less frequent, though somewhat used by both Brahmins and Buddhists. The singing of poems is universal, from the old Sanscrit odes to the ballads of modern origin. Dancing to music is very popular, and professional dancing-girls are a feature at social functions. Music is often employed in pantomimes and plays having a mythical, social or fantastic subject.

The training of the Bayaderes or Nautch girls is usually managed as a business by Buddhist priests, and is often associated with immorality.

The tone system rests upon a primary division of the octave into seven steps, but more exactly into twenty-two nearly equal 'srutis' or quarter-steps. These latter are not all used in any single scale, but serve to define with precision various seven-tone scales that differ in the location of the shorter steps (as in the mediæval modes of Europe). Theory has been so refined as to name almost 1000 possible varieties of scale (not to mention the 16,000 of mythical story). In practice not more than twenty of these appear, the usage varying with locality and tribe. Most of these scales are somewhat akin to ours, so that melodies in them often suggest our common modes. But the intonation is usually obscured by plentiful melodic decorations. Many songs are pleasing and expressive to Occidental taste, the ancient ones having much dignity, but popular singing often runs off into weird and curious effects, probably due to Mohammedan influence.

Triple rhythms are at least as common as duple. The metric schemes are apt to be varied and complicated, corresponding to those of poetry. Variations in pace and accent are frequent. Both the pitch and duration of tones, with various points about execution, are indicated by a notation of Sanscrit characters for notes, and signs or words for other details.

The art of making instruments has been as minutely studied as the theory of scales. Almost every species of portable instrument is known, and in many varieties. Native writers indicate four classes — those with strings, those with membranes sounded by striking, those struck together in pairs, and those sounded by blowing. Of these the stringed group is by far the most characteristic and admired. Percussives include various drums, tambourines, castanets, cymbals, gongs, etc. Wind instruments include many flutes (though not often of the transverse kind), oboes, bagpipes, horns and trumpets.

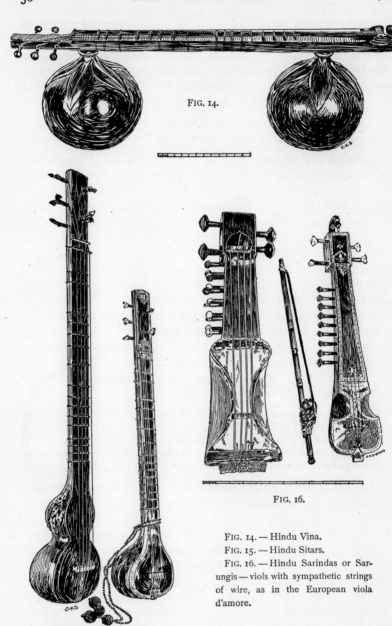

FIG. 14.

FIG. 15.

FIG. 16.

FIG. 14. — Hindu Vina.
FIG. 15. — Hindu Sitars.
FIG. 16. — Hindu Sarindas or Sar-
ungis — viols with sympathetic strings
of wire, as in the European viola
d'amore.

Certain forms are peculiar to special classes, like priests, traveling beggars or dancing-girls.

The characteristic instrument is the 'vina,' which is made in various ways, usually with a cylindrical body of wood or bamboo reënforced by 1–3 gourd resonators, and having 6–7 wire strings, played normally as a zither or lute, but sometimes with a bow. This shades off into the 'sitar,' which is a true lute, and many other related forms. Among the numerous viols, the 'sarinda' or 'sarungi' is typical.

Music in the several countries of southeastern Asia presents perplexing features in which Chinese, Hindu and Mohammedan elements are mingled. In Burma and Siam the connection is rather with India, while in Java the Chinese pentatonic scale is apparently dominant. Korea, of course, is connected with Japan and China. In each case there is a national system, often of great elaboration, but the details are comparatively unclear.

FIG. 17.— Hindu Sarungi.

More or less characteristic instruments are, in Burma, the 'soung,' a 13-stringed harp with a boat-shaped body and a gracefully curved neck; in Siam, the 'ranat,' a good xylophone (to which there are analogues in China and Japan); in Java, the 'galempong,' resembling the Chinese 'kin;' and in Korea, the 'kamounko,' corresponding to the Japanese 'koto.' But in each country there are many other instruments of different classes.

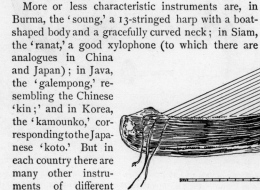

FIG. 18.— Burmese Soung.

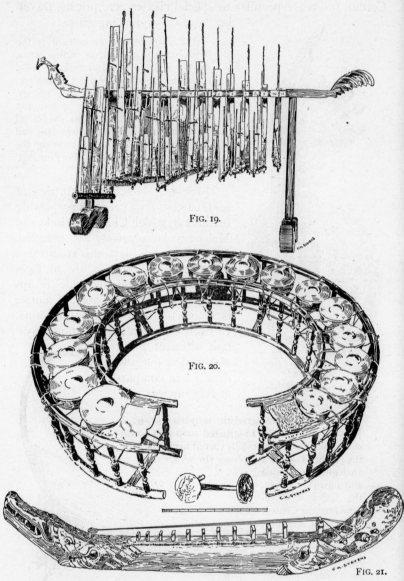

FIG. 19.

FIG. 20.

FIG. 21.

FIG. 19. — Javanese Anklong — sets of bamboo tubes sounded by striking.   FIG. 20. — Burmese or Javanese Gong-Piano — the player sits in the centre.   FIG. 21. — Burmese or Siamese Crocodile Harp or Zither.

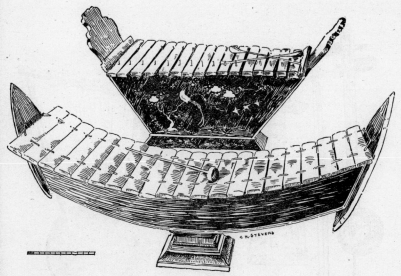

FIG. 22. — Chinese and Siamese Ranats.

13. The Mohammedans. — The music associated with Arabic culture and with Mohammedanism is more widely spread than any other of its class. Yet it is a highly composite type for this very reason. It is doubtful whether there is any real Arabian music, that is, music peculiar to Arabia itself. But in connection with the stupendous extension of Mohammedanism (from the 8th century) along the Mediterranean to the Atlantic, as well as into southern Asia and central Africa, music has often been prominent. Hence types of music called Arabic appear among the Saracens and Moors of the Middle Ages, in modern Egypt and Turkey, and elsewhere. These doubtless include features from Persian sources, from ancient Greek usages, and from all kinds of local sources. The historical puzzle thus presented is insoluble. Yet some general remarks may be hazarded.

Mohammedanism as a religion makes little use of music, though apparently stimulating it as a popular art. There is a large literature about music written in Arabic and by Mohammedan scholars, but it all belongs to the mediæval period and reflects ideas from sources not at all Arabian. This literature is particularly valuable for the light it gives upon the growth of musical theory; it is also notable for acute discussions of the psychical effects of music (see sec. 36).

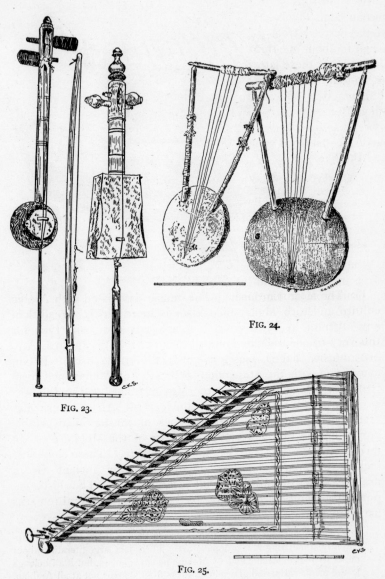

FIG. 23.

FIG. 24.

FIG. 25.

FIG. 23. — Arab Kemangehs.   FIG. 24. — Arab Kissars or Lyres.   FIG. 25. — Arab
Kanoon or Zither.

As commonly stated, the scale in characteristically Mohammedan lands involves a primary division of the octave into seven
steps, derived from a theoretical division into seventeen, each
equal to about one-third of a whole step. The exact method of
determining these latter is disputed. There are some eighteen
seven-tone scales, differing in the location of the shorter steps.
The practical effects are not obviously akin to our modes, as
they often emphasize tones that are irrational to us. But, even
more than in Hindu song, exactness of interval and fixity of
mode are disturbed by incessant slides, turns, grace-notes, shakes,
and the like.

> The rhythms and metric patterns are derived from those of poetry, and
> vary greatly. Harmony is not cultivated, except in the rudest form. Only
> a bare beginning of a notation in letters has been made.
>
> Several attempts have been made to imitate or embody Arab melodies
> in modern composition — the most famous being Félicien David's sym-
> phonic ode *Le Désert* (1844).

What are called Arab instruments have interest in several instances because they were
the prototypes of European forms in the Middle Ages. In general, the Mohammedans
in the Middle Ages were the intermediaries
between Europe and the East, and what they
introduced was called Arab without distinction.

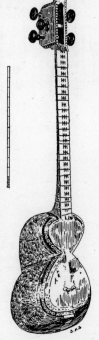

> Foremost in interest is the ''ud,' a lute with a
> broad, pear-shaped body, a rather short neck bent
> back at the head, and four or more strings. This
> was introduced into Europe by 800 A.D. at least, be-
> came popular, was imitated in manifold lutes (the
> word 'lute' being taken from *el'ud*), and still sur-
> vives in the mandolin. (See Fig. 54.) Another
> similar type was the 'tambura,' with a smaller
> body, a longer neck, and only a few strings. Of
> viols, the 'rebab' and the 'kemangeh' are important,
> because probably influencing the evolution of the
> viol and the violin.
>
> Many so-called Arab instruments are probably
> Persian. One of these is the 'santir,' a dulcimer or
> zither with many strings, akin to the 'kanoon' now
> found in Egypt and adjacent countries. (Con-
> cerning mediæval Arabic literature about music, see
> sec. 36.)

FIG. 26. — Persian
Guitar.

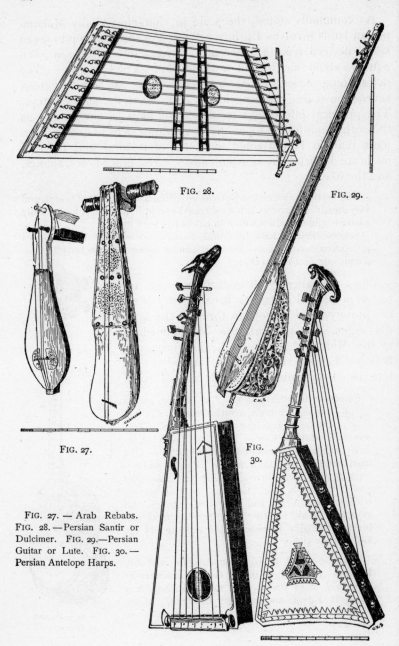

FIG. 28.

FIG. 29.

FIG. 27.

FIG. 30.

FIG. 27. — Arab Rebabs.
FIG. 28.—Persian Santir or
Dulcimer. FIG. 29.—Persian
Guitar or Lute. FIG. 30. —
Persian Antelope Harps.

ANCIENT SYSTEMS

14. Babylonia and Assyria. — We know little about music in ancient Mesopotamia, except that the monuments depict some instruments and imply the use of singing and dancing. We gather that music was a stated element in religious and civic functions, companies of performers forming parts of great processions, and infer that it was under the care of the priesthood.

> Among the instruments depicted are harps, dulcimers, lyres of several shapes, lutes, double pipes, trumpets and drums. The harps have many strings stretched obliquely from an upright body or back to a horizontal arm below, but have no pillar. The dulcimers seem to consist of a shallow box held horizontally, over which metal strings are stretched so as to be sounded by little hammers (recalling the 'santir' of the modern Persians). The lyres resemble those later found among the Greeks. The lutes are allied to those of Hindustan and the Orient generally — actual examples being found in the earlier strata at Nippur. It is likely that all Hebrew instruments were based on Babylonian prototypes.
>
> It should be noted that several of the instruments mentioned in Dan. iii. as used in Babylonia under Nebuchadnezzar (605–562 B.C.) have Greek names, whence it is inferred that the author wrote after about 330 B.C., and named instruments then in use.

15. Israel. — The origin of the Hebrews seems to have been in Arabia, but their geographical position involved close contacts with Mesopotamia on the one side and with Egypt on the other. In all matters of culture they were imitators and borrowers, so that we infer that their music was derived from outside.

> All the important data about Hebrew music come from the Old Testament, which consists of writings compiled not before about the 8th century B.C., with some (like Chronicles) hardly earlier than the 3d century. The older documents are singularly devoid of musical data.

The earliest recorded application of music in a serious way was by bands of 'prophets' (organized under Samuel before 1000 B.C.) as a means of inducing ecstasy. Probably it was used in some way in the First Temple (built c. 950 B.C.), though hardly to the extent often supposed. The services of the Second Temple (built c. 520 B.C.) certainly included singing with instrumental accompaniment by trained performers. For these latter services the Book of Psalms appears, at least in some part, to have been collected and edited as we have it. In social life music was probably common, but the references are meagre.

The actual styles can only be conjectured. Song was prob-ably in unison, loud and harsh in tone, of limited range, with rude intervals and perhaps many melodic embellishments. It is likely that recitative was common, and that many texts were rendered antiphonally, following the parallelism of the poetic text. Some forms of dance were combined with religious song.

Particular melodies are apparently mentioned in the editorial notes to a few of the Psalms, but what they were is unknown. It is supposed that various terms found with poetic texts were originally marks of musical treatment, but their date and meaning are disputed.

Many instruments are named, but in default of pictorial delineations their form cannot be determined. They include the 'kinnor' ('harp' in the English Bible, but probably a lyre, like the modern Egyptian 'kissar'), the 'nebel' ('psaltery,' but probably a lute, like the Egyptian 'nofre,' or a harp), the 'chalil' ('pipe,' either a flute or an oboe), two or three kinds of trumpets, such as the 'keren' and 'chatzotzerah,' the ''ugab' ('organ,' but probably a syrinx), cymbals, tambourines ('timbrels'), sistra, etc.

In later Judaism the importance of synagogues steadily ad-vanced, and after the fall of Jerusalem (70 A.D.) they sprang up wherever Jews settled, continuing to the present day in all parts of the world. Synagogue services to-day include the cantillation of Scripture passages and of prayers and often the singing of psalms. For these exercises many traditional melo-dies of considerable antiquity exist. But since the usages of different countries do not agree, these traditions do not appear to go back to really ancient times.

The historical importance of Hebrew music lies not in what it actually was, but in the striking influence that the fact of its existence in connec-tion with religion has exerted upon Christian thought and customs. Modern Jews have often displayed eminent musical ability, and several leading composers, like Mendelssohn and Meyerbeer, have been of Jewish extraction. Occasionally themes from synagogue music have been used in general composition.

16. Egypt. — It is evident that from early times the ancient Egyptians were extremely fond of music, especially as a social diversion, as a courtly luxury, and in religious ceremony. It was united with poetry and with many sorts of dances. Professional singers, players and dancers were common and carefully trained. Among court-officials musicians are often named as prominent. It is probable that the cultivation of music was one of the many functions of the priesthood.

The Egyptians were zealous in building and in adorning what they built with records, and the climate has preserved what they wrought as nowhere else in the world. Accordingly, in extant delineations on the monuments, as well as in papyri and in many actual objects, we have abundant data for reconstructing the actual life of the people. The use of music is thus profusely set before us, so that it is better known than in any other ancient land. But, unfortunately, we have not yet recovered any ancient Egyptian treatise on the subject. Neither is there any trace of a musical notation.

We have only disputed evidence as to the recognized types of scale, though from extant instruments it is inferred that melodies were mostly diatonic. That there was some practical use of harmony follows from the depiction of groups of performers acting in concert, and from the size of the larger harps and lyres. Singing and dancing were accompanied by hand-clapping to mark the rhythm.

The historic importance of this extensive musical activity is evident, for in the 7th century B.C., Egypt was opened to the Greeks, and intercourse with the north and west rapidly increased, until ultimately Egypt became one of the chief centres of Greek culture.   Nearly all the important Greek works on musical theory were written in Egypt, and none of them intimates that Egyptian views differed radically from the Greek. Hence we conclude that the Greek ideas of music were largely supplied or suggested by Egyptian usage or speculation. If this be so, the genesis of the mediæval system of Europe is to be traced to Egypt as well as to the Greeks.

Egyptian instruments were numerous and varied.   Apparently they were developed for tonal results, without excessive attention to outward ornamentation, though some of the harps were very rich.   They were regularly used in interesting combinations, implying attention to concerted effects.

Stringed instruments were evidently favorites. Most conspicuous are the harps, in three varieties — the small, shaped like a bow and carried horizontally on the shoulder, the medium, also bow-shaped, but held upright by a seated player, and the large, loop-shaped, with a massive body, often sumptuously decorated with color and carving, played from a standing posture. All these lack the upright pillar beyond the strings, and must have been rather grave in pitch and unstable in tune. The number of strings varies from three to twenty or more. Next in importance are the lyres, having a resonance-box below, a U-shaped frame with a cross-bar above, whence five to many strings were stretched downward ; these were held horizontally under the arm or set upright on a table or pedestal, and were played with a plectrum or the finger-tips. Less impor-- tant are the lutes, known in the Old Kingdom only from a hieroglyphic

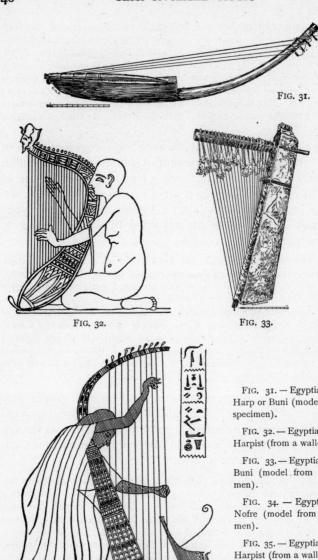

FIG. 31.

FIG. 32.   FIG. 33.   FIG. 34.

FIG. 31. — Egyptian Shoulder Harp or Buni (model from actual specimen).

FIG. 32. — Egyptian Harp and Harpist (from a wall-painting).

FIG. 33. — Egyptian Harp or Buni (model from actual specimen).

FIG. 34. — Egyptian Lute or Nofre (model from actual specimen).

FIG. 35. — Egyptian Harp and Harpist (from a wall-painting).

FIG. 35.

sign, but later found with 1-5 strings, which were stopped against a fretted neck and sounded with a plectrum. Some of these, with the trigons — triangular, many-stringed harps — were perhaps of foreign origin. Viols and dulcimers seem to be lacking.

The wind instruments include both direct and transverse flutes, the former often double and sometimes blown by the nose, and all often having several finger-holes; oboes, often double, provided with finger-holes and sounded by reeds made of straw; trumpets of copper or bronze, chiefly used for military purposes; and perhaps the syrinx. [The fact that the principle of the organ was first applied in Egypt (in the Greek period) raises the query whether perhaps it may not have been known there earlier.]

Percussives are numerous, including clappers of bone or ivory, cymbals, sistra — metal frames with loose, rattling rods — tambourines, and at least two sorts of drums, besides several trivial jingles worn by dancers. Apparently there were no true bells or gongs.

CHAPTER III

GREEK AND ROMAN MUSIC

17. In General. — The Greek mind was both analytic and constructive. In all the fine arts it seized upon styles already in existence and speedily developed them with a scope and ideality unknown before. In the case of music, this expansion was notably scientific and philosophical as well as technical. Though the conclusions reached were limited by various causes, they were yet acute for their time and have since been highly influential. In Greek music we find the immediate source of early mediæval music and thus indirectly of modern music.

Our knowledge of Greek music is, however, one-sided, being drawn almost wholly from works about music rather than from examples. Of the practical working of the system we know little, except that music was joined more intimately with poetry and with general culture than is now common.

It is not easy to mark off the historic stages in musical development, except in a very rough and general way. The following periods, however, are to be borne in mind : —

The Mythical or Heroic Age — the time of the itinerant minstrel or bard — prior to about 675 B.C., when popular contests in music and poetry began in Sparta.

The Classical Period, culminating in the 5th century B.C., but continuing till the downfall of Greek independence in 338, during which the practice of music-poetry was developed, chiefly at Athens or near by.

The Alexandrian Period, from about 325 B.C. to the Christian Era and after, in which the older versatile originality gave place to scientific criticism or mere imitation, chiefly at Alexandria.

The Roman Period, from the time of Augustus until the Roman Empire was dissolved, during which all the arts of Greece were extensively adopted, often in degenerate forms, by the dominant peoples to the west.

From all these periods we find mention of musical performers, teachers and theorists, some of whom are named below.

18. Union of Music with Poetry. — In Greek thought what we call poetry and music were intimately blended, both being held to be inspired by the Muses (whence the term μουσική, with a far wider meaning than our word 'music'). Poetry was felt to require delivery in song for its complete expression, while music had little importance except to embody poetry. So the history of Greek poetry and music is a single subject. The poets were themselves singers, and their works were meant to be chanted by readers and interpreters so as to be received into appreciation through the ear. This does not mean that the poet composed fixed melodies for his verses, but that each species of poetry had a recognized style of cantillation, well enough known to be used freely by many persons. Common education was expected to give such familiarity with these musical styles as to preserve and disseminate them. Some sort of musical improvisation was probably not uncommon in cultivated circles generally.

The first style to become established was apparently the epic, cultivated by wandering bards who intoned their verses, whether memorized or improvised, to a slender accompaniment on the lyre or some similar instrument. The historic masters here were *Homer* and *Hesiod* (9th and 8th centuries B.C.).

Later several more condensed forms became popular, such as the Ionic iambics and elegiacs — hymns and odes of a celebrative or commemorative character — represented by *Archilochos* and *Tertaios* (early 7th century); the lyrics of Lesbos and other islands — brief songs of special delicacy and point in varied verse-forms — represented by *Alkaios, Sappho* and *Anakreon* (early 6th century); and the Dorian choral songs and the dithyrambs of the Dionysiac and other mystic rites — stronger and broader festal hymns intended to be chanted by companies of people in unison — represented by *Terpander, Arion, Stesichoros, Simonides* and *Pindar* (c. 650–450).

Side by side with these latter developed the Attic drama, both tragic and comic, with a complex union of solo and choral declamation, lyric and half-epic, on the part of carefully trained performers — represented, in tragedy, by *Aischylos, Sophokles* and *Euripides*, and, in comedy, by *Aristophanes* and *Antiphanes* (from about 500).

The drama was peculiarly important, since it was a culminating and comprehensive form that utilized the best features in preceding efforts and served to make them widely popular. The social prominence of the drama is attested by the remains of splendid theatres in every part of the old Greco-Roman world.

Another institution intimately connected with the growth of music-poetry was the series of festival-contests regularly held at various places, such as the Olympian in Elis, the Pythian at Delphi, the Nemean in Argolis and the Isthmian at Corinth, at which occurred not only competitions in physical prowess, but equally strenuous rivalries in literary and musical art. These festivals were attended by great throngs, and their stimulus was felt far and wide, attracting contestants from distant lands.

> Regarding these two institutions, the Drama and the Games, it is to be noted that the impress of the former again and again affected the unfolding of the mediæval and modern drama, especially the opera, while the latter was frequently paralleled in the age of the Troubadours and Minnesinger (see secs. 38, 40).

19. Actual Effects. — We are thrown back largely upon conjecture as to the actual style of this antique song. Extant literary references are not vivid, and mostly date from long after the most productive periods. Of surely authentic melodies we have only a few mutilated specimens — the chief being the noble *Hymn to Apollo* discovered at Delphi in 1893, which was a pæan composed by an Athenian to celebrate the repulse of the Goths in 279 B.C.

It is evident that most melodies were decidedly minor, with a tonality unlike ours and some strange intervals. Doubtless most singing was by male voices in unison, the usual pitch being high and the quality somewhat strident. The rhythmic and metric patterns were certainly varied and often intricate, regulated by the quantities and accents of the text rather than by independent time-schemes as in modern music. Harmony may have been used somewhat in the union of voices, of voices with instruments, and of groups of instruments; but details are lacking.

> In the later periods the production of original poetry became steadily more feeble and less associated with music, while the latter lapsed from a dignified fine art to a careless amusement. It passed largely into the hands of slaves and vagrant minstrels, so that it fell to the status of a mere trade. Doubtless some of the refinements of early days were abandoned. Wherever Greek music went outside of Greece, it was inevitably conglomerated with local usages.

It is not clear just how instruments were employed in accompaniment or independently. Doubtless their primary purpose was to support the voice in singing, either by doubling the

melody or by adding some tones to it.   But evidently there
was some independent development of lyre- and flute-playing,
as performers are often mentioned with honor and there was a
special notation for instrumental music.

The stringed instruments were conspicuous, including the characteristic
'lyra,' consisting of a resonance-box (sometimes a tortoise-shell), a
U-shaped frame with a crosspiece, and 4–18 sinew strings; the 'kithara'
or 'kitharis' (also called 'phorminx'), apparently the older form of the
lyre, but later distinguished from it by having the strings carried partly
over the body instead of being attached to its upper edge; the 'magadis,'
an Oriental harp of varying shape and with perhaps 20 strings; and the
'barbitos' and 'trigon,' many-stringed harps of special form. All of these
were played either by the finger-tips or with a plectrum. The shape and
ornamentation of the lyres were ingeniously varied.

The other principal class was the wind instruments, including especially the 'aulos,' a direct flute of cane or bored wood, with a detachable
mouth-piece and from two to several finger-holes, in which, in later times
at least, were little movable stopples whereby the pitch could be slightly
modified. Auloi were often made double, either to give greater power
or a wider range. The player often wore a capistrum or cheek-strap to
keep the instrument in place and to support the cheeks. Sometimes
auloi were attached to a distensible bag, making a bagpipe. The 'salpinx'
was a straight, tapering trumpet of bronze, apparently without finger-
holes. The 'syrinx' or Pan's-pipe was a series of graduated tubes sounded
by blowing across the open ends — peculiarly a pastoral instrument.

A rudimentary form of organ invented at Alexandria by the mechanician Ktesibios about 175 B.C., passed into vogue among the wealthy in
different parts of the Roman Empire and was thus handed over to Christian use. The details of the first construction are unknown, but in Roman
times, as we know from various sources, including a remarkable clay model
of the 2d century A.D. found at Carthage, there were often 2–3 sets of
pipes mounted on a wind-chest, a simple keyboard or set of valve-levers,
and an ingenious device to supply compressed air by a pair of pumps
partially filled with water — whence the Latin name 'hydraulus' or 'water-
organ.'

20. Acoustical and Theoretical Research. — This side of Greek
music is far better known than any other, since most of the literature that we have treats of it extensively.   From as early
as the 7th century B.C. the physical analysis of tones and their
relations was undertaken, with studies in the formal definition
of scales.

Pythagoras, the famous philosopher and social leader — born in Samos
in 582 B.C., educated by long residence in Egypt and extensive travel, and
finally teaching in southern Italy — was the chief pioneer. He laid the
foundation of musical acoustics as a science, and started a school of inves-

FIG. 36.

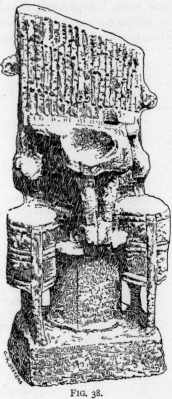

FIG. 38.

FIG. 37.

FIGS. 36, 37. — Greek Lyres or Kitharas (models of actual specimens found in Egypt).

FIG. 38. — Greek Hydraulus or Water-Organ (clay figurine, 2d century, found at Carthage).

tigators that lasted long after the Christian Era. His followers tended to regulate all musical procedure by mathematics, and the opposition long continued between them and the disciples of *Aristoxenos*, born about 354 B.C., who advocated taste and instinct as normative principles.

Through these studies, with experiments in singing and instrument-making, an extensive theoretical tone-system was gradually developed. The shaping and nomenclature of this were largely determined by the constant use of the lyre. From the first the comprehensive units recognized were the octave and the tetrachord (a series of four tones within the interval of a fourth). All tone-series were reckoned downward instead of upward (as in modern music).

Three 'genera,' or ways of dividing the tetrachord, were used : (*a*) the diatonic, consisting of two whole steps or 'tones' and a half-step or hemitone, (*b*) the chromatic, consisting of an extra long step with two half-steps, and (*c*) the enharmonic, consisting of a double-step with two quarter-steps. These arrangements may be illustrated through modern letter-names thus : —

Diatonic,	E	D	C	B
Chromatic,	E	C♯	C	B
Enharmonic,	E		CC♭B	

The diatonic genus was felt to be the most important of the three, and as it is the form that has had historic influence since, it will be the only one taken for further illustration here.

Within a diatonic tetrachord all the three possible arrangements of half-steps were utilized — the Dorian, with the half-step below, the Phrygian, with it in the middle, and the Lydian, with it above. These may be illustrated thus : —

Dorian,	E	D	C	B
Phrygian,	E	D	C♯	B *or* D C B A
Lydian,	E	D♯	C♯	B *or* C B A G

Various 'species' or octave-scales were constructed by joining two similar tetrachords together and adding one step to complete the octave. Seven such species or modes were recognized, formed in three ways, according to the position of the added step : —

Dorian species or mode,	E	D	C	B	A	G	F	E
Phrygian species or mode,	D	C	B	A	G	F	E	D
Lydian species or mode,	C	B	A	G	F	E	D	C
Hypodorian species or mode,	A	G	F	E	D	C	B	A
Hypophrygian species or mode,	G	F	E	D	C	B	A	G
Hypolydian species or mode,	F	E	D	C	B	A	G	F
Mixolydian species or mode,	B	A	G	F	E	D	C	B

Tetrachords

THE COMPLETE SYSTEM

Greek name	Description	Pitch
Nete hyperbolaion,	Last string of the extreme tetrachord,	A''
Paranete hyperbolaion,	Next to last string of the extreme tetrachord,	G'
Trite hyperbolaion,	Third string of the extreme tetrachord,	F'
Nete diezeugmenon,	Last string of the disjunct tetrachord,	E'
Paranete diezeugmenon,	Next to last string of the disjunct tetrachord,	D'
	(Also, *Nete synemmenon,* Last of the conjunct tetrachord)	
Trite diezeugmenon,	Third string of the disjunct tetrachord,	C'
	(Also, *Paranete synemmenon,* Next to last of the conjunct tetrachord)	
Paramese,	Next to the middle string,	B'
	(*Trite synemmenon,* Third of the conjunct tetrachord)	B♮
MESE,	Middle string,	A'
Lichanos meson,	Forefinger string of the middle tetrachord,	G
Parhypate meson,	Next to upper string of the middle tetrachord,	F
Hypate meson,	Upper string of the middle tetrachord,	E
Lichanos hypaton,	Forefinger string of the upper tetrachord,	D
Parhypate hypaton,	Next to upper string of the upper tetrachord,	C
Hypate hypaton,	Upper string of the upper tetrachord,	B
Proslambanomenos,	Added tone,	A

The tone *Mese* fulfills something of the office of a keynote.

The conjunct tetrachord is an extra feature, taking the place of the disjunct tetrachord when a sort of modulation is desired. The names of the two are derived from the relations to the middle tetrachord, the disjunct standing one step away from the lower, while the conjunct joins it directly.

[It should be observed that this use of letter-names is not intended to indicate the absolute pitch. For convenience, the modes are here made to begin at different points. The essential difference between them lies in the position of the short steps, and they should properly begin with the same tone.]

Of the seven species, the Dorian was the most admired, but apparently melodies were composed in all. The several species were felt to differ widely in æsthetic and moral quality, which was much discussed by thoughtful critics.

What was called the 'Complete System' was a scheme of tones comprising two octaves and composed of four Dorian tetrachords (one of which varied slightly in form). The various species or modes were understood to be imbedded in this system, each including a particular octave. While for theoretical purposes the system, with its included species, was assumed as a fixed standard or formula, its absolute pitch might be higher or lower as the performer might choose — that is, it might be transposed. But in Greek thought every such transposition had a character of its own, even though the relation of the tones was unchanged. Furthermore, similar systems were elaborated for the chromatic and enharmonic genera, as well as for the diatonic.

To each tone of the system a specific name was given, designating both the tetrachord to which it belonged and its place therein. This cumbrous nomenclature was taken from the lyre, each tone belonging to a particular string. The acuter tones were called 'last' or 'lowest' and the graver ones 'highest' simply because lyres were held with the longer strings uppermost.

21. Notation. — The modern letter-names for tones used in the foregoing sections were not used by the Greeks. Besides the long descriptive names from the lyre, however, they did employ letters and letter-like characters, so that it was possible to indicate with precision any given tone in either the diatonic, the chromatic or the enhar-

FIG. 39. — Fragment of *Hymn to Apollo*, showing notation above the text.

monic genus. For this purpose they not only used all the twenty-four letters of their alphabet, but supplemented them by the same characters inverted or turned on either side, besides a few other signs. Two different sets of such letter-signs were used for vocal and instrumental music respectively, the latter being the older and simpler. Some use was made of small marks to show the relative length of tones; and there was a sign for a silence or rest.

In teaching singing, syllable-names were sometimes given to the tones of a tetrachord (*ta, tē, to, tĕ*).

22. Roman Music. — It is not unlikely that music among the Latins derived something from the earlier Etruscans or from the enterprising Greek colonies in southern .Italy and Sicily prior to the founding of Rome, but about this nothing positive is known. Music in Italy seems to have had little importance until after the conquest of Greece in the 2d century B.C., when Greek art-works and artists were scattered far and wide. Then, and still more under the Empire, all Roman education, art and letters came under the direction of Greek teachers and models. As luxury increased, the importation of singers, players and dancers from all parts of the Orient became fashionable, though these performers were nearly all slaves and socially despised.

The Romans, therefore, contributed little to musical progress, except that under their domination immense numbers of musicians were attracted to Rome, and thus the knowledge of Greek styles was spread widely into the West. Some details of theory, of tuning, and of notation were improved, and all kinds of instruments were used and somewhat modified. But the status of musical art was not at all what it had been in Greece.

23. Literature about Music. — The total number of classical works on music that are now known is perhaps seventy, of which, however, about one-third are known only by title, author or topic, while many others exist only in brief citations or other fragmentary shape. But the bulk of writings more or less available for study is far from small.

As the data on this subject are not easily accessible, a brief summary is here appended : —

From the 6th and 5th centuries B.C. we have only some bare names, of which the chief is **Pythagoras**, the founder of a whole school of later writers on acoustics (the Canonici), but who seems himself to have left no writings.

The 4th century is far more important. Early in the century is **Plato** (429–347), the incomparable idealist, whose 'Timaios' is largely devoted to music, not to speak of allusions in other dialogues. His famous pupil **Aristotle** (384–322) is said to have written a musical treatise, now lost, besides many passages in extant works — not counting the 'Problems' once ascribed to him. Among his followers were **Adrastos**, from whose 'Harmonics' some extracts have survived; and especially **Aristoxenos** of Tarentum (b. c. 354), whose 'Harmonic Elements' is our earliest complete treatise, and of whose 'Rhythmic Elements' some fragments exist. He stands at the head of a school (the Harmonici) hostile to the extreme mathematical notions of the Pythagoreans.

In the 3d century the great name is **Euclid**, the Alexandrian geometer, to whom two complete treatises have been ascribed, that on the 'Partition of the Canon' probably with right, while the 'Harmonic Introduction' is now thought to be by **Kleonides**. The latter belongs in the 2d century, along with **Eratosthenes** and **Hero**, both Alexandrians.

From the 1st century we have **Philodemos** the Epicurean, whose diatribe on the uselessness of music was found at Herculaneum; and the Alexandrian grammarian **Didymos** (b. 63), among whose many works several on music are quoted, and to whom an account of the strife between the Canonici and the Harmonici is attributed, perhaps improperly. Here Latin writers appear for the first time, including **Lucretius** (95–51), treating the origin of music in his 'De rerum natura'; **Cicero** (106–44) and **Horace** (65–8), both evidently musical connoisseurs; and **Vitruvius**, who includes musical references in his great work 'De architectura.'

After the Christian Era, to the 1st century belongs the elder **Pliny** (22–79), whose 'Historia mundi' often mentions music. Greek writers include **Plutarch** (50–120), the author of the earliest extant historical book; **Dio**, among whose eighty orations are many musical remarks; and **Aristides Quintilianus**, who has left an important work 'On Music.'

In the 2d century the names are many and striking. Here belong **Claudius Ptolemæus** of Alexandria, whose 'Harmonics' is one of our chief sources; **Theon** of Smyrna, whose expansion of certain of Plato's ideas is partially preserved; **Gaudentios**, an Aristoxenian, whose 'Harmonic Manual' is extant; and **Bacchios** the elder, whose 'Introduction to Music' is important. Besides these appear remarks of a more or less gossipy nature from **Gellius**, a Roman dilettant, the satirist **Lucian** (125–200), and **Athenaios** (b. 160), an Alexandrian rhetor.

To the 3d century are assigned **Aelian**, whose so-called 'History' supplies some citations; **Diogenes Laertios**, who gives some biographical details; and **Porphyry** (233–305), the commentator upon Claudius Ptolemæus.

The 4th century is marked by **Alypios**, whose 'Musical Introduction,' preserved in part, is of the greatest value as the key to Greek musical notation.

The 5th century supplies **Macrobius**, whose 'Commentary' includes a fruitless discussion of 'the music of the spheres'; **Proclus** (412–485), with a commentary on Plato's 'Timaios'; and **Martianus Capella**, a Roman grammarian, the ninth book of whose 'Satyricon' is wholly on music, while other books contain quotations.

In the 6th century came **Boethius** (475–525), whose 'De musica' has been a mine for students ever since, albeit a somewhat treacherous one.

At intervals in later centuries other writers appear, mostly Byzantines, whose works furnish useful points. The long roll ends with **Manuel Bryennios** (c. 1320), whose 'Harmonics' is really a compend of extracts from earlier writers, often of great value.

FIG. 40. — Greek Lyre or Kithara and Kitharist (from a bas-relief).

PART II

MEDIÆVAL MUSIC

PART II

MEDIÆVAL MUSIC

CHAPTER IV

THE RISE OF CHRISTIAN MUSIC

24. General Survey.—The historical transition from Greek music to that of the 12th to the 14th centuries is not easy to trace or describe. Regarding both ends of the period, we have a fair amount of information, but of the intervening thousand years or more nothing adequate can be said. Certain points are clear, but how to fill the colossal period with living interest is a question. The total amount of music extant is small and the discernible personalities pitifully few. That there was considerable musical life is certain from after events, but actual vestiges of it are scanty.

The Roman Empire reached its greatest area and prosperity in the 2d century. In the 3d symptoms of decay began to appear, and in the 4th and 5th the repeated onsets of Goths, Vandals and Huns finally drove the seat of government from Rome to Byzantium (Constantinople). The later 6th century saw the rise of Mohammedanism, which in the 7th swept over Syria, Egypt and Northern Africa and in the 8th reached Spain. These cataclysmic changes destroyed the continuity of civilized life and thought, and interrupted the development of all the fine arts. The chief exceptions were in the Byzantine Empire and in regions under Moslem control, but in both cases culture was more Oriental than Occidental.

In the midst of the seething political turmoil Christianity steadily advanced. Under Constantine (c. 325) it became the official religion of the Empire. It was then propagated into the distant North and West, especially among Teutonic peoples. The Church became a mighty social institution. Adopting the Roman principle of unity in organization, it aimed to arrange its officials in perfect gradation of authority under a supreme pontiff or pope, to define 'orthodoxy' by conciliar enactments and to suppress 'heterodoxy,' and to work out a uniform, prescribed liturgy. All these efforts powerfully affected intellectual and artistic activity for centuries. Only in clerical circles, such as monastic fraternities, was continuous and peaceful mental work possible. Cathedrals and religious houses were the only repositories of learning and fountains of education, so that in the so-called Dark Ages the Church was the one persistent and shining light.

What we know of Christian music before about 1200 is involved in the complex social and political situation. It

63

is not strange that the only kind of music was ritual music and that all our information comes through ecclesiastical annalists.

25. The First Christian Songs. — Singing in public and private worship was a matter of course for the early Christians. For Jewish converts this was a continuance of synagogue customs, but, since the Church grew mostly among non-Jews, the technical forms employed were more Greek than Hebrew. The use of instruments was long resisted, because of their association with pagan sensuality. In addition to the Hebrew Psalms (in the Greek version), the new faith tended constantly to produce new hymns, at first apparently in the form of rhapsodies. From the 2d to the 4th centuries the foundations of the vast structure of Christian hymnody were securely laid, especially in the epoch-making work of certain Latin writers.

> The New Testament makes some mention of the singing of hymns. The earliest complete hymn extant is by Clement of Alexandria (d. 220), and parts of canticles like the *Gloria in Excelsis* and the *Te Deum* may have been somewhat earlier. By about 400, sacred poems have adopted accent, rhyme and stanza in a way quite novel. For two or three centuries thereafter the abundance of original hymns is a sure sign of the cultivation of religious music.

26. The Gregorian Style. — From the 4th century the strong accent upon unity of organization, fixity of creed and uniformity of liturgy led steadily to a demand for richness and stateliness. Costly edifices became common, ministrants were multiplied, and the whole ritual of worship tended to become ornate. This involved a new attention to music.

The first centre of activity was Constantinople, where Greek music was the established type of artistic song. Thus the tradition of the ancient unison melody was handed on to Italy and the West. The evolution that followed is only imperfectly traceable in detail, but in the end it provided the mediæval Church with a large and striking body of melodies, fitted to a variety of prose texts and even to metrical poetry. We must suppose that these ritual melodies grew out of manifold experiments at different places, which were only gradually wrought into a general and uniform system. Even after the system was codified, its usages continued to accumulate, and from time to time considerable modifications in style appeared.

Tradition attributes particular steps in the process to certain popes, bishops and other ecclesiastics. Two names have been specially emphasized, Bishop *Ambrose* of Milan (d. 397) and Pope *Gregory the Great* (d. 604), the latter being constantly put forth as the founder and organizer of the whole style called 'Gregorian.' But these traditions, as commonly stated, are at least doubtful. Many able scholars believe that the practical completion of the system was not earlier than the 8th century, perhaps under Gregory II. (d. 731) or Gregory III. (d. 741), and that the name 'Gregorian' either came from them or was due to the mistaken zeal of those who sought to glorify the earlier Gregory.

It should be remembered that the Gregorian style is the property of the Western or, more exactly, the Roman Church. In each of the other branches of the early Church there were analogous developments, but none of these, except to a very limited extent that of the Greek or Russian Church, has any significant connection with the story of modern music.

Since the Gregorian style originated for liturgical reasons, its home was the metropolitan cathedral or the monastic chapel, whence it spread to parish churches generally. Being cultivated only by ecclesiastics, to the common people it was remote and abstruse. Its direct influence upon the general progress of music was therefore limited. To some extent there arose an antipathy between it and secular music, which was heightened by the fact that church song was always in Latin. In the general evolution of music it has always remained a somewhat peculiar specialty, representing the persistence for a particular purpose of a style which is essentially antique. Yet it must be confessed that in its ideal perfection, as it stood in the early Middle Ages, it was a remarkable example of melodic invention and beauty.

The Gregorian style is the only form of music prescribed for use in the Roman Church, though some other styles have been allowed or tolerated. It is supposed, however, that its extensive treasures represent several stages of production, and all are not of equal validity. In a general way, the over 600 melodies belonging to the Mass and certain other principal rites have the greatest antiquity, while the almost 3000 belonging to the Breviary are later, and those fitted to hymns or sequences later still. But during the Renaissance the whole series was treated with much freedom, especially in the matter of embellishments and ornate expansions, so that in the 16th century, when Gregory XIII. and Sixtus V. ordained the service-books since in use, the style was no longer pure. Recent enactments of Pius IX. (1869), Leo XIII. (1883) and especially Pius X. (1903) have aimed not only to enforce the rules enjoining the use of Gregorian music almost to the exclusion of other styles, but to correct many abuses in its habitual rendering and ultimately to recover and restore its typical forms. Especially under the

F

lead of the monks of Solesmes (see sec. 227) fresh efforts are now being put forth to establish authentic texts and correct renderings.

Gregorian melodies vary considerably according to the kind of text for which they are designed and to the period they represent. Some are merely monotones with occasional inflections. Some, as a rule, have but one tone to the syllable and move chiefly by diatonic steps. Some abound in flowing figures to single syllables and in skips, large or small. But, whatever their form, they plainly show a desire to find a real tonal embodiment for the words and the thought. Only comparatively late came in the desire to make tonal patterns for their own sake. Being designed primarily for prose texts, they have no fixed rhythm or standard length of tones. Accents and quantities are derived from the words, after the manner of recitative, and in good rendering expressive flexibility is conspicuous. The compass is rarely greater than an octave and is often much less. The selection of tones conforms to scale-types differing from those of secular and modern music generally (see sec. 27). Properly, the unison should not be accompanied, since harmony introduces a somewhat foreign element and, unless very dexterous, totally changes the effect.

> The term 'Plain-Song,' often applied to Gregorian music, emphasizes either its lack of fixed rhythm (in contrast with 'Measured Music'), or its lack of harmony or part-writing (in contrast with 'Figured Music' or 'Counterpoint').

27. Its Technical System. — That the tone-system of the Middle Ages came from that of the Greeks is evident, though the stages of evolution are not entirely clear. But probably the formal system was at first more implicit than consciously formulated. Only after Plain-Song had reached a considerable development was an effort made to arrange its principles systematically. The basis chosen was a series of modes resembling the 'species' of the Greeks. Prior to about 1000 the accepted modes numbered eight, which later came to be known by Greek names (oddly transposed from their ancient meaning). These modes fall into two classes — the 'authentic' (straight or primary) and the 'plagal' (oblique or derived), the former having the 'final' (somewhat analogous to keynote) at the bottom and the 'dominant' (chief reciting-tone) in the middle, while the latter have the final in the middle and the dominant two or three steps above it. Strictly speaking, each pair of modes is really one, the difference between authentic and plagal being in practical application.

To these earlier modes four more were added, making twelve — the first statement of the complete series being by *Glarean* in 1547. Two more were proposed, but rejected.

THE CHURCH MODES

										ANCIENT NAMES
1. Dorian			**D**	E F	G	A* B C	D		}	*Phrygian*
2. Hypodorian	A	B C	**D**	E F*	G	A			}	
3. Phrygian			**E** F	G	A	B C* D	E		}	*Dorian*
4. Hypophrygian	B C	D	**E** F	G	A* B				}	
5. Lydian			**F**	G	A	B C* D	E F		}	*Hypolydian*
6. Hypolydian	C	D	E **F**	G	A* B C				}	
7. Mixolydian			**G**	A	B C	D* E F	G		}	*Hypophrygian*
8. Hypomixolydian	D	E F	**G**	A	B C*	D			}	or *Iastian*
9. Æolian			**A**	B C	D	E*F G	A		}	*Hypodorian*
10. Hypoæolian	E F	G	**A**	B C*	D	E			}	or *Æolian*
11. Ionian			**C**	D	E F	G* A	B C		}	*Lydian*
12. Hypoionian	G	A	B **C**	D	E*F	G			}	

In each case the final is marked by a black letter, the dominant by an asterisk.

The essential difference between the modes lies in the location of the short steps, as well as of the finals and dominants.

While melodies in the several modes were primarily intended to be sung at the pitch above indicated, they might be transposed to fit the voice. The 'ambitus' or compass of a melody properly does not exceed the octave of its mode by more than one step above or below.

In strictness, no deviations from the above scales are permitted, but the direct progression from F to B or *vice versa* (the tritone) was ruled out as unsingable, and, to avoid it, B♭ was substituted for B wherever the latter occurred in relations suggesting the above progressions. Ultimately, however, under the name of 'musica ficta,' much more extensive alterations of the modes were practised (see sec. 73).

28. The Hexachord-System. — By the 11th century, if not before, the whole series of tones found useful for song was reduced to a system like the Complete System of the Greeks (see sec. 20). But it was longer than the latter and laid out, not in tetrachords, but in hexachords — series of tones standing in the relation of C–D–E–F–G–A. To facilitate practice, the syllables *ut, re, mi,*

THE HEXACHORD-SYSTEM

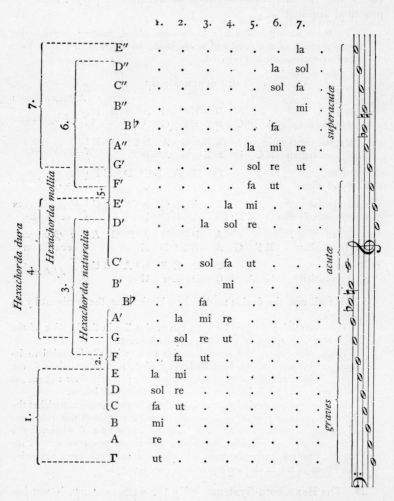

	1.	2.	3.	4.	5.	6.	7.	
E''	.	.	.	.	.	.	la	superacutæ
D''	.	.	.	.	.	la	sol	
C''	.	.	.	.	.	sol	fa	
B''	.	.	.	.	.	.	mi	
B♭	.	.	.	.	.	fa		
A''	.	.	.	.	la	mi	re	
G'	.	.	.	.	sol	re	ut	
F'	.	.	.	.	fa	ut	.	
E'	.	.	.	la	mi	.	.	acutæ
D'	.	.	la	sol	re	.	.	
C'	.	.	sol	fa	ut	.	.	
B'	.	.	.	mi	.	.	.	
B♭	.	.	fa	.	.	.	.	
A'	.	la	mi	re	.	.	.	
G	.	sol	re	ut	.	.	.	
F	.	fa	ut	.	.	.	.	
E	la	mi	.	.	.	.	.	graves
D	sol	re	.	.	.	.	.	
C	fa	ut	.	.	.	.	.	
B	mi	.	.	.	.	.	.	
A	re	.	.	.	.	.	.	
Γ	ut	.	.	.	.	.	.	

Left-side brackets: Hexachorda dura (4), Hexachorda mollia, Hexachorda naturalia (3), Hexachorda naturalia; numbered 1, 2, 3, 4, 5, 6, 7.

Hexachords 1, 4 and 7 are called *hard* because they contain B, which was distinguished as *B durum*; hexachords 3 and 6 are called *soft* because they contain B♭ or *B molle* (or *B rotundum*); and hexachords 2 and 5 are called *natural* because they contain neither B nor B♭.

fa, *sol*, *la*, were applied to the successive tones of every hexachord — the short step, therefore, being always *mi-fa*. This constituted the first form of 'solmization,' of which many new varieties and applications have appeared, all designed to represent similar tone relations by similar signs.

> These syllables were taken from a hymn to John the Baptist, the traditional melody for which began in each line with the tone corresponding to its first syllable. The hymn reads, "*Ut* queant laxis *Re*sonare fibris *Mi*ra gestorum *Fa*muli tuorum, *Sol*ve polluti *La*bii reatum, Sancte Johannes."

The system was made up of seven interlocking hexachords, covering a total range of nearly three octaves — five tones longer than the Greek. But two extra tones were provided — B♭ in addition to B, so as to facilitate a sort of modulation. The tones of the three octaves were designated respectively *graves*, *acutæ* and *superacutæ*.

> The lowest tone was called *gamma* and often *gamma ut* (whence the term 'gamut' for the scale in general). Other tones were called by their letter-names plus whatever syllables belong to them; as, for 'middle C,' *C solfaut*, or, for the uppermost or extreme tone, *E la* (whence the literary expression 'E la' for the extreme of anything).
>
> Originally the tones were not studied by means of the syllables, but later it became customary to use the syllables of one hexachord as far as they served and then to shift to those of another, if the melody went beyond. This shifting was called 'mutation,' and was somewhat analogous to modulation.
>
> Each tone was felt to derive its character from its place in a hexachord, and the similarity of the hexachords made it easy to imitate melodic effects from one to the other. The consequences of this way of regarding tones and their relations lasted long after the system as a whole was superseded by the modern system of octochords.
>
> To facilitate learning and using the system, the so-called 'Guidonian Hand' was invented — a method of assigning the various tones to the joints of the hand so as to be localized in thought. This device took its name from *Guido d'Arezzo* (see sec. 31), though that he invented it is not likely.

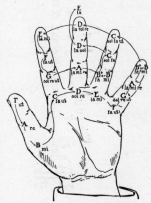

FIG. 41. — Guidonian Hand.

ut me uf dau & confiat ber a bi ullei hiui deuifme

FIG. 42.

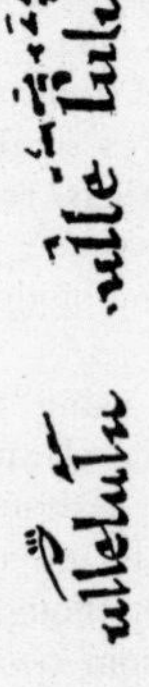

ullehutu ulle lulu v

FIG. 43.

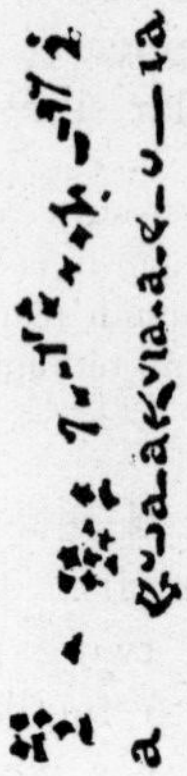

a ......ia

FIG. 44.

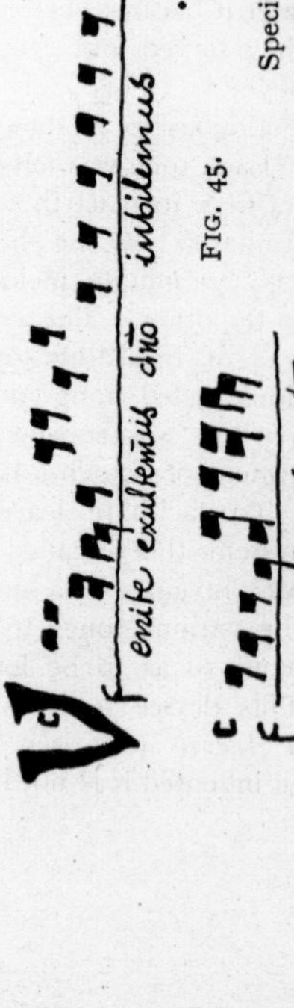

enite exultemus dno inbilemus

FIG. 45.

deo salutari nostro

Steguidao nui re   re cefi fa lan

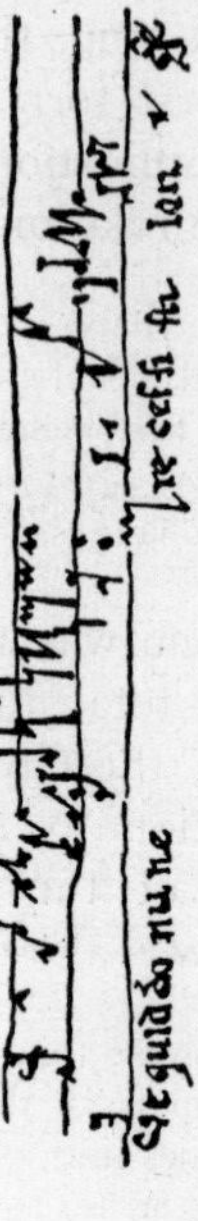

FIG. 46.

Specimens of Notation in Neumes: — FIG. 42.— 10-11th century; FIG. 43.— 11th century; FIG. 44.— 13th century; FIGS. 45-46.— 14th century. (From Spanish MSS.)

29. Notation. — One of the achievements of the early mediæval period was a partial solution of the problem of exactly representing melodies by graphic signs. For the preservation and
circulation of music a notation is as necessary as a method of
writing is for literature, but the devising of a practical system
that should be both precise and easy to use was a process
extending over many centuries.

Altogether the most important of early methods was that of
'neumes' — shorthand characters written above the words to be
sung, indicating pictorially the rise and fall of the voice in pitch.
In the early MSS., now extant, in which neumes appear (not
earlier than the 8th century), we find points and dashes used for
monotone passages, slanting strokes for upward steps, crooks
pointing downward for downward steps, compound curves for
complex motions, etc. In different places and periods these
marks took on various forms. Being a sort of cursive writing,
they naturally varied with the writer and the usage of his time.
In general, however, they tended to become more and more
regular and precise, so as to constitute not only a genuine
record, but one of fairly universal intelligibility. At a late
period they were developed into an ornate black-letter form,
harmonizing well with the finest Gothic script. Yet at the best
they were somewhat vague, serving chiefly to remind the singer
of what he had learned by rote.

> It has been conjectured that these signs were akin to the Greek
> 'accents' — marks by which the Byzantine grammarians indicated
> speech-inflections; or, more plausibly, that they were developed out of the
> marks used in Byzantine service-books to indicate the usual form of can-
> tillation. But the exact facts are uncertain.

In the 10th century a great advance was made by drawing
one or two horizontal lines across the page to mark the place of
certain tones or pitches and then adjusting the neumes to these
lines. From this beginning gradually developed the use of a
'staff' — a system of four or more such lines. To make the
significance of these staff-lines evident, one or more of them
were marked at the beginning with the letters of the tones to
which they were assigned. The letters most used were F, C
and G, and from the mediæval characters for these were
gradually developed the modern 'clefs.'

The first line to be thus used was for the tone F and was originally colored red, and the second was for C, colored yellow or green. The use of colored lines was not long continued.

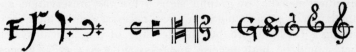

FIG. 47. — Genesis of Clefs from Gothic Letters.

Although experiments with a kind of staff began in the 9th century, its significant use dates from the 10th.

The modern arrangement of treble and bass staffs braced together is supposed to have come from an old eleven-line or 'great' staff, from which the middle line is omitted to facilitate seeing to what pitch the notes refer.

G

C

F

30. The Letter-Names. — Parallel with the growth of the neumes came the adoption of letter-names for tones. The idea had already been applied by the Greeks (see sec. 21), but the old Greek system was not directly imitated.

The Byzantines seem to have used the letters δ, φ, λ, μ (initials of Dorian, Phrygian, Lydian and Mixolydian) for certain tones, and they also applied the letters α, β, γ, δ, ε, ζ, η to the successive tones of an octave-scale — incorporating them also into a set of solmization-syllables, πα, βου, γα, δι, κε, ζω, νη. But these usages had no lasting result.

The use of Latin letters had many varieties. At one time fifteen letters were employed (A to P) to designate the tones of two octaves. More satisfactory was the use of but seven letters (A to G), repeated in successive octaves. The precise tone with which such names began was not necessarily the tone now called A, but might be any tone that was assumed as a starting-point. In all cases the series was counted upward from the gravest tone (the reverse of the Greek method). As the system reached its final form, the lowest G was added, and was called Γ (*gamma*) for distinction. (See table on p. 68.)

As the tone-system developed, the need was felt for both B and B♭, which were distinguished by differently shaped forms, B being angular (♮) and called *B durum* or *quadratum*, while B♭ was rounded (♭) and called *B molle* or *rotundum*. From the former ultimately came the modern 'natural' (♮) and also the peculiar German name H for B♮, while from the latter came the modern 'flat' (♭) and the German name B for B♭. The modern 'sharp' (♯) is simply a variation of the 'natural.'

It should be added that the letter-notation was first worked out for instruments (especially the organ) rather than for song, but its convenience soon established it for both. The first sure instances of its practical use are in the writings of *Notker* (d. 912) and of *Hucbald* (d. 930 ?). The ascriptions of the invention of the letter-system to Gregory the Great or to Boethius are not well supported.

31. Certain Pioneers. — Prior to the 11th century information regarding individual musicians is extremely scanty and uncertain. That music was made a subject of study in many ecclesiastical circles is clear, but the scope of thought about it was too narrow for the display of great originality or leadership. For convenience of reference, however, a few items are here collected. (See also sec. 36.)

Many traditions point to the early establishment of a school for church-singers at Rome, but whether this can be credited to Pope Sylvester (d. 335) is doubtful, or to any other before the 5th century. By the 9th century, however, such schools had become common, not only in Italy, but in France and England, especially in connection with strong monasteries or under the care of energetic prelates. In France the Emperor Charlemagne (d. 814) was especially interested in fostering them. From about 700, hints begin to appear of the composition of melodies by various ecclesiastics, which are suggestive of the growing attention to the art.

Flaccus Alcuin (d. 804), Abbot of Canterbury and later of Tours, supplies our earliest reference to the eight church modes; and he is echoed some decades later by **Aurelian** of Réomé.

Notker Balbulus (d. 912), a high-born and cultivated monk of St. Gall, is noted for his development of 'sequences' as a part of the musical treatment of the Mass. At first these were prose hymns fitted to the rambling codas or 'jubilations' that were added to the 'Alleluia' sung between the Epistle and the Gospel. Later the term was extended to metrical hymns, the writing of which, with appropriate melodies, became common in the later Middle Ages. (About 1000 sequences are now extant, but their prescribed use was discontinued in 1568, with four or five exceptions.) Notker also wrote upon the theory of music.

Hucbald (d. 930?), a monk of St. Amand, near Tournai, was identified with music all his life. Several works bearing his name are extant, though not all are surely his. These supply the earliest instance of staff-lines to indicate pitch (the words written in the spaces, without note-signs), use peculiar characters for the finals of the modes (often called 'the Dacian notation'), and show a clear conception of part-singing in parallel motion (*organum*).

Oddo (d. 942), Abbot of Cluny from 927, also active in music from his youth,

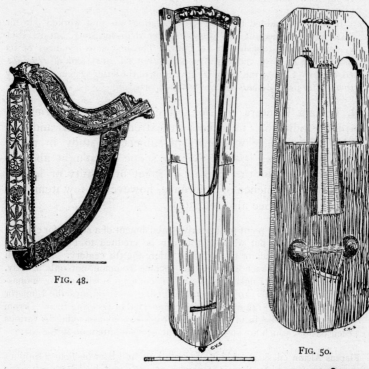

FIG. 48.

FIG. 50.

FIG. 49.

FIG. 48.— Ancient Irish
Harp.

FIG. 49.— Ancient
Rotte, of the lyre type.

FIG. 50.— Welsh Crwth,
showing the transition to
the viol type.

FIG. 51.— Modern Hur-
dy-Gurdy, with keyboard.

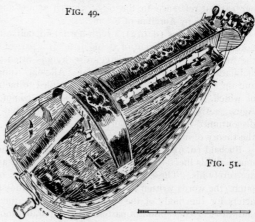

FIG. 51.

CHAPTER V

POLYPHONY AND SECULAR SONG

33. The Polyphonic Idea. — The positive achievements of the
centuries following 1200 stand in striking contrast to the timid
experiments of those before. From this point onward the art
of music becomes interestingly interwoven with progress in
other fields, being a phase of the general intellectual awakening
of Europe that preceded the Renaissance.

> Among the historic conditions to be borne in mind are (*a*) the break-
> ing up of Charlemagne's empire in the 9th century, with the gradual dis-
> integration of the feudal social system; (*b*) the Crusades in the 12th and
> 13th centuries, with their immense stimulus of thought and activity,
> especially among the lower classes; and (*c*) the new life in the fine arts
> generally, as shown by the rise of Gothic architecture about the 12th
> century and of Italian painting in the 13th.

The distinctive feature of the period in music was a profound
alteration in the aim of composition.   In Greek music and its
successor, the Gregorian style, the one desire was for a single
melodic outline to enforce and beautify a verbal text.   All
music was a specialized outgrowth or derivative of poetic speech.
A new era came in when it was seen that music might have
beauty and meaning more or less independent of its words, being built up into a fabric or edifice of tones by massing and
interweaving two or more voice-parts like strands or threads.

The transition to this new idea involved two lines of effort,
which for convenience may be taken up separately.   These
were (*a*) the reduction of melodies to regular rhythmic form,
with such accentual and durational values of the tones that
their motions could be accurately measured and mutually adjusted, and (*b*) the discovery of ways in which melodies could
be simultaneously combined so as to be concordant, or, if dis-
cordant, still satisfactory and effective.   The former effort led
to a theory of 'time,' the latter to a theory of 'counterpoint,'
and the two were mutually interdependent at every point.

34. Time and its Notation. — That the early Plain-Song had a general rhythm, often approaching regularity, was a matter of course, since all prose has some rhythm. But strict rhythm was for Gregorian melodies incidental and even objectionable. Music, however, could not avoid being affected by the rhythms and metres of poetry, in which accent and time-values were systematized. The most plausible theory of the appearance of a time-system in music is that which attributes it to certain verse-schemes that were adopted as patterns for musical phrases.

The first clear reference that we have to this subject (13th century) assumes the existence of equal measures, implying a sense of strict rhythm. It presents the notion that triple rhythm is better than duple, and in the subdivision of the parts, a long note is assumed to be equal to three shorter ones unless the contrary is specified — all different from our present view. With these fundamental conceptions of time, what was called Mensural or Measured Music rapidly developed into numerous metric patterns.

Tempus perfectum was the term for triple rhythm and tempus imperfectum for duple, while prolatio major indicated a triple division of long notes and prolatio minor a duple division. This exaltation of triple types may have been due to various causes — it was often associated with the theological doctrine of the Trinity!

Immediately arose the need for a notation corresponding to these ideas. The old neumes were still used and also the square characters derived from them. The virga, ❯, and the punctum, ◆, had passed into the longa, ◼, and the brevis, ◼. The former now came to be the standard long note, the latter the standard short note. One longa in major prolation was equal to three breves, in minor prolation to two. The system of notes was further increased by the maxima, ◼| (double longa) and the semibrevis, ◆ (half-brevis), and after 1300 by further notes of less value — the minima, ♩, semiminima, ♪, and finally the fusa, ♪, and semifusa, ♪.

These notes were written at first as above, with solid or black heads. In the 15th century open or white heads appear, and in the 16th they begin to be rounded. The derivation of the modern forms is evident: —

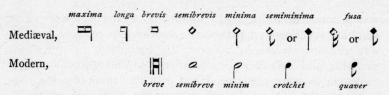

Besides these simple notes various compound characters, called 'ligatures,' were used to denote conventional note-groups.

For a time, in the transition from black to white notes, small distinctions of value were indicated by using some red notes or by retaining black heads for some notes while the rest were white. These niceties of notation were comprehended under the general term 'color,' the need for which ceased in the 16th century.

Corresponding with the various notes were equivalent pauses or rests.

Signs were early placed at the beginning of the staff to show the kind of rhythm and the prolation intended. Tempus perfectum was marked by a circle, O, tempus imperfectum by a half-circle, C; if the prolation was minor, a dot was placed within these, ⊙ or ℂ. Not until about 1600 were the measures regularly marked off, and then often only by a sort of check-mark — the rudiment of the modern bar.

The sign for imperfect time or duple rhythm survives in the modern time-signatures for quadruple and duple rhythm : —

It should be added that the growth of notation was much influenced by the use of various forms of 'tablature' — special notations devised for certain instruments (see sec. 52).

The first traces of attention to time-problems occur in the 10th and 11th centuries, long before we have a statement of the mensural system in full.

35. Organum, Discant and Measured Music. — The germ of counterpoint lay in experiments with combining two voices. Even the Greeks had a special term, 'magadizing' (from the instrument, the *magadis*, on which octaves could be played), for the singing together of two voices in octaves ; and such melodic duplication was felt by them and by their successors to differ essentially from pure unison. So in the Middle Ages another step was taken by adding to a given melody what was called an *organum* (from the instrument on which it was possible), which was a series of tones a fifth higher or a fourth lower. The resulting succession of parallels — atrocious to modern taste — was slightly interfered with by the limitations of the scales available and by other considerations, so that gradually other consonances were recognized and also the value of some contrary motion. These experiments were at first confined to but two voices, the one with a Plain-Song melody to which the other added consonances in either similar or contrary motion; but occasionally one or two more voices were added to these, thus preparing the way for some apprehension of harmony proper. For the union of two voices the terms 'diaphony' or 'discant' (or 'descant') were used. It appears that experiments of this sort were freely made before 1200 and were not unknown before 1000.

But much progress with discant was possible only through some recognition of accent and stress and of the groupings of tones that they generate. When not under the accent, occasional dissonances were permitted among the prevailing consonances, and even some chromatic alterations of the modes to avoid the suggestion of the tritone. For a time thirds and sixths were classed as dissonances, but they were soon permitted if duly supported by consonances. Gradually a number of rules of voice-leading became fixed, which have remained in force ever since. Combined with these were certain recognized time-schemes for phrases and sections that were thought to be typical. It is likely that the groping after principles of organization in time and accent had much to do with determining those of voice-part writing.

Among these tentative efforts certain special forms or methods of writing were favored, such as fitting a flowing melody to a reiterated burden or drone-bass, or arbitrarily uniting two melodies not originally meant to go together, or devising a second part by mere extemporization. The latter process may explain some of the seemingly lawless handling of added voices. The use of a burden gave obvious unity and a degree of 'form.' The forced union of incongruous melodies may have suggested the 'rondel' or 'rota.' These latter terms sometimes referred to a brief three-part song fitted to a poem of the rondeau type, sometimes to a three-part 'round' in which all the voices began together and proceeded by exchanging phrases, and in one famous instance to a true four-part canon which rests on a brief two-part canonic burden that is repeated over and over while the chief canon proceeds.

This last instance is the noted piece, " Sumer is icumen in," found in a
MS. in the British Museum, which on internal evidence is thought to date
from between 1225 and 1240, and to have emanated from Reading Abbey
(35 miles west of London).   The principal words celebrate the spring as
follows : —

> " Sumer is icumen in,   Lhude sing cuccu;
> Groweth sed and bloweth med,   And springth the wode nu;
> Awe bleteth after lomb,   Lhouth after calve cu;
> Bulluc sterteth, bucke verteth,   Murie sing cuccu.
> Wel singes thu cuccu;   Ne swik thu naver nu." —

though there are also Latin words — a hymn to the Virgin.   The theme
or subject is a flowing and joyous melody, sung in strict imitation (canon
at the unison) by four equal voices entering at intervals of four measures.
The burden swings monotonously back and forth between tonic and dominant harmony.

The questions raised by this specimen are not readily answered.   Its
probable date and place are not easily reconciled with its strictly modern
scale and form, its secular charm, and its almost flawless part-writing.
Perhaps it is a union of ecclesiastical counterpoint with a theme and a
style belonging to Trouvère music (see sec. 39).

36. Literature about Music. — While until about 1400 we do
not find much actual composition above the level of experiment,
the amount of literary discussion of music is significant.   The
topics most treated are naturally the practical handling of
Plain-Song, the problems of notation and of Mensural Music,
with questions about consonance and the rudiments of counterpoint.   Almost every one of the writers known to us by name
was an ecclesiastic, especially of the Benedictine Order.   A
large number of works, however, are anonymous and not
certainly attributable as to either country or exact period.

As will be seen from the following table, the geographical distribution of
the writers that can be identified changes about 1100.   Before then the
greater number belong to Germany or parts of France — roughly speaking, to the valleys of the Rhine and the Rhone.   After that time the
greater number are from northern France or England, with Germany
again and finally Italy added in the 14th century.   From the 12th century
Spain is more important than the table indicates, since most of the extant
works there are anonymous.   A glance at the places indicated will show
what localities were musically most active.

For convenience, all the chief writers up to the appearance of printed
books are here included, beginning with the pioneers, some of whom have
already been named, and crossing over into the 15th century.

Only a few brief notes can here be made upon the many names in this
table.

G

MEDIÆVAL WRITERS ON MUSIC

(Date of death in parenthesis)

Century	England	France and Netherlands	Germany and Switzerland	Italy and Spain	Century
8th		Alcuin (804) *Tours*			8th
9th		Amalarius (837?) *Paris* Agobardus (840) *Lyons* Aurelian *Réomé*			9th
10th		Hucbald (930) *St. Amand* Oddo (942) *Cluny*	Notker Balb. (912) *St. Gall* Regino (915) *Prüm*		10th
11th	Osbern *Canterbury*	Adelboldus (1027) *Utrecht* Bernelinus *Paris* Pseudo-Hucbald ? Raoul *Laon* Joannes Presbyter	Notker Labeo (1022) *St. Gall* Berno (1048) *Reichenau* Aaron (1052) *Cologne* Hermann Contr. (1054) *Reichenau* Aribo (1078) *Freising* Wilhelm (1091) *Hirschau* Theogerus *Hirschau, Metz*	Guido d' Arezzo (1050 ?)	11th
12th	Ælrede (1166) *Rivaulx* John of Salisbury (1180)	Joh. Cotton *Brussels* Bernard (1153) *Clairvaux* Guido *Châlis* Pseudo-Aristotle ? Alanus (1203) *Clairvaux*	Eberhard *Freising* Udalschalk (1151) *Augsburg*		12th

Century					Century
13th	Gregory *Bridlington* Simon Tailler William de la Mare Roger Bacon(1294) *Oxford*	Garlandia[1] (1245?) *Paris* Petrus de Cruce *Paris* Franco[1] Petrus Picardus Hieronymus de Mor. *Paris* Elias Salomo *St. Astière* Vincent de *Beauvais* (1264?) Garlandia[2]	Franco[2] *Cologne* Albert Magnus (1280) *Ratisbon*	Ægidius Zamorensis Marchetto di Padua	13th
14th	Odington(1330?) *Evesham* Robert de Handlo Simon Tunstede (1369) Theinred *Dover*	Guido (1315?) *St. Denis* Joh. de Muris[1] *Normandy* Joh. de Muris[2] *Paris* Phil. de Vitry (1361) *Meaux* Leo Hebræus	Engelbert (1331) *Admont* Hugo (1360) *Reutlingen*	Raimund Lull (1315) Joh. Verulus *Anagni* Thedoricus de Campo	14th
15th	Lionel Power Chilston Thos. Walsyngham *St. Albans* John Hanboys	Henricus de Zeelandia Ægidius de Murino Arnulphus *St. Gilles*	Joh. Keck *Tegernsee* Rud. Agricola (1485) *Heidelberg* Adam v. Fulda (1500?) *Würzburg*	Beldemandis *Padua* Nicolò de Capua *Rome* Ugolino (1449) *Ferrara* Anselm *Parma* Antonio di Lucca Filippo da Caserta *Naples* Johannes de Mantua (1473) *Parma* John Hothby (1487) *Lucca*	15th

Among the many elucidations of, or commentaries upon, Guido, that of **Aribo** of Freising (d. 1078) is specially valuable because of the nearness of date.

In the prolix work of **Joannes Presbyter** (late 11th century) is a vocabulary of terms — the earliest known.

Johannes Cotton, probably of English birth, was a singing-teacher in a monastery near Brussels. His treatise is noteworthy for its painstaking description of the harmonic ideas of his day, especially as to organum and discant. He refers to the hexachord-system, but does not know about measured music.

The other 12th-century writers are not specially important, except that the English **Ælrede** of Rivaulx (d. 1166) and **John** of Salisbury (d. c. 1180) imply that rather free part-singing was being attempted, but without system, while the writer known as ' **Aristotle** ' is allied to the later mensuralists in his desire to classify intervals for contrapuntal use, though in his list of dissonances he counts the sixths as best, the thirds as medium, and the tritone and the seconds as worst.

All works after 1200 indicate the advance of thought regarding both the classification of intervals and the time-relations of part-writing. [Three striking cases of identical names are associated with works that are diverse in matter or period. The difficulty is roughly solved by enumerating two Garlandias, two Francos, and two Johannes de Muris.]

The first **Garlandia** shows a clear insight into systematic counterpoint, including even the principle of imitation between the voices. He, like his successors, reckons the thirds as consonances, is feeling his way towards a time-system, and uses some chromatic tones to soften harsh progressions.

Franco of Cologne (though sadly confused with **Franco** of Paris) is apparently the first to give full expression to the theories of intervals and of time that were becoming generally accepted by his time. His great treatise on Measured Music is one of the most famous and useful in the whole period before the 15th century.

Hieronymus de Moravia, a Parisian monk, makes clear the opposition between the popular instinct for duple rhythms and the arbitrary ruling of the mensuralists in favor of triple ; while **Marchetto di Padua**, somewhat later, ventures to assert the superiority of duple forms. The latter also argues against the expression *musica falsa* for chromatic alterations of the modes, claiming them to be legitimate and necessary.

For some reason English musicians and those in touch with them seem to have been more ready than others to give up the Pythagorean tuning of the thirds (major $= \frac{81}{64}$ and minor $= \frac{32}{27}$) in favor of the modern tuning (major $= \frac{5}{4}$, minor $= \frac{6}{5}$), with its utility in the forming of triads. **Walter Odington** (d. after 1330), writing about 1300, argues strongly for this latter view, and was probably the first to emphasize the major triad as a real three-part consonance. He also is the first to mention the minim ($\flat$).

The most significant theorists in the 14th century were **Johannes de Muris** (two writers) and **Philippe de Vitry**. The first Johannes de Muris, ' the Norman,' trained at Oxford, is now distinguished from the second, ' of France,' who from 1321 was teacher and later rector at the Sorbonne. The former supplies the most extensive of mediæval treatises, treating of intervals, consonances and dissonances, ancient music, the church modes, solmization, measured music and discant, all regarded with decided conservatism. The latter, represented by several works, is much more radical, and, like Philippe de Vitry, advocates counterpoint for several voices, with free use of chromatics and rhythmic variety. Indeed, it is now queried whether the 'Ars nova' ascribed to Philippe de Vitry does not belong to this second Johannes de Muris.

Arabic writing upon musical topics was voluminous during the mediæval period. The earliest theoretical writer was **Chalil** (d. 776), followed in the 9th and 10th centuries by writers like **al-Kindi** (d. 862) and the illustrious **al-Farabi** (d. c. 950), the latter of whom was a diligent student of Greek authorities. Much later, especially in the 14th century, came a host of writers under Persian influence, prominent among whom were **Saffieddin** and **al-Khadir**. In their writings there seems to be a mingling of some ideas derived from Arabian tradition with a large amount from other sources. How these elements are to be disentangled is not clear. The doctrine of the 'messel' (proportion or measure), expounded by **Mahmud Shirasi** (d. 1315) and others, was a noteworthy effort to systemize the mathematics of intervals, including the earliest-known recognition of both major and minor thirds and sixths as consonances. Among the discussions of æsthetics mention may be made of a striking essay by **al-Ghazzali** (d. 1113) on the relation of music to religious emotion.

---

37. Secular Song. — At just the period when the scholastic music of the Church was clumsily struggling with the problem of polyphony, came the first signal outcroppings of secular song as an equally important part of musical development. These instinctive efforts of the popular spirit to find an outlet in music, though without far-reaching purpose, achieved some striking immediate results and at length contributed much to the enrichment of the art.

For convenience, the successive movements are treated summarily, though the last of them runs over into the 16th century.

38. The Troubadours. — The first definite movement occurred in Provence (now southeastern France), probably soon after 1100. This was presently paralleled in northern France by a similar, though distinct, movement. The first was that of the Troubadours, the second, of the Trouvères (both words meaning 'finders' or 'inventors'). As will be seen, these were poet-singers, at first wholly of the upper or wealthy class, and their impulse was more literary than musical. The musical consequences of their work appeared later.

The geographical range of the Troubadours was from northern Spain eastward to Venice, and from the Mediterranean northward in France to Lyons and Poitiers. The headquarters was in the basin of the Garonne and the lower valley of the Rhone — the region of which Toulouse is the centre.

The first celebrated name among the Troubadours is that of **William,** Count of Poitiers (d. 1127), and conspicuous later were princes like **Alfonso II.** of Aragon (d. 1196), **Richard I.** of England (d. 1199), and **Thibaut IV.** of Navarre (d. 1253), with Queen **Eleanor** of France, later of England (d. 1204), not to speak of scores of others with every kind of lordly title. At the outset, then, the movement was confined to the leisurely and elegant class, though its influence speedily spread to other classes.

In a peculiar sense the songs of the Troubadours embodied one side of the idea of chivalry or knightliness. They especially expressed the sentiment of love, but the form of love chiefly magnified was one almost impossible for modern thought to accept as wholesome, since it was the praise and even adoration of married women by others than their husbands. While doubtless this notion was fantastic and often ran to lawless extremes, yet it was by no means essentially or inevitably base. It was the effort of an age not fully emerged from barbarism to glorify the attraction of sex and even to etherealize it. It exalted womanhood as perhaps never before, and it unlocked the door of literary expression for intense feeling of every kind. The style of poetry thus generated was not only sentimentally extravagant, but often stilted and manneristic.

The themes most chosen were the beauty and worth of the lady to whom the knight gave his homage, the exploits of gallantry, labor or peril on her behalf, the joy of meeting or the pain of absence, the many phantasies and yearnings of the lover, the look of nature in all its aspects to the eye that love had quickened, and sometimes flights of martial, heroic or even religious ecstasy.

Certain forms were favorites, like the *canson* or stanza-song in general, the *tenso* or dialogue, the *sirvente* or narrative, with many special varieties, like the *alba* or morning-song, the *serena* or evening-song, the *balada* or dance-song, the *planh* or complaint, etc. Great ingenuity was shown in the elaboration of curious verse-forms, with reiterated rhymes, studied effects in assonance and the like, and highly complicated stanzas. Yet, in spite of the tendency to mere technique, the lyric impulse was so strong that in these efforts was the source of the entire modern art of lyric verse. The impetus thus given lasted long after the Troubadour period ended, explaining many a feature of poetry in Italy, France, Spain and England. In Italy, for example, the style of *Dante* (d. 1321) and of *Petrarch* (d. 1374) is clearly based on Provençal originals.

With the verse-making impulse ran a musical one. The Troubadour songs were meant to be sung, not recited or read. Probably some of them were written for popular airs already in use, but most of them necessitated new melodies. The forms chosen were essentially different from the traditional Plain-Song. They show a fairly clear sense of tonality as now understood, often in the major mode. Their phrases are well defined, corresponding to the lines of the words, usually with but one tone to a syllable, ending with a cadence, and based upon a regular accentual rhythm. Many airs, therefore, have attractiveness to the modern ear. Their historic importance is obvious. Wherever this minstrelsy penetrated, it fixed a taste for styles quite diverse from that of the Church, one close to the feeling of the common people and apt for their use. It thus prepared the way for the transformation of scholastic music in the 16th century. In viewing the musical situation prior to 1500 this factor cannot be neglected.

It is not clear what was the source of the musical side of the Troubadour song. It has been thought that in Provence and northern Italy traditions of the ancient popular song of the Romans may have lingered. Keltic influences were strong in Provence, and the Kelts have always been musical. It is likely, too, that something came from the experiences of the Crusaders, possibly hints from Saracenic or Byzantine songs or from reports of the Moorish culture in Spain.

The Troubadours made increasing use of 'joglars' or 'jongleurs,' singers or players who might or might not have independent poetic genius. These helpers were of various classes and served for pay. Through them the scope of the movement was greatly extended, so that it ultimately reached the lower classes generally. Thus a style that was at first aristocratic became truly popular.

Probably the jongleurs were often drawn from the itinerant mountebanks that were numerous in southern and western Europe. These artistic 'tramps' had varied accomplishments, like singing, dancing, gymnastic and sleight-of-hand tricks, etc.—as their English names, 'juggler' and 'gleeman,' signify. They thrived on the popular craving for diversion at a time when diversions were few.

Incidentally, the use of hired assistants served to differentiate a class who made music a business or occupation—of which curious consequences have continued ever since.

Both poets and singers made use of portable instruments,

especially the harp, lute and viol, though none of these was yet
technically advanced. We do not know precisely how accompaniments were played, whether giving detached tones or chords
merely to sustain the voice, or doubling the melody of the song
itself, or here and there giving an additional melody, or supplying enrichment by preludes, interludes and cadenzas. But we
may infer that the fresh genius that expressed itself in words
and song was not wanting in the accompaniment.

> The period of the Troubadours proper came to an end in the 13th
> century, primarily because of the political turmoils over the Albigensian
> heresy — that strange revolt against the abuses and the autocracy of the
> Church which reached such proportions about 1200 that Innocent III. pro-
> claimed a crusade against it. From 1208 to 1220 a furious war ensued,
> into which most of the nobles of southern France were drawn in self-
> defense, whether or not interested in Albigensian views, and which
> resulted in the total spoliation of the country. This practically destroyed
> the wealthy class that sustained the Troubadours and ruined the entire
> civilization of which they were a part. By the middle of the 13th cen-
> tury what traces remained of literary life in Provence and Languedoc
> had begun to be absorbed into the rising current of French literature
> proper.

39. The Trouvères. — The Trouvères of northern France
seem to have caught their first inspiration from the Troubadours and to have imitated them largely in choice of themes,
treatment and general spirit. But the differences were also
notable. The Trouvères, for example, loved to compile and set
forth the rich treasures of legend in Brittany and Normandy, to
accumulate the myths of Charlemagne and other traditional
heroes, and to exalt the romantic tales of the Crusades. The
language of the north was not so varied and musical as that of
Provence, and the warmth of passion and vivacity of fancy
were also slighter. There was less organization of effort
among the Trouvère poets, less competition among themselves
for technical approbation, and less class-exclusiveness. Around
them, too, were many strong monasteries and abbeys, where
ecclesiastics were leaders in literature and art, and where poetry
and music had long been valued in religious worship. Naturally, then, the Trouvère poetry often turned to sacred themes,
and its melodies were not always sharply different from those
of the Church. From this it followed that while the Troubadours stimulated poetic literature in general without much

direct musical effect, the Trouvères helped to shape and direct
the great school of composition in Flanders and England that
became conspicuous after 1400 (see sec. 43).

> The region of the Trouvères included all of northern France from
> Tours and Angers on the Loire to Arras in the north and also down the
> valley of the Moselle to the Rhine. Since the interchange between
> France and England was close, the art spread readily across the Channel.
> Paris was a natural centre, as it had been the capital of the kings of
> France since about 1000, and boasted a royal musical establishment —
> the Royal Chapel.

> To this region belonged many of the theoretical writers already named
> (sec. 36). In the 12–13th centuries **Leoninus, Perotinus, Robert de Sabilon**
> and **Petrus de Cruce** were successively choirmasters at Notre Dame in
> Paris, and all contributed to the advancing art of polyphonic writing for the
> Church.

> The best-known of the Trouvères proper was **Adam de la Hâle** (d. 1287),
> born at Arras in 1240, at first employed in church music, but later attracted
> to a roving life, living at Paris and finally at Naples. His genius was shown
> in lyric songs in Trouvère style, in polyphonic rondeaux and motets, and in
> several song-plays, chief of which was *Robin et Marion* (Naples, 1285), which
> is often called the first comic opera. His works are most interesting as
> representing the complex styles of the period that presaged the era of the
> Netherlanders.

40. The Minnesinger. — Soon after the rise of the Troubadours
in France a somewhat similar movement began in Germany,
though whether the two were directly connected is disputed.
Perhaps they were simply parallel expressions of the spirit of
the time. The poets of this order were called Minnesinger
(love-singers, from *minne*, love). It is thought that their art
was much more an expansion of the mediæval adoration of the
Virgin as the ideal of womanhood than in the case of the Troubadours, but it was also an expression of the spirit of chivalry, for
their verses were full of the same fanciful gallantry, though
their objects were not so constantly married women.

> The leaders and patrons of this school of poesy and song were of noble
> rank, notably all the Hohenstaufens from Barbarossa (d. 1190) to Con-
> radin (d. 1268), with Wenceslaus I. of Bohemia (d. 1253) and many
> princes of eastern Germany generally.

> The Minnesinger flourished chiefly in the region of southern Germany
> included in a triangle whose base extends eastward from Strassburg or
> Basle on the Upper Rhine to Vienna on the Danube, the apex being in
> Thuringia or Franconia. Celebrated headquarters were Freiburg in the
> Breisgau on the west, Vienna in the east, and several points in Thuringia.

This region abuts on the west upon that affected by the Trouvères. Hence the western Minnesinger were often influenced by French models, while those in Austria or Bohemia were rather dominated by indigenous popular song.

The early strength of the movement, with its connection with courtly pomp, was evinced in a notable song-contest said to have been held at the stately fortress of the Wartburg (Thuringia) in 1207 under the patronage of the Landgrave Hermann—an occasion celebrated in a half-mythic way by a curious narrative poem (whence came part of the plot of Wagner's opera *Tannhäuser* in 1845).

In general, the Minnesongs differ from those of Provence in more emphasis upon the beauty of nature, upon religious feelings, and upon abstract qualities of character, though many are not wanting in passion, pure fancy and even jocularity. Their versification is far less conscious and artificial. They are often less lyric than epic or reflective in style, verging more upon heroic or bardic poetry than the casual songs of the light-hearted Troubadours. Being akin to the sagas and runes of the North generally, materials in them have often been sought for dramatic treatment.

The melodies were more austere and stately than those of Provence, though ultimately marked by the same modern rhythm, phrase and tonality, with the indescribable naïveté that belongs to Germanic folk-music. At first, however, they adhered more to the formless style of Plain-Song, not very different from a modulated recitative. The text was primary and the melody subordinate, so that, like the Greeks, the Minnesinger have been called 'rhapsodists' rather than song-singers. Yet the principle of the true song was not absent, finally shaping melodies into forms related to the popular airs that in the 16th century led to the Protestant chorales.

Performance depended much on the warmth and depth of expression imparted by the singer rather than on the essential charm of the tone-design. Hence Minnesongs can seldom be reproduced with the same pleasurable effect as, for instance, some of the Trouvère songs.

As a rule, the Minnesinger avoided the help of jongleurs, probably from a sense of the dignity of their art. They were their own interpreters and accompanists, and, though using the same classes of instruments as in France, were not apparently urgent about instrumental effects. The true Minnesong, there-

fore, did not pass readily into forms of popular song. Its character and associations kept it mainly in the hands of a limited,
aristocratic class. Its direct influence upon music in general
was less than in the case of the Troubadours.

> Yet there is evidence that it contributed to the early development of the
> Meistersinger movement, which belonged to the middle classes. Possibly,
> too, back of the Minnesong, particularly in Austria, lay forms of popular
> song, now lost.

The chronological limits of the Minnesinger period are somewhat disputed.
Some include in it only poets of the later 12th century, ending the list with
Heinrich von Meissen [Frauenlob] (d. 1318), while others add some names in
the early 13th century.

41. The Meistersinger. — Following the Minnesinger came the
Meistersinger. The exact relation between the two is not clear,
though the Meistersinger were wont to look back to certain of
their predecessors as authorities, and there is an evident kinship
between the more formal Minnesongs and the mechanicalness
of the typical Mastersongs.

> The name Meistersinger came from the notion that only those who
> had won the technical title of 'masters' or experts were competent to
> fix the standard of verse and song. It also recalls the fact that among
> the Minnesinger a poet of less than noble rank was called *Meister* (in
> distinction from *Ritter*, knight).

Unlike their forerunners, the Meistersinger were wholly drawn
from the rapidly rising burgher or tradesman class, often from the
humblest and rudest artisans. Their prominence from the 14th
to the 16th centuries was an incident in the evolution of society,
when the old régime of country life under feudal conditions was
being replaced by manufactures and trades in organized towns.

> A striking characteristic of the Meistersinger was their custom of
> forming local societies, more or less secret and exclusive, like the many
> guilds or trades-unions into which craftsmen of every sort were begin-
> ning to be organized in the strong commercial towns of Germany.
> These clubs were governed by elaborate rules. Entrance was by a kind
> of initiation. The members were divided into classes, from the novices
> or 'scholars' up to the accepted 'masters,' and were presided over
> by several kinds of officers. Each guild had its hall, its insignia of
> membership, its special rules and traditional ceremony or procedure.
> Some of their gatherings were of the nature of drills or singing-schools,
> while others were formal contests or trials of skill. In the latter the
> function of the judges or 'markers' was important, since by their rulings

a standard of effort was set up, often in a way to discourage all freshness of invention.

Starting from Mayence on the Rhine soon after 1300, the guilds multiplied rapidly throughout central Germany, the noted centres in the 14th century being Frankfort, Colmar, Nuremberg, Zwickau and Prague. To these were added in the 15th Strassburg, Augsburg, Ratisbon, Ulm and Munich. In the 16th the centre of activity shifted more to the east and north. Although after 1600 the significance of the movement rapidly declined, yet organizations continued in many places. Indeed, it was not until 1839 that the last of the guilds, that of Ulm, disbanded, and the last person who had been a member did not die till 1876.

Among the many Meistersinger known to us by name the only one of lasting renown was the cobbler of Nuremberg, **Hans Sachs** (d. 1576), whose homely but sturdy genius has been widely recognized.

The historic influence of the Meistersinger movement was considerable, since it affected all Germany and spread somewhat to adjacent countries. In many quarters it was supposed to represent a real form of art. In the later 15th century and afterward, some of its strange melodies were adopted as subjects for treatment by composers, and probably they exercised some influence upon the beginnings of popular religious song at the Reformation. But, on the whole, the movement was devoid of that ideality, freedom and spontaneity that make for genuine artistic progress. Its only positive utilities were its indirect emphasis upon music as a dignified and worthy pursuit and the dissemination among its adherents of a certain degree of technical knowledge.

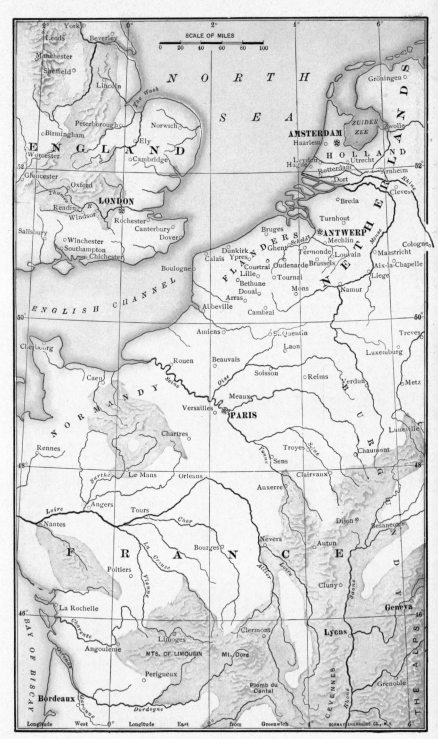

SCALE OF MILES

0   20   40   60   80   100

MAP I. — FRANCE, THE LOW COUNTRIES AND ENGLAND.

CHAPTER VI

THE FIFTEENTH CENTURY

42. In General. — We now turn back to the unfolding art of polyphony, which, from about 1400, was at length thoroughly mastered and fully applied to religious uses. From this time the mere invention and sharpening of implements gave place to positive artistic production. Though few of even the best works of the 15th century remain in use now, simply because the musical world has entered paths then quite unimagined, their real importance remains unquestionable. No just view of any art is possible without conceding all honor to its pioneers.

While the growth of secular song from the 12th century was widespread, the conditions of society indicated that the chief application of music as an art must be first in the Church, which was the only social institution of general stability. The age was dominated to a peculiar degree by religion. All social life revolved about ecclesiastical observances, and the best thought took its stimulus and guidance thence. Music, like the other arts, remained emphatically the protégé and servitor of the Church.

But in the new developments we find the centre of interest shifted to the extreme west of Europe, where secular and sacred song had full opportunity to react upon each other.

43. The Netherlands the New Art-Centre. — The headquarters of progress is now found in the region north of the Seine in France and west of the Meuse — the provinces of Flanders and Brabant, with part of Burgundy.

> The reasons for the prominence of this little section were largely political — its comparative peace and the wisdom of its rulers. But they were also economic, its many populous towns being already launched on that fascinating career of commercial prosperity that presently made their people the merchant-princes of western Europe. The Netherlanders now began to display a civic and national spirit like that of the best modern nations, and their interest in music was simply a part of their general enterprise and independence.

Other parts of Europe were also moving along similar lines, though with more interruption. Northern Italy presents many analogies, especially in the prominence of large commercial towns, but there was much less unity of effort. England, too, was coming forward as a home of free enterprise, though not equal to her neighbor across the North Sea.

The period is here called that of the Netherlanders. It has also been called Flemish or Belgian, neither of which is quite satisfactory. It might also be called Burgundian, since from 1363 for over a century it owed much to the four great dukes, Philip the Bold (d. 1404), John the Fearless (d. 1419), Philip the Good (d. 1467) and Charles the Bold (d. 1477), all of whom were friends of culture, especially music and painting. Their territory varied in extent, often reaching from Antwerp on the north clear to the Mediterranean, including fully half of modern France, favorite seats of the court being Ghent or Bruges. In the struggles between France and England the dukes usually sided with the latter — which throws light on the close connection in music between the Netherlanders and the English.

The Netherland school of sacred composition took its rise in some way from the later developments of secular song in northern France. If all the facts could be gathered, it is likely that from the ablest Trouvères, like Adam de la Hâle (d. 1287), to the earliest of the contrapuntists, like Dunstable and Dufay (active by about 1420), a series of works could be found with a continuous advance in method. While we cannot adequately fill this gap of almost one hundred and fifty years, it is clear that the transition from the solo minstrel-song to the polyphonic mass was made through the form known as the 'chanson' (the same word as the *canson* of the Troubadours, but a different thing). This was a secular piece in which a central melody or air was enriched by one to three other voice-parts so as to make a rude part-song.

> The composer's object was not to produce a true chord-sequence (which would have involved more harmonic knowledge than the age possessed), but simply to match together two or three melodies as such. The foundation melody or *cantus firmus*, selected from the stock of existing songs, sacred or secular, was usually given to a middle voice (ultimately called the 'tenor,' because it 'held' or carried the theme), and the added voices were the 'bass' below and the 'alto' or 'soprano' ('treble') above, sometimes both, giving four-part effects.

From the 13th century we have a considerable list of chansonniers, with many works of varying complexity. It is evident that the art of composition is converging upon part-writing of a novel kind. In the 14th century for some reason the number

of names and works extant is not so large, but they are enough
to show that the style is being cultivated with growing assurance. At the opening of the 15th century we are suddenly
confronted by an imposing array of composers, represented
by many works in several varieties, especially masses, motets
and chansons, all showing plain connections with previous
styles, but with an artistic quality that is new. Apparently, then, the 14th century saw the gradual transmutation
of the secular part-song, often hardly more than a fugitive
improvisation, into the extended mass, wrought out with careful study and fully written down so as to secure the intended
effect. From the original stage, when the aim was the mere
amusement of some courtly circle, to the final one, when the
enrichment of the cathedral service was attempted, was a striking transition, though not unparalleled in later musical history.

Into this transition were gathered up all the discoveries of the
ecclesiastical theorists who for two or three centuries had been
at work upon the rudiments of polyphony as a science. But it
appears that only when these monkish speculations had been
touched by the spirit and spontaneity of popular song could a
genuine type of fine art emerge.

As a hint of the richness of the 13th-century chanson period it may be
noted that in the dictionaries are the names of more than a score of writers
from whom at least 300 pieces exist — all, of course, mere songs or ballads, not
developed part-songs. The origin of these was in northern France. In the
14th century we have fewer names, like **Jehannot Lescurel**, the earliest to pre-
figure the Netherland style, and **Guillaume de Machau** (d. c. 1372), from whom
many works are extant, including two- and three-part chansons, rondeaux and
motets, with one mass. All these worked in the neighborhood of Paris.
In the early 15th century we still hear of important Parisian déchanteurs —
Cesaris, Tapissier, Carmen — thought worthy to rank with the leading Netherland pioneers, besides the able **Henricus de Zeelandia**, whose writings are cited
as fully introducing the developed style of Dufay. His name shows that he
was himself a Netherlander.

44. Secular Melodies and the Mass. — Among the signs of
the dependence of the Netherland school upon the traditions
of secular music were the tendency of leading composers to
write purely secular pieces and their constant use of secular
melodies as 'subjects' for their masses and other church works.
The absolute invention of 'subjects' being almost unknown,
some favorite theme was selected as the thread about which

the counterpoint should crystallize. This 'subject,' or parts of it, was used over and over in the successive movements of a mass, supplying in the tenor a fixed nucleus more or less familiar, while the ingenuity of the composer consisted in adjusting to it manifold figures and phrases in the other voices, occasionally in imitation.

> In consequence, masses were known by the titles of their 'subjects,' as the Mass '*L'omme armé*' or '*Se la face ay pale*' (popular songs used in unnumbered instances), or Eloy's Mass '*Dixerunt discipuli*' (from Plain-Song). Later, practice-phrases from the singing-school were similarly used, as in Des Près' Mass '*La, sol, fa, re, mi*.'
>
> It should be added that this practice of mixing words and styles seems to have been one of the early characteristics of the form known as the 'motet' (see sec. 55).

Not only were the tunes of well-known songs thus incorporated, but in many cases their words were actually sung by the tenor while the other voices were proceeding with the prescribed Latin text — a practice so open to abuse, especially when frivolous or immoral thoughts were suggested, as to call out in the 16th century the formal rebuke of the Church. In the beginning, however, this free use of secular materials in the most solemn works was not irreverent, but simply a token of the source whence the whole style of writing came.

> Here is a suitable place to state once for all that wherever a musical 'mass' is mentioned, it includes only those specific exercises in the liturgy that are traditionally assigned to the choir, acting as an auxiliary to the officiants at the altar. It does not include any of the many passages recited or intoned by those officiants themselves — these being in Plain-Song. Neither does it properly include any variable parts of the service, the text of which depends upon the day or the season — these being rather 'motets.'
>
> The invariable choir exercises include (*a*) the *Kyrie eleison* or general cry for mercy that follows the Introit, (*b*) the *Gloria in excelsis* immediately succeeding, which is often divided into distinct sections, beginning respectively with the words *Dominus Deus*, *Qui tollis*, and *Quoniam tu solus*, (*c*) the *Credo* or Nicene Creed, usually divided into sections at the words *Incarnatus est*, *Crucifixus*, *Et resurrexit*, and *Et in Spiritum Sanctum*, (*d*) the *Sanctus*, with the *Hosanna*, before the Elevation, (*e*) the *Benedictus qui venit*, after the Elevation, and (*f*) the *Agnus Dei*, at the Commixture, the latter part of which, the *Dona nobis pacem*, being often treated by itself. To these are often added a setting of the *Gradual*, the hymn intervening between the Epistle and the Gospel, and of the *Offertorium*, the hymn following the Credo — both of these being variable. There is an obvious difference of intention in the various num-

bers, the Sanctus, Benedictus and Agnus Dei being naturally the most solemn and tender, since they accompany the ceremony of the Communion itself.

45. First Group of Masters. — About 1420 three young composers stepped forth into activity who inaugurated an era in music-history, namely, Dunstable, Binchois and Dufay. Of these, Dunstable is usually reckoned the pioneer, though Dufay for various reasons has the greater fame as distinctive of the period. Which happened to have been earlier is of no great moment, since they did not so much create a new art as achieve the special advance that had long been foreshadowed. They all pushed forward along similar lines — in secular chansons for two or three voices, in motets of somewhat similar construction, and in formal and stricter settings of the mass (though here Dunstable is not represented by works now extant).

The problem before them was, under the stimulus of secular song, to take the principles of polyphony that theorists had already worked out and to produce definite compositions that should contain enough compressed reflection and sentiment to be artistic. The only method of procedure known was contrapuntal, not harmonic in the modern sense — the interweaving of independent voice-parts around some 'subject' or thread of melody adopted as a basis, rather than the unfolding of chord-sequences as such or the exposition of a conspicuous homophonic melody. All the effects in view were strictly vocal, instruments being employed, if at all, only to double the voice-parts, and much depending upon the singers' purity of intonation and sympathy of rendering. Real solo effects were unknown, though usually the voices entered one by one for the sake of individuality. The value of 'imitation,' often strictly canonic, was appreciated. But there was only a vague sense of the utility of dividing works into clear and somewhat commensurate sections as dictated by the modern doctrine of 'form.' Since, then, these early works lack several features now universal, they seem angular and crude to modern taste. But they contained the germ of much that is precious.

John Dunstable (d. 1453) is known only through a few scattered references and a fair number of compositions. We infer that he was born at Dunstable (35 m. northwest of London), but when is not known. He is mentioned by a

H

French poet, Martin le Franc (probably before 1440), who cites him as the model of Dufay and Binchois. By this time, too, works of his had been copied as far away as the Tyrol. Later writers call him the first contrapuntist. He was buried in London, and two epitaphs extol his skill in music, mathematics and astrology. His existing works are all motets or secular songs, mostly in Continental libraries. Davey (Hist. Eng. Mus., 1895) pleads strenuously for Dunstable as the inventor of counterpoint and for England as the birthplace of the new style in general. Yet from 1350 to 1450 the relations between England and northern France were extremely close, so that neither was independent. Davey conjectures that Dunstable was in the English Chapel Royal, supposed to have been organized under Henry V., and that he took part in the musical services incident to Henry's victories in France in 1418–9.

With Dunstable are associated several other English names, with similar works, such as **Lionel Power, John Benet, Richard Markham,** etc.

Gilles Binchois (d. 1460) was born near Mons in Hainaut. In youth he was a soldier, but about 1425 he is named as a singer in the Ducal Chapel of Burgundy and about 1437 choirmaster. He died at Lille. Tinctor (c. 1475) said that his name would "endure for ever." Extant works of his, however, are rather few — fragments of masses and chansons.

Guillaume Dufay (d. 1474) was born somewhere in Hainaut and was trained as a choirboy at Cambrai, where the church music was famous. He seems to have written polyphonic songs for weddings in Italy in 1416 and 1419. In 1428 he entered the Papal Chapel at Rome, remaining till 1437. After this, besides spending seven years in Savoy, he held office in the cathedrals of Cambrai, Mons and Bruges, residing finally at Cambrai, where he died, highly honored throughout Europe. His extant works are numerous, including many masses, motets, chansons, etc. In range and amount of production he far outstrips his contemporaries. Adam von Fulda (c. 1500) asserts that he decidedly improved notation. [Through a serious error of Baini (1828) the dates of his life are often given as 1380–1432.]

To the middle of the 15th century also belong many other names, including **Petrus de Domart,** whom Tinctor apparently cites and from whom some masses remain; **Philippe Caron,** perhaps a pupil of Dufay, represented by some masses and many four-voice chansons; **Vincent Faugues,** from whom come several masses, copied at Rome about 1450; **Anthoine Busnois** (d. 1492), perhaps a pupil of Binchois, from 1467 a singer in the Burgundian Chapel, noted as one of the best of the early school, from whom are preserved a number of works, sacred and secular; **Eloy,** whose career is entirely unknown, unless, perhaps, he was a singer at Milan about 1475, but of whose able style some samples exist; and **Hayne van Ghizeghem,** in the Burgundian Chapel in 1468, known by several chansons of merit.

46. Second Group of Masters. — Late in the 15th century it is clear that a decided advance took place in skill and in breadth of influence. While distinguishing between two groups of composers, the authorities do not agree as to the assignment of

names. The 'new school' found its culmination in the commanding genius of Okeghem, who became the pattern for a multitude
of talented disciples, through whom the Netherland traditions
were disseminated far and wide. Obrecht follows close upon
Okeghem in importance.

The salient characteristic of this group was the pushing of
the technique of contrapuntal construction to an extreme.
Every device of imitation between the voices was worked out
with infinite ingenuity and patience, from the plain canon at
various intervals to canonic imitation by augmentation, diminu-
tion, inversion and reversion, thus preparing for the much later
fugue. The number of voices was frequently five or six, occasionally twelve, sixteen, twenty-four or even more. Though
the custom of borrowing 'subjects' still obtained, the ability to
invent them increased, often with some gain in expressiveness.
The handling of details was more certain and varied, avoiding
the stiffness of earlier works and often aiming at effects somewhat grand and imposing.

> The skill of the period tended to expend itself on the purely intellectual
> side of composition. The heaping together of intricacies was often so
> great that sentiment and beauty were lost in merely curious feats of poly-
> phonic dexterity. The texts were often treated as if of slight account —
> single words, for example, being spun out over long passages until wholly
> unintelligible. Too little care was taken to adjust the general effect to
> the spirit of the words.

This second school, in spite of its extremes, rendered immense
service to the progress of composition through its conquest of
certain materials and methods. If it had done nothing more, it
would deserve respect for making later achievements possible.
But it also left a notable array of works that are still remarkable
as artistic monuments.

> The expansion of the geographical range of composers attracts notice.
> In the Netherlands themselves a new centre appears at Antwerp. Several
> Italian cities begin to rival those of the west, while Germany, Austria and
> England exhibit independent musical life.
> Many other princely courts besides that of Burgundy acquired renown
> as musical centres. The maintenance of a musical establishment be-
> comes a more regular feature of royal or princely luxury. Such estab-
> lishments were technically known as 'Chapels,' and the chief musician
> in them, who was both composer and conductor, was 'Chapel-master'
> (Chapelain, Maître de chapelle, Maestro di cappella, Kapellmeister, etc.).
> In time the Papal Chapel at Rome became the most famous, but earlier

the Chapels Royal of England and France were prominent. Most large bishoprics, also, aimed to maintain at their cathedrals musical forces of ability. This dependence of music upon the official patronage of the Church and of courts remains conspicuous until the 19th century. [For convenience, the head of a chapel will in following pages be designated as 'choirmaster.']

Jean de Okeghem (d. 1495), born at Termonde in East Flanders soon after 1430, had his first training as a choirboy at Antwerp in 1443-4, entered the Royal Chapel at Paris in 1452 and was soon made choirmaster, in which post he apparently continued till his death, though also serving for a time as cathedral-treasurer at Tours. He was employed by three kings in succession, is said to have taught many pupils, and was often styled 'Prince of Music.' His genius set Paris in the first rank as a musical capital. His extant works include about 20 masses, many motets and chansons, etc., of unquestioned importance. In technique and genius he rises above all his contemporaries.

It is impossible to arrange the names of the period in any satisfactory order, or to be sure which most deserve mention, since so many details are unknown. The following, at least, should be named : —

More or less associated with Antwerp were **Jacques Barbireau** (d. 1491), born in Hainaut, for more than forty years choirmaster at Antwerp and highly honored as an authority elsewhere, but whose known works are few; **Jacob Obrecht** (d. 1505), who was born at Utrecht about 1430, probably was choirmaster there in 1465, later visited Italy, taught at Cambrai in 1483-5, later at Bruges and at Antwerp in 1492–1504, dying of the plague at Ferrara, and whose numerous works show a genius that has much to attract a modern taste, including one of the earliest Passions known; **Antonius Wyngaerde** (d. 1499), also born at Utrecht, and a singer at Antwerp Cathedral, whom Glarean names as a fine contrapuntist, but whose works have nearly all vanished; and **Jean Regis**, who taught at Antwerp as early as 1463. Possibly **Philippon de Bourges** and others should here be added.

In Italy, Netherland musicians begin to be in request, like **Guillaume Guarneri**, who worked first at Milan and later at Naples, besides serving in the Papal Chapel in 1474-83 ; **Gaspar Weerbecke** (d. 1514), born about 1440 at Oudenarde, who made his reputation from 1472 as teacher and court-choirmaster at Milan, and was in the Papal Chapel in 1481-9, and again in 1499-1509, returning to Milan in the interval, and whose extant works are many; and **Alexander Agricola** (d. 1506 ?), an eccentric writer, probably born about 1446, long a singer at Milan, from 1474 in southern Italy, later at Mantua, then from 1500 choirmaster at Brussels, and finally in Spain.

In Spain should be noted **Francisco de Peñalosa** (d. 1535), who was court-musician to Ferdinand V. of Castile, and of whose works much remains.

In Germany, also, talented contrapuntists begin to appear, among the earliest being **Traugott Eugenius**, cantor at Thorn (on the Polish border) about 1490, who wrote some fifty part-songs, and **Heinrich Finck** (d. 1519 ?), who was born at Bamberg, studied at Leipsic, served long in Poland, where he was royal choirmaster in 1492-1506, and then removed to Stuttgart — represented by many notable German part-songs and much sacred music of a lower order.

47. Third Group of Masters. — Immediately following the preceding group or interlocking with it was a third group which belongs partly to the 16th century.   On the one hand, the extraordinary skill in the niceties of polyphonic technique continues and is still sometimes pedantically overemphasized.   But, on the other, under the lead especially of Josquin des Près, Okeghem's greatest pupil, a new drift set in toward beauty and sentiment as the crown of musical learning.   While the final culmination of the Netherlanders' art waited for certain later masters, the group now in view helped to make an important transition from the comparatively archaic styles of the 15th century to the more flowing and emotional ones of the 16th. The line between the two groups is not easy to draw, but as we move forward into the next generation after Okeghem, we begin to feel the peculiar stimulus that the new century certainly gave to all music, so that in the works of these masters we catch the quality of enduring vitality and elevation by which the whole 16th century is characterized.   The art of music was beginning to take a place side by side with the arts of design.

It is usual, following a single and rather ambiguous reference, to name several composers as actually pupils of Okeghem.   These may well be grouped together as exhibiting a maturer style.

Josquin des Près (d. 1521) was by far the greatest.   He was born about 1445, probably at Condé in Hainaut, went to Italy, where he held important posts at several courts and in the Papal Chapel till towards 1500 (the exact dates are disputed), when he went to Paris as choirmaster.   His Italian life seems to have associated him with Florence, Ferrara, perhaps Milan and Modena, as well as Rome.   He is to-day represented by a larger number of works than any earlier composer, including manifold specimens in all the usual forms. His style still arouses delight, since it is not only full of technical skill, but charged with a delicate appreciation of the sense of the text and of tonal beauty and richness.   He exercised a profound influence upon succeeding writers, many of whom were his pupils.

Pierre de La Rue (d. 1518) was born in Picardy, was in the Burgundian Chapel from 1492, was prebendary at Courtrai and Namur, and enjoyed high esteem, as is shown by the unusual care lavished upon the MSS. of his works. He excels most of his contemporaries in profundity and seriousness.

Antoine Brumel was born in French Flanders, was employed by the Duke of Sora at Lyons and from 1505 by the Duke of Ferrara.   He was a prolific composer, with less warmth than Josquin and less depth than La Rue, but with as great command of method as either.

Loyset Compère (d. 1518) was also of Flemish birth, perhaps from St. Quentin, where he died as canon.   From his remaining works it appears that his genius had a peculiarly romantic and tender quality.

Other names in the series are **Jehan Cousin, Guillaume Crespel, Jean Prioris,** probably organist at St. Peter's in Rome from 1490 and in the French Chapel about 1507, and **Jean Verbonnet,** probably from about 1491 at Ferrara — the details of whose lives and works are not abundant.

Of the many other known contemporaries of Josquin, only a few can here be specified. Connected with Antwerp were **Jacotin Godebrye** (d. 1528), choirmaster as early as 1479, and **Noël Baulduin** (d. 1529), choirmaster in 1513–8. Possibly the earlier **Philippe Basiron** and the talented **Jean Ghiselin** also belong here. **Mathieu Pipelare** and **Marbriano de Orto** (d. c. 1516) are both well represented by existing works, but their careers are not known, except that the latter was in the Papal Chapel in 1484–94 and Burgundian choirmaster from 1505.

The further progress of the Netherland style was mainly under masters whose spheres of work were not only outside the Netherlands, but conditioned by new influences.

----

48. Folk-Music. — In immediate connection with the story of the perfecting of counterpoint by the Netherlanders should be set a sketch of the informal popular music that developed by its side, sometimes serving merely as a background for it, sometimes touching it with positive impetus. In the 15th century the expression of life in song and dance began to become influential, with results scattered through all the centuries since. A just estimate of the changes of the 16th century is impossible without some sense of the popular tendencies at work.

As far back as we may go in the story of European civilization we find traces of the use of song in common life. The same instinct for musical expression that is universal among uncivilized men persists in civilized conditions. Song springs forth spontaneously as the voice of the ordinary sentiments of domestic and communal life, embodying the feelings belonging to whatever occupies man's interest with intensity. It beguiles labor and loneliness, and enlivens all social festivity. It gives outlet to exuberant vitality, interacts with all sorts of bodily and mental effort, and brings to light that love for the beautiful and the ideal that is latent in healthy natures. It passes over readily into dancing — the rhythm and motion of the voice fitting closely with expressive movements of the body. It also turns easily to the use of whatever instruments the singer's wit suffices to fashion.

Folk-music tends to associate itself with several lines of effort that in more highly developed conditions are quite distinct from music. Thus it is often mimetic or epic, suggesting incipient stages of the drama or of history. It is always related to rudimentary literature of every kind. It is apt to reflect vividly religious beliefs, superstitions and practices. It belongs to a grade of culture where the many modes of expression are not yet differentiated.

Folk-music has been more notable at certain times than at others and among certain peoples. In the later Middle Ages among such racial groups as the Kelts, the Teutons and some others the interest in popular songs and dances was so widespread that formal music was finally forced to reckon with it. This mediæval influence became important as the 16th century approached and continued potent long afterward.

The various branches of the Keltic stock have always been singularly musical. This influence has been strong in France from the Troubadour time, and to it is to be attributed some part of the French capacity for gay, piquant and brilliant song and dance that has been notable since the 14th century. The Keltic genius is also evident in Wales, Ireland and Scotland. Here the interference of formal styles has been so slight or so long delayed that extensive literatures of folk-music have accumulated and have been highly valued. Just what relation this has to the history of English music is not clear, but that it has been a useful factor can hardly be doubted.

Still more important is the gift for folk-music among the Germans. The healthy sturdiness of the ancient Teuton — virile, assertive, masterful, yet also tender, reflective and religious — continued for centuries to express itself in every sort of music with an earnestness and grace that have become proverbial. This was the soil in which the Minnesinger flourished. This gave character to the first German experiments with counterpoint. This determined the form of the music of the Reformation. Even now, in spite of the prevalence everywhere of more artistic forms, the peasantry in many parts of Germany and in Switzerland and the Tyrol continue to cherish songs and dances that are full of artless charm. The value of this to the general art of music cannot be computed. Again and again the standard types of melody, harmony and form have been modified by the impress of these humble styles.

Somewhat similar remarks might be made about the folk-music of Romance countries like Italy and Spain, or of the several Scandinavian countries, or of the vast regions where the Slavs have gradually pushed their way into the circle of modern civilization.

That which distinguishes all folk-music is its essential naïveté. Its production is unconscious, unstudied, unfettered by rules. Although particular specimens often acquire a precise and permanent shape, they can seldom be traced to an individual author, and their preservation does not depend upon any process of transcription. They seem to spring up by common consent, to be perfected by common effort, and to persist by mere tradition.

49. Its Technical Features. — No attempt can be made here to indicate the peculiarities of particular national styles, but certain general remarks may be offered. Most characteristics follow from the necessary simplicity of all folk-music, which is the product, not of formal analysis or patient working out on paper, but of instinct and taste operating extempore, and which depends for its success upon the ease with which it can be caught, remembered and repeated by the unstudious mind.

Folk-songs are normally melodies of moderate length, laid out in more or less symmetrical lines and strophes that correspond with the plan of a verse-text. Each line is usually somewhat complete in itself, having a specific figure or pattern that ends with a cadence or 'fall.' The lines usually tend to form couplets or other simple groups that are so similar or contrasted that the mind as easily associates them together as it does rhyming verse-lines. Usually the text is in parallel stanzas, all of which can be sung to a single musical strophe. Even in the oldest specimens there is a tendency to adhere throughout to a single key or tonality, though often with a clear perception of the value of dominant closes in the middle cadences. The kind of tonality preferred varies considerably in different countries. Keltic and Scandinavian songs, for example, show a predilection for minor scales, sometimes of the pentatonic variety. The older French and German songs are not seldom based upon the mediæval church modes, but as a rule drift toward the minor or major as now recognized. The evident appreciation of the major mode is the more notable because found at a time when scientific music was still unwilling to desert the arbitrary tone-system that it inherited from antiquity. The popular mind seems to have had an instinct for tone-relation as we know it to-day.

Folk-dances as such are properly made up of steps and motions in brief series of equal duration — following the idea, now the basis of musical 'form,' that phrases should be two or four measures long. These figures are sometimes simply repeated over and over, sometimes strung together in sets, making a kind of dance-stanza. Each particular sort of dance is characterized by some special step or similar device. The songs or instrumental airs intended to accompany and guide these motions are fitted to them at every point, indicating musically what the dancer executes orchestically.

In both songs and dances the fundamental rhythm is emphatic and regular, either duple or triple, and the phrase-structure is so built upon it that the 'form' is plain and easily kept in memory.

All these features are of historic importance, since they are traceable at periods when formal composition was timidly groping its way, and when the supposed value of the old modes and of contrapuntal structure, with its lack of 'form,' was keeping musicians from these more natural methods. All of them were noted in the Troubadour and Minnesinger periods (secs. 37–40), but their decided influence belongs rather to the 15th and 16th centuries. Even until 1600 some features of folk-music seemed to educated musicians rather vulgar. To-day we can see that there was no more valuable element in the evolution of modern styles than this same despised music of the people's instinct.

50. The Minstrel Class. — Popular music in a settled community involves a somewhat organized class of persons who make their living by it. Like the bards of the older time, the mediæval itinerant minstrels constituted a significant type. Such rude musicians were the medium through which folk-music was disseminated and preserved. By them the songs and dances of one locality were mingled with those of other places. They often wrought what they found into a finer shape or added to it from their own invention. They were usually skillful players, and often greatly improved musical instruments. Their business was not to theorize about music or to play the rôle of formal composers, but to render it with voice and finger so as to make it socially attractive and indispensable. They were bound to keep in touch with strictly popular taste. The minstrel, as his name implies, was the 'servant' of his audiences. Yet, wherever he was also something of a genius, he was incidentally a leader and teacher as well.

> Throughout the Middle Ages the popularity of traveling singers and players is constantly indicated. Perhaps they may have been the successors of the tricksters and mountebanks of the later Roman domination. The line between the clown and the minstrel proper was seldom sharply drawn. Often there was a strong prejudice against all such itinerants because of their lawlessness — a prejudice that took shape in edicts, civil and religious, which sometimes attempted to suppress them altogether. But the popular craving for amusement — all the stronger because of the hard and narrow conditions of life — gave them employment and a measure of wondering admiration. Part of the contempt that has pursued the whole art of music even to modern times is due to the mediæval association of it with coarse buffoonery, athletic tricks and shows of trained

animals. Vagrant minstrels were too often mere beggars or thieves or corrupters of public morals. Yet it is only just to remember that the minstrel class was artistically serviceable in many ways.

Attention has been called to the guilds of the Meistersinger in Germany (sec. 41). Somewhat similar institutions appeared much earlier in England, France and the Low Countries, though they were not governed by such fantastic rules, nor were they ordinarily so secret and exclusive. They remind us of the bands of Gipsies that still exist in many parts of the world. Indeed, it seems that between them and the modern Gipsies there is some real connection.

The earliest mention of a personage called 'The King of the Jugglers' is in England at the time of William the Conqueror (before 1100). Several such 'Kings' are named in the 13th century at different places. For over four centuries the same title recurs, often with civil privileges conferred by statute. The name implies the existence of organized societies. Several such brotherhoods are matters of record, notably the *Confrérie de St. Julien*, first recognized in Paris in 1331, and the *Musicians' Company*, established in London in 1472, the latter of which still exists in honor. These are but samples of a multitude of such organizations that were once common in France and neighboring countries, and which varied widely in character, from the almost casual group of mere itinerants to the permanent town or city union that assumed to dictate within its boundaries who could ply the musical trade or profession. The connection of these mediæval institutions with the later guilds of town-musicians, especially in Germany, can be traced in considerable detail, as also with the modern learned and artistic musical societies and academies in various lands.

51. Instruments. — Folk-music and minstrelsy were prolific in the invention and application of instruments. The multitude of records here is bewildering, especially in illuminations of manuscripts, architectural carvings, and poetic and other literary references. In the search for novel effects the variety of instrumental forms in widespread use was probably greater than ever since, for with the rise of scientific instrument-making in the 17th century and of real instrumental styles of composition a few main types drove the rest from the field. It is likely that dancing stimulated this attention to instruments, since they were useful for marking its rhythm and figures and for enriching its interest. But another stimulus was the desire for genuine accompaniments for singing — a desire which, like the notion of the solo song itself, was lacking in the current contrapuntal

system.   There are some indications, too, that independent instrumental music was attempted, though this was slight.

> No exhaustive catalogue of mediæval instruments can be
> given.   The list is too long and complicated.   Various
> shapes and names are known to us, but they cannot always
> be brought together with certainty, and evidently both were
> liable to curious and capricious variations.   In the stringed
> group we find elementary forms of all the well-known types —
> harps, lyres, dulcimers, lutes, viols, etc., in countless modi-
> fications, with peculiar special types, like the 'trumscheit'
> or 'nun's-fiddle'—a derivative of the monochord, and
> the 'organistrum,' 'bauernleier,' or 'hurdy-gurdy,'—essen-
> tially a viol sounded by a revolving wheel and fitted with
> a rude keyboard (see Fig. 51).   In the wind group, also,
> there are many representatives of the flute, oboe and trumpet
> families, with bagpipes and Pan's-pipes, besides the organ
> and its petite varieties.   In the percussive group there are
> drums, bells, castanets and clappers of all sorts.   The key-
> board as a means of controlling a complex instrument like
> the organ was already well known (see sec. 101), and its
> application to stringed instruments of the lyre or viol kind
> was understood, though it had not been combined with
> the dulcimer as in the pianoforte.   All these instruments,
> except the organ, were mainly the products of popular in-
> genuity, though at the end of the 15th century they began
> to engage the serious attention of thoughtful musicians.

The more favorite instruments were often made in
several sizes, so that of each there might be a graded
series from treble to bass, making an instrumental
choir.   It seems that before learned musicians had
fixed upon the notion of true harmony as the basis of
composition popular music had recognized it and had
begun to apply it in solid chord-effects from instruments of differing pitch.   Similar experiments were
of course made with voices.   Such efforts were essentially diverse from those of true counterpoint, since
the several voice-parts were not developed independently or equally, but as constituents in the massive
or total effect.   It would appear, therefore, that the
mediæval eagerness for concerted instrumental effects

FIG. 52.—
Nun's-fid-
dle, with one
string, on
which melo-
dies could be
played by se-
lecting tones
from the se-
ries of natural
harmonics.

is memorable, not simply because it hastened the maturity of
leading solo instruments, like the violin, but because it involved
some recognition of true harmony as distinct from counterpoint.

52. Tablatures. — Incidental to the free use of instruments were systems of notation for them, called 'tablatures.' Several systems were in wide use, varying with the instrument in view and also with the country of their origin. They were alike in that they did not employ the staff, which belonged to vocal music. Yet the experiments with tablatures evidently had much to do with the perfecting of the staff-notation. Indeed, the latter is essentially a kind of tablature, whose ultimate supremacy is due to its adaptability to every species of music, instrumental as well as vocal.

What was called German or organ tablature was meant for keyboard instruments generally, and consisted of the letter-names of the intended tones written in horizontal lines that were broken at regular intervals by vertical bars to mark the measures — the whole resembling the modern Tonic Sol-Fa notation, except that the letters referred to the keys of the keyboard and not to solmization-syllables. Notes meant to be sounded together were ranged one above the other, and over each vertical column stood a sign to indicate the desired duration (a point for a breve, a stroke for a semibreve, a stroke with a side-pennant or hook for a minim, one with two hooks for a crotchet, etc. — all these signs being transitional forms from the old mensural notation). Rests were shown by dashes in the part where they were needed, with a duration-sign as before.

For other instruments, especially the lute, the same general scheme was used, but the notes were named, not by their letter-names, but by some letter or other character indicating what string and what finger were to be used. In these latter forms what looked like a staff was often employed, but its lines referred to the strings of the instrument, all the notes to be played on a given string being marked by letters on its particular line.

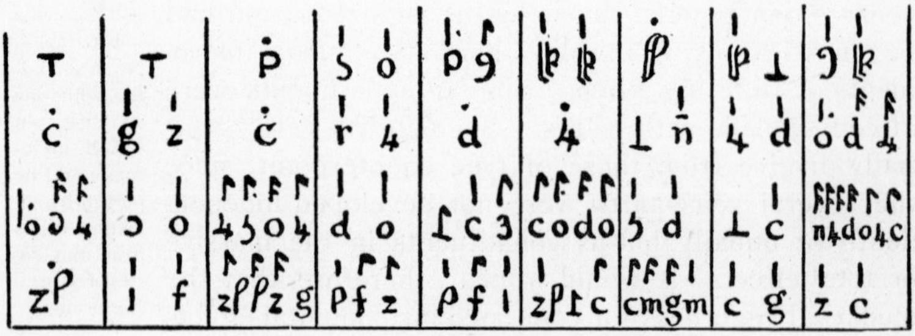

FIG. 53. — Lute Tablature (16th century).

PART III

THE SIXTEENTH CENTURY

PART III

THE SIXTEENTH CENTURY

CHAPTER VII

THE VENETIAN AND ROMAN SCHOOLS

53. General Survey. — The 16th century is perhaps the most fascinating of any before the 19th, since it was the meeting-point of mediæval and modern life. Into it as towards a focus various lines of progress converged, only to be recombined and redirected. All Europe was stirred by the great mental movements of the Renaissance and the Revival of Letters, which originated further back, but were now hastened to maturity by certain events that gave an unexampled expansion to intellectual and artistic interests.

Note especially (*a*) the Fall of Constantinople in 1453, which sent a wave of Byzantine learning into the West, making real the richness of ancient literature and art, (*b*) the invention of printing with movable types about 1450, making it possible to multiply and distribute the tools of culture indefinitely, (*c*) other inventions that tended to alter society, like gunpowder, changing the whole aspect of war and politics, and the mariner's compass, opening the door to explorations beyond the sea, and (*d*) startling discoveries of far-off geographical facts, as of America (1492), the Cape of Good Hope and the sea-route to India (1498), the Pacific (1513), etc., enlarging men's horizons, awakening adventurous zeal, and provoking dreams of foreign domain and fabulous wealth.

In place of the stiff and abstract scholasticism of the Middle Ages the New Learning now asserted itself, being really the first expression of the modern historical and scientific spirit. Other signs of the mental vigor of the age were the advances of arts like painting and poetry under masters of permanent importance.

As illustrations, note that Erasmus, the leader of the Humanists, was born in 1465 and died in 1536, that here belong typical Italian painters of the first rank, like Da Vinci (1452–1519), Michelangelo (1475–1564), Raphael (1483–1520) and Titian (1477–1576), with the German Dürer (1471–1528), and that here was the brilliant blossoming of the Elizabethan Era in England.

As the century opens, we find ourselves on the verge of the tremendous upheaval of the Reformation, appearing just before

1520 in Germany and Switzerland.   As this movement spread in northern and western Europe, besides its theological and religious effects, it produced extraordinary political, social, literary and artistic results, stirring all society to the depths.

> The century was an age of great sovereigns, like Charles V., Emperor in 1518–56, Francis I., King of France in 1515–47, Henry VIII., King of England in 1509–47, Philip II., King of Spain in 1556–98, and Elizabeth, Queen of England in 1558–1603.   The relations of these to the power of the Papacy and to Protestantism were often extremely important to the progress of all culture.

It is not strange that the century was rich in musical significance.   The great musical events were the application of printing to the reproduction of music, the culmination of the art of mediæval counterpoint, the rise of Protestant church music, the obliteration of the old line between sacred and secular music, the shift of emphasis in theory from polyphony to monophony, with a new sense of harmony and of 'form,' and the discovery of the musical drama, with its emotional possibilities.

> In these developments several countries participated, but Italy easily leads in all but one.   Although the impetus everywhere is largely from Netherlanders, native genius comes steadily to the front.   Germany and England compete with Italy for attention, while France and the Low Countries are less important.

Individual composers and theorists now exert a wider and more lasting influence, especially since musical publication becomes a potent factor in progress.   Their dignity and worth as members of society are better recognized, and the variety of demands upon them increases.   The manufacture of instruments, also, now begins to afford room for the exercise of positive genius.

> The dependence of music upon the Church and upon the patronage of rulers continues, but there are signs that the art in its higher forms is coming closer to the people generally.   Just as it is becoming more cosmopolitan, so it is also becoming more evidently democratic.

54. Music-Printing. — No single event in the evolution of music in its social applications is more important than the invention of a practical method of printing its products.   The same men who conceived the notion of movable types for letters advanced almost at once to that of movable types for notes, and, just as the use of typography led immediately to book-publish ing and book-selling as standard branches of commerce, so it led also to music-publishing and music-selling. The value of this new agency was at once apparent. Though the early editions were small and the copies relatively expensive, yet through them masterworks now began to circulate in authentic form and to be studied and used as never before. An immense incentive was thus supplied both to producers and to users.

Throughout the Middle Ages the drafting of musical manuscripts and even the pursuit of musical calligraphy as an art were common occupations in monasteries and similar institutions. Every cathedral and large church was obliged to supply its priests and choir with all needed service-books, which were often marvels of laborious patience and interest. But the time and effort required upon them were excessive, so that they were costly or priceless. Naturally there was no effort to circulate them. The knowledge of the larger musical works was therefore limited to a few places and persons.

To relieve this difficulty, experiments were made in the 15th century with printing music from engraved wooden blocks, a whole page to a block. When movable types were first tried for letters by Gutenberg (c. 1440), the question at once arose whether the same device was not practicable for music, but the extreme difficulty of printing both staffs and notes at one impression postponed the solution of the problem. For a time the musical portions of books like missals were printed from blocks while the text was printed from type, and this continued till 1520 and occasionally after.

The earliest known printing of music from types was in 1476 by Ulrich Hahn of Rome, in 1481 by Jörg Reyser of Würzburg and Ottavio Scotto of Venice, and during the next twenty years by several others. In all these cases only Plain-Song was attempted, and the process involved two impressions, the staffs being in red, the notes in black. The first application of this process to the more difficult problem of contrapuntal music was in 1501 by Petrucci of Venice, followed in 1507 by Oeglin of Augsburg, and before 1512 by Schöffer of Mayence. The first to work out a one-impression process, notes and staffs together, was the type-maker Pierre Haultin in 1525, whose types were used from 1527 by Attaignant of Paris. Further progress consisted in devising better types (as, for example, the round-headed notes invented in 1530 by Briard of Avignon). The publishing of music as a trade was now undertaken in various places. Venice, being the chief centre of publishing in general,

I

was naturally prominent, but many other cities took up the new industry with success.

The mechanical difficulties of music-printing are not generally appreciated. The staff-lines should be continuous across the page, and yet upon and between them must stand notes and other signs. It is easy to make uniform types for all the latter, but not easy to apply them without breaking the lines. Making two impressions not only increases cost, but is mechanically delicate, since even a small variation in 'register' (location on the paper) between the two printings vitiates the result. Petrucci's success with this method is extraordinary in view of the fact that even on modern presses it is practically abandoned. The problem was solved by making the types for notes, bars and other characters with small portions of the staff-lines attached to them (in all desired combinations) and then setting these, with other types for the remaining portions of the staffs, in a complicated mosaic, so exact in adjustment and so closely compacted that when the whole is inked and applied to the paper, both notes and staffs are produced in apparent continuity and perfection. (See an excellent account in Grove's Dict. under 'Music-Printing.')

The above remarks apply only to printing from types, which can be cast in large quantities, set up in any desired combination, printed from, and then separated or 'distributed' so as to be used again in other combinations. To-day this process is employed mainly for books containing much literary matter or 'letter-press.' Sheet-music is usually printed from engraved plates — a wholly different process, which also began to be used in the 16th century (by Verovio of Rome in 1586). The first plates were made of copper and the engraving was laborious. The modern plan of using soft-metal plates and punching the notes and other characters by dies did not appear till about 1700.

As a clue to the spread of the new art and a help to tracing the many collections thus put into circulation, some of the pioneers may be enumerated: —

At Venice we have **Ottaviano dei Petrucci** (d. 1539), born at Fossombrone in 1466, who went to Venice in 1491, secured a monopoly of music-printing there in 1498, issuing his first book in 1501, and returned to his birthplace in 1511, where he prosecuted work till 1523, completing a monumental series of over 30 collections of masses, motets, frottole and pieces for the lute (some in more than one volume or edition) by a great variety of composers; **Andrea Antigo** (d. 1539), who began at Rome in 1510, but moved to Venice in 1520; **Girolamo Scotto** (d. 1573), from 1539 one of the most prolific publishers of the time, as well as a composer of madrigals and canzone; **Antonio Gardano**, who began business in 1537, was soon in fierce competition with Scotto, and was succeeded in 1571 by his almost equally enterprising son **Angelo** (d. 1610); and **Francesco Rampazetto** (d. 1579), at work from about 1562. At Rome we note **Valerio Dorico** (d. 1567), with two books in 1531–3; **Antonio Barré**, at work in 1555–8; **Alessandro Gardano** (d. 1623), son of Antonio above, at work in 1584–91; and **Simone Verovio**, at work (with his copper-plate process) in 1586–1604.

In Germany we have at Augsburg **Erhart Oeglin,** whose first book in 1507 was printed from wooden type and another in 1512 from copper type, the latter being a collection of folk-songs — the first of many by other printers. At Mayence **Peter Schöffer** first appeared as the colleague of Gutenberg and Faust in general printing, but turned to music-printing before 1512, after which he worked first at Worms, issuing one of the earliest Protestant hymn-books in 1525, and from 1534 at Strassburg. At Wittenberg was another important Protestant publisher, **Georg Rhaw** (d. 1548), who began business in 1525. At Nuremberg were many printers, like **Johannes Petreius** (d. 1550), at work from 1536, **Johann vom Berg** (d. 1563) and **Ulrich Neuber** (d. 1571), a firm whose first book was issued in 1531, **Hans Ott** (d. 1550 ?) and **Hieronymus Grapheus** (d. 1556), another firm nearly as old, and **Dietrich Gerlach** (d. 1575), beginning about 1566. At Frankfort mention should be made of **Christian Egenolff** (d. 1555), at work from 1532, whose technique was notoriously poor, but whose books are historically valuable. At Munich **Adam Berg** was diligently at work in 1567–99.

In France music-printers were notable for zeal in the improved cutting of types as well as for their work as publishers. **Pierre Haultin** (d. 1580), beginning work at Paris in 1525, was followed at Avignon by **Étienne Briard** and **Jean de Channay,** and later at Paris by **Guillaume Le Bé.** **Robert Granjon,** at work from about the same date, published books at Lyons in 1559 and at Rome in 1582. At Paris **Pierre Attaignant** used Haultin's types in 1527–49, followed by **Nicholas du Chemin** in 1549–68, and **Adrien Le Roy** (d. 1599), a lutist and composer, who began publishing in 1540, and from 1552 was joined by **Robert Ballard** (d. 1606), the first of a family of publishers that lasted till the 19th century.

In the Netherlands a prominent name at Antwerp is that of **Tylman Susato** (d. 1564), whose work began in 1543, succeeded in 1572 by **Jean Bellère** (d. 1595) and his partner **Pierre Phalèse** (d. c. 1579), the latter having worked at Louvain from 1545.

In England slight specimens of musical typography are traceable as early as 1495. Petrucci's two-impression process began to be imitated in 1530, apparently by **Wynkyn de Worde.** The Prayer Book with music was printed in 1550 and the metrical Psalter in 1562. In 1575 **Tallis** (d. 1585) and his pupil **Byrd** (d. 1623) secured a monopoly, and they were followed in 1588 by **Thomas Este** (d. 1609 ?) and others.

55. The Rise of Italian Music. — Between the strictly Netherland writers of the 15th century and those of the 16th in other countries there was no absolute line of separation, though the divergences gradually became marked. The transfer of activity to Italy and Germany was made by those who were either Netherlanders themselves or their pupils. But at once the line of progress was taken up by others and carried forward with increasing independence. In Italy we now note two large groups, set apart geographically and artistically. These centre

about Venice and Rome respectively.   Both served to develop
the Netherland art, but in different directions.   The Roman
school adhered to the stricter traditions, dominated by the
demands of the Church, while the Venetians were far more
ready for innovation, especially in secular and sensational effects.   The former brought the older style to its natural consummation ; the latter laid foundations for new developments.

There was an increasing differentiation of the forms of composition.
These were all essentially polyphonic, though varying greatly in elaboration, and all at first vocal, though soon instrumental forms begin to
appear.

For the church service the 'mass' was of course the most stately and
constant form, and its treatment followed the traditions of the 15th
century, though with some technical modifications.   But the 'motet' was
now more appreciated, since its variety of text encouraged originality of
treatment.   For both of these the words were Latin, and the handling
was clearly contrapuntal, usually learned and intricate, avoiding the extreme or the sensational (but see sec. 44).

In secular writing the 'madrigal' was the analogue of the motet — a
finished contrapuntal setting of secular words, often in Italian and usually
amatory, into which gradually crept qualities of sensuous piquancy and
lightness that were out of place in sacred writing.   The old French
chanson, also, was followed in Italy by the 'canzona' or popular part-song
(often called by local names, as Venetian, Neapolitan or Sicilian, accord
ing to the style adopted), having much more freedom and outward charm
than the madrigal.   Next came the 'frottola,' a variety of the canzona,
usually following a fixed plan of stanza with a refrain.   This shaded off
into the 'villanella' or street-song, often with a rough and even coarse text,
a prominent melody and comparatively little attempt at part-writing.
These latter forms, though often despised, were beneficial in breaking up
the heaviness and formlessness of stricter writing (see sec. 69).

As instrumental writing was taken up, several names were used that
were not at first clearly distinguished, all of them referring to pieces in
which some thematic treatment was decorated with much aimless passage-work and the like.   Sometimes the term 'fantasia' was used much
as now, but 'ricercare,' 'toccata' or 'sonata' were more common.   Stricter
pieces were occasionally given the name 'fuga,' though the true fugue
hardly began before the 17th century.

56.   Willaert and the Venetian School. — For various reasons
Venice stands out in the 16th century as one of the most interesting cities.   She had long been foremost in commerce, her
trade reaching far into the Orient on the one side and over all
western Europe on the other.   With her wealth came an ag-
gressive and productive culture.   Notable among her national

institutions was the Church of St. Mark's, founded in the 9th
century, and, from the 11th, famous as one of the richest and
most splendid of cathedrals.   Here the powerful patronage of
the state developed a musical establishment that in the 16th
century attained fame in all Europe.

The excellence of the music at St. Mark's first became notable in the 14th
century.   The successive organists after 1400 were **Zuane** (1406–19), **Bernardino** (1419–45), **Bernardo di Stefanino Murer** (1445–59), **Bartolommeo Vielmis**
(1459–90 and later), **Francesco d' Ana** (1490– ?), **Zuan Maria** (1504–7), **Baldassare da Imola** (1533–41), **Jachet de Buus** (1541–51), **Annibale** (1552–66),
Merulo (1557–84), **Andrea Gabrieli** (1556–86), **Giovanni Gabrieli** (1585–1612),
Vincenzo Bell'Haver (1586–88) and **Gioseffo Guami** (1588–91).   From 1490
there were two organs, and the overlapping dates above signify terms of
service beginning on the second organ and passing to the first.   The list of
choirmasters begins in 1491 and includes **Pietro de Fossis**, a Netherlander
(1491–1525), **Willaert** (1527–62), **De Rore** (1559–65), **Zarlino** (1565–90) and
Donato (1590–1603).   From 1403 there was a special school for choristers.

The peculiar eminence of Venice in the early 16th century
was due to the extraordinary genius of Willaert, choirmaster at
St. Mark's for thirty-five years from 1527, who is commonly
called the founder of the Venetian school.   In all the technical
mysteries of counterpoint he was fully as expert as his predecessors, while he excelled in interesting extensions of their style.
Chief of these advances was the free use of double-choir effects,
probably suggested by the fact that St. Mark's had two organs
facing one another across the chancel.   Antiphony of this
kind involved important changes in current method — partition
into sections, with some symmetry between them, more clear
cadences, more massing of voices in pure harmony, conciser
handling of the words, etc.   Progress in all these was novel
and a grateful addition to the older procedures.   In general, emotional effects were pushed forward, with richer combinations of
chords and more freedom with chromatic tones, while mere precision or intricacy of imitation was less prominent.   In all this
we see the working of the typical Italian love of color, warmth
and sentiment.   Though not the first to grasp the possibilities
of the madrigal-form, Willaert was one of the first strong
writers in it, exercising a dominant influence on its development (see sec. 69).   For all these reasons Willaert is counted
as, on the whole, the ablest master between Des Près and
Palestrina.

Adrian Willaert (d. 1562) was born at Bruges or Roulers before 1490. His first training was at Paris and for the law, but he also studied music with Mouton and Des Près to such effect that in 1516, when he went to Rome, it is said that he found the Papal Choir using a motet of his under Des Près' name. After some years, of which we have no record save that he was employed for a time by Louis II. of Bohemia, in 1527, the Doge of Venice, in the face of some opposition, installed him as choirmaster at St. Mark's, where he remained in the greatest honor till his death. In 1542 and 1556 he paid visits to the Low Countries. He was in request as a teacher and trained a long list of talented pupils. His published works (1536–71) include only 5 masses, but are rich in motets, hymns, etc., for the church and very numerous secular part-songs and madrigals, besides some instrumental ricercari. Further masses, motets and songs were left in MS.

In following down the long line of Willaert's contemporaries and successors at Venice we note the recurrence in their works of the same tendencies of style, with many individual peculiarities as well. The drift was strong toward such uses of contrapuntal art as should be less diffuse and abstruse than formerly, with emphasis upon depth of feeling, charm of detail, richness of impression, in place of the older delight in puzzle-working. The potent influence of secular music was taking hold of all music, rendering its more studied products more beautiful and human.

Jachet de Buus was certainly a Netherlander. He came early to Venice and in 1541 was chosen from many competitors for the second organ at St. Mark's, whence in 1551 he went to Vienna, and became court-organist there, remaining in service till 1564. He is notable as one of the earlier writers for the organ. His works (1543–50) consist of some canzone, ricercari, and motets.

Ciprian de Rore (d. 1565), also a Netherlander, born at Mechlin or Antwerp in 1516, was brought up as a choirboy at St. Mark's as one of Willaert's earlier pupils. He began to publish madrigals in 1542. Before 1553 he was made choirmaster at Ferrara, but in 1558 returned to the Low Countries, spending some time at Antwerp and Brussels. There he was sought as choirmaster by the Duke of Parma, but in 1563 became Willaert's successor at Venice. The next year, being discontented with his post, he moved to Parma, where he died. His long series of works (1542–73) includes several masses, many motets, an abundance of beautiful madrigals for 4–5 voices, and some ricercari. Their popularity is shown by the numerous editions demanded. He went much beyond his master and his school in the free and dexterous use of chromatic tones and harmonies, and his style has a novel richness and geniality.

Gioseffo Zarlino (d. 1590) was born in 1517 at Chioggia. After training as a Franciscan, he came in 1541 to Venice, studied under Willaert, and in 1565 succeeded De Rore as choirmaster, serving 25 years. There is no doubt that he was eminent as a composer, but comparatively few of his works remain (motets and madrigals, 1548–70). His chief fame is as a theorist (see sec. 72).

Annibale Padovano was born in 1527 at Padua, succeeded De Buus as organist at St. Mark's in 1552, and remained till 1566, when he became ducal choirmaster at Gratz (Austria). He had great repute as a player on the organ and other instruments. His relatively few works, in all the usual forms, appeared in 1556–73, with a probably posthumous collection of organ-toccate and ricercari in 1604.

Baldassare Donato (d. 1603) was a Venetian who seems to have spent his entire life at St. Mark's, first as singer, from 1562 as trainer, and finally, from 1590, as Zarlino's successor. Most of his known works are madrigals (1550–68), in which much originality appears, with one book of motets (1597). The long gap between these publications is unexplained.

Claudio Merulo (d. 1604), born in 1533 at Correggio and trained there, early displayed conspicuous genius. He began his career in 1556 as cathedral-organist at Brescia, in 1557 came to the second organ at St. Mark's, was promoted to the first in 1566, remaining almost 20 years, and in 1586 began another 20 years' service as court-organist at Parma, where he died. Besides being interested (from 1566) in music-publishing and in organ-building, he stands out as one of the chief organists of the period, excelling both as player and as composer. With the two Gabrielis, he marks an epoch in the separation of organ from vocal music. His masses, motets and excellent madrigals are many (from 1564), but his best works are his organ-ricercari, toccate and canzone. In 1579 he coöperated in the drafting of a madrigal-play, one of the precursors of the opera.

Andrea Gabrieli (d. 1586), born in Venice about 1510 and trained by Willaert, became a singer at St. Mark's in 1536 and second organist in 1566. Like his younger predecessor Merulo, his fame rests upon the stimulus he gave to organ music, but his publications were at first all vocal (several volumes of motets, masses and madrigals from 1565), while his concerti and organ-pieces appeared posthumously (1587–1605). He wrote much for 5–6 voices or more — his *Penitential Psalms* for 6 voices (1583) being specially notable. He also collaborated on a madrigal-play (1574). Among his eminent pupils were his nephew Giovanni and Hassler, the South German pioneer. The new forms of organ-writing later conspicuous in Germany are finely prefigured in his works.

Giovanni Gabrieli (d. 1612), Andrea's nephew and pupil, born in Venice in 1557 and first organist at St. Mark's from 1585, stands on the same high plane as player, composer and teacher. His published works appeared first (from 1587) with those of his uncle. He was fond of polychoric effects (3–4 choirs treated more or less independently), and in his organ-writing advanced toward the fugal form with success. He seems not to have produced much secular music, but he had a profound sense of richness and variety of tonal effect. His most famous pupils were Sweelinck, the founder of the North German school, and Schütz, the great Dresden master.

Giovanni Croce of Chioggia (d. 1609) was first a choirboy at St. Mark's under Zarlino, then leading singer and finally, from 1603, choirmaster. Growing up amid the accumulated traditions of the century, his numerous works of every description (from 1585) have much breadth and variety. Notable are his humorous part-songs or mascherate (1590).

Several other names might be added, such as **Giovanni Ferretti** of Ancona (canzone, 1567-91), **Vincenzo Bell'Haver** (d. 1588 ?), and **Giovanni Bassano**, long a choir-trainer at St. Mark's (works, 1585-1602).

57. Other North Italian Masters. — The Venetian school reaches far outside of Venice itself. With the whole of northern Italy Venice, as the metropolis, was in the closest commercial and social relations, so that the whole valley of the Po constituted a region musically united.

> In the 16th century the Venetian Republic stretched along the north bank of the Po almost 150 miles, including cities like Padua, Vicenza, Verona, Mantua, Brescia, Cremona and Bergamo, while on its borders were Ferrara, Bologna, Modena, Parma and Milan.

Throughout this whole region the drift of composition by the best masters was strongly toward forms like the madrigal, the canzona and the like, in which fresh, varied and piquant sentiment might find expression. In sacred music the motet was much more cultivated than the mass, apparently because its treatment was not so conventional and its topics were more diversified. In the search for splendor and charm of effect there was a tendency to increase the number of voices and to introduce more and more license in their handling — all looking toward the later emancipation of harmony from the tyranny of the modes and of strict contrapuntal rules.

> Connected with Padua is the name of **Costanzo Porta** (d. 1601), who was born at Cremona about 1530 and studied with Willaert. He was a Minorite who was constantly in request as choirmaster. His longest terms of service were at Osimo from 1552, at Ravenna from 1567, and at Loreto from 1578, but he was twice at Padua, from 1565 and 1595, where he died. His works (from 1555) range from sacred to secular in a style of dignity and beauty. Among his pupils was **Lodovico Balbi** (d. 1604), also a Minorite, a singer at St. Mark's and at Verona, and choirmaster at Padua in 1585-91 (works from 1570). A later writer of some power was **Giulio Belli** (d. 1613?), who was choirmaster from 1582 at many different places, including Padua from 1607 (works from 1584).
>
> At Vicenza we note **Giovanni Matteo Asola** (d. 1609), choirmaster from 1581, with many able sacred works (from 1570), and **Leone Leoni**, from 1588 cathedral-choirmaster, whose many works, sacred and secular (1588-1622), were much used.
>
> At Mantua was **Jachet de Mantua** [Jacques Colebaud] (d. before 1559), a Frenchman who appeared about 1527 as a singer and later became both ca-

thedral and ducal choirmaster, producing only sacred works (1539–67) in a conservative style. [He is seriously confused with Jachet de Berchem, as well as both of them with De Buus.] **Jacob van Wert** (d. 1596), also a foreigner, born in 1536, was a choirboy at Mantua and from 1566 choirmaster for 30 years, except for a short term at Novellara from 1568. Though he seems to have had strenuous difficulties with his co-workers, he was highly honored. He was a prolific madrigalist (11 vols. 1558–95), but left also many motets. **Giovanni Giacomo Gastoldi** (d. 1622) was in the ducal service from 1582, producing a large number of works, sacred and secular (from 1581), including some balletti (5–6-part dances) that became widely known. Other Mantuan musicians were **Benedetto Pallavicino**, Van Wert's successor in 1596 (11 vols. of madrigals, 1579–1612), **Girolamo Belli** (12 vols. 1583–1617), and **Alessandro Striggio** (d. 1587), born about 1535, a famous violist, from 1560 at Florence and from 1574 at Mantua. His works (from 1560 and finally published posthumously by his son) include several intermezzi in madrigal style (1565–85), which were connected with the Florentine innovations (see sec. 70).

At Brescia we note **Costanzo Antegnati**, born in 1557, who, like his father, was a celebrated organ-builder, also in 1584–1619 cathedral-organist, with masses and madrigals (1571–92) and a book on the organ (1608), with pieces of his own.

At Cremona the chief name is **Marc' Antonio Ingegneri** (d. 1592), born at Verona about 1545, a pupil of Ruffo at Verona, and from 1576 choirmaster at Cremona, with many noble works (1573–87). The excellence of his style appears from the fact that his *Responsoria* (1588) were long ascribed to Palestrina. Monteverdi was his pupil.

At Bergamo mention should be made of the Sicilian **Pietro Vinci** (d. 1584), cathedral-choirmaster from 1571 (10 vols. of madrigals, besides other works, from 1563).

At Ferrara, south of the Po, music began to flourish early in the Middle Ages under the patronage of the powerful dukes of the Este family. In the 13th century their court was the headquarters of the Italian troubadours, and later a centre for painting as well — an artistic eminence that lasted till the 18th century. Many of the later Netherlanders worked here, like Des Près and Isaac before 1500 and Brumel from 1505, besides **Johannes Gallus** [Jean le Cocq], who died before 1543 as ducal choirmaster, and **Jachet de Berchem**, from 1555 ducal organist (works, chiefly secular, 1546–61). Other choirmasters were **Francesco Viola**, at Modena from 1530 and at Ferrara from about 1558, who edited some of Willaert's works (1559), besides issuing madrigals of his own (from 1550); **Alfonso della Viola**, notable for his incidental music for several plays (from 1541), of which only the words remain; and **Paolo Isnardi**, with many masses, lamentations, psalms, etc., besides madrigals (1561–98).

At Modena the outstanding name is **Orazio Vecchi** (d. 1605), where, after holding church offices at Correggio, he became choirmaster in 1596. From 1580 he put forth a long series of beautiful madrigals and canzonetti, depicting varying moods, grave and gay, and in 1594 a notable madrigal-comedy, *Amfiparnasso*. Almost equally fine were his sacred works.

At Milan, among the later Netherlanders, **Weerbecke** was a teacher from 1472, **Simon de Quercu** in the cathedral choir before 1508 and **Matthias Hermann** choirmaster in 1538–55. Among the madrigal-writers were **Vincenzo Ruffo**, born at Verona and choirmaster there from 1554 and at Milan from 1563, except six years at Pistoia, whose works (1542–88) were highly esteemed, and the organist **Giuseppe Caimo** (works, 1564–85). More important was **Orfeo Vecchi** (d. before 1604), choirmaster at Sta. Maria della Scala, prolific as a church writer (from 1590).

58. The Papal Chapel. — While northern Italy was thus cultivating composition, especially in secular directions, with enthusiasm and brilliance, important progress was taking place at Rome, but usually with a different spirit and emphasis. In Rome advance was practically confined to establishments identified with the papal court — the Papal or Sistine Chapel, St. Peter's, St. John Lateran, Sta. Maria Maggiore, and one or two others of the basilicas. While secular writing was not neglected, the accent fell upon ecclesiastical music and upon such a conservative handling of it as befitted the churches that stood as models for the Catholic world. Furthermore, the drift of Roman taste and manners was at the time less toward sensuous display and less vivacious and impressionable than in cosmopolitan and luxurious Venice.

> The 15th century closed with a decided decline in the prestige of the Papacy, owing to the evil lives and violent intrigues of certain pontiffs, but the 16th opened with a reassertion of dignity and power by Julius II. (1503–13) and Leo X. (1513–22), the latter of whom was called upon to meet the beginnings of Protestantism. After these the longer pontificates were those of Clement VII. (1523–34), Paul III. (1534–50), Gregory XIII. (1572–85) and Clement VIII. (1592–1605). During the 16th century it is notable that none of the popes was chosen from Venice or its dependencies.

The Papal Chapel is an institution with a long and peculiar history, reaching back to the singers' schools of the early popes. During the Middle Ages its traditions developed until it became a fixed feature of the papal court. Election to it was a great honor, being for life and including a moderate salary, with many curious perquisites. The rule was that none but priests or those who might be priests were eligible. Elderly members were usually removed by promotion to more lucrative church positions.

> The number of singers varied — 9 about 1450, 12–16 a little later, 20 about 1510, 36 about 1520, 24 through most of the century, then 18–32 for a time. As the need grew for competent sopranos and altos, much

skill was used in the culture of the higher tones of the male voice (a specialty remarkably developed in Spain). After 1600 even castrates or *evirati* were admitted to some extent.

The leadership of the Chapel was ordinarily intrusted to the oldest singer, but special choirmasters were sometimes designated. At first sight it would seem curious that during the 16th century so few of the choirmasters known by name were eminent composers, but it appears that the choirmaster of St. Peter's usually had oversight of the choir in the Sistine Chapel as well.

Naturally here sacred polyphony was developed to its highest perfection. It is customary to single out the great Palestrina as the chief agent in this, but it should be remembered that he was one of a series of masters, some of whom preceded him, and that the quick recognition of his power implies a considerable preparation. It was inevitable that the best works of current styles should be desired by the papal authorities, and that able composers should be eager to compete for approval.

Among masters already named, two were members of the Papal Chapel — **Dufay** in 1428–37 and **Des Près** in 1486–94?. Probably others were active there also. Certainly the initial impetus for the Roman school came direct from the Netherlands. From about 1515, composers of Italian birth began to be prominent.

Eleazar Genet [Carpentras] (d. 1532?) was born near Avignon, joined the Papal Choir in 1508, ultimately becoming choirmaster, and in 1521 returned to Avignon as a papal agent. His masses, lamentations and hymns, in a style antique and austere, were printed by Channay at Avignon in types cut by Briard (from 1532).

Costanzo Festa (d. 1545), a Roman born, on the other hand, was a writer of original power. From 1517 he sang in the Papal Chapel, for which his sacred works (printed posthumously) were written, including the Te Deum still used at the election of a pope and other great occasions. His style, with its sweet and earnest fidelity to the text, foreshadows Palestrina, whence Ambros calls him the "morning-star" of the new epoch. He issued one book of madrigals (1537).

Ghiselin Danckerts, a Zeelander, was in the Chapel in 1538–65, then retiring on a pension. Besides composing skillfully (few works extant), he took the conservative side in the debate between Vicentino and Lusitano in 1551 (see sec. 72).

Jacob Arcadelt (d. c. 1560), born in the Netherlands about 1514, was in the Chapel in 1540–9, went to Paris probably about 1555, and died there as royal musician (see sec. 65). He is best known by his five books of exquisite madrigals (1539–44), which rank among the best. His sacred works came later.

Cristobal Morales (d. 1553), born at Seville in 1512, after serving in the Chapel in 1535–40, was probably choirmaster at Toledo and Malaga. He stands out, not only as the ablest of the Spaniards who now begin to appear at Rome, but as one of the greatest of Palestrina's immediate predecessors, and his works are still somewhat in use. His style was serious, but eminently tasteful and free from secularities (masses and magnificats from 1542).

Giovanni Animuccia (d. 1570?), born at Florence, was choirmaster at St. Peter's in 1555-71, filling the interval between the terms of Palestrina. He is notable as the first to write *laudi spirituali* (1563-70) for Neri (see sec. 76), besides madrigals (from 1547) and masses (from 1567). His brother, Paolo Animuccia (d. 1563), was choirmaster at the Lateran in 1550-2.

59. Palestrina. — The finest tendencies of the time were summed up in the achievements of Palestrina, whose half-century of activity was almost wholly spent at Rome. Even in his own lifetime his genius was seen to be of the highest order, at once representative and original, with an exaltation that remained unmatched for more than a century. Yet, wonderful as it was, its permanent impress upon musical art has been limited, because chiefly put forth in a form of church music which in theory holds itself aloof from other music and which was not an ultimate type. Both the greatness and the limitation of Palestrina's work are evidenced by the fact that it had comparatively little sequel. In its own field it was a consummation that could not be surpassed, but it came at a time when musical progress was turning with avidity to other fields.

The Palestrina style commands admiration, not for its mere technical dexterity as polyphony, though it is full of extreme skill, nor for its stupendous or startling effects, though it is eminently sublime, but for its rejection of intellectual cleverness for its own sake, its instinctive avoidance of secular elements and a secular spirit, its success in finding ways of expression perfectly germane both to the solemn texts treated and to the conditions of the Roman liturgy, and an indescribable ideality or etherealness of conception. This ideality makes it to the modern taste somewhat cold and impersonal. Yet, when properly rendered and properly considered, its representative works stand among the noblest triumphs of religious art. While the Venetian styles were facing forward toward the more passionate forms of the 17th and later centuries, the Palestrina style belonged rather to the mediæval world, with its emphasis upon monastic reveries and contemplation, so that it can be fully appreciated only through sympathy with that unmodern realm of belief and sentiment.

Giovanni Pierluigi da Palestrina (d. 1594) acquired his name from the village where he was born (in 1526) and had his early training. At 14 he probably went to Rome for four years, studied with a Netherlander, Gaudio Mell (not Goudimel), and in 1544 returned to Palestrina as organist, marrying there in 1547. In 1551 he was called to St. Peter's as choirmaster, whence in 1555 for about six months he was taken into the Papal Chapel, being thrown out, with others, by a change of popes and an enforcement of the rule against married singers. He then became choirmaster successively at the Lateran and in 1561 at Sta. Maria Maggiore, besides being employed by the Pope from 1565 to supply various works for his Chapel. In 1571 he was called back to St. Peter's, where, in spite of attractions elsewhere (as to Mantua in 1583), he remained till his death, over twenty years later. In 1581, having lost his wife, he was married again to  a wealthy widow. Though probably of humble origin and perhaps early struggling with hardship and the jealousy of rivals, his later years were spent in ease and honor. It is said, however, that of his four sons, the three more promising died young. His renown was both attested and enhanced by his connection with the debate before the Council of Trent (see below) and by his position as composer to the Papal Choir — a dignity conferred only upon him and upon his successor Anerio.

His works were probably more numerous than of any other Italian writer of the period, including over 90 masses (12 books, 1554–1601), over 500 motets (7 books, 1563–84), and other church pieces, such as hymns, lamentations, litanies, offertoria, laudi and madrigali spirituali, etc., and over 100 madrigals (from 1555). They are now republished complete in a standard edition of 33 vols. (1862–1903). His *Improperia* have been sung in the Sistine Chapel on Good Fridays since 1560, and many other works are still in use.

In the middle of the century there arose a sharp debate about the whole method of ecclesiastical music. As has been noted (sec. 44), the Netherlanders evolved their praxis out of secular music, not hesitating to take 'subjects' for masses and motets from popular song, even those with vulgar or jocose words. They even tolerated the singing of these phrases to their original words, while the counterpoint proceeded with the Latin text. When these customs were transplanted to Rome, they were bound sooner or later to be challenged. When, therefore,

at the end of the memorable Council of Trent the general subject of music in public worship came up, a strong presentation
was made against all figured music and in favor of Plain-Song
only.   After hearing from a committee chosen to indicate
abuses, the Council simply voted against the use of whatever
was "lascivious or impure," and the matter was left to the provincial synods with a general warning.

The definition of what was "lascivious or impure" remained an open question.   The drastic action originally proposed was powerfully combatted by
the influence of various members, among them the Emperor Ferdinand I., who
sent a formal notice that in his judgment figured music should not be excluded,
"since it often arouses the feeling of piety."

In 1564 Pius IV., himself a music-lover, brought the subject before the
cardinals, and a small committee was named to consider it.   They speedily
agreed to the exclusion of all words except those of the prescribed Latin
texts, with all careless alterations of the latter, and to the importance of so
restricting the expansion of musical phrases upon single syllables and the
confusion of conflicting voice-parts as to leave the words and sense of the
text obvious to the hearer.   Many works conforming to these principles were
already in use, but, to make the matter sure, a recent work of Palestrina's was
named by the Pope as a model.   This is the one now known as the *Mass of
Pope Marcellus* (from the Pope who, in 1555, had made a special effort to
purify church music).   Hence came in later times an exaggerated estimate of
Palestrina as "the saviour of church music," with many perversions of the
story.   From this time there was a marked improvement in the character of
the works regularly used in the Papal Chapel, but it was one that really began
before 1564 and to which many composers contributed.   In Palestrina's own
style there was a distinct advance from about 1560.   In 1576 Gregory XII.
intrusted the revision of the Gradual and Antiphonary to Palestrina, but most
of the actual work was done by his pupil *Giovanni Guidetti* (d. 1592).

60. Other Roman Masters. — The composers who wrought at
Rome after about 1570 were necessarily influenced by the new
ideals that had been set up, and this period is justly considered
as the best of the Roman school.   Within certain natural limits
the forms in which Palestrina and his immediate successors
worked and the methods they used were thought to be the acme
of musical art.   This special type continued into the 17th and
18th centuries, and is still supported by the official approval of
the Catholic Church.   But, as will be seen, progress in absolutely
new directions became so absorbing that the Palestrina style was
presently overtopped in popular interest and historic importance
by styles belonging to a totally different sphere.

In the long list of Palestrina's contemporaries and followers these are most worthy of special mention : —

Giovanni Maria Nanino (d. 1607), born at Tivoli about 1545, after study probably with Gaudio Mell, Palestrina's reputed teacher, became a singer at Sta. Maria Maggiore in 1571 and choirmaster at S. Luigi dei Francesi in 1575 and at Sta. Maria Maggiore from 1579. He founded an important sing-ing-school in which Palestrina was a teacher, with a noble line of pupils. He was in the Papal Chapel in 1577-9, and its choirmaster from 1604. He is ranked as a composer of high order, belonging to the conservative school like Palestrina, though not equaling him in originality or productiveness. His relatively few remaining works (from about 1571) are largely secular, but include some masses, motets and lamentations. With him was associated his nephew, **Giovanni Bernardino Nanino** (d. 1623), a less striking, but more enterprising, genius (works from 1588).

Tomas Luis de Victoria [called **Vittoria** in Italy] (d. c. 1613) was born at Avila (Spain) about 1540, came to Rome, studied under Morales, in 1566 became singer and later choirmaster at the German College and later at S. Apollinare, and from 1589 served in the Royal Chapel at Madrid. He was a close friend of Palestrina and their styles were similar, though he had a warmth peculiarly his own. His extant works are all sacred and are numerous and powerful (from 1576). He often wrote for many voices.

Felice Anerio (d. 1614), born at Rome, a pupil of G. M. Nanino, was so closely affiliated with Palestrina that their works have been confounded. After holding lesser positions, in 1594 he succeeded him as composer to the Papal Choir — the only other appointee to this post. His known works are not many (1585-1606).

Giovanni Francesco Anerio (d. c. 1620), perhaps the brother of Felice, was born about 1567, and in 1575-9 was a choirboy at St. Peter's under Pale-strina. In 1609 he was royal choirmaster in Poland and in 1610 at Verona, but returned to Rome in 1611. His fertility was great and his works (from 1599) were extremely varied, the later ones being quite out of the recognized *a cappella* styles. He arranged Palestrina's *Marcellus Mass* and two others for four voices (1619).

Francesco Soriano (d. 1620), born at Rome in 1549 and a pupil of Zoilo, G. M. Nanino and Palestrina, held several posts as choirmaster — from 1581 at S. Luigi dei Francesi, soon after at Mantua, from 1587 at Sta. Maria Mag-giore and again from 1600, in 1599 at the Lateran, and from 1603 at St. Peter's. His motets, masses, psalms, passions and madrigals (from 1581) show a versatile and powerful genius ; he also rearranged the *Marcellus Mass*.

Tiburtio Massaini is an example of representatives of the Roman school whose activity was mainly elsewhere. He was in Rome in 1571, at various places in Italy afterward, and also in imperial service in Austria (many works from 1569).

Lesser names are **Annibale Zoilo**, choirmaster at the Lateran in 1561-70 and then in the Papal Chapel (works from 1563) ; **Annibale Stabile** (d. c. 1595), a pupil of Palestrina, choirmaster in Rome from 1575 (works from 1572) ; and **Giovanni Andrea Dragoni** (d. 1598), also one of Palestrina's pupils, choir-master at the Lateran in 1576-94 (works from 1575).

CHAPTER VIII

CHURCH MUSIC IN NORTHERN AND WESTERN EUROPE

61. In General. — The story of music in northern Europe at this time gathers about three centres, Austria, the seat of the Hapsburg line of emperors, Bavaria, more or less associated with it, and Saxony, the headquarters of the Protestant Reformation. The first two were intimately affiliated with Italy and shared in all Italian tendencies, while the last tended to strike out into new paths in sacred music. It is convenient and valid to consider them somewhat apart. Chronologically it would be better to begin with Austria, but topically it is more useful to turn at once to the rise of Reformation music in Saxony. This will lead on, finally, to a survey of musical progress in France, the Low Countries and England, all of which were affected by the Reformation.

62. The Lutheran Reformation. — Lutheran Protestantism began in Saxony and took its name from Martin Luther, a highly educated Augustinian monk, well versed in music, who at Wittenberg, in 1517, publicly protested against the sale of indulgences and other abuses in the papal system as then administered, and who by 1520 had become so outspoken as to be excommunicated. His action was a symptom of a widespread feeling that was waiting for organization. Luther at once attracted able coadjutors, and under their leadership a complex revolution of thought swept over northern Germany, winning support from all classes.

> The issue between the Protestant and the Catholic parties was fully defined by 1520 (the Diet of Augsburg), but was not held to be irreconcilable till about 1550. The progress of the movement during its first century, owing to the extreme partition of Germany into many petty states, all overshadowed by the Empire, was involved in complicated political entanglements, by which its character was often distorted its well-wishers split into hostile factions, and its advance checked. In consequence, its features escape succinct statement.

From his doctrines of salvation by faith, the right of private judgment, and the universal priesthood of believers, Luther deduced radical conclusions regarding public worship, including special emphasis on congregational participation in the service in the vernacular language (instead of Latin). Although holding closely to the outlines of the Roman service, he undertook to reduce some features that he held objectionable and to make the people's part conspicuous. He seized upon common song as indispensable, and in 1523 and 1526, with the aid of Walther and others, issued orders of service with this element emphasized. The hymns provided were as a rule specially written in metrical form. For them melodies were either borrowed from favorite folk-songs or part-songs or were newly written in similar style, thus linking the new style with forms already universally popular. These melodies were later called 'chorales.'

Though at first the musical treatment of chorales was more or less contrapuntal, with the melody in the tenor, before 1600 the style advanced to a definitely harmonic form, with a solid progression of chords, the melody in the treble and the lines sharply defined by cadences and controlled by a coherent tonality.

The chorale became the nucleus of Protestant church music generally, and it is of historic importance because its wide acceptance hastened and popularized the new tendency to base composition on harmony rather than counterpoint, and because from its extensive literature German organ music later derived an inexhaustible fund of suggestion. What the treasures of Plain-Song had been to Catholic music, the new treasures of the chorale style became to Protestant music. This innovation, then, contained the germ of great subsequent developments.

Luther's strong interest in congregational music involved no hostility to choir music. He himself knew and loved a wide range of mass and motet music, and he advocated the free use of whatever was excellent, believing that, with slight exceptions, there was no distinction between Catholic and Protestant standards. Thus much of the rich polyphonic accumulation, so far as accessible in northern Germany, passed over at once into Protestant usage. With it came not a little Plain-Song.

It is a curious fact that presently the Catholic world lost the power of further advance in the style of which Palestrina was master, while in Protestant Germany contrapuntal theory and practice were cultivated to such purpose that in the 18th century a second culmination was possible. It is idle to speculate whether this transfer of artistic vitality was due to religious or racial causes.

K

On the whole, the Reformation tended to awaken a new energy in society, whence the art of music on all its sides received benefit. But the political confusions and distresses that accompanied it were unfavorable to all art, and these were not overpast till late in the 17th century. Yet, even from the first, the liberation of thought and feeling made popular expression in song and with instruments more spontaneous, varied and heartfelt. Much of the wealth and depth of modern music may surely be traced in large measure to the mental and spiritual stimulus accompanying the rise of Protestantism.

The various Saxon states, including cities like Dresden and Leipsic on the east, Erfurt and Mühlhausen on the west, and Wittenberg and Magdeburg on the north, may be regarded as a region musically distinct at this time. Here may be noted the following individuals : —

Martin Luther (d. 1546), born at Eisleben in 1483, was educated at Magdeburg, Eisenach and Erfurt, entered the priesthood in 1507, became professor of theology at Wittenberg in 1508, where in 1517 his 95 theses against indulgences were put forth. In 1521 he appeared before the Diet of Worms, where his views were rejected by the Emperor. To save his life, the friendly Elector of Saxony seized him and kept him hidden for a year at the Wartburg, where he completed the first part of his epochal translation of the Bible. In 1524 appeared his first hymn-book, later augmented. In 1525, having renounced the priesthood, he married. In 1529-30 occurred his controversy with the Swiss Reformers, and the important Diet of Augsburg. The control of the movement then gradually passed into the hands of others. His original hymns grew from 4 in 1524 to 35 in 1545, and for a few of these he perhaps wrote melodies. He was fond of music, a good flutist and lutist, and highly appreciative of good polyphony, but was not a composer. His literary references to music are enthusiastic and discriminating.

Johann Walther (d. 1570), Luther's chief musical adviser, was electoral choirmaster at Torgau from 1525 and at Dresden from 1548, retiring in 1554 on a pension. The musical editor of the first hymn-book (1524 and later editions to 1551), he was the composer or arranger of many chorales. He also wrote motets and sacred part-songs (from 1538).

To meet the demand for German church music, a multitude of writers now began to appear throughout northern Germany, some of whom displayed skill in so combining contrapuntal learning with popular types that their choir music had a certain kinship with the new congregational music. The texts used were often the same as those of the Roman liturgy, though generally in a German version. It is interesting to observe occasional settings of the story of the Passion — the germ of a form later of great importance.

The following names may be taken as illustrations : —

Sixt Dietrich (d. 1548), born at Augsburg, spent his early life in Switzerland, not developing his decided musical talent till about 50 years old, when he came to Wittenberg (motets, hymns, etc., from 1535).

Matthæus Le Maistre (d. 1577), a Netherlander, was court-choirmaster at Dresden in 1554–67. His works (from 1563) include masses, motets and many part-songs. As early as 1566 he arranged chorales with the melody in the treble. [Not to be confused, as by Fétis and Kade, with Hermann Matthias of Milan.]

Antonio Scandello (d. 1580), born at Brescia about 1517, came to Dresden before 1553 as court-trumpeter and assisted Le Maistre from 1566, succeeding him in 1568. He was a notable writer of sacred and secular part-songs (from 1551), also of masses, motets and several Passions (from 1550).

Elias Nikolaus Ammerbach (d. 1597), organist of the Thomaskirche in Leipsic from 1560, was a composer for organ and clavichord, and author of a handbook (1571) on organ tablature, with important data about tuning, fingering, etc.

Leonhardt Schröter (d. c. 1600), from about 1572 cantor at Magdeburg, left a cluster of sacred part-songs, etc., (from 1562), that mark him as one of the able Protestant contrapuntists.

Joachim à Burck [Moller] (d. 1610) also made a name as a prolific composer, being organist at Mühlhausen from 1566. His works, nearly all sacred, included three Passions (from 1568), a Communion Service, psalms, many *Odæ sacræ* or part-songs.

To this general region also belong **Jobst vom Brant**, governor of Liebenstein from 1549 ; **Nikolaus Rosth**, court-musician at Heidelberg, Altenburg and Weimar (works from 1583, including a Passion, 1598) ; **Henning Dedekind** (d. 1628), cantor and pastor at Langensalza (works from 1588) ; and **Valentin Haussmann**, a busy organist at Gerbstedt, whose talent lay rather in developing the resources of secular music, especially dances (works from 1588). The first known members of the great Bach family also belong here — **Hans Bach** of Wechmar (near Gotha) and his son **Veit Bach** (d. 1619) being direct ancestors of J. S. Bach, besides others whose relationship is not clear.

Outside of the Saxon circle were —

Franz Elers (d. 1590), who spent his life at Hamburg as teacher, from 1529 cantor and finally choirmaster at the cathedral. His large and important Gesangbuch (1588) contains much Protestant ritual music.

Johann Eccard (d. 1611), born at Mühlhausen in 1553, a friend of à Burck, was first in the service of Baron Fugger of Augsburg, from 1579 choirmaster at Königsberg (Prussia), and from 1608 in the Electoral Chapel at Berlin. His many part-songs (from 1574), mostly sacred, show him to have been one of the more original writers of the time.

Bartholomäus Gesius (d. 1613), born about 1555, first studied theology, but from 1595 was cantor at Frankfurt-an-der-Oder. His important works (from 1569) include a Passion (1588), a great number of sacred part-songs, motets, psalms, several masses, festival anthems and a popular handbook (1609).

Hieronymus Prätorius (d. 1629), born at Hamburg in 1560, studied there and at Cologne, was cantor at Erfurt in 1580-2, and then returned to Hamburg to succeed his father as organist at the Jacobikirche. His masterly style resembles that of the best Venetian contrapuntists, passing to the use of as many as 20 voices (works from 1599). The earlier **Christoph Prätorius** (d. 1609) was cantor at Lüneburg in 1562-82 (works from 1560).

63. The Imperial Chapel. — The musical importance of Austria at this time arose from its relation to the Holy Roman Empire, which was the inheritor of the prestige and romantic interest of the ancient imperial idea, combined with the mediæval idea of Catholic unity. From 1438 the Emperors were all of the Hapsburg line, and the imperial capital was usually Prague or Vienna. The dignity of the court required the maintenance of a musical establishment or Chapel, which naturally came to have international significance. The close relations of the Empire with the Papacy brought their musical activities into the same class. During the 16th century most of the leading imperial musicians were Netherlanders. Yet with these were others who illustrated the native genius once shown by the Minnesinger and again to become famous in the 18th century. While most of these composers devoted themselves to the current Catholic types of composition, many of them were so successful in simpler part-writing of the German type that their works were often adopted into Protestant use.

The list of emperors for the period includes Maximilian I. (1493-1519), Charles V. (1519-56), Ferdinand I. (1556-64, also sole ruler of Austria from 1522), Maximilian II. (1564-76), and Rudolf II. (1576-1612).

Among the musicians in the imperial service were the following: —

Heinrich Isaac (d. c. 1517), who was born in Flanders before 1450, but won his first fame in Italy, especially as organist and choirmaster at Florence in 1477-89. From 1497 he was court-musician to Maximilian I. at Innsbruck. From him we have many important masses, motets and part-songs (from 1506), the former in the older Netherland style, the latter akin to the early Protestant music. Among his pupils was Senfl.

Paul Hofheimer (d. 1537) was born near Salzburg in 1459. From about 1480 he was imperial organist and composer, first at Innsbruck, from 1496 at Vienna. About 1515 he was made a noble and received other honors, being held as the foremost German musician of his time. He returned to Salzburg after 1520, perhaps by way of Augsburg. As a player he was unrivaled, but of his compositions little remains.

Jakob Clemens (d. 1558?) was a Netherlander who is usually supposed to have been imperial choirmaster under Charles V., but of his career nothing is certain. This is the more remarkable because he was one of the finest contrapuntists after Des Près, artistic, rich in melody and harmony, versatile and highly productive. His known works (from 1543, most apparently posthumous) are numerous, including a series of noble masses, over 150 motets, many chansons on French or Flemish popular songs, etc. [He was called *Clemens non Papa* to distinguish him from *Clement VII.* (pope, 1523–34), who was himself a good musician.]

Arnold von Bruck (d. 1545), born at Bruges, was choirmaster to Ferdinand I. from 1534 — to-day known through some 60 scattered motets and part-songs with Latin or German words (from 1538).

Philippe de Monte (d. 1603), born at Mechlin in 1521, after serving in the Chapel Royal of England, became imperial choirmaster in 1563, at first assisting Vaet. His long term of service and his extant works (from 1554) indicate something of his eminence as one of the ablest Netherlanders. His publications (from 1554) included over 35 volumes of madrigals and chansons for 3–7 voices, 10 volumes of motets for 4–12 voices, 3 volumes of madrigali spirituali, 1 of masses, with many more in MS.

Jakob Vaet (d. 1567), another Netherlander, was in the Royal Chapel from 1562 and choirmaster from 1564. He is supposed to have served as an early promoter of the strict style (many motets, some masses and magnificats, a fine Te Deum for 8 voices, from 1562).

Alexander Utendal (d. 1581), of Netherland origin, spent his life in Innsbruck as choirboy, singer and assistant choirmaster under the Archduke Ferdinand. He wrote psalms, motets, masses, German and French part-songs (from 1570).

Alard du Gaucquier, born at Lille, was in the Chapel in 1564–76 and later ducal choirmaster. His reputation rests on several masses and magnificats (from 1574).

Jakob Regnart (d. c. 1600), still another Netherlander, one of five brothers, born in 1540, was choirboy, then court-singer and assistant choirmaster at Prague, about 1582 under the Archduke Ferdinand at Innsbruck, returning in 1595 to Prague again. His varied works (from 1574) were much esteemed, especially his canzone and German part-songs.

Jakob Handl [usually called **Gallus**] (d. 1591), born about 1550 in Carniola (southwest Austria), in 1578, after some travel, became choirmaster at Olmütz, whence in 1585 he went to Prague. He stands out as one of the best German contrapuntists during the Palestrina epoch, belonging, however, rather to the Venetian school. His masses, motets and moralia or 4-part songs (from 1580) were long in high repute in Germany.

A few lesser names are **Leonhardt Paminger** (d. 1597), rector of a school at Passau and a good motettist (cycle for the year, posthumous) ; **Valentin Bacfart** [**Graew**] (d. 1576), a Hungarian lutist, from 1566 alternately at the courts of Vienna and Poland, author of two works in tablature, with many pieces (1564–8) ; **Blasius Ammon** (d. 1590), a Tyrolese singer at Innsbruck and Vienna (sacred works from 1582) ; and **François Sale** (d. 1599), about 1589 choirmaster at Hall (Tyrol), and from 1593 singer at Prague (works, mostly sacred, from 1589).

64. Lassus and the South German Masters. — In the 16th
century Bavaria was almost as potent a factor in the Empire
as Austria.   Religiously it was strongly Catholic in sympathy
and in close communication with Italy.   Some of its cities, like
Nuremberg, Augsburg and Ulm, were musically known throughout Europe, not only as Meistersinger centres, but as headquarters of music-printing and instrument-making.   About 1550
Munich rose to eminence under the culture-loving Dukes
Albrecht and Wilhelm.   Furthermore, here as elsewhere, the
native power of German genius was beginning to compete on
equal terms with that of the Netherlands.   Even Protestant
Württemberg and other states to the west, though less active,
were not without worthy musicians.

> In the early development of South German music are seen certain
> musical traits that are more or less distinctive of all German music.
> Perhaps most valuable among these is a remarkable sincerity and direct-
> ness of sentiment, heartfelt and wholesome, combined with imaginative
> and creative energy.   From the outset German composers realized the
> unequaled capacity of music for the real embodiment of human life on all
> its sides, and strove to fuse together in their works the intellectuality of
> the Netherland school with their own richness of experience and phan-
> tasy.   In illustration, it is enough to adduce the German fondness for the
> song-type, from the homely folk-song with its artless earnestness up to
> the studied part-song.   The religious bent of the German mind, also, is ex-
> ceptional in its heartiness of conviction, its independence and its practical-
> ity.   Hence, while the mere working out of forms suited to the mediæval
> ritual was elsewhere accomplished, the broader application of music to
> religious utterance was first conceived in the atmosphere of German life.
> Even in the 16th century, when music was acquiring its first self-con-
> sciousness as an art, the later German leadership in it can already be
> descried, asserting itself in both vocal and instrumental writing.

Historically, it was important that so gifted an artist as
Orlandus Lassus was brought to spend the productive part
of his career in Germany.   His genius towered above that of
all his contemporaries except Palestrina.   Both were in full
command of the resources of polyphonic construction, and both
aspired to compositions of the grandest magnitude and quality.
But the differences between them are noteworthy.   Lassus exhibited the greater breadth and fertility, though he was not
as essentially ideal in purely ritual music.   His warmth of
human feeling and readiness of sympathy made his impress
upon progress wider and more genial.   He was more truly a

man of the time, and the fact that he lived at a princely court, with its free and shifting society, in the heart of the music-loving German highlands, gave him great influence. But the musical strength of South Germany was not dependent upon him alone. Other geniuses appeared to give at this point an impetus that did not cease for centuries.

The line of distinguished Bavarian masters includes —

Ludwig Senfl (d. 1556), born about 1492 at Zurich, a pupil of Isaac at Innsbruck and his successor there for a short time. In 1519 he was in the Imperial Chapel at Vienna and from 1520 in Augsburg, and from 1526 court-choirmaster at Munich, remaining till his death. His works (from 1526) were masses, motets, hymns, German part-songs, etc., in a style that united the old strictness with something of Venetian richness. Although a Catholic, he was a friend of Luther, and the latter greatly admired his music.

Ludwig Daser (d. 1589), born at Munich in 1520, was from 1552 court-choirmaster there till displaced by Lassus in 1560, then from 1571 court-choir-master at Stuttgart. Though a worthy composer, his works, mostly masses, remain in MS., except a Passion (1578).

Orlandus de Lassus [Orlando di Lasso] (d. 1594) was born at Mons (Hainaut) in 1532. His boy's voice gave him a dangerous notoriety, so that about 1544 he was abducted and taken to Palermo and Milan in the service of Ferdinand Gonzaga. About 1550 he passed into another noble's service at Naples and Rome. He is said to have visited England, but settled at Antwerp. Called thence in 1556 to Munich, he became court-choirmaster in 1560, and continued in office and in great honor till about 1590, when he broke down mentally through overwork. His life and Palestrina's were almost exactly contemporaneous, but it is not known that they ever met. Lassus had the great advantage of travel and of constant contact with culture amid unbroken appreciation. Though his office was laborious and difficult, requiring great executive ability, his patron spared nothing to keep the Chapel one of the best in Europe. The duke being a stanch Catholic, most of Lassus' sacred works were of the mass or motet class, but freedom of treatment was encouraged. His most celebrated work was the *Penitential Psalms* (1584). Secular works of every description were also welcomed, including not only stately madrigals, but also sprightly canzonets, drinking-songs — even musical jokes. The list of his compositions (from 1552) is enormous — almost 2500 separate works, now published in a standard edition. He had many pupils, of whom Eccard and Reiner were perhaps the foremost.

Of Lassus' co-laborers, mention may be made of **Ivo de Vento** (d. 1575), a Spaniard, organist from 1569 (motets and good German part-songs from 1569).

Not far west of Munich is the much older Augsburg, the capital of Swabia, prominent in the 16th century as a centre for music-publishing. Here a notable patronage came from the wealthy Barons Fugger. Among earlier composers were **Sigismund Salbinger**, an ex-monk, who edited valuable collections of part-songs (1540-9); **Jacob van Kerle** (d. c. 1583), a Netherlander, first in service at Cambrai, then in Italy, from 1562 under the Cardinal of Augsburg (sacred works from 1558); and the able Eccard (d. 1611), already mentioned (sec. 62).

Adam Gumpeltzhaimer (d. 1625), born in 1559, was musically trained in an Augsburg monastery, was then a general teacher, and from 1581 cantor at one of the churches, being also employed by the Duke of Württemberg. Besides a theoretical work (1591), he produced a quantity of motets, psalms and part-songs (from 1591) that show him to have been a careful student of both old and new styles.

Hans Leo Hassler (d. 1612), born in 1564 at Nuremberg, was one of the earliest Germans to seek instruction in Italy, where he studied with A. Gabrieli at Venice. In 1585 he became organist to Baron Fugger at Augsburg and later also at the cathedral, whence, in 1601, he was called to Nuremberg and in 1608 to the Royal Chapel at Dresden. His diversified works, sacred and secular (from 1590), not only show Venetian influence, as in the use of double choirs, but indicate the German genius for harmony, with important efforts to utilize artistically the folk-music of various peoples. His was a singularly enterprising and influential genius, sometimes ranked with that of Palestrina and Lassus. His two brothers, Jakob Hassler (d. c. 1611), a famous organ-virtuoso at Hechingen and Prague, and Kaspar Hassler (d. 1618), organist at Nuremberg (sacred collections from 1598), are also to be named.

Gregor Aichinger (d. 1628) was long organist to Baron Fugger (from 1584) and later vicar-choral at the cathedral. His motets and part-songs (from 1590) are praised for their elegance and simplicity.

Christian Erbach (d. 1635), born in 1573, was also organist to Baron Fugger and succeeded Hassler at the cathedral in 1602. He was a motettist of importance (works, 1600-11), and another leader in the direction of harmonic treatment.

North of the Danube in Franconia is the interesting city of Nuremberg. Among the many instrument-makers here were Konrad Gerle (d. 1521), whose lutes were famous before 1470, Hans Gerle (d. 1570), his son, known for good lutes and violins from 1523 and for important works in tablature (1532-52), and Hans Neusidler (d. 1563), also the compiler of lute-books (1536-44). Georg Forster (d. 1568), a physician here from about 1544, was one of the earliest and best collectors of folk-songs (5 parts, 1539-56) and of motets; and Friedrich Lindner (d. 1597), cantor of the Egidienkirche, was another useful editor of masses, motets and madrigals, adding examples of his own (1585-91).

At Ansbach we note Kaspar Othmayr (d. 1553), canon in the church of St. Gumbert from 1547, a worthy composer of part-songs (1546-9), and Jakob Meiland (d. 1577), court-choirmaster, afterwards at Frankfort and Celle, a strong contrapuntist (works from 1564).

Passing now westward into Württemberg, Hohenzollern and Baden, we add the names of Arnold Schlick, the blind court-organist at Heidelberg, whose books on organs and organ music (1511-2) are curious and valuable, indicating a genius ahead of his time; Bernhard Schmid (d. 1592), famous as one of the founders of the German organ style (with Sweelinck and Scheidt), organist at Strassburg, first at St. Thomas and from 1564 at the cathedral (organ-book, 1577), in both of which posts he was succeeded by his son

Bernhard Schmid (organ-book, 1607) ; **Wolf Heckel**, a Strassburg lutist (book, 1556) ; **Sebastian Ochsenkuhn** (d. 1574), court-lutist at Heidelberg and author of a valuable lute-book (1558) ; **Leonhard Lechner** (d. 1604), first a choirboy under Lassus at Munich, teacher at Nuremberg from 1570, and from 1584 court-choirmaster at Hechingen and from 1587 at Stuttgart — a versatile and gifted composer (works from 1575) ; **Melchior Schramm**, another good contrapuntist, long in the court chapel at Sigmaringen, afterwards organist at Offenburg (works from 1576) ; **Jakob Reiner** (d. 1606), one of the best pupils of Lassus, music-master all his life (though not a priest) in the monastery of Weingarten, with a varied list of works (from 1579) ; **Jakob Paix** (d. c. 1590), organist at Lauingen, whose collections of organ-pieces and motets (from 1583), with some original masses and a history of sacred music (1589), are important ; and **Lucas Osiander** (d. 1604), the son of the distinguished Nuremberg theologian, himself early noted as a Protestant leader in Wurttemberg and finally abbot at Adelsberg, with an important Choralbuch (1586) having the melodies in the treble (as by *Le Maistre* in 1566 and by *David Wolkenstein* in 1583).

65. France and Spain. — The 16th century was a stormy period in French history, made so at first by the craving of successive kings to widen their boundaries in the face of strong rivals, and later by the bitter contests between Catholics and Huguenots. What notable musical life there was appeared in the Royal Chapel at Paris, to the advancement of which the ambitious Francis I. devoted special attention. The styles there most cultivated were those of the Netherland masters, with gradually more and more chansons and lute music. Originality in composition was almost wholly confined to writers born in the Netherlands.

The chief kings (House of Valois) were Louis XII. (1498–1515), Francis I. (1515–47), who was the rival of Charles V., Henry II. (1547–59), Charles IX. (1560–74) and Henry III. (1574–89). The latter's successor, Henry IV. (1589–1610), the first of the Bourbons, was of Huguenot sympathies.

The information about most of the musicians in the Royal Chapel is scanty, but the following should be named : —

Jean Mouton (d. 1522), born near Metz, studied with Des Près, early entered the service of Louis XII., continuing under Francis I., and became canon of St. Quentin, where he died. His many works exhibit not only the utmost polyphonic facility, but an expressiveness singularly like his master's. They include some masses, many motets and chansons (from 1505). He was Willaert's teacher, and thus a link with the Venetian school.

Antoine de Riche [Divitis], a singer first at Bruges, then in the Burgundian Chapel, before 1515 in the Royal Chapel at Paris, is favorably known by a few works (from 1514). **Claude de Sermisy** (d. 1562) is still more famous as from 1508 singer, then about 1532–60 choirmaster in the Chapel, and a strong writer (works from 1529). **Pierre Colin,** singer in the Chapel in 1532–6, was later choirmaster at Autun (masses and motets from 1541). **Pierre Certon** (d. 1572), a pupil of Des Près, had the name of being one of the best writers of the day (works from 1540).

Clément Janequin, also a pupil of Des Près, is entirely unknown except from his many striking chansons, over 200 in number (1529–59), many of which bear descriptive or pictorial titles like ‘La bataille,’ ‘La chasse au cerf,’ ‘Le caquet des femmes,’ ‘L’alouette,’ etc., introducing a new element of depiction into composition.

Jacob Arcadelt (d. c. 1560), who has already been noted at Rome (sec. 58), much more celebrated than the foregoing, spent the last years of his life at Paris as royal musician, leaving some motets and masses (1545–57).

François Eustache du Caurroy (d. 1609), born near Beauvais in 1549, was in the Chapel from about 1568 for 40 years, perhaps as choirmaster throughout. His extant works (from 1569) are few and not equal to his reputation; they include a Requiem which for a century was the only one used for the kings of France.

Claudin Lejeune (d. c. 1600) was court-composer toward the end of the century. It has been thought that he resigned on account of his Huguenot opinions, but this is uncertain. His works (from 1564) are mostly chansons and madrigals, except his settings of metrical Psalms, which are important in early Calvinistic music.

Lesser names are **Jean Courtois**, choirmaster at Cambrai in 1539 (works from 1529), **Pierre Cadeac** of Auch (works from 1556), and **Guillaume Belin** (d. 1568), singer in the Chapel about 1547 (chansons from 1539).

Among the renowned lutists of the century who published music for their instrument were **Orance Finé** (d. 1555), with two books (1529–30); **Alberto da Rippa** (d. c. 1550), court-lutist from 1537 or earlier, with pieces from 1536 and two books (1553, ’62, each 6 parts); **Guillaume Morlaye,** with three books (1552–8); **Adrien Le Roy** (d. 1599), the publisher, with several books of his own, an instruction-book and very many valuable collections (from 1551); and **Jean Antoine de Baïf** (d. 1589), a much-traveled Venetian who about 1566 gave popular concerts at Paris, with several books (1562–80).

The Swiss Reformation, beginning before 1520 at Zurich under Zwingli, won the adherence of the Frenchman Calvin before 1530 and about 1535 came under the latter's leadership at Geneva, which was thenceforth the fountainhead of Protestantism in western Europe. Before 1550, Calvinists or Huguenots became numerous in France. They increased in power so rapidly that from 1562 for thirty-five years civil war between them and the dominant Catholic party went on, including in 1572 the notorious Massacre of St. Bartholomew, and closing in 1598 with the granting of toleration by the Edict of Nantes. The musical influence of the Huguenot movement was confined to the encouragement of chorales, often finely harmonized. These were adopted into Scottish and English use to some extent after 1558.

> Zwingli was a musical amateur and not averse to music in church worship, but his party went far beyond him in antipathy to all existing usages. In their onslaughts upon churches they ruthlessly destroyed organs and choir collections. Calvin's influence was cast on the other side, especially in favor of congregational singing of the Psalms. Hence arose a demand for metrical versions of the latter and for practicable tunes.

The evolution of the Calvinistic hymns and tunes, though analogous to that of the Lutheran chorales, presents peculiar features. The treasury of popular song from which they drew their inspiration was much smaller, their total number was less, and they were disseminated through several countries of varying traditions. They were not made the source of as much subsequent treatment by organ-writers, and in general their influence was much more restricted. Yet in themselves they were often eminently excellent.

> *Clément Marot* (d. 1544) was the first Calvinistic psalmist. He was introduced to Huguenot ideas as a boy and suffered imprisonment for them about 1525. Later, however, when court-poet to Francis I., he prepared some 30 psalm-versions in ballad style, which were forthwith taken up as a novelty by the gay court circle and sung to popular airs. But they were condemned by the Sorbonne, and Marot fled to Geneva, where he added 19 more Psalms (the first 30 were published in 1541, 35 in 1542, 49, with 40 by Beza, in 1555). It is supposed that Marot arranged some of the melodies used. His version was gradually completed at Calvin's desire by *Théodore de Beza* (d. 1605), who became a Huguenot in 1548. The most famous of those who fitted music to these versions were Bourgeois and Goudimel, but others experimented with the new and popular style.

> **Loys Bourgeois,** born at Paris, became a Huguenot and was a singer at Geneva in 1545-57, going thence to Lyons and probably later to Paris. He issued chorales (1547, 1554, 1561), harmonized for 4 voices, himself composing many of the melodies. Besides thus being the first writer of Calvinistic music, he issued a theoretical work (1550) that improved solmization and otherwise simplified the hexachord-system. (Cf. *Waelrant*, sec. 66.)

> **Claude Goudimel** (d. 1572) was born at Besançon about 1505. [It has been commonly said that he was a Netherlander, a pupil of Des Près, the founder, about 1540, of a school at Rome where Palestrina, G. Animuccia, G. M. Nanino and other composers were taught, and therefore ' the father of the Roman school; ' but it is now thought that he was never in Rome, and was confused with Gaudio Mell.] From at least 1551 he was in Paris, for a time a partner

of the publisher Chemin, in 1557 lived at Metz, and was killed in the St. Bar-tholomew massacre at Lyons, though whether actually a Protestant is not clear. His masses, motets and chansons (from 1549) are written in a masterly style, and he was diligent in producing motet settings of metrical Psalms for 4-5 voices (1551–66), the melodies of which, usually in the tenor, were not original with him. These latter were important additions to early Calvinistic music, though too elaborate for congregational use.

Philibert Jambe de Fer (d. 1572) also published a complete Psalter (1561, possibly in part as early as 1549). He also was killed at Lyons with Goudimel.

It is natural that Spain, with its intense devotion to the me-diæval Church and under princes like Charles V. (1515–56) and Philip II. (1556–98), should show a strong interest in church mu-sic. But the notable musicians of the Royal Chapel were Neth-erlanders, the most famous being Gombert.

In both Spain and Portugal, also, the influence of the Trou-badours lingered long, showing itself in a special taste for gay songs and dances and the use of a great variety of instruments. Not much of this is preserved in detail, but we know that the social interest in poetry and song was considerable.

Nicolas Gombert, born at Bruges, was perhaps a pupil of Des Près. From 1530 he taught at Brussels and in 1537 entered the Royal Chapel at Madrid, first as trainer, then as choirmaster, though apparently with absences at Tournai. His works (1539–57), numbering about 250, range over all the usual forms, sacred and secular, in a style specially clear, solid and full of feeling.

Francisco Guerrero (d. 1599), born at Seville in 1527, was early a singer there, and in 1555 competed successfully for Morales' post as cathedral-choir-master, remaining 45 years. His works (from 1555) are all sacred, unless, possibly, one book of Spanish part-songs is his.

The only Portuguese composer to be named is **Damião de Goes** (d. 1560), born in 1500, trained at Padua, who lived at various places in Europe as royal envoy and was finally employed at home in historical writing. He had high repute as a composer, but hardly any works remain. He is said also to have written a theoretical treatise, now lost.

Among the early lute-books (from 1546) were those of **Enriquez de Valderravano** (1547), **Miguel de Fuenllana** (1554) and **Antonio de Cabezon** (1578).

66. The Netherlands. — While in the 16th century the leader-ship in contrapuntal music passed from the Low Countries to Italy and Germany, yet the land of its origin not only provided teachers for all the rest of Europe, but preserved her own in-terest as well. In some cases, late in the century, the study of Italian models is evident, but on the whole the Netherlands continued to be a fairly independent musical region. The chief centre of activity was Antwerp. The commercial instinct of the nation showed itself in decided success with music-printing and organ-building throughout the century.

From the accession of Philip II. of Spain in 1556 the political and social condition of the country became very unfavorable for artistic advance, since for almost half a century the energy of the people went into struggles for freedom from Spanish tyranny. In 1579 the Utrecht Union of seven of the northern provinces was the beginning of the later Republic, but this led the Catholic provinces in the south to ally themselves either with Parma or with Spain itself.

After the death of Jacotin in 1528 (see sec. 47), the traditions of Antwerp Cathedral were sustained by a few leaders, such as : —

Antoine Barbe (d. 1564), who was master of the choir-school from 1527 and later choirmaster. His extant works are very slight (1540-51). His two sons were in the choir, and a daughter married **Séverin Cornet** (d. 1582), who, after service at Mechlin, was from 1577 one of the choir-trainers at Antwerp.

Gérard de Turnhout (d. 1580), born about 1520, entered the choir as a singer in 1545 and succeeded Barbe in 1563, but in 1592 was called to Madrid, where he died (few works, from 1568). During his service at Antwerp the cathedral was plundered by a fanatic mob, the organ destroyed, and the choir-library scattered or burnt. Turnhout was active in restoring both. His son, **Jean de Turnhout** (d. after 1618), was choirmaster to the Duke of Parma at Brussels from about 1586.

Benedict Ducis (d. c. 1550?), probably born about 1480 at Bruges and a pupil of Des Près, was about 1510 head of the Musicians' Guild at Antwerp and for a time organist at the cathedral, later, perhaps, migrating to England. His many motets and chansons (from 1532) are unfortunately much confused with those of **Benedictus Appenzeller**, choir-trainer at Brussels in 1539-55.

Thomas Crecquillon (d. 1557) from 1544 was choirmaster to Charles V., probably at Brussels, besides holding church offices elsewhere. He is ranked among the strong composers between Des Près and Lassus (many works, from 1542).

Hubert Waelrant (d. 1595), born about 1517, entered the University of Louvain in 1529, perhaps studied under Willaert at Venice and in 1547 established a music-school at Antwerp, engaging also in music-publishing. He advocated solmization with the syllables *bo, ce, di, ga, lo, ma, ni* (known as the *voces belgæ* or 'bocedization'), from which modern usage probably derived its *do* and *si*. His style was melodious and clear (works from 1554).

André Pevernage (d. 1591), born at Courtrai in 1543, where he was first choirboy and then choirmaster, about 1577 became choirmaster at Antwerp, where his decided gifts as composer were displayed (works from 1574).

Cornelis Verdonck (d. 1625), born in 1564, was a choirboy in the Royal Chapel at Madrid from 1572, continuing till 1598, when he returned to Antwerp in the service of wealthy patrons. His facility gave him repute for a time (works, mostly secular, from 1584).

Peter Phillips (d. 1624), born about 1560 in England, emigrating because an earnest Catholic, became canon at Béthune, visited Rome in 1595, and from 1596 was viceroyal organist at Antwerp or Brussels. His madrigals (from 1591) and sacred music (from 1612) show him to have been a contrapuntist of great ability in the Palestrina style. His fame as the first writer of a true fugue on one subject (Burney) is now disputed in favor of his countryman Bull (Davey). After 1610 he wrote somewhat in the new monophonic style and with a basso continuo.

Other composers were **Petit Jan Delâtre**, from 1552 choirmaster at Liège (works from 1539); **Christian Hollander** (d. before 1570), choirmaster at Oudenarde in 1549–57 and then in the Imperial Chapel at Vienna (works posthumous); **Noé Faignient** (works from 1567); and **Emanuel Adriaensen**, a compiler of lute-books (1584–92).

Amsterdam came into prominence late in the century through the genius of **Jan Sweelinck** (d. 1621), born in 1562, the son of the organist of the Old Church. He was trained at Venice by Zarlino and G. Gabrieli, and on his return in 1580 became organist at the Old Church. He soon became famous as one of the great players and teachers of the age, being the real founder of the true fugue, with its development from a single subject through the use of double and triple counterpoint. He had a sure instinct for the essential differences between vocal styles and those suited to the organ, and by example and precept served as the pioneer for the whole North German school of organists. His works, vocal and instrumental, were but partially published during his life, but are now collected in a standard edition (1895–1903).

67. England. — English music in the 16th century stands by itself, and has not always been justly appreciated. Its isolation was due primarily to geographical reasons, but also to England's peculiar relations to the Papacy. The neglect of the subject has resulted from the difficulty of getting at the documents, which are now better known. The more the story is studied, the more interesting and even astonishing it becomes.

The very early and efficient share of England in the origin of counterpoint has already been noted (sec. 45). In the second half of the 15th century English music suffered a check, perhaps because of the unsettled conditions during the Wars of the Roses (1455–85). But even then some interest was indicated by the maintenance of the Chapel Royal (flourishing from at least 1465), by the conferring of musical degrees at both Oxford and Cambridge (from 1463), by the number of monastic and cathedral choirs and organs, by the chartering of a monopolistic Minstrels' Guild (1469), and by popular interest in singing of all kinds.

The Tudors were all music-lovers, and during the reigns from Henry VII. (1485–1509) onward the Chapel Royal remained the chief rallying-point for musicians, a model and incentive to cathedral and private establishments, and an object of astonished admiration from foreign visitors. As the century went on, English players were more and more drafted into service on the Continent, even when the existence of good English compositions was but slightly known.

Whether or not at the opening of the 15th century true counterpoint was first invented by Englishmen and by them handed over to the industrious Netherlanders may be a question. But in the 16th century England deserves credit for much progress peculiarly her own. She seems to have led the way in writing for keyboard instruments. Her development of counterpoint early in the century was distinct from that of the later Netherlanders or their disciples, and quite as remarkable. In the remodeling of styles under the influence of Protestantism she made an original combination of polyphony with the new materials of Protestant liturgies. The English cultivation of the madrigal and its relatives was also strikingly original.

The pre-Reformation period ended under Henry VIII. (1509–47) with his impulsive break with Rome about 1535 and the suppression of the monasteries and religious houses in 1536–40. An outbreak of iconoclastic zeal against the old order followed, which wrought havoc in choir-libraries and organs and which condemned all elaborate service-music. Then came, especially under Edward VI. (1547–53), the first steps in the full organization of the Anglican Church, with the drafting of new liturgies in English. Under Mary (1553–8) the old usages were somewhat revived. During the long reign of Elizabeth (1558–1603) sacred music again became notable in connection with the new Prayer Book, leading to contrapuntal achievements of remarkable power. The encouragement then given brought out a long line of talented madrigalists which continued into the troubled time of the first Stuarts.

The number of early composers known is large, among whom the following may be mentioned : —

Henry Abyngton (d. 1497), organist at Wells in 1447, Mus. D. at Cambridge in 1463, Master of the Chapel Royal from 1465; Gilbert Banastir, Master of the Chapel in 1482–1509; Richard Davy, organist at Magdalen College, Oxford, in 1490, who is said to have written the earliest Passion known; Robert Fayrfax (d. 1529), the leading genius of the earliest group, Mus. D. at Cambridge in 1501 and at Oxford in 1511, Master of the Chapel from 1510, later organist at St. Alban's; Nicholas Ludford, probably in the Chapel about 1510–20; and John Taverner, organist at Boston till 1530 and then at Oxford, who was one of the few to write a mass on a secular melody after the Netherland style. Hugh Aston (d. 1522), probably in the service of the Countess of Richmond, later Archdeacon of York, is known by instrumental pieces (before 1510) that are the first of the kind anywhere. Henry VIII. (d. 1547) was not only a patron of music, but played on several instruments and composed masses, motets and ballads (probably before 1530).

Christopher Tye (d. 1572) began as a choirboy at King's College, Cambridge, in 1497, was organist at Ely from 1541, perhaps also in the Chapel Royal for a time, and became a clergyman in 1560. Besides his curious metrical version of the Book of Acts with varied musical settings (1553), he left extensive works in MS., including masses, Latin and English motets, a Passion, etc. (before 1560). His style was singularly able and unartificial.

John Redford (d. before 1559), organist and choirmaster at St. Paul's, London, about 1535, was the best instrumental writer of his day, leaving many organ-pieces of historic interest.

Thomas Tallis (d. 1585), born about 1510, organist at Waltham Abbey till 1540 and in the Chapel Royal till 1577, obtained a monopoly of music-publishing in 1575 (with his pupil Byrd). Besides the tunes, canticles and motets published during his life (1560-75), he left a mass, many more motets (including a gigantic one for eight 5-voiced choirs), several remarkable anthems and a few madrigals. He is sometimes called 'the father of English cathedral music,' since he was the link between the old and the new schools (see sec. 68).

68. The Prayer Book and Music. — A reconstructed liturgy was one of the earliest undertakings of the new national Church. Edward VI. authorized two successive forms (1549, 1552) and Elizabeth still a third (1559), the last of which remained in use for more than a century. While in these the outlines closely resembled those of Roman services, yet in practice Morning and Evening Prayer (corresponding not to the Mass, but to Breviary offices) received a special accent, with a musical treatment equal to that of the Communion itself. In consequence, Anglican ritual music has always tended to be quite distinct in its texts and spirit.

The English Reformation was a peculiarly complicated movement. Although the reactions on the Continent under Luther and Zwingli were immediately known in England and approved by many, the secession of Henry VIII. was occasioned by his personal pique at the Pope's attitude toward his marriages. At first the English love of independence was quite as influential as any convictions about doctrine. But later, when Mary had exasperated the nation by her cruelties and when the refugees returned from Geneva at Elizabeth's accession, the Anglican position became decidedly Calvinistic. Thenceforward two parties began to form — the moderates, who would keep all possible continuity with the ancient church, and the radicals (later called Puritans), who preferred to sweep away all traditions and begin afresh. The latter were more and more inclined to oppose ritual music because of its associations with the Catholic system.

For a time it was demanded that whatever music was used should so fit the syllables with solid chords that every word of

the text should be obvious to the hearer — a not unnatural reaction against the profuse and intricate style of many contrapuntal settings.   For short texts it was entirely applicable, but
for the longer canticles it was heavy and hampered musical expression overmuch.   Before the end of the century, then, this
plain harmonic type of writing was again supplemented by
ample counterpoint.

Among the famous early settings of parts of the liturgy were the Litany
(*Stone*, 1544), the Canticles, Creed, Psalms and Communion in Plain-
Song (*Merbecke*, 1550), and the Preces, Versicles and Responses (*Tallis*,
1552?).   The composition of whole Services — settings in .notet style of
all the canticles, etc., required in Morning or Evening Prayer or in the
Communion (analogous to the Mass) — became frequent after 1560.
With these, as variable parts, came the writing of 'anthems,' the English
counterpart of the older Latin motets.   This latter form has had a
remarkable modern development.

The first venture in hymn-tunes was the *Goostlie Psalmes* of Coverdale
(1539), derived from Lutheran sources.   This was overshadowed by the
metrical Psalter begun by Sternhold in 1548 and gradually enlarged
in England and at Geneva until 1559, when three very different variants diverge — the Genevan, much influenced by Marot's French version
and discontinued after 1570, the English (or 'Old Version'), completed in
1562 and supreme in the Anglican Church till about 1700 or after, and
the Scottish, completed in 1564 and used till 1650.   The English variant
was almost wholly in 'common metre' and at the best had but about
40 tunes of a plain type, while the Scottish used many metres and had
over 140 tunes in a much richer style.   The readiness of Knox and his
circle to utilize the best Calvinistic music is curiously in contrast with the
English reluctance.

Although the Elizabethan composers pass over without break into those
of the early 17th century (see secs. 69, 99), the earlier leaders should be
given here :—

John Sheppard, first a choirboy at St. Paul's, London, in 1542 became
organist at Magdalen College, Oxford, and from 1551 was in the Chapel
Royal.   He left services, motets and anthems (from 1550).

John Merbecke (d. 1585?), born in 1523, was a choirboy at St. George's,
Windsor, and later organist there.   In 1550 he issued his famous Plain-Song settings of the Prayer Book services, besides leaving a mass and a few anthems.
In 1544 he was almost martyred for his Protestant views, and in later life he
was more theologian than musician.

Richard Edwards (d. 1566), also born in 1523, was both a poet and a musician of high order.   From 1561 he was Master of the Chapel Royal, a post
then involving dramatic as well as musical gifts.   His madrigals are famous.

Robert Whyte (d. 1574) was highly esteemed in his time, but strangely
forgotten afterwards.   He succeeded Tye at Ely in 1562, removing to West

L

minster in 1567. He is supposed to have been Tye's son-in-law. He left numerous motets and anthems, with some instrumental fantasias, all showing great ability.

Richard Farrant (d. 1580) was in the Chapel Royal from 1564. His services and anthems (some possibly by other Farrants), with 20 organ-pieces, show him a worthy contemporary of Tye and Tallis.

William Byrd (d. 1623), born in 1543 and a pupil of Tallis, became organist at Lincoln in 1563, was in the Chapel Royal from 1570 and later its organist, and was joint-publisher with Tallis from 1575, succeeding to the monopoly in 1585. He was often in trouble because of his strong Catholic sympathies. Though perhaps not absolutely unexcelled at every point, his works (from 1575) are so many, varied and superior that he is counted not only the greatest English composer of the century, but a compeer of Palestrina and Lassus. The list includes masses, motets, anthems, psalms, madrigals, songs and remarkable virginal-pieces, including some true variations. As an instrumental writer he was long unrivaled.

John Bull (d. 1628), born about 1562, was organist at Hereford from 1582, soon entered the Chapel Royal and in 1591 became its organist, and in 1597–1607 was the first professor of music at Gresham College. In 1601 he traveled on the Continent as a virtuoso, and in 1613 migrated to Brussels, becoming in 1617 organist at Antwerp Cathedral. He was a remarkable performer, an expert contrapuntist and a prolific composer of keyboard-pieces of decided historic importance.

Italian madrigals began to be reprinted in England in 1588 and strengthened the national interest in secular composition. Under this stimulus a long series of further composers appeared (see sec. 69), though the earlier of them were immediately connected with those here mentioned.

CHAPTER IX

SECULAR MUSIC. INSTRUMENTS. THEORY

69. The Madrigal and Part-Song. — The early indebtedness of the Netherlanders to secular music has already been noted (sec. 43), and the number of chansons that they produced side by side with more pretentious works. This aspect of early counterpoint was never lost. But it was reserved for their disciples in the 16th century to lift it into prominence and thus to transform the spirit of all composition. In the hands of certain Italian masters both the French chanson and its analogue, the Italian frottola, passed over into the madrigal, which steadily advanced into a distinct and brilliant history of its own.

> The word 'madrigal' came from the Troubadours and meant originally a pastoral song, but in later usage it was applied to any lyric poem of decided artistic value. Its musical sense followed when such poems were taken as texts for vocal treatment.

The madrigal was simply the lighter and gayer type of standard part-writing. Its spirit came from secular poetry, which, especially in Italy, was learning how to set forth topics of sentiment, wit or passion in the language of common life with delicacy and charm. The lyric beauty of the words called for lyric music, but this, in the absence of any due recognition of the artistic solo, could only be supplied contrapuntally, though, to match the sparkle and play of the words, evidently there needed to be some departure from the ponderous style of the motet. It was natural that the Italians should lead in developing this lighter style.

> No strict definition of the madrigal-form is possible, simply because in all the older counterpoint what is now called 'form' was either lacking or extremely irregular. The laying out of the music was governed by the flow and balance of the text, though without any close adherence to the mere syllables or lines. Indeed, though occasionally the advance of the voices might be checked and then begin again, real strophe-like divisions were usually avoided. The counterpoint was sometimes developed about a borrowed 'subject,' but usually passed from theme to theme, specially devised for the phrases of the words as they came, each then

handled imitatively, often with strictness and dexterity, but aiming constantly at beauty of effect rather than a show of learning. Properly a madrigal was based upon one of the mediæval modes, but with the gradual change of view about harmony usage tended toward the modern major or minor, with points of real modulation. In later examples the rhythmic side of the form became more definite, catching more or less of dance-movement. Many a license of treatment crept into the madrigal before it was accepted in stricter writing.

The historic importance of the madrigal is evident. It raised secular music to honor and afforded a chance for genius to exercise itself in fields otherwise untouched. Although essentially polyphonic, it really prepared the way for other vocal forms, even for dramatic monodies and arias, since it revealed the expressive possibilities of melody. The earliest attempts at dramatic construction were chains of madrigals, and in the early opera madrigals were long a usual feature. In both Germany and England it amalgamated with the true part-song, to the latter's great enrichment. On the other hand, it served as a step toward independent instrumental music, which at the outset was merely the transcription of what was written to be sung, but which presently set off on analogous lines of its own. Hence it is just to say that the madrigal was the 16th-century representative of what is now called chamber music (Riemann).

In a number of cases what were called *madrigali spirituali* were put forth — motets in a style that sought to bring into church services more of the warmth, flexibility and grace of secular music than had been customary. These prefigured the Protestant motets and anthems of Germany and England.

The origin of strong madrigal-writing was with the Venetians. Willaert is often named as the inventor, but it is impossible to say exactly who was the first writer in the form, since it was evolved gradually.

Among Petrucci's earlier collections (1502-8) were about 900 frottole by North Italian writers, largely from Verona and Padua. These slight works were the forerunners of the madrigal. Soon after 1530, madrigals proper begin to appear in print in rapidly increasing numbers, the leading writers entering the field in about this order: Willaert in 1519, Festa in 1531, Arcadelt in 1538, A. della Viola in 1539, Jhan Gero in 1542, De Rore in 1542, Lassus in 1552, De Monte and A. Gabrieli in 1554, Porta and Palestrina in 1555, Van Wert in 1558, Striggio in 1560, Annibale in 1562, Merulo and Caimo in 1564, G. Gabrieli in 1575?, G. M. Nanino in 1579, Marenzio in 1580, Monteverdi in 1583, Orazio Vecchi and G.B. Nanino in 1586, and the German Hassler in 1590. This list gives but a hint of the magnitude of the subject, since almost every active writer in Italy was a madrigalist, and the fertility of several of them was enormous.

All the above have been noted in earlier sections except **Monteverdi** (see sec. 77) and **Luca Marenzio** (d. 1599), who was born near Brescia and a pupil there of Contino, in the service of Cardinal Luigi d' Este, first at Triest and from 1580 at Rome, where from 1595 he was organist in the Papal Chapel. Although also a sacred writer, his renown rests on his incomparable madrigals, canzonette and villanelle (almost 20 vols. from 1580).

The English development of the madrigal was prompt and rich, but marked by an instinctive effort to merge the madrigal proper with the lighter and gayer styles of the part-song and the dance. For convenience, the more famous writers are here grouped together, though their activity reached far into the 17th century.

The earliest MS. specimens date from about 1560, but the greater number come after 1590, being stimulated by reprints of Italian works. During the next 40 years about 2000 madrigals were published, and more remain in MS. In many cases competent composers wrote little else, so that at the opening of the 17th century the English school really devoted itself to this form. To the pioneers **Edwards** and **Byrd**, already mentioned, the following should be added : —

Thomas Morley (d. c. 1602), born in 1557 and a pupil of Byrd, entered the Chapel Royal in 1592, after being for a time organist at St. Paul's, and succeeded to Byrd's monopoly in 1598. His canzonets (from 1593), madrigals (from 1594), ballets (1595) and ayres (1600) constitute the best of his work, though his instrumental pieces and limited sacred music are also notable. His theoretical treatise (1597) was influential.

John Dowland (d. 1626), born in 1563, was exclusively a secular composer, and famous as a virtuoso upon the lute. Partly because of his Catholic associations in early life, he spent much time abroad from 1580, visiting France, Germany and Italy, besides being employed in 1598–1606 with peculiar honors at the Danish court. On returning to England, he held two or three positions, the last as court-lutist. His madrigals and ayres (1596-1621) have remained in use to the present. He also issued a popular set of instrumental pavans (1605) and a translation of Ornithoparchus' book (1609), with a short addition of his own.

George Kirbye (d. 1634) is known from one book of fine madrigals (1597) and others scattered in collections or MS. **Thomas Weelkes**, who also entered the field with success in 1597 with several books, was organist successively at Winchester College and at Chichester. **John Wilbye** gained the title of 'the chief of English madrigalists' by some 65 famous specimens (from 1598). **John Bennet** issued one book (1599) of exquisite beauty, with some other pieces, including a few anthems and hymn-tunes (till 1614) **Thomas Bateson** (d. 1630), organist at Chester from 1599 and at Dublin from 1609, was almost equally expert (works, 1604–18). **Michael Este**, choirmaster at Lichfield, not only wrote many fine madrigals (1604–38), but considerable instrumental music and some anthems. **Francis Pilkington** was connected with Chester Cathedral (ayres and madrigals, 1605–24). **Thomas Ford** (d.

1648), music-master in the royal household and in the Chapel from 1625, was both a secular composer (from 1607) and a writer of anthems (in MS.).

Thomas Ravenscroft (d. 1635?), born about 1582 and a choirboy at St. Paul's, though not greater than several of the foregoing, exerted a wider influence through his madrigals (from 1609), motets and canons, his collection of tunes (1621) and his treatise (1611) on Measured Music.

Orlando Gibbons (d. 1625), born in 1583 and a choirboy at King's College, Cambridge, organist at the Chapel Royal from 1604 and at Westminster Abbey from 1623, is by far the greatest name in the series after Byrd. His abundant works (from 1611) range from services, anthems and hymn-tunes to remarkable madrigals and instrumental pieces (see also sec. 99).

While musicians were thus discovering the latent capacities of the madrigal as a branch of counterpoint, what are more properly called 'part-songs' were not neglected and, especially in Germany, were often still more cultivated. The part-song differs from the madrigal in derivation and character, being primarily an attempt to arrange a folk-song or similar melody for three or more voices with little more than note-for-note part-writing. The madrigal was the secular counterpart of the motet, the part-song the companion of the chorale. In the latter there was usually a continuous dominating melody in either the tenor or the treble, a division into lines or strophes with cadences, and a tendency to use the form over and over for successive stanzas, while the harmonic basis was not confined to the ecclesiastical modes. Yet in practice everywhere the madrigal and the part-song lay so close together that they influenced each other and often coalesced.

Thus in Italy the 'villanella' or 'villota' was explicitly a part-song based upon a popular air, and even the 'frottola' was not strictly a contrapuntal form, though developed thus for a time. In Germany true part-songs were the rule and reached a notable prominence with both secular and sacred words. In France and the Low Countries the 'chanson' often veered toward the part-song, probably reverting thus to its primitive type. In England the line between the madrigal and the part-song was always fluctuating, and finally disappeared in what was called the 'glee.'

The part-song, then, illustrates a process of evolution common in 16th-century music — a form that originated almost within the circle of unconscious folk-music, was adopted into artistic use without a full sense of its significance, and then proved so consonant with the trend of technical progress as to become typical. In most countries the pursuit of the strict madrigal died out in the 17th century, but the part-song, both in its normal form and with contrapuntal elaboration, has survived with unlessened vigor to the present day.

70. The Florentine Monodies. — Throughout the later 16th century composers were groping toward dramatic music. So long as the only recognized type of writing was contrapuntal, nothing significant could be accomplished, since without the solo the element of personality in song was kept at a minimum.

Several experiments were tried with incidental music for plays (*intermezzi*) in madrigal style, as by A. della Viola (1541-63), Striggio (1565-85), Merulo (1579), A. Gabrieli (1585) and Orazio Vecchi (1594). Only the last of these was specially successful, and one of them, at the wedding of Duke Francesco of Tuscany at Venice in 1579, led to a war of pamphlets between Venetian and Florentine critics.

About 1575 there began at Florence a movement that had important consequences. A wealthy and cultivated nobleman, Giovanni Bardi, Count of Vernio, himself a poet and amateur musician, drew about him a group of dilettanti in literature and art who were all inquiring after some method of dramatic expression of an intenser form than was then known. Their ambition was to restore the Greek drama in its entirety. This raised the question of musical declamation as a means. Such declamation was practically a lost art, and numerous attempts were made to rediscover it. These experiments were called 'monodies,' the first of which were simply recitatives with a slight accompaniment.

The circle of Florentine dilettanti was originally a social club drawn together by common tastes, but before long became animated by a positive purpose of revolution in the direction of solo music. The chief names, besides Bardi, were Jacopo Corsi (d. 1604), a rich patron of the arts and a good player on the gravicembalo, who from 1592 was the head of the movement, Bardi having moved to Rome; the poet Ottavio Rinuccini (d. 1621), afterwards most serviceable as librettist; Emilio del Cavaliere (d. 1602), a Roman noble, at the time Ducal Inspector of Art at Florence, who was well versed in musical work and later one of the composers in the new style; Vincenzo Galilei (d. c. 1600), not so famous as his son, the astronomer, but a talented lutist and a good student and writer, who led the way in practical experiments and zealously defended the new ideas in pamphlets (from 1581); Giulio Caccini (d. 1618), singer in the Ducal Chapel from 1565 and a lutist whose versatile skill powerfully aided the movement; Jacopo Peri (d. 1633), also a well-trained musician, ducal choirmaster at Florence and later at Ferrara, who likewise served notably as a composer in the new style; Pietro Strozzi, who took part with Merulo and Striggio in the wedding music at Venice mentioned above and later heartily accepted the new ideas; Marco da Gagliano (d. 1642), at the time a young student for the priesthood, but later a composer in the monodic form.

Galilei and Caccini were probably the first to write monodies, with such success that by 1585 attention was strongly attracted to what seemed like a new style of decided value. Just what these monodies were is not clear, but they certainly contained the germ of both the recitative and the aria.

The monodic style was at once applied in musical plays, with plot and personages. After some tentative essays (with more or less madrigal material), in 1594 was produced the first real musical drama, *Dafne*, with words by Rinuccini and music by Peri and Caccini, followed in 1600 by two more significant works, commonly known as 'the first opera' and 'the first oratorio' respectively (see sec. 76).

71. Instruments and Instrumental Music. — The 16th century inherited from its predecessors a bewildering variety of instruments, most of which it continued to use, pending the time when experience should determine which contained the largest artistic possibilities. The keyboard instruments — the organ, clavichord, harpsichord and their relatives — stood in a class by themselves, having obvious capacity for concerted effects. The remaining forms were small and portable, representing the standard stringed, wind and percussive groups. These were utilized variously, and the artistic importance of some of them, especially the lute and the viol, were more and more perceived.

Virdung's *Musica getutscht* (1511) is an invaluable source on this subject near the opening of the century, giving both descriptions and woodcuts. His list includes, besides the keyboard instruments (omitting the harpsichord proper), in the stringed group, the lyra (hurdy-gurdy), two forms of lute, two viols (tenor and bass), harp, psaltery, hackbrett (dulcimer) and trumscheit (nun's-fiddle); in the wind group, the schalmey and bombarde (oboes), several varieties of flute or recorder, zinken, cromornes and other horns, bagpipes, trumpet, clarion and trombone; and among percussives, drums and some nondescript forms. Other similar sources are Agricola's *Musica instrumentalis* (1528) and, about a century after Virdung, Prätorius' *Syntagma musicum* (1615–9), which latter is the most elaborate of all.

The lute was the characteristic instrument of the period, since it gave opportunity for concerted effects and for variety of force and color. Much pains were taken with its construction. All kinds of music were arranged for it, most musicians sought proficiency in playing it, and socially it was more fashionable than any other instrument. That it contributed powerfully to the awakening of a taste for true instrumental composition is obvious, but its mechanical limitations were such that gradually it was supplanted by the viol, though it continued in some vogue till the 18th century.

Its essential features were an oval or pear-shaped body, flat in front and vaulted behind, strengthened within by a soundpost under the bridge and by one or more longitudinal sound-bars, the belly being pierced by 1–3 carefully shaped and located soundholes and bearing the bridge (usually placed obliquely and to one side) to which the lower ends of the strings were fastened; a neck of varying width and length, with a fretted fingerboard, and a head, either flat, curved or bent sharply back, containing the tuning-pegs; usually about 13 strings of gut or wire, of which the uppermost or chanterelle was single, but the others tuned in pairs, the lower pairs being sometimes carried off at the side of the fingerboard and used without stopping. The customary sizes varied greatly, from the little 'chiterna,' with but 4 strings, up to the big 'theorbo,' 'archlute' and 'chitarrone', all properly with a double or extended neck and head and 20–24 strings. The accordatura or method of tuning varied somewhat, with a range of 3–4 octaves or even more. The tone, produced by twanging with the finger-tips, was incisive and slightly nasal, but was capable of fine gradations in skillful hands. Dexterous players got good effects in melodies with accompaniment, in chord-sequences and even in polyphonic passages. (The modern derivatives of the lute are the guitar and the mandolin, the latter most resembling it in shape.)

FIG. 54.—Italian Lute.

The viol was not yet as much valued as the lute, chiefly because incapable of concerted effects, but its unique singing-tone was appreciated and its possibilities were being diligently studied. Late in the century several varieties had become distinct, including the true violin. Brescia and Cremona in Lombardy were already the headquarters of the best manufacture. But the full development of viol music was delayed until the 17th century (see secs. 110–112).

The recognition of instrumental music as distinct from vocal was one of the striking advances of the 16th century. Previously, true accompaniments and all independent writing for

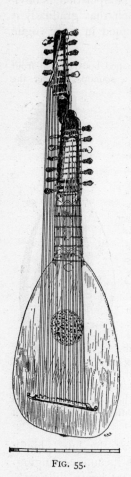

FIG. 55.

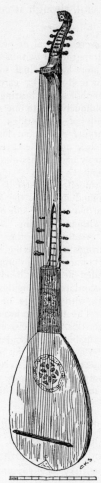

FIG. 56.

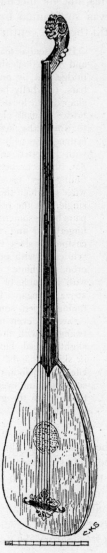

FIG. 57.

FIG. 55.— Theorbo, with
five pairs of strings off the
fingerboard. FIG. 56.— Arch-
lute, also with part of the
strings off the fingerboard. (The terms 'theorbo' and
'arch-lute' are used rather indiscriminately for the above
forms.) FIG. 57.— Bass-lute or Chitarrone, the largest of
the lute family.

instruments had been either unknown or used only casually. With the unfolding sense of the range of musical art this neglect could not continue. Two different lines of experiment appeared early in the century — on the one hand, contrapuntal works of the motet or chanson class were written to be either sung *or* played ; and, on the other, dances or similar pieces were drafted for purely instrumental use. In either case the desire was first for concerted effects upon a single instrument, but the further notion of combining instruments together followed speedily, though with vague and shifting ideas of what combinations were most serviceable. So far as the production of particular works or the settling of specific forms of composition went, this movement is significant only as regards music for the organ, but the mere fact that a beginning was made in other keyboard music, in pieces for the lute and viol, and in rudimentary chamber music, is important, since from these tentative efforts came great results later.

The earliest publication of lute-music was by Petrucci (1507–8), made up largely of dances. An English MS., presumably of earlier date, contains three virginal-pieces, also in dance style. Printed lute-books in tablature appeared frequently through the century. Of these the leading German, French, English and other examples have already been noted. It remains to enumerate a few of the earlier Italian editors : **Francesco da Milano** (7 books, 1536–63) ; **Julio Abondante** (2 books, 1546–8, perhaps more) ; **Giovanni Maria da Crema** (perhaps 3 books, 1546) ; **Melchiore de Baberijs** (at least 9 books, only partially preserved, 1546–9) ; **Giacomo Gorzanis** of Triest (at least 4 books, 1564–7).

Virginal-books begin to be found in England toward the end of the century, though not in printed form, the earliest large one being that in the Fitzwilliam Collection, which was once associated with Queen Elizabeth. The real pioneer in secular writing for the keyboard was *Byrd* (d. 1623).

The dances most in vogue were the 'pavan' (*padovano*, from Padua), a slow movement in duple rhythm, with the 'galliard' (*gaillarde*, a gay or merry piece), a quick movement in triple rhythm, also called 'saltarello' (from its springy steps) — these two being frequently united into a two-movement form resembling the suite in miniature. The 'passamezzo' or 'passepied,' a triple movement prefiguring the minuet, was also common, with the 'allemande' (German dance), a flowing movement in quadruple rhythm. Other instrumental forms were of rambling structure, often made up largely of passages, and were variously called 'fantasias' (or, in England, 'fancies'), 'ricercari,' in which was much thematic imitation, occasionally approaching the fugue, 'toccate' (pieces to be touched on the key-board), or 'sonate' (pieces to be sounded by instruments instead of sung) — both of the latter being usually of the nature of free preludes (later called 'sinfonie' or 'ritornelli ').

72. Literature about Music. — To give an adequate account of the many musical books from the invention of printing to 1600 is here impracticable. Fifty or more authors might be named, chiefly Italians or Germans, writing upon standard subjects like Plain-Song, Solmization, Counterpoint, Intervals, Notation, etc., with reference to the practical needs of singers and composers. A few, however, were constructive theorists, dealing with musical procedure in more than a routine or annalistic manner. There were traces, too, of the dawning historic spirit, seeking to describe how the art had been evolved and how it differed in different countries, with some summaries of composers, works and instruments. Almost all treatises were still written in Latin, and many writers (like many composers) were known under the often curious Latin paraphrases of their real names.

Jean Tinctoris (d. 1511), choirmaster in the Royal Chapel of Naples in 1475–87, then in the Papal Chapel till 1500, and finally at Nivelles (Brabant), issued about 1475 the first printed dictionary of musical terms and left a large number of tractates in MS., besides some compositions.

Franchino Gafori (d. 1522), from 1484 connected with Milan Cathedral, published his first treatise in 1480, his greatest in 1496 and others later. A strong supporter of the older views of theory, he was drawn into the strenuous debate opened in 1482 by Bartolomeo Ramis de Pareja, a Spanish teacher at Bologna, later at Rome, to whom Nicolò Burzio of Parma (d. 1518) responded in 1487, followed in 1491 by Ramis' pupil Giovanni Spataro (d. 1541), who was then attacked by Gafori in 1518–20, and who responded with emphasis in 1521–31. Ramis took positions about the scale, interval-ratios and chromatic tones that were far ahead of his day, prefiguring the maturer theory of the 18th century.

Passing over Jacques Le Febvre [Faber Stapulensis] (d. c. 1537), royal tutor at Paris and later at Navarre, Michael Keinspeck of Nuremberg (both writing in 1496), Nicolaus Wollick of Paris (works, 1501–12), Joannes Cochlæus [Joh. Dobnek or Wendelstein] (d. 1552) of Worms, Mayence, Frankfort and Breslau (works, 1507–11), and Simon de Quercu of Vienna (1509), we come to Sebastian Virdung, organist at Basle, who published in 1511 (in German) his invaluable treatise on keyboard and other instruments (illustrated), with practical directions about notation and tablature, which Ottomarus Luscinius [Nachtigall] (d. c. 1536) of Strassburg, Augsburg and Freiburg translated into Latin in 1536, besides his own theoretical book in 1515.

Again passing over Wenceslaus Philomathes of Vienna (1512) and Sebastian von Felstein of Cracow (1515), several leading names follow: —

Pietro Aaron of Venice (d. 1545) issued works (1516–'45) that resemble Gafori's in scope, but take the progressive side of the famous dispute. His last work contains a list of various musicians, men and women.

Heinrich Loriti [**Glarean**, from his birthplace in Switzerland] of Cologne, Basle and Freiburg (d. 1563), published two works (1515,'47), the second of which, the *Dodecachordon*, contains his noted contention that the whole fabric of mediæval music rests upon 12 modes instead of 8, as ordinarily taught, with many examples cited from leading composers — the whole set forth with acumen and clearness. This work was epitomized by his step-son **Wonnegger** in 1557. Glarean also edited the works of Boethius (1570).

Andreas Ornithoparchus, an extraordinary traveler, is known by his excellent general treatise (1517), which **Dowland** translated into English (1609).

Martin Agricola of Magdeburg (d. 1556) by a series of works (1528–45) achieved a unique reputation as a scholar, the first being a masterly account of all kinds of instruments, and the others discussions of theory and notation. He also edited collections of Protestant music. With him worked **Georg Rhaw** (d 1548), the enterprising Wittenberg publisher, who himself issued a theoretical handbook (1518).

Sebald Heyden of Nuremberg (d. 1561) issued important treatises on mensural music (1532, '37), besides psalms and a Passion.

Ludovico Fogliani of Rome (d. 1539) was a careful student of ancient musical writings, and is notable for a work (1529) in which the major third is correctly fixed with the ratio 5 : 4, as against the prevalent Pythagorean theory, with other useful acoustical distinctions. (Cf. *Ramis* above.)

Names of less significance are **Hans Judenkunig** of Vienna (d. 1526), with a text-book for the lute (1523); **Stefano Vanneo** of Ascoli (1533); **Matheo de Aranda** of Portugal (1533); **Silvestro di Ganassi** of Venice, with methods for the flûte-à-bec, viola and violone (1535–43); **Antonio Francesco Doni** (d. 1574), a cultivated Florentine, author of two books (1544–50), the second of which is a valuable bibliography of Italian musical books and MSS.; **Heinrich Faber** of Naumburg (d. 1552), with very popular handbooks (1548–50), the earlier of which was expanded by **Gumpeltzhaimer** of Augsburg (1591) and by **Vulpius** of Weimar (1610); **Juan Bermudo** of Portugal, on instruments (1549); **Adrian Petit Coclicus** of Wittenberg and Nuremberg (d. 1563), pupil of Des Près and ex-member of the Papal Chapel (1552); and **Hermann Finck** (d. 1558) of Wittenberg (1556).

Nicolò Vicentino, a pupil of Willaert in the service of the Este family at Ferrara and Rome, in his enthusiasm over the revival of the Greek chromatic and enharmonic genera, was opposed by the Portuguese **Vicente Lusitano** (1551), and, though unsuccessful in a public debate, defended his views in a book (1555) and by the invention of the complicated 'archicembalo,' thus helping forward the reaction against the older diatonic theory of the modes. The chief arbiter of the debate was **Ghiselin Danckerts**, a Netherlander in the Papal Chapel, who left a written opinion (1551), which about a half-century later was indorsed by Artusi (see below).

Gioseffo Zarlino (d. 1590), the Venetian composer and choirmaster (see sec. 56), was altogether the greatest theorist of the age. His works (1558–88) for the first time wrought out the distinction between the major and the minor as two complementary types of harmonic structure (developed with great fullness in the 19th century), and set forth the principles of counterpoint in its higher and more intricate applications, with numerous illustrative examples.

Antonius Gogavinus, a Flemish physician in Venice, deserves special mention as the first editor of important Greek treatises (1552).

Franciscus Salinas (d. 1590), court-organist at Naples from 1558 and later of Salamanca (Spain), issued in 1577 a finely written treatise in which musical rhythm is discussed in relation to rhythm in poetry, aiming to develop the ancient theories as the author understood them.

Vincenzo Galilei of Florence (d. c. 1600), in his zeal for a return to the dramatic monody of the Greeks, published several works against Zarlino (1581–9) in connection with the memorable Florentine movement, besides an earlier book on lute-playing (1568).

William Bathe (d. 1614), an Irish Jesuit of Salamanca, is known from a handbook (1584) in which, among other things, the octave is accepted in place of the hexachord as the norm of scales.

Giovanni Maria Artusi of Bologna (d. 1613), an industrious but highly conservative writer, issued extensive works (1586–1603) in which he vainly strove to check the tendencies away from the strict counterpoint of the old school.

Cyriak Schneegass of Friedrichsroda (d. 1597) was a somewhat useful writer of small text-books (1590–2), the first of which was the earliest printed work on the monochord.

Sethus Calvisius (d. 1615), from 1582 the distinguished cantor at Schulpforta (near Naumburg) and from 1594 at Leipsic, issued several able books (1592–1612), one of which contains an advocacy of bocedization, while part of another is devoted to a genuine history of music. He was useful in directing thought into harmonic channels.

Lodovico Zacconi of Venice (d. 1627), also for a time in court service at Vienna and Munich, published in two widely separated parts (1592, 1622) a celebrated treatise on contrapuntal composition, including a valuable account of instruments.

Ercole Bottrigari of Ferrara and Bologna (d. 1612), an erudite classical scholar, wrote three elaborate works (1593–1602) designed to combat views held by various friends about harmonic questions, the third reasserting Vicentino's contention about chromatic tones. He also left in MS. extensive other writings, including translations of ancient authors and a work on the theatre.

Girolamo Diruta (d. after 1612) issued in two parts (1593, 1609) an elaborate discussion of organ-playing — an indication of the advance in that branch of music.

Thomas Morley (d. c. 1602), the noted madrigalist, shares with Bathe the honor of leading the way in England with a general theoretical work (1597) which exerted a wide influence.

Cyriak Spangenberg of Strassburg (d. 1604) is to be remembered for an important MS. work on the Meistersinger (1598), which was first published in 1861.

73. Summary of the Century. — The most salient external feature of the 16th century is the sudden expansion in magnitude of the world of music. Composers of importance now number some hundreds — almost as many as in the 17th century — and they are scattered through all the leading countries. Their known works count up into the thousands, chiefly designed for the church, but with a goodly proportion of secular compositions as well. The forms adopted are often extended and complex, so that into many single works went a large amount of effort and skill. In mere bulk of composition, then, the century is marked by an outburst of extraordinary artistic abundance.

But other features command attention. The period was instinct with the spirit of enterprise. Musicians were not content to go on doing the like of what had been done, but must needs strike out new paths. Even those wedded to the old lines of ritual composition usually supplemented or modified the old methods, and the few ultra-conservatives were unable to hold a following. The area of strict counterpoint, for example, was widened in various ways — by increasing the vocal forces and gathering them in contrasted choirs, by cunningly developing new beauties of close imitation (even by novel applications of the pure canon), by introducing more frequent harmonic passages as a foil for polyphony, by heightening the expressiveness of individual voice-parts and playing them off against each other more effectively, by reaching out after revolutionary extensions of the modes through chromatic tones, by experimenting with alternating tonalities or modulations, and by adopting into serious writing rhythmic and accentual refinements from secular sources.

The practice of what was called 'musica ficta' reached its climax in this century. This was an instinctive recognition that chromatic modifications of the modes were not only permissible but necessary in certain situations, both for the better forming of the melodic phrases and for the smoother articulation of the harmonic drift. At first the insertion of irregular semitones was left to the singers' discretion without written mark, but ultimately the necessary sharps or flats were written above or in the staff. It is impossible to tell how early or how far this license was applied before 1500, but from that date it became the subject of formal rules, especially in the formation of final or other cadences, in final chords (making them regularly major), in cases where the tritone or other objectionable intervals occurred either melodically or harmonically, and in the treatment of thirds and sixths in certain connections.

All regular composition had been for voices in chorus. It now began to be seen that the chorus of instrumental tones was equally valid. Instrumental writing branched off from vocal with timidity, at first following the vocal type slavishly, but presently noting that every instrument capable of concerted effects has a genius of its own, so that a piece for organ, virginal or lute ought to be essentially diverse from one for a choir, since the tonal and mechanical elements are different. While instrumental styles for a time floundered helplessly in their search for proper forms or types, the future of such styles as a great department of musical art was prefigured in the lute-music, the organ-fantasias and the clavichord-dances of this experimental period.

Furthermore, the genuine harmonic idea of composition now disengaged itself from the purely contrapuntal, and the handling of tones in simultaneous masses or chords was felt to be of importance. The old notion had been that the individual voice in its progress was the unit of reference and that what chords were produced were incidental. Now it was felt that the chord as such was another unit and that such massive units might be joined in series, making the voice-part motion incidental to the harmonic sequence. Thus a revolution of procedure gradually came to pass — one that did not so much destroy or drive out the old as reveal a deeper principle with which the old might be associated without losing its own value.

Associated with this recognition of chords as working units was a new analysis of scales and tonality, whereby was disclosed the imperfection of the modes as formulæ (embodying the ancient tetrachordal idea) and of the hexachords. Room was made for the instinct of secular music for major or minor scales laid out in octochords (or heptachords), with a positive keytone, a cadential leading-tone, and a dominant and subdominant that were accessory chord-centres with the tonic. Hitherto melodic procedure had rested on arbitrary assumptions as to the principality of tones; now it circled inevitably about natural foci to which certain primary chords belonged. Melody and harmony were thus found to be twin faces of the one truth of tonality. The unique importance of the leading-tone as establishing the tonic and providing for obvious cadences now attained its full significance.

The acknowledgment of a full scale with its absolute tonality as a unit of thought led onward toward a still more momentous possibility. If a cluster of tones might be thus unified about a single centre, it followed that by altering one or two of them the centre could be changed, and, since the alteration might be smoothly introduced, a fresh sort of progress might be worked out, whereby, besides passing from chord to chord, the harmony might move from scale to scale or from key to key without losing continuity and with a decided gain in expressional and structural value. Though the modern theory of free modulation in all directions was still impossible, owing to current methods of tuning, yet definite advances toward it now began.

The increasing study of popular music tended constantly to alter theory in other ways. It brought to the front the question of 'form'—the lay-out of movements in sections or phrases, each with some completeness in itself, and all with some definite relation of length to the others. This was directly opposed to the genius of contrapuntal structure as usually conceived, and was probably resisted as vulgar and mechanical. But its utility as a principle of organization gradually became clear, especially in lighter composition. In dances and popular songs it was indispensable. The problem was to use it without sacrificing the general continuity and unity of the whole movement. This higher unity, it was already seen, could be secured only through resemblances or contrasts of melodic and harmonic design between successive strophes.

Popular music also brought into view the artistic possibilities of the solo. Not only might a melody have beauty in itself and be highly expressive, but, as the doctrine of tonality unfolded, it appeared that a melody carried within itself the implication of an harmonic sequence, which was its essence. This threw a new light upon accompaniments, showing that the primary office of the latter was not to supply further independent melody, but to declare the chord-foundation that the melody implied.

This chord-foundation, it was found, could be outlined by means of a continuous bass upon which the desired chord-series could be built up in accordance with a few simple rules. To suggest a whole effect, then, it was necessary only to indicate the intended melody and the appropriate bass with some conventional signs attached, and the proper harmony could be supplied at sight. This was the principle of the 'basso continuo' or 'thorough-bass' that came into use immediately after 1600.

M

Finally, attention to structure as defined by melody wrought a revolution from polyphony, as the primary type of design, to monophony. Perhaps strictly this was hardly a revolution, since polyphony presupposed a melodic 'subject,' yet practically the shift of emphasis from a mesh of many voice-parts to the thought that at every point there should be a dominating melody, to which all else should contribute, was indescribably novel. Here lay the key to full lyric and dramatic expression, and until this key was in hand, entrance into the whole vast field of the artistic aria and of the lyric drama was impossible.

MAP II.—ITALY, AUSTRIA AND SOUTH GERMANY.

PART IV

THE SEVENTEENTH CENTURY

PART IV

THE SEVENTEENTH CENTURY

CHAPTER X

THE EARLY MUSICAL DRAMA

74. General Survey. — In general history the 17th century has less distinctive character than the 16th, being a time of extensive readjustments in politics, society and thought along lines previously indicated. So, although the actual amount of artistic activity was great, it was not marked by the most distinguished achievement, except, perhaps, in literature.

> In Germany the devastating Thirty Years' War (1618–48) almost paralyzed social energy, not only for the time, but long afterward. England was racked for an equal time by the struggles between the Stuarts and the Puritans, ending in 1660 with the restoration of the monarchy. In France the great feature was the long reign of the autocratic, ambitious and luxurious Louis XIV. (1643–1715), in which took place the lamentable exodus of the Huguenots before and after the revocation of the Edict of Nantes (1685). Italy was comparatively peaceful. Striking events were a new repulse of the Turks in the east, the reduction of the Empire to a merely nominal character, the rise of Sweden, and the colonization of America, but none of these had immediate relation to musical progress.

In the musical world the energy already developed had momentum enough to proceed in spite of external conditions. Early in the century the most notable new fact is the rapid evolution of dramatic music, especially the opera, which was soon propagated from Italy into Germany, France and England with interesting results. To this followed the vigorous advance of instrumental music, again from Italy as a centre. Indeed, Italy now fully replaces the Netherlands as the musical headquarters of Europe. In Germany, however, independent genius is displayed in sacred music, especially for the organ, and in France a special aptitude for concerted instrumental writing. Musical theory continues to crystallize towards its modern form. The manufacture of instruments like the violin, the organ and other keyboard instruments is perfected or decidedly improved, so that music of a higher order is demanded and scope given for instrumental as well as vocal virtuosity. Performance now becomes differentiated as a significant branch of musicianship, especially on the vocal side. Correlative with this is the tendency to transfer certain forms of music from private to public patronage, with consequent changes in the standards of musical ambition and in the social influence of the art. While the century presents no composer of the first order, it is of great interest as a preparation for the creativeness of the 18th century.

75. The Mediæval Plays. — All the fine arts have been powerfully affected sooner or later by the universal craving for dramatic impression. Dramaticness is a quality in art not easily defined. It usually involves features or arrangements that represent or suggest a story, with personages, action, developing situations and a dénouement of some sort, predestined or unexpected. The fascination of dramatic art in all forms rests upon the fact that it recalls living experiences, continually piques curiosity as to the outcome, and in its climaxes is sensationally exciting. The impulse to it is universal in all ages.

> In modern society the drama stands as a separate and independent fine art. But it is not always remembered that other fine arts are constantly handled dramatically, even the static arts of sculpture, painting and architecture, and of course the mobile arts of poetry and music in all their larger forms. This general thesis may be extensively developed. It is here mentioned simply to justify references to the general taste for drama, of which the musical drama was a result and by which at first it was dominated.

The entire modern drama — theatre and opera — is immediately descended from practices in the Middle Ages that were instituted and sustained by the Church. The beginning was doubtless in the liturgy itself — the Mass, for instance, being a sort of reënactment of the sacrifice of Christ. But the connection is clearest with the particular undertakings known as Mysteries, Miracle-Plays and Moralities, all of which were originally designed to give religious instruction and edification, though from the first tending to pass over into secular diversions. These were the direct precursors of the opera and the oratorio, even though originally they may have contained no important musical features whatever.

> The Mystery was properly a representation of some Biblical story. Its development was most natural in connection with the stories of Easter,

including all the events from the Betrayal to the Resurrection, and of
Christmas; but it was early extended to subjects like the Creation, the
Flood, the Exodus, the lives of Biblical characters, and the Last Judgment.   The words were taken from the Bible direct as far as possible.
The earlier renderings were by ecclesiastics in churches or monasteries.
Gradually these expansions of church services became protracted performances, occupying parts of several days, which tended more and more
to swing away from the Church.   The common tongue replaced the
Latin, liberties were taken with the narratives, and by-play of a comic
kind was slipped in, with not a little superstition as well.   These
features, with the accent upon mere amusement, from the 13th century
caused the form to be less approved by the church authorities, so that it
betook itself to the market-places or the fields, where large crowds could
gather and every kind of topic and treatment could be tolerated.   The
further development of these public plays varied in different countries.
In many cases their maintenance became a municipal function, while in
others they were undertaken by the various guilds of craftsmen.   As a
rule, Mysteries ceased with the Reformation, but survivals exist even now,
as the Passion-Play at Oberammergau in Bavaria.

The Miracle-Play was an offshoot of the foregoing, its materials being
taken from the legendary lives of the saints.   Its tendency was to emphasize heroic, romantic or magical incidents, often with great freedom
of treatment.   Though not so closely liturgical in origin, its first purpose
was ecclesiastical, and one variety of it consisted in elaborations of formulæ like the Lord's Prayer or the Creed.   It passed over readily into
mythological or historical dramas, varying widely in subject.

The Morality was an allegory in which qualities or other abstract
notions were personified.   It was properly religious or moral, but occasionally assumed didactic forms of a more general sort.   Bunyan's
'Pilgrim's Progress' is a well-known literary example of the Morality idea.

In all these the staple procedure was dialogue between the personages,
but among the accessories were passages for narrators (supplying parts
of the story), comment-passages, somewhat after the fashion of the ancient
Greek chorus (often arranged for the audience as a participant in the
action), and interludes and by-plays of all kinds.   The use of music
became frequent, either as a vehicle for the dialogue or as a comment or in-
terlude.   In such cases the forms used were either borrowed from Plain-
Song or folk-song, or prepared in similar styles.   There was no distinct
recognition of the peculiarly dramatic types of musical writing until near
the end of the 16th century.   There was little real scenery, but somewhat
elaborate stages were often provided — one of the favorite forms being
one separated into stories, heaven above, hell beneath and earth between.
These stages were often mounted on wheels and drawn from place to place.

By the 16th century, then, the street-play had become a common institution in all leading countries, and was well on its way toward the modern
theatre.   The differentiation of the opera began when it was perceived
that the vehicle of impression might be musical throughout and when
appropriate musical styles were devised.

It should be added that back of the mediæval drama, much of whose history is illustrated by literary remains, especially in Teutonic Europe, lay multifarious Byzantine undertakings, sometimes within the Church, sometimes in hostility to it. These seem to have represented every type and quality, from the classic tragedy or comedy down to the rudest vaudeville. Music and dancing were used so freely that certain works were at least virtually operettas. By way of Constantinople, then, a continuous dramatic tradition and practice in Greek extended from ancient times even till the 15th century. But about all this, as about analogous dramatic traditions in Latin here and there in the West, the available data are meagre. Apparently, the remarkable Byzantine interest in the drama and its musical accessories had no direct connection with the rise of Italian opera, for Italy was slow to adopt the culture that expressed itself in the Greek language.

76. Musical Experiments. — While the use of music in some way as a dramatic accessory was common in the 16th century, a peculiar interest attaches to two Italian experiments. One of these was made about 1560 by the Roman priest Neri, who employed singing in popular gatherings for instruction in Biblical topics, and the other from about 1575 by the Florentine dilettanti (see sec. 70). The former slightly prefigured the oratorio, while the latter pointed clearly toward the opera. Both of these lines of progress were profoundly influenced by the prevailing types of dramatic effort, but at first their importance lay in discovering strictly musical ways and means for dramatic expression, and in bringing poetic styles into conjunction with musical expression.

Filippo Neri (d. 1595) was a zealous Florentine who from about 1550 was prominent at Rome in philanthropic and educational work conducted at the oratory (*oratorio*) first of the S. Girolamo monastery and later of Sta. Maria in Vallicella, his efforts being so successful as to lead in 1564 to the formation of a brotherhood for popular instruction, called the Congregation of the Oratory (which has had many distinguished members in Italy, France and England, and still exists). Singing was magnified by Neri as a help in his meetings, and from 1565 he enlisted the services of G. Animuccia and Palestrina of the Papal Chapel in the preparation of *laudi spirituali* — plain settings of sacred words, to be sung after his addresses. From this practice came later the name 'oratorio' for a sacred musical drama, though Neri's efforts were not themselves dramatic.

We know little of the details of the first Florentine experiments, because the works are not preserved. Galilei is said to have been the pioneer with a solo scene from Dante's *Inferno* and some settings from Lamentations. Cavaliere followed in 1588–95 with works on classical topics, and in 1594 Peri, perhaps with Caccini, wrote music for Rinuccini's *Dafne*, privately given at Corsi's house. In all these the style was monodic, probably a crude recitative.

In 1594 Orazio Vecchi's *Amfiparnasso* was produced at Modena, a comedy wholly in madrigal style, which was either an unconscious demonstration of the ineptitude of that style for dramatic use or a satire (this work is extant). A similar work was Banchieri's *La pazzia senile*, given in 1598 at Venice.

In 1600, however, for the marriage of Henry IV. and Maria de' Medici at Florence, Rinuccini's poem *Euridice* was set to music independently by both Peri and Caccini, the performed version being made up from both and the two at once published. Peri's version opens with a seven-stanza prologue in recitative style, with ritornelli. The dialogue proceeds in recitative with brief interjected choruses, a long passage for a triple flute and a final dance. The accompaniment is written for a gravicembalo (harpsichord), two large lutes and a lira grande (large viol), with only bare indications of the chords intended. Caccini's version is in the same style, except that he writes more freely for the voices, actually indulging in florid runs or fioriture. These works mark the beginning of the musical drama, the joint production being usually called 'the first opera.' They also, like their many successors, illustrate the combination of the Mystery with stories of classical mythology.

In 1600, also, but some ten months earlier, Cavaliere's *Rappresentazione di anima e di corpo* had been produced at Rome, apparently as one of a series of sacred musical dramas under the auspices of the Oratorians, all the others of which are lost. This work is not only more extended than the above (some 90 sections), but technically more elaborate. It includes recitatives, solos, short choruses, an instrumental intermezzo, part-song movements, etc., with a final chorus in two alternative forms, one in four parts with dancing and the other contrapuntal. The sense of the text is often musically expressed with effectiveness and evidence of latent power. The accompaniment is designed for a gravicembalo, a large lute, a double lira and two flutes, with a violin suggested to strengthen the soprano throughout. Cavaliere died the year before his work was given, but he left explicit directions that show his artistic sense of dramatic values. This is often called 'the first oratorio,' though its adherence to the Morality type was not at all characteristic of its successors — and, indeed, no successor appeared for almost a quarter-century (unless possibly Agazzari's small pastoral *Eumelio*, 1606, is to be assigned to this class).

The principles of dramatic singing embodied in the above works were set forth by Caccini in 1601 in the preface to a book of accompanied solos called *Le nuove musiche* — a phrase which is still used to describe the many features in which theory and praxis about 1600 were consciously departing from the old traditions. The general thesis of Caccini's preface is that singing should be guided by the desire to bring out the meaning and artistic force of the words. Emphasis is put upon vocal execution in all its parts, including tone-formation, correct intonation and enunciation, the use of the three principal registers, text-interpretation, freedom of delivery, etc. Embellishments of various kinds are carefully explained and illustrated, though their excessive use is deprecated. Two extended examples of solos are appended for study. The whole forms a well-reasoned guide to the new art of solo-singing, and shows how rapidly ideas about its technique had matured.

In the direct Florentine succession was the setting, in 1607, by **Marco da Gagliano** (d. 1642) of Rinuccini's *Dafne*, a work cognate in style with those of Peri and Caccini, but slightly more expanded.

77. Monteverdi. — While the Florentine enthusiasts are to be honored as pioneers in the New Music, their efforts might not have had at once so large an influence if a new factor in the situation had not been introduced. The movement presently lost its local character and was transferred to Venice, where, through the genius of the mature and experienced musician Monteverdi it achieved a success that brought it before the whole musical world. Part of this was due to the readiness of Monteverdi to cast aside whatever was not serviceable for his immediate dramatic purpose, and part to the peculiar musical eminence of Venice. His series of dramas (1607–42) made the opera the most popular form of composition in Italy and started an interest that gradually spread everywhere. He stood forth as an innovator in his disregard of the customary conjunct voice-writing so far as dramatic effect demanded sudden and even difficult leaps, in his vigorous pushing of the solo beyond the tame and timid limits of the early recitative to at least the stage of the arioso, in his sense of the value of a somewhat symmetrical phrase-plan, and in his experiments with instrumentation. Gradually his efforts incited imitation and further advance by other composers. They also led, in 1637, to the establishment in Venice of the first opera-house — the beginning of a long line elsewhere.

Monteverdi's fame spread speedily throughout Europe, and he must still be regarded as one of the formative geniuses of musical history. This fame was different from that of any of his great predecessors. They were invaluable students of the structural texture of composition as an end in itself, while he brought to the front the importance of so adapting musical procedure, even by revolutionary changes, to the utterance and delineation of every phase of warm emotion that it might become a many-sided rescript of life in all its intenser aspects. The old polyphony was apt for certain kinds of feeling only. The New Music now became at least the promise of a voice for many more, and for those closest to the popular heart.

Claudio Monteverdi (d. 1643) was born of humble parents at Cremona in 1567, early showed musical aptitude, studied under Ingegneri, became violist to the Duke of Mantua (where he was choirmaster from 1601), and began publishing canzonets and madrigals in 1583, showing sympathy with the newer features of composition. After at least thirty years' experience as player and composer, and after great success in 1607–8 with his first three dramatic works, in 1613 he was made choirmaster at St. Mark's in Venice, where he remained in honor till his death. For several years he was engrossed in sacred music, though continuing secular writing in small forms, but returned to the opera in 1627–30 and again in 1639–42 (after the opening of the first opera-house). Of his 12 dramas only 4 are extant, *Orfeo* (1607, text by Striggio), *Il ballo dell' ingrate* (1608, dance-play, text by Rinuccini), *Il ritorno d' Ulisse* (1641, text by Badoar, known in a form perhaps not authentic), and *L' incoronazione di Poppea* (1642, text by Busenello). Of the most famous, *Arianna* (1618, text by Rinuccini), only a fragment remains.

Orfeo marks a great advance on previous experiments. The staple form is still the recitative, but it is more declamatory, with passages of sustained melody looking toward the later aria, and there are frequent choruses and instrumental numbers, a fanfare prelude and many ritornelli. The accompaniments are diversified, including hints of novel effects and some interesting contrasts between groups of instruments, but the parts are not usually written out — simply indicated by a figured bass. The orchestra was extraordinary — 2 harpsichords, 2 large lutes, 2 violins, 10 tenors, 2 viole di gamba, 2 bass viols, a double harp, 3 trumpets, 2 cornets, a clarion, a small flute and three portative organs.

In the later works special effects appeared for the first time, like the tremolando and the pizzicato, and in the last there are dialogues, duets and a trio, besides many solos, but no chorus.

At the outset the musical drama was wholly dependent upon the extravagance of wealthy individuals, and was strictly private. With the establishment of opera-houses it became a public amusement and a source of musical education. Thus was opened a new field for singers and instrumentalists, since every opera-house made up its company afresh at intervals. Thus, too, was called into being a new class of organizers, the managers or impresarios, whose business it was to cater to the public taste, especially by 'discovering' new works or performers. The development of the musical drama and the opera-house business have been closely interdependent ever since.

The first Venetian opera-house (1637) was that of S. Cassiano, under the management of Ferrari and Mannelli, respectively the librettist and the composer of the first work given. Before 1700, no less than 16 opera-houses had been started in Venice, half of them before 1670. Other cities followed much more slowly — for example, Rome had but 3 in 1700 (the first founded in 1661), while Bologna had none till 1680. But operas were often given in theatres, so that the institution spread more rapidly than its edifices.

Contemporaries of Monteverdi, as a rule represented each by but one work, were (besides Gagliano noted above) **Girolamo Giacobbi** (d. 1630), probably the first native opera-writer in Bologna (intermezzi, 1608, operas, 1610, '17); **Paolo Quagliati** (d. before 1623), whose play was produced at Rome (1611) from a movable stage; **Stefano Landi** of Rome (1619); **Filippo Vitali**, a Florentine, temporarily in Rome (1620); **Francesca Caccini**, the talented daughter of Giulio Caccini of Florence (1625); **Domenico Mazzocchi** (1626), **Giacinto Cornachioli** (1629), **Michel Angelo Rossi** (1635), and **Loreto Vittori** (1639) — the last four all of Rome. In the same period was **Schütz**, the pioneer in Germany (*Dafne*, 1627, and a later ballet, 1638).

78. The Intermezzi. — The dramatic fertility of the age was shown not simply in extended and serious operas, but in many entertaining pieces of small dimensions and often humorous tone, meant to be performed between the acts of literary plays. Such entr'actes were common in the later 16th century in the madrigal or dance style, and were called 'intermedi' or 'intermezzi,' sometimes 'balletti' when dancing predominated. After 1600 these turned steadily from the older contrapuntal style to monophonic solos and dances, usually with a slight plot and some personages. They served to popularize the new monodic style, to afford composers a chance for experiment, and finally to lead the way toward the opera buffa (see sec. 126). The Florentines were prompt to use such forms, followed soon by others in northern Italy, who were not ready for the sustained effort of the real opera.

Among the many famous instances of the early use of intermezzi mention may be made of a comedy by Bardi at Florence in 1589, for which several intermezzi were prepared, the texts mostly by Rinuccini, the music by **Bardi** himself, **Cavaliere, Caccini, Peri, Marenzio** and **Cristofano Malvezzi** (d. 1597). **Adriano Banchieri** (d. 1634), the organist and church composer of Bosco, Imola and Bologna, wrote a number of works of this class (1603–28), one of which (1607) was a pendent in the new style to his *La pazzia senile* (1598). **Giovanni Boschetto Boschetti** brought out at Viterbo in 1616 his *Strali d'amore*, which illustrates not only the rapid advance of the new style toward questionably sensuous representations, but also the tendency to treat intermezzi as parts of a secondary drama in spite of their detached use in the pauses of another play. A similar example is a series by **Ottavio Vernizzi** in 1623 — the first of the kind in Bologna. From this time intermezzi were certainly as numerous as operas, though usually far less important.

79. Cavalli, Carissimi and Cesti. — Among perhaps twenty-five dramatic composers who entered the field before 1670, three were decidedly the most influential in fixing the characteristic

forms to be used in both opera and oratorio. These were Cavalli of Venice, pupil and successor of Monteverdi, Carissimi of
Rome, who devoted himself to sacred music, and Cesti of Florence, Rome and Vienna, a pupil of Carissimi, but as an opera-
writer chiefly associated with Venice. These three, though
strict contemporaries, became important in succession.

Cavalli's special service lay in the full recognition of the aria as
distinct from the recitative. The latter had been the type from
which more flowing or declamatory passages had been developed
without evident differentiation, thus retaining the literary standpoint that marked the first experiments. Cavalli realized that
in every strong dramatic situation room should also be made
for absolutely lyric expression through solo song, having great
musical interest and value in itself. This was the true aria,
not an elaborate variety of recitative, but a song embedded in
the action. Cavalli thus brought to the front an element that
before long came to dominate the opera completely. His own
arias were not carried much beyond folk-song patterns, though
occasionally they suggest the *da capo* form that later became
the rule. At first he also clung to the chorus, but gradually
omitted it altogether. Instead, he did much to develop the
duet or dual aria, often with interesting imitations between the
voices.

Carissimi, while pursuing similar lines of advance in the
oratorio, added a valuable appreciation of the essential powers
of the voice as an instrument, and led the way more positively
toward the freedom and brilliance of effect that later made dazzling vocalization the crowning feature of the opera. He was
specially able in what came to be known as the 'cantata' —
usually a short solo work in which variety was secured by skillful alternations of style, but also sometimes one in which several
voices were handled characteristically as if they were personages.
He was important, too, for attention to the chorus and to the
harmonic enrichment of accompaniments (see sec. 82).

Cesti went beyond these in the technical variety and vigor
with which he developed what they had begun. His power of
genuine invention was more conspicuous, both in breadth and in
abundance, with more of charming and vivacious brilliance, including much of the comic element. He transferred to the opera
all that Carissimi had wrought out in the cantata, with a better

binding of the movements into a balanced whole, and advanced the plan of scenes and acts toward its later completeness. The chorus he used sparingly, but with ability. His accompaniments and instrumental numbers were carefully and freshly conceived, though without special increase in orchestral resources. In mere number of works he falls much behind Cavalli, but he did more to set forth the opera as a permanent type of musical art, thus rounding out the first stage of progress that had been begun by the Florentines almost a century before.

Francesco **Cavalli** (d. 1676) was born at Crema about 1600, and was trained at Venice, probably under Monteverdi. His real name was Caletti-Bruni, but he owed his education to a noble, whose name he took in return. His whole career was spent at St. Mark's, as singer from 1617, second organist from 1640, first from 1665, and choirmaster from 1668. He married into a wealthy family and enjoyed much esteem. His operas numbered about 40 (1639–67), two-thirds of them crowded into the years 1642–55. Nearly all were first given at Venice. The most famous was *Giasone* (1649), which was widely reproduced elsewhere, but only one, *Xerse* (1654), was published. In 1660 he was called to Paris to assist in the festivities at the marriage of Louis XIV., giving *Xerse* (with incidental music by Lully), and again in 1662, giving *Ercole amante*. He was likewise called upon to grace other occasions, as to Milan in 1653 and to Innsbruck in 1662. Besides operas, he wrote some church music (from 1645), including an 8-voice Requiem.

For **Carissimi**, see sec. 82.

Marc' Antonio Cesti (d. 1669) was born at Florence about 1620 and studied with Carissimi at Rome. In 1646 he became ducal choirmaster at Florence, in 1660 returned to Rome as tenor in the Papal Chapel, and from 1666 was second choirmaster of the Imperial Chapel at Vienna, dying at Venice while bringing out his last opera, *Genserico* (finished by Partenio). He wrote some 12 operas (from 1649, all but two after 1663). One, *La schiava fortunata* (1667), was written jointly with P. A. Ziani, and, with about half the others, was first produced at Vienna, the rest appearing mostly at Venice. The most noted were *La Dori* (1663), *Il pomo d'oro* (for the marriage of Leopold I. at Vienna, 1666), and the comic *Le disgrazie d'amore* (1667), while the initial work, *Orontea* (1649), held the stage at Venice till 1683. He left, besides, some solo cantatas, but almost no church music.

80. The Early Operas as Dramas. — The first blossoming of the opera at Venice involved more than the opening of a new method of musical expression. It fixed a type of musical drama that for almost two centuries was extremely popular, and hence determinative of all progress in secular music. A special word should therefore be said about the dramatic treatment adopted.

While the early opera derived its topics and material from the ancient drama and its form from the mediæval Mystery, it early settled into an arbitrary style of its own. The stories were at first wholly taken from Greek mythology, but tales from Roman, Jewish, Oriental or early Christian history were soon added, especially those that had already been used by Italian poets. The same subjects and the same plots constantly recurred with slight variations. Intrigues, entanglements through disguises and tricks, applications of magical or superhuman power, and the like, abounded. The dénouement was always happy, however tragic the story, while absolute comedy became more and more frequent. Personages were usually multiplied, both as actual participants and as a dumb spectacle. The action was divided into three or more acts, each containing many scenes with shifts of setting, while at the beginning was usually a considerable prologue by mythological characters or personified ideas and at the end a *licenza* or epilogue of a dedicatory or apologetic nature. Occasionally, poets of ability served as librettists (Busenello being named as the most gifted), but, as a rule, the texts were hack-work, often hasty, ill-conceived and bombastic. Especially where works were given as parts of lavish private festivities, but more or less in all cases, the expenditure for costumes, scenery and manifold accessories tended to be enormous. Great numbers of soldiers, slaves, citizens, etc., were introduced for spectacular effect, with quantities of animals, birds, plants and other natural objects. Huge or grotesque machines or figures were devised to heighten the illusions.

As an illustration, at the performance of Cesti's *Il pomo d'oro* at Vienna (1666) a special theatre, seating 1500 persons, was built in the castle courtyard, the scenery included landscapes and a harbor view, the open sea with tritons, the nether world, and the Olympian heaven, each with its respective divinities, and the number of characters was bewildering. In the prologue appeared the personified divisions of the Empire, Spain, Austria, ·Hungary, Bohemia, Germany, Italy — even America! There were 5 acts and 67 scenes. The cost of production was said to be 100,000 thalers. Freschi's *Berenice* at Padua (1680) was another example of prodigious display.

As a rule, the opera season was limited to the time of Carnival (Epiphany to Lent), but supplemental seasons after Easter and in the autumn were sometimes undertaken. Novelties were constantly demanded — which explains the immense number of works written and emphasizes the cases in which certain of them were given more than once.

The difficulties with scenery necessitated long waits between acts or scenes, to offset which the intermezzo or the ballet was a relief — the former tending to be a second play within the main one, and the latter becoming ultimately a somewhat permanent addition to the spectacle as a whole.

> Until about 1675 the orchestra was usually rather meagre, but brief preludes, ritornelli and independent numbers in the midst of the action steadily increased in importance, necessitating a gradual expansion of the forces. This had a decided influence upon the entire development of instrumental music (see sec. 112).

81. The Earlier Venetian Opera-Writers. — During the sixty years from 1637 to 1700 an extraordinary number of operas appeared in Italy — at least 700. When the list is analyzed, it appears that about 1670 a decided expansion took place, due to the rise of independent interest at Bologna and Naples, and to the fertility of certain writers. Prior to 1670 the new works averaged four or five per year, but later at least three times as many. Till long after 1700 Venice kept far ahead of all other cities in the number of first productions, and the Venetian style dominated everywhere. The most important name, after those mentioned, is that of Legrenzi.

In this first period important writers were the following : —

Francesco Mannelli, Ferrari's associate in the first opera-house, where his *Andromeda* (1637) was the first work, presented 6 others (till 1666) at Venice, Florence, Piacenza and Ferrara.

Benedetto Ferrari (d. 1681), born in 1597 and probably trained at Rome, was early famous as a theorbist and later as a poet (dramatic works, 1644), being the librettist of Mannelli's first two operas and all of his own. After a short term at Vienna, he spent most of his life in court service at Modena. His 8 operas or lesser dramas were mostly given at Venice (1639–64), and the earlier ones were repeated at various places.

Paolo Sacrati (d. 1650), born at Parma, probably lived at Venice, but was finally choirmaster at Modena. To his credit are 7 operas, all at Venice (1639–48). The most famous was the comedy *La finta pazza* (1641), repeated under his direction at Paris (1645) at the request of the Premier Mazarin.

Andrea Mattioli, from 1646 choirmaster at Imola, from 1653 at Ferrara, and later at Mantua till at least 1671, produced 7 operas (1650–66), mostly at Ferrara, and also issued collections of church music (from 1639).

Antonio Sartorio (d. 1681), born at Venice, was long at the court of Bruns-wick, but from 1676 was second choirmaster at St. Mark's. He brought out 14 operas at Venice (from 1652, mostly from 1666), besides psalms (1680).

Pietro Andrea Ziani (d. 1711), born at Venice, from 1657 choirmaster at Bergamo, from 1669 organist at St. Mark's, and from 1676 at Naples, was more prolific, producing over 20 operas (from 1657), mostly at Venice, besides 2 oratorios, church works (1640–60) and instrumental pieces (1691). With him the growing interest in instrumental writing becomes notable in connec-tion with the opera.

Giovanni Legrenzi (d. 1690) was born near Bergamo about 1625 and studied with Rovetta and C. Pallavicini. From 1654 he was organist at Bergamo, in 1657–64 (if not longer) choirmaster at Ferrara, from 1672 head of one of the Venetian conservatories, from 1681 also second choirmaster at St. Mark's, and chief from 1685. His 18 operas (from 1664, mostly 1675–84) were nearly all produced at Venice. He was highly extolled in his own time, and is conspicu-ous for a decided development of the orchestral accompaniments and for suc-cessful handling of comic scenes and plots. He was also eminent for many sacred and instrumental works (see sec. 94). With him begins the transition to the fertility of the last part of the century. His distinguished pupils were many, including Lotti and Caldara.

To these may be added at Venice **Giovanni Rovetta** (d. 1668), Monteverdi's successor at St. Mark's in 1643 and a distinguished church composer, with 2 operas (1645–9) ; **Giambattista Volpe** (d. 1692), his nephew and pupil (hence called **Rovettino**), from 1665 organist at St. Mark's, with 3 (1659–64) ; **Carlo Grossi**, a conceited singer at St. Mark's, with at least 6 (1659–77), besides church works ; and **Giovanni Antonio Boretti** of Parma, with at least 8 (1662–73).

Outside of Venice before 1670 may be noted, at Rome, **Luigi Rossi**, one of the many protégés of the Cardinals Barberini, with 1 (1642), besides another at Paris (1647), **Marco Marazzoli** (d. 1662), a famous harpist and from 1637 in the Papal Chapel, with 3 (1642–58), **A. M. Abbatini** (d. 1677), with 2 at Rome and Vienna (1650–66), and **P. F. Valentini** (d. 1654), with 2 favole, each with intermezzi (1654), besides learned canons, etc. ; at Genoa, **Francesco Righi**, with 1 (1653) ; at Ferrara and Vienna, **Giuseffo Tricarico**, with 2 (1655–62) ; at Naples, **Francesco Cirillo**, with 2 (1654–5) ; at Viterbo, **Giovanni Battista Mariani** (1659) ; and at Palermo, **Vincenzo Amati** (1664).

82. The Early Oratorio. — Although the musical drama began in both secular and sacred varieties, the Venetian attention to the former left the latter undeveloped. The one Italian oratorio-composer to be emphasized is Carissimi. Before his time the difference between the two forms (so far as both were attempted) lay only in topic and text, both being given with scenery, costume and action, and with the same musical materials. Carissimi set aside the theatrical presentation, often committed dramatic details to a ' Narrator,' emphasized the function of the

N

chorus, and fully recognized the value of a distinct oratorio manner. His own oratorios were short, but are still decidedly interesting. He also, as has been noted, developed the cantata — a work utilizing the dramatic forms of recitative and aria, with a more or less dramatic plan, but designed either for a single voice or for a few voices, and available for use in actual church services, often with organ accompaniment.

Giacomo Carissimi (d. 1674), born near Rome about 1604 and probably trained there, was from 1624 choirmaster at Assisi and from 1628 at S. Apollinare in Rome, remaining till his death. His oratorios number 15 or more, the most famous being *Jephta* and *Jonas* (dates unknown). His church music includes many motets and some masses (one for 12 voices on the old melody *L'omme armé*, said to be the last written on that hackneyed ' subject '). He left many cantatas, together with some secular and half-humorous pieces, with a treatise on singing (known only in German, 3d ed. 1689). His contributions to the monodic style have already been mentioned. As a contrapuntist he was notable, not as a follower of Palestrina, but for the accommodation of the old facility to the new conceptions of tonality. He is commonly reckoned as next to Monteverdi in importance in the century.

Carissimi stands almost alone in his adherence to Biblical subjects in his oratorios — the Flood, Abraham and Isaac, Jephtha, the Judgment of Solomon, Ezechiel, Job, Jonah, Daniel, Belshazzar, the Last Judgment, the Joy of the Blessed. Among other oratorios up to 1670, only a few are strictly Biblical, while several celebrate the life of some saint (especially Loyola), and some are moralities or similar works.

The meagre list of Italian oratorio-writers in the early period includes Johannes Hieronymus Kapsberger (d. 1650 ?), a pretentious German theorbist who pushed himself into church circles at Rome, writing 2 oratorios (c. 1630), an opera, madrigals, solo works and several lute-books (from 1604); Domenico Mazzocchi, a Roman lawyer, the first to mention the signs for crescendo and diminuendo, with 2 oratorios (1631); Stefano Landi (1634); Luigi Rossi, an early Roman writer of cantatas; Loreto Vittori (d. 1670) of the Papal Chapel (1647), besides cantatas; Francesco Bazzini (d. 1660), a noted theorbist of Bergamo (c. 1650); Marco Marazzoli (d. 1662), one at Rome (1658), besides others in MS.; Giovanni Antonio Boretti of Parma; Giuseffo Tricarico at Vienna (1661); P. A. Ziani (d. 1711) of Bergamo, later at Vienna, with 2 (1662); Giovanni Antonio Manara of Bologna, with 3 (1665–85); and Maurizio Cruciati, also of Bologna (1667).

It will be noted that what interest existed was chiefly at Rome.

As the century went on, attention to the oratorio continued in Italy to a considerable extent, but the early types persisted without special improvement, though the use of Biblical subjects increased. As compared with the genius for oratorio-writing that presently developed in Germany, the Italian composers in this form from the first displayed but moderate zeal and power, and the public interest in it was slight. Yet the total number of works produced was not small.

After about 1660, passing over those with but one or two works, the following oratorio-composers may be noted : **Provenzale** of Naples, with 3 (from c. 1670) ; **Colonna** (d. 1695) of Bologna, with 11 (from 1677) ; **Stradella** (d. 1681), with perhaps 8 (c. 1680), of which *S. Giovanni Battista* is the best-known ; **A. Scarlatti** (d. 1725), the great Neapolitan, with 14 (from 1683) ; **Pasquini** (d. 1710), the organist of Rome, with 5 (1685-9) ; **Perti** of Bologna (d. 1756), with over 10 (from 1685) ; **Gianettini** (d. 1721) of Modena, with 4 (1687-1704) ; **G. B. Bononcini** (d. c. 1750) of Bologna, Vienna, London, etc., with 4 (from 1688) ; **Bassani** (d. 1716) of Ferrara, with 3 (c. 1689) ; **Aldrovandini** (d. after 1711) of Bologna and Mantua, with 5 (1691-1706) ; **Pistocchi**, the eminent singing-master of Bologna, with 3 (from 1692) ; and **Polaroli** (d. 1722) of Venice and Vienna, with at least 3 (from c. 1700).

At Vienna, Italian workers in this field included **Bertali** (d. 1669), with 3 (1663-5) ; **Sances** (d. 1679), with 4 (1666-72) ; **Draghi** (d. 1700), the prolific opera-writer, with over 30 (from 1669) ; **Ariosti** (d. c. 1740), with 5 (1693-1709) ; **Badia** (d. 1738), with 16 (1694-1717) ; **M. A. Ziani** (d. 1715), with 10 (1700-13) ; and **M. A. Bononcini** (d. 1726), with 3 (1707-11).

Most of these were chiefly famous as opera-writers (see secs. 90-91).

CHAPTER XI

THE EXPANSION OF DRAMATIC MUSIC

83. In General. — Although the rise of the Italian opera under Monteverdi, Cavalli, Carissimi and Cesti has unique historic importance, the story of the early opera was by no means confined to Italy. Italian musicians visited other countries or migrated to them, carrying with them the styles to which they were wonted. The Italian opera thus came into contact with native styles of drama that were on the verge of a definite musical development and that needed only a slight impulse to advance to national types. The Italian *dramma per musica*, with its accent on grandiose recitative, was but one of several forms that were capable either of independent evolution or of varied combination. Prominent among these were the French ballet, the German singspiel and the English masque — all secular derivatives in some way of the mediæval Mysteries and Miracle-Plays, but with differences of traditional treatment. With these the Italian opera either competed or coalesced, and out of their varied interactions were gradually shaped the types of opera found in the 18th century. The age was eager to adopt or create the musical drama in any available form. The strong influence upon musical progress of the later opera is clearly due to the intricate blending of several tendencies that first attracted attention in the 17th century. While the works produced were presently overshadowed by later ones, the interest of the lines of experiment then initiated is unquestionable.

84. The French Ballet. — The distinctive feature of the ballet as a dramatic form (to which it owes its name) was its emphasis upon actual dancing and upon the kinds of structure, action, verse and song that dancing favored. From at least the 14th century the trend of French taste in this direction had been manifest. It showed itself in a liking for pantomimic spectacles, in which situations and events were illustrated by dance-ensembles, for dialogue cast in the form of reciprocal verses that could be sung to dance-steps, and for a general shaping of words and music by the neat and exact form of dance-patterns.

The reaction of all this upon musical method was decided. The French mind was not content with the more or less form-less Italian recitative or any treatment of the arioso not dis-tinctly rhythmic — that was not a clear 'tune.' It tended at first to exalt piquancy of tonal effect above truth to the text.

While not avoiding serious themes, it frankly sought to devise captivating entertainments rather than to evolve a grand form of monumental art. Ere long it seized eagerly upon instru-ments as specially effective means for the decoration and elabo-ration of dance-themes of all kinds. Thus was early laid the foundation of that sprightly and brilliant type of composition that has always been characteristic of the French opera — a type of great utility to musical progress even when its works were not of the highest intrinsic value.

The evolution of the French drama is traceable with exceptional com-pleteness. Only a few points need here be mentioned. The Trouvère play, *Robin et Marion* (1285), was peculiar because wholly devoid of re-ligious elements, these being replaced by the secular features of amusing story, light song and dancing. It is suspected that there were other simi-lar works, now lost. For over two centuries afterwards the performances of Mysteries and Miracle-Plays were common and ambitious in various French towns, usually under the care of societies like the Confrérie de la Passion, Les Clercs de la Bazoche, Les Enfants sans Souci, etc., in whose hands the free use of music and dancing increased.

The 'mascarade' or mimetic ballet was not a French invention, but after 1500 it became specially associated with French court festivities, and in some form has remained peculiarly characteristic of the French drama. Though what is now called the ballet has fallen to the low estate of a mere divertissement in the grand opera or been transformed into the orchestic farce, its historic prototype was significant as a dramatic form that might have been the forerunner of the modern opera had circumstances favored it. The notable performance in 1581 of the *Ballet comique de la reine* (properly *Circé et ses nymphes*) was almost as early as any like undertak-ing in Italy and much more pretentious. Its scenic scale is shown by its expense — over 3,600,000 francs. Its arranger, though not the composer of its incidental music, was the Italian violist Baltazarini. Its music re-sembled that of the Italian madrigal-plays in that it did not include solos. The popularity of the form, especially because of its unlimited spectacular possibilities, is evidenced by the record that under Henry IV. (1589-1610) about 80 ballets were produced at court. If some constructive genius had appeared, this early ballet might have become the progenitor of the opera proper. As it was, progress paused for almost a century.

A few attempts were made to import musical plays from Italy, as Sacrati's *La finta pazza* (1645), Rossi's *Orfeo* (1647) and Cavalli's *Xerse* and *Ercole amante* (1660–2), and French imitations seem to have been attempted in 1646–7. But, though French taste for theatric spectacles had long been supported by players and managers from Italy, the Italian musical drama commanded but scant applause.

Meanwhile, the ballet advanced from its early miscellaneous plan to a more sustained unity. In this the literary leader was *Isaac de Benserade* (d. 1691), the court-poet, whose first work was given in 1651. But the progressive musical workers were Italians. Detached solo songs and part-songs began to be put forth in 1661 by *Michel Lambert* (d. 1696) the first important French singing-master, father-in-law of Lully.

85. Cambert and Lully. — Opera in French and according to French ideas took shape in the hands of the mediocre poet Perrin and the composer Cambert, the former of whom supplied much of the constructive impulse, while the latter was the executive genius. Their first joint experiment in 1659 was not followed up till 1671, when a more pretentious work was given in the first public opera-house in Paris.

> Notable features in the plan adopted were these: an overture in three movements, the first and last slow and sonorous, the second quick and fugal; a grandiose and irrelevant prologue; a loose and rather miscellaneous plot on a subject from Greek mythology, with more attention to scenic display than to musical coherence or dramatic power; a constant tendency to handle the recitative and arioso with emphasis on the declamatory possibilities of the text; and a marked readiness to suspend the action for ensembles of the ballet class. Whether Perrin or Cambert originated any of these features is doubtful. It is more likely that they were features to which French taste was already committed.

At this point appeared the Italian Lully, whose cleverness, versatility and instinct for popularity presently made him the leading figure. Securing the royal favor and a monopoly of opera-production and occupying a new opera-house (built in 1672), he put forth a surprising series of works, both ballets and real operas, which united the Italian and the French styles so successfully as to establish the opera in Parisian regard, with himself as its chief and almost only exponent. Without being a genius of a high order, Lully was certainly talented on the dramatic side, with a keen sense of the values of musical means. At the same time when the Italian opera was already tending to develop the music at the expense of the drama, he exalted the forcible delivery of the words, even when he thus missed the richer and more affecting uses of melody, especially as characterizing personages or sentiments. This improved the technique of the recitative and restrained the drift toward merely pretty tunes. He sought to captivate by ingenious ensemble climaxes, by using dances freely, and by a novel amount of instrumental numbers. He did much to unfold the latent possibilities of the overture, incidentally advancing the capacity of the operatic orchestra. As a composer, he often showed power in stately and noble effects, and not a little ingenuity in devising fresh accompaniments. In practical success with the public he far outshone all his contemporaries and immediate successors, remaining a dominant influence for many decades.

Pierre Perrin (d. 1675), born in Lyons, came to Paris about 1645, was a dependent of the Duke of Orleans, was involved in many difficulties and spent some time in prison, published poems, wrote several librettos that Cambert set to music, and died in poverty. He was a clever dancer and singer, with some musical ability.

Robert Cambert (d. 1677), born at Paris in 1628, was a pupil of the court-clavichordist Chambonnières, served as organist at St. Honoré, and in 1665 became musician to the Queen Dowager. Besides writing various detached pieces, including motets, songs and preludes, he joined Perrin in some operatic works, first in 1659–61 (*La pastorale, Ariane, Adonis*), and again, after Perrin in 1669 had secured an opera-monopoly and the first public opera-house had been built, in 1671 (*Pomone, Les peines et plaisirs de l'amour*). In 1672 Lully wrested the monopoly from Perrin, and Cambert betook himself to London, where he died in some court position. Only fragments of his works have survived, but these show him as a correct and careful writer for the time.

Jean Baptiste Lully (d. 1687) was born in Florence in 1633, probably of noble parents. He was taught the violin and lute as a child. Catching the notice of the Duke of Guise, he was taken to Paris and installed in the household of Mlle. de Montpensier, at first as a kitchen-boy. His musical talent soon led to his advancement, finally into the private band of Louis XIV., of both divisions of which he became leader, raising the whole establishment to high efficiency. From 1653 he was court-composer, becoming through his ballets one of the king's chief favorites. In 1672 he secured the exclusive privilege held by Perrin, and, in a new theatre specially built, began the series of about 15 operas by which his fame was made. In 1681 he became court-secretary and was ennobled. His death was occasioned by a blow upon the foot from his cane or baton while conducting a rehearsal. In character he presents a curious mixture of unquestionable ability and mere dexterity as a courtier. He was indefatigable, excitable, imperious, proud and unscrupulous, but he had such gifts as player, composer, organizer and director that he is called the founder of the French opera. His leading operas were *Alceste* (1674), *Isis* (1677), *Persée* (1682) and *Armide* (1686). The success of some of them was due to the skillful librettos of Quinault (d. 1688). From 1658 he wrote over

30 ballets and similar works, some to texts by distinguished poets, like Molière. He also composed some church music and many violin-solos and pieces for instruments. He is sometimes named the inventor of the minuet, and his place in the history of orchestral music is almost as important as in that of the opera proper. All of his three sons were musically gifted.

Although Lully's vogue long prevented the success of others, several names should be mentioned : —

Marc Antoine Charpentier (d. 1704), born at Paris in 1634, went to Italy to study painting, but became a pupil of Carissimi and returned to France as choirmaster to the Dauphin. Driven out by the intrigues of Lully, he entered the service of Mlle. de Guise, of the Duke of Orleans and of the Jesuit College, finally becoming choirmaster at the Sainte Chapelle. He was Lully's special rival, but in spite of real ability was unable to compete with him in royal favor. He wrote many ballets (from about 1675), a few operas (as *Médée*, 1694), and 18 oratorios, with psalms and masses.

Pascal Colasse (d. 1709) was Lully's pupil and long his assistant in completing his operas. A royal favorite, from 1677 he was concertmaster at the Opéra and from 1683 held court positions, besides an operatic privilege at Lille. Of his 10 operas (1687–1706) the best was *Thétis et Pélée* (1689). The failure of some, with other trials, drove him to alchemy and finally into insanity. **Marin Marais** (d. 1728), another pupil of Lully, from 1685 in the royal orchestra, wrote 4 operas (1693–1709), with many pieces for the gamba (see sec. 112). **Henri Desmarets** (d. 1741) began his career as a musical page to the king, competing unsuccessfully for a higher position in 1683, and after 1700 was choirmaster to Philip V. of Spain, returning later to serve the Duke of Lorraine. He wrote several operas and ballets (1693–1704, '22).

André Campra (d. 1744) was much more important. After long service (from 1679) as choirmaster at Toulon, Arles, Toulouse, the Jesuit College, the Sainte Chapelle and Notre Dame, from 1697 he turned to secular music and from 1722 was court-conductor. Of his perhaps 20 popular operas (1697–1718, '35) the most noted were *Hésione* (1700), *Tancrède* (1702) and *Les festes vénitiennes* (1710). His style showed Italian influence and had richness in ensemble and instrumental effects.

André Cardinal Destouches (d. 1749), in youth undecided between the priesthood and the army, finally took up music. His *Issé* (1697) was so successful that he began serious study and produced about 10 operas (till 1726), though without reaching special eminence, except for the time. From 1697 he was royal inspector of music.

86. The German Singspiel. — The term 'singspiel' has no precise meaning, being used of any of the German derivatives of the mediæval plays in which songs were introduced in the midst of the spoken dialogue without distinctly adding to the dramatic effect by their musical treatment. The taste for both part-songs and solo songs was so early developed in Germany under the impress of folk-music, that it was inevitable that all dramatic experiments should seek such musical extensions and decoration. It was natural, also, that an effort should ultimately be made to construct a play out of a chain of vocal numbers almost or quite without spoken dialogue. In this case the singspiel differed from the opera in the form of music adopted, which was not dramatic, but lyrical, often laid out upon the strict strophe-plan.

Song-plays of some sort are traceable in Germany as early as the 13th and 14th centuries, when they gradually detached themselves from the original church plays. In the 15th century they dropped into great vulgarity, from which in the 16th they were lifted again into dignity by the poets *Paul Rebhun* (d. 1546?), *Hans Sachs* the Meistersinger (d. 1576), and his follower *Jacob Ayrer* (d. 1605) — the last of whom is sometimes called the inventor of the singspiel.

In the 17th century the stimulus of the young Italian opera was early felt, and what are often styled the first German operas (Schütz' *Dafne*, 1627, and Staden's *Seelewig*, 1644) were really singspiele. From this time the singspiel becomes merged in the opera, though late in the 18th century came a notable effort to revive it as a distinct type (see sec. 158) — the result being analogous to the English ballad-opera, the French vaudeville and the modern operetta. Until this later development the singspiel exerted no important general influence, except to modify slightly the earlier German imitations of the Italian opera. For the most part the early story of German opera is simply that of the Italian type transplanted.

87. The Opera in Germany. — As in Italy, the early cultivation of dramatic music was wholly under the patronage of powerful princes as a court luxury. Among the establishments where the opera was thus taken up, that of the Emperor at Vienna was the most conspicuous, but other courts, like Dresden and Munich, were early important. About 1680 Hamburg became the chief centre in northern Europe for operatic music, a position of leadership which it retained until almost 1740.

Ere long the erection of theatres or opera-houses, more or less public, was undertaken — Munich, 1651, Vienna, 1659, Dresden, 1667, Nuremberg, 1668, Hamburg, 1678, Hanover, 1689, Brunswick, 1691, Leipsic, 1691, with Berlin not until 1742. Until about 1690 the works given were either those imported from Italy or those of the singspiel class.

The number of singspiele produced during the century was probably considerable, but nearly all of them have disappeared.

Heinrich Schütz of Dresden (d. 1672), altogether the strongest German composer of his age (see sec. 96), showed his sympathy with the new Italian dramatic style by setting a German version of Rinuccini's *Dafne* (1627) and by a ballet, *Orpheus und Eurydice* (1636), the music of which is lost. **Sigmund Staden** (d. 1655), a Nuremberg organist, wrote the earliest German musical drama that is now extant, *Das geistliche Waldgedicht, Seelewig* (1644), nominally 'in the Italian manner,' but lacking many usual Italian features, while showing the German taste for orderly and expressive song. There are but scattered references to other works before 1675.

Important advance waited for the opening of the Hamburg opera-house in 1678, where the writers of singspiele included **Nikolaus Adam Strunck** (d. 1700), an extraordinary violinist employed at various courts (Brunswick, Celle, Hanover, Dresden), and writing for Hamburg several German dramas (1678–83) and for Leipsic, where in 1691 he built an opera-house, about 15 more in Italian; **Johann Theile** (see sec. 96), supplying 2 singspiele (1678); **Johann Wolfgang Franck** of Hamburg, who wrote 14 (1679–86), besides many sacred songs (1681–1700); **Johann Georg Conradi**, court-choirmaster at Oettingen and Kusser's predecessor at Hamburg, with 7 (1691–3), one or two of which were later revived by others; and **Philipp Krieger** (d. 1725), organist or choirmaster at various courts (Copenhagen, Bayreuth, Halle, Weissenfels), where from 1679 he brought out a great many singspiele, two of which were repeated at Hamburg (1694).

The prominence of Vienna as a headquarters of Italian opera was due to the exceptional musical enthusiasm of the Emperors during the 17th and 18th centuries. In the 17th, two of these, Ferdinand III. (1637–57) and Leopold I. (1657–1705), were composers of ability, besides being lavish in their patronage. The court singers and players sometimes numbered as many as a hundred. Besides the chief organist and director and their assistants, toward the end of the century a court-composer was appointed. Distinguished composers and performers were often brought to Vienna by imperial invitation for special undertakings.

Besides the imported performances of works by **Cavalli** (possibly in 1642, '50, certainly in 1662, at Innsbruck) and by **Cesti** (1665–9), the following resident composers, all Italians, are noteworthy: —

Antonio Bertali (d. 1669), for over 30 years in the imperial service, with 8 operas (from 1653); **Antonio Draghi** (d. 1700), still longer at the court, with the incredible number of over 170 operas, festal plays, serenatas, ballets, prologues, etc. (from 1661, mostly 1669–95), in many cases with arias by the Emperor Leopold inserted; **Giovanni Felice Sances** (d. 1679), in the Chapel from 1637 and Bertali's successor as choirmaster in 1669, with 1 (1670); and **Carlo Agostino Badia** (d. 1738), the first court-composer, with 20 operas and many lesser dramatic works (from 1697) — not to mention others whose stay at Vienna was briefer. In 1696 the powerful composer **Fux** appeared, opening the series of important 18th-century writers (see secs. 121, 125).

At Munich the list is also striking — **Johann Kaspar Kerll** (d. 1693), most famous as an organist, who as court-choirmaster led the way with 4 operas (1657–68) ; **Giuseppe Ercole Bernabei** (d. 1688), choirmaster from 1671, with 5 (1674–86), though chiefly engaged in church music ; **Giuseppe Antonio Bernabei** (d. 1732), his son and successor, with 15 (1678–91) ; **Agostino Steffani** (d. 1728), a protégé of the Elector from boyhood, court-organist in 1675–88 (see Hanover below), a highly trained and efficient composer, who brought out here his first operas (from 1681) ; and, as a link with the next century, **Pietro Torri** (see sec. 125).

At Dresden the dominant influence in the middle of the century was that of **Schütz**, whose two early dramas have been mentioned. But the Italian **Giovanni Andrea Bontempi** (d. 1705), coming from Venice to be court-choir-master about 1650, brought out here 3 operas (1662–73) ; and **Carlo Pallavicino** ended his career here in 1688, his last work being completed by Strunck. For a quarter-century operatic interest was slight, until revived by the important works of **Lotti** in 1717.

At Hanover the one name of importance is **Steffani**, already named at Munich, who was court-choirmaster from 1688 till succeeded in 1710 by Handel, producing some 10 operas with signal success, his mature style comparing favorably with that of his greater contemporaries. It was here that his gifts as a political agent secured him honors from the Elector and a bishopric from the Pope.

At Brandenburg and Berlin under the patronage of the Prussian court the giving of operas began just before 1700 with some small works by **Karl Friedrich Rieck** (d. 1704), the royal choirmaster, and a few by visiting musicians. Progress then waited till the opening of an opera-house and the advent of **Graun** about 1740.

That which gave Hamburg its peculiar eminence in opera at the opening of the 18th century was the marked ability of two composers, Kusser and Keiser, both Germans, but both sensitive to cosmopolitan influences.

Johann Sigismund Kusser [Cousser] (d. 1727), a musician's son at Pressburg, received his first training there and at Stuttgart. He moved much from place to place in his career, being from 1682 court-musician at Stuttgart, from 1683 at Strassburg, from about 1690 at Brunswick (or Wolfenbüttel), from 1693 director of the Hamburg opera, from 1698 at Stuttgart again, from 1704 teaching singing in London, and from 1710 viceroyal choirmaster at Dublin. His talents as organizer and leader immediately advanced the Hamburg opera to importance, so that he is said to have been the first really to establish in Germany the well-developed Italian art of dramatic singing. He wrote 11 operas, of which 7 were produced at Brunswick (from 1690), 3 more at Hamburg (from 1693) and 1 at Stuttgart (1698). Only one, *Jason* (1697), has survived entire. His style was not far removed from that of the singspiel.

Reinhard Keiser (d. 1739), born near Weissenfels in 1674 and trained by his father and at the Thomasschule in Leipsic, stands out as the most famous name in the early German opera, though in absolute genius not of the highest rank.   Before he was 20, he won applause by an opera at Brunswick (1692), so that he aspired to be heard at Hamburg.   Most of his subsequent career was passed there, except 3 years at Weissenfels (from 1706), 2 at Ludwigsburg (from 1719), and 7 at Copenhagen (from 1722).   His official positions varied, but he was always a leading spirit in musical enterprises.   He is said to have written 116 operas or similar works, 4 Passions, many solo cantatas and songs, motets, etc.   His most brilliant period was about 1700, noted works being *Adonis* (1697), *La forza della virtù* (1700), *Claudius Cäsar* (1703, with Italian arias for the first time), *Crœsus* (1710), etc.   In 1706 he put forth a statement of his dramatic principles, which, however, he did not always observe.   Though the subjects and the style of his librettos were often poor, his readiness as a melodist and his clever handling of effects gave him a hold upon popular attention.   He devoted himself chiefly to the aria rather than to recitative, choruses or orchestration, though dances were used freely.   His popularity stimulated other musicians, and he contributed to Handel's early growth (see sec. 120).   With him German subjects first came to the front.

Lesser composers at Hamburg were **Johann Philipp Förtsch** (d. 1732), a versatile physician, with about 10 operas (1686–90); and **Georg Bronner** (d. 1724), Keiser's predecessor as director, with 6–7 (1693–1702).

In Copenhagen the first opera (1689) was by **Paul Christian Schindler** (d. 1740).

88. The English Masque. — In England the dramatic form that led toward the opera was the 'masque,' originally imported from Italy in the 16th century, but specially developed by English poets.   This was a piece of private theatricals in which members of high society in disguise (whence the name) acted out a mythological or other fanciful story with dialogue and declamation, much dancing, elaborate scenic effects and, as time went on, considerable singing and incidental pieces for instruments.

> Though resembling the French ballet at first, the masque came to differ in its greater literary finish, since many of the best poets undertook it (like Ben Jonson, Chapman, Fletcher, Milton, etc.).   The fashionable court attention to it under the Stuarts checked the advance of the more serious drama.   Under the Commonwealth masques were at length suppressed because of their tendency to coarseness, but with the Restoration in 1660 they came in again.

Throughout the century almost all leading English composers wrote masque music, and thus gradually the musical masque became important (sometimes under the Italian name 'opera').   Its development into a national type of musical drama hardly came to pass, but the operatic genius Purcell was influenced by it more or less.

It should be added that in England, as elsewhere, there was much writing of detached songs or scenes either as incidentals to some spoken drama or in a similar style, so that any list of masque-writers might be reasonably extended to include many composers of 'ayres' and the like.

It has been the fashion to say that the Puritans were hotly opposed to all music, simply because they objected to the ornate cathedral services and to the abuses of the theatre. Yet all the Puritan leaders were interested in music itself, many of them, like Milton, being expert in it, and it seems that the revival of public concerts and even of some sort of musical plays in 1656 was either by direction of the Protector or with his implied approval. During the Commonwealth there was a notable amount of music-printing.

The better-known composers of masques or similar plays were all either in court service or engaged in church music — in 1607–13 Thomas Campion (d. 1620), poet and physician; in 1609 (*Ayres*) Alfonso Ferrabosco (d. 1628), the second of the name, born in England of Italian parents; in 1613–4 John Coperario [Cooper] (d. 1627), lutist, gambist and court-teacher; in 1613 Nicholas Lanier (d. 1666), royal choirmaster from 1640, who is said to have been the introducer of the recitative into England; in 1613 William Lawes (d. 1645); in 1634 (*Comus*) Henry Lawes (d. 1662), his brother; in 1653–75 Matthew Locke (d. 1677); in 1667 Pelham Humphrey (d. 1674); in 1667–77 John Banister, Sr. (d. 1679), an eminent violinist; from 1675 Henry Purcell (d. 1695), the crowning genius of the period; in 1676–1706 Jeremiah Clarke (d. 1707); in 1681–1707 (over 40 works) John Eccles (d. 1735); in 1695–1707 Daniel Purcell (d. 1717); and in 1700 John Weldon (d. 1736). Masques continued to be written much later, as by Arne (d. 1778) in 1733 and after, but they were overshadowed by the Italian opera under Handel and others.

89. Purcell. — The one master with both dramatic and musical gifts was the extraordinary Purcell, whose fertile originality, in spite of the brevity of his career, brought the century to a brilliant close. Making up for the lack of travel by intuition and assiduous study, he seized upon the finest points in the Italian style, combined them with some features (especially in choral writing) strangely neglected, and applied them to the treatment of plots that were essentially strong. Purcell's use of Continental methods had been prefigured by Humphrey, who might have been another strong opera-writer if his life, too, had been longer, but he himself outstripped all before in true melody, in characteristic and telling accompaniments, in delineation of personages and situations, and in daring innovations in constructive detail. His many-sidedness is remarkable, since he worked with equal power in stately and thoughtful church music, in festal odes and tributes, in purely chamber music, and in every grade of opera. The culmination of his dramatic efforts came when he was joined by Dryden as a poetic collaborateur. Even before he died, his superiority was well discerned, while now he appears as one of the most creative geniuses of the century. It is a tragedy of history that his career was not only so short, but so utterly devoid of consequence. After him no native English writer appeared to fill his place or continue his work.

Pelham Humphrey (d. 1674, aged 27) was a choirboy in the Chapel Royal when it was organized afresh in 1660, and wrote anthems before he was 17. In 1664 the king sent him to France, where he was a pupil of Lully. In 1666 he reëntered the Chapel for a year, and in 1672 became choirmaster, with the title of composer as well. His compositions include 25 anthems and many songs, some written for the masque *The Tempest* (1667). In these appears that taste for declamatory passages which suggests his latent operatic talent.

Henry Purcell (d. 1695, aged 37), the most famous of a musical family, early left an orphan, became a choirboy in the Chapel Royal, first under Cooke,

then under Humphrey, later studying also with Blow. His evident genius led in 1675 to his setting a play by Tate (later poet-laureate), and its success encouraged him to put forth songs and musical dramas in quick succession. In 1680 he became organist at Westminster and in 1682 also at the Chapel, turning his attention for a time to anthems, chamber music and numerous festal odes. His compositions include, besides 3 services and at least 100 anthems, a great number of solo and other songs and some good chamber pieces, almost 40 dramatic works, both masques or plays with incidental music and full operas, of which *King Arthur* (1691) is chief. The number of important poets who furnished texts is extraordinary, including Shadwell, Tate, Beaumont and Fletcher, Congreve, D'Urfey and Dryden, and the versatile instinct with which he supplied settings for their varied plays shows a dramatic artist of the first order. While claiming that his wish was to introduce the "seriousness and gravity" of "the most famed Italian masters," and catching from the French also a taste for dances, he contributed powerful ideas peculiar to himself.

90. Venetian Opera-Writers after 1670. — The increase in the number of Italian operas about 1670 was due to the popularity of the style, which stimulated the composers already at work, called out others in Venice itself, and gradually aroused emulation in other cities, especially Bologna and Naples. In this second period of the Venetian school there is no name of high rank, though many composers eminent in other fields worked worthily in this. Several were extremely prolific, but their ambition was simply to win immediate success by catering skillfully to the taste of the time. In the eagerness for effective melodies and many of them, dramatic power and truth were more and more neglected.

For reference, the more notable writers of Venice and Bologna are here enumerated : —

In 1670 there were already at work **Carlo Pallavicino** (d. 1688), from 1667 court-choirmaster at Dresden, but with many absences at Venice, where his over 20 operas (from 1666) were mostly produced, with 2 oratorios; and **Giovanni Domenico Partenio** (d. 1701), from 1666 a singer at St. Mark's, and Legrenzi's successor there and at the conservatory, with 4 (1669–82).

Giovanni Domenico Freschi (d. 1690), born at Vicenza and from about 1660 choirmaster there, brought out 14 operas at Venice (from 1671) and an oratorio, besides earlier masses.

Antonio Gianettini [the same as *Zannettini*] (d. 1721), early a singer at St. Mark's and pupil of Legrenzi, from about 1676 was court-organist and later choirmaster at Modena, with about 10 operas at Venice (1674–1705), several oratorios, cantatas and motets.

Marc' Antonio Ziani (d. 1715), choirmaster at Mantua till 1686 and from 1700 in the Imperial Chapel at Vienna, made his early reputation by over 20 operas at Venice (1674–99), with half as many more and about 10 oratorios at Vienna, besides many church works.

Giuseppe Felice Tosi, born at Bologna about 1630 and organist there till 1683, then choirmaster at Ferrara, wrote about 10 operas for Bologna, Venice and other cities (1679–91), besides some cantatas and psalms.

Francesco Antonio Pistocchi (d. 1726), born at Palermo in 1659, was also associated with Bologna, where he was early a singer at the cathedral and the opera. From 1687 at Parma, about 1697 at Ansbach (Bavaria), in 1700 at Vienna, in 1701 he returned to Bologna and presently founded the famous singing-school that soon became a model for others. He wrote several operas (1679–1700), mostly for Venice, with 3 oratorios, many cantatas and motets. A curious book of his pieces for instruments was published when he was but 8 years old (1667).

Jacopo Antonio Perti (d. 1756), born at Bologna in 1661, is chiefly distinguished as a church composer, being choirmaster at Bologna from 1690, after service at Modena and Rome. He wrote about 20 operas (1679–1717) for Modena, Bologna and Venice, with over 15 oratorios and 4 Passions.

Domenico Gabrieli (d. 1690), an eminent 'cellist of Bologna, from 1688 at Modena, brought out 11 operas (from 1683), mostly at Venice, with an oratorio (1687), besides cantatas and instrumental dances.

Antonio Lotti (d. 1740), born about 1667, a pupil of Legrenzi, was all his life connected with St. Mark's, being singer from 1687, second organist from 1692, first from 1704, and choirmaster from 1736. He was strongest as a church composer and teacher, but in opera-writing he was also one of the links between the older style and that of Scarlatti and Handel. At Venice he produced over 20 operas (1683, '93, '96, 1707-17, '36), and, invited to Dresden in 1717-9 with his wife (who was an able singer) and a competent company, he added 3 more, besides 1 at Vienna (1716) and 2 oratorios (1712). He was rather a melodist and a master of finished style than a dramatist, beauty of external effect being uppermost. He was cautious with instruments, lest they should overpower the voices.

Carlo Francesco Polaroli (d. 1722), born at Brescia and a pupil of Legrenzi, preceded Lotti at St. Mark's, being singer from 1665, second organist from 1690 and vice-choirmaster from 1692. Entering the operatic field, he far outstripped Lotti in prolificness, producing nearly 70 operas (1684-1721), besides 3 oratorios for Vienna (c. 1710). Though writing rapidly and superficially, his talent was above the average. His *Roderico* (1684) was widely repeated, and in *Faramondo* (1699) are found arias in *da capo* form, accompanied recitatives, etc., analogous to those of Scarlatti.

Attilio Ariosti (d. c. 1740), born at Bologna in 1660, left the priesthood to devote himself to the viola d' amore and the opera. In Italy he wrote 4 operas for Venice and Bologna (1686-1706) and a Passion (1693). He was court-choirmaster at Berlin in 1698-1705, where he added 2 more (1700), with 4 at Vienna (1703-8) and 4 oratorios. In 1715 he went to London, composing 8 more (1723-7), winning success especially with *Coriolano* (1723) and *Lucius Verus* (1726), but was outclassed by Handel and returned to Italy. He was a well-trained musician, but in opera imitated Lully and Scarlatti.

Other North Italian opera-writers whose work extended into the 18th century were **Caldara** (d. 1736), later eminent at Vienna, with several operas at Venice (from 1689); **Albinoni** (d. 1745), a fine violinist, with about 50 (1694-1741), besides many other works; **Aldrovandini**, a pupil of Perti, with 15 at various cities (1696-1711) and 5 oratorios (1691-1706); and **M. A. Bononcini** (d. 1726), with 19 (1697-1710). This list might be indefinitely extended, as the period was excessively prolific in works of short-lived influence.

91. The Opera at Rome and Naples. — While at the end of the century operatic enthusiasm was keen at Venice and Bologna, so that new works were put forth in large numbers with great popular success, the rest of Italy was content to take its operas mostly from these two cities. But there were signs of a dramatic development at Naples, especially when the genius of Alessandro Scarlatti began to reveal itself. With him properly begins the Neapolitan opera, which was destined in the 18th century to supersede the Venetian and to give the law for all Italian opera throughout Europe (see sec. 125). A few opera-writers also appeared at Rome.

The rise of the Neapolitan school was due not only to the genius of particular composers, but to the steady and diffused influence of four conservatories, all founded in the 16th century, which were important centres of instruction till the 18th. These were *Sta. Maria di Loreto*, founded in 1566 (though begun as a small enterprise in 1535), *S. Onofrio a Capuana*, 1576, *De' Poveri di Gesù Cristo*, 1589, and *Della Pietà de' Turchini*, 1583 (but not definitely devoted to music till late in the 17th century). These were all originally designed as charity-schools for poor children, but in time they became notable institutions of popular art. They attracted large bequests and distinguished teachers, and often counted their pupils by hundreds. Nearly all the great musicians later associated with Naples were students at one or more of these schools. In 1744 the third was transformed into a theological school, in 1797 the first and second were united, and in 1808 the fourth was discontinued. Immediately after was established the *Real Conservatorio di Musica*, which took the place of all and still continues worthily the noble traditions of three centuries of musical fruitfulness.

Alessandro Stradella (d. 1681 ?) should probably be named here, though biographically he is an enigma. It is conjectured that he was born at Naples about 1645, and that he was murdered at Genoa. An extensive romance has grown up about him that may or may not be true, at least giving a fictitious interest to his career, while some music has been attributed to him that was really later. He is said to have been a fine singer and harpist. He left a notable number of works, about 150 in all, including 10 operas (c. 1665–81), 8 oratorios (from 1676), numerous cantatas, duets and madrigals, which show him to have been correct and skillful, but not specially profound. His oratorio *S. Giovanni Battista* (published 1676) is his best-known work.

Bernardo Pasquini (d. 1710), the famous Roman organist (see sec. 104), wrote 7 operas (1672–92), one for the opening of a new opera-house and one for the private circle of the famous ex-Queen Christina of Sweden, then resident in Rome.

Francesco Provenzale is the first prominent composer at Naples, where he produced 2 operas (1670–1) and some oratorios elsewhere, besides being a successful teacher and church writer.

Alessandro Scarlatti (d. 1725) is also to be mentioned because his active career began some time before the century closed, first at Rome, later at Naples. About 10 of his operas and at least 3 oratorios appeared before 1700 (from 1679), mostly at Rome (see sec. 125).

o

CHAPTER XII

PROGRESS IN CHURCH MUSIC

92. In General. — As compared with the 16th century, the 17th was much less productive of church music of a high order, since the new zeal for dramatic music absorbed the best attention of both musicians and the public. In Italy, in spite of the efforts of a small number of conservatives, the drift toward secular works and a secular handling of sacred ones was overwhelming. In Germany, however, amid many changes observable in the treatment of sacred music, a worthy development began in Protestant choir and organ music on the basis of the chorale. This movement was augmented by that vigorous interest in the problems of inner musical construction which has always marked German music as compared with Italian. These efforts pointed toward the culmination of Protestant music under Bach in the 18th century. In England, also, there were interesting, though not remarkable, movements.

Dramatic music inevitably affected all church music, working an emphatic revolution from the severe polyphony of earlier times and often leading to a questionable sensuousness or sensationalism. In many instances whatever was successful on the operatic stage was transferred to the church (of course with religious words). The oratorio was recognized as the link between the two fields, and it was frequently undertaken in both Italy and Germany, though with contrasted results. All these efforts, also, were important in relation to progress after 1700.

More distinctive was the attention to organ music as a specialty. Here the impulse came from Italy, but the greatest progress was in Germany. The organ itself now became more complete, virtuosity became gradually common, and steady gains were made in devising forms of composition germane to the instrument. Through them the wealth of suggestion in chorale music was taken up and under polyphonic manipulation wrought into works of abiding value.

93. The Roman School. — It was natural that at Rome an effort should be put forth to maintain the traditions of the Palestrina style, with its strictly *a cappella* effects, its restraint and purity of structure, and its quality of unworldliness, and that some new writers should seek to add to its repertory. Their success was relatively small, so that it is commonly said that the Palestrina style ceased by 1650. This is not strictly true, since worthy names in the succession can be cited beyond the 17th century, but the style was no longer a positive historic force.

Certain changes in style crept in more and more, though often resisted. Chief of these was the use of the organ for accompaniment, which became a matter of course in most cases (though not in the Papal Chapel, where there was no organ). Another was the Venetian device of several groups of voices, producing what are called 'polychoric' effects. Another was the introduction of solo passages and the handling of voices in ways not strictly choral. This involved the use of song-forms and often florid vocal ornaments, neither of which were germane to the older style. As far as possible the Roman school sought to avoid the powerful drift toward the concertistic or theatrical style, thus recognizing a distinction that has been a subject of debate ever since.

> None of the pontificates during the century were of musical importance, though Urban VIII. (1623–44) took pains to complete certain service-books, and Alexander VII. (1665–7) was a noted patron of literature and the fine arts.

Without attempting an exhaustive catalogue, certain composers should be enumerated : —

Agostino Agazzari (d. 1640), born at Siena in 1578, was from about 1609 choirmaster at various Roman churches and later perhaps at Siena. A prolific composer of motets, masses and madrigals (from 1596), he is notable as one of the first to use organ-accompaniments with a figured bass and to indicate rules for the latter (1607). He also published a tract aiming to elucidate the edicts on church music of the Council of Trent.

Antonio Cifra (d. c. 1638), born in 1575, a pupil of Palestrina and G. M. Nanino, was choirmaster at Loreto in 1613–21 and again from about 1628, in the interval being two years at the Lateran and five in Austria. His very numerous and excellent works (from 1600) included masses, motets, psalms, madrigals, part-songs and ricercari.

Romano Micheli (d. c. 1655), a pupil of Soriano and Nanino, was choirmaster at S. Luigi dei Francesi from about 1625. In his writings (from 1610) he emphasized complicated canons in a style that he claimed to be his own.

Vincenzo Ugolini (d. 1626), born at Perugia, was choirmaster at Sta. Maria Maggiore from about 1603, though partly laid aside by illness (and somewhat an invalid thereafter), at Benevento from 1609, at S. Luigi dei Francesi from 1615, and at St. Peter's from 1620. Recognized as an authority on the Palestrina style, he was much sought as a teacher. In his masses, motets, psalms and madrigals (1614–30) he often used organ-accompaniments with figured bass.

Gregorio Allegri (d. 1652), born in 1584 and another of G. M. Nanino's pupils, after serving as singer at Fermo, entered the Papal Chapel in 1629, remaining in honor till his death. His works are chiefly motets (partly published from 1618, but largely in MS.). The most famous, though not the best, is his Miserere for 9 voices in two choirs, officially sanctioned for use on Wednesday and Friday of Holy Week in the Sistine Chapel, the reproduction of which was ultimately forbidden. The charm of this as there rendered and the barriers thrown about it have given it a fictitious renown. [At least 13 such settings of the Miserere have been authorized, from that of Festa (1517) to those of Baj (1714) and of Baini (1821).]

Stefano Landi (d. after 1639), born about 1590, was choirmaster at Padua and from 1629 in the Papal Choir. He was an expert in the old style (works from 1618), but also wrote solos and duets, besides two dramatic works.

Paolo Agostini (d. 1629, aged 36), the pupil and son-in-law of G. B. Nanino, had a short life, but one full of activity. After being employed in different Roman churches, in 1627 he succeeded Ugolini at St. Peter's. His motets, masses and psalms (partly published from 1619) were technically able, involving extreme contrapuntal skill and sometimes using as many as 48 voices.

Antonio Maria Abbatini (d. 1677), born about 1595, was choirmaster of various Roman churches and at Loreto all his active life, beginning with the Lateran in 1626–8, and including three terms at Sta. Maria Maggiore. Besides church music (from 1627), he wrote cantatas, madrigals and dramatic works.

Virgilio Mazzocchi (d. 1646), after one year at the Lateran, was from 1629 choirmaster at St. Peter's. The author of many motets (from 1640) and 2 oratorios, he is notable as a leader in the change from the stricter style to one more sensuously effective, and as the founder of a music-school of repute.

Pier Francesco Valentini (d. 1654), a pupil of G. M. Nanino, was, like Micheli, a specialist in canon-writing of the highest intricacy and considerable artistic value (from 1629). In one of his books he proposed a theme of which over 2000 solutions are possible, samples of which are given for 2, 3, 4 and 5 voices ; in another are canons for 6, 10 and 12 voices ; in another, some for 96 voices! He also wrote motets, madrigals and 2 slight dramas (1654).

Orazio Benevoli (d. 1672), born in 1602, studied under Ugolini and was his most able successor in learned polyphony. Beginning as choirmaster at S. Luigi dei Francesi, he was called to Vienna, but returned in 1646 to St. Peter's, following Mazzocchi. All his works were sacred, but partly published (from 1628). He was amazingly skillful in works of gigantic structure, employing many voices (up to 48), disposed in 4–12 groups or choirs, and often added extensive polyphonic instrumental parts.

Francesco Foggia (d. 1688), born in 1604, was trained by Cifra, G. B. Nanino and Agostini, and married the latter's daughter. In his youth he held court positions at Cologne, Munich and Vienna, followed by short engage

ments in Italy.   From 1643 he was choirmaster at the Lateran, from 1661 at
S. Lorenzo in Damaso and from 1678 at Sta. Maria Maggiore.   His abundant
works (from 1642 or in MS.) are written in a pure and noble style, almost
untouched by the concertistic drift.   He was one of the first Italians to use
the tonal as distinct from the real fugue (see sec. 103).

Bonifacio Gratiani (d. 1664), born in 1605, from 1649 choirmaster at the
Seminario and the Jesuit Church, composed a prodigious amount of sacred
music (published posthumously), which was highly regarded at the time.

Antimo Liberati (d. after 1685), after study with G. Allegri and Benevoli,
is said to have worked at Vienna until about 1650, when he returned to Rome.
In 1653 he was in the Papal Chapel, and later served two of the city churches.
He left considerable church music, several oratorios and some literary remains.

Matteo Simonelli (d. after 1688), pupil of the same masters and a patient
student of Palestrina's works, entered the Papal Chapel in 1662 and later was
choirmaster elsewhere in Rome.   His many works (left in MS.) were so
finished and noble in style as to give him the name of 'the Palestrina of the
17th century.'

Giuseppe Ottavio Pitoni (d. 1743), born in 1657 and living far into the next
century, was at once the last of the old school and the connecting link with a
much later period.   Musically precocious, he studied with Natale and Foggia,
and was minutely acquainted with Palestrina's works.   From the age of 16 he
was choirmaster in provincial towns, from 1677 in the collegiate church of S.
Marco at Rome, from 1708 at the Lateran and from 1719 at St. Peter's, besides connections with several other churches not fully explained.   His works,
besides being marvels of erudition and skill, were extremely numerous, but,
with one exception (1697), they were not published, and are still not generally
available.   Like Benevoli, he excelled in immense compositions for many voices
in separate choirs — at his death he was working on a mass for 48 voices in 12
choirs.   For St. Peter's he prepared a complete set of masses, motets and vespers
for an entire year, including every service in the calendar.   Among his masses
some are *a cappella*, some with organ and other instruments.   He also left a
MS. account of all the Roman polyphonists from 1000 to 1700, on which Baini
based his monograph upon Palestrina (1828), besides a small manual on composition (c. 1690).   He was an important teacher, as of Durante, Leo and Feo.

A few lesser names may be added, like Francesco Severi (d. 1630), in the
Papal Chapel from 1613 and notable as the author of psalms (1615) exemplifying the overlaying of the voice-parts with florid embellishments;
Lorenzo Ratti (d. after 1632), nephew and pupil of Ugolini, with motets, litanies, graduals and offertories for the whole year (from 1617) ;   Agostino Diruta
(d. after 1668), from 1622 choirmaster at Asola, and from 1630 at S. Agostino
in Rome (works from 1617) ;   Giuseppe Giamberti (d. after 1650), pupil of
G. B. Nanino and Agostini, in 1629 the successor of D. Allegri at Sta. Maria
Maggiore, who was useful as the editor of the new standard antiphonary, besides writing motets (from 1628) ;   Domenico a Pane, pupil of Abbatini,
from 1654 in the Papal Choir and from 1669 its leader, whose works (1672–87)
include masses on themes from Palestrina ;   and Giovanni Battista Giansetti,
choirmaster at the Lateran from about 1670, whose most noted work was a
mass for 48 voices in 12 choirs (1675).

94. Venetian Church Composers. — In the 17th century the general contrast between the Roman and the Venetian schools of sacred music that was noted in the 16th (see secs. 55–60) not only continued, but took on a new and pronounced form as the Venetian opera advanced.

This contrast is naturally viewed by different critics differently. To the enthusiast for objective *a cappella* polyphony of the purest Roman type every deviation towards warmer and more subjective forms of expression, especially with complex instrumental accompaniments and vocal solos, seems an echo of the theatre and a concession to vulgar taste. But, on the other hand, to many practical artists an absolute church style, unconnected with all current secular music, seems a visionary and self-defeating ideal, so that to them the problem is not so much to keep church music uncontaminated by whatever is popularly powerful as to treat it in any available way that secures devotional elevation. For them the end justifies the means, provided only that the end is fairly estimated and actually attained. This brief statement may serve as a key to the profound antagonism between two great schools of Catholic music that dates from the 17th century and is still conspicuous. It is clear that there is reason on both sides and also that each view has dangers — the one of such abstraction as to miss practical utility, the other of such yielding to transient drifts as to lose dignity and depth. The papal authorities have striven to uphold an extremely conservative style, following in all their official rules (including those of Pius X. in 1903) the dictum of the Council of Trent in favor of nothing but Plain-Song and strict *a cappella* polyphony. But the common usage of the Church, even from about 1600, has constantly slipped away from the standards, often running off into rather wild vagaries.

The innovating tendencies included several points. With the development of the organ and of organ-playing the desire for freely handled accompaniments steadily grew, presently reaching out after orchestral effects as well. With the uncovering of the emotional and even passionate capacities of the individual voice came the increasing use of solo passages and solo settings of entire texts (with accompaniment), passing over into concerted forms for two or more solo voices. With the general interest in secular music as normative of all musical style came experiments with settings of sacred words in rhythmic and even dainty styles that recalled the grace of the folk-song, the popular part-song, and even the dance. All these were essential innovations. Not all of them were first attempted by Venetians, since even Palestrina himself was not afraid of slight developments in these directions. But, on the whole, what was known as the *concertato* style was chiefly Venetian, receiving its impulse from Monteverdi and becoming established in honor under Legrenzi and Lotti, with Colonna of Bologna. This free style naturally commended itself strongly to popular taste.

Claudio Monteverdi (d. 1643) published comparatively little church music, but left more in MS. Never in sympathy with pure polyphony, he tended to try new methods, sometimes in a harsh or immature way. His 30 years' service as choirmaster at St. Mark's, however, gave him great influence (see sec. 77). His first printed work was a set of madrigali spirituali (1583), and a collection of motets, psalms, etc., with instrumental accompaniments was one of the last (1641).

Alessandro Grandi (d. 1630), began as choirmaster at Ferrara in 1610, entered the St. Mark's choir in 1617, becoming vice-choirmaster in 1620, but in 1627 removed to Bergamo. His many works (from 1607) include masses, motets, psalms and varied secular pieces, the motets being accompanied from the first, and *concertato* methods becoming obvious later.

Giovanni Rovetta (d. 1668) was early a choirboy at St. Mark's and succeeded Grandi as vice-choirmaster in 1627 and Monteverdi as chief in 1643. He also wrote freely in all forms (from 1626), his style being strongly marked by the new ideas and continuing the traditions of his predecessors.

Francesco Cavalli (d. 1676), pupil of Monteverdi and Rovetta's successor in 1668, though almost 50 years at St. Mark's (see sec. 79), wrote relatively little church music (from 1645).

Natale Monferrato (d. 1685) also spent his life at St. Mark's, being a pupil of Rovetta, from 1639 a singer in the choir and Cavalli's unsuccessful rival for one of the organs, from 1647 vice-choirmaster and Cavalli's successor in 1676. He was also a favorite teacher and engaged in music-publishing. His many motets and psalms, with some masses (from 1647), are in the free style of his school.

Giovanni Legrenzi (d. 1690) studied with Rovetta and succeeded Monferrato in 1685. During his administration the orchestra was increased to 34 players, including 24 strings, 4 theorbi, 2 cornets, 1 bassoon and 3 trombones. One of the best early opera-writers (see sec. 81), he is counted even better as a church composer (works from 1654), besides being one of the earliest writers of chamber music (from 1655).

After him came as choirmasters **Rovettino** in 1690 (organist since 1665), **Partenio** from 1692, and **Biffi** from 1702 — all better opera-writers than church composers.

Antonio Lotti (d. 1740), also a fine opera-writer (see sec. 90), though not choirmaster till 1736, following Biffi, is really next in the succession at St. Mark's, since he was singer there from 1687. Though largely occupied till 1718 with operas, he wrote much church music (left in MS.) of great dignity and beauty, marking him as the culmination of the Venetian school, as well as the model for many followers in the 18th century.

Only second in influence as a centre for church music in the later 17th century was Bologna, where the following composers may be emphasized: —

Adriano Banchieri (d. 1634), born about 1565, a pupil of Guami, and a highly educated Olivetan monk, was not only a learned author, but a practical musician of influence. He was organist in 1599-c. 1615, chiefly at Bosco (near Bologna) and Imola, and founded a musical society which later became the famous *Accademia filarmonica* of Bologna (still existing). His compositions, at first secular (from 1593), including several madrigal-plays, also ranged over the usual sacred forms. In these he showed a keen sympathy with the semi-dramatic style as against *a cappella* polyphony.

Ercole Porta was one of the early users of orchestral support for sacred music (works from 1609).

Giovanni Paolo Colonna (d. 1695), well trained at Rome under Abbatini and Benevoli, was cathedral-organist at Bologna from 1659 and choirmaster from 1674. His numerous sacred works (from 1677, with many in MS.) are in a style that puts him in the front rank of the church composers of the latter part of the century.

Jacopo Antonio Perti (d. 1756), another opera-writer, was cathedral-choir-master from 1690 and wrote fine sacred works (from 1681).

Other North Italian sacred composers were **Guglielmo Lipparino**, choirmaster at Como from about 1619 (works, 1600-37); **Pietro Lappi**, choirmaster at Brescia (works, all sacred, 1601-27); **Giovanni Ghizzolo**, from 1613 successively at Correggio, Ravenna, Padua and Novara (works, sacred and secular, 1608-25); **Stefano Bernardi** (d. 1638?), choirmaster at Verona from about 1615 and at Salzburg in 1628-34 (sacred and secular works from 1611); **Ignazio Donati** (d. 1638?), at various places from 1612, and at Milan from 1631 (works, all sacred, from 1612); **Francesco Bellazzi**, also of Milan, perhaps a pupil of G. Gabrieli (works, all sacred, from 1618); **Galeazzo Sabbatini**, choirmaster at Mirandola, noted as a madrigalist (works, 1625-40); **Orazio Tarditi** (d. after 1670), organist at various places from 1622 and from 1647 choirmaster at Faenza, a very prolific writer, with fully 25 collections (from 1628) of masses, motets, psalms, litanies and madrigals, usually with free use of *concertato* methods; **Giovanni Antonio Rigati** (d. c. 1649), early a singer at St. Mark's, and from 1636 choirmaster at Udine (works from 1640); **Francesco della Porta** (d. 1666), choirmaster at Milan from 1645 (works, all sacred, 1637-57); **Francesco Petrobelli**, choirmaster at Padua in 1651-77 (works from 1643); and **Giovanni Battista Bassani** (d. 1716), an able violinist, organist at Ferrara from 1677, choirmaster at Bologna in 1680-5, and then at Ferrara again, with many sacred works, secular songs and some chamber music (from 1677) — the teacher of Corelli.

95. In Germany. — It was inevitable that in Germany there should be two diverse tendencies in church composition, the one perpetuating the older Catholic traditions, the other seeking to adapt music to the new Protestant services and spirit. Though for a time the distinction between these was more nominal than real, except regarding the chorale, and the earlier German motets and other liturgical pieces were modeled upon their Latin prototypes, the separation of Protestant music gradually became more obvious. Chorales were immensely popular and their number rapidly increased. Their harmonic style pushed its way into choir music, though never driving out counterpoint, for which German writers now began to show their eminent capacity. While Italian power in this field was on the wane, the Germans were preparing not only to preserve the old skill, but to open up new achievements for it. This development was upheld and furthered by the growth of organ composition (see Chapter XIII.).

> The Thirty Years' War (1618–48) interfered with the steady flow of musical progress. In many places musical establishments were wholly suspended (notably at Dresden) and social life generally was unsettled. The momentum of the early part of the century, however, enabled the art to resume its place promptly after 1650.

The Palestrina style in its purity was never dominant in Germany, though it had its isolated disciples. But the connection with northern Italy was close, and, so far as definite influence went, the Venetian type of church music was more likely to be followed. Schütz of Dresden, the ablest German composer of the century, studied at Venice and was fully alive to the new movements there. Under his lead and that of some others, a notable tendency set in to apply *concertato* writing to church use in a more wholesome and suitable way than was common in Italy. The German church cantata and oratorio soon began to be more significant than their Italian prototypes, prefiguring the nobler work of the 18th century. Thus the new methods of accompaniments, solos, concerted passages and every device of formal disposition was brought into the church without such operatic sensuousness as to be debilitating. It is from these beginnings that modern German and English church music really took their rise.

> As samples of Catholic composers, mostly in Austria or South Germany, these names may be noted: **Asprilio Pacelli** (d. 1623), who, after service at Rome, was from 1603 royal choirmaster at Warsaw (motets and psalms from 1597); **Johann Stadlmayr** (d. 1648), at Salzburg in 1603–7, then court-choir-master at Innsbruck, with masses, motets, psalms and hymns (from 1603); **Giovanni Felice Sances** (d. 1679), of Roman birth, in the Imperial Chapel at Vienna from 1637, second choirmaster from 1649 and first from 1669, with many motets, psalms and secular songs (from 1633); **Felicianus Schwab**

[Suevus], a Franciscan of Weingarten and Constance (works, 1634–56) ; Ambrosius Reiner (d. 1672), archducal choirmaster at Innsbruck, with masses, motets and litanies (1643–56), in some of which instruments were combined with novel effect; Georg Arnold, organist at Bamberg (works, 1651–72) ; J. K. Kerll (d. 1693), the great organist at Munich and Vienna (see sec. 105), with important masses, etc. (1669–89), besides dramas and keyboard works ; Johann Melchior Gletle, choirmaster at Augsburg, with many masses and motets (1667–84), often including elaborate vocal and orchestral combinations ; and Steffani (d. 1728), the opera-writer (see sec. 87), pupil of Kerll, from 1667 at Munich and court-organist from 1675, and from 1688 choirmaster at Hanover, with important works (few published, 1674–85).

The centre of activity in Protestant music was naturally Saxony and the neighboring states. Here we encounter a series of composers who united great technical skill with a deep insight into the possibilities of sacred song apart from the Catholic ritual. Being without controlling traditions, they experimented freely with many forms from simple part-songs and solos to extended counterpoint. They evidently felt that there was no fixed boundary between the sacred and the secular, and many of them were eminent in both fields. Yet few of them had to do with the opera, though not wholly averse to dramatic styles. Even when they essayed to treat church music dramatically, their innate German earnestness held them back from triviality or excess.

In the annals of German Protestant music the title 'Cantor' often appears. This is practically equivalent to Kapellmeister as earlier used, except that it belongs not to a princely court or a cathedral, but to a municipality, implying some measure of responsibility for civic education. The office has existed in most German towns and cities, sometimes with duties confined to a single church or school, sometimes involving the care of all the official music of the community — churches, schools, choral societies and bands of players — the incumbent often having the title of 'Town-Musician.'

In many ways the most famous instance has been in the Thomasschule at Leipsic (see secs. 117, 193), where the list of cantors begins early in the 15th century and is complete from 1531 to the present time. In the 17th century the cantors here were from 1594 *Calvisius*, from 1616 *J. H. Schein*, from 1631 *Tobias Michael*, from 1657 *Sebastian Knüpfer*, from 1677 *Johann Schelle*, followed in 1701 by *Kuhnau* and in 1722 by *J. S. Bach* — all dying in office after an average term of 22 years.

Christoph Demantius (d. 1643), from 1597 cantor at Zittau and from 1604 at Freiberg (Saxony), was an abundant and versatile composer of both Latin and German church music (from 1602), many secular songs and canzonets (from 1594) and various dances, together with a Passion (1620) and popular text-books for singing (1592, 1607).

Melchior Franck (d. 1639), from 1603 choirmaster at Coburg, was also prodigiously fertile and a notable master of melody, with church music, both harmonic and contrapuntal (from 1601), a Choralbuch (1631), secular songs, part-songs and dances — all in a style attractive to a modern taste.

Erhard Bodenschatz (d. 1636), pastor near Eisleben, edited invaluable collections of Protestant motets (1603–21) and of chorales (1608), besides writing some works of his own.

Michael Prätorius (d. 1621), from 1604 choirmaster at Wolfenbüttel, was a gifted and prolific composer in many styles, besides being an author of capital importance. His sacred music (from 1605) includes numerous motets, psalms and other choir-pieces, some polychoric for as many as 30 voices, with numbers of chorales and songs, besides secular works, both vocal and instrumental. His *Musæ Sioniæ* (1605–10) is a gigantic collection of religious part-songs, some original. His style was eclectic, ranging from the purely polyphonic to concertistic solo-writing, and richly illustrates the lines of progress going on in Germany. (For his literary work, see sec. 113.) Prätorius was a personal friend of Schütz, as well as his artistic relative.

Johann Staden (d. 1634), from 1609 organist at Bayreuth and from 1616 at Nuremberg, wrote varied sacred and secular works (from 1606), including many part-songs and dances, evincing power as a harmonist.

Johann Hermann Schein (d. 1630), early a choirboy at Dresden and a law-student at Leipsic, was from 1616 cantor of the Thomasschule there. His smooth, melodious and masterly style was shown in a vast number of vocal and instrumental works (from 1609), including many *concertato* pieces for many parts and a notable Choralbuch (1627). His genius was so superior in every way that he, with Schütz of Dresden and Scheidt of Halle (see secs. 96, 106), were called ' the three great S's ' of the century.

Christoph Thomas Walliser (d. 1648) was professor and musical director at Strassburg, with varied vocal works (from 1602), including incidental music for student-plays, besides theoretical books.

Johann Crüger (d. 1662), variously educated by study and travel, was from 1622 cantor of the Nikolaikirche at Berlin. Besides being important as a theorist, he was famous as the editor of hundreds of choir-pieces and chorales (from 1619) and of Choralbücher (1644), adding works of his own.

Thomas Selle (d. 1663), from 1637 cantor at Hamburg, was a fertile writer of part-music in the Italian style (from 1624), largely secular, but including sacred songs by Rist and a quantity of motets and madrigals (in MS.).

Less important, perhaps, though also productive, were **Melchior Vulpius** (d. 1615), from 1602 cantor at Weimar, with varied works (from 1602), including a Passion (1613), chorales and settings of the Gospel pericopes ; **Johann Stobæus** (d. 1646), a pupil of Eccard, cantor at Königsberg from 1602, with some finely wrought motets (from 1624) and festal choral works ; **Michael Altenburg** (d. 1640), pastor at Erfurt from 1608, with a Passion (1608) and choir-pieces (1613–21), often many-voiced ; **Johann Schop** (d. c. 1665), an accomplished player on the violin, lute and wind instruments, who was at the Danish court from 1618 and town-musician at Hamburg from 1621, a composer (from 1630) of melodious church music, including noted settings of religious poems (especially by Rist), besides dances and other instrumental pieces ; and **Johann Dilliger** (d. 1647), from 1619 cantor at Wittenberg and from 1625 at Coburg, with abundant works in many forms (from 1620). Later writers will be grouped under *Schütz*.

96. Schütz and the Oratorio Style.— While the new impetus in German music in the 17th century was certainly not due to the genius of any one man, yet Schütz stands out as a typical and dominating figure. Besides equaling or excelling his contemporaries at various points, he had something of that prevision as to musical progress that marked his greater successor Bach just a century later. He was familiar with Italy and plainly influenced by Venetian models, especially as to polychoric forms, richness of effect and a tendency to dramatic methods. Yet the tone of his work is essentially German as well in its seriousness and solidity. With him begins a style that is intensely religious without having a necessary connection with the usual church services. At intervals through his life he produced works in which may be seen the outlines of the German oratorio — a form that is not a sacred opera, but a religious concert-drama, suitable either for the church or elsewhere.

> Besides the general use of recitative and other solo melodies, as in all works of the dramatic species, Schütz emphasized the function of Narrators in addition to the personages in action, also of interjected chorales (as it were, the voice of the audience), and also of noble choruses, declamatory, reflective or contrapuntal. Often, too, he made the instrumentation a strong accessory.
>
> The earlier works of this class had been all Passions or the like, based properly upon the narratives in the Gospels, but sometimes upon chapters like Isaiah liii. — the whole built out poetically in various ways.

Heinrich Schütz (d. 1672) was born in 1585 at Köstritz (Thuringia), was a choirboy at Cassel and a law-student at the University of Marburg. In 1609 he was sent to Venice by the musical Landgrave Moritz to study under Giovanni Gabrieli, returning in 1613 to be court-organist at Cassel. From 1617 (really from 1615) till his death 55 years later he was electoral choirmaster at Dresden, his long service being broken, especially during the Thirty Years' War, by several trips to Italy and by three extended visits to Copenhagen to act as court-conductor. His life is said to have been beset by many domestic bereavements, from which artistic production was his chosen recourse. His striking success with the Dresden Chapel and his gifts as a composer brought him fame and many accomplished pupils. (His official stipend, however, was never equal to that of Italians in the court employ.) His eminence has lately been recognized afresh, and his works are now accessible in a great standard edition (1885-94). They are numerous and extensive, all being sacred except some early madrigals (1611), various pieces for court festivities, and the singspiel *Dafne* (1627, but score lost), often called the first German opera. To the list in the oratorio style belong the *Resurrection* (1623), the *Seven Words* (1645) and the four Passions, to which may be added the Psalms (1619) and the *Symphoniæ sacræ* (motets, 1629-50), in which the treatment of choruses often rises to concert grandeur.

From about 1650 there was a striking increase in originality in all German music, affecting both sacred and secular writing. In the vocal field a notable feature was the attention to solos more or less of the folk-song pattern, which, however, as dramatic impulses became stronger, tended to give way before the concertistic aria. The use of instruments in combination was free and often ingenious, especially as concerns the handling of certain wind instruments (like *krummhörner* and *zinken*). Almost all leading composers began to pay attention to dances of several sorts as offering scope for artistic development. All this new life had important historic relations to the work of the next century. The achievements, then, of the greater Bachs rested upon extensive earlier experiments.

Leading names among the many in the period following Schütz are these : —

Heinrich Albert (d. 1651), Schütz' nephew and early pupil, who, though trained for the law, was from 1630 cathedral-organist at Königsberg. Himself a good poet, he became famous as one of the first real song-composers (8 collections, 1638-50, besides other works), and is often called the father of the German 'Lied.'

Andreas Hammerschmidt (d. 1675), a Bohemian, was from 1635 organist at Freiberg (Saxony) and from 1639 at Zittau. His works (from 1639) range from dances and other instrumental pieces to many-voice masses, and include interesting melodic and concerted effects as well as some good counterpoint. Specially noted are his *Dialogues between God and a Believing Soul* (part-songs, 1645).

Johann Rosenmüller (d. 1684), educated at Leipsic and teacher in the Thomasschule there in 1642-55, under a charge of immorality fled thence to

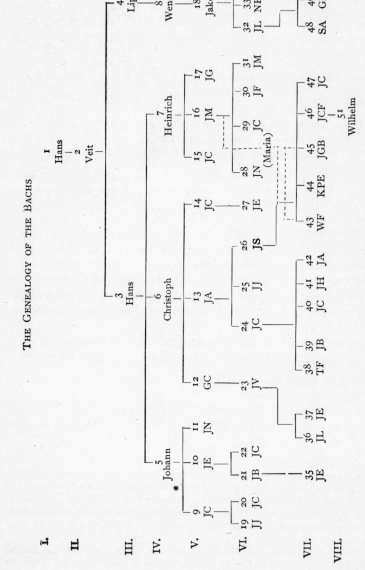

The Genealogy of the Bachs

Hamburg and Venice. In some way cleared, he became ducal choirmaster
at Wolfenbüttel in 1667. His published works (from 1645) were mostly
dances, with some motets (more in MS.), and were valued at the time for
their originality.

Johann Rudolph Ahle (d. 1673), trained at Göttingen and Erfurt, was from
1646 cantor at Erfurt and from 1654 at Mühlhausen. Besides text-books, he
wrote choir music of moderate value (from 1647), with about 120 religious
songs or arias, paralleling Albert's secular songs. His son, Johann Georg Ahle
(d. 1706), succeeded him at Mühlhausen, and was in turn followed by J. S.
Bach. His many works (from 1671) were like his father's, but advanced to
the aria as distinct from the song. He was named poet-laureate by the Emperor in 1680.

Samuel Bockshorn (d. 1665), after teaching at Pressburg and Nuremberg,
was from 1657 court-choirmaster at Stuttgart, where his strictness involved
him in some difficulties. Besides both Latin and German church music (from
1655) and a kind of Passion (1660), he also wrote part-songs and dances.

Christoph Bernhard (d. 1692), helped by generous friends to his education
under Schütz and in Italy, was second choirmaster at Dresden from 1655, became in 1664 cantor at Hamburg, and returned to Dresden in 1674 as Schütz'
successor. Though an able contrapuntist, he left but few works (1665-7 and
in MS.).

Wolfgang Karl Briegel (d. 1712), from 1650 cantor at Gotha and from 1671
choirmaster at Darmstadt, was very prolific (at least 25 large books, 1652-1709),
chiefly in religious works, using all forms with a strong leaning to concert
styles. His instrumental accompaniments were also good.

Johann Theile (d. 1724), probably a pupil of Schütz, had a restless career
at Stettin, Lübeck, Gottorp, Hamburg, Wolfenbüttel, Merseburg and Naumburg. His works included, besides singspiele at Hamburg, a Passion (1673),
a Christmas oratorio (1681), over 20 masses, other sacred works, and a set
of instrumental pieces, all showing immense skill in counterpoint. He had
many able pupils and issued text-books.

97. The Bach Family.

Throughout the 17th century the
Bachs of Thuringia steadily became more notable as musicians.
Although always of humble station and often sufferers from the
ravages of war, they thriftily made their way, lived earnest and
upright lives, and so generally cultivated music that in some
places town-musicians were actually called " the Bachs."

As they multiplied and won place as singers, players, town-musicians,
organists and cantors, their intense family feeling united them in a sort
of Bach guild. Their chief headquarters were Eisenach, Arnstadt or
Erfurt (besides a collateral branch at Meiningen), and they finally
established the custom of an annual family reunion at one of these
largely devoted to music.

Most of them emphasized sacred composition—for choir or
organ—but almost all worked freely in secular forms as well,

especially for instruments. Until far into the 18th century, none of them enjoyed opportunities for travel or study at musical centres outside their own region, but their enterprise and intuition enabled them to keep well abreast of progress in their art. It is hard to describe the massive value of their cumulative influence, not only in Saxony and its neighborhood, but far beyond. Certainly no family of artists in any field can be named that rivals them, if, indeed, there be any equal instance of hereditary genius on record. Their varied activity in the later 17th century led worthily toward their supereminent renown in the 18th in the careers of Johann Sebastian Bach and his talented sons.

During the three centuries from 1550 to 1850 perhaps 400 Bachs are known. Of these about 60 occupied positions of some official importance. The full genealogy is intricate, being complicated by the intermarriage of cousins. In general, it is to be noted that in the third generation two great branches separate, the first of which splits into three — giving four principal lines. For reference, the names are tabulated on page 206, each person being marked by his initials.

I. 1. Hans of Wechmar.

II. 2. Veit (d. 1619).

III. 3. Hans 'the Player' (d. 1626).
     4. Lips (d. 1620), presumably his brother.

IV. *Sons of Hans* (3) —
     5. Johann of Erfurt (d. 1673).
     6. Christoph of Erfurt and Arnstadt (d. 1661).
     7. Heinrich of Arnstadt (d. 1692).

   Son of Lips (4) —
     8. Wendel of Gotha (d. 1682).

V. *Sons of Johann* (5) —
     9. Joh. Christian of Erfurt and Eisenach (d. 1682 ?).
    10. Joh. Egidius of Erfurt (d. 1717).
    11. Joh. Nikolaus of Erfurt (d. 1682).

   Sons of Christoph (6) —
    12. Georg Christoph of Schweinfurt (d. 1697).

    13. Joh. Ambrosius of Eisenach (d. 1695).
    14. Joh. Christoph of Arnstadt (d. 1694).

   Sons of Heinrich (7) —
    15. Joh. Christoph of Eisenach (d. 1703).
    16. Joh. Michael of Gehren (d. 1694).
    17. Joh. Günther of Arnstadt (d. 1683).

   Son of Wendel (8) —
    18. Jakob of Ruhla (d. 1718).

VI. *Sons of Joh. Christian* (9) —
    19. Joh. Jakob of Eisenach (d. 1692).
    20. Joh. Christoph of Gehren (d. 1727).

   Sons of Joh. Egidius (10) —
    21. Joh. Bernhard of Eisenach (d. 1749).
    22. Joh. Christoph of Erfurt (d. after 1735).

Son of Georg Christoph (12) —

23. Joh. Valentin of Schweinfurt (d. 1720).

Sons of Joh. Ambrosius (13) —

24. Joh. Christoph of Ohrdruf (d. 1721).
25. Joh. Jakob of Stockholm (d. 1722).
26. Joh. Sebastian of Leipsic (d. 1750).

Son of Joh. Christoph (14) —

27. Joh. Ernst of Arnstadt (d. 1739).

Sons of Joh. Christoph (15) —

28. Joh. Nikolaus of Jena (d. 1753).
29. Joh. Christoph of Erfurt and England.
30. Joh. Friedrich of Mühlhausen.
31. Joh. Michael.

Sons of Jakob (18) —

32. Joh. Ludwig of Meiningen (d. 1741).
33. Nikolaus Ephraim of Gandersheim.
34. Georg Michael (d. 1771).

VII. *Son of Joh. Bernhard* (21) —

35. Joh. Ernst of Weimar (d. 1777).

Sons of Joh. Valentin (23) —

36. Joh. Lorenz of Lahm (d. 1773).
37. Joh. Elias of Schweinfurt (d. 1755).

Sons of Joh. Christoph (24) —

38. Tobias Friedrich of Uttstädt.
39. Joh. Bernhard of Ohrdruf (d. 1744).
40. Joh. Christoph of Ohrdruf.
41. Joh. Heinrich of Oehringen.
42. Joh. Andreas.

Sons of Joh. Sebastian (26) —

43. Wilhelm Friedemann of Halle (d. 1784).
44. Karl Philipp Emanuel of Berlin and Hamburg (d. 1788).
45. Joh. Gottfried Bernhard of Mühlhausen (d. 1739).
46. Joh. Christoph Friedrich of Bückeburg (d. 1795).
47. Joh. Christian of Milan and London (d. 1782).

Sons of Joh. Ludwig (32) —

48. Samuel Anton of Meiningen (d. 1781).
49. Gottlieb Friedrich of Meiningen (d. 1785).

Son of Georg Michael (34) —

50. Joh. Christian of Halle (d. 1814).

VIII. *Son of Joh. Chr. Friedrich* (46) —

51. Wilhelm of Berlin (d. 1846).

Son of Joh. Christian (50) —

52. Joh. Philipp of Meiningen (d. 1846).

Of the 15–20 names belonging to the 17th century the greatest were the two sons of Heinrich [7] : —

Johann Christoph Bach [15] (d. 1703) was born at Arnstadt in 1642 and most carefully trained by his father (who was organist there for over 50 years). From 1665 he was for 38 years town-organist at Eisenach. He was probably the most original of the motettists of the time, as well as one of the ablest organists, having an unusual instinct for form and great facility in handling many voices and in organ extemporization. He was not in sympathy with the prevalent dramatic styles, though one of his motets for double chorus and orchestra belongs remotely to the oratorio class. He was simple, earnest and painstaking, and won universal respect as man and artist. He educated his

P

four sons, and possibly slightly influenced Johann Sebastian, his cousin's son, who lived at Eisenach till his tenth year.

Johann Michael Bach [16] (d. 1694), born at Arnstadt in 1648, was similarly trained.   In 1673 he became organist at Gehren, remaining till his death. His genius resembled his brother's, especially as regards invention, though he was less gifted in form.   His more numerous motets and organ-pieces are not only learned, but rich in ideas and feeling.   He was one of the earliest of the family to take up instrument-making.   Of his five daughters, the youngest, Maria Barbara (d. 1720), became the first wife of Johann Sebastian in 1707, so that her four surviving children, including three sons, were descended from both the second and the third lines of the great family.

Mention should also be made of the two sons of Christoph [6] : Johann Ambrosius Bach [13] (d. 1695) and Johann Christoph Bach [14] (d. 1693), who were twins (b. 1645) and almost indistinguishable.   Ambrosius was a good violinist, in request at Erfurt from 1667 and at Eisenach from 1671. Johann Sebastian was the last of his eight children.   Christoph was court-violinist and town-piper at Arnstadt from 1671, living a curiously troubled life.   Of his five children, Johann Ernst [27] (d. 1739), though of but average talent, was Johann Sebastian's successor as organist at Arnstadt in 1707.

98. In France, Spain and Portugal. — Although church music was naturally cultivated in every cathedral and principal church in France, yet the trend of musical interest under both Louis XIII. and Louis XIV. was so strong in other directions that few masters of sacred music appeared.   The tendency was to go on using old works or simply adopt Italian works as they came out.

Two composers, however, may be mentioned : —

Arthur AuxCousteaux (d. 1656), teacher at St. Quentin and later in the Royal Chapel, was a somewhat prolific writer of masses, motets, psalms and part-songs (from 1631) in the Italian style.

Michel Richard Lalande (d. 1726) won notice as a choirboy at Paris and secured instruction in playing various instruments.   Developing special talent for the organ, from about 1675 he served several churches, would have been made royal organist except for his youth, became teacher in the king's household, and from 1683 was one of the royal superintendents of music.   He was the strongest French church composer of the time (fine motets, 1695–1712), besides writing many ballets (from 1678).

The same remarks apply to Spain at this period so far as lack of originality is concerned, though there was no other musical interest of importance.   It should be said, however, that from the 17th century a special form of motet, the 'vilhancico,' arose in both Spain and Portugal, in which choral opening and closing movements were combined with a middle movement for a solo voice (analogous to many English anthems).

Almost all Spanish works of this period are unpublished, the MSS. being widely scattered. Little is therefore known generally of their value. Apparently notable composers were few. Bare mention may be made of **Sebastiano Aguilera de Heredia,** choirmaster at Saragossa early in the century, with superior magnificats (1618) still in use; **Carlos Patiño** (d. 1683), choirmaster at Madrid from perhaps 1633, with many works, mostly polychoric, that are still highly regarded; and **Juan Perez Roldan** (d. 1722), Patiño's successor, also with many works (in MS.).

Portugal, on the other hand, enjoyed in the 17th century a time of decided musical activity, beginning during the Spanish domination (from 1580), but reaching its height after independence was recovered in 1640. From that time to this the monarchy has been in the hands of the House of Bragança, of which the first king, João IV., was an eager and accomplished musician ("more musician than king," says Von Waxel). Under him church music was cultivated with assiduity, large numbers of works for the Catholic service were produced, and talented composers were encouraged — none of them exerting notable influence on general progress, but worthy of remembrance nevertheless.

João IV. (d. 1656), besides writing theoretical treatises (1649–54), collected an enormous musical library, probably the best in its day, including rare MSS. from all countries, besides a comprehensive collection of Spanish and Portuguese works up to that time. Of this a partial catalogue was prepared. Almost exactly a century later (1755) this library was totally destroyed in the great earthquake at Lisbon. This catastrophe doubtless wiped out hundreds of works of which no other copies now exist, and rendered a thorough survey of Portuguese music impossible.

Of some scores of composers whose names are known and whose works lie hidden in various cathedral archives, the following are important : —

Duarte Lobo (d. 1643), a pupil of the famous music-school of **Manoel Mendes** (d. 1605) at Evora, was from about 1594 choirmaster at Lisbon. He was an active teacher, with important work (1602–39) in the intricate style of Benevoli.

Manoel Cardoso (d. 1650), also trained at Evora, was choirmaster there and from 1628 at the Carmelite monastery in Lisbon. His works (1613–48) include three collections of masses.

João Lourenço Rebello (d. 1661) was the most eminent composer in the middle of the century. He left many works for large numbers of voices, also madrigals. He was the teacher of João IV.

Felipe da Magalhães studied at Evora and was court-choirmaster at Lisbon and a good teacher (works, 1635–91).

Many other names perhaps equally deserve record, such as **Felipe da Cruz**, twice choirmaster at Lisbon; **Andre da Costa** (d. 1685), singer in the Royal Chapel; and **Antonio Marques Lesbio** (d. 1709), royal choirmaster at Madrid from 1698 (works, 1660–1708).

99. In England. — English church music in this century passed through varied vicissitudes. Under James I. (1603–25) the heavy harmonic style was replaced for a time by a return to the old counterpoint, the ablest composer being Orlando Gibbons. But with the overpressure of prelatical authority after 1630 came the Puritan reaction and the Civil War, during which a fanatical onslaught was made on choirs, organs and all the apparatus of 'curious music,' not because it was music, but because associated with a hated system (see sec. 88). This crusade made a gap in sacred music till the Restoration in 1660, when cathedral choirs and the Chapel Royal were reinstated. Services and anthems now began to adopt French and Italian features, such as dramatic solos and generally homophonic treatment. The widespread lack of interest in religion reduced the popular power of all sacred music, though the genius of Humphrey and Purcell was respected.

Among the madrigalists (see sec. 69) were many good church composers, like **Morley, Weelkes, Este, Ravenscroft** and **O. Gibbons**. With them are to be named **Nathaniel Giles** (d. 1633), from 1597 in the Chapel Royal; **Thomas Tomkins** (d. 1656), organist at Worcester; **John Amner** (d. 1641), from 1610 organist at Ely; **Martin Pearson** (d. 1650), choirmaster at St. Paul's from 1604; **John Milton** (d. 1647), the father of the poet; and **Adrian Batten** (d. 1637), from 1614 singer at Westminster and from 1624 organist at St. Paul's.

Many musicians who were prominent after 1660 began their activity before the Civil War, like **William Child** (d. 1697), organist at Windsor from 1636 and in the Chapel from 1660; **Benjamin Rogers** (d. 1698), from 1639 at Dublin, from 1641 at Windsor, and from 1664 at Magdalen College, Oxford; and **Christopher Gibbons** (d. 1676), son of Orlando and pupil of Edward, from 1638 organist at Winchester and from 1660 of the Chapel, as well as of Westminster in 1660–5. During the political turmoils, what interest there was in church music centred at Oxford and Cambridge.

Of the many church composers after 1660, besides **Humphrey** and **Henry Purcell** (see sec. 89), may be noted **Henry Cooke** (d. 1672), the famous Master of the Chapel Royal from 1660; **Matthew Locke** (d. 1677), royal composer from 1661 and later in the service of Queen Catherine; **Michael Wise** (d. 1687), organist at Salisbury from 1668 and in the Chapel from 1676 — one of the best of the series; **John Blow** (d. 1708), organist at Westminster in 1669–80 and from 1695, preceding and following Purcell, besides being organist to the Chapel from 1674 and royal composer from 1699, an able player and a prolific writer of the ornate order; **Thomas Tudway** (d. 1730), from 1670 organist at King's College, Cambridge, and from 1704 Professor of Music; **William Turner** (d. 1740), in the Chapel Royal all his life; **Daniel Purcell** (d. 1717), from 1688 organist at Magdalen College, Oxford, and after 1695 in London, who wrote dramas and odes as well as anthems; **Henry Aldrich** (d. 1710), dean of Christ Church, Oxford, from 1689, a versatile scholar, architect and musician, whose library of music was the finest outside the British Museum; and **Jeremiah Clarke** (d. 1707, suicide), organist at Winchester from 1692, in the Chapel Royal from 1700 and its organist from 1704. Several other composers of services and anthems that belong to the next century began active work before 1700.

Among the important collections of church music were those of **Barnard** (1641), **Clifford** (1661, '63), and **Tudway** (MS., about 1715–20).

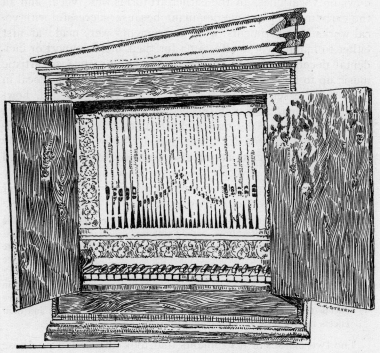

FIG. 58. — German Positive Organ (17th century).

CHAPTER XIII

THE ORGAN STYLE

100. The Rising Importance of Instruments. — Although in all stages of musical progress instruments are interesting, in the formal evolution of the art they were long remitted to a strictly subordinate place, vocal music supplying the ideal norms of procedure. All the fundamental rules of composition were first laid down on vocal lines, all the earlier art-forms were vocal, and all the early masters became dominant because successful with vocal works. Experiments with instruments were made at first either to imitate vocal effects or for their mere support or incidental decoration. The entire theory and practice of artistic music up to the second half of the 16th century was vocal in basis and essence. As the 17th century approached, however, and much more as it proceeded, a new tendency asserted itself. Without giving up emphasis upon the voice as the primary musical implement, it was perceived how advantageously mechanical implements might also be used by themselves and in ways essentially unvocal. In consequence, instrumental music now shook itself clear and set out upon a vigorous development that had marvelous later consequences.

The new tendency had many causes. Perhaps chief of these was the mighty swing of interest from sacred to intensely secular music, with the exaltation of objective forms over subjective, and of whatever could excite and pique attention by its impact upon the listener rather than merely give outlet for the feeling of the composer or performer. But combined with this was the stimulus derived from the technical improvement of certain particular instruments. The taste of the time called for more impressive effects and more elaborate implements, and these implements and their effects in turn reacted powerfully upon taste.

The two classes of instruments that took the lead were those with a keyboard, especially the organ, and those sounded by a bow, that is, the entire viol family. The former were prominent because capable of concerted, polyphonic and massive effects, the latter because capable of the finest solo effects and because, when combined, they constitute the most flexible and expressive instrumental chorus — the natural nucleus of the orchestra. Though notable achievements with both classes were delayed till later, the 17th century is remembered for its persistent endeavors to perfect them and to discover styles appropriate to them.

101. The Keyboard.— The genesis of the modern keyboard cannot be fully traced. Its essential mechanical principle (that of the lever) has always been obvious, but its special adaptation to the hand and to the production of tone must have been gradually worked out. By the 16th century the keyboard as now known had become well established, though some niceties of measurement and disposition were not fully settled.

> In modern usage 13 (white) keys occupy the lateral space of one foot, so that an octave is about 6½ in. wide. The white keys are ⅞ in. wide on top, and the black keys ⅜ in., the latter being about 2 in. behind the former and about ½ in. higher. The dip of all is usually about ⅜ in. All these details are the result of centuries of experiment (see sec. 32).

The peculiar disposition of the longer and shorter keys — the latter interspersed among the former in twos and threes alternately — is really arbitrary, but it clearly records a stage in the evolution of musical theory to which the staff-notation is also accommodated. Although both keyboard and notation are mediæval, they are so imbedded in musical praxis and terminology that apparently no more scientific substitutes are likely to come into general use.

> So long as the mediæval modes were used in their purity, only what are now white keys were required. The need of the chromatic semitones probably arose both from the desire to transpose diatonic melodies and from the growing use of *musica ficta*, with its virtual acceptance of what is now called modulation. Possibly the semitones came in gradually in some such order as this — B♭, F♯, C♯, E♭, G♯. Their tuning offered a problem not well solved till the 18th century. To avoid harshness, alternative semitones were sometimes provided, as both G♯ and A♭ between G and A. The diatonic keys were often colored black and the semitones white — the reverse of present-day practice. Semitones were at first not introduced throughout, but were confined to the middle octaves.

The length or compass of the keyboard has varied greatly. In early organs simply a single octave or an octave and a half was not uncommon, since only this limited range was needed to carry Plain-Song melodies. But as the notion of harmony and

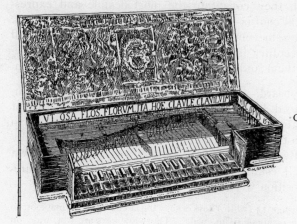

FIG. 59. — Italian
Clavichord (1537).

FIG. 60. — German
Regal (16th century).

FIG. 61. — Italian Virginal or Small
Spinet (17th century).

FIG. 62. — Italian
Portative Organ
(17th century?).

the desire for concerted effects grew, the compass was gradually stretched to three or four octaves or even more.

> In most early organs, to avoid expense, the lowest octave was usually 'short,' that is, not only without all of the semitones (or even without some of the diatonic keys), but with the keys disposed in some peculiar order so as to bring them close together.   This was specially common in pedal keyboards.

The original application of the keyboard was probably to the organ proper.   But it was early extended to small portative organs or 'regals,' which were very popular through the later Middle Ages; and it was on such domestic instruments that the modern measurements of the keys became established.   From at least the 14th century it was also applied to the monochord, producing the rudimentary clavichord, and to some form of harp or lyre, producing the spinet, virginal and harpsichord.   Finally, as the 17th century closed, it was applied to the dulcimer, producing the first form of the pianoforte.   When all the artistic consequences of these applications are considered, the keyboard is seen to be most interestingly related to musical progress (see sec. 135).

102. The Organ. — Among mediæval instruments the organ was conspicuous because used in church services.   At least as early as the 13th century it appeared in several forms or sizes. The largest were those permanently set up in churches as part of their fixed furniture.   Next came the 'positives,' which were of moderate size and could occasionally be moved as convenience required.   Next were the 'portatives,' which were small enough to be carried about in processions or applied to purely private and secular entertainment.   Finally, there were still smaller forms, often called 'regals,' which were made so as to fold together, often in the shape of a large book (hence often called 'Bible regals').   It is natural to think of the larger forms as connected with the historic importance of the organ, but the portatives and regals were really more significant.   While church organs were meant solely to support and intensify the unison Plain-Song or some stiff counterpoint, and were coarse and strident in tone and awkward to play, the smaller forms could be used for all sorts of tonal experiments, were often sweet in quality and relatively easy to play, being distinctly conducive

to the advance of keyboard technique.   The arts of organ-playing and of composition for the organ were doubtless developed
largely outside the churches, though in the 16th and 17th centuries they came into important use in church worship.

Organ-making was originally in the hands of monks, but by about
1500 it began to be widely undertaken as a general trade, so that we encounter from that time the names of many organ-builders.   No sure estimate can be made of the number of instruments in use at any given period,
but it is clear that by the 17th century they were common and that the
ambition for mechanical improvement was thoroughly awakened.

The mechanical problems of organ-making are manifold.   They are
usually grouped under three heads — the pipe-work, the wind-supply, and
the action.   Under the first belong questions regarding the selection and
preparation of metal and wood for the pipes, the exact shape and proportions of the pipes with reference to pitch and quality of tone (including
the invention of those varying types of structure that belong to distinct
'stops' or 'registers'), and many niceties in the adjustment of the
'mouth' or the reed by which the tone is actually produced.   Under the
head of wind-supply fall the problems of pumping air into a reservoir or
'bellows,' where somehow it can be brought under a steady pressure
and then distributed by tubes to the 'wind-chests' under the pipes
so as to be ready for delivery into the pipes as wanted.   It is remarkable how much difficulty has been encountered in avoiding leak-
age and maintaining a uniform pressure.   Under the 'action' comes
the adjustment of one or more keyboards to the valves admitting the air
to the pipes, with the control of the several sets of pipes by stop-handles,
every connection having to be made easy, prompt and noiseless.   Not
until about the 17th century did the modern notion fully emerge of uniting several distinct organs, each with its own keyboard, into one instrument, though more than one keyboard had often been used before.
The addition of a pedal keyboard was common from the 15th century.
Among special devices, that of the 'swell' in some form (to vary the loudness of some of the tones) is of great utility, but it is doubtful if it appeared before the early 18th century.

The making of large organs differed from other branches of instrument-
making in that most or all of the work was originally done not in fixed
factories, as now, but on the spot, so that organ-makers moved from place
to place as their services were required.   Each maker had his own
patterns or models, and details varied indefinitely.

103. The Rise of the Organ Style. — The problem of forms of
composition for the organ remained unsolved far into the 17th
century.   The earlier experiments were strictly contrapuntal
and modeled closely upon vocal styles.   Yet it was seen that
the instrument was capable of much more — massive chord-suc-

cessions, manifold unvocal passages and figures, striking effects of contrasted tone-color. The trend of invention was long toward chaotic fantasias or ricercari with much use of aimless scales and embellishments, and of tedious or ill-organized imitations. As an offset, various dance-patterns were often transferred bodily to the organ, though these did not fully comport with its dignity or its church associations.

In the 17th century better standards came in, especially in the adoption of definite 'subjects' for exposition, in the invention of appropriate 'figures' for elaboration, and in the devising of harmonic and modulatory plans with real coherence and progress. In Germany we now find increasing emphasis on two particular forms, the true fugue, with its systematic unfolding of a 'subject' and its 'answer,' and the chorale-elaboration, with its orderly and ingenious treatment of the melodic and harmonic substance of church songs. The genius of Germany began to exercise itself in a new sort of counterpoint, one based upon the keyboard and the organ tone instead of upon the voice, and hence far freer in details and more sensuously impressive than the old polyphony. This was a legitimate advance, though distinctly novel, and pointed toward the extremely liberal and majestic contrapuntal styles of the 18th century. Its reaction was profound upon choral music and upon all keyboard writing.

The 'fugue' is the most elaborate of contrapuntal forms. Its technical basis is the principle of strict imitation that was first wrought out by the Netherlanders in vocal works, especially in the 'canon'—a work or passage in which a 'subject,' after being stated by one voice, is repeated note for note or interval for interval by another voice or by several voices in succession, each voice proceeding in counterpoint as the others enter, and the imitation continuing throughout. (If the imitation uses the same tones as the 'subject,' the canon is 'at the unison,' if those a tone higher, 'at the second,' etc.) Experiments with this kind of writing early showed that there is a peculiar value in a canon 'at the fifth,' that is, one in which the imitation is in the key of the dominant or at least circles about the dominant as the 'subject' does about the keynote. This species of canonic imitation is characteristic of the true fugue. If the dominant relation is regarded somewhat as in the mediæval relation of plagal to authentic modes or *vice versa*, so that both the tonic and the dominant series utilize the same scale-tones, the fugue is called 'tonal.' If, however, the imitation is literally in the key of the dominant, using one tone not in the original scale, the fugue is 'real.'

Throughout the 16th century the name 'fuga' was not uncommon, usually designating what would now be called a canon. The derivation

of the word is in dispute, Italian usage favoring the meaning 'flight' or
'pursuit,' German usage, that of 'fitting together.' Meanwhile, fugal
passages were frequent in all sorts of writing, though very rarely expanded
to entire works based upon a single 'subject,' as in the true fugue. In
the 17th century instrumental writing generally tended often to adopt the
fugal form, as in many Italian 'sonatas' and French 'overtures.' The
final eminence of the organ fugue was due to the aptness of the organ
for strong and majestic polyphony under the hands of a single performer.
(For some other features of the completed fugue-form, see sec. 139.)

The influence of organ music, then, was highly beneficial to
the whole theory of composition, powerfully advancing the art
of pure harmony, maintaining interest in counterpoint, and
to some extent counterbalancing the drift toward captivating
superficiality that the opera was fostering with alarming success.

All the favorite forms of writing were essentially fantasias, having no
fixed method. On the whole, the 'ricercare' was the closest and strongest, the 'toccata,' more devoted to passages and other points of virtuosity,
the 'canzona in the French style,' usually based upon a special metric
pattern and disposed in short sections like a song, and the 'capriccio,'
midway between the ricercare and the toccata, with frequent changes of
theme. The treatment was at first almost wholly contrapuntal, though
not confined to a single or extended cantus. Later more solid harmony
came in, but it was hampered by the imperfect theory of tuning, which
made only certain chords satisfactory and precluded free modulation. In
Spain writing was much influenced by the frequency of 'divided stops,'
inviting antiphonal or dialogue passages. Until after 1600 the independent use of the pedals was unusual. Not until then was there any clear
sense of using solo melodies with accompaniment.

Among the many early organists known, a few stand out in prominence : —
In the 14th century worked **Francesco Landino** (d. 1397), a blind Florentine
of noble family, whose genius as both poet and musician won him renown and
of whose varied works many specimens remain; besides several players at
St. Mark's in Venice, and one or two in France, like **Robert Labbé** (d. c. 1432),
at Rouen from 1386. Among organ-builders were **Jacobello**, the reputed
builder of the first organ at St. Mark's, **Joachim Schund**, the maker in 1356
of what became the nucleus of the organ of the Thomaskirche in Leipsic, and
Nicol Faber, whose famous organ at Halberstadt (1361) was described by
M. Prätorius in 1618.

In the 15th century attention to the church organ increased, and with it the
freer use of pedals. In Italy, besides the players at St. Mark's (see sec. 56),
appeared **Antonio Squarcialupi** (d. 1475), a high-born favorite of Lorenzo
de' Medici at Florence and organist of the cathedral. Contemporary with
him was **Konrad Paumann** (d. 1473), the blind player at St. Sebald's in
Nuremberg from before 1446 and at Munich from 1467, a notable pioneer,
famous throughout Germany, Austria and Italy, from whom come the earliest

known organ-studies. Later German organists were **Schlick** of Heidelberg (also blind) and **Hofheimer** (d. 1537) of Salzburg and Vienna (see sec. 63). Both of these inspired many pupils. By this time the number of organ-builders had become large, as instruments were in great demand.

In the 16th century two notable lines of advance appeared, the one in Italy under the Netherlanders and the Venetians, the other in South Germany. In the former were many composers already mentioned (see Chapter VII.), especially **Willaert**, **De Buus**, **De Rore**, **Merulo**, the **Gabrielis** and **Antegnati**, with some others — their general style being gradually evolved into forms like the toccata, the ricercare, the French canzona, the capriccio, etc., in which the tendency was to alternate between solid chord-successions and flights of scales, sometimes with some semblance of a persistent 'subject,' sometimes with a capricious shifting from theme to theme. In the latter were some already named (see Chapter VIII.), like **Ammerbach**, **Hassler**, the **Schmids** and **Paix**, with many others — their general style, especially in the second half of the century, tending toward a peculiar treatment of thematic material by an excess of mere figuration (*coloraturen*, whence the writers were called *coloristen*), the presentation of structural ideas being choked or hidden under a mass of ingenious, but petty, detail. (The last notable publication of the 'colorist' school was the collection in 1617 by **Johann Woltz**, for 40 years organist at Heilbronn, the third part of which consists of pieces in tablature for church use.)

In other countries, also, the organ was studied with success, especially by **Sweelinck** of Amsterdam and by several Englishmen, like **Byrd**, **Bull** and **Phillips**, with some others. While these scattered workers often went beyond their Italian and German contemporaries in independence and in the perception of the styles suited to the instrument, they were as a rule less influential (except Sweelinck). Late in the century Italian writers began to publish collections of strictly church pieces, thus marking the separation of the ritual use of the church organ from that of small, private organs. An example is that of **Antonio Valente** of Naples (1580).

Among Italian organists not already named were **Florentio Maschera**, from 1557 at Brescia, with popular canzone (1584) ; **Luzzasco Luzzaschi** (d. c. 1607), at Ferrara from 1576, highly praised as a player ; **Sper' in Dio Bertoldo** of Padua (d. c. 1590), with toccatas, ricercari and canzone (1591) ; and **Gioseffo Guami** (d. 1611), from 1568 at Munich, from 1579 at Genoa, from 1588 at St. Mark's, Venice, and from 1591 at Lucca, with canzone (1601), besides earlier madrigals and motets.

In northern countries should be added **Leonhard Kleber** (d. 1556), for over 30 years at Pforzheim (Baden), who edited an important collection (1522–4), mostly in a style prefiguring the 'colorists'; **Charles Luyton** (d. 1620), a Netherlander, court-organist at Prague from 1576, an original composer (from 1582) and the inventor of a clavichord with divided semitones (19 keys to the octave), facilitating varied harmony in pure intonation; and **Pieter Cornet**, organist to the Spanish Infanta at Brussels (few works extant).

In Spain, also, were **Antonio de Cabezon** (d. 1566), the blind organist of Philip II., represented by a large collection (1578), edited by his son; and **Bernard Clavijo**, professor at Salamanca, and later royal organist at Madrid. with many works (mostly burnt in 1734).

104. Italian Organists. — After 1600 the number of competent players rapidly increased and their equipment became more varied, since both the capacity of the instrument and interest in its music were developing. As styles of writing became better defined, its dignity, with its aptitude for intricate part-writing and for tonal variety, was more appreciated. Gradually the stiff effects of the earlier period were softened by more real melody and a richer harmony, and decorative elements were gradually reduced from undue prominence.

In Italy the leadership plainly fell to Frescobaldi of Rome, one of the noblest geniuses of organ-history, whose influence was widely felt. His works were many and diversified. While adhering to the old modes in ritual pieces, he was enterprising with modern tonality elsewhere. His use of chromatics and modulation was often free, implying the existence of unusually advanced tuning. He discarded the real for the tonal fugue, and revived effective double counterpoint. His pieces abound in technical difficulties, but subordinated to a firm general conception. His style often has an energy and even impetuosity that betokens an absolute mastery of his materials.

Besides **Agazzari**, **Cifra** and **Ugolini** of the Roman school and **Banchieri** and **Bassani** of Bologna (see secs. 93-94), the following are notable : —

Girolamo Diruta (d. after 1612), pupil of Merulo and organist from 1597 at Chioggia and from 1609 at Gubbio, besides being a good player and composer, edited an important organ-book (1593-1609), in which, besides valuable specimens of works by several hands, the organ style is for the first time extended to other instruments.

At Ferrara was **Alexandre Milleville** (d. 1589), French by birth, from 1544 at Modena and from 1575 at Ferrara, with his son **Francesco**. **Antonio Mortaro** (d. 1619), successively at Milan, Novara and Brescia, wrote good canzone, etc. (from 1599). **Giovanni Paolo Cima** of Milan (works from 1606), and his brother **Andrea Cima** of Milan and Bergamo, a famous player, now known only by vocal works (from 1614), are also noteworthy.

Girolamo Frescobaldi (d. 1644), born at Ferrara in 1583 and a pupil of Luzzaschi, probably began his career at Antwerp, but from 1608 was organist at St. Peter's in Rome, except for brief sojourns at Mantua in 1614-5 and as court-organist at Florence in 1628-33. His playing attracted great admiration, and his works (from 1608) include every variety of form already named, with partite (variations), preludes and dances, many of them meant for either the organ or the clavichord. They are written in the prevalent notation for the latter (a 6-line staff for the right hand and an 8-line for the left), with comparatively little use of the pedals. Among his greater pupils were the Germans Froberger and Tunder.

Giovanni Maria Trabacci, royal organist at Naples, issued two books of ricer-cari (1603, '15), besides vocal works; and Giovanni Battista Fasolo, a Fran-ciscan of Palermo, published a collection of pieces (1645) for every part of the church year, displaying ability within the old modes.

Bernardo Pasquini (d. 1710), a Tuscan, born in 1637 and a pupil of L. Vittori and Cesti and a student of Palestrina, besides writing dramatic works, became famous as organist of Sta. Maria Maggiore at Rome (works from 1702). He taught Durante and Gasparini.

Giulio Cesare Arresti (d. c. 1695), pupil and successor of Vernizzi at Bologna, collected a notable series of organ-pieces by various 17th-century composers, with some of his own.

105. The South German School. — In Germany the century opened with two lines of succession already established, the southern, stimulated by Italian influence at the outset, and the northern, chiefly shaped by the genius of Sweelinck. Between these developed later the Saxon or Thuringian school, influenced by both and ultimately the greatest of all. In Austria Italian models were naturally followed, as in other regions where the organ was connected with Catholicism, but elsewhere the Protes-tant chorales and their polyphonic elaboration, with the study of the fugue, absorbed attention. In general, organ music avoided secular themes and forms.

In the south the most brilliant masters were Froberger of Vienna and Pachelbel of Erfurt and Nuremberg.

Johann Jakob Froberger (d. 1667) was sent in 1637 by the Emperor to Rome to study with Frescobaldi, served in 1641–57 as imperial organist and clavecinist at Vienna with immense success, but with long intermissions, probably for travel, and later settled at Héricourt (E. France). As a player he was quite as important on the harpsichord as on the organ, delighting in such forms as brilliant toccatas, capriccios and suites of a secular character. His many works were published posthumously (from 1693).

Johann Kaspar Kerll (d. 1693), born in Saxony in 1627, was court-choirmas-ter at Munich in 1656–73, and then, displaced by the jealousy of the Italian singers, removed to Vienna, becoming court-organist in 1677 and returning to Munich in 1684. Like Froberger, he divided his attention between the harp-sichord and the organ, besides producing much vocal music. His organ style was solid and strong, foreshadowing that of the Bachs. Of his many instrumental works little was published during his life (one collection, 1686).

Georg Muffat (d. 1704), of Scottish descent, but German by birth (c. 1645), was trained at Paris under Lully's influence, was organist at Strassburg till 1675, then at Vienna and Salzburg, whence he went to Rome to study with Pa-squini, and from about 1687 at Passau. His interesting instrumental works (from 1682) were largely for the organ, and show a mixture of French and Italian manners.

Early in the century Nuremberg became a centre of Protestant music, and the organists of its churches were often influential and productive in styles appropriate to the Protestant service. Among them, though not all composers of eminence, were **Johann Staden** (d. 1634), at the Sebalduskirche from 1620; **Johann Erasmus Kindermann** (d. 1655), from 1630 at the Egidienkirche, who not only published good preludes and fugues (from 1645), besides other instrumental works, but was an excellent teacher; **Sigmund Staden** (d. 1655), the son of Johann above, who, after work at Berlin, was from 1635 at the Lorenzkirche; **Heinrich Schwemmer** (d. 1696), a pupil of Kindermann, and, though only late in life an active organist, a teacher of important pupils; **Paul Heinlein** (d. 1686), from 1655 at the Sebalduskirche, a prolific and admired composer; **Georg Kaspar Wecker** (d. 1695), a pupil of Kindermann and his successor in 1655 and also of Heinlein in 1686; not to mention others, like the brothers **Philipp Krieger** (d. 1725) and **Johann Krieger** (d. 1735), both born at Nuremberg and more or less trained there, both organists at Bayreuth, and the one from 1680 at Weissenfels and the other from 1681 at Zittau.

Johann Pachelbel (d. 1706), born in 1653 at Nuremberg, was trained at Altdorf and Ratisbon. His official life was a broken one — from 1674 at Vienna, from 1677 at Eisenach, from 1678 at Erfurt, from 1690 at Stuttgart, from 1692 at Gotha, and from 1695 at Nuremberg, succeeding Wecker at the Sebalduskirche. His abundant organ-works were left mostly in MS., except some good preludes and variations (1683–99). His style was diversified, uniting the brilliance and effectiveness of the southern school with much of the solidity of the northern. He was one of the pioneers in the competent development of the chorale-prelude. He was diligently studied by the great Bach, and was clearly one of his early models, though lacking in the power of extended and sustained treatment. While at Erfurt, he taught many good pupils, like Vetter, Buttstett and J. C. Bach (J. S. Bach's elder brother), who were later prominent in central Germany.

Other names are **Johann Ulrich Steigleder** (d. 1635) of Stuttgart, a contemporary of Scheidt, with ricercari and variations (from 1624), and **Sebastian Anton Scherer**, cathedral-organist at Ulm, with organ-pieces (1664) and other works.

106. The North German School. — The extent of Sweelinck's personal influence was exceedingly wide, his most distinguished pupils being scattered from Hanover and Hamburg on the west to Danzig on the east and to Halle in Saxony. From him came a sound perception of the special qualities of treatment germane to the organ, a vigorous conception of the fugue as the greatest single form available, with its capacity for every phase of contrapuntal art, and an enterprising and genial breadth of view as to the possibilities of organ progress. Several of his pupils were really greater than he, but to him is due the impulse that later made Germany the home of the noblest organ style. His connection with Italy has already been noted (see secs. 66, 103).

Sweelinck's greater pupils include the following: —

Samuel Scheidt (d. 1654), born at Halle in 1587, where, after his study with the Dutch master, he became in 1609 court-organist at the Moritzkirche and for a time choirmaster as well, continuing till his death almost half a century later. His works were largely vocal, but included the much-lauded *Tabulatura nova* (1624), sinfonie (1644), and chorale-preludes, etc. (1650), which show him to be one of the founders of the art of chorale-elaboration that replaced the older 'colorist' style. He was not so daring an innovator as his close contemporary Frescobaldi, nor perhaps as great a genius as his followers thought him, but his eminence is unquestionable. His traditional place as one of 'the three S's' (with Schütz of Dresden and Schein of Leipsic, all three being nearly of an age) is, however, probably due to his success with vocal works.

Jakob Prätorius (d. 1651), the son of Hieronymus (see sec. 62), though born in 1586 at Erfurt, was brought up at Hamburg, where, after studying with Sweelinck, he was from 1603 for almost 50 years organist of the Petri-kirche. His virtuosity was famous, but little is known of his compositions.

Heinrich Scheidemann (d. 1663?) came of a family of organists at Hamburg, and, after being trained by his father and by Sweelinck (at the city's expense), he succeeded the former at the Katharinenkirche in 1625, remaining till his death. Most of his works are lost, except a few settings of poems by Rist (1651) and some scattered pieces, but laudatory references to his skill are preserved, and he taught Reinken, his more famous successor, and Fabricius of Leipsic.

Melchior Schildt (d. 1667) is sometimes called Sweelinck's best pupil. After brief terms of service at Wolfenbüttel from 1623 and at Copenhagen from 1626, he was from 1629 at the Marktkirche at Hanover. His style is said to have been peculiarly expressive, but his extant works (from 1642) are meagre.

Paul Siefert (d. 1666), born at Danzig, after working with Sweelinck, was in the Royal Chapel of Poland for some years. Returning to Danzig, he became organist in 1623 at the Marienkirche, being succeeded at his death by **Ewald Hirsch**, a pupil of Froberger. Besides some MS. organ-pieces, his only known works are two sets of Psalms (1640, '51), the first of which was the occasion of a sharp attack by **Marco Scacchi** (d. before 1685), royal choirmaster of Poland, to which Siefert replied in 1645. If traditions are right, Siefert was opinionated and quarrelsome.

Delphin Strunck (d. 1694), born in 1601, was organist at Wolfenbüttel in 1630–2, then at Celle, and from 1639 at the Martinikirche in Brunswick. A few chorale-preludes of his remain, showing the beginnings of the line-by-line treatment that was frequent later.

Franz Tunder (d. 1667), born in 1614 and a pupil of Frescobaldi, was from 1641 at the Marienkirche at Lübeck. From him we have a few chorale-elaborations and some motets with accompaniment.

Johann Martin Rubert (d. 1680), also born in 1614 at Nuremberg, studied at Hamburg and Leipsic, and in 1640 became organist at the Nikolaikirche at Stralsund. His style is said to have been dignified and even austere, but no organ-works of his are now known, though we have part-songs, violin-duets and short cantatas (from 1645). Contemporary with him at Stralsund in the

Q

Marienkirche was **Johann Vierdanck,** with dances, capriccios and many motets (from 1641).

Matthias Weckmann (d.1674), a Thuringian, born in 1621 and a pupil of Schütz, J. Prätorius and Scheidemann, assisted at the Dresden Chapel in 1641–2 and in 1647–54, serving in Denmark in the interval, in 1655 won appointment at the Jacobikirche in Hamburg, and founded an important series of concerts there in 1668. His extant works are mostly motets and some chorale-elaborations, with remarkable harpsichord-sonatas, toccatas and suites.

Jan Reinken (d. 1722), born in 1623 in Lower Alsace, studied with Scheidemann at Hamburg and in 1663 followed him at the Katharinenkirche, where he remained almost 60 years, the Nestor of North German organists. Though doubtless over-conceited, his ability cannot be gainsaid, since he aroused extraordinary interest on the part of J. S. Bach, whom he hailed as his true successor in chorale-treatment. Of his works we have only a few elaborations, a toccata, and some variations and chamber music. His will directed that his MSS. should be burnt.

Dietrich Buxtehude (d. 1707), the greatest of the whole school, was born in 1637 at Helsingör (Denmark), where his father was organist 32 years. After thorough training from the latter, in 1668 he succeeded Tunder at Lübeck (marrying his daughter according to custom). Provided with one of the best organs in Germany and enthusiastically appreciated, he won international fame, especially through his handling from 1673 of the annual series of musical vespers in November and December which were perhaps instituted by Tunder and which continued till the early 19th century. At these, famous singers and players assisted, and for them Buxtehude wrote many *Abendmusiken.* Nearly 70 organ-works of his have survived, largely chorale-elaborations, with 13 fugues, 3 toccatas, etc., also some wedding-hymns. He was a thorough virtuoso, facile and brilliant in technique (on the pedals as well as the manuals), and original in registration, while as a composer he excelled in the invention of characteristic themes and in their intricate, but effective, development into closely-knit movements of almost modern solidity. His influence upon Bach was profoundly stimulating.

Vincent Lübeck (d. 1740), born near Bremen in 1654 and trained by his father, served from 1674 at Stade for almost 30 years, and from 1702 at the Nikolaikirche in Hamburg. His works have almost all vanished (clavier-suite, 1728), but the fact that Bach repeatedly took pains to hear him indicates his ability.

Georg Böhm (d. 1733), born in 1661 near Gotha, was first trained in Pachelbel's style and at Hamburg under Reinken, besides studying French instrumental music. From 1698 he was at the Johanniskirche in Lüneburg, so that Bach in his school-days there came directly under his influence. With him the art of chorale-elaboration appears in full maturity. Of his works we have several chorale-variations, a fugue, and some clavier-suites and sacred songs. He also wrote a Passion, not now known.

Nikolaus Bruhns (d. 1697), a pupil of Buxtehude, was organist first at Copenhagen and later at Husum (Schleswig). His reputation in his day was almost equal to his master's. He was also a remarkably expert violinist.

107. The Thuringian School. — In central Germany (mainly Thuringia and Saxony) there was a considerable interlocking of influences. Workers here were affected by traditions from both the Catholic and the Protestant sides. While their more natural affiliation was with the South German school, especially as Pachelbel was for a time at Erfurt, the stronger northern styles were eagerly studied and adopted, so that by the end of the century this middle school presented an amalgamation of the best from all sources. Conspicuous among the masters here were many of the Bachs.

The long line of organists in the **Bach family** includes, in the fourth generation, **Johann** (d. 1673), town-musician at Erfurt from 1635 and organist at the Predigerkirche from 1647, and **Heinrich** (d. 1692), his brother and pupil, town-musician and organist at Arnstadt from 1641, a worthy worker in chorales and the teacher of his two sons ; in the fifth generation, **Joh. Christian** (d. 1682), who succeeded Johann at Erfurt in 1673 and was in turn followed by his brother **Joh. Egidius** (d. 1717) — with the distinguished brothers **Joh. Christoph** of Eisenach (d. 1703) and **Joh. Michael** of Gehren (d. 1694), Heinrich's sons (see sec. 97) ; and several in the sixth generation who belong rather to the 18th century. Here the influence of Pachelbel became marked.

Werner Fabricius (d. 1679), born in Holstein in 1633, won notice as a clavichordist when not 12 years old, was taught by Selle and Scheidemann at Hamburg, studied law as well as music at Leipsic, and became organist of the Nikolaikirche there in 1657, being famous both as a virtuoso and as an organ-expert. His extant works (from 1657) are motets, chorales, some dances and a handbook on organ-examination (1656).

Andreas Werckmeister (d. 1706), born in 1645 in the Hartz, trained by two uncles, was from 1664 organist at Hasselfelde, from 1675 at Quedlinburg (where he wrote his best works), and from 1696 at Halberstadt, where he was also city-councilor and royal organ-inspector. His importance lay in his unequaled knowledge of organ-building, his hostility to inartistic and ill-made instruments, and his theoretical writings (see sec. 113), of which those on the organ were the *Orgelprobe* (1681), the pioneer study of equal temperament (1691), and an account of the organ at Grüningen.

Friedrich Wilhelm Zachau (d. 1712), born at Leipsic in 1663, pupil of his father, in 1684 became organist at the Marktkirche at Halle. As player and composer he was careful and exact. His fame rests on the fact that for several years before 1702 he was Handel's teacher, firmly grounding him in the technique of composition.

Johann Heinrich Buttstett (d. 1727), born near Erfurt in 1666 and a pupil of Pachelbel there, began as organist in 1684 and followed his master at the Predigerkirche in 1691. His works (1705–20) include chorale-variations, fugues, 4 masses, etc. He sought to withstand the drift toward freer styles in church music by a pamphlet (1717).

Among many other names may be mentioned **Johann Kuhnau** (d. 1722), organist at the Thomaskirche in Leipsic in 1684–1701 and Bach's predecessor at the Thomasschule ; **Johann Philipp Bendeler** (d. 1708), cantor at Quedlinburg and an important writer on organ-making (c. 1690) ; and **Nikolaus Vetter** (d. 1710), pupil of Wecker and Pachelbel, from 1691 court-organist at Rudolstadt, later an organ-teacher as well as lawyer.

108. In Western Europe. — As compared with the portentous development in Germany, which was laying broad foundations for still greater production later, the advance of organ music elsewhere was much less significant, though some excellent masters may be cited. Only in England were these numerous enough to affect the national style as a whole. In France keyboard music tended rather to styles suited to the clavichord instead of the organ.

In France there were no noted players till toward the end of the century. In 1678 the post of royal organist was divided between four incumbents, each serving three months at a time. Among these were **Giullaume Gabriel Nivers** (d. after 1701), pupil of Chambonnières, with many works, theoretical and practical (from 1646), including choir- and organ-pieces for the Catholic service, **Nicholas Antoine Le Bègue** (d. 1702), with some similar works (from 1675), and **Jacques Thomelin**. [Nivers and Le Bègue, with the elder **François Couperin** (d. 1698), were among those who successfully opposed the bizarre pretensions of *Guillaume du Manoir* to rule the profession as 'Roi des violons' in virtue of a patent originally granted in the 14th century (book on music and the dance, 1664).] Another able composer for organ and clavier was **André Raison** (works, 1687–1714).

In Spain and Portugal were **Manoel Rodrigues Coelho** of Lisbon (important collection, 1620) ; **Francisco Corrêa de Arauxo** (d. 1663), organist at Seville, professor at Salamanca, finally Bishop of Segovia (theoretical treatise, 1626) , **Andrés Lorente** (d. 1703), organist at Alcala (treatise, 1672) ; and **Josef Cavanillas** (d. c. 1725), cathedral-organist at Urgel, a famous virtuoso.

In England almost every church composer during the century was an organist (see sec. 99), and several of them, like **Bull, O. Gibbons, Rogers, Blow** and **H. Purcell**, attained permanent distinction.

CHAPTER XIV

THE VIOLIN. MUSICAL LITERATURE

109. Stringed Instruments in General. — Of all musical instruments, those with strings for the sounding material have always been chief. They may be roughly classified under generic names like harp, lyre, zither (psaltery), dulcimer, lute and viol, though cases occur which are difficult to assign.

The 'harp' and the 'lyre' are distinguished by having the strings either wholly or partially free from the soundbox (except at or near their lower attachment), the string-plane being at right angles to the face of the soundbox in the harp, but parallel to it in the lyre. Each string is properly capable of but one tone, the pitch of which is not controlled by 'stopping.' In both cases the strings are sounded by plucking or twanging, with or without a plectrum. Harps are usually held with the strings upright, but lyres (unless very large) are held more or less horizontally, with one edge of the soundbox down, so as to present the strings to the player's right hand.

The 'zither' and the 'dulcimer' have the strings stretched from end to end over the soundbox or soundboard. Upon the latter, frets or bridges may be placed so that some or all of the strings can be shortened by pressure and thus made to yield more than one tone. Historically, this device of 'stopping' has been confined to the zither or psaltery. Zithers are sounded by plucking, dulcimers by blows from a rod or hammer. Both are usually placed horizontally, the strings running either across or away from the player.

The 'lute' and the 'viol' are peculiar in having a slender neck or fingerboard projecting from the soundbox, along which all or most of the strings extend to tuning-pegs in the head. All such strings can be 'stopped' so as to yield more than one tone. Lutes are sounded by plucking, sometimes with a plectrum, but viols by the friction of a bow or something analogous. Both are held horizontally and turned sidewise like the lyre, except some larger varieties of the viol.

Harps of various kinds are shown in figs. 6, 18, 30–34, 48, 107; lyres in figs. 24, 36–38, 49; zithers in figs. 6, 13, 14, 21, 25, 66; a dulcimer in fig. 28; lutes in figs. 7, 8, 10, 15, 26, 29, 35, 54–57, 65, 67–69, 108; and viols in figs. 9, 16, 17, 23, 27, 50, 52, 64, 70–77, 87, 93.

Each of these types has had a distinct history, often of great artistic importance. *Harps* were conspicuous in ancient times

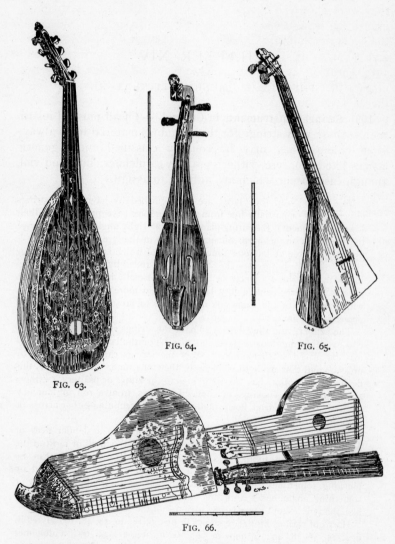

FIG. 63.

FIG. 64.

FIG. 65.

FIG. 66.

FIG. 63.— Moroccan Kouitara, a modern survival of the old lute type. FIG. 64.—
Old French Rebec, made of a single piece of wood (cf. Fig. 27). FIG. 65.— Modern
Russian Balalaïka or Guitar. FIG. 66.— Modern German Zithers.

in Assyria, Egypt and Greece; throughout the Middle Ages they were known in manifold shapes and sizes, among the most interesting being those of the Kelts; and from these has come the modern orchestral harp, whose perfecting as a chromatic and transposing instrument was not achieved until the early 19th century. *Lyres* were characteristic in Egyptian and Greek music; they continued in the Middle Ages as variants among the more common harps; in modern times they have generally been discarded. *Zithers* were known in ancient times, though not prominent; in mediæval usage they were common because of their relatively great sonority in proportion to size; and as highly artistic instruments their advance was then delayed till the 19th century. *Dulcimers* were known to the Assyrians and the Greeks; and they persisted into the Middle Ages in varied forms. With a keyboard added, the zither type passed over into the harpsichord, and the dulcimer type into the pianoforte. The clavichord, the other stringed instrument with a keyboard, was de- rived from the 'monochord' (uniting features from both zither and dulcimer), from which also the curious 'nun's-fiddle' or 'marine trumpet' was descended (see Fig. 52). *Lutes* were certainly used in ancient Egypt and probably by many Oriental nations; thence, especially through Mohammedan channels, they came into great prominence in mediæval Europe; in the 16th century they were chief among portable instruments in artistic valuation, but have since lost place, being now represented only by the guitar and mandolin. *Viols*, which seem not to have been known to the ancients, began to compete with other types sometime in the Middle Ages, were more and more considered in the 16th century, and in the 17th assumed an artistic leadership among solo instruments that has since not been questioned. Experi- ments have often been made with keyboard viols, like the hurdy- gurdy (see Fig. 51) and many complicated forms, but none of these has had success.

110. The Genesis of the Violin. — Infinite discussion has been had regarding the remote ancestry of the violin, but without satisfactory results. It is likely that several early forms yielded suggestions which were gradually combined. Among these probably were varieties of the 'crwth,' some of which were lyres or lutes, though one has a striking likeness to the viol proper,

FIG. 67.

FIG. 68.

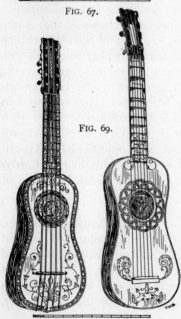

FIG. 69.

FIG. 67. — Milanese and Neapolitan Mandolins.

FIG. 68. — Cittern, or 'English Guitar.'

FIG. 69. — Italian Guitars.

in spite of its rectangular frame (see Figs. 49–50). Important influence doubtless came from some Oriental forms, but precisely which of them and when is not certain. In the 16th century every effort to improve the lute reacted on the viol, and the early makers of the latter were generally luthiers. Yet the critical difference of the viol as to the method of sounding tended always to keep the number of the strings small and decidedly to modify its outer contour.

A few of the transitional steps may here be noted. The mediæval ' vielle ' or ' fiddle ' had a body more or less pear-shaped, following that of the Troubadour rebec. In the 15th century more than one size began to be made, so as to imitate the parts of the vocal choir. Naturally the tenor size was held to be typical, and to this the name ' viola ' was especially attached. (Hence later the treble or discant viol was called ' violino ' or 'little viola,' and the bass, ' violone ' or ' big viola '; while still later come the term ' violoncello ' or ' small big viola.' Similarly ' viola da braccio ' or ' arm-viola ' and ' viola da gamba ' or ' leg-viola ' were designations both of size and of position in playing.)

The larger the viol, the greater the need of providing means of free access to the strings for the bow and of augmenting the strength and rigidity of the body. The true violin type appeared only when the outline of the body was broken by a ' waist ' with corners reinforced within by blocks. Probably before this, that is, early in the 16th century, decided gains had been made in details — in shaping the bridge, in fixing it upon a soundpost, and in settling the place and form of the longitudinal bass-bar. But the models were still relatively thick from front to back, had flat backs, sloping shoulders and very variable contours, and the shape and placing of the soundholes were capricious. In the typical viol the fingerboard was provided with frets, as in the lute, but in the violin these were ultimately discarded.

Besides the three or four standard sizes of the viol proper, experiments were tried with more complicated forms, such as the ' lyra ' in several sizes, which was double-strung and required a broad, high-arched bridge, and the ' viola d' amore,' also in more than one size, which had from seven to many sympathetic strings of metal under or beside the fingerboard. Some of these transitional forms remained in use till about 1800, but they were steadily being replaced by the true violin.

The perfected violin-model presents many points of technical interest, which cannot be briefly described. Every detail has been exhaustively studied, and the results of small variations in form and adjustment are fully understood. The genius of the great makers lay in gradually conquering every problem involved, and then in perfecting one of the several possible combinations of the factors. While adhering to the certain broad lines of

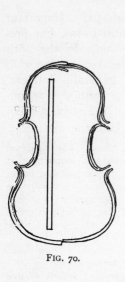

FIG. 70.

FIG. 71.

FIG. 72.

FIG. 70. — Violin-Making — the linings and unfinished bass-bar.

FIG. 71. — Violin-Making — neck and head, ribs, linings and corner-blocks, bass-bar and soundpost.

FIG. 72. — Violin-Making — completed instrument.

FIG. 73. — Stradivari Violin (1679) — side view, showing contours, scroll and inlaid ornamentation (from Hipkins).

FIG. 74. — The same — front view, showing contours, f-holes and inlaid purfling.

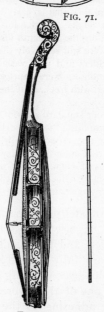

FIG. 73.

FIG. 74.

construction that are common to all, each maker had marked individuality of method and often applied his own method in peculiar or unique ways.   It is certainly most remarkable, however, that in the main the art of violin-making reached a culmination so long ago as 1700 which seems to be unsurpassable.

> The niceties of the art include not only the choice and proper seasoning of the woods for every part and the minute determination of the shape, size and placing of the nearly 60 pieces, with their perfect modeling, joining and gluing, but the very important treatment of the whole with beautiful varnishes and the decoration of the head with its carved 'scroll' and of the edges of the back with 'purfling.'   Critical attention is required for the location of the soundholes and of the soundpost, since these determine the centre and character of the vibrations transmitted from the strings through the bridge to the body.   Individuality is shown in the quality of tone secured and in the grace and harmony of the outlines, the one appealing to the ear, the other to the eye.   Similar niceties enter into the making of the bow by which the strings are sounded (see sec. 149).

111. The Great Violin-Makers. — The evolution of the violin took place between the middle of the 16th century and the first third of the 18th, culminating with the work of geniuses like Stradivari and Guarneri.   The chief makers worked at Brescia or Cremona in northern Italy — a region offering superb materials, established traditions in fine instrument-making, and nearness to Venice, then the headquarters for artistic secular music. Bavaria, Austria and the Tyrol also had able masters, and their disciples gradually became frequent throughout western Europe. Many instances occur of families of makers whose skill descended from generation to generation, since success in the art depended on the inheritance not only of patterns and models, but of delicate manipulation.

> Several makers are often named in the early 16th century and even in the 15th, but it is doubtful whether any true violins much antedate 1550, though artistic viols were common.
>
> At Brescia the most noted names are **Gasparo da Salò** [Bertalotti] (d. 1609), perhaps the first to note the value of the corners, who had many pupils, though his relation to the Cremonese makers is not clear;   **Giovanni Paolo Maggini** (d. c. 1640), pupil of Da Salò, specially successful with the larger viols and with violins of a full, rich tone;   and his son **Pietro Maggini** (d. c. 1680), often quite his father's equal.
>
> At Cremona the great makers are more numerous and renowned.   First stands the **Amati family,** especially **Andrea** (d. 1611), his two sons **Antonio** and

FIG. 75.

FIG. 76.

FIG. 77.

FIG. 75. — Viola da Gamba and Alto Viol—the latter called in France 'haute contre.'

FIG. 76. — Viola d'Amore, with sympathetic strings.

FIG. 77. — Pochettes — miniature or pocket violins, often used by dancing-masters.

Geronimo (d. 1638, 1635), and the noted son of the latter, **Nicola** (d. 1684), all of whom generally preferred a small model and sought sweetness of tone more than power or brilliance, though Nicola's 'grand' pattern is of the highest rank. Greatest among their successors, probably Nicola's pupil, was **Antonio Stradivari** (d. 1737), whose style had several stages, the best of which extended about a quarter-century from 1700, and whose achievements then, both as to refinement and brilliancy of tone, and as to grace of form, mark the acme of the art — with his sons **Francesco** and **Omobono** (d. 1743, 1742). The **Guarneri family** includes **Pietro Andrea** (working till c. 1695), his son **Giuseppe** (till 1730), his grandson **Pietro** and his nephew **Giuseppe Antonio** (d. c. 1745), usually called ' del Gesù ' (from his use of ' I. H. S.' on his labels), whose best work equals Stradivari's. The **Ruggeri family**, beginning with **Francesco** (d. 1720), probably a pupil of Nicola Amati, includes **Giovanni Battista** (till 1723), with several others. Among Stradivari's pupils were **Carlo Bergonzi** (d. 1755), and **Lorenzo Guadagnini** (till 1740), with his son **Giovanni Battista** (d. 1786) and other descendants. In the Guarneri line was **Lorenzo Storioni** (d. 1799). Later Cremonese makers of note were the **Ceruti family** and others, reaching far into the 19th century.

From Cremona the developed art passed to other places. Thus in Piedmont was **Gotofredo Cappa** (till 1640), whose instruments are often confused with those of the Amatis. At Milan were **Paolo Grancino** (till 1692), and his son **Giovanni** (till 1720), with others of the same family, representing Amati traditions ; and **Carlo Giuseppe Testore** (till 1720), and his sons, followers of Guarneri. At Venice were **Francesco Gobetti** (till 1715) ; **Domenico Montagna** (till c. 1740), a pupil of Stradivari ; and **Santo Serafino** (till 1748), famous for the beauty of his varnish and finish. At Naples the **Gagliano family**, beginning with **Alessandro** (till 1730) and continuing for two or three generations, upheld for a time the Stradivari tradition. The same derivation is still clearer in **Vincenzo Panormo** (d. 1813), who worked first at Palermo and later at Paris and London. Still another of the same school was **Giovanni Francesco Pressenda** (d. 1854) of Turin.

Violin-making of an advanced type did not begin in South Germany until far into the 17th century, though lutes and viols were manufactured with singular ingenuity. Of the many makers who then appeared the most original was **Jakob Stainer** (d. 1683), a Tyrolese who studied with the Amatis and whose violins now rank only second to those of the best Cremonese artists. **Matthias Albani** (d. 1673), also a Tyrolese, was one of Stainer's best pupils, and his son **Matthias** (d. after 1709) studied at Cremona and finally worked at Rome. **David Tecchler** (d. 1743), coming to Rome from Salzburg, strengthened his style by incorporating Italian features.

Among the closest students and cleverest imitators of the great Italians have been some Dutch and many French makers. Leading names are **Peeter Jacobs** (d. 1740) of Amsterdam, whose work follows that of Nicola Amati ; and **Nicholas Lupot** (d.1824), the chief of a large Parisian family that followed Stradivari. Other well-known Parisian makers are **F. L. Pigue** (d. 1822), **Pierre Silvestre** (d. 1859), who settled finally at Lyons, and **J. B. Vuillaume** (d. 1875), whose instruments are extremely many.

Violin-making in England began early and was at first more indebted to German than to Italian influence. Prominent names are **Benjamin Banks of Salisbury** (d. 1795), **Richard Duke** (till 1780), **Charles Harris** (c. 1800), **William Forster** (d. 1807), and several descendants, **Bernhard Fendt** (d. 1832), a Tyrolese, and his sons, and **John Frederick Lott** (d. 1853).

112. Early Violin Music and Violinists. — The rapid improvement of the violin and its larger relatives was due to the recognition of their remarkable artistic possibilities. These lay in two directions, concerted or orchestral combinations and solo effects. The more these were appreciated and the better became the instruments themselves, the greater was the stimulus to composers to devise and work out special effects, and to players to overcome the technical difficulties involved. The 17th century, therefore, witnessed the foundation of violin music and violin-playing, using both terms in the wide sense that includes all bowed instruments.

In the later 16th century manifold experiments had been made with strange aggregations of instruments for concerted effect. All these lacked a settled principle of organization. But with the rise of the opera, particularly under Monteverdi (himself a violist of long experience), the true orchestra began to take shape with viols of different grades constituting almost half the total force. For more than a century further, however, solidity of harmonic structure was secured by the almost constant use of the harpsichord, though more and more the viol-quartet was pushed into the foreground. The complete emancipation of the orchestra as a body of solo instruments was delayed until after 1750.

It is instructive to compare the make-up of orchestras at different periods. As early as 1565 we hear of accompaniments for intermezzi in which 7 viols contended with three or four times as many wind instruments and 2 harpsichords. In 1600 Peri did not use viols for 'the first opera,' and Cavaliere only one for 'the first oratorio.' But in 1608 Monteverdi in his opera *Orfeo* employed 16 viols (including 2 violins) with 14 wind instruments, a harp, 2 large lutes and 2 harpsichords. Late in the century works by Legrenzi, Lully and A. Scarlatti show a preponderance of bowed instruments, often with clear signs that the value of the string-quartet as a nucleus was appreciated, if not always consistently maintained. In the 18th century Bach and Handel applied the orchestra in very different ways, each for his own purposes, but they contributed little to the settling of the modern orchestra on its present lines. It remained for Haydn and Mozart to make a permanently satisfactory adjustment.

Prior to about 1650 there was little consensus as to the forms in which purely instrumental music should be written, though isolated works showed thought and skill. After that date composers tended to apply the term 'sonata' to pieces for a small group of instruments or for a solo instrument with accompaniment. Two varieties were distinguished, the 'sonata da chiesa,' usually consisting of a slow, stately introduction, a quick fugal movement, a flowing melodic section, and finally a lively, dashing movement, all treated with considerable contrapuntal detail; and the 'sonata da camera,' which was practically a set of dances, the selection and order varying, though with a tendency toward the later plan of, first, pavan or allemande, second, coranto, third, sarabande, and fourth, gigue, all treated with emphasis on some metric figure and on brilliant touches of executive effect. Thus instrumental composition worked itself free from the old imitation of vocal styles and launched out into forms that were perfectly suited to the instruments used. We cannot name precisely the pioneers in these innovations, since many minds worked upon the problem.

The germs of the later styles appeared somewhat before 1600 in works by G. Gabrieli, the Venetian organist, and from 1620, violin solos were attempted, with stringed chamber music soon after. It is conjectured that some important composers of this period may have been forgotten, since later works imply so much of settled procedure. Among the known names are these : —

Carlo Farina, a Mantuan at the Saxon court, published (1626–8) 5 sets of chamber-pieces, interesting for their attempts at imitative effects or tone-painting. Marco Uccellini of Modena followed (from 1639) in a stronger style. Still abler was Massimiliano Neri, organist at St. Mark's, Venice (works from 1644), who may have been the first to distinguish between the two kinds of sonata. Legrenzi (d. 1690), the eminent Venetian, not only strengthened the orchestra, but wrote valuable chamber-sonatas (from 1655). Further advance was made by Giovanni Battista Vitali (d. 1692), violist at Bologna from 1666 and choirmaster at Modena from 1674 (chamber-works from 1666); Tommaso Vitali, his son, one of the best violinists of the time, with striking sonatas (from 1693) ; and G. B. Bassani (d. 1716), the vocal composer of Bologna and Ferrara, a notable player and composer for strings (from 1677).

Arcangelo Corelli (d. 1713), born near Imola in 1653 and a pupil of Bassani, after some years in Germany, before 1685 became the protégé of Cardinal Ottoboni at Rome, where he won immense renown as violinist, composer and teacher, in spite of his simplicity and modesty. His extant works (from 1683) are not many and from a modern point of view not ambitious, but they show that he was an artist of true feeling, a skillful consolidator of style rather than an innovator, and with real insight into the genius of his instrument. From him has developed by direct artistic descent a long line of violin masters of the greatest significance.

Giuseppe Torelli (d. 1708), self-taught at Bologna and long violinist there, but after 1696 at Ansbach, was not only a close contemporary of Corelli, but with him was instrumental in defining the 'concerto' and the 'concerto grosso' — forms in which either a solo violin or a solo group is thrown into contrast with a concerted accompaniment.

Other Italian writers in the first half of the century were **Biagio Marini** (d. c. 1660), who worked variously in Italy and Germany (works from 1617, including much vocal music); **Giovanni Battista Fontana** (d. 1630) of Brescia and elsewhere in Italy, with a few pieces (1641); and **Tarquinio Merula** of Bergamo and Cremona (chamber-works from 1626, besides madrigals and motets from 1615). In the second half, were **Carlo Ambrogio Marini** of Bergamo (many works from 1687); **Bartolomeo Girolamo Laurenti** (d. 1726) of Bologna (works from 1691); **Antonio Veracini** of Florence (works from 1692); and the fertile opera-writer **Tommaso Albinoni** (d. 1745) of Venice (many works from 1699?).

It will be noted that all these, except Corelli, belong to northern Italy.

In Germany, though writing for bowed instruments was somewhat abundant during the second half of the century, especially in dance-forms and accompaniments for vocal works, no commanding master or historically important style was developed.

Almost all the works produced were sets of dances, representative composers being **Briegel** of Darmstadt (d. 1712), a very facile writer (works from 1652); **Nikolaus Hasse** of Rostock (1656); **Johann Heinrich Schmelzer** (d. 1680), from 1649 a player in the Imperial Chapel at Vienna and from 1679 choirmaster, with chamber music (from 1662) and many ballets for operas; **Johann Pezel** of Leipsic, notably industrious (from 1670) in writing for various combinations of instruments, both bowed and wind; **Heinrich Franz von Biber** (d. 1704), court-musician at Kremsier (Moravia) and from 1675 at Salzburg, whose works (from 1673) rank fairly with those of the Italians; **Johann Jakob Walther** of Dresden, an ingenious player, very celebrated in his time, but not a remarkable composer (works from 1676); **Johann Schenk** of Düsseldorf and Amsterdam, a noted gambist, with works for the gamba (from 1685); and **Strunck** (d. 1700), the Hamburg opera-writer (see sec. 87), whose playing won Corelli's admiration and honors from several courts (sonatas, 1691, mostly lost).

In France interest in pure chamber music was not usually dissociated from that in the orchestral side of the opera. Concerted suites of dances were frequent, but developed more as parts of operas than as independent works. The operatic overture also became steadily more significant, being laid out in three or four distinct movements. These two instrumental styles were essentially analogous to the two kinds of Italian sonata. In them progress tended gradually toward clearness,

interest and artistic organization of detail and plan.   In all this
the influence of Lully was dominant, and radiated more or less
into Germany and England.

It is to be remembered that **Lully** (d. 1687) first won recognition at
Paris as a violinist about 1650 and that his works began soon after (see
sec. 85).   He was most successful with his overtures, which were usually
laid out with a slow, massive first movement, then a lively fugal movement, then a melodious slow movement.   Mention should also be made of
Marin Marais (d. 1728), an extraordinary gambist, in the royal orchestra
for 40 years from 1685, with much gamba and chamber music (from 1686),
and **Jean Rousseau,** author on and composer for the gamba at Paris (1687).
Nicolas à Kempis, organist at Brussels, put forth chamber-works as early as
1644.

In England the established national zeal for secular vocal
music passed over more or less into a care for instrumental
works, especially late in the century.   Several composers experimented with concerted pieces even before the Commonwealth, resuming with zest after it.   Early pieces were often
called 'fancies,' which were somewhat contrapuntal fantasias,
generally of slight value, but better suites of dances were common after 1660.   No single composer of chamber music became historically eminent, but the diffused interest is to be noted
as illustrating the tendency of musical thought.

Many writers elsewhere named (secs. 88, 89, 99) put forth chamber music,
from **O. Gibbons** (d. 1625) and **W. Lawes** (d. 1645) to **Rogers** (d. 1698) and
H. Purcell (d. 1695).   Mention may also be made of **Christopher Simpson**
(d. c. 1677), a good gambist, with several instruction-books (from 1659);
John Jenkins (d. 1678), a lutist and violist, teaching before the Civil War and
in the royal band after 1662, with much chamber music (from 1660), including sonatas, fancies and 'rants' (dance-tunes);   **John Banister, Sr.** (d. 1679),
called the first significant English violinist, who left the royal band because
of friction with the French players in it, afterward a teacher and the leader
of public concerts (perhaps the first in England);   his son **John Banister,
Jr.** (d. 1735), violinist from 1668 to Charles II., James II. and Queen Anne,
and concertmaster at the opera (works from 1688);   and **Nicola Matteis,**
an Italian settled in London (works from 1687).

It should be added that the strong 16th-century interest in the
lute and theorbo, both as solo instruments and as parts of concerted combinations, continued to some extent into the 17th,
and that lute-books were still issued from time to time.   But the
developing family of viols steadily supplanted these older and
feebler instruments.

R

113. Literature about Music. — The growth of intellectual interest in music, which began so fruitfully in the 16th century,
was maintained and increased in the 17th The widespread
teaching of practical music called forth numerous manuals and
text-books, with several philosophical treatises on composition,
instruments and performance. The instinct for historical investigation grew stronger and more productive, and the drafting
of dictionaries and similar compendiums began. Scholarship
busied itself still further with questions of ancient musical
theory, assisted now by notable republications of Greek treatises.
Musical acoustics appeared as a specialty, though its strong
development was deferred till the 18th century. In these varied
lines of study and literary production all the leading countries
participated more equally than before, England now taking her
place with the rest.

　　No exhaustive catalogue of works will be attempted, only a rapid
　enumeration of those temporarily or permanently influential. For con-
　venience, the century will be taken up in two parts. The usual language
　is still Latin, but other languages begin to be used with freedom.

　　Technical manuals of varying scope during the first years of the century
were issued in 1598 by **Orazio Scaletta** of Padua (d. 1630) ; from 1601 by
Scipione Cerreto of Naples ;　in 1606-10 by **Antonio Brunelli** of Florence ;　in
1611-3 by **Johann Heinrich Alstedt** of Herborn (d. 1638), who also wrote
encyclopædia articles ;　in 1611 by **C. T. Walliser** of Strassburg (d. 1648) ;
in 1618 by **Giovanni Battista Rossi** of Genoa ;　in 1618 by **Thomas Campion** of
London (d. 1620) ;　in 1620 by **Francesco Rognoni-Taegio** of Milan ;　in 1626 by
Arauxo of Seville (d. 1663) ;　and in 1626, on solmization, by **Nikolaus
Gengenbach** of Zeitz.　An early exposition of figured bass (1607) was by
Agostino Agazzari (d. 1640) of Rome and from 1630 at Siena, who also wrote
(1638) on church music in the light of the action of the Council of Trent.
The earliest treatise on conducting as a specialty (1611) was by **Agostino Pisa**
of Rome.　**Georg Leopold Fuhrmann** of Nuremberg wrote upon the lute and
its music (1615).　**Erycus Puteanus** [Hendrik van Put] (d. 1646), from 1607
professor in Louvain University, issued two or three works (1599-1602) in
which history and theory mingled.　He opposed solmization.

　　Adriano Banchieri (d. 1634), the eminent organist and composer of Bologna,
treated importantly of organ-playing and composition (1601-28).　**Domenico
Pietro Cerone** (d. after 1613), for about 15 years at Madrid and from about
1608 at Naples, issued two theoretical treatises (1609-13), the latter containing almost 1200 closely printed pages — now known only by a few copies.
Heinrich Baryphonus [Pipegrop] of Quedlinburg (d. 1655) wrote extensively
(from 1609?), including elaborate mathematical discussions, many now lost.

　　Michael Prätorius (d. 1621), choirmaster at Wolfenbüttel (see sec. 95),
was the most important writer in the early part of the century.　His *Syntagma*

musicum (3 vols., 1615–19, appendix, '20) is a mine of information. Vol. i. treats of sacred music from the earliest times and of ancient music in general; Vol. ii., of every kind of musical instrument then in use or historically known, with carefully executed illustrations; Vol. iii., of all the recognized forms of composition and of technical signs and terms, with details about the training of choirs and bands; and Vol. iv. (not completed) would have discussed the whole art of counterpoint. In scope and execution this work is one of the monuments of musical scholarship.

Marin Mersenne (d. 1648), a monk at Paris, pursued similar lines. His *Harmonie universelle* (1627, enlarged, 1636–7) deals with acoustics, singing, harmony and counterpoint, instruments, etc. He also discussed Hebrew music (1623), and supplemented his *magnum opus* by several lesser works (1634–48).

Johann Crüger (d. 1662), for 40 years at Berlin (see sec. 95), published several useful treatises on composition (from 1624?), besides important chorale-collections (from 1640).

Notable among works on ancient music were those (from 1635) of Giovanni Battista Doni (d. 1647), the distinguished Florentine. Before this, Joannes Meursius (d. 1639) had published texts by Aristoxenos, Nikomachos and Alypios (1616), besides writing on ancient dancing (1618). The monumental work (1652) of Marcus Meibom of Upsala and Utrecht (d. 1711) gave texts and translations of Aristoxenos, Euclid, Nikomachos, Gaudentios, Bacchios, Aristides Quintilianus and Capella. At intervals followed still better works by John Wallis (d. 1703) of Oxford, giving texts of Ptolemy, Porphyry and Bryennios, with discussions (1657–99).

Athanasius Kircher (d. 1680), a Jesuit at Rome, put forth several volumes (from 1641) as the results of his antiquarian studies, partly valuable, partly grotesque. The chief of these was the *Musurgia* (2 vols., 1650), treating of ancient music, acoustics and general composition. Other books dealt with the medical use of music, Egyptian music and still further with acoustics. His handling of ancient music was sharply challenged by Meibom.

Technical treatises were numerous in the middle and later parts of the century, such as from 1640 by Lorenz Erhardi of Strassburg and Frankfort; in 1640–66 by Otto Gibel of Minden (d. 1682); in 1642–53 by Johann Andreas Herbst of Frankfort and Nuremberg (d. 1666); from 1646 by G. G. Nivers of Paris (d. after 1701); in 1648 by J. R. Ahle of Mühlhausen (d. 1673); from 1649 by King João IV. (d. 1656); posthumously by Gerhard Johann Voss of Leyden and Amsterdam (d. 1649); in 1654 by John Playford (d. 1693), the London publisher; in 1657 by Giovanni d'Avella of Naples; in 1658–67 by Christopher Simpson of London (d. c. 1677); in 1665–79 by Jean Jacques Souhaitty of Paris; from 1656 by Lorenzo Penna of Mantua and Parma (d. 1693); in 1673 by Matthew Locke of London (d. 1677), the first English work on figured bass; in 1673 by G. M. Bononcini of Bologna (d. 1678); in 1673, also, a notable treatise on Plain-Song by Pierre Benoît de Jumilhac of Rheims (d. 1682); in 1681–93 by Angelo Berardi, successively of Viterbo, Tivoli, Spoleto and Rome; in 1683 by Francesco Gasparini of Venice (d. 1727); from 1687 by J. G. Ahle of Mühlhausen (d. 1706); and in 1696 by Étienne Loulié of Paris.

In the field of history, church music was extensively treated (1653-73) by Cardinal **Giovanni Bona** of Rome (d. 1674) ; and the Meistersinger by **Johann Christoph Wagenseil** (d. 1708) of Altdorf (in his History of Nuremberg, 1697). General histories were attempted in 1690 by **Wolfgang Kaspar Printz** of Sorau (d. 1717), and in 1695 by **Giovanni Andrea Bontempi** of Dresden (d. 1705), both of whom had previously written on composition ; and MS. works of the same class were prepared by **Liberati** (d. after 1685) and by **Pitone** (d. 1743), both of Rome. Some lists or catalogues giving historical data were issued, as, for example, an account of 13 Venetian musicians (1605) by **Giacomo Alberici**, general bibliographies (1611-25) by **Georg Draud** (d. c. 1636), an important catalogue of dramas and operas (1666) by **Leo Allacci** (d. 1669), accounts of Milanese writers and musicians (1670) by **Filippo Picinelli**, and of about 20 Brescian composers (1685) by **Leonardo Cozando**. **Thomas Mace** (d. 1709) of Cambridge published (1676) a quaint book on church music, the lute and its music, viols, etc.

Sieur Ducange (d. 1688), a Parisian lawyer, published (1678) a valuable glossary of mediæval Latin, including many musical terms ; and **Matthias Heinrich Schacht** (d. 1700), a Danish scholar, prepared a dictionary of composers (1687), which Gerber used a century later.

Andreas Werckmeister (d. 1706), the able organist of central Germany, besides his works on the organ and on temperament, issued several on composition (from 1686).

Acoustical questions were discussed by **Salomon de Caus**, a Heidelberg architect (1615) ; by **René Descartes** (d. 1650), the famous mathematician and philosopher, in his treatise on music (1618, publ. 1650) and his letters (publ. 1682-3) ; by **Johann Kepler** (d. 1630), the great astronomer (1619) ; by **Mersenne** (from 1635), **Kircher** (from 1650), **Wallis** (from 1672) and **Werckmeister** (from 1687) ; and by **Daniele Bartoli** (d. 1685). **Loulié** of Paris invented the metronome in 1696.

To the important collections of church music already mentioned may be added those by **Abraham Schade** (d. c. 1617) of Speyer (1611-7), **Berthold Spiridio** of Bamberg (1665), besides a guide to organ-playing, etc. (1670), and by Cardinal **Giuseppe Maria Tommasi** (d. 1713) of Rome (1680-97).

114. Summary of the Century. — In one sense the 17th century presents no such essential novelty as the 16th, since it brought no further revolution in the fundamentals of composition. Yet, in another sense, it was more notable, since what had been tentatively attempted before now advanced into confident maturity, and since the popular applications of musical art now became more conspicuous.

The mere fact that the art-form known as the opera was extensively undertaken signified a prodigious change. The opera is distinctively secular, and, to succeed, it must appeal powerfully to the popular craving for amusement. Hence, when it replaced church music as the principal object of pro fessional ambition, it altered the whole social bearing of the art, besides affecting its inner character. Music now competed for social regard in a new way, unsupported by the sentiments or institutions of religion, in a form essentially public and democratic. While it is true that the opera has always had grave possibilities of misuse in that it tempts to superficial methods and tends to degenerate into a vulgar diversion, yet from the first it has also afforded room and incentive to great artists to give voice to certain profound and intense emotions for which church music makes no demand. It has therefore never failed to be counted one of the consummate tonal art-forms.

The hectic cultivation of the opera brought into prominence one or two sides of music that were but imperfectly developed before. For example, the art of solo-singing received an altogether new impetus. It is true that fine vocalization was required in the Palestrina type of choral writing, but such music demanded nothing like the versatility and magnetic self-expression essential to stage-declamation and the delivery of elaborate arias. The 17th-century opera was necessarily sensational in method and aim, for vocalists quite as much as for librettists and stage-managers. Hence came an art of singing not heard before, or perhaps since. Every latent power of dexterity and compass, of sonority and delicacy, of color and chiaroscuro, was not only diligently cultivated, but enthusiastically applauded, until the display of virtuosity became the be-all and end-all of the musical drama. Though this excessive glorification of vocal technique at length made necessary a revolution in operatic methods, it yet served a purpose in revealing once for all the possibilities of the voice as an artistic instrument.

The opera also brought out the values of certain instrumental voices. Especially notable was the rapid advance of the violin family. The utterance of passionate feeling and the depiction of thrilling situations were impossible without appliances very different from the feeble and colorless instruments of the 16th century. Hence suddenly this new group of instruments came into view, with presently a new order of performers, and then a new style of writing suited to the new resources. In all this lay the promise of the modern orchestra, of modern chamber music, and of the modern use of the violin as the solo instrument *par excellence*.

In connection with these movements the theory of composition made steady advance, especially in the freedom and solidity of harmony proper as distinguished from counterpoint, in the production and varied embellishment of pure melody, and in the establishment of 'form' in general and of certain forms in particular. Dance-types pushed more and more into evidence in serious writing, with their clearness of plan, individuality of figures and energetic momentum. Out of them, it was clear, were to come still further enrichments of style. Already the 'sonata' and the overture were settling down into complex series of movements in which larger conceptions could find expression than are possible in an extended work without such separated and contrasted divisions.

Meanwhile, the pursuit of choral styles and of organ music was not given up, but, especially in the latter, was keeping alive that feeling for counterpoint and thematic development generally which in the 18th century was to attain a fresh culmination under Bach and Handel. In this field German musicians proved themselves more apt than all others, thus laying deep the foundations on which their country's later eminence was to rest. In these more serious and thoughtful sides of the art, the leadership had already passed from Italy to northern Europe.

PART V

THE EARLY EIGHTEENTH CENTURY

PART V

THE EARLY EIGHTEENTH CENTURY

CHAPTER XV

CHURCH MUSIC IN BACH'S TIME

115. General Survey. — The number of musicians of note in the 18th century is at least three times as great as in the 17th, but of these the majority belong to the time after 1750. For this reason and because then distinctly new points in musical procedure become prominent, the century may well be divided into two parts, the first related closely to the 17th century, the second looking forward toward the 19th. The first is popularly known as the age of Bach and Handel, the second as that of Haydn and Mozart, though in both a host of other masters demand attention and in neither was the historical movement dictated by individuals, however great.

The political conditions from about 1690 were extremely complicated. Only the barest hints of these are needed, since music was but indirectly affected by them. The longest reigns were those of Louis XV. of France (1715–74), Peter the Great of Russia (1696–1725), George II. of England (1727–60), Maria Theresa of Austria (1740–80), and Frederick the Great of Prussia (1740–86). The mediæval vision of a Holy Roman Empire was vanishing. Salient events were the dynastic changes in England in 1688 and 1714, the latter involving entanglements with Germany; the War of the Spanish Succession, ending with the Peace of Utrecht (1713) and the success of the Bourbons; the brilliant, but short-lived, influence of Sweden under Charles XII. (1697–1718); the rise of Russia under Peter the Great (St. Petersburg founded in 1703); the strong advance of Prussia that began with Frederick I. (d. 1713) and that forthwith tended to displace the waning eminence of the Empire; the complicated War of the Austrian Succession (1741–8); and the Seven Years' War (1756–63), incidental to which were repeated collisions between France and England on both sides of the Atlantic.

Probably the widespread political unrest and the economic disorders of the time somewhat checked musical enterprise. All the fine arts, too, suffered temporarily from the diffused spirit of intellectual doubt and criticism that now set in. The age was one of readjustments of thought, and, while important gains were made in preparing for the science and literature of the future, the immediate impulse to creation in art was for the time lessened.

The conspicuous happenings in music before 1750 were these. In Germany the advance of church music, both for voice and for organ, came to a mighty culmination in Bach, the first of the triumvirate of superlative geniuses now universally recognized. The older type of the Italian opera was perfected by Alessandro Scarlatti and Handel, the one working in Italy itself, the other mostly in England. Connected with this was the establishment by Handel of the English oratorio as a concert-form. The means of instrumental music were greatly improved. As has already been seen, during the first third of the century the violin was perfected. The invention of the pianoforte belongs to the same period, though its special influence came much later. In the field of clavier music Domenico Scarlatti stands out as a pioneer. Chamber music continued to grow, with a fuller recognition of the individuality of particular instruments. Musical theory and science exhibited fresh activity in accordance with the analytic spirit of the age. The possibilities of harmonic expression were much increased by the growing acceptance of the doctrine of tuning in equal temperament. The half-century before 1750, then, shows itself as a new meeting-point between the old and the new, rising in a few of its achievements into comparison with the 16th century.

116. German Church Music at its Culmination. — While in Italy sacred music revolved about the Catholic liturgy and drew its materials from Gregorian sources, in Germany it was based upon the chorale, which was the product of a different race and faith. The chorale, unlike Plain-Song, was vitally connected with popular life and feeling, and its fund of material was constantly growing. Hence Protestant composition instinctively advanced on lines quite unknown in Italy. In the face of the rage for the opera it preserved its integrity, proceeding with two great styles which Italy presently forgot, namely, chorus music and organ music, both contrapuntal in structure. As has been noted, a multitude of writers in the 17th century labored earnestly and fruitfully upon the chorale-elaboration, the fugue, the motet and the immature liturgical oratorio. Church music in Germany was an intensely living art.

The great Bach led all this progress to a consummation so complete that no later period has been able to add much

within the lines then established.   Bach's work stood squarely
upon that of several preceding generations.   The technical
foundations were already provided.   It remained for him to fill
the style with further vitality and to apply it to the utterance of
grand ideas.

> The Lutheran liturgy, like the Roman and Anglican, was favorable to
> musical art.   The annual calendar was the old Church Year, though with
> few saints' days.   The outline of services closely followed the Catholic,
> except in the use of the German language, the frequent congregational
> chorales and the prominence of the sermon.   For every Sunday and
> other special day were prescribed, not only the Bible lessons, the versicles
> and the prayers, but most of the chorales and some other musical exer-
> cises.   The observance of high festivals was fuller in regular services,
> often spreading over more than one day.   Even on ordinary Sundays the
> morning service was nearly four hours long, beginning at seven o'clock,
> including an hour's sermon and the Eucharist.   Its order was like that of
> High Mass, and some parts of it were in the old Latin forms.   The mu-
> sical features were an extended organ-prelude, a motet (usually in Latin),
> the Kyrie, the Litany, the Creed, the 'principal music' (either a motet or
> a cantata), many chorales, often embellished with prelude and interludes,
> and often another motet in the Communion Service.   Pains were taken to
> vary the method of the musical exercises, some being either *a cappella* or
> very simply accompanied, others lavishly supported by the organ or other
> instruments.   The afternoon service was also elaborate, but without the
> Eucharist.   While such services were not universal, in the chief town-
> churches they were a conspicuous item in municipal oversight and expen-
> diture, and emphatically popular.   The use of the vernacular and of
> chorales kept them in the understanding and affection of the people gener-
> ally.   Into this system, with its free use of music, all the Bachs threw
> themselves with enthusiasm, none more so than the greatest of the family.

117. Johann Sebastian Bach.— The accumulated artistic capacity of the Bach family found manifestation in the genius of
Johann Sebastian.   He grew up and did all his mature work in
Thuringia and Saxony, in towns and cities full of traditions of
the Bachs and where several noted relatives were still at work.
He thus entered by inheritance into the heart of the richest
musical life of Germany as it stood at the opening of the 18th
century.   By indefatigable study he made himself master of
the literature of German music, especially that for the organ
and the choir, welcoming impressions from every school.   His
catholicity enabled him to absorb much from the styles of other
countries, especially Italy and France.   He was keenly conscious of the best tendencies of the time, notably in the general

theory of composition and in instrumental music as a specialty. It was no narrowness that led him to disregard the opera, for from the first he was probably conscious of his power to surpass what was for the time exalted and to reach levels of constructive intricacy and of gigantic expression for which his age was not ready. Accordingly, he chose more and more to labor for the satisfaction of his own intuitive aspirations, regardless of immediate success. In certain quarters and on some sides his greatness was understood and reverenced during his life, but not until almost a century after was there any adequate recognition of all that he was and that he did for musical art. Now he is clearly seen to have been not only the consummation of the best progress of previous times, but also the source of the strongest tendencies of all modern music outside of the dramatic field. He trained many excellent pupils, but his greater legacy to musical progress is the far larger number of geniuses that have rejoiced to own him as master simply from the study of his works.

Johann Sebastian Bach (d. 1750) was born in 1685 at Eisenach, the eighth child of Ambrosius Bach, a respected violist there since 1671. Losing both parents before 1695, he was given a home by his brother Christoph, organist at Ohrdruf. From his father he received instruction on the violin and from his brother on the harpsichord and organ, with schooling at the academy at Ohrdruf, where his soprano voice was valued. In 1700 a place was secured for him in the choir and school of St. Michael's at Lüneburg (near Hamburg), where his gifts as a player saved him when presently his voice broke. Here he had practice in the best church music, access to the fine school library, and fruitful contact with Georg Böhm (d. 1733), the organist. He often visited Hamburg to hear Reinken (d. 1722), but cared little for the opera. He also learned much of French chamber music from hearing the ducal orchestra at Celle. At the school he gained a fair classical education. In music, having no special master, he began the indefatigable independent study that continued through his life. From the first he was grounded in the contrapuntal style as used by various schools of German organists, and his taste set toward church and chamber music.

In 1703 his skill as a violinist gave him a place at Weimar in one or both of the court-bands, but he was soon made town-organist at Arnstadt, with a large new organ and opportunity for study and writing. Here he began composition in earnest. Late in 1705 he had leave to visit Lubeck (traveling the 225 m. thither on foot) to hear the organ and choir music of Buxtehude, the veteran Danish organist, whose style powerfully influenced him. He long outstayed his leave, and this, with some differences about details in his work, led him to remove in 1707 to Mühlhausen, succeeding J. G. Ahle. In 1707, also, he married his cousin Maria, daughter of Michael Bach of Gehren. He began to reorganize the church music and to have the organ greatly improved, but in 1708 was called to be court-organist and violinist to the Duke of Weimar. His celebrity had already begun to attract pupils.

His new patron at Weimar was a model ruler, a strict Lutheran and a great lover of church music. The court organ was small, but excellent, and the Kapelle competent; in the town-church the organist was the contrapuntist J. G. Walther, for a time Bach's intimate friend. This period was one of the happiest and best of his life. Here he attained absolute command of organ technique, perfected his knowledge as an organ-expert, and wrote most of his finest organ-works. He studied Italian chamber music, both solo and con-certed, and entered deeply into its de-veloping sense of extended form. He derived much from the works of certain Italian masters, like Frescobaldi and Al-binoni. He began writing fugues and clavier-suites, using both Italian and French styles, but with great inde-pendence. He also began producing church cantatas, combining some

features of operatic style with his immense resources in thematic writing. Occasionally he made trips to a distance, especially to examine or exhibit important organs, as to Cassel, Leipsic and Halle, where in 1714 he was sought as town-organist, and to Meiningen and Dresden, where in 1717 he challenged the boastful French clavier-player Marchand to a trial of skill which the latter lost by default. In 1717, however, probably because not fully appreciated at Weimar, he accepted the place of court-choirmaster at Cöthen.

The Prince of Anhalt-Cöthen was highly cultivated and an enthusiastic musician; he favored the Reformed Church, for which church music was un-important, but chamber music of various sorts was in constant demand. Bach now had no organ, but every incentive in other directions. Here he matured his views as to clavier technique and as to temperament, and composed most of his greater works for the clavichord and harpsichord, including part of the *Well-Tempered Clavichord* (1722). His mastery of stringed instruments became prominent, guiding him in works for violin, gamba and 'cello that only a practical player could have produced (besides leading him to invent the 'viola pomposa,' a form between the viola and the 'cello, but held like the former). He wrote somewhat for other instruments, like the flute. Here he proceeded to deal strikingly with ensemble music, including suites, concertos and similar extended forms, adopting traditional outlines in part, but trans-forming them by prodigious contrapuntal enrichment. He made trips away at intervals, as to Leipsic in 1717, to Halle in 1719, where he just missed seeing Handel, to Carlsbad several times with the Prince, and to Hamburg in 1720, where he won the admiration of the aged Reinken. In 1720, while he was at Carlsbad, his wife died so abruptly that he did not know the fact till his return three weeks after. In 1721 he married Anna Wülken of Weissenfels, fifteen years his junior, a beautiful singer, and so deeply interested in music that she engaged in detailed study, served much as his copyist and shared fully in his ideals. In 1723, partly to enlarge his artistic field, partly to get better schooling for his children, he secured appointment as cantor at the Thomasschule in Leipsic, where he remained till his death. He continued, however, to be honorary choirmaster at Cöthen and also at Weissenfels.

Technically, his new position at Leipsic was not a promotion, though its traditions were honorable (see sec. 95). Its duties were laborious and complicated. The school was administered as the choir-school for the four town-churches, and the cantor was responsible to both the Town Council and the Church Consistory. Besides living at the school and sharing in its discipline, he was expected to teach Latin as well as music. While Ernesti was rector (till 1729), the pupils were few and poor, the equipment and discipline neglected, and the interest of the Council in the musical work narrow. Bach asserted his authority as supervisor of music in the two leading churches, besides composing much for them and attending to all occasional music (processions, weddings, funerals), and also claimed his legal rights as musician to the university which his predecessor, Kuhnau, had allowed to lapse. This latter contention he carried up to the Elector of Saxony himself, and was sustained. Yet the situation was trying, for the drift of popular interest was toward the opera and even the school pupils were continually being drafted as operatic singers. It is pathetic to realize what inefficient resources he had for his public work — organists that disliked his ideas, a body of immature singers and players, seldom more than twenty in number, and a popular hostility to all serious styles. In 1730–4, however, under the new rector, Gesner, a fine scholar and disciplinarian, matters were better, but lapsed again under his successor. In spite of Bach's increasing renown, circumstances combined to make the later part of his life unhappy on its public side and to drive him into seclusion. His delights lay in his home-life, in his many pupils, in his visitors from abroad, and in incessant composition of the most ambitious sort. The Leipsic period is marked by the writing of an enormous number of cantatas and several oratorios, usually devised with reference to the Lutheran liturgy and calendar. He also diligently revised many of his earlier works. He made many trips, especially to Dresden, where Hasse was in high honor, to Weimar and Cöthen, and to the various gathering-places of the Bachs in Thuringia. In 1747 he was invited to Potsdam by Frederick the Great, in whose band was Bach's son Emanuel, and was received with the greatest favor. Late in 1749 he underwent an operation upon his eyes which resulted in total blindness. In 1750 he died of apoplexy. His grave in the yard of the Johanniskirche was later obliterated in municipal improvements, but his supposed remains were discovered in 1894 and reinterred in the church on the 150th anniversary of his death. His wife and his three unmarried daughters struggled on in poverty, part of the time as dependents upon the town; Anna Bach died in 1760. The surviving sons, with one exception, attained renown and importance. Of seven children by his first marriage, three remained; and of thirteen by the second, six — in all, five sons and four daughters.

In appearance Bach was stalwart, with a full face dominated by keen eyes, arching brows and an ample forehead. His expression was grave, but brightened readily into kindliness or humor. In manner he was courteous, but decidedly dignified. He was reserved in conversation, but wrote with clearness and pungency. He formed intimate and loyal friendships with those whom he could respect. He was considerate as a critic, especially for earnest students, but had small patience with pretension. While perfectly aware of his abilities and dogged about his official rights, he hated parade and boasting. He was a prodigious worker, rising to supremacy as executant and composer by persistent self-discipline, sparing no effort to acquaint himself with all styles except that of the opera, and becoming also an expert in organ-building and a good musical engraver. He was a devout and orthodox Lutheran, and many facts show the depth of his religious sentiments and their bearing on his musical and social life.

118. His Style and Works. — The centre of Bach's art was organ music. Though first trained as a violinist and always eminent in dealing with stringed instruments, he instinctively fastened upon the concerted style of the organ as the field for his fullest expression. Here, in the union of several keyboards, each with its varied stops, and in the continuity and majesty of tone characteristic of the instrument, he found room for solid harmony, for manifold polyphony, for unlimited development, and for immense climaxes suitable to the noblest conceptions. Up to his time music had been groping after the formal means for sustained and cumulative effects. Bach realized the necessity for strong thematic material, for contrapuntal organization, and for marshaling parts and sections with the utmost artistic strategy. In his hands the chorale-elaboration, the toccata and the fugue attained an unsurpassed grandeur. And in whatever other direction he chose to work the influence of his organist's method of thinking and writing is obvious, whether with the smaller resources of the clavier, or with solo instruments in combination, or with voices as such instruments or in chorus.

In the details of structure Bach never fails to be a contrapuntist, but analysis shows how far his polyphony transcends that of the mere pedant. Its subject-material is almost all original, has character and meaning in itself, suggests more or less clearly a harmonic idea, and often achieves decided melodic beauty. As the subjects are unfolded, interwoven and combined with episodical matter, it is clear that the whole is greater

than its parts, having an organic unity to which all details contribute. All music of this sort is intensely intellectual rather
than sensuous, but Bach's works never lack an obvious overrul-
ing sentiment that lifts them out of the merely learned level
into that of living art. But the means chosen demand mental
maturity and experience in both performer and listener. Hence
his works are not fully appreciated except by those of advanced
culture.

Yet Bach's works are almost incredibly varied. He was not
only a prince of polyphonists, but far ahead of his times in the
grasp of melodic invention, of every device of form, and of the
application of rhythmic and metric energy. He had begun
to foresee the sonata-form, with all its symphonic possibilities.
The marvelous ductility of melodic material in his hands pre-
sages the plastic part-writing of the later 19th century. With the
latent artistic capacity of dance-forms he was perfectly familiar. Technically, he was thoroughly radical regarding modulation and technique. He threw aside the conventional notions
as to 'proper keys,' and demanded the new systems of tuning
and of key-relation so as to open for use the whole range of
tonal possibility. Instead of writing down to players and singers or making technique an end in itself, he imperiously called
for a new method of keyboard fingering and for a vocalization
that is extreme in its difficulty, simply because technique for
him was subordinated to conception and construction.

The grandest quality of his larger works cannot be described
in words. It lay in the mental view of the tonal material and
its handling with reference to the embodiment of ideas and sentiments. Like all artists of the highest class, he had an intuitive sense of the relation of formal structure to the expression
of the mind and soul in universal terms. His music, therefore,
is a true rescript not only of his own personality, but of ideal
personality. Its significance has proved too great to be exhausted by later generations. Hence it is natural to class him
with creators like Michelangelo, Shakespeare and Goethe.

Very few of his works were published during his life. Most of them
remained in MS. for more than a century after his death, while many are
known to be lost. The recent authoritative edition (1851–96) numbers
over fifty large volumes, presenting many hundreds of distinct compositions, from brief chorales to gigantic choral or orchestral works.

The greater organ-works include nearly 20 extended preludes and fugues, a few toccatas, a passacaglia, and many chorale-preludes and elaborations.

The chief works for clavier alone are the *Das wohltemperirte Clavier* (48 preludes and figures, Pt. I., 1722, Pt. II., 1744), 12 suites, many inventions, partite, etc., besides *Das musikalische Opfer* (1747) and *Die Kunst der Fuge* (1749), the latter of which requires other instruments in part. To these are to be added about a dozen concertos for one, two, three, and even four claviers with orchestra.

The chamber and orchestral works comprise a multitude of sonatas and concertos, (*a*) for violin, viola pomposa or 'cello alone, (*b*) for flute, violin or viola da gamba with clavier, (*c*) for violin with orchestra, (*d*) for varied combinations of solo instruments, and (*e*) several overtures for orchestra.

The vocal works include (*a*) many secular cantatas, serenatas and complimentary pieces, (*b*) over 200 motets and cantatas for the Sundays and festivals of the Lutheran Church Year (being about two-thirds of five complete annual cycles of such works), (*c*) 5 Passions, including the St. Matthew (1729), the St. John (1724), together with similar church oratorios for Christmas (six parts, 1734), for Easter and for Ascension, (*d*) 2 Magnificats, 5 large masses (that in B minor, 1733-8, being the chief) and several shorter ones.

In two directions these works involved technical procedures that were comparatively novel. The first related to the method of keyboard fingering. Bach threw his influence in favor of employing equally all the fingers instead of mostly the middle three, as had been the tendency, and hence of adopting the curved or curled position for the hand instead of a flat or rigid one. In this he anticipated and guided the practice of the later 18th century, when the question of pianoforte technique became urgent. While he himself seems not to have approved of the pianoforte in the types first presented to his attention, by thus increasing dexterity, as well as by his methods of composition (largely induced by his liking for the delicate clavichord), he contributed to the advance of pianoforte music. The second principle was that of equal temperament in tuning, so that modulation might take place freely in all directions (see sec. 136). So strenuous was Bach for this that wherever possible he insisted upon himself tuning the clavichords or harpsichords that he was to play, and many of his works were almost unplayable otherwise. The *Well-Tempered Clavichord* was a conspicuous fruit of this conviction. Here, again, he was ahead of his age, although he did not originate the principle itself.

119. The Church Cantata and Oratorio. — Bach's relation to the use of extended vocal works of a more or less dramatic type in Lutheran church worship is so important that it requires treatment by itself. As has been noted, his church cantatas probably amounted to about 300 in all, while his Passions and similar church oratorios and his masses (which belong to an allied class) number 15 or more. Among these are many of his greatest works, and it is evident that into them was put much of his choicest thought and feeling, since they offered an outlet at once for his musical skill and his sincere religious nature.

The word 'cantata' has been variously used. In the 16th century it meant simply any vocal work as distinguished from one for instruments. In Italy, for about a century from about 1650, it meant specifically a solo scena, secular or sacred, in which recitatives and arias alternated, often with elaborate accompaniments for a solo instrument. This was clearly an offshoot from the prevalent opera. This form became popular in the services of the Catholic Church, and all the leading composers from Carissimi onward used it, often abundantly. Its artistic importance, however, was not great, since it had little independent development.

In Germany, on the other hand, the word cantata came to be applied in the 17th century to a work in which Bible passages delivered by a solo voice in recitative or arioso were interspersed with congregational chorales or with choruses in similar style. The first impetus here came from Schütz of Dresden The effort was usually to unite some thread of story or some logical series of ideas with expressions of devotion or meditation. The peculiarity of the whole lay in its congregational point of view, and herein it differed radically from the operatic Italian cantata. In its correspondence to the warm Protestant piety of the German people it was often intensely subjective and even extravagantly sentimental.

The new interest in the opera about 1700 throughout Germany reacted promptly upon this immature form of cantata. Hence arose a demand for poetical texts specially prepared for semi-dramatic musical treatment and at the same time connected with the special character of the Sundays and other days of the Lutheran calendar. The first noted poet was *Erdmann Neumeister* (d. 1756), a clergyman of Weissenfels and Sorau, who wrote five complete annual cycles (1704–16), starting from the free style of the Italian poetical madrigal, but exemplifying many variations of handling. Similar texts were soon attempted by others outside the church circle, as from 1711 by *Salomo Franck* of Jena and Weimar (d. 1725), and from 1724 by *Christian Friedrich Henrici* (nom-de-plume, *Picander*) of Leipsic (d. 1764). The musical setting of such texts at once became common with musicians and decidedly popular.

Bach's handling of the cantata varied much in different cases, and the elements emphasized came from many sources. Thus the recitatives and arias are of operatic origin, the chorales from the Protestant service, the form of the preludes and often of other numbers from chamber music, and the polyphonic choruses and accompaniments built on the lines of organ composition. But his genius succeeded in fusing these diverse elements into unity and applying them to the exposition of sustained religious conceptions. Almost always the chorale is conspicuous, often serving as the musical text for the whole, usually presented strongly in the opening and closing numbers at least, and in its detailed treatment often carried to the extreme of contrapuntal elaboration. The form of the solo numbers varies greatly, showing that he was not only fully aware of the current style of *da capo* aria, but ready to adopt other plans as well; usually there is a detailed development of the sentiment of the words, though often with a profundity of interpretation that escapes the casual hearer. The accompaniments, usually for at least some solo instruments besides the organ, are full of learning and originality, and constitute important parts of the total effect. Sometimes there is a prelude or overture. The enormous extent of Bach's work in this field indicates how much it engaged his interest. Yet, unfortunately, the intimate connection of all these works with the specific type of Lutheran service of the period makes it impossible to maintain them in general popular knowledge and appreciation.

> In selecting his texts Bach often used those of inferior literary quality, evidently feeling that the dignity of the total impression would be determined by the music. Yet in editing these texts and in laying them out for treatment he was guided by a fine dramatic instinct.

The Passions and other festival oratorios of Bach are really expanded cantatas. They involve the same structural elements, but rest on texts that are still more evidently dramatic or historical in substance. Here again we find him taking forms and materials that had been used before, either in similar or different connections, and remodeling them into a novel and powerful unity all his own. He thus contributed notably to one branch of the development of the oratorio as a significant art-form.

> As soon as extended musical treatment of the mediæval Mysteries became common, the preparation of settings of Gospel stories of the sufferings and death of Christ, or of other texts based upon these stories, naturally aroused peculiar interest. The methods adopted at different periods in the history of the musical Passion vary widely. The text selected might be wholly Biblical, or might contain verses of hymns suitable for chorales or part-song settings, or might consist entirely of a freely composed narration and elaboration of the Gospel incidents. The musical form might be Plain-Song melodies throughout, or such melodies alter-

nating with chorales or polyphonic numbers. Throughout the 16th century expert composers undertook settings in full motet or part-song form, often with madrigal numbers. Experiments followed in more or less dramatic form, with some distinction of personages, after 1600 with recitatives and ariosos, and after about 1675 with true arias. Special texts for dramatic Passions began to be written with care soon after 1700, the most popular of them being that by *Barthold Heinrich Brockes* (d. 1747) of Hamburg (1712). The regular use of such texts with varying musical settings continued to be a feature of Good Friday services until late in the 18th century, and irregularly till much later.

Among the older polyphonic or motet Passions were those by *Davy* (before 1500), *Obrecht* (before 1505), *Galliculus* (1528), *De Rore* (1557), *à Burck* (1568–74), *Daser* (1578), *Handl* (1587), *Gesius* (1588), *Machold* (1593), *Demantius* (1623), *Glück* (1660), and some others.

Of dramatic works, including more and more solo material and about 1700 tending to pass over fully into the style of the Italian oratorio, there were many, as by *Walther* (1530–52), *Scandello* (1550–70), *Meiland* (1568–70), *Lassus* (1573–82), *Asola* (c. 1580), *Reiner* (?), *Victoria* (1585), *Vulpius* (1613), *Mancinus* (1620), *Harnisch* (1621), *Schütz* (1623–66), *Chr. Schultz* (1653), *Sebastiani* (1672), *Theile* (1673), *Funcke* (1683, with the first true arias), *Rothe* (1697), *Keiser* (1704–12), *Handel* (1704–16), *Telemann* (1716–66), *Mattheson* (1717), *Kuhnau* (1721), and others.

In the German Passions there came to be a tendency to adhere to fixed plans of text and treatment that amounted almost to a liturgical formula. The use of chorales varied greatly, and towards 1700 their congregational rendering was largely replaced by solos.

Bach's treatment of the Passion-form was in a sense eclectic, in that he combined elements from various styles, including chorales of different degrees of elaboration, polyphonic choruses, often of gigantic proportions, recitatives, both plain and accompanied, arias in extended form, and dramatic choruses, with the fullest use of instrumental resources for accompaniments and even for independent movements. He approached the matter from the liturgical or devotional side, rather than the purely dramatic, but he was also ready to employ intensely dramatic methods at certain points. With his five Passions proper belong his festival oratorios for Christmas, Easter and Ascension, the plan of which was analogous, though their emotional content was different. In these works the liturgical oratorio reached a culmination that has not since been surpassed.

The more famous of this group are the *St. Matthew Passion* (1729) and the *Christmas Oratorio* (1734), both of which remain in the repertory of competent choral societies.

Bach's attitude toward the musical mass, especially as shown in that in B minor (1733-8), was extremely original. Traditionally, the form had been so closely identified with the actual Catholic liturgy that its treatment had been either fully subordinated to its ritual surroundings, or, if elaborate, developed along conventional lines of method and sentiment. Bach, a Protestant and apparently not writing for ritual use in a Catholic service, followed neither of these types, though influenced somewhat by the second. In the text of the mass (all of which was in some use in Lutheran services) he saw possibilities of gigantic artistic expression. The result is a monumental sublimation of ritual music, treated not as an accessory of a church service, but as an end in itself. Hence his masses, especially the great one, belong properly to the church oratorio class, with the Passions, etc., but have a range of abstract topic and idea not often reached by the historical oratorio.

> It has been supposed that Bach's attention to the mass was partly in connection with his official relations to the Catholic court of Dresden, but it is not clear that any of his works of this class were actually used as wholes in Catholic services. Parts of them were used at Leipsic, however.
>
> With the *B minor Mass* is to be classed the great *Magnificat in D* (1723 ?), since it, too, is a setting of a Catholic ritual text.

120. Other German Church Music. — The general interest among German Protestants in music for the organ and the choir in the later 17th century continued into the 18th, but artistically it was confused by the rapid advance of the opera on the one hand and of diverting chamber music on the other. While Bach, by virtue of his mastery of technique, his profundity of thought, and his independence of mere popularity, pushed on to achievements of enduring value, his contemporaries generally sought to gratify the taste of the time, sometimes with inventive ability, sometimes in slavish complaisance. The revolt from the older severity became steadily stronger, though for a long period without leading to the invention of new styles of positive importance. In vocal music the prevalent forms were of the cantata or Passion class, usually treated after the sentimental fashion of the opera. Organ music persisted longer along the serious paths of the fugue and the chorale-elaboration, but with constantly diminishing vigor. With but few exceptions, the drift of the period was against church music in its purity.

The century opened with a large number of great organists in service, like Joh. Christoph Bach of Eisenach (d. 1703), succeeded there by Joh. Bernhard Bach (d. 1749), Pachelbel (d. 1706) at Nuremberg, Buxtehude (d. 1707) at Lubeck, Joh. Egidius Bach (d. 1717) and Buttstett (d. 1727) at Erfurt, Reinken (d. 1722) and Lübeck (d. 1740) at Hamburg, and Böhm (d. 1733) at Lüneburg. There were also noted vocal contrapuntists, like Theile (d. 1714) at Merseburg, and the two Kriegers (d. 1725, '35) at Weissenfels and Zittau respectively. Kuhnau (d. 1722), organist at Leipsic from 1684 and cantor of the Thomasschule from 1700 (preceding Bach), is also remembered for many cantatas and a fine Passion (1721) in a flowing style.

The opening of the century is further marked at Hamburg by three strong composers of nearly the same age, who gave at least part of their talents to church music : —

Reinhard Keiser (d. 1739) took up church music first from 1704, when at the height of his operatic career, and again from 1728, when cantor at Hamburg (see sec. 87). Several of his Passions are known, written to poems by Hunold (1704), König (1711) and Brockes (1712), the latter text being also set by Telemann and Handel in 1716, by Mattheson in 1717 and by Stolzel (d. 1749). His solo cantatas were numerous and exhibited the facile melodic skill shown in his operas. Neither his experience nor his character fitted him to enter deeply into sacred music.

Johann Mattheson (d. 1764) began his musical life at Hamburg as a choir-boy in 1690. After writing several operas (from 1699), he was cantor at the cathedral in 1715–28 (preceding Keiser), retiring because of increasing deafness. Though best known for his critical writings, he is credited with some 25 oratorios and cantatas, at least 2 Passions and a mass, written during his cantorate. His style was less melodious and effective than Keiser's, but decidedly stronger in scholarship and churchly sympathy. His oratorios were a serious attempt to utilize the new dramatic methods in connection with sincere public worship. For a short time he was a friend of Handel, but nearly killed him in a hasty duel (1704) ; later he was a fairly cordial judge of the latter's greatness.

Georg Philipp Telemann (d. 1767) was superior to Mattheson in versatility and enthusiasm, though almost wholly self-taught. In 1701, while studying at Leipsic University, he began to write cantatas and to serve as organist. At this time he was intimate with Handel. After short terms as court-musician at Sorau from 1704 and at Eisenach from 1708, he became in 1712 choirmaster at Frankfort and in 1721 town-musician at Hamburg, where he continued till his death over 40 years later. His activity as a church composer began at Frankfort and continued side by side with his operatic and instrumental work. His fertility and rapidity were almost incredible, his sacred works including 12 annual cycles of cantatas (said to comprise about 3000 numbers), besides many detached ones, 44 Passions (1716–66), several oratorios, about 65 installation-pieces, about 25 anthems for weddings and funerals, and numerous accompanied solos of various sorts. His style naturally tended to be superficial, but was popularly so effective that he was one of the most famous composers of his day.

Regarding Handel's works of this class, see secs. 129–130.

In central Germany the drift away from contrapuntal methods was delayed by the influence of a few masters more or less of the older order : —

Johann Gottfried Walther (d. 1748) and J. S. Bach were closely related through their mothers, were intimate friends and artistically akin. Walther was brought up at Erfurt, where he was organist from 1702, removing thence in 1707 to be town-organist and later court-musician at Weimar. He war famous as a player and traveled much to perfect his knowledge of organ styles. Most of his extant works are chorale-elaborations, in which he was almost ᴀ̱ successful as Bach. He was the author of the first musical dictionary (see sec. 141).

David Heinichen (d. 1729) attended the Thomasschule at Leipsic, studied law there and practised at Weissenfels, but from about 1709 devoted himself to music at Leipsic. In 1713, wealthy patrons, one of whom was the Prince of Cöthen whom Bach later served, enabled him to travel and work in Italy, whence in 1718 he returned to Dresden as court-choirmaster. Besides his operatic and instrumental works and a manual of figured bass (1711), he wrote much church music, chiefly masses and motets for the Catholic service, with 2 oratorios. At first he cultivated the older styles, but ultimately adopted the easier Italian methods. Technically he preceded Bach in advocating free fingering and the entire circle of keys in modulation. His assistant from 1719 and his successor was **Johann Dismas Zelenka** (d. 1745), a Bohemian whose tireless industry produced over 20 masses, 3 requiems, 100 psalms, 3 oratorios, many motets, etc. (from 1712).

Gottfried Heinrich Stölzel (d. 1749), after good training at Schneeberg, entered Leipsic University in 1707 and profited by the musical opportunities of the city. From 1710 he was busily engaged, chiefly upon opera-writing, at Breslau, in Italy, at Prague, Bayreuth and Gera successively, and in 1719 became court-musician at Gotha. He produced a prodigious amount of music, chiefly sacred, including 8 double annual cantata-cycles, 14 Passions, many masses, festival music, etc., besides secular works. He was an accomplished contrapuntist, especially notable for the vigor of his accompaniments and often for the difficulty of his voice-writing, and his work commanded the respect of Bach.

Johann Friedrich Fasch (d. 1758), fellow-student with Stölzel at Leipsic from 1707, diligently cultivated the popular style of Kuhnau and Telemann, was variously employed for some years at Naumburg, Darmstadt, Gera and Zeitz, and from 1722 was court-musician at Zerbst (having failed to win the cantorate at Leipsic which Bach secured). His church compositions include many Passions, oratorios, cantatas, etc., besides instrumental works.

Christoph Förster (d. 1745), pupil of Heinichen, from 1717 was court-composer at Merseburg. He is said to have written over 300 works, including a cantata-cycle and many other cantatas in the Italian style, but his works are confused with those of the earlier **Kaspar Förster** (d. 1673).

Two other prolific and learned writers of the period, in eastern and southern Germany respectively, were **Georg Gebel [Sr.]** (d. 1750), organist at Breslau from 1713, and **Meinrad Spiess** (d. 1761), of the monastery of Irrsee.

It is to be noted that all these composers were close contemporaries of Bach and Handel, and serve with them to characterize the important transitional period in German church music from 1700 to 1750.

In the next group of composers are several whose fame is greatest in other fields than that of church music, though some of them were industrious in the latter. The increase in the number of Catholic musicians of note is striking. In general, monophonic methods predominate over polyphonic, with more or less of the theatric sensuousness that is essentially diverse both from the classic restraint of the old Palestrina style and from the intellectual depth of the later German counterpoint.

Johann Adolph Hasse (d. 1783), the popular opera-writer (see sec. 125), was the most brilliant of the Catholic writers of the time in Germany, represented by numerous masses, Te Deums, Magnificats, motets, cantatas and about 12 oratorios, mostly written after he became court-musician at Dresden in 1731. His style was attractive melodically, but lacked energy and sublimity.

Other Catholic composers in various parts of northern Europe were **Valentin Rathgeber** (d. 1750), a monk of Banz in Franconia, more fertile than distinguished; **Henri Jacques de Croes** (d. 1786), trained at Antwerp and first active there, from 1729 choirmaster at Ratisbon, but from 1749 again in Belgium (at Brussels), of whose many works few remain; and **G. A. Ristori** of Dresden (d. 1753), who, besides his operas, wrote many masses, motets, psalms, etc., with 3 oratorios (see sec. 126).

Christoph Gottlieb Schröter (d. 1782), on the other hand, continued the Lutheran traditions as organist and church composer at Minden from 1726 and at Nordhausen from 1732. Best known by his theoretical and critical writings (see sec. 165) and for his relation to the development of the pianoforte (see sec. 135), he was also able and fertile in sacred music, his works including 7 cantata-cycles, 5 Passions, many festival and other cantatas, together with fugues and chorale-preludes for the organ. His learning as a harmonist gave his style a decided richness.

Johann Schneider (d. 1787), a pupil of Bach and organist from 1721 at Saalfeld, from 1726 at Weimar and from 1730 at Leipsic, was one of the best players and improvisers of the day, with some organ-compositions.

Karl Heinrich Graun (d. 1759), beginning as a choirboy at Dresden, won his first success in opera, but also early undertook church composition. After ten years at Brunswick, he became in 1735 the protégé of Frederick of Prussia, and from 1740 was royal choirmaster at Berlin — a post more conspicuous than stimulating, since the king demanded mainly French and Italian styles. He wrote many cantatas, including 2 annual cycles, many Latin motets, 5-6 Passions, several masses and a fine Te Deum (1756), with some organ-pieces (see sec. 128). His Passion cantata *Der Tod Jesu* (1755) remains in annual use at Berlin, and enjoys therefore a peculiar renown. His style was fluent, but without decided originality or force.

Johann Peter Kellner (d. 1788?) was from 1728 organist and cantor at Gräfenroda in Thuringia. A devoted admirer of both Bach and Handel, as both player and composer he served to perpetuate the noble organ style, his works including many fugues, preludes and suites, besides some cantatas and a Passion.

Georg Gebel [Jr.] (d. 1753), the precocious son and pupil of the Gebel named above, was from 1729 organist at Breslau, from 1735 court-choirmaster at Dresden, and from 1747 at Rudolstadt, much admired for his facile style. Besides operas, he wrote many cantatas and 2 Passions. (His works, however, are confused with his father's.)

Johann Heinrich Rolle (d. 1785) began church composition as a boy of 13 (1731) at Magdeburg, becoming organist there the next year. From 1736 he studied law at Leipsic and began practice at Berlin, where in 1740 he resumed musical work at the court of Frederick the Great. From 1746 he was again organist at Magdeburg and succeeded his father as town-musician in 1752. His works were exceedingly many, mostly sacred, including several cantata-cycles, at least 10 Passions and several other similar works, 15 or more oratorios (*Der Tod Abels*, 1771, being the most admired), and many songs. His invention was not equal to his dramatic ideas.

Among the many pupils of the great Bach who in the latter part of the century attained eminence in church composition were his eldest son **Wilhelm Friedemann Bach** (d. 1784), organist at Dresden from 1733 and at Halle in 1747–64, who was a player of the first order and a powerful writer for both organ and choir, but whose later life was spent in poverty and disgrace, due to dissipation; his third son **Karl Philipp Emanuel Bach** (d. 1788), most eminent as the founder of the forms of instrumental composition that characterized the period of Haydn and Mozart (see sec. 140), but notable also for worthy church music, including many cantatas, over 20 Passions and similar works, a few oratorios, etc.; **Johann Ludwig Krebs** (d. 1780), under Bach's care for about 10 years and esteemed by him his best organ pupil, from 1737 at Zwickau, from 1744 at Zeitz, and from 1756 at Altenburg, with many fine organ works and some cantatas, besides clavier-pieces, mostly in the homophonic style; **Johann Philipp Kirnberger** (d. 1783), from 1741 a teacher in Poland and from 1752 prominent at the Berlin court, a prolific but dry composer, and a theorist of importance, though not of insight (see sec. 165); **Johann Friedrich Agricola** (d. 1774), court-composer at Berlin from 1751 and Graun's successor as royal choirmaster in 1759, a fine organist and popular singing-teacher, but not eminent as a composer, though he wrote considerable sacred music, besides several operas; and **Gottfried August Homilius** (d. 1785), organist at Dresden from 1742 and cantor at the Kreuzschule from 1755, a good player and favorite church composer, with a cantata-cycle, Passions, motets, chorales and organ-pieces, all in a style remote from that of his master.

Here may be added, though not in the above series, **Matthias van den Gheyn** (d. 1785), from 1741 organist and carillonneur at Louvain, whose fame as a player was extensive.

121. The Imperial Chapel. — While under Bach and his contemporaries Protestant music was attaining its great culmination, the current of composition in Catholic countries went on tending steadily into new channels of expression, mostly theatric but not wholly forsaking the old ways of *a cappella* polyphony.

In both church and dramatic music at the opening of the century Vienna was one of the most notable centres, in touch with Germany on the one hand and with Italy on the other. Under three successive Emperors, Leopold I. (d. 1705), Joseph I. (d. 1711) and Charles VI. (d. 1740), the Imperial Chapel, with the Chapels of the two Empresses Dowager, and of the cathedral church of St. Stephen's, attracted a host of great directors, composers, players and singers. Talented Italians were naturally in constant request, but masters of other nationalities did not wholly fail of honor. In spite of the fact that in the middle of the century, under Maria Theresa, there was a decided lapse of imperial interest, this earlier time presaged in several ways the remarkable eminence of the Viennese school in the later period of Haydn, Mozart and Beethoven.

In the Imperial Chapel itself the number of active musicians, vocalists and instrumentalists rose to fully 100 under Joseph I. and to about 135 under Charles VI., the offices of choirmaster, assistant choirmaster, composer, organist and chief singers commanding good salaries. The list of choirmasters includes *Antonio Pancotti* (d. 1709), singer from 1665, assistant from 1697, chief from 1700, *M. A. Ziani* (d. 1715), assistant from 1700, chief from 1712, *Fux* (d. 1741), assistant from 1713, chief from 1715, *Caldara* (d. 1736), assistant from 1716, *L. A. Predieri* (d. 1769), assistant from 1726, chief in 1746–51, *Georg Reutter, Jr.* (d. 1772), assistant from 1746, chief from 1751, *F. L. Gassmann* (d. 1774), chief from 1772, and *Josef Bonno* (d. 1788), chief from 1774. The title of court-composer was held by *Badia* in 1696–1738, by *Fux* from 1698, by *G. B. Bononcini* in 1700–11, by *Francesco Conti* in 1713–32, by *Giuseppe Porsile* in 1720–40, by *Reutter* in 1730–46, by *Matteo Pallota* in 1733–41 and 1749–58, by *Bonno* in 1739–74, by *G. C. Wagenseil* in 1739–77, and by *Gassmann* in 1763–72. This latter office yielded no special salary after 1770, but the title continued to be conferred, as upon *Gluck* in 1774–87 and upon *Mozart* in 1787–91.

During the first forty years of the century the most influential leader was Fux, a composer emphatically of the old Palestrina school, more learned than original, but a theorist and teacher of exceptional ability, as well as an organizer who knew how to hold in some sort of harmony the diverse elements of the large imperial musical establishment. Prominent among his coadjutors were the Italians Caldara, F. Conti and Porsile.

Georg Reutter [Sr.] (d. 1738) served at St. Stephen's as organist from 1686, and as choirmaster from 1715, while at the court he was theorbist in

1697–1703 and organist from 1700. His works are confused with those of his more talented son and successor.

Johann Joseph Fux (d. 1741), a Styrian by birth, but of whose early training nothing is known, appeared at Vienna as organist at the Schottenkirche in 1696–1702, was assistant choirmaster at St. Stephen's from 1705 and chief from 1712, and in court service as composer or choirmaster from 1698. It is curious that he still clung to the old mediæval system of modes and to the strict *a cappella* methods of writing, with little yielding to the prevalent operatic and homophonic styles (except in his dramatic experiments). His best works were all sacred, including 54 masses, several, like the *Missa canonica* (1718), of great learning, 3 requiems, 2 Te Deums, many motets and psalms, etc., with 10 oratorios in the Italian manner, but including more attention to the chorus. He also wrote 8 operas and 12 other dramatic works, mostly for court festivities; of these *Costanza e fortezza* (1723, at Prague) was the most brilliant. His use of the orchestra was vigorous and rich, and he contributed worthily to chamber music. His great theoretical work was the *Gradus ad Parnassum* (1725), which remained for almost a century a standard treatise.

Antonio Caldara (d. 1736) was born at Venice and began opera-writing there as early as 1689. Apart from brief terms at Mantua and Rome, his work is wholly associated with Vienna, where he was greatly admired. Though most fertile in operas and oratorios (32 in 1712–35), he was also a strong writer of masses and other church music in contrapuntal style, with many cantatas, ranking with the masters of the Italian school. He also wrote much secular part-music and important chamber music.

Carlo Agostino Badia (d. 1738) was also a Venetian, well trained, but of no great genius. Besides numerous operas, he wrote some 15 oratorios (from 1694) and many cantatas.

Francesco Conti (d. 1732) came from Florence in his twentieth year (1701), being in request for his gifts as a theorbist. Except for a period of eight years (1705–13), he remained in the imperial service, producing, besides operas and serenatas, 9 Italian oratorios (1706–36) and over 50 cantatas. His style followed that of Scarlatti.

Gottlieb Muffat (d. 1770) was the son of Georg Muffat (see sec. 105), born at Passau. He was trained under Fux and served as court-organist and harpsichordist in 1717–63. His works include valuable fugues, toccatas, etc., for the organ, besides many clavier-pieces.

Matteo Pallota (d. 1758) was born at Palermo, and was favorably known as a church composer by 1720, though not called to Vienna as court-composer till 1733. Of his works several masses and motets remain, besides a MS. treatise on Plain-Song.

Georg Reutter [Jr.] (d. 1772), the son of the earlier Reutter above, had a long and distinguished career at St. Stephen's and the court from about 1725. He was a facile composer of some brilliance, especially in opera. He left a large number of masses and motets, with 8 oratorios (1727–40). He discovered Haydn in 1740 and was his master till 1749, when he turned him off abruptly because his voice was no longer available.

Franz Tuma (d. 1774), a Bohemian theorbist, studied under Czernohorsky of Prague and Fux of Vienna, was choirmaster to the Empress Elizabeth in

1741-50, and was later connected with monasteries. He was chiefly a church composer, with about 30 excellent masses and other works, besides some instrumental pieces.

A few other Austrian church composers should be mentioned, such as **Bohuslaw Czernohorsky** (d. 1740), a Bohemian Minorite, who worked successively at Padua, Assisi and finally Prague, and who was not only a noted teacher (as of Tartini, Gluck and Tuma), but a superior sacred composer (works mostly destroyed by fire in 1754) ; and **Johann Ernst Eberlin** (d. 1762), a Swabian of whose life little is known except that from 1725 he was in the service of the Archbishop of Salzburg as organist and choirmaster, and whose able organ and church works, including fugues, toccatas, masses, etc., and 13 oratorios, rank among the best of the period.

122. In Italy. — As will be seen, the spirit and methods of the opera were overwhelmingly dominant in Italy throughout the century. Between these and the older ideals of *a cappella* church music there was a gap so wide that hardly any composers could bridge it successfully. A limited number essayed to resist the prevailing drift toward theatric music entirely and to confine themselves to sacred works in something like the old style, but without notable success. Many of the leading opera-writers, no doubt, were diligent composers of masses, litanies, psalms and other ritual music, but only a few of them proved fully sensitive to the differences between church and concert music, or equally expert in both. Most of them, however, undertook oratorios and cantatas upon Biblical subjects or episodes in the legends of the saints, but the reason for this was evidently that such works called for methods that were at least partially dramatic.

As contrasted with their German contemporaries, all Italian composers of this and later periods show the lack of those remarkable restraining and modifying influences in sacred writing that were influential in northern Europe. They had behind them no such traditions of majestic organ polyphony or of fervent congregational singing, and the public they addressed was not permeated by any similar breadth of religious thoughtfulness or depth of homely piety. The conditions of their practical work were different, and it is not strange, with all their artistic ability, that their church compositions seldom rise to the height of permanent value.

In the following notes, details are given only where the emphasis of the composer's work was wholly or mainly laid upon sacred composition. In other cases such details will be found in later sections regarding the opera.

Tommaso Baj (d. 1714), a Bolognese singer in the Papal Choir from the latter part of the 17th century, is almost exclusively known by the beautiful Miserere which shares with those of G. Allegri and of Baini the honor of annual rendering on Good Friday. A few other works remain in MS.

Pompeo Cannicciari (d. 1744), choirmaster at Sta. Maria Maggiore in Rome from 1709, wrote many masses, psalms and motets in strict style (from c. 1690).

Francesco Antonio Vallotti (d. 1780), best known as a learned theorist (see sec. 165), made his first reputation as an organist at Padua from 1722, being considered the most able of his time in Italy, and was also a masterly writer of contrapuntal church music (mostly unpublished).

Giambattista Martini (d. 1784), still better known as the most important theorist of the age and the first of the great musical historians (see sec. 165), became choirmaster at Bologna in 1725 and produced from that time a vast amount of church music of every description, largely in the pure Roman style, but including several oratorios and cantatas also. He further wrote nobly for the organ.

To these may be added the names of **Domenico Zipoli**, a Neapolitan, who was organist at the Jesuit Church in Rome from 1696 and the author of a collection of organ-pieces (1716); **Emanuele d'Astorga** (d. 1736), a native of Palermo, who lived a roving life, including short residences in Spain, in England, at Parma, at Vienna, and finally in Bohemia, and who wrote over 100 solo cantatas of much beauty, with a fine Stabat Mater (1713); **Benedetto Marcello** (d. 1739), a well-born Venetian lawyer and official, thoroughly trained in music (though he called himself a dilettante), who wrote a large number of solo cantatas, a famous set of Psalms (1724-7) for from one to four voices, together with chamber music and part-songs; and **Bartolomeo Cordans** (d. 1757), from 1729 an opera-writer, but from 1735 choirmaster at Udine, where he composed an incredible amount of masses, motets and psalms in a rather eccentric style (many said to have been purposely destroyed, but many still preserved).

Most prolific and characteristic in the field of church music were several masters of the Neapolitan school, all of them renowned in opera (see sec. 125). While they tended always to depart widely from the patterns of the earlier time, they are to be ranked with the great Germans for successfully effecting a compromise between the needs of the form of church worship with which they were connected and the new styles of composition, without altogether throwing away the dignity and ideality of the older styles. It was in the hands of this group of writers especially that gradually a new conception of melody began to emerge — one not dependent upon either a contrapuntal or a strenuous and restless harmonic sequence, but evolved more flowingly and simply from a plain chord-series. Melodies of this type, though apparently devoid of learning, were more and more appreciated as genuine vehicles of feeling, suitable for the expression of both religious and other sentiments. This transition opened the way for much that was most valuable in the styles of later periods.

Alessandro Scarlatti (d. 1725), the first of the great Neapolitans, a pupil of Carissimi about 1680, though most influential through his operas, was even more prolific in sacred works. He cultivated both fields at once from the outset of his career at Rome. Thoroughly at home in all the intricacies of counterpoint, he held his own with the best Roman masters of the later 17th century, and was esteemed at the Papal Chapel and at Sta. Maria Maggiore (where he was assistant or chief choirmaster in 1703–6). He is said to have written 200 masses, set for as many as ten voices, a great variety of psalms, motets and vespers, with literally hundreds of cantatas, mostly solo, and 10 oratorios (from 1693). His extraordinary readiness was supported by ample learning and genuine heartiness of feeling, so that his works seldom lack worth.

Nicola Fago (d. c. 1736) was a pupil of Scarlatti and of Provenzale at Naples, succeeding the latter as teacher at one of the conservatories. Numerous church works (from about 1700) remain, including masses and motets, cantatas, a Stabat Mater and an oratorio, written in a good, but not specially notable, style.

Niccolò Porpora (d. 1766), the most famous singing-teacher of his day, though working ultimately outside of Italy, was trained at Naples, probably under Scarlatti. He wrote in all the usual sacred forms, including many cantatas and 6 oratorios (*Sta. Eugenia*, 1721, being the most famous). His gifts as a vocal expert show in the suave writing of his cantatas (see sec. 125).

Francesco Durante (d. 1755) was also a Neapolitan, studying under Greco and Scarlatti, succeeding the latter as teacher and educating a multitude of great pupils. Being without dramatic ambitions, he devoted himself to sacred composition, leaving a great number of works in all forms, elegantly and attractively written, but, except for their harmonic richness, not particularly strong. His repute throughout Europe, however, is attested by the unusually wide distribution of his works. His best-known work is a Magnificat in B.

Leonardo Leo (d. 1744), ten years younger than Durante, was a pupil of Scarlatti, Fago and the Roman master Pitoni, and served as choirmaster at Naples from 1716 and also as the teacher of several noted pupils. His ablest work was in opera (see sec. 125), but he also wrote abundantly for the church in a rich and imposing style, his *chef d'œuvre* being an *a cappella* Miserere for double choir. He wrote 4 oratorios (1713–32) and some fugues for organ.

Francesco Feo (d. after 1740) studied under the singing-master Gizzi and with Pitoni of Rome. Though the composer of 6 operas, he is better known for considerable sacred music, chiefly in the Roman manner, with one oratorio.

Pasquale Cafaro (d. 1787) was the pupil and successor of Leo as teacher, and, like him, was a church composer as well as opera-writer, his best work being a Stabat Mater (1785).

Giovanni Battista Pergolesi (d. 1736), pupil of Greco, Durante and Feo, though his career was very short (see sec. 126), won renown for the simple and unaffected charm of his church works (from 1731), of which a Stabat Mater for two voices (finished just before his death) and a Salve Regina are the best.

Later composers of this group, whose works fell mostly in the middle or latter half of the century, were the great **Jommelli** (d. 1774), who was from 1749 choirmaster at St. Peter's in Rome and from 1754 in Württemberg (see sec. 125), **Perez** (d. after 1782), and **Abos** (d. 1786).

123. In England. — The declining school of English church music has nothing to show in the 18th century that compares with Germany or Italy. The taste for services and anthems of the 'verse' or solo sort, which set in powerfully towards the end of the 17th century, continued, though for a time it was slightly offset by the genius of a few worthy choral writers, mostly in the Chapel Royal. That there was vitality left in English church music is evidenced by the fact that Handel contributed to it to a small extent. But before the middle of the century came a period of barrenness in which musicians were more interested in glee-writing than in anthems and when the latter were largely concocted by adaptation from various sources.

Among the more prolific anthem-writers whose work began before 1700 were **James Hawkins** (d. 1729), organist at Ely from 1682, with 75 verse and full anthems; **Vaughan Richardson** (d. 1729), pupil of Blow and organist at Winchester from 1693, with 21 anthems; **John Weldon** (d. 1736), pupil of Purcell and organist at Oxford from 1694, and from 1701 connected with the Chapel Royal, succeeding Blow as organist in 1708 and named 'composer' from 1715, besides serving at two of the city churches, with 35 anthems, some of which are still prized; and **John Goldwin** (d. 1719), pupil and in 1697 successor of Child at Windsor, with 24 anthems.

William Croft (d. 1727), trained in the Chapel Royal under Blow and its organist from 1704, besides being organist at Westminster and choirmaster in the Chapel Royal, was the composer of nearly 100 anthems (30 published in 1724), written mostly in a manly and sterling style. From 1700 to 1703 he also wrote some incidental theatric music.

Maurice Greene (d. 1755), a pupil of King at St. Paul's, where from 1718 he was organist, followed Croft in 1727 as organist and composer to the Chapel Royal, and Tudway in 1730 as professor of music at Cambridge. Accounted the leading church musician in England, and for a time the intimate friend of Handel, he is known by almost 100 anthems, often of decided strength (especially 40 published in 1743), a service and a Te Deum, 2 oratorios (1737, '44), 3 light operas (1737-48), many songs and catches, etc. He assisted in founding the Royal Society of Musicians in 1738. His collection of *Cathedral Music* was completed by Boyce.

Minor composers of the period were **James Kent** (d. 1776), pupil and close imitator of Croft, organist at Cambridge from 1731 and at Winchester from 1737, with 23 anthems and 2 services; **John Stanley** (d. 1786), a famous blind organist in London from 1724 (at the Temple Church from 1734), a pupil of Greene and a warm admirer of Handel, with 6 anthems, 3 oratorios (1757–74), organ and chamber works; **John Travers** (d. 1758), pupil of Greene and Pepusch, organist in London from 1725 and at the Chapel Royal from 1737, with 25 anthems, a service, a Psalter, and a favorite set of part-songs; **William Hayes** (d. 1777), organist at Shrewsbury from 1729, at Worcester from 1731, at Magdalen College, Oxford, from 1734 and professor of music there from 1742, with 45 anthems and many secular pieces; **James Nares** (d. 1783), pupil of Pepusch, organist at York from 1734 and in 1756 Greene's successor at the Chapel Royal, with 53 anthems, 2 services, many harpsichord-pieces, etc.; and **John Alcock** (d. 1806), pupil of Stanley, organist in London from 1738, at Lichfield in 1748–60, etc., with 38 anthems, 3 services and considerable secular music.

William Boyce (d. 1779), pupil of King, Greene and Pepusch, began his active career as organist in 1734 in London, became composer to the Chapel Royal in 1736 and its organist in 1758, was conductor of the Three Choirs (West England) for several years from 1737, became increasingly deaf and turned much to editorial work. His compositions include about 70 anthems, 5 services, 2 oratorios, several masques and odes (from 1734) many songs and similar pieces, and some chamber music. His style was solid and noble, often with picturesque color and beauty. He is commonly ranked as the last of the older group of masters. He is gratefully remembered for a great collection of *Cathedral Music* (3 vols., 1760–78), the materials for which were partly collected by Greene and bequeathed by him to Boyce.

It is notable that none of these contemporaries of *Handel* showed a marked tendency to imitate his style.

CHAPTER XVI

THE CULMINATION OF THE EARLY ITALIAN OPERA

124. The Completed Art-Form. — In spite of undeniable genius on the part of several opera-writers in the 17th century, with their hundreds of works, that century was little more than a time of experimentation. It was only toward its close that the form of the opera became definitely settled by a consensus of usage. The particular form chosen was due to a variety of considerations, partly artistic from a really dramatic or musical point of view, and partly due to the demand of the public for an exciting entertainment, whether highly artistic or not. Out of these combined influences a strangely rigid set of rules for procedure was developed by which both librettists and composers were governed, sometimes in defiance of dramatic sense and truth. The observance of these rules was general during the early 18th century, and certain features resulting from them continued into the 19th. It must be admitted that the plan adopted had points of practical effectiveness, however it may be judged as a type of strict dramatic art. At all events, as a popular form it was enormously successful for the time.

The musical elements contributed by the 17th century were the recitative as the best method of developing active situations and expressing trains or sequences of feeling, the aria as the lyrical embodiment of moments of peculiar interest or states of intense emotion on the part of individual characters, and the orchestral accompaniment, lending color and vividness of characterization and enhancing the interest of all vocal numbers, besides occasionally enriching the plot by purely instrumental numbers. The chorus remained almost unutilized except in a subordinate and artificial fashion, and ensemble effects of many voices were for the time rare. Scenery and costuming, with many stage accessories and devices, were employed lavishly, often with more spectacular singularity than the highest taste could approve.

The recitatives were either 'secco,' supported only at intervals by a few chords on the harpsichord, or 'stromentato,' accompanied throughout by various instruments in forms having some musical individuality of their own. In the former style, declamation was utilized in any way that the story or the character speaking happened to suggest, and ranged all the way from simple narration or conversation up to passionate declamation. In the latter style, the recitative verged more or less upon the 'arioso' or informal song, in which rapid or vehement advance in the plot was less possible.

The arias had come to be cast usually in the *da capo* form — a first section mainly in the principal key and some homogeneous manner, a second section contrasted with the first in key and manner, and a third section which was either a repetition of the first or an intensified variant of it. This type of solo has great values as a purely musical form, and is cognate with the longer song-forms generally, but it has obvious dramatic drawbacks if used too persistently and stiffly, since, if its text harmonizes with it, it arrests action and exaggerates emphasis on some single incident, situation or sentiment. For musical reasons, also, in this early usage not only were arias introduced by a short instrumental prelude or 'sinfonia,' but at intervals in each of the sections, especially the first, interludes or 'ritornelli' were inserted, echoing or imitating the melodic figures of the vocal part. These instrumental expansions increased the musical interest of the whole, regarded as a highly developed song, but also increased the difficulty of its satisfactory dramatic application. Arias were properly solos, but duets in similar form gradually became recognized as affording room for musical and dramatic climax. In such duets the voice-parts were often handled in somewhat exact contrapuntal fashion.

As media for expression, arias tended to fall into somewhat distinct classes according to their melodic and harmonic treatment and their consequent fitness for certain types of feeling. Thus, the 'aria cantabile' was characterized by a flowing melody, usually in slow tempo, with few skips, and supported by compact harmony, expressive of placid or meditative emotion; the 'aria di portamento' was similar, but with a much bolder melody, marked by sweeping skips and more prominent accents, expressive of heightened, but not agitated, feeling; the 'aria di mezzo carattere' was more declamatory or descriptive in the voice-part and usually provided with an accompaniment of greater importance, particular species being the 'aria parlante' or talking aria, in which the forcible enunciation of the text was the special feature, the 'aria all unisono,' in which the voice was either unsupported altogether or merely doubled by a few instruments, and which depended for its effectiveness upon the vigor and harmonic suggestiveness of the melody alone, and the 'aria d'imitazione' or imitative aria, in which a point was made of the imitation (usually more in the accompaniment than in the voice) of such sounds as those of bird-song, moving water, festal pomp or warfare; and the 'aria di bravura' or 'd'agilità,' in which every device of vocal virtuosity was employed, including elaborate runs or 'divisions,' prolonged and intricate figures or 'roulades' to single syllables, every sort of embellishment, like grace-notes, trills and turns, and rapid variations or contrasts of register, with tones at the extremes of the vocal compass. The 'aria parlante' might also pass over under certain dramatic conditions into the 'aria strepitosa' or 'aria infuriata,' in which the acme of agitation or of violent passion was expressed. So urgent was the demand for all these types as exhibitions of vocal dexterity that it became the rule that in each main division of an opera there should be at least one example of each of the principal classes, and also that no two successive arias should come from the same class. The principal singers in the cast acquired the right to have opportunity to parade themselves in all the more difficult and showy forms, especially in the final portion of the work, and usually the climax of interest included a grand duet between the leading characters. All these conventional usages arose from the popular conception of the musical drama as a grand concert-entertainment rather than a drama pure and simple.

The use of the orchestra also tended to become stereotyped. At the opening of a work was usually an overture of varied dimensions. Sometimes it was a mere tonal introduction in but one movement, but in larger works it consisted of three to four movements, each of a distinct character. Two main types of overture were distinguished, the French, which originated with Lully, having a first movement in full harmony, stately and even grandiose, the second in quick tempo, more or less fugal and with more distinction of instruments, the third a flowing melody in moderate tempo, and the fourth, if present, a dance like a gavotte or minuet; and the Italian, which was first established by Scarlatti, having a first movement in quick and incisive style, a second like the third above, and a third again quick and often contrapuntal. The relation of the overture to the topic and spirit of the work as a whole was so slight that overtures were often transferred from work to work, and even from operas to oratorios. Besides the overture, opportunities were seized to introduce instrumental numbers into the progress of the action, such as marches, dances, pictorial scenes — anything to enhance the tonal variety and interest. Accompaniments were more and more made a special study, particularly as the capacities of the orchestra became better understood. Yet they were strictly accompaniments, designed to support and set off the voice, rather than to supply an independent development of the dramatic situation in any large way. The harpsichord remained the basis or centre for the whole ensemble, filling in all harmonic gaps and often serving alone.

The general plan of disposing the dramatic and musical resources involved properly three or four male and three female characters, the hero or 'primo uomo' being a high tenor and the heroine or 'prima donna' a soprano — the latter until well on into the 18th century being an artificial male soprano, since the opposition to women-singers on the stage was outgrown only with difficulty. Voices of low register, such as altos and basses, were not considered important. The chorus was little more than a piece of stage-furnishing, performing in dumb show for the most part. The plot was regularly laid out in three acts, each composed of alternate recitatives and arias in long series — sometimes as many as twenty to an act. At the end of the whole or of each act a madrigal or dance in ensemble was used somewhat like an epilogue; occasionally similar numbers served as prologues. Except for these and the orchestral numbers, if any, the play might consist entirely of solos.

Obviously, a plan like this was hostile to dramatic freedom and truth. Librettists were constrained to force every story into a single mould and to prepare their lines wholly with reference to the arbitrary musical schedule in view. The subjects most in vogue were those of ancient history or mediæval romance, and the same story was worked again and again. Naturally, the texts were of the most mechanical and tasteless description. Composers were equally constrained on the dramatic side, and were forced to win success by a one-sided cultivation of sensuous or sensational melody alone.

The early Italian opera, therefore, was simply a concert-scheme of great artificiality, designed to provide an arena for the display of virtuoso vocalists. It was perhaps a natural reaction from the pedantry and heaviness of the contrapuntal period, but as a reaction it was extreme. If in the 18th century new ideas had not presently made themselves felt, the opera would never have ranked as a great art-form.

The trade of librettist flourished long and was lucrative, since new texts were in demand. But it had little to attract poets of merit until the opera began to break away from its conventional rigidity. Early in the 18th century, however, three court-poets at Vienna secured renown by works of real power, namely, *Silvio Stampiglia* (d. 1725), a Roman by birth who worked at Vienna from about 1700 till 1711; *Apostolo Zeno* (d. 1750), a Venetian at Vienna till about 1730; and, more influential still, *Pietro Trapassi* or *Metastasio* (d. 1782), a Roman who was court-poet at Vienna for a half-century from 1730, the author of about 35 librettos.

The position of opera-singer was one of enormous éclat and pecuniary profit. It presupposed decided vocal gifts, developed by the most exacting discipline, which often involved no slight genuine musicianship. The vocal accomplishments demanded were astonishing, but a capacity for *tours de force* was more valued than artistic endowment. Under the old régime the arrogance and conceit of singers were proverbial. The general employment of 'evirati' for female parts was demoralizing.

The work of the singing-master naturally became of the utmost importance, and many notable composers were equally famous as trainers. The greatest teacher of the century was undoubtedly *Porpora* (d. 1766).

The above description applies to the traditional *dramma per musica* or 'opera seria' — the serious or tragic opera. Gradually, as will be seen, there branched off from this another form, the 'opera buffa' or comic opera, which was a revolt from the mechanical plan and the sentimental monotony of the opera seria. In the opera buffa many of the old rules were deliberately set aside, and thus the way made easier for the reconstruction of the serious opera that occurred after 1750.

> Many light works were often written, often in one act and for but two or three soloists, in which all sorts of deviations from rules were practised. Common names for such works were 'serenata,' 'festa teatrale,' etc. In Germany the singspiel was not abandoned, while in France the ballet was decidedly popular, as was the masque in England. In England, too, the 'ballad-opera' had a sudden vogue. All these implied some degree of dissatisfaction with the fixed form of the typical Italian opera.

Furthermore, what is here said applies strictly only to that form of opera which was essentially Italian, especially that which during the first half of the 18th century emanated from Naples or was under the sway of its school. The Neapolitan opera was the direct descendant of the Venetian, and the latter continued in active existence, though not so impressive in its personnel as it had been. With these two Italian centres Vienna was closely associated. Operas written in Italian were also produced abundantly at several points in northern and western Europe, notably at Dresden, Hamburg, Paris and London. In many cases these were similar to those produced in Italy. But there was an evident tendency to modify the Italian type in directions determined by other ideas, so that German, French and English writers should be regarded somewhat by themselves, especially as operas in the languages of these countries now began to be numerous.

125. The Rise of the Neapolitan School. — The brilliance of the operatic development at Naples from about 1700 was due to the genius of a series of masters, of whom Alessandro Scarlatti was the first and one of the ablest. But behind this leadership lay an awakened popular enthusiasm under the influence of the four conservatories already mentioned (sec. 91), with possibly some stimulus from altered political conditions.

> The Kingdom of Naples, founded in the 13th century, was ruled by Spain throughout the 16th and 17th, often with much oppression. In the War of the Spanish Succession, Naples passed over to Austria (1707), and in 1735 regained its relative independence and its intellectual importance under Charles I.

Although data as to Scarlatti's early training are meagre, it is clear that he was thoroughly grounded in the harmonic and contrapuntal learning of his age and was able to handle it in traditional forms.   His eminence, however, was due to his gifts as a melodist and his instinct for the ordering of extended operatic works so as to achieve a maximum of sustained interest.   While not himself the inventor of the main types of operatic procedure, he is commonly regarded as the father of the completed opera seria — certainly one of its earliest and most successful exponents.   He was influential, also, as a teacher and the stimulator of other geniuses.   Thus around him grew up a circle of gifted artists, who together gave a memorable impetus to composition. Though the salient feature of the opera at this stage was its attention to affecting and distinctive melody, yet the structure of melody was still so closely associated with polyphonic procedure that broad musicianship was required at every point. It is noticeable that almost all the Neapolitan opera-writers were writers of noble church music as well, in styles that show their descent from the masters of the preceding century.

> **Alessandro Scarlatti** (d. 1725) was born in 1659 at Trapani (Sicily). He is supposed to have studied at one of the schools at Naples and also under Carissimi at Rome (before 1674).   In 1680 he produced an opera at Rome under the patronage of the well-known Christina, ex-queen of Sweden, whose choirmaster he was till 1689.   Soon after, he became choirmaster to the Spanish Viceroy at Naples, but returned to Rome in 1703 to assist Foggia at Sta. Maria Maggiore, succeeding him there in 1707.   In 1709 he went again to Naples, was visited there by Handel, was teacher at three of the conservatories successively, and was for a short time royal choirmaster under the new régime.   It is not clear that he ever traveled, except to visit Venice in 1707, where he produced two operas.   His musicianship was many-sided, for he was eminent as singer, harpsichordist, teacher, conductor and composer in every style then in use.   His most famous pupils were his son Domenico Scarlatti, Durante, Leo, Greco, Feo, Logroscino and Hasse.   His handling of the orchestra won the astonished praise of Corelli.   His methods and style

contributed much to Handel's development, and his works secured him universal renown among thoughtful critics.   His fertility of composition verges upon the incredible.   Besides his almost innumerable sacred works (including 200 masses), he wrote at least 115 operas (*Griselda*, 1721, being numbered 114), mostly for Naples, but some for Rome ; of these only about one-third are extant. Among the most famous are *La Rosaura* (1690), *Teodora* (1693), *La caduta de' Decemviri* (1697), *Laodicea e Berenice* (1701), *Il Medo* (1708) and *Tigrane* (1715).   While his usual plan included little more than a series of arias, with a rare duet or terzet, strung together with recitatives, without much dramatic continuity or special characterization of the personages, the vigor and beauty of his arias is generally notable, the recitatives are often fully accompanied, and the orchestral writing, especially for the

strings, is able and enterprising.   His liking for the *da capo* form of aria did much to establish that form.   Wind instruments he used sparingly, because not satisfied with their purity of intonation.   His overtures, usually in three movements, with a slow movement between two quick ones, fixed a type that rivaled that of Lully in popularity.   Besides his operas, he wrote many secular cantatas, serenatas and madrigals, besides a number of oratorios.

Other opera-writers of this early time were **Francesco Mancini** (d. 1739), a good teacher, assistant royal choirmaster from 1709 and chief from 1728, with 20 operas from 1697 (as *Ariovisto*, 1702) and 4 oratorios ;   **Domenico Sarri** (d. after 1741), Mancini's successor at court, with over 15 popular operas and some oratorios from 1702 (as *Didone abbandonata*, 1724) ;   **Domenico Scarlatti** (d. 1757), the great harpsichordist (see sec. 140), with a few operas from 1704 ; and **Nicola Fago** (d. c. 1736), an eminent teacher and sacred composer, with several operas from about 1709 (as *Eustachio*) and an oratorio.

Niccolò Porpora (d. 1766) was born at Naples in 1686 and studied at one of the conservatories under Greco and Mancini.   His first three operas appeared in 1709–11, including one at Rome.   About 1711 he began to be known as an expert singing-teacher, and the renown of his many pupils, like Farinelli, Caffarelli, Senesino and others, indicates his efficiency.   Later he resumed opera-writing, largely for Rome and Venice, and in 1733 was called to London to assist in the combination against Handel, but without great success.   From 1736 he was at the head of one of the music-schools of Venice, and from about 1745 taught at Vienna, where Haydn sought his help. From 1748 to 1750 he competed unsuccessfully with Hasse at Dresden, and ultimately returned to Naples.   Altogether he wrote about 45 operas and several oratorios, characterized by little real genius, though considerable cleverness, particularly in the orchestration.   Some solo cantatas rank higher because of their adaptation to the voice. He was a master of the art of vocalization, the typical exponent of the old Italian school of singing.

Other important singing-teachers were **Domenico Gizzi** (d. 1745), and his pupil **Francesco Feo** (d. after 1740), an accomplished composer of church music, 6 operas (1713–31) and an oratorio (1739), his learning and versatility giving him much renown.

Francesco Durante (d. 1755), though not himself a secular composer (see sec. 122), stands with Scarlatti and Leo as a leader in shaping the Neapolitan style, because under him as head of one of the conservatories were trained almost all the versatile opera-writers by whom that style became powerful throughout Europe. His influence told for clearness and elegance of melody, with attention to breadth and brilliance of general effect. He helped also to raise the standard of orchestral writing, especially as concerns the wind parts.

Leonardo Leo (d. 1744), born near Naples in 1694, pupil of Fago and Scarlatti at Naples and of Pitoni at Rome, won renown by an oratorio in 1712 and an opera in 1714, rapidly advanced as a teacher and was welcomed as a gifted composer. Among his many pupils were Pergolesi, Jommelli and Piccinni. Besides excellent sacred music (see sec. 122), he wrote about 60 operatic works, with a few oratorios, in a style of expressiveness and charm, rising often to grandeur and passion. His success extended to other Italian cities besides Naples. In the handling of the orchestra he surpassed Scarlatti, as well as in suavity of melody. He often utilized texts by librettists like Zeno and Metastasio.

Giuseppe Porsile (d. 1750), born at Naples, after serving for a short time at the Spanish court, from about 1711 was at Vienna, employed by the Empress Amalie. In 1715, at the suggestion of Fux, he entered the Imperial Chapel, where from 1720 he was 'composer.' His works (from 1719) were almost wholly dramatic, including perhaps 20 operas or similar works (as *Spartaco*, 1726) and 13 oratorios (as *Giuseppe riconosciuto*, 1733), all written for Vienna and representing a fusion of styles.

Leonardo Vinci (d. 1732), a pupil of Greco, for a time royal choirmaster at Naples, and finally a monk, left a surprising number of works, almost all dramatic (from 1719), which were very popular, especially at Naples and Venice. They include nearly 40 operas, the earlier comic (as *Lo cecato fauzo*, 1719), and the later serious (as *Ifigenia in Tauride* and *Astianatte*, 1725), besides oratorios and some church music.

Other composers after 1725 include **Girolamo Abos** (d. 1786), a pupil of Leo and Durante, with 14 operas (from 1730) at Naples, Venice, Rome, London, etc.; **Francesco Araja** (d. c. 1767), who was at St. Petersburg in 1735–59, with over 10 operas (from 1730), first at Florence, Rome and Venice, but mostly at the Russian court, including (1751–5) the first operas in Russian; **Gaetano Latilla** (d. c. 1789), pupil of Gizzi, for a time from 1738 choirmaster at Sta. Maria Maggiore in Rome and from 1756 teacher at Venice, later at Naples, with over 35 operas (from 1732); **Nicola Sala** (d. 1800), famous as a theorist (see sec. 165), with a few operas and oratorios (from 1737); **Giuseppe Scarlatti** (d. 1777), Alessandro's grandson, with 27 operas (from 1740) at Naples, Venice and Vienna; **Pasquale Cafaro** (d. 1787), pupil and successor

of Leo, with almost 20 operas and oratorios (from 1745) ; and the two Spaniards **Dominico Terradeglias** (d. 1751), pupil of Durante and choirmaster in
Rome, with 13 operas (from 1736) in Italy and at London, and **Davide
Perez** (d. after 1782), pupil of Mancini, from 1739 choirmaster at Palermo and
from 1752 at Lisbon, with about 30 operas (from 1740) at various places,
of which *Demetrio* (1752) and *Solimanno* (1757) were specially successful at
Lisbon.

It will be observed that gradually the vogue of Neapolitan
works spread far away from Naples. Leading composers were
beginning to travel more and Italians were in request at all musical centres in Germany and at London. Chief among these
apostles of the school was Jommelli, who for a time had great
renown from his many works for both theatre and church. He
brought an access of emotional intensity into the style that increased its dramatic power, broke up somewhat the formal regularity of its aria forms and improved some technical details.
The German Hasse matched him in fertility and in melodiousness, but fell below him in vigor and brilliance. In a distant
way, also, the far greater Handel belonged to this group, though
his early style was formed before he came in contact with the
Neapolitans and was always too individual to be treated with
theirs.

Nicola Jommelli (d. 1774) was born in 1714 near Naples, was trained there
in the schools, especially under Durante, Leo and Feo, and, besides some
slighter works, produced with success his first operas (1737-8), the earliest,
L'errore amoroso, under an assumed name. His sudden fame led to extensive
travels as a favorite opera-writer. At Rome from 1740 he was patronized by an
English noble, at Bologna in 1741 he came under Martini's influence in counterpoint, at Venice in 1741 and later he received honors from the Council and
began notable writing for the church, at Vienna in 1748 he was intimate with
Metastasio, and in 1749 he was again at Rome, for a time as choirmaster at
St. Peter's, producing much church music. From 1754 he was court-choirmaster at Stuttgart with extraordinary privileges and salary, and by his
abundant new works and his accomplished leadership made the musical
establishment famous. In 1769, however, the court interest having flagged,
he returned to Naples, bringing out several further operas, but with a startling want of success, due to the change of style that his long German
residence had produced. This failure shattered his health. Among his
about 50 dramatic works were *Ezio* (1741, Bologna), *Merope* (1741, Venice),
Eumene (1747, Naples), *Artaserse* (1749, Rome), *Achille in Sciro* (1749,
Vienna), *Ifigenia in Aulide* (1751, Rome), *Pelope* (1755, Stuttgart), *Alessandro* (1757), *Demofoonte* (1764) and *Armida* (1770, Naples). His style
was too dignified and forceful to serve well in comic works, and his best writing depended on the inspiration of a good text. Quite as important were his

church works, written in a smooth, thoughtful style, including some oratorios, as *Isacco* (1755), a Passion (1749), many masses, motets and cantatas, a famous *Laudate pueri* (1746), a great Requiem (1756), a Miserere (1774), etc. He also left some instrumental works, of much less value.

Johann Adolph Hasse (d. 1783) was older than Jommelli, but outlived him. He was born in 1699 near Hamburg, where he came under Keiser's influence. In 1721 he produced his first opera, *Antiochus* (German text), at Brunswick. In 1722 he went to Italy for a ten years' sojourn, receiving from the Neapolitans his permanent style, partly from Alessandro Scarlatti himself, and writing operas for both Naples (from 1723) and Venice.   In 1730 he married the prima donna *Faustina Bordoni* (d. 1781), to whom much of his later success was due. From 1731 he was court-choirmaster at Dresden, enjoying great local honor and having leave frequently to travel, as to London in 1735 (to compete with Handel), in 1740 to Paris, in 1746 to Munich, in 1753 to Berlin, besides many trips to Italy, everywhere in request as a popular favorite. In 1748-50 occurred a series of operatic contests with Porpora at Dresden.   In 1760, in the siege by the Prussians, his property was destroyed, including most of the MSS. for a complete edition of his works.   From 1764, the Saxon Chapel being broken up, he moved to Vienna, continuing composition, and from 1773 lived in Venice, where he died. At Dresden he was often visited by Bach, at Vienna he came into rivalry with Gluck, and at Milan along with his last opera, *Ruggiero* (1771), was given a serenata by the boy Mozart. His fertility was enormous, touching almost all branches of composition, though slight in contrapuntal forms. He essayed every variety of Catholic church music, and was prolific in sonatas and concertos for harpsichord, small orchestra or solo instruments — most of these without distinction, though always fluent and graceful. His dramatic works included some 10 oratorios and about 70 operas. He set about 25 librettos by Metastasio, some of them twice or thrice over. His more famous operas were *Sesostrate* (1726), *Attalo* (1728), *Artaserse* (1730, '40), *Arminio* (1731, '45), *Alessandro* (1731), *La clemenza di Tito* (1737, '59) and the intermezzo *Piramo e Thisbe* (1769). His style was melodious and singable rather than marked by dramatic or structural vigor. Its success was due to its perfect adaptation to the taste of the time.

Ignazio Fiorillo (d. 1787), a pupil of Leo and Durante, after some years of wandering, with operas at Venice and Milan from 1736, was from 1754 choirmaster at Brunswick and in 1762-80 at Cassel.   He wrote some 14 operas in a style resembling Hasse's, besides church music. Another composer of the same class was **Giovanni Battista Lampugnani** (d. c. 1790), a Milanese who succeeded Galuppi at London in 1744 and lived at Milan from 1770, writing in all about 20 operas (from 1737).

While the Neapolitans were thus developing the opera, especially on its melodic side, the later writers of the Venetian school were not idle, though their numerous works added little to real progress.

Among the composers already mentioned (sec. 90) who worked on into the 18th century were **M. A. Ziani** (d. 1715), **Perti** (d. 1756, no operas after

1717), **Lotti** (d. 1740, no operas after about 1720), **C. F. Polaroli** (d. 1722), **Ariosti** (d. c. 1740) and **Caldara** (d. 1736).

Besides these the following should be mentioned : —

Giovanni Battista Bononcini (d. c. 1750), the ablest of the three composers of the family, lived a long and checkered life, of which the details are in part obscure. Born about 1660 at Modena, trained at Bologna, where in 1688 he was choirmaster, and connected with the court music at Vienna in 1691-1711, he was also at Rome, Berlin and other cities before 1716, when he was called to London first as Handel's operatic colleague, later as his bitter rival. In 1731, being convicted of plagiarizing from Lotti, he left London, moved from place to place, and was last heard of at Vienna and Venice. He was a clever writer along conventional lines, with some gifts as a melodist. His works include over 30 operas, of which the series in London are the best, from *Astarto* (1720) to *Astianatte* (1727), several oratorios (as *Ezechia*, 1737), some church music, cantatas and many instrumental pieces.

Francesco Gasparini (d. 1727), pupil of Corelli and Pasquini at Rome, from about 1700 chorusmaster at one of the Venetian conservatories, wrote about 50 operas (from 1694). **Luc'Antonio Predieri** (d. 1769), a leader in the Accademia filarmonica at Bologna and probably choirmaster at the cathedral, from 1739 assistant choirmaster at Vienna and from 1747 chief, and from 1751 at Naples on a pension, produced 14 operas (from 1711), largely for Italian theatres. Among the Venetians were **Giovanni Porta** (d. 1755), at first a teacher at Venice, from 1720 in London, and from 1738 choirmaster at Munich, with about 30 operas (as *Numitore*, 1720, London) ; **Giovanni Battista Pescetti** (d. 1766), pupil of Lotti, active in London in 1737-40, but principally associated with Venice, finally as organist at St. Mark's, with about 10 (from 1726) ; and **Fortunato Chelleri** (d. 1757), brought up at Piacenza, where his first opera was produced (1707), followed by about 15 more (till 1722) at various Italian cities and in Spain, and from 1725 court-choirmaster at Cassel.

At Vienna were also notable the contrapuntist **Fux** (d. 1741), with nearly 30 dramatic works (from 1702), the strongest being oratorios ; **Francesco Conti** (d. 1732), from 1713 court-composer, with even more (from 1706) ; **Josef Bonno** (d. 1788), court-composer from 1739, with about 20 (from 1732) ; and **G. C. Wagenseil** (d. 1777), the clavier-virtuoso, in the imperial service from 1739, with perhaps 10 (from 1740). (See secs. 121, 140.)

At Munich were **Pietro Torri** (d. 1737), from 1689 court-organist and the successor of Bernabei as choirmaster, with about 25 operas (from 1690) ; and **Andrea Bernasconi** (d. 1784), born at Marseilles and educated at Parma, but first known as an opera-writer at Vienna (1738) and Venice (1741), from 1753 at Munich and in 1755 Porta's successor, with about 20 operas, chiefly for Munich, besides considerable church music.

With Breslau are associated **Antonio Bioni** (d. after 1739), pupil of Porta, opera-director from 1726, with about 25 operas (from 1721) ; and **Daniel Gottlieb Treu** (d. 1749), born at Stuttgart, pupil of Vivaldi at Venice, choirmaster at Breslau from 1725, at Prague from 1727, and at Hirschberg from 1740, with about 15 operas, besides other works.

126. The Opera Buffa. — Soon after 1730 the many experiments with the comic opera, which had been going on from the opening of the century, attained signal importance. Comic pieces had long been used as intermezzi, slipped in for sheer diversion between the acts of the opera seria. Often two utterly disconnected works were thus united at a single performance, an opera seria in three or more acts interlarded with an opera buffa in two or more acts — producing an anomalous dramatic mixture. These humorous pieces had been esteemed lightly, but now they began to compete upon more equal terms with the opera proper, especially because in them the conventional restrictions were not applied. The number and disposition of the characters in the cast were elastic, the low voices, especially basses, were favored, piquant dialogue and acting were essential, with vivacious differentiation of the personages, concerted numbers and climaxes in ensemble were in demand — in short, the type came to be as much vitalized by dramatic sense as the serious opera was dominated by the spirit of the concert. The popular and artistic success of some of these works tended to diversify and revolutionize the prevailing notion of the opera in general. Thus, from a source at first unrespected, began the reclamation of the opera to its true dramatic mission. The impulse was given by certain Neapolitans, followed by several who belong rather to the Venetian group.

Giovanni Battista Pergolesi (d. 1736, aged 26), born at Naples, after study with Greco, Durante and Feo, appeared from 1731 as the composer of an oratorio, 2 operas, 2 intermezzi, some string-trios and a grand mass for 10 voices. Besides writing much church music, in 1733 he scored an epoch-making triumph with the comedy *La serva padrona*, though it was drafted with but two characters in the cast and a simple string-accompaniment. No others of his 14 operatic works, about half of them comedies, were notably successful during his brief life, because of the delicacy of their workmanship, but were later revived to some extent. But his exquisite sense of characterization and his novel evolution of melody from simple harmonies did much to indicate dramatic possibilities. His career was cut short by consumption while he was working on his Stabat Mater. He left some important trio-sonatas.

Egidio Romoaldo Duni (d. 1775), a pupil of Durante, competed successfully with Pergolesi at Rome with his *Nerone* (1735), traveled widely as an opera-writer, and finally (from 1755) took up the French operetta, first at Parma and then at Paris, with such clever adaptation to popular taste that he is often called the founder of the opéra bouffe. He wrote over 30 works.

Nicola Logroscino (d. 1763) was also one of Durante's pupils, but nothing is known of him until 1738, when the series of his over 20 operas, all comedies except one (1750), began.   In 1747 he went to Palermo as a teacher of counterpoint, but later returned.   His special contribution to the advancing opera buffa was the climacteric ensemble at the close of the acts, which was later introduced into serious opera.   Among his best works were *Il Governatore* (1747) and *Il vecchio marito*.   He preferred subjects that were farcically humorous, and wrote almost exclusively in the Neapolitan dialect.   His works retained their vogue till displaced by those of Piccinni.

Giovanni Alberto Ristori (d. 1753), born at Bologna, made his entire career outside of Italy, being engaged from 1715 at Dresden.   He was an accomplished player on the organ and harpsichord, besides writing freely in secular and sacred forms.   Among his 15 or more dramatic works, the comic operas *Calandro* (1716) and *Don Chiscotte* (1727) are notable.

Baldassare Galuppi (d. 1785), born near Venice, was from 1722 a pupil of Lotti and the organist of various churches.   He was also a clavier-virtuoso. His first opera (1722, Vicenza) failed, but showed his gifts as a buffo writer. In 1729, however, *Dorinda* made a hit at Venice, and further works were extremely popular.   From 1741 he was in London, where airs from his works were in demand.   Except for two sojourns in Russia (1743–8, 1765–8), the rest of his life was spent at Venice, where from 1748 he was second choirmaster at St. Mark's and in 1762–5 chief.   His 115 operas had a great vogue.   About one-third of them were comic (mostly after 1750), and their verve and jollity won for him the name of 'the father of the opera buffa.'   He also wrote church music and some interesting instrumental pieces (see sec. 148).

127. The Opera in France. — No special progress took place in French opera during the first third of the century.   The works of Lully continued to be regarded as typical, with some additions by Destouches and especially Campra.   But popular interest in the serious opera was constantly hindered by the craving for scenic divertissements of an ephemeral sort.   The styles in vogue varied from the 'ballet' or dance-spectacle, with its accent upon studied alternations of movements set to brilliant orchestral accompaniments, or the 'intermède' and 'vaudeville,' which were often analogous to the German singspiel or the English ballad-opera, up to the later 'opéra comique,' in which genuine dramatic interest was developed by the essential humor of the plot or the text, often treated to some extent through spoken dialogue.   The glitter of costuming and staging, the sensuous charm of dancing evolutions and the catchy lilt of light song were far more prized than noble or impassioned declamation, sustained arias, well-considered scenes or dramatic force and unity in the whole.   What gains there were lay in increased skill with accompaniments and in a more piquant handling of the voices. It is notable that many writers of operas at this period were drawn from the ranks of the orchestra. The dominant composer after 1735 was Rameau.

While the serious opera had its home under royal patronage at the *Académie* (later the *Grand Opéra*), several other theatres became exceedingly popular, like the fluctuating *Théâtres de la foire* and the more established *Comédie Française* and *Comédie Italienne* (the forerunners of the *Opéra-Comique*).

Several of the opera-writers already named (see sec. 85) produced works after 1700, notably **Campra** (mostly before 1718) and **Destouches** (till 1726). To these the following may be added : —

Jean Claude Gillier (d. 1737), a violinist at the Comédie Française, brought out perhaps 20 operettas (from 1696), of which *Les dieux de la foire* (1724) and *Sancho Pança* (1727) are examples. They did much to fix the taste of the Parisian public for the light style.

Baptistin Stuck (d. 1755), born at Florence of German parents, was long employed as 'cellist by the court and at the Opéra, being a pioneer on his instrument in the operatic orchestra. He wrote some 20 operettas, ballets and operas (from 1709), notably *Méléagre* (1709), *Manto la fée* (1711) and *Polydore* (1720), with many solo cantatas (from 1706).

Other temporarily popular composers in the light vein were **Joseph Mouret** (d. 1738, insane), from 1707 in the service of the Duchess of Maine, later conductor of the Concerts spirituels and composer to the Comédie Italienne (works from 1711) ; **Jean Baptiste Maurice Quinault** (d. 1744), in 1712-33 an actor and stage-singer at the Comédie Française (many works, one produced at the Opéra, 1728) ; **Colin de Blamont** (d. 1760), superintendent of music at Versailles from 1719, with over 15 ballets (from 1721), solo cantatas and some chamber suites ; and several instrumentalists, like **Jacques Aubert** (d. 1753), with several ballets, etc. (from 1713), and **Michel Pignolet de Montéclair** (d. 1737), the pioneer double-bassist.

François Francœur (d. 1787) and **François Rebel** (d. 1775), both first appearing as boy-violinists at the Opéra in 1710 and 1714 respectively, were life-long friends and collaborateurs in a series of court offices, including the supervision of the Opéra from 1736, and produced jointly 10 operas (from 1726), such as *Pyrame et Thisbé* (1726) and *Tarsis et Julie* (1728), which were the vogue for a time. Francœur also wrote some violin-sonatas.

Jean Philippe Rameau (d. 1764), born at Dijon in 1683, was a precocious clavier-player, attracting attention when but 7 years old. After a good general education and becoming noted as an organist, at 18 he was sent to Italy, but was uninterested in Italian music. After visiting Paris in 1705 and touring in southern France as a violinist in an opera-troupe, in 1717 he went to Paris, where he studied with Marchand, but soon incurred his jealousy. For a time he was organist at Lille and Clermont, devoting himself to theoretical study and the writing of church works and clavier-pieces. Returning to Paris in 1721, he steadily advanced in reputation, though his views on harmony were too novel to be readily accepted, and became recognized as the foremost

French organist. Under wealthy patronage he first attempted a Biblical
opera (libretto by Voltaire), which was not accepted at the Opéra, and his
Hippolyte et Aricie (1733), though undeniably powerful, so far failed that he
almost gave up dramatic writing. From 1735 till 1760, however, he wrote
opera after opera with increasing success, *Castor et Pollux* (1737), *Dardanus*
(1739) and *Zoroastre* (1749) being the largest, with nearly 20 others of the
ballet-opera type, of which *Les Indes galantes* (1735) was the most popular.
Gradually his prestige displaced that of Lully, though their styles were not
radically different. Both used much declamatory recitative, many dance-num-
bers, the tripartite overture, many arias with more decoration than organic
strength, etc. Lully had the keener dramatic sense, but Rameau was musically
more gifted. He also made a freer use of the chorus. He was beset by
continual controversy and intrigue, but his industry and vigor were unflagging.
(For his other works, see secs. 138, 141.)

Other names are **Jean Joseph Cassanea de Mondonville** (d. 1772), a violinist
from 1737, leader at the Concerts spirituels and from 1755 conductor, in the
royal band and from 1745 at its head, with 9 light operas, 3 oratorios and
some motets (from 1742); **Jean Jacques Rousseau** (d. 1778), the philosopher
and theorist (see sec. 141), of whose few dramatic works (from 1745) *Le
devin du village* (1752) achieved a signal success, while his later *Pygmalion*
(1770) became the prototype of the melodrama, both being marked by melodic beauty; **Antoine Dauvergne** (d. 1797), a violinist at the court and the
Opéra from about 1740 and Mondonville's successor at the Concerts spirituels in 1762, with 15 works (from 1752), chief of which were *Les troqueurs*
(1753), usually called the first opéra comique (with spoken dialogue), *Énée et
Lavinie* (1758), etc.; and the Italian **Duni** (d. 1775), who arrived in 1755 and
exerted a strong influence on the opéra bouffe in general (see sec. 126).

In 1752 broke out the curious strife between Italian and French partisans, known as the 'Guerre des buffons,' which was occasioned by the
advent of an Italian troupe with their own repertory of works and with
singers trained in the fine art of vocalization. Their side was championed by the critics Grimm, Diderot and Rousseau, and the court, the
press and the public for two years or more were sharply divided into two
parties, between which the literary and social antagonism was intense
(expressed, for instance, in some 60 pamphlets). The Italians ranged
themselves under the name of the queen, the French under that of the
king, and each sought by every means to discredit the other. The
French party ultimately triumphed and the historic opéra comique followed. In this contest a prominent figure was *Jean Georges Noverre* (d.
1810), known throughout Europe as a dancer, who strengthened the
dramatic quality of the ballet and wrote a noted book on dancing (1760).

128. The Opera in Germany. — It seems as if Hamburg should
have led in significant operatic progress in northern Europe,
since there were brought together the singspiel, the Italian
opera and certain French ideas as to instrumental music. It is
true that in some cases German opera-writers showed dra-

matic force, vigorous harmonic structure, based on sound contrapuntal experience, and a virile use of the orchestra, but as a
rule they surrendered themselves to a facile copying of Italian
melodious conventionality.   In details the German style differed
somewhat from the Italian, but in general spirit and method it
tended to treat composition as a stereotyped trick which could
be learned by any one once for all.   Hence became common a
lifeless, but outwardly correct, style which is often called that
of the ' zopf ' or ' perruque ' — an official, perfunctory, mechanical style.   This was not wholly bad or useless, since it favored the
wide extension of many sorts of works in many places, but in
historical perspective it seems tame and flat.   Much that has
already been noted really belongs to this monotonous class.
Unfortunately, the tendency of the Hamburg circle was mainly
toward making it universal in Germany.   It was from this that
Bach turned in discouragement, from which Handel vigorously
broke away, and against which at length came a revolt in the
second half of the century.   Until that time there was little
German opera of distinctive quality.

Brief reference, however, is due certain composers of renown, if not all of
much originality : —

Both **Mattheson** (d. 1764) and **Telemann** (d. 1767), already named as industrious church writers (sec. 120), wrote operas from about 1700, the former
sparingly and with angularity, the latter freely and superficially.   Of Mattheson's 8, the chief were *Cleopatra* (1704) and *Henrico IV.* (1711), and of Telemann's 40 or more, *Damon* (1724), *Flavius Bertaridus* (1729) and *Genserich*
(1732).   Telemann also wrote at least 600 overtures!   His wide popularity
led many lesser writers to imitate his style.

The relation of **Keiser** (d. 1739) to the Hamburg opera, his fertility and his
power have already been noted (secs. 87, 120).   From him the youthful
Handel received in 1703-6 an impulse to dramatic work that bore immediate
fruit (see sec. 129).   In a limited sense, therefore, Handel belongs to the
Hamburg group, though he had no later connection with it except as he gave
one of his Passions there in 1716.

Christoph Graupner (d. 1760), almost exactly contemporary with Handel,
had a similar connection with Hamburg.   After training under Schelle and
Kuhnau at Leipsic, in 1706-9 he was in Keiser's orchestra as cembalist, and
then went to Darmstadt, where in 1712 he succeeded Briegel as choirmaster.
In 1722 he was one of the aspirants for the cantorate of the Thomasschule at
Leipsic, and would have been appointed before Bach came into the competition had not his Darmstadt patron objected.   In 1750, like Handel, he became
totally blind — the penalty of excessive application, partly to music-engraving.
He was enormously prolific, especially in church music (1300 pieces left in

MS. at Darmstadt), and in works for harpsichord and orchestra. Early in his
career he also wrote about 10 operas (1707-11, '19), mostly at Hamburg. His
genius was much admired and was certainly above the average.

Gottfried Heinrich Stölzel (d. 1749), the eminent church composer (see sec.
120), produced over 20 operas (1711-23) at Breslau, Naumburg, Prague, Bayreuth and Gotha, among which *Valeria* (1712) was specially popular. He
united learning with a gift of tunefulness, which he cultivated by travel in
Italy.

Karl Heinrich Graun (d. 1759) was the remaining prominent opera-writer of
the time, though, like Stölzel, not directly connected with Hamburg (see sec.
120). His operas numbered over 30 (from 1726), chiefly for Berlin, where he
was director under Frederick the Great, whose taste was imperious for French
and Italian styles, and who himself edited many librettos and often contributed
some numbers. Popular examples after the erection of the new opera-house
in 1742 were *Artaserse* (1743), *Catone in Utica* (1744), *Adriano in Siria*
(1745), *Demofoonte* (1746), etc. Graun's style resembled Hasse's in agreeable
melody and clever workmanship.

129. Handel.—The historic position of Handel is peculiar. To
a certain degree he appears, like Bach, as a natural consummation
of movements that had been long in progress in Italy and Germany, since he stands out as the most powerful opera-writer in
the early Italian manner, and was also an organ contrapuntist in
the direct German line. But the final application of his energetic and sturdy genius to the oratorio was unprecedented, and
the fact that this took place in England and acquired concentrated influence there has linked him closely with modern choral
music. Although he was keenly alive to the dominant tendencies of his age and facile with conventional writing for immediate
popular success, he also often broke through traditions with the
confident independence that betokens original conviction and
creative invention of high order. The circumstances of his
career developed artistic characteristics very different from those
of Bach, setting him in another category, artistically not so high,
but practically for a long time more effective. His individual
works usually do not bear such minute analysis as those of Bach,
but his popular impress has been infinitely greater and in its
sphere thoroughly healthy and noble. Certainly he towers in
dignity above all others of his contemporaries except Bach.

Georg Friedrich Handel (d. 1759) was born in 1685 at Halle. [The family
name was properly Händel, later commonly anglicized into Handel.] There
is no record of musical ability among his ancestors. He was the son of a respected surgeon and his second wife (28 years younger), the daughter of a
Lutheran pastor. His father destined him for the law, but the boy's eager-

U

ness for music was irrepressible, and finally, after attracting the notice of one
of the father's patrons, was met by careful instruction under the organist Zachau

(d. 1712). His mastery of playing
(clavier, organ, violin and oboe) and
of strict composition was rapid. At 11
(1696) he was taken to Berlin as a
prodigy. From 1697, his father having
died, his education was guided by his
mother, a quiet and earnest woman.
In 1702 he entered the new University
of Halle, besides becoming organist at
the cathedral. In these early years he
is said to have written much, but few
traces of this remain. In 1703, in search
of experience, he entered Keiser's orchestra at Hamburg as second violin.
Soon he appeared as a composer, producing 4 operas, *Almira* (1704) being
the first, besides winning applause as
an organist. Becoming intimate with
Mattheson, they went together in 1703
to Lübeck to visit the aged Buxtehude. In 1704 he produced his first Passion.
The same year, after a quarrel with Mattheson, he narrowly escaped being
killed by the latter in a duel. After about three years he betook himself to
Italy for further operatic work.

His Italian sojourn extended from 1707 to 1710, with repeated stays at
Florence, Venice, Rome and Naples. Everywhere he was honored by musicians, patrons and the public. He wrote some notable church music, 2 immensely successful operas, *Rodrigo* (1707, Florence) and *Agrippina* (1708,
Venice), and 2 Italian oratorios. His style became externally accommodated
to Italian traditions, though without sacrificing its native freshness and force.
In 1710, returning to Germany and introduced by Steffani, he succeeded him
as choirmaster to the Elector of Hanover, with leave for further travel. Proceeding at once to London, he made a hit with *Rinaldo* (1711), followed on a
second visit by *Teseo* (1713) and later by a few other dramatic works. In 1713
he began writing sacred music to English words, especially the so-called
Utrecht Te Deum and *Jubilate*. In 1714, at the sudden death of Queen Anne,
the Elector succeeded as George I., and Handel was for a time in disgrace both
for his long absence from Hanover and for his part in the Utrecht celebration,
which the new king disapproved. In 1715, however, regaining favor, he was
assigned court salaries that continued till his death. In 1716 he composed
his second Passion for Hamburg. Till 1719 or 1720 he was choirmaster to
the wealthy Duke of Chandos, producing a noble set of anthems, his first
English oratorio *Esther* (1720), the serenata *Acis and Galatea* (1720) and
some harpsichord-pieces. His power as a choral writer was already clearly
visible.

In 1720 an aristocratic stock-company, The Royal Academy of Music, was
formed to give operas, with Handel and G. B. Bononcini as directors, and a

powerful troupe. For this Handel wrote 14 operas, including *Radamisto* (1720), *Muzio Scevola* (1721, 3d act only, the others being by Bononcini and Mattei), *Ottone* (1722), *Tamerlano* (1724), *Rodelinda* (1725), *Scipione* (1726), *Alessandro* (1726), etc. From 1721 the bitter rivalry between him and Bononcini was taken up by numerous partisans, became entangled with the political antipathy between Whigs and Tories, was inflamed by intrigues and competitions between leading singers, especially Senesino and the prime donne Cuzzoni and Bordoni (later Hasse's wife), finally led to disgraceful riots in the theatre, and in 1728 ruined the enterprise. Handel's self-respect then impelled him to organize a company of his own, for which he wrote 13 more operas, including *Lotario* (1729), *Poro* (1731), *Ezio* (1732), *Arianna* (1733), and several pasticcios and hasty works. The hostility of Bononcini, backed by the prominent Marlboroughs, led in 1733 to the formation of a rival company, to which Senesino deserted, and in which, after Bononcini's disgrace, Porpora, Hasse and other famous opera-writers coöperated. In 1737 the two enterprises ruined each other, Handel losing all his savings and suffering a partial stroke of paralysis. In his efforts to hold his public he had revived *Esther* with dramatic action, also *Acis and Galatea*, had produced the oratorios *Deborah* and *Athaliah* (both 1733), and had also written fine court anthems and considerable instrumental music.

He was now 53 years old. From this time he practically gave up operatic music, turning with a sure instinct to oratorios. He now produced about 15 choral works, on which his modern renown almost wholly rests, including *Saul* (1739), *Israel in Egypt* (1739), the serenata *L'Allegro, etc.* (1740), *The Messiah* (1742), *Samson* (1743), *Judas Maccabæus* (1747), *Joshua* (1748), *Solomon* (1749), *Theodora* (1750) and *Jephtha* (1752) — *The Messiah* being produced on a concert-tour to Dublin. These works vary in method, the majority being modeled in dramatic form, while *Israel in Egypt* is unique for its gigantic series of pictorial ' plague ' choruses, and *The Messiah*, following its masterly libretto (by Charles Jennens), is almost wholly contemplative and devotional. In them all the choral numbers are lifted to a chief place and developed with extraordinary variety and vigor, thus constituting a musical type of great importance. The appeal of these works to English religious feeling and their eminent intrinsic value secured for them not only immediate popularity, but an enduring influence upon subsequent English composers. Their recognition by Continental critics was slow, however, so that their general influence came much later. In his later years Handel's enemies disappeared and his powers as composer, conductor and organist were universally acknowledged. In 1753 he became almost totally blind, but continued active till within ten days of his death. He was buried in Westminster Abbey with notable public honor.

Personally, Handel was bluff and hearty, much inclined to society and with keen insight into character. He was blunt, outspoken, sometimes caustic, yet generous and strictly honorable. His handling of singers and players was imperious, but often shrewd and clever. As life progressed, his inborn German seriousness became more apparent, and it is clear that his religious works were expressions of earnest conviction and feeling. He was an indefatigable worker and in composition exceedingly rapid, since his command of resources was absolute and his flow of invention unlimited. He accumulated a considerable fortune, and was never married. From 1726 he was a naturalized British subject.

130. His Style and Significance. — Since Handel lived through the whole first half of the century, he was contemporary with all the masters who have been considered. Yet his contact with most of them was casual or altogether lacking. His youth was spent in the atmosphere of German church music and the Hamburg opera. In Italy for a time he was intimate with musicians at Venice, Rome and Naples. Later he made several hurried trips to the Continent in search of singers. Many good performers worked under him in London, and a few composers competed with him. Up to the middle of his career he was probably cognizant of the chief tendencies of the operatic world.

> The closest personal influences upon Handel in Germany came from Zachau, his first teacher, from the Hamburg triumvirate, Keiser, Mattheson and Telemann, though only the first was old enough to be significant, and from Steffani, who was a close friend for years. In Italy he certainly met Lotti, Corelli and the two Scarlattis, competing with Domenico on the harpsichord and organ. The Neapolitan school was then only just taking shape. In England he must have encountered the memory of Purcell's career, which had ended 15 years before his arrival. Just prior to his coming a few Italian operas had been given in London (M. A. Bononcini's *Camilla* in 1706 and *Almahide* in 1710, Scarlatti's *Pirro e Demetrio* in 1708, Mancini's *Idaspe* in 1710, G. B. Bononcini's *Etearco* in 1711), besides several nondescript pasticcios. At intervals afterward various Italian composers were represented at London, usually in rivalry to Handel, as Dom. Scarlatti (*Narcisso*, 1719), Porta (*Numitore*, 1720), G. B. Bononcini (seven works, 1720–7), Ariosti (seven, 1723–7), Porpora (four or more, 1733–5, '42), Hasse (a few from 1734), Galuppi (1741–3), Lampugnani (1743–5), Gluck (1746) and Terradeglias (1746–7). The predominating school in vogue was certainly the Neapolitan.

Granting whatever may be necessary for the bent given him at Hamburg and in Italy and for the influence of his later conditions, his development was mainly an independent one, guided by his own desires and the possibilities of his public. He was fortunate in choosing to work in England, where traditions were unformed. This made it possible to deal freely with all forms and to devise new ones. Hence he was able to be the founder of a special English tradition which still continues. But his comparative isolation kept his works from being widely known elsewhere and delayed the full recognition of his genius.

Handel was first of all a dramatic musician, his ambition centring upon the opera. Under this impulse he took such forms as his age provided, such librettos as he could get, and then put his music together as he thought dramatic effectiveness required. His originality was shown more in the essential truth, beauty and energy of particular numbers than in any remodeling of accepted methods. His resources of melody were unrestricted, evolved out of a complex, nervous harmony, rather than from a simple chord-scheme, as in later writers. He much excelled his contemporaries in characterization, embodying in phrase, movement and figure the general quality and the personal reactions of a dramatic situation. And his instinct for arrangement was unerring, so that effective contrasts and climaxes were never wanting. His operas are no longer known because based on poor librettos and written in an obsolete musical and dramatic dialect, but, measured by the standards of their own time, they were masterly.

> The full list of his operas (1704-41) includes over 40 full operas, over 10 pasticcios, and several serenatas. The subjects are almost all from classical mythology or history, with some from mediæval romance. The librettos came from various hands — 7 each by *Paolo Rolli* and *Niccolò Francesco Haym* (d. 1729), 3 by *Metastasio*, 1-2 each by 10 others, with some unassigned.

The step from the opera to the oratorio was a short one, since Handel's notion of the oratorio was primarily dramatic and not liturgical. He transferred to it precisely the same methods, except in the one feature of the chorus. He perceived that in a concert-form the chorus was feasible as it was not in the theatre, and that for the expression of the profound and collective emotions of religion its use on a grand scale was inevitable. Here he applied the resources of his contrapuntal skill with a lucidity, breadth and sublimity seldom since surpassed. This fusion of the dramatic recitative and aria with the ecclesiastical motet, being made by one who was at once a veteran popular musician and a truly devout man, resulted in a new composite type for the English oratorio that has ever since persisted. Although much of his success in this field was due to the excellence of some of his librettos, his masterly use of choral means — not so original or learned as Bach's, but far more immediately effective — gives his works of this class a commanding interest.

His oratorios, including a few early works, number about 20, and to these may well be added one or two of the serenatas (especially *L'Allegro*, in spite of its jocularity in part) and a few of the larger church works. His principal librettists were *Chas. Jennens* and *Thos. Morell*, but the pith of two works (*Samson* and *L'Allegro*) came from Milton, and other poets, like Dryden, Pope and Gay, were represented. The substance of most of the works was, of course, Biblical.

It would be quite impossible to mention all the noted singers to whom much of Handel's popular success was due, but a brief enumeration of some may be of interest. In addition to the two mezzo-sopranos, **Francesca Cuzzoni** (d. 1770), in London in 1722–8 and 1734, and **Faustina Bordoni** (d. 1781), in London in 1726–8, whose rivalry lasted about 20 years, the most famous male sopranists were **Antonio Bernacchi** (d. 1756), in London in 1716–7 and 1729–30, later a great teacher at Bologna, **Senesino** [Francesco Bernardi] (d. c. 1750), in London in 1720–7 and 1730–5, finally engaged against Handel, **Giovanni Carestini** (d. 1760), in London in 1733–5, **Gioacchino Conti** (d. 1761), in London in 1736, and (in the hostile company) two pupils of Porpora, **Farinelli** [Carlo Broschi] (d. 1782), in London in 1734–6, later in court service at Madrid, and **Caffarelli** [Gaetano Marjorano] (d. 1783), in London in 1738. These last were life-long rivals for the highest place in the operatic world.

These are but examples of the many singers of the age whose dexterity as vocalists and interpreters made them long renowned.

It remains to refer to Handel's services to instrumental music. He was a superior organist, and to most of his oratorio performances contributed what were called ' concertos,' partly probably extemporaneous, partly later published. These works are distinctly concertistic, rather than churchly, and they stand detached from the German school, to which they technically belong, in their disregard of chorale-material. He used the orchestra of his day with dramatic variety and power, in accompaniments, in many overtures and in some incidental numbers. Without distinctly advancing established forms, he brought into them the freshness of idea, effectiveness of plan and vigor of treatment that marked his vocal writing. His clavier style was much less important, though often interesting.

In all, he wrote some 70 overtures, usually on the French plan. The orchestra as he found it was much stronger in the wood-wind than is now common, and the harpsichord or organ far more indispensable. Unfortunately for historic accuracy, several of his best-known works have been greatly modified by later adapters (as, notably, *The Messiah* by Mozart in 1789).

A special word should be added about the charges of plagiarism that have been made against Handel. It is clear that he occasionally

adapted whole passages from other composers to his own uses, just as he
transferred sections from one to another of his original works. But it
was an age in which pasticcios or medleys abounded, strict creativeness
being subordinated to concertistic success. We may doubt whether
Handel's intent was deceptive, and surely there is no doubt about his
capacity for origination. Many of the cases are merely those of ' borrowed
subjects,' which was and is an established artistic practice.

131. The English Ballad-Opera. — Incidentally connected with
the general course of musical events, though in itself insignificant, was the appearance in Handel's time of a kind of English
singspiel, called the 'ballad-opera.' This was an amusing,
often satirical, play in which well-known popular songs or similar
numbers were strung together by a spoken dialogue into a loosely
connected story. Essentially it was an inferior sort of comic
opera, and its popularity from 1728 interfered with the success
of more serious music. Most of the writers in this style, however,
contributed also to others.

In all, about 45 ballad-operas were produced in a little over 15 years.
Around the mention of their arrangers may be grouped some notes of other
dramatic music in Handel's period : —

John Christopher Pepusch (d. 1752), born at Berlin, came from the Royal
Chapel there to London in 1700 as cembalist and compiler of Italian music at
the Drury Lane Theatre. In 1710 he founded a society for the study of the
older composers, and from 1712 preceded Handel in the service of the Duke
of Chandos. From 1715 he brought out several masques and later 3
ballad-operas, of which *The Beggar's Opera* (1728, words by Gay) was the
first of the style. From 1737 he was organist at the Charterhouse. His
musicianship was excellent, as his *Harmony* (1730) shows, but his invention
was slight.

Johann Ernst Galliard (d. 1749), another German, pupil of Steffani at
Hanover, was teacher in the royal family under Queen Anne and succeeded
G. B. Draghi as court-organist. Besides some church music and many in-
strumental pieces, he produced the opera *Calypso* (1712), from 1717 a number
of masques or pantomimes (somewhat akin to the ballad-operas), and left an
Italian opera in MS. In 1742 he translated Tosi's work on Figured Song.

Henry Carey (d. 1743), often called the author of "God Save the King," a
music-teacher in London, was from 1715 both librettist and composer of many
successful ballad-operas and similar works. He was one of several able
satirists of the bombastic style current in the Italian opera.

John Christopher Smith (d. 1795), the son of a German who came to England
in 1716 to be Handel's assistant, was Handel's pupil, later his organist, copyist
and conductor, the legatee of his MSS., and the author of *Anecdotes* about
him (1799). From 1732 he wrote several operas in Italian or English (as
The Tempest, 1756), and also oratorios (as *Paradise Lost*, 1758), besides clavier-
pieces.

Thomas Augustine Arne (d. 1778), the most fertile of the series, was born in London in 1710. From 1733 he wrote numerous operas, masques and other dramatic works, of which *Artaxerxes* (1762) is counted the best, though the masque *Comus* (1738), the oratorio *Abel* (1743) and some lighter pieces were very successful. In his oratorio *Judith* (1761) women-singers were used in the chorus for the first time. He was essentially a song-writer, but he cultivated all styles up to the Italian recitative and the florid aria. His settings of some of Shakespeare's songs are classic.

The English colonies in America, being in constant communication with the mother-country, naturally copied many features of its social life. Thus English ballad-operas and similar half-musical entertainments began to be given in a few American cities certainly from 1735, if not earlier, and became fairly frequent after 1750.

The first ballad-opera drafted in America was *The Disappointment* (1767), the libretto (by Andrew Barton) involving the use of 18 popular airs. The projected performance of this at Philadelphia was given up because its satire was too personal. By whom the songs were to be arranged is not known. (See also sec. 164.)

CHAPTER XVII

INSTRUMENTS AND INSTRUMENTALISTS

132. Solo Instruments. — One of the signs of a broadened view regarding methods of musical procedure was the closer attention to the artistic use alone of various instruments that before had been chiefly ancillary to vocal effects. The great development of the vocal solo aroused an analogous development of the instrumental solo, and this tended more and more to bring out their contrasted possibilities. In the 17th century, under the opera régime in its early stages, the voice had often been used as if it were first of all a marvelous machine, capable under training of dazzling feats of tonal legerdemain. From this extreme the 18th century gradually reacted in favor of something more normal, namely, the expression through the voice of intimate, profound or intense personality. Thus the more external accomplishment of the mere vocalist gave place to the fine art of the true singer, and the noblest field of the vocal solo began to be fully perceived. Meanwhile the less personal voice of certain instruments was more carefully studied, and to it was transferred much that was possible for the singing voice, with much, too, which was quite unvocal, but suggested by the genius of the instrument itself. Thus the instrumental solo began to advance as a distinct art-form.

The solo instruments thus used were chiefly those of the viol family, especially the violin, the old gamba and the new violoncello, but the flute was also somewhat considered, and the oboe, with occasionally the trumpet and other wind-instruments. Furthermore, interest in the lute and the theorbo had not yet ceased, especially as they were capable of concerted effects of moderate dimensions. The stringed keyboard instruments, finally, now stepped forward into decided prominence as independent implements, giving clear tokens of their later immense influence. Hints of all this had appeared before 1700, but the early 18th century rises much above preceding periods in definite achievements.

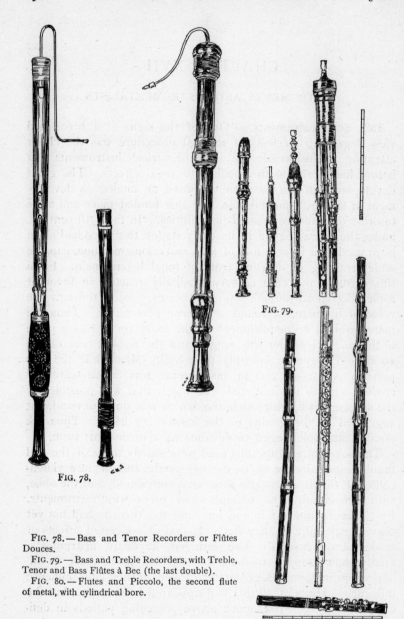

FIG. 78.

FIG. 79.

FIG. 80.

FIG. 78. — Bass and Tenor Recorders or Flûtes Douces.

FIG. 79. — Bass and Treble Recorders, with Treble, Tenor and Bass Flûtes à Bec (the last double).

FIG. 80. — Flutes and Piccolo, the second flute of metal, with cylindrical bore.

The perfecting of the violin took place in the first part of the 18th century (see secs. 110–111). Violin composition of importance began earlier, receiving its first strong direction from Corelli (d. 1713); but its wide expansion in the hands of many able composers and players belongs to the 18th century, establishing for the instrument the eminence among all solo types that still obtains. Among the technical advances in playing was that from only the first three positions (Corelli) to the seventh, with gains in finger-dexterity and in bowing.

Of the older forms of viol, the only one to hold its place was the 'viola da gamba,' a large viol with flat back and 6–7 strings (usually tuned D G c e a d' — a'). Its tone was a cross between that of the tenor violin and the violoncello, but weaker and tamer than either. Probably because of its many strings and its relative ease, it continued in use long after it was really superseded by these finer forms. J. S. Bach (d. 1750) was the last of the strong writers for it, and virtuoso playing upon it ceased before 1790. In Italy it became obsolete much earlier than in Germany, France and England. Gambas were often made in several sizes, so as to form a family by themselves.

The 'violoncello' is properly a bass violin, having 4 strings tuned in fifths (C G d a), the lower two covered with wire, the accordatura being an octave lower than that of the tenor violin. It was first made early in the 17th century, but did not become common for nearly a century, since its fingering involved considerable stretches — a difficulty not fully overcome till after 1750. From early in the 18th century, however, scattered virtuosi upon it appeared, and it steadily pushed its way to the front. Both Bach and Handel clearly perceived its value.

Occasionally for solo purposes a form called the 'octave-violin' was made intermediate between the tenor and the 'cello, its tuning being an octave below the violin proper. Bach's 'viola pomposa' was a small type of 'cello with 5 strings and a compass equal to that of the 'cello and the above octave-violin combined.

The flute, though in use everywhere from time immemorial, did not become artistically prominent till the early 18th century. From that time the German or transverse variety steadily superseded the older recorders, galoubets, flageolets and other direct forms having a beak or mouthpiece. Most of the older cross-flutes had a cylindrical bore, but in the 18th century it was usually conical; since about 1840 the modern flute has reverted to the cylindrical type. The number of finger-holes was rarely more than 8, chromatics and upper tones being secured by cross-fingering and increased force. The scale had many inequalities, so that certain keys and successions were difficult. Every variety of flute was made in different sizes or pitches, forming a full family. Modern music retains only the treble, which has always been the chief form for solos, and the still higher 'piccolo.' From 1700 the sweetness and brilliance of the flute tone, with its capacity for rapid execution, were more and more appreciated. Bach was specially successful with the flute, and his younger contemporary Quantz (d. 1773) was indefatigable in developing its music, being unsurpassed in his voluminous writing for it.

The oboe (or hautboy) and the bassoon, likewise, belong to a large group of double-reed instruments known from the earliest times. In the 16th and 17th centuries various kinds were common, such as the schalmey, chalumeau or shawm, the bombarde or pommer, etc., all with a conical bore, about 8 finger-holes, and made in sets or families of different sizes. The bassoon proper or fagotto dates from the 17th century; it, too, was made in graded sets. The krummhorn or cromorne differed from these in having a cylindrical bore and hence a lower pitch. All these were gradually consolidated in the 18th century into a single family with three chief representatives, the oboe (treble), the cor anglais or English horn (tenor), and the bassoon (bass). The older instruments had broad, thick reeds, and gave a loud and rather coarse tone, but, as solo use became greater, the reeds were made more delicate and the tone sweeter and more refined, so that ultimately the oboe achieved artistic importance, especially regarded for its pungency, its expressiveness and its adaptation to pastoral or idyllic themes.

FIG. 81. — Serpent — a wood-wind instrument allied to the zink or wooden cornet, sounded by a cup-shaped mouthpiece. In use from the early 17th century.

133. The Rise of the Virtuoso. — Better instruments imply better players. In the 18th century the instrumental virtuoso or concert-expert became for the first time conspicuous. Exceptional performers on any instrument had always commanded attention and often good positions in courtly or private establishments. But they could hardly become a fully distinct class among musicians until several steps were taken in the public use of the art. First of these was the full recognition by composers of the value of purely instrumental writing, such as came to pass in the later 17th century. Another was the development of the orchestra as a special agency for accompaniments, as in the progress of the opera. Still another was the free use of the public concert as an institution distinct from the church service, the theatric opera, or the private entertainments of a court or a wealthy patron. From early in the 18th century such public performances, with miscellaneous programs by singers and players specially secured for the occasion, became increasingly popular, prefiguring the universal modern custom.

Important early instances of concerts are the 'Abendmusiken' of Buxtehude and his successors at Lübeck (from 1673 or earlier); those of the Tonkünstlersocietät of Vienna (from 1672); those by Keiser at Hamburg (from about 1700); those of the Musikverein of Leipsic (from 1743, following the lines of an earlier club at the University), which later (from 1781) became famous as the Gewandhaus Concerts; the 'Concerts spirituels' on feast-days at Paris under the management of the Opéra (from 1725), followed by several other similar enterprises; those of Banister at London (from about 1675) and of the Academy of Ancient Music (from 1710), etc., with the festivals of the Three Choirs in West England (from 1724) and the oratorio performances of Handel (from 1739 and earlier) — the prototypes of many others throughout England.

These are simply conspicuous instances of a public musical institution previously unknown, of which every variety was possible in many places under diverse auspices. This new institution joined with the opera to make music on a large scale a function of society in a way the historic significance of which cannot be overestimated.

The order in which the various kinds of instrumental virtuosi appeared is approximately as follows: in the 16th century the lutist and theorbist, in the 16th and 17th the organist, in the 17th the gambist and violinist, and in the 18th the 'cellist, flutist and oboist. In the 17th, also, accomplished clavichordists and harpsichordists or cembalists became notable, followed in the later 18th by pianists.

In previous chapters some pioneers and leading representatives in the earlier classes have been indicated. Such lists in the other classes cannot be made exhaustive, but certain leading names demand mention.

Of the many violinists of the period the following were either the ablest or important as pioneers: —

Antonio Vivaldi (d. 1743), born at Venice, from about 1707 choirmaster to a German prince at Mantua, was from 1714 in the orchestra of St. Mark's, Venice, and director of one of the conservatories. He was a very fertile writer, producing about 80 concertos, many sonatas, cantatas and arias, besides over 35 operas (from 1713). He supplemented the influence of Corelli by accenting brilliancy of technique with the impulse of the true virtuoso, in addition to solidity of construction. He pushed the concerto toward orchestral dimensions. Bach arranged and expanded 16 of his concertos for clavier and organ

Johann Georg Pisendel (d. 1755), who had been a player at Dresden since 1712, became one of Vivaldi's pupils, toured through Italy as a virtuoso, and from 1728 was concertmaster at Dresden, serving as a pioneer of style in Germany (concertos in MS.).

Francesco Maria Veracini (d. 1750) was from 1714 a pupil and colleague of Vivaldi at St. Mark's, from 1717 chamber-composer at Dresden, after 1722 at Prague, in Italy again, and in 1735–47 at London, where he produced 3 operas and competed for popular favor with Geminiani. He was an able player, with a keen sense of effect, and contributed to the growth of an intense and passionate style, giving a powerful impulse to the great Tartini. His works (from 1716) included sonatas and concertos of considerable difficulty and worth.

Giuseppe Tartini (d. 1770), who shares with Corelli the renown of heading the list of the greatest violinists, was an Istrian, but educated at Padua, whence, because of a secret marriage with Cardinal Cornaro's niece, he fled to the monastery of Assisi. After studying composition for two years, his marriage was forgiven and he returned to Padua, but soon came under Veracini's influence at Venice and retired to Ancona to master the violin. In 1714 he discovered the acoustical phenomenon of 'combination-tones' and began to apply it practically. From 1721 he was violinist and director at S. Antonio in Padua, remaining till his death a half-century later, except for two years (1723–5) at Prague. In 1728 he established a famous violin-school, training many great players. His style united the finish of Corelli with greater vigor, passion and daring, and he excelled in double-stopping, trills and other special devices of effect. His practical works (from 1734) included at least 100 sonatas and as many concertos, though incompletely published. Many of these are still classics ; the most celebrated is the sonata *Il trillo del Diavolo*. His *L' arte dell' arco* is a set of 50 variations on a gavotte of Corelli's. He was also a significant student of musical acoustics (see sec. 139). His theory of bowing was an advance on previous usage, and to facilitate it he coöperated in improvements in the structure of bows (see sec. 149).

Francesco Geminiani (d. 1762), born at Lucca, was a pupil at Rome of Corelli. From 1707 he was employed at Lucca, and from 1710 toured Italy as a virtuoso, going in 1714 to London, where, except for a sojourn at Paris (1748–55), he lived for almost 50 years, at first being slightly associated with Handel. His ardent and eccentric temperament interfered with his success as an orchestral leader. In later life he rarely played in public, devoting himself to teaching and some foolish business ventures. His works (from 1716), in the usual forms, were many and ambitious, but not equal to Tartini's. He also wrote one of the earliest violin-methods (1751), embodying Corelli's principles, with several other less important instruction-books.

Pietro Locatelli (d. 1764), a pupil of Corelli (before 1713), from 1725 at Mantua and probably from 1732 at Amsterdam, was one of the earliest of the clever jugglers with the violin in the display of dexterity and peculiar devices of tuning. His works (from 1721), however, setting aside the studies and show-pieces, contain some strong passages.

Giovanni Battista Somis (d. 1763) studied under both Corelli and Vivaldi and then worked wholly at Turin, founding a noted school of players in that

part of Italy and serving as an important link between Italian and French
players (sonatas, 1722–34).

Jean Marie Leclair (d. 1764, murdered) was originally a dancer at Rouen
and then at Turin, where he became a pupil of Somis. From 1729 he was
in the Opéra orchestra at Paris and from 1731 in the royal orchestra, but soon
turned to composition and teaching. He was influenced by Locatelli, but had
marked gifts of grace and invention of his own. His works (from 1723) included fine sonatas, concertos, trios, an opera (1747) and a ballet.

Johann Gottlieb Graun (d. 1771), the elder brother of K. H. Graun, studied
with Pisendel at Dresden and with Tartini at Padua. After short terms at
Merseburg and Arolsen, he became in 1732 leader for the Crown Prince
Frederick at Rheinsberg, following him at his accession in 1740 to Berlin,
remaining in his employ over 40 years. By his own playing, his training of the
conspicuous royal orchestra and his many works (from about 1725) he contributed much to the sound establishment of German violin music. He also
wrote cantatas and a Passion (MS.).

Franz Benda (d. 1786), the eldest of a talented family, was a choirboy at
Prague and Dresden, and early became one of the finest virtuosi in Germany,
excelling not only in dexterity, but in profound expression. He entered
Frederick's orchestra in 1733, soon after Graun, and in 1771 succeeded the
latter as leader. His beautiful and affecting style, somewhat akin to Tartini's,
became a model to many successors. His works (from about 1733) included
sonatas, trios, concertos, études, etc. (many in MS.).

Felice de' Giardini (d. 1796), a pupil of Palladini at Milan and of Somis
at Turin, early developed virtuosity, appearing at Rome and Naples before
1730. In 1748 he went to Germany and from 1750 had immense success
in London, where at intervals during the next 40 years he conducted the
opera and various choral festivals, besides teaching singing. He died (80
years old) while managing an operatic troupe in Russia. He was a skillful
player, somewhat given to display in his early days, and an industrious composer in a good style (from about 1750). He also wrote several operas
(1756–64), but had more success with the oratorio *Ruth* (1763–8). His
significance lay in his stimulus to English players.

Johann Stamitz (d. 1757), a self-taught player, appeared at Frankfort in
1742 and from 1743 was leader of the Mannheim orchestra, which under his
direction became famous for its unanimity, shading and verve. He wrote
much both for violin alone and for orchestra (see sec. 147).

Less notable names are **Pietro Castrucci** (d. 1769), one of Corelli's pupils,
who came to London in 1715 and later was Handel's first violin (till 1737),
and who invented the 'violetta marina' (a form of viola d' amore for which
Handel wrote obbligati) ; and **Carlo Tessarini** (d. after 1762), from 1729 a
player at St. Mark's in Venice and from 1741 at Urbino, whose extensive
works, including concerti grossi, are in the Corelli style, besides a method
(1741).

Giovanni Pietro Guignon (d. 1774), a player in the royal band at Paris from
1733, secured the revival for himself in 1741 of the grotesque mediæval office
of ' Roi des violons,' with monopoly-rights in the whole practice of music as a
profession. In 1750, in view of the general censure of this act, the office was

emptied of its rights and emoluments, and Guignon resigned the title before his death. (See under *Manoir*, sec. 108.)

Among the gambists **Marin Marais** (d. 1728) was the most famous (see sec. 112), and he was succeeded in the royal band at Paris by his son **Roland Marais** (pieces, 1735–8). Without adding further names, it may be noted that the last great player on the gamba was **Karl Friedrich Abel** (d. 1787), a choir-boy under J. S. Bach at Leipsic, from 1746 court-player at Dresden, and from 1759 in London, where in 1765–81 he collaborated with Christian Bach in concerts. He was an able musician and wrote good chamber music and popular symphonies.

Among the violoncellists an Italian pioneer was **Franciscello** (d. after 1730), known only through the reports of able critics who visited Rome between 1715 and 1730. Another eminent Italian player was **Salvatore Lanzetti** (d. c. 1780), who was trained at Naples, but spent his life at Turin, publishing sonatas and studies (1736) and visiting Frankfort in 1751. One of the earliest players in France was **Batistin Stuck** (d. 1755), the opera-writer (see sec. 127) ; but the real founder of the French school was **Martin Berteau** (d. 1756), originally a gambist, who appeared in the Concerts spirituels in 1739 and taught many fine pupils. The 'cello was introduced into England in 1728 by **Giacomo Bassevi** [Cervetto] (d. 1783, over 100 years old), followed by his son, known as **James Cervetto, Jr.** (d. 1837).

While the rise of artistic violin-playing took place in Italy and spread thence to other countries, flute- and oboe-playing seem to have been earliest developed in France. Foremost in this process were the many members of the **Danican-Philidor family,** beginning with **Jean** (d. 1679), who was royal piper from 1659, and his sons **André** (d. 1730), who entered the king's band probably about 1670 as oboist, bassoonist and cromornist, and later served as a patient copyist of musical works for the royal library at Versailles (dances and ballets from 1687), and **Jacques** (d. 1708), also a player of various wind instruments in the royal band. Each of these brothers had four sons who were more or less noted as players and composers, the chief being **Anne** (d. 1728), André's eldest son, who was flutist in the royal band from 1702, wrote several operas (1697–1701), and founded the Concerts spirituels in 1725 as a monopoly (in 1728 bought back by the Opéra), **Pierre** (d. 1731), Anne's cousin, highly honored by Louis XIV. from before 1700 as oboist, flutist and violinist (flute-pieces, 1717), and **François André** (d. 1795), Anne's brother, who first distinguished himself as a chess-player, but later developed into a popular opera-writer (from 1759). Omitting the last-named, at least ten members of the family contributed to the advance of music for wood-wind instruments.

Similarly, **Henri Hotteterre** (d. 1683), a celebrated maker at Paris of wood instruments, especially flutes and oboes, had two sons, **Nicholas** (d. 1695), from 1668 a noted oboist and bassoonist in the king's band, and **Louis,** who probably lived for a time at Rome (whence called *le Romain*), but made a great name as a flute-player before 1700, also publishing a method (1699?), many solos, suites, etc. (from 1708). Another impulse proceeded from **Pierre Gabriel Buffardin** (d. after 1749), a Provençal who from 1715 for almost 35 years was court-flutist at Dresden, with his pupil, the many-sided **Johann**

Joachim Quantz (d. 1773), whose original training was as an expert trumpeter and oboist, as such entering the court-band at Dresden in 1718 ; but who there took up the flute so successfully that he was sent to Italy, Paris and London for further experience, returning to Dresden as flutist in 1727. At this time the Crown Prince Frederick heard him and had him at Berlin twice a year to give lessons, and from 1741 made him chamber-musician at a high salary. Quantz was a cultivated musician, a theorist and a critic of ability. For the flute he wrote at least 500 pieces of every description (from 1734), besides a method (1752). To him are attributed some additions to its mechanism. The extraordinary interest of **Frederick the Great** (d. 1786), who was himself a player and composer, did much to call attention to the flute, to stimulate composition for it and improvements in it. From 1750 its artistic importance was fully established.

An important oboist was **Alessandro Besozzi** (d. 1775), in court service at Turin from 1731, who with his two brothers made many concert-tours. His nephew, **Carlo Besozzi,** was in the Dresden court-band in 1755–92 (oboe-sonatas and concertos).

As further illustrating the interest in various other solo instruments, mention may be made of **François Campion,** in 1703–19 theorbist at the Paris Opéra, with methods for the guitar, lute and theorbo (1705–30) and some pieces ; **Ernst Gottlieb Baron** (d. 1760), from 1728 court-lutist at Gotha, from 1732 at Eisenach, and from 1734 in Frederick's employ as theorbist at Rheinsberg and Berlin, writing well-known, but not remarkable, treatises on instruments of the lute class (1727, '56) ; **Fabio Ursillo** (d. 1759), a Roman arch-lutist, flutist, guitarist and violinist who worked at Tournai from 1725 (string-trios from about 1735) ; and **Henri** and **Charles Baton,** players on the musette (bagpipe) and vielle (hurdy-gurdy) at Paris, the latter with pieces (from 1733) and a work on the vielle (1757).

134. Instrumental Ensembles. — With the improvement of solo instruments and the growth of virtuosity came notable advances in concerted music for particular groups, like the string-trio or quartet, for the small or chamber orchestra (strings and some wood-wind), and for the large orchestra. The orchestra proper still continued to be mainly used as a part of the opera ensemble, so that distinct writing for it was rare except in the way of overtures and special dramatic numbers. But throughout the early 18th century chamber music in the proper sense steadily advanced. Herein lay the germs of orchestral composition, for through it were made the necessary technical experiments for determining how best to favor the peculiarities of the various instruments, and how to combine and contrast them. Through it, too, the outlines of practicable concerted forms began to be discerned. All this bore fruit in the next period in the practice of the early symphonists.

x

As regards the mastery of technical details, the opera orchestra was decidedly important, since accompaniments and detached movements inserted in the dramatic action gave room for great variety of effect and expression. The finer operawriters realized this, but there were evident dangers and drawbacks also. In the opera as then conceived the instrumental forces were quite subsidiary to the vocal. It was easy to fall into merely conventional ways of supplying instrumental backgrounds and accessories, embodying nothing original or forceful. Furthermore, for the opera the orchestral instruments were necessarily much used in large masses, with many players to a part, a condition somewhat hostile to delicacy of treatment. Operatic music, then, told less for the minute internal improvement of instrumentation than for its massive popularity.

In the small or chamber group, on the other hand, there was as a rule but one player to a part, the total effect required that each player and each instrument should be above the average, and individuality of detail was far more indispensable. Hence chamber music, though not influential upon the broad outlines of scoring, constantly stimulated attention to its fine inner texture.

The make-up of the operatic orchestra now became practically what it is to-day, with the important exception of the clarinets and their relatives (see sec. 147). But the quality of some of the instruments was somewhat different, especially that of the oboes and of the brass, the former being more masculine and the latter more dominated by the true trumpet tone. The balance of qualities was generally very different, since throughout the early 18th century, and to some extent afterward, the wood-wind was very strong in proportion to the strings. In particular, oboes and bassoons were multiplied, somewhat as clarinets are now in a military band. The full or *tutti* effects were therefore very different in timbre from those now heard. But skillful writers, like Handel, made much of contrasts in successive movements between groups of instruments, variously selected. Furthermore, many passages were written for only the slender resources of the string-quartet or of the chamber band, each part without *ripieni* and often one of them in the rôle of a solo. Bach was fond of working out varied patterns of this kind with ingenuity and nervous vigor. It is also to be remembered that the harpsichord or the organ was still essential to the orchestra, filling in many passages alone and coöperating in the *tuttis*. The conductor almost invariably led from this central instrument.

For chamber music many slightly different schemes were used, selected usually from violins, 'cellos, flutes, oboes, bassoons, horns and trumpets, generally not more than two of any one sort. The frequent absence of the viola or tenor violin is somewhat notable.

135. Keyboard Stringed Instruments. — Throughout the 18th century three main types of stringed instruments with a keyboard were in constant and conspicuous use — the clavichord, the harpsichord and the pianoforte, the first two in more than one form. The clavichord and the harpsichord were inheritances from previous centuries, while the pianoforte was new. So far as the keyboard itself went, the three were not distinguishable. Their mechanical differences lay in the way in which the strings were sounded, and, incidental to this, in the method of stringing. Tonally and artistically they differed considerably. For a time each was felt to have its own special utility, but, as the pianoforte was gradually improved, its superiority became so manifest that finally, at the close of the century, it had practically driven the others from the field.

The clavichord was a keyboard application of the principle of the mediæval monochord, which was not so much a musical instrument as a device for the study of intervals. The monochord (as its name shows) had properly but one string, stretched by a weight over a soundboard, and a movable bridge by which the string could be divided into parts having some desired mathematical ratio to each other and hence giving tones in the corresponding harmonic relation. The essential feature was that the pitch of the tones was fixed by the placing of the bridge. In the clavichord each key of the keyboard brought to bear upon some string a metal (brass) 'tangent,' which was driven against the string and held there like the monochord bridge, the point of its impact determining the pitch of the tone. (The vibration of the string took place only on one side of the tangent, the other part of the string being deadened by a strip of cloth.) The strings were all of about the same length, and often two or even three keys operated the same string so far as this could be managed without interference, thus diminishing the total size of the instrument and facilitating its tuning. In the earliest clear references to the clavichord (16th century) the number of keys was about 20, and in the 18th century the compass seldom exceeded four octaves (that is, less than 50 keys), but the number of strings might be much less. In time, however, clavichords were often made with a string for each key. These were called 'bundfrei' or 'unfretted,' while the others were 'gebunden' or 'fretted.' The outward shape of the instrument was that of a simple rectangular box (usually without legs), not too large to be carried under the arm. The case and inside of the cover were often ornamented.

The clavichord tone was thin, metallic (since both strings and tangents were made of brass), and never powerful. Since, however, its character was directly dependent upon the pressure of the key, it could be delicately graded as to force, and even be prolonged and given a peculiar wavy effect by rocking or pulsating the finger ('bebung'). Accordingly,

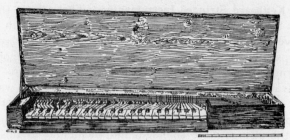

FIG. 82. — German Clavichord
(17th century).

FIG. 83. — Italian Harpsichord (17th century).

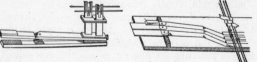

FIG. 84. — Diagrams of
Harpsichord and Clavi-
chord Actions.

composers like J. S. Bach and his sons, Haydn, Mozart and Beethoven admired the clavichord because of its sympathetic expressiveness. But it was distinctly a private or domestic instrument, lacking the sonority and ictus for public use. Late examples, however, sometimes had two strings to a note for greater power. Its manufacture ceased before the 19th century, though instruments lingered in use long after 1800.

The harpsichord was simply a keyboard zither or psaltery. For each key of the keyboard there was a corresponding string, past which depressing the key pushed a jack from whose side projected a small quill or spine by which the string was snapped or twanged. When the key was released, the quill, which was jointed, slipped back into its first position and a damper fell upon the string. The strings varied in length according to pitch. Hence the frame tended to be roughly triangular or wing-shaped (whence the German name 'flugel'), resembling a modern grand piano. The smaller varieties, known as 'spinets' or 'virginals,' had the strings running from side to side, but in larger ones they stretched away from the keyboard. An upright form, the 'clavicytherium,' was also occasionally made. Large instruments, for the sake of varied qualities, often had two or more keyboards, each provided with a special form of jack and quill. The cases and covers were often highly ornate, and, when the instrument had legs, these, too, were often elaborate.

The harpsichord tone was vigorous and sonorous, especially in the larger varieties, with a peculiar reedy quality. It had a decided ictus from the snap of the quill past the string. But it could not be reduced in power below a certain point without 'blocking' (though variations in power were often secured by some sort of opening and closing shutter or lid, controlled by a foot-lever). Neither could its character be much varied. Until late in the 18th century the harpsichord was the standard instrument for the theatre and concert-room, and for all chamber combinations. For public use it was often made with two or three strings to the note. It was no longer made after 1800, though its use continued later.

The early history of both the clavichord and the harpsichord cannot be traced. It seems likely that both were known as early as the 14th century, but definite data begin with the 16th. Their manufacture was more or less associated with that of the organ till the 17th, when the famous *Ruckers family* of Antwerp raised harpsichord-making to the grade of a fine art. In the 18th century Paris and London were the leading headquarters of good makers. The excellence of the best instruments lay chiefly in the perfection of their soundboards and the delicacy and precision of the action.

The pianoforte (or 'fortepiano,' as at first called) is essentially a keyboard dulcimer. Each key has its own string, sounded by a blow from a recoiling hammer that has a padded head. Its invention was delayed until the making of clavichords and harpsichords was well advanced, since its success depended on mature experience in constructing frames, soundboards and key-action, as well as in the drawing of heavy wire. In the clavichord and harpsichord the strings needed to have some lightness

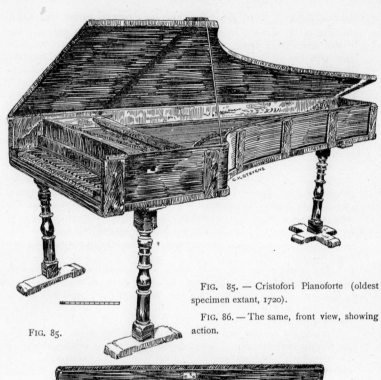

FIG. 85. — Cristofori Pianoforte (oldest specimen extant, 1720).

FIG. 86. — The same, front view, showing action.

FIG. 85.

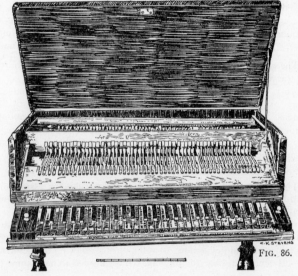

FIG. 86.

and flexibility, but in the piano they had to be much heavier and drawn very taut. In the latter, too, the space required for the hammers necessitated a gap in the soundboard at one end. The hammer-action was more complicated than any of the direct jack-actions, since the hammer must be thrown freely against the string, must then recoil instantly, and the damper meantime must be kept off the string till the key was released. The devices employed to secure all these results in the smallest space and with the minimum of resistance and noise have been far too many to be here enumerated. The earliest instruments resembled the harpsichord in shape, like the modern 'grand,' but from perhaps 1760 they were made after the clavichord style, like the modern 'square'; still later the now popular 'upright' was added. Most of the great improvements in detailed mechanism, including the introduction of a metal frame, strengthened by braces, and of steel wire of the finest quality in place of the original brass, as well as the gradual development of a perfect action, belong to the 19th century.

The pianoforte tone is quite distinct from that of its predecessors, since it uses the latent sonority of a tense and heavy wire, actuated by a stroke from a soft, yielding hammer-head. It has a vigorous ictus, and, if the hammer-heads be good, an almost vocal roundness and sweetness. Its loudness can be indefinitely varied (whence its name) and the character of its tone considerably modified by varying the touch. Hence the piano has proved to have all the excellences of both the clavichord and the harpsichord, with several peculiar to itself. To increase its power and breadth it is now commonly made with two or three strings to the note, and has pedals by which the dampers may be held up at will, the number of strings affected by the hammers reduced, felts inserted between the hammers and the strings, etc. On account of its mechanical immaturity, it did not come into public use until about 1765, but before 1800 it had already become accepted as the keyboard instrument *par excellence*.

Some experiments toward a hammer-instrument may have been made early in the 17th century, but what they were is unknown. About 1695 **Pantaleon Hebenstreit** (d. 1750), a dancing-master at Merseburg, devised an enlarged and improved dulcimer (with 185 strings), which in 1705 he exhibited before Louis XIV. at Paris. His success with it secured him court-positions at Eisenach from 1706 and at Dresden from 1714. His dulcimer, commonly known as the 'pantaleon' or 'pantalon' (from his first name), was without a keyboard. Before 1709 **Bartolomeo Cristofori** (d. 1731), an able harpsichord-maker, originally of Padua, but from about 1687 of Florence, began to make hammer-claviers which were described by *Scipione Maffei* (d. 1755) in 1711. Cristofori, then, appears to have been the inventor of the true pianoforte. The only extant specimens of his work, dating from 1720 and 1726, have all the essential elements of the complete action, even to the check to catch the hammer on its recoil. They have two strings to the note and a compass of 4⅓ and 4 octaves respectively. How many pianos Cristofori made is not known, but his fame as an inventor extended to Germany as early as 1720. Other pioneer experimenters were the Parisian harpsichord-maker **Marius**, who exhibited models of hammer-actions in 1716, and **Christoph Gottlieb Schröter** (d. 1782), from 1726 organist at Minden and from 1732 at Nordhausen, who in 1738 claimed that he had made models between 1717 and 1721. Neither of these efforts seems to have been connected with Cristofori's or to have had any result. The next practical step was taken by **Gottfried Silbermann** (d. 1753), a noted organ-builder at Freiberg, who at intervals from 1726 made several pianos on the Cristofori model (mostly, it seems, for Frederick the Great). But it was not till after 1755 and in England that piano-making became a business of importance (see sec. 160).

136. Tuning and Temperament. — The practical problem of tuning all keyboard instruments is an intricate one, unless playing is to be confined to but a single scale or tonality, or unless the number of keys to the octave is many more than twelve. Back of it all lies the question of the true theory of intervals, which began to be discussed six centuries before the Christian era (by Pythagoras). And, however this question is answered, the moment that the fundamental scale is augmented by chromatic tones or the slightest modulation attempted, difficulties begin to multiply. Hence discussions of tuning steadily increased from the 16th century onward. The earliest-known formal system of tuning dates from 1571 (Ammerbach), though this came far from solving the problem.

The Pythagorean theory of intervals, which ruled until the 16th century, rested on the assumption that the perfect fifth ($\frac{3}{2}$) is the only unit, beside the octave, to be used in laying out scales. The theoretical objection to this is that if, from any starting-tone, like C, a series of twelve fifths is laid out (C–G, G–D, etc., disregarding octaves), the final C will be almost a quarter of a semitone too sharp. The most serious practical difficulty began to be felt as soon as the progress of harmonic feeling revealed the beauty and utility of the major triad, for, to be smooth, this required a major third ($\frac{5}{4}$) distinctly flatter than the Pythagorean third ($\frac{81}{64}$). The recognition of this true third (beginning early in the 16th century) gave a major scale with the ratios, 1, $\frac{9}{8}$, $\frac{5}{4}$, $\frac{4}{3}$, $\frac{3}{2}$, $\frac{5}{3}$, $\frac{15}{8}$, 2, that is, one made up of three exactly similar triads, 1–3–5, 5–7–2, 4–6–8 (*e.g.*, C–E–G, G–B–D, F–A–C).

But this perfected scale, admirable as it was for diatonic harmony without modulation, proved difficult to use in determining chromatic tones; for if F♯, for example, was taken as the third of D in the triad D – F♯ –A, then A proved to be flat by a 'comma' ($\frac{81}{80}$), and if B♭, similarly, was deduced from F, then D was a comma sharp, and so on. Modulation by one remove in either direction always made at least one tone in the new scale slightly false, and every further remove made matters steadily worse. Any attempt, therefore, to tune a keyboard instrument, like the organ or the harpsichord, by first making some one scale true and then making some other scale also true and then another, broke down at the first step and ended in total confusion.

The removal of the difficulty had to be sought through some system of 'temperament,' that is, by deliberately falsifying some tones by a very small amount so that practical effects might either be truer or that the error might be so distributed as to be unnoticeable.　Two principal systems of temperament or practical tuning have had historic importance, the 'mean-tone' system, which was in general use through the 18th century, and often held to, especially for organs, till much later, and the 'equal' system, which was first suggested just before 1700, came into more or less use during the 18th century, though not for the organ, and has now become universal.　The former system sought to make certain selected keys or tonalities as good as possible at the expense of certain others which were outlawed.　The latter system seeks to make all keys alike and therefore equally usable, but in doing so is forced to make all of them equally incorrect by small amounts.

The 'mean-tone' system is so called because it assumed that the interval of a 'tone' (as C – D) is in tuning to be made halfway (or a 'mean') between the larger or Pythagorean 'tone' ($\frac{9}{8}$) and the smaller ($\frac{10}{9}$), or, in other words, that the major thirds were as far as possible to be true, but the fifths a quarter-comma flat.　The result of this, if C is taken as the starting-point, is that E and A♭ are correct, C♯, F and A a quarter-comma sharp, E♭, G and B a quarter-comma flat, D, F♯ and B♭ exactly midway between their two possible values, and D♭, D♯, G♭, G♯ and A♯ more or less unusable.　(By a slightly different application of the system, however, G♯ might be made correct, but A♭ unusable.)　The deviations of the worst intervals approached a half-semitone, and these collectively were known as the 'wolf,' to 'drive' which 'out' of the other intervals and into them was the object of tuning.　This system was admirable so long as composers confined themselves to certain scales or keys.　The major keys of C, G, D, F, B♭, E♭, and the minor keys of C, G, D, were very good, but all others bad (if G♯ were favored instead of A♭, A major would take the place of E♭ major and A minor that of C minor).　Free modulation was impossible, especially in the use of minor keys.　On the other hand, the sweetness of the major thirds in the 'good' keys was a decided advantage.

The 'equal' system is so called because it assumes that the octave is to be divided into twelve exactly equal semitones, making every interval in every scale or key equal to the same interval in all other scales or keys. The result of this, if C is taken as the starting-point, is that F and G are almost exactly correct, D and B♭ very good in certain relations, but the one sharp and the other flat in others, C♯, D♯, G♯ and A♯ decidedly sharper than they should be, D♭, E♭ and A♭ rather flatter than they should be, and F♯ and G♭ either moderately sharp or flat in some relations or seriously so in others.   Exactly what is true of the scale of C is true of every other possible key.   This system is admirable for music in which all keys, major and minor, are liable to be used, since whatever effect is produced in one is exactly reproduced in the rest.   It also favors enharmonic shifts of every sort.   It is noticeable, also, that the sharped intervals are sharper and the flatted intervals flatter than they should be, thus accentuating the alterations from the diatonic scale which led to the nomenclature of the chromatics (a process often observable in the playing of instruments of free intonation, like the violin, and also in singing). On the whole, however, the restfulness of the major thirds is sacrificed to the brilliance and perfection of the fifths and fourths.

It must be added that the above theoretical comparison of the two systems holds good only so far as each is perfectly carried out by tuners and as the instruments stand as they are tuned.   Under either of them unconscious or intentional deviations may be made by the tuner, and the structure or condition of the instrument may speedily introduce further changes.   It is an uninvestigated subject, how much the peculiarities of the two systems or of their traditional use by tuners has to do with the asserted differences between keys in emotional character.

If it were practicable to make keyboards with fifty-three keys to the octave, it would be possible to play in all scales in pure intonation.

Tuning as a distinct occupation seems to have begun early in the 17th century, and was especially concerned with the harpsichord. In the 18th it steadily became more important, especially as harpsichords and pianos were multiplied. Organ-tuning was still held as a branch of organ-making. Players on all keyboard instruments, however, long continued to act as their own tuners to a large extent.

In the 17th century tuning usually proceeded from F, but in the 18th and since from C or A.   The standard pitch of the 18th century was decidedly lower than now, if the few data can be trusted — A=405–422 vibrations per second, as compared with Scheibler's pitch of 1834 (A=440), the now generally accepted 'French pitch' of 1859 (A=435), or the practice of many orchestras till about 1880 (A=450–455).   The 'tuning-fork' as a device for preserving a standard pitch is said to have been invented in 1711 by *John Shore* (d. 1753), a London lutist.

CHAPTER XVIII

FORMS OF COMPOSITION. THEORY AND LITERATURE

137. The Larger Forms in General. — The problem of method or form in composition, especially for instruments, attracted increasing attention throughout the 18th century. It was clearly seen that no long and elaborate work can be intelligible unless either divided into comparatively short sections, each relatively complete in itself, or developed in such stages and by such orderly processes that the mind can regard it as an organic whole. Several notable forms were brought over from the preceding period in a fair degree of advancement. These were either perfected or greatly improved, so that about 1750 the way was open for certain further steps that were reasonably final.

A complete and satisfactory classification of all the extended forms in use after 1700 is not possible, since some of them were variously construed by different writers, so that they overlapped. Any survey of them must consider two points, first, how far and how they are built up out of more or less distinct 'movements,' and second, what internal method of treatment is used within single movements.

> Works in several separate movements are often called 'cyclical,' though this term is better applied to a circling or recurrent treatment within a movement, as in a rondo or in a stanza-song.

In all large works the division of the whole into movements was common. Thus the opera and the oratorio were regularly made up of distinct recitatives, arias, choruses, etc., the recitatives usually serving as rather formless introductions to the formal aria or chorus that followed. Thus the overture was regularly split up into three or four sections, each with its own scheme and subjects. Thus sets of dances were frequent, in which the individual components were often so complete in themselves that they could be used alone or recombined in other orders without special inconvenience. In all these cases the total effect in view was plainly one of orderly variety or contrast, different methods of handling being used in succession so as to maintain interest and give scope for diverse procedures.

Within movements at least four general methods of treatment were recognized, of which the first belonged especially to vocal music and the rest were more associated in this period with instrumental music. First was the method of the *da capo* aria, a form in three principal sections — the first and second in considerable contrast as to key and style, and the third repeating the first more or less literally — all homophonic in essence, that is, organized with a dominating melody and an accompaniment mainly harmonic. This method was not only universal in the solos and duets of operas, oratorios and cantatas, but was creeping into instrumental works somewhat. It was distinctly the creation of the later 17th century, with its strenuous activity in dramatic music. Second was the method of various dances, in which some characteristic rhythm was worked out in two groups of sharp-cut strains of some definite number of measures (strictly eight), the two set in some contrast, usually with a drift in the first from tonic to dominant harmony and back again in the second. This method was typical in the suite and in all movements in dance style. Its origin was plainly in the field of folk-music and it had been steadily making its way into artistic music since the 15th century. Third was the method of formal or virtual counterpoint, in which several voice-parts were introduced with much individuality and made to proceed according to established rules of imitation or combination. This method was that of all strict church music of the old school and of organ music generally. It had already reached its climax in the formal fugue, both vocal and instrumental, but was liable to appear in the fugal handling of any sort of movement or of a passage within a movement. In it a tripartite division was well recognized — exposition (of the subject or theme), development, recapitulation. Fourth was a new method which may be called the free thematic, which was not controlled by the conventional rules of counterpoint, but operated more homophonically or harmonically in a variety of ways. The lay-out was usually tripartite, as in the fugue, but the artistic effect was strikingly different. This method was becoming common for certain movements of forms like the overture, the sonata and the concerto, and was the one that finally ousted the old contrapuntal methods from their long-held position of supremacy. In the next period it passed over into what is now known as 'sonata-form.' Prior to 1750 composers had not quite perceived the value of a second subject or of certain points of harmonic procedure.

> The above summary statement is evidently not exhaustive. It does not include certain comparatively formless types, like the recitative or the arioso, nor the variable form applied in preludes or 'sinfonie' of various degree, in which the emphasis fell either upon the bold enunciation of a few chord-sequences or melodic figures without any orderly treatment of them, or upon a rather vague harmonic musing before the serious discussion of materials was begun.

The details of some of these larger forms are so important as to call for special statement, together with references to the composers who were prominent in determining them or in using them with evident power and distinction.

138. The Suite. — Among the forms in which regularity of outward character was conspicuous, was the 'suite' or series of dance-tunes. Such chains of dances had been used since early in the 16th century, but more as helps to actual dancing or as capricious diversions than as a recognized form of pure composition. Somewhat before 1700 and still more during the first third of the 18th century, the use of them in an artistic manner became notable, since they gratified the desire for a form consisting of several entirely separate movements, each with a clear, definite pattern. Gradually the plan and treatment became fixed.

> The name 'suite' did not acquire its technical meaning at first. Similar works had been called 'lessons' in England, 'sonate da camera' in Italy, 'ordres' in France, and 'partien' or 'partite' in Germany.
>
> Attention has already been called (sec. 71) to the early association of 'pavans' and 'galliards.' This tentative plan was finally altered and extended to include at least four movements : — (a) a flowing 'allemande' in quadruple rhythm, (b) a more lively and emphatic 'courante' in triple rhythm, (c) a melodious and often serious 'sarabande' in slow triple rhythm, and (d) a lively and brilliant 'gigue' either in triple rhythm or at least with triplet divisions of the beats. To this scheme was often prefixed a prelude of some sort, not usually in dance-form. After the sarabande other dances were often inserted according to fancy, sometimes in great profusion. Conspicuous among these were the lively 'passepied' and the stately 'minuet,' both in triple rhythm, the energetic 'gavotte' and the virile 'bourrée,' both in quadruple rhythm, or the more

complicated 'chaconne' and 'passacaglia,' both elaborations upon a
ground-bass.   The original patterns of the principal dances came from
various countries — the allemande probably from southern Germany, the
courante in one of its forms from France, in the other from Italy, the sarabande from Spain, the gigue from England.   The added forms were
chiefly French.

In the choice and order of the movements the primary purpose was
variety.   The allemande was usually understood to be introductory (even
when there was a prelude besides) ; the courante included matter requiring more close and technical attention ; the sarabande had greater
lyrical and emotional value ; and the gigue was originally the fullest of
life and humor, but often was handled with much contrapuntal intricacy.
All were usually in the same key.

The suite was the earliest of composite forms to reach maturity.
It stands apart from analogous forms in the comparative rigidity
of the inner structure of its movements.   Hence it cannot properly be called the direct ancestor of the modern sonata and
symphony, though it undoubtedly influenced them.

The dance-form that dominates the suite is somewhat akin to song-form
in that it consists of definite and balanced sections or strains.   In the
simplest examples there are two such strains, each eight measures long
and both repeated.   These are properly somewhat contrasted in style,
the first often ending in the key of the dominant.   But this rudimentary
structure was generally much expanded, though tending always to retain
the sharp partition into brief strains.

That which distinguished these dances from songs was the prominence
throughout of the special rhythmic or metric pattern that belonged to the
given dance.   Whether or not decided melodic themes were adopted was
immaterial, though in artistic examples such themes were sometimes conspicuous.   The treatment might be homophonic, harmonic or contrapuntal, or any mixture of the three.   Much ingenuity was needed to keep
within the strict bounds of the strains and to maintain the characteristic metric pattern, and yet to achieve continuity, variety and positive
interest.

Somewhat analogous to the suite in structural plan was the
'double' or 'variation,' which also came to be prominent in
the early 18th century.   This was a series of movements developed out of a simple song or dance taken as a theme, each
successive movement presenting the theme either intact, but
with manifold decorations, or under varying disguises of treatment.   Another allied form was the 'rondo,' in which a melodic
theme recurs at intervals without substantial change, the appearances being separated by varying episodes or digressions.

Both doubles and rondos were sometimes inserted among the extra movements of the suite.

> The formal unity of both these forms inheres in the identity of the theme. Hence both are merely analogous to the suite.

All these were preëminently forms of chamber music, and hence were felt to be especially suitable for keyboard instruments. Their development was a symptom of the growing importance of the clavichord and harpsichord. While all of them had evident artistic limitations and tended always toward an extreme of formal precision, yet their popularity served a useful purpose. In the hands of a few masters they attained distinction and real power.

> In the treatment of the suite different countries showed varying tendencies. In France the essential dance-patterns were exalted for their own sake and their adaptation to the keyboard was prompt and able, but, instead of developing the architectonic possibilities of the form as a whole, composers tended to make merely picturesque or piquant series of sketches conceived in a half-dramatic spirit and strung together like the scenes in a pantomime. In Germany, on the other hand, the suite was early seized by organ-composers as a field for the exercise of polyphonic skill, though with a true sympathy for the dance idea underlying it. In Italy, again, the strictness of the dance-patterns was notably neglected in favor of a free thematic treatment, and the violin was more employed as a vehicle than the keyboard.

> **François Couperin** (d. 1733) came of a family of organists and clavecinists celebrated from about 1650 till 1800, all of them at some time players at St. Gervais in Paris. Born in 1668 and trained by the organist Thomelin, he became organist at the king's private chapel in 1693 and at St. Gervais in 1698. Though most famous in his day as an organist, he is now counted one of the founders of harpsichord music. Besides an early set of pieces (probably before 1700), he issued four notable collections (1713-30), an instruction-book (1717), and considerable chamber music. His pieces are grouped in ' ordres' of very varied plan, usually fancifully entitled and arranged in a half-theatric ' program.' They are a link between the operatic ballet and the keyboard suite. Their style attracted wide notice and imitation. With them begins the exuberant development of keyboard 'graces ' or embellishments that continued through the century.
>
> **Louis Marchand** (d. 1732), a close contemporary of Couperin, was also a leading Parisian organist before 1700 and soon known as a clavecinist (books, 1702-3). Exiled in 1717, he visited Dresden, where he ignominiously ran away from a contest in organ-playing with Bach. Later he was allowed to return to Paris, and taught many pupils. He was notoriously conceited, but had ability as player and composer.

Jean Philippe Rameau (d. 1764), the great opera-writer (see sec. 127), began his career as a clavecinist, and among his works are several collections of pieces (1706, '24–41) which rank close to Couperin's in interest and importance, though he, too, failed to develop the full capacities of the suite.

In Germany many organ-composers used the suite-form with originality, bringing out more and more its possibilities of delicate and intricate inner structure. Data fail for an exhaustive list, but prominent names just before and just after 1700 were those of **Kuhnau** of Leipsic (pieces, 1689, '95), **Johann Krieger** of Zittau (1697), **Böhm** of Lüneburg (before 1700), **Mattheson** of Hamburg (1714), **Buttstett** of Erfurt (1716), **Telemann** of Hamburg (many suites for small orchestra, in MS.), **Graupner** of Darmstadt (1718, '22, '37), **Muffat** of Vienna (c. 1735), and **J. P. Kellner** of Gräfenroda (1739–49). It is known that Bach made careful study of the suites of some of these, as well as of French writers about 1700.

J. S. Bach (d. 1750) wrote over 20 works of the suite class, which are justly counted among his ablest. Most of them are in the sets known to-day as the 'French,' the 'English' and the 'German' (orchestral partite), all written probably between 1720 and 1730. In the second and third of these the suite reached its highest point of significance and dignity.

Handel (d. 1759) wrote four books of suites (1720–33), which, though less typical than Bach's and much slighter in essential value, are yet interesting as illustrating the varied applications of which the form was capable.

After about 1750 the suite became almost obsolete, and was not revived till well into the 19th century.

139. The Fugue. — Among the many types of contrapuntal writing, the fugue became in the later 17th century easily the chief (see sec. 103). Its development was sought primarily upon the organ, of which it has remained the characteristic master-form, but it was extended in the early 18th century to the clavier and to oratorio choruses. Fugal treatment tended to appear frequently in all kinds of writing, since the artistic feeling of the period was still dominated by the old idea that polyphony was the noblest method of musical construction.

The 'fugue' itself is not a composite form — does not consist of separate movements. But with it is very commonly associated a prelude of some kind, the two together making a work in two movements. Yet the completed fugue-form included somewhat distinct sections. These are (*a*) the enunciation or exposition, in which a theme ('subject,' 'dux,' 'proposta') is given out by some one voice-part in the tonic key, followed in a second voice-part by a restatement of it ('answer,' 'comes,' 'risposta') literally or approximately in the key of the dominant, while the first voice-part proceeds in counterpoint, usually forming a subsidiary theme ('counter-subject'), followed by similar alternating propositions by the remaining voice-parts till all are in action; (*b*) the development or free fantasia, in which the thematic material thus presented is elaborately discussed by the several voice-parts in various contrapuntal ways, with much freedom of key and usually with the insertion of episodes, often of considerable extent, the whole section culminating in an extended passage on a stationary bass, usually the dominant ('pedal-point' or 'organ-point') ; (c) the recapitulation, in which the theme as subject and answer is again presented by all the voices in turn, often in reverse order and usually with a crowding or overlapping of the entries ('stretto'), the whole leading to a climax of intricacy and intensity. The ideal method throughout is to keep to strictly polyphonic devices and to use many varieties of imitation, so as to unfold fully the striking possibilities of the theme.

A 'fugato' is a movement or passage treated with some selection of the above features, often with many omissions, compressions and licenses.

Every important composer of the period, except some of the opera-writers, was a fugue-writer as a matter of course, and the number of fugues produced was enormous, especially for the organ. The best of them have hardly been surpassed since. Thus the old art of counterpoint began a new life, but chiefly now in the instrumental rather than the vocal field.

It would be entirely impossible to give any satisfactory résumé of the many fugue-writers. Of course, Bach overtops all his contemporaries in the organ-fugue, and his *Wohltemperirtes Clavier* (1722–44) was a monumental demonstration of the suitability of the form to the clavichord and hence to the pianoforte. Both he and Handel wrote majestic fugues for voices also.

140. The Overture, Sonata and Concerto. — Besides the suite and the fugue, there were several other large composite forms that manifested an increasing tendency to utilize principles of development in a different way. These were the overture, originally a part of dramatic composition, the sonata, originally a chamber-work for solo instruments, and the concerto, originally a similar work with orchestral collaboration. All of these were properly laid out in three or more distinct movements. While some of these movements or passages in them were in dance-form and so like extracts from a suite, and some were polyphonic and so fugues or at least fugal, others were homophonic or harmonic in ways that demand special notice.

The 'overture' was properly an orchestral form, intended as the introduction to a dramatic work. Of the two existing plans for it, the French and the Italian (see sec. 124), the latter had the greater subsequent influence, since, with the insertion of a minuet as a third movement and with some modifications of the final movement, it led to the plan of the modern sonata and symphony. But the inner structure of the first and second movements often presented points of fresh importance, because

Y

the former tended to employ distinctly harmonic methods in the building up of strong chord-series without conspicuous thematic detail, and the latter often passed over into the homophonic presentation of a melody with accompaniment. Both of these methods offered opportunities not presented by set or strict forms like the suite or the fugue.

The 'sonata' had already passed through several stages before 1700. Of these that of the later 17th century, when the 'sonata da chiesa' was distinguished from the 'sonata da camera,' is specially important. This 'church' sonata, as perfected by Corelli and his contemporaries, was usually written for from one to three solo stringed instruments, with an accompaniment on a figured bass, the material distributed in four movements (sometimes three), alternately slow and quick. Just before 1700 the type was used for the harpsichord as well, so that in the early 18th century sonatas were written either for a solo instrument, especially the violin, or for a very small group of such instruments, or for the clavier alone, the details of treatment differing considerably according to the vehicle adopted. The order of movements, if there were four, was slow, quick, slow, quick, or, if three, quick, slow, quick, and, as a rule, the first quick movement was chief in intrinsic interest. Within the movements, the material was generally presented either in two sections, progressing from tonic to dominant and back again, as in dance-forms, or in three stages of exposition, development and recapitulation, but with no such schematic regularity as in the fugue. The treatment was predominantly thematic, but with a constant tendency to escape from the comparative formality and learning of polyphony and to utilize methods that were homophonic or harmonic. In all this are to be seen premonitions of the method of the later and modern sonata, though the importance of a second subject was not yet generally recognized, nor the need of a comprehensive harmonic plan controlling the process of development (see sec. 146). The total unity was sometimes increased by having some relation between the subjects proposed for treatment in the different movements. But in many cases dance-forms or fugues or variations were used as movements without evident connection with the rest.

The 'concerto' was not sharply distinguishable from the sonata, except in the vehicles of expression used. Originally, concertos were instrumental pieces in which different orchestral instruments or groups of such instruments were employed successively in combination or contrast (whence the name *concerto*, a working together). Later, the term was limited to works in which a solo instrument, especially a violin, appeared in successive contrasts with a concerted accompaniment, the part of each element being elaborated. In the early 18th century, the name was also given to extended works for either the clavier or the organ alone, or for all sorts of ensembles of orchestral instruments. The number of movements was variable, but tended to be three or four. In the plan and treatment of these there was no constant distinction from the sonata. It was not until the next period that the concerto in precisely its modern sense was undertaken. Yet experiments with the form were contributing to the establishment of the modern type.

The fertility of the period in forms of this character was notable in itself and in its prefiguring of the completed sonata-form that followed. Instrumental music was approaching a great culmination, to the success of which many minds contributed and in which several lines of previous effort were united and fused. In practical advance the Germans and the Italians took the lead, the former being strongest in contrapuntal methods, the latter in suggestions derived from operatic and purely secular styles. All were feeling their way toward architectonic types of the greatest breadth.

Here, again, no exhaustive survey of workers is possible. But certain pioneers require special mention : —

Domenico Scarlatti (d. 1757), born at Naples in 1685, the son of Alessandro Scarlatti, the opera-writer, studied with him and with Gasparini at Rome. His genius as a clavecinist developed early, but his first known works were operas at Naples and Rome (from 1704). In 1709 at Rome he and Handel were pitted against each other on the harpsichord and the organ, and were adjudged equal on the former. From 1715 he was Baj's successor as choir-master at St. Peter's in Rome, from 1719 opera-cembalist at London, from 1721 court-cembalist at Lisbon, and from 1729 in court service at Madrid. Of his many clavier works, all notably compact, he himself published only two collections (probably between 1730 and 1745). Though not fully appreciated in Italy, his extreme originality was widely known elsewhere. He contributed to the range of keyboard execution, especially in the use of the crossed hands, double runs, repeated notes, wide skips, etc., and also to the emancipation of keyboard composition from its contrapuntal trammels in the direction of a free style that was essentially modern in its homophonic and harmonic point of view. He thus distinctly advanced the tendency toward the modern sonata, though his own works were usually dances in fantasia-form, and are regularly cast in one movement only.

J. S. Bach (d. 1750), whose life covered almost exactly the same years as the foregoing, was a diligent worker in this field. In it, as elsewhere, he stood preëminent for depth of intuition and freshness of invention. His greatest strength was put forth in the sonatas and concertos in which solo instruments and the clavier were combined in a semi-orchestral manner. In these, as in many preludes, toccatas, etc., for the organ or the clavier alone, he showed a prescient sense of the contrast in subjects and the progress in keys that mark the later sonata, though his prevailing idiom of expression was too intricate in texture for a permanent type.

Karl Philipp Emanuel Bach (d. 1788), the second surviving son of the great Bach, was the most important link between this period and the next in the use of extended forms. Born at Weimar in 1714, thoroughly trained in music by his father and finally educated otherwise at Leipsic and Frankfort, from before 1740 he was clavecinist to Frederick the Great. In 1767 he followed Telemann as cantor at Hamburg, where the balance of his life was spent. He was the best keyboard performer of the middle of the century, and through his remarkable instruction-book (1753–62) exerted a profound influence upon the development of technique. He was also a facile composer, chiefly for instruments (over 200 clavier-solos and 50 concertos, etc., from 1731), as well as many Passions and cantatas, and 2 oratorios. His style differed greatly from his father's, since it concerned itself far more with elegance of outward form than with strength of content, and since he turned to more homophonic means of expression. His genius lay in the application of the rudimentary sonata-form that later was powerfully developed by Haydn. It was the study in 1749 of one set of his sonatas (1742) that gave Haydn his first strong impetus.

Passing mention may be made of **Giovanni Battista Sammartini** (d. 1774), a choirmaster and organist at Milan, who is said to have written almost 3000 works of all kinds, among which are numerous sonatas, concertos and 'symphonies' (from 1734) that are sometimes called prototypes of Haydn's; and **Georg Christoph Wagenseil** (d. 1777), a favorite pupil of Fux at Vienna and court-composer and teacher to the royal family there from 1739, an able clavecinist and the composer of many chamber works (from 1740), besides 10 operas, 2 oratorios and some church music, combining manners derived from Leo, Hasse and Rameau.

As the middle of the century approached there was a notable increase of production in chamber music, indicating a widespread interest in both the harpsichord and the small orchestra. To this movement many composers contributed, though generally in styles so perfunctory and formal that it is needless to specify further names.

141. Literature about Music. — A distinguishing feature of the literary treatment of musical subjects in the early 18th century was the persistent and fruitful attempt to reach a sound theory of harmony on the basis of physical facts inductively studied. The critical spirit of the age was actively displayed in the domain of acoustics, which then assumed its modern form. Out of the acute investigation of the physical basis of music came new conceptions of intervals, tonality and chord-building which are the nucleus of all present theory. Many manuals of composition continued to be put forth in larger or smaller shape, more and more conforming to these fresh ideas and tending to push harmony into the place of supremacy formerly held by counterpoint. Another significant feature of the time was the rise of criticism as a distinct line of effort, though its principles were not yet systematized or its spirit made judicial. Significant advances were also made in the way of encyclopædic compendiums, like dictionaries, and of valuable historical studies, with a few essays in biography. All these

developments indicated the increase of that searching intellectual handling of musical structure, methods, products and
workers which in the later 18th century and still more in the
19th was to become prominent.

Joseph Sauveur (d. 1716) was the founder of the modern science of acoustics, which he first called by that name. His work is astonishing, since he was
a deaf-mute from infancy, hearing never but a little and acquiring but a partial
use of his voice. Early evincing mathematical genius, he came to Paris in
1670, taught mathematics, from 1680 in the Dauphin's household, and from
1690 was employed by the government upon fortification-plans. From about
1696, with the aid of musical assistants, he became absorbed in acoustics,
joined the Académie, and published in its Transactions several epoch-making
studies (1700–13). He fully established the vibrational character of all
sound, examined the phenomena of vibrating bodies, elaborated the theory
of partial-tones and sought to base a system of consonance on them, determined the vibration-numbers of tones of fixed pitch, suggesting 256 as a
standard number for middle C, studied the range of audibility, etc. Contemporaneous with him in the Académie was Louis Carré (d. 1711), a pupil of the
metaphysician Malebranche, with essays on sound and instruments (1702–9).
The contending views of temperament were reviewed by Johann Georg
Neidhardt of Königsberg (d. 1739) in several works (1706–34), that of 1724
containing the first use of logarithms in calculating intervals, and by Christoph
Albert Sinn, a Brunswick surveyor, advocating the equal system (1717).
Louis Bertrand Castel (d. 1757) attempted the futile task of presenting
musical effects to the eye by the use of colors (1725–35), besides other
essays. Leonhardt Euler (d. 1783), from 1727 a prolific mathematical writer
at St. Petersburg, reëxamined the general physics of sound, and sought to
frame a fresh theory of harmony from numerical principles, with rather
grotesque results in part, though his studies of vibrations were valuable
(about 25 works, 1727–74). Useful additions were made in 1732 by Johann
Bernoulli of St. Petersburg (d. 1747), and in 1753 by his son Daniel Bernoulli
(d. 1781). Georg Andreas Sorge (d. 1778), from 1722 court-organist at
Lobenstein, wrote extensively (from 1741) upon sound, intervals, temperament,
instrument-making, etc., often with ability, but in an obscure style and a con-
tentious spirit; his work on composition (1745–7) led about 1760 to a bitter
debate with Marpurg. Levens of Bordeaux sought (1743) to readjust scales
by a theory of reciprocal overtones and undertones, followed by others.
Robert Smith (d. 1768), professor of astronomy at Cambridge, published a
good general treatise (1749). Both the chief editors of the famous *Encyclopédie* (1751–80), Denis Diderot (d. 1784) and Jean le Rond d' Alembert (d. 1783),
were acousticians, the former known (from 1748) through essays, including one
on a mechanical organ, and the latter (from 1747) through many articles and
an exposition of Rameau's theory of harmony (1752) ; both contributed musical
articles to the *Encyclopédie*. Tartini (d. 1770), the violinist, was an original
investigator, as his theoretical works (from 1754) show, being the discoverer
of combination-tones, as also Sorge (above), Romieu of Montpellier (1751)
and Jean Adam Serre of Geneva (1753) claimed to be.

In the field of theory, the period was notable for several general writers of originality, basing their discussions upon the new acoustics and seeking a feasible system of true harmony rather than of counterpoint, the fundamental questions being as to the construction and relations of chords as such. Chord-inversions are now for the first time clearly recognized.

Rameau (d. 1764), the distinguished composer and player (see secs. 127,138), was the first and long the chief of the new harmonists. His views were developed through reading and reflection before he settled at Paris. When first published (1722, '26), they were not fully wrought out, but in some 20 later works (1730–62) were fashioned into a system. Some of these works dealt with musical acoustics, including temperament, some were mere attempts to popularize harmonic arguments, some treated of the musical defects of the *Encyclopédie*, and some were of a general philosophic character. Rameau's style was often difficult, his ideas novel, and some of his positions forced; but his historical importance cannot be gainsaid. The main points of his theory were that all chords are deducible from the harmonic series (partial-tones), are to be built up in thirds, often appear as inversions without loss of identity, and, however presented, imply a 'fundamental bass' (which may not be the actual bass), by which they are to be classified. The brilliant perception of the truth about inversions and the new search after the roots of chords opened the way for later advance, though some points were still unsatisfactory. The system was finely elucidated by d' Alembert (1752) and extensively commented upon by others.

Fux (d. 1741), the Viennese master (see sec. 121), took an entirely different course in his *Gradus ad Parnassum* (1725). Holding still to the old modes and not catching the drift of the new acoustics, he presented a system of counterpoint as the centre of composition, the value of which in its field is shown by its being translated from the original Latin into German (1742), Italian (1761), French (1773) and English (1791), and by its constant use by the best students.

Other publications until 1745 or later were mostly text-books of varying degree, often treating of the practical use of the basso continuo, as by Friedrich Erhardt Niedt (d. 1717) of Jena and Copenhagen, a larger work (3 parts, 1700–17, the last edited by Mattheson) and a smaller one (1708); by David Heinichen (d. 1729), from 1718 at Dresden, a considerable treatise (1711, much enlarged, 1728); by Mattheson (d. 1764), the versatile Hamburg critic and composer, several practical manuals, largely on the same (1719–39), the most important being the last, *Der vollkommene Capellmeister*; by Buttstett of Erfurt (d. 1727), advocating the old hexachord solmization (1717); by Giovanni Francesco Beccatelli (d. c. 1734), choirmaster at Prato, some 12 essays on various subjects (from 1725), mostly dealing with special points, with some historical notes; by Pepusch (d. 1752), the London ballad-opera-writer, a useful text-book on old-fashioned lines (1731); by Francesco Antonio Calegari (d. after 1740) of Padua and Venice, a general treatise, one of the best in Italian till much later (MS., 1732); by David Kellner, a German lutist who was cantor at Stockholm, on figured bass (1732), which, though not valuable, was often republished and translated; by Lorenz Christoph Mizler (d. 1778), one of Bach's pupils, a student and later lecturer at Leipsic University, the founder in 1738 of the Society of Musical Sciences there, and from 1743 a teacher at Warsaw, a handbook on figured bass (1739) and some others, with a translation of Fux' *Gradus* (1742); by Johann Daniel Berlin (d. c. 1775), organist at Copenhagen from 1730 and at Drontheim from 1737, an instruction-book in Danish (1742); by Geminiani (d. 1762), the violinist, practical directions for modulation and accompaniment (1742-55); by Meinrad Spiess (d. 1761), prior of the monastery at Irrsee, a thoughtful, but execrably written *Tractatus* (1746); and by Charles Henri Blainville (d. 1769), a 'cellist and teacher at Paris, a brief text-book (1746), a plea for a third or 'Hellenic' mode (1751) and a so-called *Histoire* (1767), which is mostly on theory.

The situation in theory from about 1745 onward is hard to put briefly, since lines of controversy crossed and recrossed. Rameau's system was becoming known and to it new features or new emphases were being added. The chief contributors to the literature, besides Rameau himself, were Sorge of Lobenstein (d. 1778), with an able general treatise (1745-7) and several later works, usually polemic; Joseph Riepel (d. 1782), a widely traveled musician, from 1751 working at Ratisbon, with a series of books (1752-86, the last edited by Schubarth), partly on counterpoint; Jean Adam Serre of Geneva, with two acute critiques (1753, '63); Friedrich Wilhelm Marpurg (d. 1795), a scholar of superior training, from 1746 at Paris and from 1763 lottery-superintendent at Berlin, whose masterly treatises on the fugue (1753-4) and on general composition (1755-8), with other works, were widely influential because of their excellent style and forcible thought; Tartini (d. 1770), the veteran violinist of Padua, with a notable compendium (1754) that strove to carry further the analysis of chords, with some other works; Johann Friedrich Daube (d. 1797), successively at Stuttgart, Augsburg and Vienna, with several text-books (from 1756); Jakob Adlung (d. 1762), in 1727 Buttstett's successor at Erfurt, with two thoughtful works (1758, '68); and Pietro Gianotti (d. 1765), a double-bass-ist at the Paris Opéra, with a redaction of Rameau's system (1759). Further writers in the succession will be noted under the next period (see sec. 165).

More or less connected with the above were the various manuals or methods for singers and players. Thus vocal music was treated by Michel L'Affilard (d. after 1717), from 1683 in the French Royal Chapel, on sight-singing (1691); by Michel Pignolet de Montéclair (d. 1737) of the Paris Opéra (1700); by Kaspar Calvör of Klausthal (d. 1725), on church music (1702); by Martin Heinrich Fuhrmann (d. after 1740), cantor at Berlin, two text-books (1706, '15); by Jean Le Beuf (d. 1760), abbé at Auxerre, many essays on Plain-Song (from 1725); and by Marpurg (d. 1795), on singing (1763). Methods for the violin were put forth by Montéclair (1711), Geminiani (d. 1762), several short books (from 1740), including rules for guitarists and other players, and Tartini (d. 1770), brief posthumous essays; for the flute (1752) by Quantz of Berlin (d. 1773), including accounts of his improvements in the instrument; rambling writings on the lute (from 1727) by E. G. Baron (d. 1760), also of Berlin; a valuable compendium of the various instruments of the day (1732) by Joseph Friedrich Bernhardt Kaspar Majer, cantor at Hall (Württemberg), which is a historical source as well; and for the clavier (2 parts, 1750, '61) by Marpurg (d. 1795), and the epoch-making treatise (1753-62 and later enlargements) by K. P. E. Bach (d. 1788).

Also intimately connected with theory were various discursive writings, often controversial, that now began to appear, indicating the rise of true criticism.

Johann Matteson of Hamburg (d. 1764) was much the most prolific writer of this class, his books on musical topics alone aggregating about 8000 pages. His purpose vibrated between the didactic, the polemic, the critical and the historical. His works on theory or method extended through 20 years (1719–39). Of the rest, the first was *Das neu-eröffnete, Das beschützte*, and *Das forschende Orchester* (3 vols., 1713, '17, '21, over 1700 pp.), treating didactically of music as a part of elegant culture, satirizing those who still clung to the antiquated scales (especially Buttstett), and discussing problems of intervals. Then came the *Critica musica* (1722–5, 748 pp.), essays in part reprinted or translated from various sources, issued periodically (including a diatribe against Handel's first Passion), and *Der musicalische Patriot* (1728, 376 pp.), a similar publication, issued weekly for a short time (including an account of the Hamburg opera). To the new interest in biography he contributed through his *Ehren-Pforte* (1740, 475 pp.) and his *Life of Handel* (1761). His vigorous attacks on conventional notions did good, but his judgment was not infallible and his method often spiteful, while his pedantry and prolixity are wearisome. Matteson's advocacy of dramatic church cantatas stirred up a strenuous debate between Joachim Meyer (d. 1732) of Göttingen (1726–8) and Fuhrmann (d. after 1740) of Berlin (1728–30), the latter on Matteson's side. Matteson's experiment with periodical publications was imitated by Mizler of Leipsic and Warsaw (d. 1778), in his *Bibliothek* (monthly at intervals, 1736–54), containing much valuable matter, often directed against Matteson, and another short-lived venture (1739–40) ; and also by Johann Adolf Scheibe (d. 1776), from 1736 at Hamburg, in his *Der critische Musicus* (weekly, 1737–40, enlarged ed. 1745), made up of superficial and often bitter original articles (as an attack on Bach's vocal writing, 1737), aiming in part to combat the growing use of acoustics in theory.

Friedrich Wilhelm Marpurg (d. 1795) was a much abler critic than Matteson. His *Der critische Musicus an der Spree* (weekly, 1749–50) was succeeded by the important *Historisch-critische Beyträge* (at intervals, 1754–62, '78), which, besides contributed and original discussions, included notices of events and persons, with some careful biographies. His *Critische Briefe* (weekly, 1759–63), besides similar matter, also included extensive theoretical essays. .

Other critical writers of varying importance were Benedetto Marcello (d. 1739), the sacred composer, with an attack upon Lotti as a madrigalist (1705) and a satire on the Italian opera (1720 ?), besides a MS. work on theory (1707) ; J. J. Rousseau (d. 1778), always too ready with his pen, with articles and pamphlets (1743–54) ; Charles Avison (d. 1770), organist at Newcastle, with an *Essay on Musical Expression* (1752), which William Hayes (d. 1777), professor at Oxford, criticised (1753) ; Christian Gottfried Krause (d. 1770), a Berlin lawyer, with good discussions of lyric poetry (1753) and other essays ; Colin de Blamont (d. 1760), superintendent at Versailles, with an essay on French opera-texts (1754) ; and Francesco Algarotti (d. 1764), an erudite Italian, from 1739 under the patronage of Frederick the Great at Rheinsberg and Berlin, with a notable book on the opera (1755).

The making of dictionaries was now taken up by several hands, as by
Thomas Balthasar Janowka, organist at Prague, with his *Clavis ad thesaurum*
(1701, 324 pp.), containing terms only ; by Sébastien de Brossard (d. 1730), a
musical priest, from 1687 at Strassburg and from 1698 at Meaux, with a *Dictionnaire* (1703, 300 pp.), terms only ; by J. G. Walther (d. 1748), the Weimar
organist, with a *Lexicon* (1728-32, 659 pp.), including biographies, terms and
bibliography ; by an unknown editor (possibly the publishers *C.* and *J. D.
Stössel* of Chemnitz), a *Lexicon* (1737, 430 pp.), names, terms, history, etc. ;
and by Rousseau (d. 1778), with a *Dictionnaire* (1768, 548 pp.), being his
articles in the *Encyclopédie* revised and increased.

In the field of history only minor works are to be noted. Nominally comprehensive, but really fragmentary, were those of Jacques Bonnet (d. c. 1724),
using material by Pierre Bourdelot (d. 1685), both of Paris, (1715, increased
to 4 vols., 1721) ; and of Philippe Joseph Caffiaux (d. 1777), also of Paris
(MS., 1754). On ancient music there are valuable data in the bibliographical
collections (1705-34) by Johann Albert Fabricius (d. 1736) of Hamburg ; in
essays (from 1705) by Pierre Jean Burette (d. 1747), professor at the University of Paris ; in many dissertations on Hebrew music by various authors,
collected (1744-69) by Blasio Ugolini of Venice ; in an essay on the Greek
genera (1746) by Pepusch (d. 1752) ; and in one of the works (1759) of
Marpurg (d. 1795). Andrea Adami da Bolsena (d. 1742) wrote on the
methods of the Papal Chapel (1711) ; Pierre François Godard de Beauchamps
(d. 1761), two works on the French theatre and opera (1735, '46) ; Francesco
Saverio Quadrio (d. 1756) on poetry, including the opera and oratorio
(1738-59) ; Bonnet on dancing (1723) ; Jean Georges Noverre (d. 1810) on
the same (1760) ; John Parry (d. 1782), a blind Welsh harper, made collections, with notes, of British, Welsh and Scottish songs (1742-81) ; and Scheibe
(d. 1774) contended for the origin of harmonized song among Northern
peoples (1754).

The famous firm of Breitkopf & Härtel in Leipsic (see sec. 193) was started
in 1719 by Bernhard Christoph Breitkopf (d. 1777) as a general printing business, which undertook music-printing also from 1754 by the aid of new methods of making type invented by his son, J. G. Immanuel Breitkopf (d. 1794),
whose scholarship brought forth several books on printing (from 1779). Gottfried Christian Härtel (d. 1827) did not enter the business till 1795. It
may be noted that Pierre Simon Fournier of Paris (d. 1768) introduced
round-headed notes into music-type in 1756, later issuing a history of music-
type (1765).

142. Summary of the Half-Century. — The early 18th century,
taken as a whole, presents many of the contradictory features
of a transitional epoch. Even more than the 17th century, it
was the meeting-point of tendencies old and new, so that it was
characterized by qualities that were intricately mixed. A just
summary must try to take account of all of these.

On the whole, the greatest feature of the age was the second culmination of the polyphonic idea of composition which had begun in the Netherlands in the 14th and 15th centuries, had come to a first culmination in the Italian *a cappella* style of the late 16th century, and had then gathered itself for a new and vigorous growth in the German organ schools of the 17th century. This majestic evolution now reached an unapproachable height in the comprehensive and unique genius of Bach. Its influence told mightily upon most of the German composers of the period, bringing forth numerous works in strict style and affecting the treatment of all sorts of other works. Its applications were on the whole more instrumental than vocal, thus supplying the counterpart to the earlier climax before 1700, but the advance of the contrapuntal chorus under Bach, Handel and others is significant, since it made vocal polyphony parallel in breadth and vigor of expression to that of both the organ and the orchestra. The facility displayed has remained a model and an inspiration for all later periods.

Meanwhile the expansion of dramatic music continued, with its distinctly unpolyphonic methods and its appeal to the popular taste for enjoyment and excitement. The vogue of the opera in all countries was not at once productive of works of enduring value, for reasons to be noticed in a moment, but it was useful in making the art of music a still more extensive popular power, in forcing composers to study persistently the ways and means of tonal effect, and in stimulating vocal and orchestral technique. It kept to the fore questions about vocal melody, about articulated harmonic and rhythmic accompaniment and about instrumental color. As dramatic music came to include the more elastic type of the opera buffa and as it gave birth to the Handelian oratorio, it gave tokens of a new vitality that was to rejoice many later generations.

Side by side with these movements and influenced by both, the advance of chamber music went on, calling to its aid the latest improvements in the members of the violin group, stimulating the betterment of other solo instruments, especially of the wood-wind class, and of keyboard instruments, especially the harpsichord and the immature piano, and differentiating the virtuoso as a new variety of musician. This type of composition had behind it no extensive traditions, but its progress in this period was notably rapid. The vigor of a few masters,

of whom Bach was easily chief, sufficed to push it toward maturity, outlining for it forms and principles that needed but little
to make them permanently satisfactory. The freedom of this
whole type of music made it peculiarly attractive. Into it might
go the exactest contrapuntal learning, the extreme of concertistic spirit and brilliance, and any degree of personal imagination and ingenuity besides. While the tendency of the age to
formality held it back for a time, its accomplishments presaged
the later glory of the piano and the orchestra as vehicles for
monumental expression.

But the 18th century in all its activities drifted toward formalism and mannerism. This was apparent in its literature, its
philosophy and its ethics, and was bound to affect its art. By
the middle of the century all musical art showed tendencies
toward routine conventions of various sorts. Thus much polyphonic writing became to a surprising degree a knack or trick,
as it had been in the time of Okeghem at the opening of the
16th century. Thus even the opera became for too many writers
a matter of rule and formula, manneristic and mechanical. Thus
there was a constant search for regular ways of writing instrumental music that could be applied without inspiration or real
invention. The greater geniuses, who mostly escaped these
tendencies, were outnumbered and often hidden by the host of
lesser workers who conceived of their art as mere artisans.
Hence the scornful epithets ' pigtail music ' and ' capellmeister
music' that are often given to much 18th-century composition.
It was the prevalence of this superficiality and heartlessness
that constituted the call and the opportunity for the great masters of the next two periods.

In the domain of theory and criticism the period was significant for the opening up of several new lines of thought. For
the first time harmony begins to get down to basal physical
principles, and thus to take on the aspect of a true science. It
was really not until this time that harmonic coherence and drift
began to be controlling influences in the lay-out of extended
works, thus bringing actually to bear the innovations begun in
the 16th century. And the whole literary side of musicianship
now begins to be cultivated, though without much system, with
considerable oddity and partisan bias, and so without producing
works of permanent influence. But the mere fact that writers

were active in discussing questions of acoustics, of structure, and of artistic value, is significant.

Throughout the century the social status of music as an art left much to be desired.   As a rule, musicians, unless attached to the church or employed in the opera, were forced to occupy a menial relation to some titled patron.   But the rise of instrumental music turned attention to the public concert as a frequent social event, gave employment and stimulus to the independent virtuoso, and ultimately led to the organization of fixed orchestras.   Gradually these changes wrought a change in the character of music as a calling or profession.   They also tended to lift musical art to a place of greater dignity in popular estimation.   To these results every extension of the literary and scientific discussion of musical subjects through publication was a distinct contribution.

PART VI

THE LATER EIGHTEENTH CENTURY

PART VI

THE LATER EIGHTEENTH CENTURY

CHAPTER XIX

HAYDN. THE SONATA AND THE ORCHESTRA

143. General Survey. — The half-century following 1750 proved to be in several ways extremely important in music-history, but we look in vain for much evident connection between its events and those of general history, or rather, to put it more exactly, the conditions of the time affected music most on its lower and commonplace level, which was not the plane upon which vigorous and constructive geniuses were at work. The latter were the agents that made the period memorable, simply because they rose so much above their fellows.

The world of politics was full of turmoil, but with little effect upon musical art except to subject its exercise to local and temporary interruptions, as, for example, in parts of Germany and Austria during the exhausting Seven Years' War (1756–63), and at Paris at the time of the Revolution (1789–95). The effects of the latter upon art in general, as of the complications connected with the achievement of American Independence (1761–83), were naturally not apparent until after 1800.

The long reigns were those of Louis XV. of France (1715–74), Maria Theresa of Austria (1740–80), Frederick the Great of Prussia (1740–86), George III. of England (1760–1820), Catharine II. of Russia (1762–96), and Louis XVI. of France (1774–92). The remarkable figure of Napoleon appeared in 1795, but his accession as emperor did not come till 1804.

The time was one of controversy and criticism in the world of thought, with a tendency to negations rather than construction. Morals and manners were artificial, and religion tended to lapse into deism or atheism. The average pessimism was relieved only by the display of ideality or of practical efficiency on the part of individuals. Altogether, the period was not one that might be supposed favorable for important artistic advance. Yet, on the other hand, it was precisely here that the truly modern spirit took its rise, breaking away from outgrown formulæ, throwing off restraints, and catching sight of far-off goals.

Briefly summarized, the chief movements of the period in music were these — the establishment of the principles of what is now called 'classical' form by a group of masters of whom Haydn and Mozart are typical examples; the reformation of the manneristic Italian opera upon new and much nobler lines of development, in which Gluck was the pioneer; a rising interest in the song as an art-form of importance, and the reappearance of the singspiel; the recognition of the piano as the keyboard instrument *par excellence*, with advances in virtuosity upon it and in methods of instruction for it; the definition of the orchestra in its modern form, and of standard groups for chamber music; and a steady progress in theory, with the disappearance of most of the remnants of the old ideas and the complete supremacy of modern tonality. As the period merges in the next are seen the beginnings of the famous contrast between the 'classical' and the 'romantic' spirits in composition, with the consequent tokens of a coming revolt from mere regularity of outward form in favor of greater truth and variety of subjective expression.

144. Haydn.— By a curious coincidence, during the last months of Bach's life at Leipsic in 1750 a young musician at Vienna, as he faced the problem of his future career and sought to lay foundations for it by methodical private study, was fitting himself to become the next great leader in the musical world. This was Haydn, a poor peasant boy, just discharged from the choir of St. Stephen's and searching eagerly for musical opportunity. It was still some years before the opening came, but, when it did, he stepped into a place of singular influence, which he occupied for the whole later half of the century. His genius was strikingly different from Bach's and his special contribution to progress at first sight utterly diverse. Yet between the two there was a real bond of connection, and the work of the later master was a real supplement to that of the earlier. And Haydn had what Bach lacked, a vital hold upon the admiration and following of the rank and file of musicians in his own day, so that what he did had an immediate effect upon standards of style. To him belongs the honor of fixing a type of instrumental composition that not only became characteristic of the period, but is still decidedly influential. He also was helpful in settling the form of the modern orchestra as the crowning implement of musical expression. The circumstances of his mature life were favorable to his orderly development and to the production of a noble list of works, for which he is still held in affectionate regard.

Joseph Haydn (d. 1809), born in 1732 at Rohrau, a village not far from Vienna on the Hungarian border, was a wagon-maker's son, the second of twelve children. His parents were simple folk, industrious, upright and devout (Catholics). From his father he derived a taste for rustic music, from his mother practical habits of order and thoroughness. Evincing early a passion for music, when 6 years old he was sent to the near-by town of Hainburg to study with a musical relative, J. M. Frankh, a good but severe master. Here in 1740 he was discovered by Reutter, the Viennese organist, and taken into the choir of St. Stephen's, where for 9 years he had constant practice in singing, both at the cathedral and often at the court, with free support and instruction of a sort at the choir-school. He supplemented the meagre school training by much independent study. In 1745 his brother Michael came into the choir and, when the elder boy's voice broke, succeeded him as chief soloist. In November, 1749, Joseph was abruptly dismissed and literally turned out into the city streets. Kept from starving by a few kind friends, he began to secure some means of self-support. He drilled himself assiduously in playing the clavichord and the violin and in composition, using at first a set of six sonatas by K. P. E. Bach as models. In 1751 he wrote his first mass, in 1752 a comic opera (music now lost), and in 1755 his first quartet. He learned to know Metastasio the poet, Porpora the singing-master and composer (whom he served as valet in return for instruction), Gluck the opera-writer, and Dittersdorf the young violinist. Some teaching and irregular work as a player brought money for music and theoretical books, and the process of tireless self-discipline went on. Among his early patrons were the amateur Von Fürnberg, for whom he wrote 18 quartets, the cultivated Countess Thun, who became his pupil, and in 1759 Count Morzin of Bohemia, who made him his choirmaster. Here he had a good orchestra, for which in 1759 he wrote his first symphony. At this juncture (1760) he married a wig-maker's daughter, whose extravagance and bad temper caused him infinite irritation for 40 years.

His powers as composer and conductor being now matured, in 1761 he became assistant choirmaster to Prince Paul Esterhazy, the head of a family long famous for wealth, culture and musical enthusiasm. At his country-seat at Eisenstadt the Prince maintained a small but choice musical establishment. In 1762 Prince Nicholas ('the Magnificent') succeeded his brother and greatly improved the musical forces, of which Haydn became director in 1766. Soon after this the Prince built a new palace at Esterház, whose furnishings and surroundings were so superb that it was called 'the second Versailles.' Here till the death of the Prince in 1790 Haydn lived and worked. For the

z

daily routine of family concerts, services in the palace chapel, and performances in the private theatre he had a first-rate orchestra and good singers. The Prince was cordial, generous and scholarly, and his demand for new music was incessant. Here Haydn wrote most of his orchestral and chamber works, his clavier-pieces, his songs and operettas, his masses and other church music (excepting works mentioned below). His many gifts were called into constant activity under extremely favorable conditions. The drawbacks were the distance from musical centres, the lack of absence-leaves, and the consequent monotony of stimulus to which he was subjected. Yet his development was happy, independent and symmetrical. He was idolized by his musicians and his fame spread far and wide. Occasionally the establishment was taken to Vienna and other cities for performances, but none of these trips went beyond the limits of Hungary and Austria. While the imperial court circle affected to disdain his style, the publication of many of his works by Artaria of Vienna, Forster of London, and many others, brought him recognition from a distance, even from Italy, France and Spain. Numerous musicians sought him out, and in particular his relations with the much younger Mozart were most cordial.

In 1790, Prince Nicholas having died, Haydn accepted an invitation from Salomon the violinist to visit London and give a series of concerts. Though almost 60 years old, this was his first considerable journey. Arriving in England in January, 1791, he was welcomed with universal enthusiasm. At his concerts and otherwise a long list of his works was given, including 6 new symphonies — all with enormous success. He was overwhelmed with attentions, professional and social, was made Mus.D. by Oxford, was received by royalty, and generally lionized. In July, 1792, he returned to Vienna, where he was now exalted, and spent a year and a half, among other things giving lessons to the young Beethoven. Early in 1794 he again journeyed to London, where his reception was as hearty as before, giving many concerts and adding 6 more symphonies to his English series. Late in 1795 he was again in Vienna. His connection with the Esterhazys continued and he served occasionally as composer at Eisenstadt. In 1797 he wrote his *Emperor's Hymn*, now the national hymn of Austria. In London he had been deeply impressed by hearing much of Handel's oratorio music, and finally undertook *The Creation* (words from the Bible and from Milton), which was first given at Vienna in 1798 and rapidly taken up elsewhere. This was followed by *The Seasons* (words by Thomson), which for a time was almost equally successful. The last ten years were uneventful, as his strength failed and his productivity almost ceased. He was much sought after by musicians and tenderly cared for by admirers. The occupation of Vienna by the French in 1805 and 1809 distressed him greatly, and during the second he died of old age. He was buried at Vienna, but in 1820 his remains were transferred to the Esterhazy estate at Eisenstadt, whence they have recently been removed again to Vienna.

Haydn's personality was singularly sunny and lovable. He was simple-hearted, generous, painstaking, indefatigably industrious, almost finically precise, a devout Catholic, honorable and manly. His music he regarded as a divine gift. His own powers had been developed by exacting labor, and he demanded similar fidelity from his assistants. The reverence he inspired is shown by the sobriquet 'Papa' generally given him during his later years.

He left a considerable property, carefully bequeathed to relatives and the many persons who had shown him kindness.

145. His Works and Style. — Haydn was first of all an instrumental composer, primarily for the chamber or orchestral ensemble. His style was matured in this field, as Bach's was in that of the organ. It is his achievements here that have given him his place in history. Yet he was also an accomplished writer of vocal music, including masses, oratorios, operas and songs. In addition he contributed worthily to clavier literature. The total number of his works must be over 1000 (depending on how the count is made), of which fully two-thirds are instrumental. The one prominent field that he did not enter was that of organ music, and, as will be seen, his predilections led him away from certain customary methods in several of the fields he did cultivate. So far as his experience and opportunities went, he compassed the whole range of musical effort, but his position as an Austrian, with his isolation until past middle life, kept him from feeling various strong influences that were at work elsewhere.

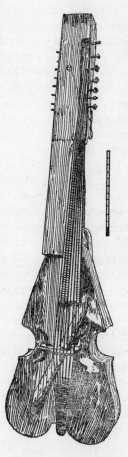

FIG. 87. — Baryton or Viola di bordone, having sympathetic strings like the viola d'amore.

Without attempting an exhaustive summary, the following statistics are useful. Among his nearly 700 instrumental works are 125 symphonies (for an orchestra varying in size from strings with 2 oboes and 2 horns up to the full band, including clarinets), 30 trios, 77 quartets, about 100 pieces for various chamber combinations, 31 concertos for sundry solo instruments, 175 solos for baryton (Prince Esterhazy's favorite instrument), about 50 sonatas and similar works for clavier alone, and as many for clavier with other instruments. Of these, many of the symphonies, with the trios and quartets, are the most important. (A number of the symphonies are known by special names.)   His vocal works include 14 masses and over 30 motets and other church pieces, the largest of which is *The Seven Words* (1785), written for the Cathedral of Cadiz, at first as an orchestral work, 3 oratorios, chief of which are *The Creation* (1798) and *The Seasons* (1801), several cantatas, 13 operas in Italian (from 1769), including *L' isola disabitata* (1779) and *Orlando paladino* (1782), several operettas, etc., and a large number of songs, part-songs, etc.

Haydn's entire style proceeds from the homophonic and harmonic point of view rather than the contrapuntal. Here he followed Emanuel Bach instead of the elder Bach. This was due partly to his nationality and early circumstances, and partly to his instinct as to the trend of musical progress. He was by no means lacking in contrapuntal power, as his choral works and the details of many other works attest, but his artistic interest lay in other directions. He was conspicuously a melodist, and his mind was saturated with the forms and spirit of folk-music. His gifts on this side involved not only a keen appreciation of beautiful tone-figures, but a strong sense of the sweeping harmonic drifts and balanced form that underlie them. His harmony is not so much the consequent of voice-part texture as a dominating plan or scheme from which the part-writing is developed. And his clarity and precision of form are so conspicuous as to seem to-day almost excessive. His works have a crystalline sharpness, every melodic outline, every harmonic mass or progression and every element of internal structure being presented with absolute distinctness. But his love of exactitude and perspicuity is kept from mechanicalness by the pervading healthiness, animation and humor of his imagination, and by his fine sense of large total effects and of the color-contrasts essential to them. His method emphasized the objective side of composition, but it could not conceal the warmth and elevation of his personality. Technically, his works marked an epoch in instrumental style, but they never would have done so if they had not been the vehicle through which a really artistic nature expressed itself.

The conspicuous achievements of Haydn were two — the full definition of 'sonata-form' as the basis for a variety of extended works for keyboard, chamber groups and orchestra, and the settling of instrumentation upon better principles than had hitherto obtained. Each of these requires separate treatment, because they became characteristic of the half-century as a whole (see secs. 146-147).

As a vocal composer Haydn was not so striking, though his works were neither few nor without merit. His operas were tuneful and entertaining, but his dramatic power was slight and his conception of the form (as he well knew) was limited. Of his oratorios *The Creation* was much the best, overflowing with naïve and sincere feeling. His masses are unequal, some being thoughtful, some showy, but as a rule they represent a view of sacred music too external and even theatric to be typical. This remark applies in some degree even to his serious *Seven Words*. In his songs he shows affinity with the movement toward lyric expression in small forms that at length became one of the valuable legacies of the 18th century to the early 19th, though in his case the tendency to nicety of form overweighted his spontaneity.

146. The Classical Sonata and Symphony. — Haydn can hardly be called the inventor of anything absolutely new in musical usage, but to him belongs the honor of so combining various points in procedure and so exemplifying them in masterly works that they became norms for a considerable period and, indeed, are still recognized as superior. This service of his concerned both the plan of movements in extended works and the particular form of each of them. The use of movements had been common for a full century, but the exaltation of one particular order as standard was a fresh step. Composition had long been tending toward homophonic and harmonic ways of conceiving and handling materials, but not until now were these made unquestionably supreme. The treatment of the first and last movements had been approximating its final stage of development, but essential points had usually been lacking that were now regularly supplied. All through the 17th century the 'sonata' had been properly a form for a solo instrument, and the transfer of such forms to the keyboard or to a concerted group had been becoming frequent since 1700, but henceforth this concerted use became typical. In this advance, so significant for modern style, the influence of Haydn was immediately reinforced by that of Mozart, Beethoven and others of the Viennese group.

Without trying to trace the growth of practice in full, the broad outlines should be stated of the general plan and specific form, as ultimately established not only for the keyboard works known as sonatas proper, but for trios, quartets, symphonies and even concertos. For all these the same general principles of structure became in Haydn's time standard. His personal influence was exercised more in chamber or orchestral works than in those for the keyboard.

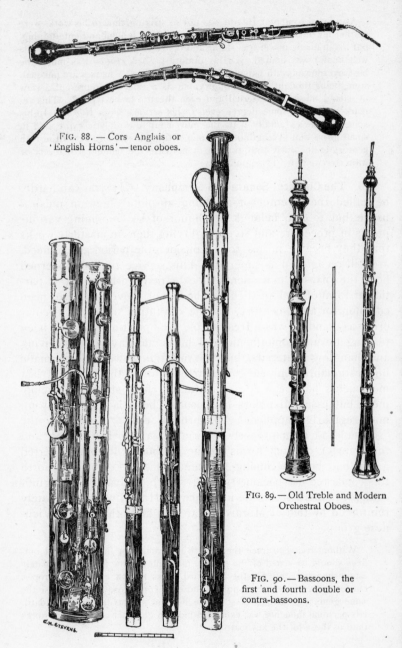

FIG. 88. — Cors Anglais or 'English Horns' — tenor oboes.

FIG. 89. — Old Treble and Modern Orchestral Oboes.

FIG. 90. — Bassoons, the first and fourth double or contra-bassoons.

The ' classical ' plan of movements included either three or four — the latter number being the more common in quartets and symphonies. Of these the first and the last were the longer and more essential. The first is properly in ' sonata-form ' and the last either in that or in ' rondo-form,' and both are brisk in tempo, the last often a presto. The second, in slow tempo, is either in ' song-form ' or at least eminently lyrical, and the third, if there are four, is properly a sprightly or even humorous minuet. The keys of the first and last movements are the same, of course, but those of the others may vary.

' Sonata-form' as a type of structure within a movement involves the familiar three divisions of exposition, development and recapitulation (see sec. 137), but, as understood in the ' classical ' period, it also involves the principle that in the exposition there shall be either two distinct ' subjects,' the one in the tonic, the other in the dominant or (if the tonic is minor) in the relative major, or the same subject presented in the two keys successively. Haydn's practice was not consistent in requiring two different subjects. Ultimately the second subject was usually of a flowing, song-like character, contrasted with the more incisive and brilliant first subject. The ' exposition' tends to subdivide into parts — sometimes a brief introduction, then the first subject (often reiterated), leading to a transition into the contrasting key, in which is the second subject (also often reiterated), culminating in its key, often with a coda. For emphasis and clearness the whole exposition is regularly repeated. The ' development' is naturally the test of originality and musicianship. In it the materials presented in the subjects are freely handled, torn apart, combined anew, mixed with new material, interrupted by episodes or connective passages, and passed from key to key. Here the advance of the Haydn period over its predecessor was marked, since the need of definiteness and coherence was better felt, and the ways of working were better understood. The development properly ends in the contrasting key, but with an immediate and emphatic return to the original key, introducing the ' recapitulation' or ' reprise,' in which both subjects are restated, with a final climax and often a coda. Sonata-form is characteristic of the first movement, and hence is often called ' first-movement-form.' But it is also common in the last movement, and may occur even in the other movements.

The materials taken for ' subjects ' from Haydn's time onward are almost always different in character from those used for contrapuntal treatment. Often they are distinctly lyrical, as if from a song, or solid harmonic progressions, as if from a part-song or chorale, or, if more distinctly instrumental, are employed rather for their pithy decoration of a metric pattern or a chord-sequence than for their adaptation to polyphonic unfolding. In a word, they are decidedly homophonic or harmonic in essence. And all the treatment given them is dominated by homophonic or harmonic principles. In details, of course, the part-writing must be careful and significant, and occasionally there are passages that recall the polyphony of the organ style, but in general there is some supreme melody or controlling harmonic progression that determines the form. Where exceptions occur, they are felt to be exceptions.

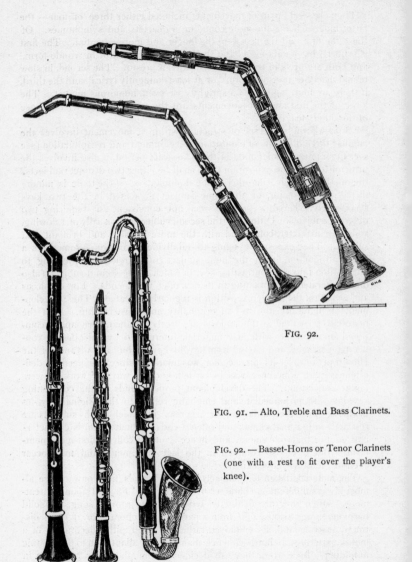

FIG. 92.

FIG. 91. — Alto, Treble and Bass Clarinets.

FIG. 92. — Basset-Horns or Tenor Clarinets
(one with a rest to fit over the player's
knee).

FIG. 91.

147. The Perfected Orchestra. — The contrast between the orchestra of the early 18th century and that of the later is remarkable, the change being due both to the rapid advance of chamber music and to the shift in methods of musical construction. In the Bach-Handel period the wood-wind rivaled the strings in number of players, the deliberate antithesis of tone-colors in groups was comparatively rare, and the massive effects desired were more indiscriminately vigorous than artfully calculated. Design in composition was far more valued than coloring, and the interplay of parts more than refinement in treating them individually. The polyphonic ideal gave but slight spur to expressiveness of delivery. But in the Haydn-Mozart period the string-quartet was made supreme in fact, the number of woodwind players reduced, though variety of tone was greatly increased by the addition of clarinets (especially after 1775), the study of the tonal groups energetically begun, and the principle perceived that sonority depends less upon complexity of scoring or loudness of playing than upon a judicious disposition of the tones and upon purity of quality in each instrument. Color or timbre began to stand on a more equal footing with design as a means of expression and effect. The emphasis on expressive melody forced a new attention to elasticity and shading.

As now balanced for the first time, the modern orchestra comprises three divisions: (*a*) the strings, including first and second violins, violas (tenors) and double-basses — a quartet; (*b*) the wood-wind, including first and second flutes, first and second oboes, first and second clarinets, first and second bassoons — a quartet with interchangeable upper parts; (*c*) the brass, including first and second horns, first and second trumpets, and two kettledrums — a partial quartet. It is to be noted that the violoncello was not yet commonly used, certainly not in differentiation from the basses, but that the piccolo (octave flute), the cor anglais (tenor oboe), the basset-horn (tenor clarinet), the bass clarinet, more than two horns or two trumpets, two to three trombones, and even four kettledrums were occasionally introduced for special effects.

It should be remembered that till about 1800 the old custom persisted of using the harpsichord or piano with the orchestra both to fill in some of the harmony and to fix the tempo. The conductor usually led from this instrument, though the use of the baton had been known, though rarely employed, for at least a century.

It would be interesting if the exact time could be given when particular instruments began to be used orchestrally, but the data are few. The following summary remarks, however, may be given upon each division of the ensemble. (*a*) The whole violin family came into view during the

FIG. 93. — Viola da gamba.

17th century, its members being slowly perfected out of the earlier viols and gradually supplanting them. The double-bass alone retained the old viol contour. Violins were used perhaps before 1600, certainly by Monteverdi in 1608. Tenors doubtless followed soon, but were commonly combined with the basses till about 1750. The violoncello seems not to have been recognized till after 1700, and not specially esteemed till towards 1800. (*b*) The transverse flute was used by Lully in 1677, but not brought into wide acceptance till about 1720. The oboe was the gradual derivative of several forms of double-reed instruments that were common in the Middle Ages, especially the schalmey, but its mechanism was improved early in the 17th century. The cor anglais (possibly a corruption of *cor anglé*) was similarly evolved from the tenor pommer of olden time, and the bassoon from the bomhart. (The invention of the bassoon is doubtfully attributed to Afranio of Ferrara before 1539.) The clarinet, with but one reed, was invented by J. C. Denner of Nuremberg (d. 1707) just before 1700, but did not make its way into the orchestra till after 1750 and was not common till about 1775. Its mediæval prototypes are obscure, though one of them, the chalumeau, persisted in use till the time of Gluck. (*c*) The horn is the descendant of the mediæval hunting horn; its orchestral use began early in the 18th century against some opposition on account of its alleged harshness! The trumpet, which differs from the horn in mouthpiece and tube, is a military instrument which came into orchestral use without much change. The trombone, as its name implies, is a big trumpet (*tromba*). The kettledrums or timpani have an ancient pedigree, largely military.

FIG. 94. — Orchestral or 'French' Horns.

Although experiments with larger or smaller aggregations of instruments had been going on for two centuries, especially for accompaniment, the true orchestra as a large ensemble for independent use, and a true theory of orchestration as a distinct branch of musicianship, hardly began before 1750. Two factors coöperated in this advance — the cultivation of chamber music, which brought out the capacities of particular instruments, and the growing custom of public concerts, for which the orchestra became the favorite artistic apparatus. In this period the excellence of particular orchestras became a powerful factor in musical progress, as they offered adequate means for giving extended works, stimulated virtuosity on various instruments, and set a standard of artistic quality generally.

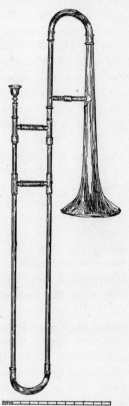

A striking instance was the Kapelle of Karl Theodor, Elector Palatine from 1743, residing at Mannheim, and Elector of Bavaria from 1778, residing at Munich. He was devoted to good music, as to other arts and sciences, and his band became the best in Europe under the able leadership of **Johann Stamitz** (d. 1757), concertmaster in 1743–57, **Ignaz Holzbauer** (d. 1783), choirmaster from 1753, and **Christian Cannabich** (d. 1798), concertmaster from 1759. These leaders developed a unanimity, a balance of tone and a perfection of shading entirely unknown before. The influence of this establishment was felt far and wide, being, for example, one of the potent factors in the unfolding of Mozart's genius. In it, indeed, the whole modern idea of concert orchestration may be said to have taken its rise (see sec. 148).

FIG. 95. — Trombone. The pitch of the tone is partly determined by sliding the lower crook out or in upon itself, thus altering the length of the tube.

A somewhat similar instance was the impulse given at Paris from 1751 by the original genius of **François Joseph Gossec** (d. 1829), who antedated Haydn as a symphonist, founded the Concerts des amateurs in 1770, reorganized the Concerts spirituels in 1773, etc., besides winning fame as an opera-writer, sacred composer and teacher (see secs. 154, 177). His endeavors were more or less hampered by the absorption of the Parisian public in the opera rather than concerts, and after 1790 the unfolding of all musical art in France was temporarily checked by the outbreak of the Revolution.

148. The Early Symphonists. — The largest forms of orchestral writing in this period were the symphony and the concerto, the latter being distinguished by the prominence given to a solo instrument. No precise date can be named for the invention of the symphony, since it was gradually evolved from the operatic overture (taking its name from the old term 'sinfonia'), the suite and the solo sonata. The scheme of movements and the use of two subjects in at least one of them, with some details of handling, are traceable before 1750, though not systematically maintained. It has been common to call Gossec and Haydn the pioneers, with Emanuel Bach or his father foreshadowing both. It now appears that special emphasis should also be placed upon the improvements in technical style made by the Mannheim group of composers, under the lead of Stamitz and others. It was at Mannheim that the refinements of orchestral expression were first brought fully into view and that a series of composers was stimulated to produce ambitious works employing these new resources. Few works of this class can be exactly dated, so that the historic sequence cannot be satisfactorily worked out. We simply know that, from about 1750, symphonies more or less upon modern lines began to multiply, that soon the number of composers engaged upon this form decidedly increased, and that from 1780, especially under the touch of Mozart's genius, the quality of the style became permanently significant. It is true that among the hundreds of symphonies written during the half-century many are devoid of interest except as tokens of a general movement that we now know had a grand destiny. As in other cases, the first efforts were largely directed toward the perfecting of tools and methods. In only a few examples was the content of the form rich enough to compete with the finer works of the next period.

Among the composers in this field before 1750, the Venetian opera-writer **Galuppi** (d. 1785) deserves mention for his overtures (from about 1740). More important was **K. P. E. Bach** (d. 1788), the Berlin and Hamburg composer, with almost 20 symphonies (from 1741), besides many works in related forms, all prefiguring later developments (see sec. 140).

The Mannheim violinists **Johann Stamitz** (d. 1757) and **Franz Xaver Richter** (d. 1789) exerted a wide influence through their attention to contrasts and nuances in performance, as well as to the improvements in structure that these made effective. Stamitz himself, though dying when only 40 years old, wrote nearly 50 symphonies, besides other works, in a style that supplies the

basis for the entire Viennese school. Richter, at Mannheim from 1747 and
choirmaster at Strassburg from 1769, wrote about 65 symphonies and much
other music in an almost equally original and suggestive manner.

The amount of production called forth under the Mannheim stimulus
was enormous, embodied not only in symphonies, but in every other variety
of ensemble instrumental music. Among the composers directly connected
with Mannheim were the Bohemian 'cellist **Anton Filtz** (d. 1760), with
nearly 40 symphonies; **Christian Cannabich** (d. 1798), Stamitz' successor
as conductor in 1759, with about 100 ; **Ignaz Holzbauer** (d. 1783), with
a multitude of works, including 11 operas; the bassoonist **Ernst Eichner**
(d. 1777), with 40 symphonies; **Giovanni Battista Toeschi** (d. 1800), the
third member of a talented family, with over 60; the violinist **Franz
Beck** (d. 1809), from 1777 at Bordeaux, with about 25; **Karl Stamitz**
(d. 1801), Johann's son, early noted as a virtuoso, concertmaster at
Paris from 1770, making extended tours, with 70; and his brother **Anton
Stamitz** (d. c. 1820), also at Paris from 1770, with 13.

More or less closely under the Mannheim influence were the following: —
François Joseph Gossec (d. 1829), otherwise noted as an opera-writer
(see sec. 154), was a Belgian violinist, in Paris from 1751 (see sec. 147),
who wrote over 25 symphonies (from 1754) and many quartets of real
value. Besides raising the orchestral standard at Paris, at the Revolution he wrote much popular patriotic music. Another Belgian was **Pierre van
Maldere** (d. 1768), from 1755 in service to Charles of Lorraine, with quartets
(from 1757) and nearly 20 symphonies (from 1769), which had vogue prior
to Haydn's popularity.

Luigi Boccherini (d. 1805), born at Lucca in 1743, stands still higher.
Trained as a virtuoso 'cellist, he worked first at Lucca, writing oratorios
and an opera, made tours into France, Spain and Germany, securing
honors at several courts, and then lived mostly at Madrid. He wrote
nearly 350 chamber works (from 1768) and about 20 symphonies, often
with distinction, but sometimes carelessly. His later style was influenced by Haydn.

Here belong also **Johann Christian Bach** (d. 1782), the youngest of the
great Bach's sons, with a large number of symphonies (see sec. 151); and
Karl Ditters von Dittersdorf (d. 1799), with about 50 (see sec. 154). Only
Boccherini and Ditters are counted as equaling the first Mannheim masters.

A direct link between Mannheim and Vienna is furnished by **Leopold
Hoffmann** (d. 1793), who from 1772 was choirmaster at St. Stephen's and who,
besides much church music, wrote for the orchestra so cleverly as to delay
the recognition of Haydn.

Joseph Haydn (d. 1809), as already stated (sec. 145), wrote in all about
125 symphonies (from 1759), the best after he had begun to feel the impress
of Mozart (especially after 1790). **Michael Haydn** (d. 1806), his younger
brother, chiefly noted as a church composer (see sec. 163), was an able
orchestral writer, with 30 symphonies (from 1762) and other works. Those
issued in 1785 and a quintet, long attributed to Joseph, are counted the
best. For some reason he avoided publication, so that his influence was
much less than his brother's.

Wolfgang Amadeus Mozart (d. 1791) as a symphonist was not so prolific as many others (see sec. 157), but the materials and the elaboration of his best works, such as the 3 symphonies in 1788, are richer and stronger. The themes have more warmth and character, the harmony and part-writing more variety and daring, and the articulation of the whole is more full of animation. He had a sure grasp of instrumental effects, delighting, for example, in charming uses of the wind groups, with clarinets and horns in a novel prominence. His best work was his latest, suggesting how much further he might have gone if his life had been prolonged.

Rapid mention may be made of **Friedrich Schwindl** (d. 1786), with some 15 symphonies (from 1765); **G. C. Wagenseil** (d. 1777), the Viennese organist and clavecinist, with over 30; **Johann Baptist Wanhal** (d. 1813), a Bohemian at Vienna, the producer of a prodigious amount of facile music, including descriptive pieces; **Wenzel Pichl** (d. 1805), also a Bohemian, court-composer at Milan in 1775–96 and then at Vienna, with about 700 works, including about 90 symphonies; **Franz Anton Rössler** (d. 1792), still another Bohemian, from 1776 serving Prince Esterhazy, from 1781 Prince Wallerstein, and from 1788 at Schwerin, with over 20 symphonies and much chamber music that won Haydn's respect; **Paul Wranitsky** (d. 1808), who was in Haydn's orchestra and became court-conductor at Vienna, with numerous works, including over 25 symphonies that competed in popular favor with Haydn's; the colorless **Ignaz Joseph Pleyel** (d. 1831), at one time a pupil of Haydn, the holder of good positions at Vienna, Strassburg and London, and finally (1797) the founder at Paris of a famous piano-factory, with 30 symphonies and other works, as many " as the sands of the seashore " (Eitner); and **Ernst Wilhelm Wolf** (d. 1792), from 1761 violinist and leader at Weimar, with about 15 symphonies, many piano-concertos and chamber pieces.

149. Instrumental Virtuosi. — The period was notable for the steady increase in the number and importance of solo players on various orchestral instruments, whose genius not only expanded the range of technique and the impressiveness of performance, but made worthy contributions to composition. The instrumental voice was becoming generally recognized for its tonal value and its power of expression, and its masterly use in concert ways was winning a place as a distinct branch of musical art. Naturally the violin and its relatives aroused the greatest interest, but there was notable advance in the wood-wind group as well. The frequent tours of players from city to city, and their consequent calls to service here and there, did much to extend and unify musical taste in different lands.

Although the earlier impetus to artistic violin-playing had been given by the Italians **Corelli** and **Tartini**, and radiated from them through various lines of tradition, in the later 18th century the centres of greatest activity were not in Italy, but at Paris and in Germany.

Following the Corelli tradition the greater names were these : —

Gaetano Pugnani (d. 1798), who was a pupil both of Somis at Turin and of Tartini at Padua. He set forth as a virtuoso in 1754, lived much at London, and from 1770 served at the Turin court and as a teacher. His style was broad and strong, and he wrote copiously for his instrument and for the orchestra, his works including many sonatas, much chamber music and 13 symphonies, besides several operas. Regarding his merits as a composer opinions differ.

Giovanni Battista Viotti (d. 1824) was Pugnani's greatest pupil, and is often called 'the father of modern violin-playing.' In 1780, with his teacher, he toured in Germany, Poland and Russia, receiving honors at St. Petersburg. Later he aroused intense enthusiasm at London and Paris, but, offended at a fancied coolness in the Paris audiences, abruptly left the concert-stage for a time. In 1789 he began giving Italian opera at Paris, at the Revolution was forced to resume touring and appeared at London and Hamburg, then went into business for several years, though without losing his consummate skill as a player, and finally (1819-22) was director of the Paris Opéra. As an artist he excelled in every way, in composition as well as in technique. His abundant works, ranging from solo sonatas up to quartets, quintets and nearly 30 concertos, are still admired. He was the first to apply true sonata-form and the use of the full orchestra to the violin-concerto. He was in request as a teacher, his greatest pupils being Rode and Baillot.

In the direct Tartini line were the following : —

Pietro Nardini (d. 1793) was a constant pupil of Tartini till 1746. Then, after some years at Livorno, he served as soloist at Stuttgart in 1763-7, was with his old teacher at Padua till the latter's death, and from 1770 was court-director at Florence. Good critics testify to the purity and nobility of his style, though he cared little for showy effects. His works comprise sonatas, quartets, concertos, etc. His best pupil was **Bartolomeo Campagnoli** (d. 1827), who came to Germany in 1776, touring extensively, was concertmaster at the Gewandhaus in Leipsic in 1797-1818, and finally choirmaster at Neustrelitz. He left some works, especially good studies and a Method (1797).

Johann Peter Salomon (d. 1815), a pupil of Franz Benda, began as a boy (1758) in the orchestra at Bonn, from 1765, after a short tour, was concertmaster to Prince Heinrich of Prussia at Rheinsberg, and in 1781 moved to London, where his superiority as a quartet-player and leader brought him long-continued success. He was quick to appreciate the works of Haydn and Mozart and to introduce them to the London public. In 1790 he induced Haydn to visit England, and between them a warm friendship resulted. His powers as a performer continued till his last years, and in 1813 he was the first conductor of the newly founded Philharmonic Society. His compositions were few and unimportant.

The founder of the notable Mannheim group (see sec. 148) was **Johann Stamitz** (d. 1757), first violin in the electoral orchestra from 1743. Early among his pupils was **Christian Cannabich** (d. 1798), in the orchestra from 1747 and Stamitz' successor in 1759. His renown was greatest as player and trainer. **Karl Stamitz** (d. 1801), son of Johann, after 8 years in the orchestra, began touring in 1770, was for many years in a ducal band at Paris, and later held office at Cassel, Jena and St. Petersburg. **Rodolphe Kreutzer** (d. 1831), a pupil of Anton Stamitz, made his début at Paris at 13 (1779), soon entered the royal band, from 1790 produced many operas (see sec. 177), from 1796 taught at the Conservatoire, from 1801 was soloist at the Opéra and from 1817 its director, besides court service under Napoleon and Louis XVIII. He wrote about 20 concertos, many chamber pieces and solos, 40 masterly études and (with Rode and Baillot) a standard Method. The Mannheim traditions were also spread by **Ignaz Fränzl** (d. 1811), who entered the orchestra in 1747, from 1774 was concertmaster and remained at Mannheim when the orchestra went to Munich, by **Christian Danner** (d. 1807?), in the orchestra from 1770 and leader at Carlsruhe from 1787, and by **Ferdinand Fränzl** (d. 1833), who, after about 15 years at Frankfort and on Russian tours, in 1806 succeeded Cannabich at Munich — all these being fruitful composers as well as significant players.

Here may well be mentioned **Leopold Mozart** (d. 1787), brought up at Augsburg, who in 1743 entered the service of the Archbishop of Salzburg and there remained till his death, devoting his whole energy to the development of his son (see sec. 156). He was a broadly trained composer, writing oratorios and church music, symphonies, sonatas, etc., and a famous *Violinschule* (1756).

Pierre Gaviniés (d. 1800), mostly self-instructed at Bordeaux, appeared at Paris in 1741, became a favorite player and teacher, and was called by Viotti 'the French Tartini.' He wrote concertos, sonatas and studies (from 1760). **Antonio Lolli** of Bergamo (d. 1802) first became famous from 1762 as leader at Stuttgart, but from 1774 moved from place to place throughout Europe. He had amazing technique. Among his pupils, both of the showy order, were **Giovanni Mane Giornovichi [Jarnowic]** (d. 1804), appearing at Paris in 1770 (numerous concertos), and **Michel Woldemar** (d. 1816), a Frenchman who lived a wandering life.

From the many other names that might be given the following may be selected because of their influence or the number of their contributions to orchestral literature : — **Friedrich Wilhelm Rust** (d. 1796), the highly cultivated director at Dessau ; **Niccolò Mestrino** (d. 1790), first at Vienna, then at Paris ; **Fedorigo Fiorillo** (d. c. 1823), who was from 1788 associated with Salomon at London ; **Franz Christoph Neubauer** (d. 1795), never long settled anywhere ; **Franz Krommer** (d. 1831), highly honored by several Hungarian noblemen and finally by the Emperor at Vienna ; and **Andreas Romberg** (d. 1821), famous as a virtuoso at different places, living longest at Hamburg, who was also known as a vocal composer (operas and cantatas).

Among the numerous 'cellists that now began to be prominent as virtuosi and composers were **Pierre Duport** (d. 1818), appearing first at Paris in 1761 and from 1773 in royal service at Berlin ; **Louis Duport** (d. 1819), his brother and an abler player, working at Paris till the Revolution and again after 1812 (excellent Method, 1806-19) ; **Christoph Schetky** (d. 1773) of Darmstadt (many works) ; **B rnhard Romberg** (d. 1841), cousin of Andreas above and his constant companion from 1774 as a virtuoso, in the court orchestra at Berlin in 1805-19 (numerous and excellent works) ; **Anton Kraft** (d. 1820).

pupil of Haydn, and in the Esterhazy orchestra in 1778–90 and in that of Lobkowitz from 1796; **Nikolaus Kraft** (d. 1853), his son and also in the Lobkowitz band, at Stuttgart from 1814 (important works); and **Jakob Christian Michael Widerkehr** (d. 1823), at Paris from 1783, playing several instruments and teaching singing. Here may be added the extraordinary double-bassist **Domenico Dragonetti** (d. 1846), a Venetian, famous at 13 (1776) for his unexampled skill, from 1794 at London, preserving for a full half-century his singular eminence.

A distinguished flutist was **Johann Georg Wunderlich** (d. 1819), prominent at Paris from 1779 as player, composer and teacher.

Among the oboists may be named **Christian Samuel Barth** (d. 1809), when a boy a pupil of J. S. Bach; **Johann Christian Fischer** (d. 1800), from 1760 at Dresden, from 1780 at London; and especially **Ludwig August Le Brun** (d. 1790), from 1764 in the Mannheim and Munich orchestra, but widely known through tours.

François Devienne (d. 1803), a noted Parisian player on both the flute and the bassoon, was an abundant composer for ensembles that called for great advances in the technique of the wind instruments, and also issued a good flute Method (1795).

From the noted early clarinettists we select **Franz Tausch** (d. 1817), one of a large family of players, in the Mannheim and Munich orchestra from 1770, and from 1789 at the Berlin court; **Joseph Beer** (d. 1811), from 1771 in service in France, later also at the Berlin court — the inventor of the fifth key on his instrument; **Michel Yost** (d. 1786, 32 years old), pupil of Beer at Paris, from 1777 a favorite concert-player (many works); **Jean Xavier Lefèvre** (d. 1829), pupil of Yost, public player from 1787, at the Opéra in 1791–1817, teacher in the Conservatoire from 1795, for which he prepared a Method (1802) — inventor of the sixth key; and **Johann Heinrich Backofen** (d. 1830), first appearing about 1789, a specialist on several instruments and from 1815 head of a factory of wind instruments at Darmstadt.

Famous among players on the horn, and composers for it and kindred instruments, were **Johann Wenzel Stich** [Italianized **Punto**] (d. 1803), a Bohemian who appeared as a virtuoso about 1775, was in Paris in 1782–99, then returned to Vienna and Prague (numerous facile works and a Method, 1798); **Johann Andreas Amon** (d. 1825), pupil of Stich and long his companion on tours, from 1789 at Heilbronn, from 1817 at Wallenstein; and **Georg Abraham Schneider** (d. 1839), in Prince Henry's orchestra at Rheinsberg from 1790, from 1802 in court service at Berlin, an expert on wind instruments and a prolific composer of varied works, including operettas and sacred music.

Here may be mentioned the fact that about 1750 **Johann Anton Mareš** (d. 1794), a Bohemian, introduced in Russia the peculiar form of horn-music in which each player in the band plays but a single tone (just as in old English change-ringing there was a ringer for each bell).

Reference should also be made to the noted harpist **Johann Baptist Krumpholtz** (d. 1790), who appeared at Vienna in 1772, worked for a time with Haydn, from 1776 settled in Paris, where he influenced Érard in the improvement of his instrument (important works).

2 A

For convenience, sundry notes upon improvements in instruments may here be inserted : —

François Tourte (d. 1835), one of a family of bow-makers at Paris, about 1775–80, perhaps with the aid of the violinist Viotti, perfected a novel type of violin-bow which has not since been improved.   The material is straight-grained Brazilian lancewood or snakewood, delicately tapered and slightly bent inward (by heating), and it is fitted with about 100 white horse-hairs, the tension of which is controlled by a screw at the 'nut.' This invention imparted a new value to all violin-playing.

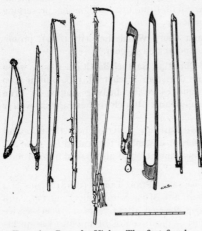

Anton Bachmann (d. 1800), a Berlin instrument-maker, in 1778 introduced the machine-head for 'cellos and basses, and also invented a keyboard attachment for guitars.

Charles Clagget (d. 1820), an Irish violinist, from 1776 in London, devised a number of curious improvements or novelties (book, 1793), which, however, met with no acceptance.

Georg Joseph Vogler (d. 1814), the eccentric organist and teacher,

FIG. 96.—Bows for Viols. The first five belong with savage or semi-civilized instruments, the sixth and seventh with double-basses, the eighth with the 'cello, the ninth with the violin.

in 1789 exhibited at Amsterdam his 'orchestrion,' a portable organ that included many new ideas, such as the imitation of orchestral effects, largely by the use of free-reed pipes.   Similar instruments were made in 1796–8 at Prague by **Thomas Anton Kunz**, and in 1800 at Vienna by **Johann Nepomuk Mälzel** (d. 1838) — the last better known for his 'metronome' (1816, Paris).   Vogler's advocacy of free reeds is supposed to have arisen from his seeing a Chinese 'cheng' (see sec. 11), or hearing of its principle, at St. Petersburg in 1788 — the idea having been used there by Kirschnigk and Rackwitz.   Since his day free-reed pipes have been sparingly used in pipe-organs.   The principle had notable application in the 'orgue expressif' or 'harmonium,' developed later in France.

CHAPTER XX

GLUCK AND THE DRAMATIC REFORM

150. The Operatic Situation. — The latter half of the 18th century was a time of enormous activity in operatic music. At least seventy-five composers might be named whose ability or practical success gave them prominence. So intense was the popular demand that perhaps as many as 2500 operas of all sorts were written, of which many hundreds were produced. The field may be roughly divided between three principal groups — the Neapolitans, whether working in Italy or abroad, the Viennese (including some belated Venetians), and the French. Other national groups, however, were beginning to appear as offshoots from these, though none of them, not even the German, was yet of much importance.

At first Italian models were almost everywhere supreme, though in Paris they were in competition with styles of French origin. The opera seria was at its extreme of structural formality and showy heartlessness — a procession of conventional arias designed to exhibit the dexterity of vocalists and to feed the popular craving for sensation. Except in the hands of a few writers, the musical structure was meagre and commonplace, lacking both harmonic and contrapuntal life, and unsupported by any broad sense of orchestral treatment. Opera-writing was largely a knack or a trade, which many an aspirant felt he could acquire at short notice and then honorably exercise as long as public favor could be shrewdly cajoled. The principal exception in the prevailing flatness was the opera buffa, with its tendency to transgress traditions by developing real personification, pithy and animated action, and extended ensemble or concerted effects. The reaction of this upon the opera seria was beginning to be felt, so that the line between the two was growing fainter — one of the signs of a new era.

Between 1760 and 1780, however, came the revolution proclaimed and executed by Gluck, which aimed to uproot established traditions, to emancipate the opera from its long slavery to the mere concert ideal, and to make it again what its early progenitors had meant it to be, a true drama in music. Gluck reached his convictions by slow processes of study and reflection, and he advanced them by argument as well as by illustration, thus precipitating a violent discussion that extended over many years. But the time was ripe for new views, and they were consciously or unconsciously adopted by other composers after 1780. Foremost in this number was Mozart, whose effective period immediately succeeded that of Gluck.

One of the minor features of the period was the reversion in Germany to the old singspiel type, with its freedom to use spoken dialogue and its predilection for simple songs.

151. The Later Neapolitans. — The popularity of the concert-opera in the sensuous melodic style of southern Italy was upheld by a large number of prolific and often talented writers, and their works were in favor all over Europe. In one case, that of Piccinni, by the exigencies of a Parisian partisan debate this type was brought into direct and disastrous competition with the stronger ideas of Gluck, but elsewhere it encountered little opposition until about the time of the French Revolution (1792–5). After that time the Neapolitan school as such followed the Venetian and the Bolognese into oblivion, its best representatives, like Cherubini, becoming merged in new groups, characterized by tendencies that belong rather to the 19th century.

Several of the composers mentioned in secs. 125–126 continued at work after 1750 — notably Jommelli (d. 1774) at Stuttgart and Naples, Duni (d. 1775) at Paris, Hasse (d. 1783) at Dresden and Vienna, Bernasconi (d. 1784) at Munich, and Galuppi (d. 1785) at St. Petersburg and Venice. At Paris, also, was the veteran Rameau (d. 1764), representing the best of the native French style (see sec. 127).

Tommaso Traetta (d. 1779), born in 1727 at Naples and trained for nine years under Durante, began as a church composer, but from 1751 became noted as an opera-writer, working in 1758–65 at Parma, then at Venice, and in 1768–75 at St. Petersburg (following Galuppi), with visits to Vienna (1759, '60), Munich (1767) and London (1775–6). As examples of his over 35 operas may be mentioned *Ezio* (1754, Rome), *Ippolito ed Aricia* (1759,

Parma), *Ifigenia in Aulide* (1759, Vienna) and *Armide* (1761, Vienna). He was gifted musically and dramatically, and has been credited with some fore-gleams of Gluck's ideas.

Nicola Piccinni (d. 1800), born in 1728, studied about twelve years under Leo and Durante, and then (1754) risked competition with Logroscino in opera buffa, displacing the latter as the popular favorite at Naples and Rome, and becoming famous far and wide. Before 1775 he produced at least 60 operas, serious and comic, as a rule with success, since his gift of melody was ample and his power in ensemble-finali unique. In 1776 he was induced to move to Paris, where the enemies of Gluck seized him and pushed him forward, against his will, as representing the true lyric ideal. Hence developed the fiercest contest in music-history, that between the ' Gluckists ' and the ' Piccin-nists.' In all this Piccinni himself held aloof, except that he strove to execute worthily the commissions given him. His Parisian productions continued till 1789, some being well received, but others suffering by comparison with the vigor of Gluck or the fresh popularity of Sacchini. His direct competition with Gluck (*Iphigénie en Tauride*, 1781) was distinctly unsuccessful, Piccinni himself acknowledging his rival's greatness. From 1784 he taught in the royal music-school. Returning to Naples in 1789, he fell under suspicion of republicanism, was kept a prisoner in his house for four years, and lapsed into poverty, against which he struggled by writing some oratorios and church music. In 1798, however, he was called to Paris to receive a pension and other honors, which his broken health did not long allow him to enjoy. His operas are said to have numbered over 130, of which about 90 are still traceable. Among the most noted were *Alessandro nell' Indie* (1758, Rome), *La Cecchina* (1760, Rome), *L'Olimpiade* (1761, Rome), *La Didone* (1769, Naples), *Antigono* (1771, Rome), *Roland* (1778, Paris), *Atys* (1780, Paris) and *Didon* (1783, Paris). It is probable that some of his works were carefully studied by Mozart before 1781.

Antonio Maria Gasparo Sacchini (d. 1786), a fisher-boy, was discovered by Durante, with whom he studied eight years. From 1756 he wrote colloquial comic operas at Naples, and from 1762 undertook grand opera with rapid success at Rome and other cities, becoming a strong rival of Piccinni. In 1768 he succeeded Traetta at Venice as a teacher, writing considerable sacred music. After sojourns at Munich and Stuttgart, from 1772 he was in London, reproducing his earlier works. In 1781 he visited Paris and soon removed thither, once more competing ably with Piccinni. In all, he wrote about 60 operas, varying in size and importance, those of his youth being specially full of spirit and of simple, graceful melody, though hasty in workmanship, while those later were less spontaneous, but better finished. The leading examples are *Semiramide* (1762, Rome), *Alessandro nell' Indie* (1768, Venice), *Scipione* (1770, Munich), *Rinaldo* (1783, Paris), *Oedipe* (1786, Versailles), *Arvire et Évelina* (1788, Paris, finished by Rey). He also left some orchestral and clavier-pieces.

Pietro Guglielmi (d. 1804), born in 1727, was another pupil of Durante, though when is not clear. It is claimed that he began opera-writing as early as 1739. Winning applause in Italy by many works before 1762, he then worked for a time at Dresden and Brunswick, and in 1772-7 was in London.

competing moderately with other favorites. The next 15 years he was in Naples again, where he succeeded in reasserting his strength even against Paisiello and Cimarosa. In 1793 he became choirmaster at St. Peter's in Rome and devoted himself to oratorios and church music. He is said to have written 200 operas, of which most have vanished. Chief among them were *I viaggiatori ridicoli* (1772, London), *Pappamosca* (1783, Milan), *Enea e Lavinia* (1785, Naples), *La pastorella nobile* (1785, Naples), *I due gemelli* (1789, Milan), *La bella pescatrice* (1789, Naples) and *La serva innamorata* (1790, Naples). Of his oratorios, *Debora e Sisara* (1794) is noted as one of the best examples from the whole period.

Francesco di Majo (d. 1771), probably a pupil of Martini, died very young (31 years at most). But his brilliant promise secured him high place in the Royal Chapel at Naples, and his fine dramatic power was shown in nearly 20 operas (from 1759). He also wrote considerable church music.

Johann Christian Bach (d. 1782), born in 1735, the youngest surviving son of the great Bach, after his father's death in 1750 continued his studies with his brother Emanuel at Berlin, from 1754 with Martini at Bologna, and from 1757 partly at Naples. He became a Roman Catholic and from 1760 was organist at Milan, but was much occupied over operas, of which *Catone* was the first (1758). By 1762 his fame had spread so that he was invited to London, producing *Orione* and *Zanaida* (both 1763) and becoming music-master in the royal family. In 1764-5 occurred his memorable intercourse with the boy Mozart. He was in request as a clavier-teacher, and from 1764 collaborated with Abel in a noted series of public concerts, which continued till his death. In 1772 and '74 he gave operas at Mannheim and in 1779 at Paris (near the close of the Gluck-Piccinni contest). In all, he wrote 20 operas, with several pasticcios and cantatas, and a notable dramatic oratorio, *Gioas* (1770). He was a significant contributor to the evolution of the symphony and to chamber music, wrote extensively for the clavier, and while in Italy worked assiduously on church music (a fine Te Deum, 1759, etc.) in the strict style. He was the only Bach who was fully identified with the new styles later in the century.

Johann Gottlieb Naumann (d. 1801), born at Dresden in 1741, being early taken to Italy, secured lessons from Tartini and Martini and at Naples, bringing out his first opera at Venice (1763). In 1764 he became electoral church composer at Dresden, but soon visited Italy again as a favorite opera-writer. Though invited elsewhere, he held his place at Dresden, where from 1776 he was choirmaster. He made long stays at Stockholm (where he raised Italian opera to a high standard), Copenhagen and Berlin, securing by his facility and refinement much renown for the time. He wrote 23 operas, among which were *Amphion* (1772, Stockholm), *Solimano* (1773, Venice), *Cora* and *Gustav Vasa* (Swedish texts, 1780, '83), *La dama soldato* (1791, Dresden) and *Protesilao* (1793, Berlin), many oratorios, much church music, including several good masses and a noted Vater Unser, many symphonies, etc. It is noticeable that his prominence at Dresden dates from Hasse's departure.

Giacomo Tritto (d. 1824), born in 1733, lived a long life, almost wholly at Naples, studying under Cafaro and Sala, and succeeding them both as an influential teacher. His about 50 operas extended through a full half-century (1764–1815), and he also wrote extensively for the church. Late in life (1821-3) he published theoretical works.

Giovanni Paisiello (d. 1816), born in 1741, studied nine years at Naples under Durante, Cotumacci and Abos, the last four years himself serving as a teacher. In 1765 began the long series of dramatic works that continued for almost 40 years and made him famous throughout Europe. From 1776 he was at St. Petersburg in the employ of the Empress Catherine, returning in 1784 to royal service at Naples. In 1802–3 he was in high favor with Napoleon at Paris, after which he resumed his post at Naples. From 1772 he produced more or less sacred music as well — masses, motets, a Passion (1782, Warsaw) ; and he was a fertile instrumental composer — many symphonies, quartets, concertos, etc. But he chiefly excelled in opera, especially in buffo forms or those that mingled the comic with the serious. He was strong as a melodist, not so much in the conventional and stilted style, but in spontaneous lyricalness, and his handling of accompaniments was original and ingenious. Occasionally he rose to a degree of dramatic sublimity and force, though his best talent lay in charming and piquant effects. Of his more than 100 operas and operettas many had special success, such as *L' idolo cinese* (1767, Naples), *La serva padrona* (1769, Naples), *Il matrimonio inaspettato* (1778, St. Petersburg), *Il barbiere di Siviglia* (1782, St. Petersburg), *Il re Teodoro* (1784, Vienna), *Il molinara* (1788, Naples), *Nina* (1789, Naples), *I zingari* (1789, Naples) and *Proserpina* (1803, Paris). He was much in competition with Piccinni and Cimarosa, sharing with them the highest popularity of the period.

Several lesser names follow. **Gennaro Astarita** (d. 1803?) wrote about 35 popular operas, mostly comic (from 1765), given throughout Italy and somewhat elsewhere, including *Circe ed Ulisse* (1777). **Felice Alessandri** (d. 1798) began as both clavierist and opera-writer (from 1767), and worked at Turin, Paris, London, St. Petersburg and Berlin, producing about 30 operas of transient value. **Nicola Antonio Zingarelli** (d. 1837), born in 1752, entered the opera field in 1768, but not strikingly until 1785, whence his activity continued till 1811, with about 30 operas, the most famous being *Romeo e Giulietta* (1796, Milan). His official posts and his greater renown were in connection with church music (see sec. 163). **Pasquale Anfossi** (d. 1797), born in 1727 and a pupil of Piccinni, began writing operas in 1758, soon sought to rival his teacher at Rome, visited Paris, London, Berlin, Prague and Florence in a busy search for popularity, and from 1791 was choirmaster at the Lateran in Rome. His operas number over 70, of which *L'incognita perseguitata* (1773, Rome) was the first to show his clever talent. **Giacomo Insanguine** [or **Monopoli**, from his birthplace] (d. 1796), pupil at Naples of Cotumacci, produced 21 operas (1756–82) and also fair church music, as the *71st Psalm* (1775). **Giuseppe Gazzaniga** (d. 1818), pupil of Porpora and Piccinni, wrote about 45 operas (from 1768), among which was *Il convitato di pietra* (1787, Venice), with a libretto which influenced that of Mozart's *Don Giovanni* (same year, Prague). **Giuseppe Giordani** (d. 1798) began opera-writing in 1771 at Pisa, from 1772 taught in London and Dublin, besides giving operas, and in 1782 returned to Italy, in 1791 becoming choirmaster at Fermo. He produced about 35 operas, among them *Il bacio* (1774, London), and much instrumental and some church music.

Domenico Cimarosa (d. 1801) was born near Naples in 1749 and studied there for eleven years under Manna, Sacchini, Fenaroli and Piccinni. In 1772 began his phenomenal series of nearly 80 operas, completed often with incredible rapidity, sometimes several in a year. This facility, however, was supported by abundant melodic inspiration, especially in the expression of sparkling humor, by a sure instinct for proportion and balance, by great ability in the organization of ensemble passages, and by fine orchestral resourcefulness. He almost immediately became a strong competitor of Paisiello, then at the height of his popularity, and ultimately surpassed him, rising close to Mozart's level. Until about 1781 he divided his time chiefly between Naples and Rome. In 1788 he was invited to St. Petersburg to succeed Paisiello, receiving princely honors in many cities on the way thither. In 1792, though in high favor among the Russian nobility, he moved to Vienna, where he was made imperial choirmaster at an enormous salary. Soon he was back in Italy, still the object of prodigious enthusiasm. In 1799, having displayed at Naples his sympathy with republican ideas, he was imprisoned and sentenced to death, but was finally only banished. Going to Venice, while working on a fresh opera, he suddenly died. Of his almost 80 operas, by universal consent *Il matrimonio segreto* (1792, Vienna) was counted the best, but many other fine ones might be named, such as *La finta parigina* (1773, Naples), *Il fanatico per gli antichi Romani* (1777, Naples), which is said to have been the first instance in which concerted numbers were used in the midst of the action, *L'Italiana in Londra* (1779, Rome), *Cajo Mario* (1780, Rome), *L'Olimpiade* (1784, Vicenza), *La vergine del sole* (1788, St. Petersburg), *L'astuzie femminili* (1794, Naples), etc. He also wrote 5 oratorios and some church music, besides overtures, other instrumental pieces and numerous cantatas and solos.

Rapid reference may be made to a few later writers. **Luigi Caruso** (d. 1822), choirmaster at Perugia, composed about 55 operas (1773-1810), besides sacred music. **Pietro Carlo Guglielmi** (d. 1827), son of Pietro above, imitated his father's style in some 40 operas (1791-1819), mostly for Naples. **Giuseppe Farinelli** (d. 1836), in later life choirmaster at Trieste, wrote over 50 operas (1791-1819), mostly comic, skillfully copying Cimarosa. **Valentino Fioravanti** (d. 1837), first an opera-writer (from 1784) at Naples, Turin and Lisbon, and from 1816 choirmaster at St. Peter's in Rome, brought out over 75 comic operas, the best-known being *Le cantatrici villane* (1803, Naples).

152. Gluck as a Reformer. — The career of Gluck belongs to two periods in more than one sense. Chronologically it fell partly within the period of Bach and partly within that of Haydn. And in spirit and purpose it belonged at first to the conventional class of Jommelli, Hasse, Piccinni and the rest, while later it escaped into a wholly new class. Gluck is perhaps the most brilliant illustration in music-history of a genius that completely outgrew its original ambitions, so that it finally entered upon creation of which at the start it did not dream. His historic significance, however, lay not so much in the new ideals that dawned upon him — for these were not absent from some other minds of his day — but in his ability to bring them to tangible embodiment in works so beautiful and powerful as to arrest the attention of the musical world. He was much more than a theoretical critic. As he caught sight of new paths, he himself broke the way into them, and to such purpose that the entrance could never again be closed. It is probable, however, that his ultimate triumph as a pioneer was facilitated by his long experience in following the fashions of the age, though from one point of view the first half of his life seems almost wasted.

Christoph Willibald Gluck (d. 1787) was born in 1714 near Nuremberg, the son of a forester or game-keeper who moved from estate to estate. At 12 he was sent to a Jesuit school at Ko-

motau, where he learnt singing, violin, 'cello, clavier and organ. In 1732 he removed to Prague, partially supporting himself by giving lessons and making music for rustic gatherings. At 22 (1736) he was taken up by Prince Lobkowitz at Vienna, introduced to the musical circle at court, and thus thrown in the way of Count Melzi, who took him to Milan for lessons from Sammartini. Here he remained four years.

In 1741 he brought out his first opera at Milan, which led to commissions there and elsewhere. In 1745 he was invited to London, but without much success, owing partly to Handel's popularity. After visiting Hamburg and giving a hasty work at Dresden, from 1748 he made his home at Vienna, having the entrée into the best society. He was immediately summoned to prepare an opera at court, *La Semiramide*, which was very successful, and in 1749 was called to Copenhagen on a similar errand. Thence he went to Rome and Naples, where his *Telemacco* was well received — a work showing signs of new ideas. In 1750 he married at Vienna the accomplished Marianne Pergin. In 1751 he was made conductor to Prince Frederick at Vienna, and in 1754 was officially attached to the Opera. In 1754, also, he gave two works at Rome, being made by the Pope Chevalier of the Golden Spur. Besides fulfilling other commissions, in 1756 he produced *Il re pastore*, with new tokens of growth, especially regarding the overture, and in 1761 filled an engagement at Bologna. Several of his larger works hitherto had been on librettos by Metastasio, but he had written many slighter ones, and now essayed some texts by Favart, the distinguished French librettist of light opera — as *La rencontre imprévue* (1764). While thus far skillfully adapting himself to the standards of the operatic world as he found them, he had also already become an independent student.

In 1762, with the help of the cultivated Calzabigi as librettist, he boldly struck out on a new line with *Orfeo ed Euridice*, though his lack of full conviction is evidenced by considerable admixture of conventional methods. The public was at first bewildered with this work, but finally accepted it with interest. Though not hesitating to continue his old style and to repeat old works, in 1767 Gluck took the second step in the new path with *Alceste* (text by Calzabigi), and now used his fresh ideas with more confidence. Its reception was not enthusiastic, for the theme was gloomy, the treatment austere and the climax poor (later made worse by a French alteration). *Paride ed Elena* followed in 1770 (text by Calzabigi), with a remarkable revelation of latent power in romantic lyricism. Gluck had now secured a considerable following at Vienna, especially among the thoughtful, but his innovations were also sharply criticised.

In 1774, after considerable diplomatic correspondence with the authorities of the Paris Opéra, Gluck appeared there with *Iphigénie en Aulide* (text adapted from Racine), the fourth work in the new style and not one of the best. It was produced only after incredible difficulties, owing to the incompetence of the musical forces and the machinations of enemies, at the end overcome only by the personal intervention of Marie Antoinette (who had been Gluck's pupil at Vienna). The work made a hit, secured for the composer munificent rewards at Paris and a new court office at Vienna, and led at once to the recasting of other works for the Parisian stage, some of which succeeded, while others failed. In 1776 Gluck's opponents undertook to overthrow him by importing the veteran Piccinni as a rival, thus bringing on the brief but famous war between the partisans of the old and new ideas. In 1777 Gluck produced *Armide* (text by Quinault, written for Lully, 1686), a work of much romantic beauty, which, however, did not at once succeed. In 1778 both Piccinni and Gluck were induced to write upon the same libretto, *Iphigénie en Tauride* (by Guillard), Gluck's version being soon ready, while Piccinni's was delayed till 1781. This masterpiece crowned his success, and was really the last, for his remaining works were feeble. His health began to break and his last years were spent quietly at Vienna. After his death in 1787, Piccinni vainly tried to collect funds to establish an annual concert in his rival's memory.

In all, Gluck wrote over 30 operas, of which 7 belong to the epoch-making series. His other works, sacred or instrumental, are unimportant, though neither few nor small.

Personally, he was impetuous and strong-willed, though a tactful manager of men. Intellectually, he was gifted and his ideas were matured by careful study. That he was vain of his talents and perhaps miserly with his wealth are defects not always absent from an artistic temperament.

153. The Purpose of his Innovations. — The central purpose of Gluck's reaction was to restore to the opera its legitimate dramatic truth and power. This involved many changes from the artificial procedures that had become traditional, and a profound alteration of the entire spirit in which both the composition and the performance of a work were approached.

For example, the old detached overture or sinfonia in three movements was dropped in favor of a brief introduction suggesting the leading topics and sentiments of the play itself and passing without break into the action. The chorus was freely employed as a significant element in the vivid depiction of situations and as a setting for individual utterance. Concerted passages of any form were made lawful, if demanded by the plot, especially in the building up of climaxes. All the old rules about the structure and collocation of recitatives and arias were abrogated as rules, the employment of such formal methods being determined solely by the demands of the drama. Thus the text was elevated to primary importance. Its subject and disposition were estimated first of all from a dramatic point of view, and literary power in it became indispensable. The personages in their contrast and interplay were studied individually, and each was conceived and treated in its own proper quality. The details of expression were then elaborated from this characterization and from the development of the situations. At this point Gluck's instinct saved him from running to an extreme of declamation. Furthermore, he saw clearly that the opera called for more than merely vocal effects. He sought, therefore, to raise the orchestra from its position as a mechanical support or an occasional by-play into a genuine constituent in the total action, assigning to it a constant part in suggesting the progress of sentiment and in heightening the emotional effect. Here again, his instinct saved him from falling into the attempt to provide merely pictorial effects.

Theories like these involved a revolution in the whole process of making and giving operas. The librettist must be both poet and dramatist. The composer could no longer turn off work after work with clever versatility, but must immerse himself in the atmosphere of each new play and, if necessary, be ready to devise for each a new method of expression. The entire personnel of performance must be imbued with a new spirit, in which the petty search for chances of personal display had no place. And even the attitude of the public required alteration, so that the hearer should realize that the opera was no longer a variegated concert, but a unified and dignified piece of dramatic art. It is clear that

only an artist of experience and assured standing, of strong intellectuality and genuine musical endowment, and of indomitable
moral vigor, could have hoped alone and by one stroke, as it
were, to accomplish this radical departure from the established
traditions of the great Neapolitan school. Yet such an artist
Gluck was, and his honor lies not so much in his theory as in
his absolute success in bringing it to realization.

> We have considerable evidence of Gluck's theoretic position about his
> work in the prefaces or dedications which he had friends prepare for
> *Alceste* (1769) and for *Paride ed Elena* (1770), and in his fairly numerous
> and extensive letters. He sought to reason out a definite system of
> æsthetic thought as applied to dramatic music. His views were remarkably
> similar to those of the Italian scholar Francesco Algarotti, whose essay
> on the opera was first published in 1755 and enlarged in 1763, and which,
> therefore, he might have seen (whether he had actually done so is un-
> known). But Gluck's theory and practice do not wholly correspond,
> showing that he was more of an artist than a philosopher. In particular,
> his musical instinct led him on to greater lyric exuberance and charm
> than his bare theory indicated, so that the result was not simply a slavish
> subordination of music to the 18th-century conception of the drama, but
> an organic union on equal terms of the drama and music, each conceived
> with artistic freedom. Hence his works have an enduring value.

154. Gluck's Immediate Contemporaries. — Here is an appropriate place to insert some account of several workers in the operatic field who were not closely identified either with Naples on
the one hand or with Paris on the other. Gluck's reaction was
primarily against the ideals of the Neapolitans, but it told equally
against other groups, including those of his own Vienna and of
Venice. With these representatives of northern Italy and Austria
may well be included the few Germans who came into operatic
prominence at this time. Some of these, with the Austrians,
are the more notable because they had some share in the early
attempts to create a Teutonic type of opera as over against the
prevailing Italian type.

> **Giuseppe Sarti** (d. 1802), born in 1729 at Faenza, studied under Martini at
> Bologna, and made his operatic début in 1752 with such success that almost
> at once a place was made for him at Copenhagen, where he became court-con-
> ductor and was honored for years. In 1775 he became involved in a case of
> bribery and was banished. After teaching at Venice, in 1779 he was made
> choirmaster at Milan, whence in 1784 he went to a similar post at St. Peters-
> burg. Of his over 50 operas, the best were those written after his return from
> Denmark, such as *Le gelosie villane* (1776, Venice), *Achille in Sciro* (1781,

Florence), *Giulio Sabino* (1781, Venice), *Le nozze di Dorina* (1782, Milan) and
Armide (1785, St. Petersburg). He also wrote considerable sacred music,
especially for Russian use. Though courteously treated by Mozart, he indulged in an extraordinary attack upon the latter's quartets.

Florian Leopold Gassmann (d. 1774), a Bohemian, for a time a pupil of
Martini and then in the service of a Venetian noble, in 1762 became court-
composer and conductor at Vienna, there producing the first of his 22 operas.
Being a favorite of Maria Theresa, in 1771 he was made choirmaster, succeeding Reutter, and head of the Royal Library. He wrote also for the church
and for instruments.

Joseph Misliweczek [**Venatorini**] (d. 1781), also a Bohemian, studied at
Prague and in 1760 published his first symphonies. From 1763 he turned to
dramatic music under Pescetti at Venice, and in 1764 wrote *Il Bellerofonte*,
achieving instant popularity in the chief Italian cities. In all, he wrote about
30 operas, which were generally well received. He had a cordial friendship
with Mozart.

Karl Ditters von Dittersdorf (d. 1799), born in 1739 and trained at Vienna
under Trani and Bonno, made his first reputation as a violinist of the highest
skill. In 1765 he followed Michael Haydn at Pressburg, where in 1767 his
first opera was given, and about 1770 entered the service of the pleasure-
loving Bishop of Breslau at Johannisberg. He became a court-favorite there
and at Vienna, where he often appeared as an opera-writer, as also at Berlin.
From 1795, his patron having died, he was befriended by a Bohemian noble.
He was an abundant writer in all forms, specially famous for his comic operas
and singspiele, mostly in German, which gave an important stimulus to the
national drama. The more noted examples belong to 1786–8, such as *Doktor
und Apotheker* (which is still given), *Der Betrug durch Aberglauben*, *Die Liebe
im Narrenhaus*, *Hieronymus Knicker*, *Das rote Käppchen*. Of his oratorios,
Ester (1773) and *Giobbe* (1786) are still extant. He also wrote over 110
symphonies, including 12 on Ovid's Metamorphoses (1785), many concertos,
quartets and piano-pieces. His brilliant gifts as a composer might have been
more telling if he had not come into immediate comparison with Haydn and
Mozart, both of whom were his personal friends. In 1770 the Pope made
him Knight of the Golden Spur, and in 1773 he received knighthood from
the Emperor. Just before his death he dictated an interesting autobiography.

As opera-writers, Ditters, Mozart and Haydn were almost exactly contemporaneous. **Mozart** must be separately considered (see secs. 156–157).
Haydn's efforts in this field were inconspicuous, though not without merit
(see sec. 145). Two others of the same period follow : —

Joseph Schuster (d. 1812), the fluent composer of about 25 operas (from
1770) and much other music, from 1772 was in high favor at the court of
Dresden. He was trained in Italy, partly under Martini, was honored at
Naples, and made long sojourns in Italian cities, writing mostly in the current
Italian style. But he was also an early experimenter with German opera.

Antonio Salieri (d. 1825) was more significant. Born near Verona in 1750,
first trained at Venice and from 1766 under Gassmann at Vienna, his first
opera was produced there in 1770, followed by several more in the usual Italian manner. In 1774 he took Gassmann's place as court-composer and in

1788 Bonno's as choirmaster, acquiring a unique prestige and influence which he retained for a generation.   From the start he had attracted Gluck's interest, became his pupil, and brought out *Les Danaïdes* (1784, Paris) under the shelter of Gluck's name.   From this time he wrote frequently for the Vienna stage and occasionally for that of Paris, as *Tarare* (1787), but after 1792 produced few new operas.   Most of his 40 operas were very successful for a time, since they were less strenuous and novel than Gluck's.   His relations with Mozart were not altogether cordial, and he is supposed to have stood in the way of the latter's due recognition at court.   His long career made him an interesting link between the Haydn-Mozart period and that of Beethoven and Schubert, both of whom profited by his advice or instruction.

Matthias Kamienski (d. 1821), born in Hungary in 1834 and educated at Vienna, settled early at Warsaw, becoming the first composer of opera in Polish (from 1775).

Vincenzo Righini (d. 1812), a Bolognese, and pupil of Bernacchi and Martini, was noted first as a tenor and from 1776 as an opera-writer at Prague.   From 1780 he was teaching and conducting at Vienna, from 1788 was choirmaster at Mayence, and from 1793 at Berlin on a large salary.   His originality and vigor were slight, but several of his 20 operas were popular, like *Tigrane* (1799) and *Gerusalemme liberata* (1802).   His ablest work was a *Missa solenne* (1790).

Peter von Winter (d. 1825), was born at Mannheim in 1754 and brought up there as a violinist, going with the orchestra to Munich in 1778 and becoming in 1788 its conductor.   He was a pupil of Vogler and later of Salieri.   Beginning opera-writing as early as 1776, he was in much request at Munich, Vienna, Venice and many other cities, writing in all some 40 entertaining works, most of them originally in German, of which *Das unterbrochene Opferfest* (1796, Vienna) and *Marie von Montalban* (1798, Munich) were the most famous.   *Das Labyrinth* (1794, Vienna) is on a text (by Schikaneder) which is a pendant to Mozart's *Magic Flute*.   He disliked clavier-composers, and early took a prejudice to Mozart that he often expressed.   He was a prolific sacred and instrumental writer, leaving many oratorios and cantatas, masses and motets, and several symphonies, including the *Schlacht-Symphonie* (1814) for chorus and orchestra.   He had a certain gift for choral effects, but lacked learning and inspiration.

Vicente Martin y Solar (d. 1810), a Spaniard who made a name in Florence and Turin as an opera-writer (from 1776), went thence to Vienna, where for a time he outshone all rivals, even Mozart himself, and in 1788–1801 was in honor at St. Petersburg.   Of his about 20 comic operas, the chief were *Una cosa rara* (1786) and *L'arbore di Diana* (1787).

Among the further writers appearing before 1800, several are named under the next period (see Chapter XXVI.).

155. Operatic Progress in France. — Just after 1750 the French musical drama entered upon a period of debate and contention that was extreme enough at one or two points to become notorious.   The struggle over the Buffonists in the fifties was ostensibly between Italian and French ideas of comic opera, and the

Piccinni-Gluck quarrel in the seventies emphasized the contrast between the whole body of Italian and French conventions and a new dramatic ideal.   Yet, different as these two conflicts were, they were both symptomatic of large differences of opinion.

The elements involved were complex.   The total character and tendency of the Italian type of opera seria as represented by the Neapolitans was somewhat opposed by the specially French type as developed by Lully and more recently by Rameau, yet in both the aim was to present subjects removed from the sphere of common life and with many artificialities of dramatic treatment.   The Italians ran to an excess of extravagant lyricism, while the French tended to too much mere declamation. Against all this the rising Italian opera buffa was a healthy protest, but its broad and rough hilarity lacked the intellectual wit and the dainty handling of situations that the French genius craved. Hence one of the first products of discussion was the French opéra comique, which was a real contribution to progress. But hardly had this begun its exhilarating course before Gluck appeared with a total renovation of the operatic ideal, which was destined to affect both serious and comic styles. The effect of Gluck's work was not felt in full force during the 18th century, but it came at a time when the reactions between the opera seria and the opera buffa had progressed far enough so that the distinctions between them were breaking down and that a general advance could affect them both.   In this general improvement the work of Mozart had great influence.

The chief representatives of the native French opéra comique were Monsigny and Grétry, and of the later period, when extensive amalgamations of contrasted styles took place, Cherubini, Méhul and Le Sueur.

Pierre Montan Berton (d. 1780), an operatic singer at Paris as early as 1744 and from 1748 conductor at Bordeaux, is noteworthy because from 1759 for over 20 years he was director of the Paris Opéra and a useful agent in the renovation of the lyric drama in Gluck's time.   He himself wrote a few operas (from 1755).

François André Danican-Philidor (d. 1795), the ablest of a famous family (see sec. 133), was a precocious chess-player of international renown.   In 1759 he suddenly stepped into notice as a composer, at first of comic opera. Till about 1790 he was one of the most popular of French writers, excelling in harmony and instrumentation, though not specially strong melodically or dramatically.   Of about 25 works, the best were *Le maréchal ferrant* (1761), *Le sorcier* (1764), *Tom Jones* (1765), *Ernelinde*, (1767) and *Persée* (1780). He had much success with ensemble numbers — trios, quartets, septets, etc.

Pierre Alexandre Monsigny (d. 1817), born in 1729, in youth a self-trained violinist, also made such study of composition that, aroused by hearing Pergolesi's *La serva padrona*, he suddenly blossomed in 1759 into a writer of comic operas. In 18 years he produced, mainly at the Comédie Italienne, about a dozen operas with augmenting success, among the last and best being *Le déserteur* (1769), *La belle Arsène* (1773) and *Félix* (1777). His gifts were the reverse of Philidor's — melodic invention and dramatic instinct, but little technical or structural skill. During the rest of his life he wrote no more operas, distrusting his power of further creation. He long held a business office under the Duke of Orleans, was inspector at the Conservatoire in 1800-2, and followed Grétry as an Academician in 1813.

François Joseph Gossec (d. 1829), already mentioned (sec. 148) as important in the development of the symphony, was born in Belgium in 1734. After training at Antwerp as a choirboy and violinist, from 1751 he had success at Paris as a player. In 1761 he entered the field of light opera, making a hit with *Les pêcheurs* (1766), and soon undertook grand opera in rivalry with Gluck, writing over 15 works of various calibre. He also wrote some oratorios, much excellent church music, including a noted *Messe des Morts* (1760), and was one of the few musicians of the Revolution (festal plays and songs, 1792-3). Except in his instrumental works, Gossec was more industrious than creative, but he secured a position of great influence, which he used for wholesome results. He was an able organizer, setting up a new orchestral standard from his first years in Paris, founding the Concerts des amateurs in 1770, conducting the Concerts spirituels from 1773 and also as deputy at the Opéra in 1780-2, founding the École royale du chant in 1784, and serving from 1795 as inspector in the later Conservatoire and also for many years as one of the judges of new works at the Opéra.

André Ernest Modeste Grétry (d. 1813) was the most conspicuous figure of the period. He was born in 1741 at Liège, where as a boy he heard some Italian operas. He developed his evident talent there and from 1759 at Rome, but his eagerness to compose interfered with his studiousness. An intermezzo of his was given at Rome in 1765, and his first French comic opera at Geneva in 1767. He then went to Paris and, after producing *Zémire et Azor* (1771), entered upon a popularity of extraordinary magnitude that lasted, in spite of many checks, for 30 years. Of his about 50 operas, those most valued were *Le tableau parlant* (1769), *L'amant jaloux* (1778), *La caravane du Caire* (1783), *L'épreuve villageoise* (1784), and especially *Richard Cœur de Lion* (1784). His forte was comedy, if not cast on too large a scale. He had a great liking for musical declamation and a certain degree of melodic power, and his dramatic sense was excellent. But his harmony was feeble and his instrumentation thin, though not inapt, so that several of his works were later reorchestrated by other composers. In spite of his defects as a musician, he is counted as the founder of the modern French comedy-opera, and in his own day was loaded with honors, both within France and elsewhere. He was vain of his successes and yet understood his limitations. He wrote some church music and many instrumental pieces (6 symphonies as early as 1758), besides an egotistic work on declamation (1789) and a feeble manual of harmony (1801–2).

Luigi Cherubini (d. 1842) is a difficult figure to classify, since he was originally an Italian of the Italians, but later for more than 50 years identified with musical progress at Paris, since he was most influential as a church composer, though in his middle life (1780–1810) chiefly occupied with opera-writing, and since, finally, the type of his genius allied him more with the best of the Germans than with either Italy or France. He was born at Florence in 1760, where he was first trained by his father, who was cembalist at one of the theatres, but in 1778 went to Sarti at Bologna and was carefully instructed in contrapuntal traditions, beginning some sacred writing. From 1780 he wrote many operas in the prevalent Italian style, so that he is commonly ranked among the Neapolitans, though working in northern Italy. After a sojourn in London (1784–5), he went to Paris. Here, under the influence especially of Gluck's innovations, his operatic style was profoundly changed, becoming far richer, more dignified and more warmly dramatic, and he established himself as one of the ablest leaders in French opera. In 1795 he was made one of the inspectors at the new Conservatoire, but later, under Napoleon, was in less favor, so that for a brief time he betook himself to Vienna (1805–6). Returning to France, he gradually resumed the writing of church music, though not entirely retiring from the opera. In 1815 he paid a notable visit to London. From 1816 he was professor of composition at the Conservatoire, and from 1821 its director, continuing in active service till the year before his death. Of his almost 30 dramatic works the more celebrated were *Ifigenia in Aulide* (1788, Turin), *Lodoïska* (1791, Paris), *Médée* (1797), *Les deux journées*, called *Der Wasserträger* in Germany (1800), *Anacréon* (1803) and *Faniska* (1806, Vienna). Hardly any of his operas rest upon good librettos, except *Les deux journées*, and this had much to do with their lack of permanent success. Another blemish is that the wealth of musical ideas in them is often too abundant, so that scenes are too much prolonged and in some cases the whole work. But many of the overtures are classic masterpieces, and the refinement of the themes and the originality of the instrumentation are widely acknowledged. It is notable that in *Les deux journées* the Italian traditions are completely deserted, in that there are practically none but concerted or chorus numbers throughout. In spite of all qualifications, Cherubini must be considered one of the most potent influences, with those of Gluck and Mozart, in the essential renovation of the opera upon modern lines. (For reference to his work in sacred music, see sec. 163.)

Étienne Nicholas Méhul (d. 1817), born in 1763 in northeastern France and receiving his direction as a musician there and at Paris, under the personal guidance of Gluck, is still more a link between the older French opera and that of the 19th century. He began organ-playing at 10 and sacred composition soon after. In 1778 he went to Paris, where the hearing of Gluck's masterpiece in 1779 and the latter's advice led him to undertake opera, though his first work was not given till 1791. In spite of the political disorders, he scored a series of successes and speedily became one of the most admired composers of the time. In 1795 he was made an inspector at the new Conservatoire and also an Academician. From his more than 30 operas, leading

2 B

examples are *Stratonice* (1792), *Mélidore et Phrosine* (1795), *Adrien* (1799), *Uthal* (1806), *Joseph* (1807) and *La journée aux aventures* (1816).   He had an exquisite tastefulness, a quick and versatile imagination, and a keen appreciation of whatever gives local color.   Some of his large effects were broad and grand, his recitatives were often nobly expressive, some of his arias excel in tragic or passionate quality, and he handled the chorus and the orchestra with originality and force.   Some of his overtures surpassed those of all preceding writers, and he introduced many unheard-of instrumental effects.   But he could not compete with Cherubini in technical learning or usually in capacity for sustained effort.   Outside of his operas, he left nothing of special importance.   But in opera he pointed the way for the best writers of the next period.

Passing mention may be made of **Louis Emmanuel Jadin** (d. 1853), with about 40 dramas (from 1788) and much instrumental music;   **Jean Pierre Solié** (d. 1812), a remarkable baritone, with about 30 operettas (from 1790), such as *Le secret* (1796) and *Le chapitre second* (1799);   and **Pierre Gaveaux** (d. 1825), also with about 30 (1792–1811), such as *Le petit matelot* (1796) and *Léonore* (1798) — the latter on the same story as Beethoven's *Fidelio*.

Jean François Le Sueur (d. 1837), born in 1760, was first a choirboy at Amiens.   Till his thirtieth year he was busy with church music at Séez, Dijon, Mans, Tours and Paris (from 1786 at Notre Dame), with finally the avowed intention of introducing freely into it dramatic and picturesque effects, both vocal and orchestral.   In 1789 he retired for general composition and in 1793 produced his first opera with great applause.   He was inspector at the Conservatoire in 1795–1802, being finally thrown out by a quarrel, and from 1804 became private choirmaster to Napoleon, continuing under the later régime till 1830.   He was one of the Opéra judges in 1806–24, and from 1817 professor at the Conservatoire, besides receiving other honors.   Among his about 10 operas, the most noted were *La caverne* (1793) and *Les bardes* (1804), and he also wrote a number of oratorios and much church music. As an opera-writer, he had no such imagination as Méhul or such technical equipment as Cherubini and, in spite of his date, belonged to the 18th century, though he sought eagerly for novelty.   His lectures were popular and he had many distinguished pupils, among them Berlioz, whom he foreshadowed. His innovating ideas were much combatted, and he wrote often in their defense (from 1787).

CHAPTER XXI

MOZART AND THE EXALTATION OF MELODY

156. Mozart's Unique Position. — Mozart was born almost a quarter-century after Haydn, and lived less than half as long, so that he died before Haydn had reached the acme of his power. Yet he developed so rapidly and phenomenally as to outrun Haydn and to force him to new efforts. Thus, in spite of the difference in age, the two wrought side by side, and, as regards the establishment of the homophonic sonata and symphony, the period is rightly known as that of Haydn and Mozart.

But Mozart's genius was many-sided, much more so than Haydn's. In particular, it included, even from early years, an intense interest in the musical drama, with a ready sensitiveness to the most progressive tendencies of the age in this field. Mozart's strongest period followed immediately upon Gluck's triumph, and, since he was personally in touch with the whole controversy, both at Vienna and at Paris, he was bound to share in the new views and ambitions. Like Gluck, he had already had a wide cosmopolitan experience and was at home in all the leading operatic styles, Italian, Austrian and French. He was not specially a student or philosophical analyst, but he had keen intuition and quick versatility. Hence it is not strange that from about 1780 he stepped into a real companionship with Gluck (more than forty years his senior) and that, as regards the renovation of the opera, the period is further called that of Gluck and Mozart. This is the more fitting because Mozart excelled Gluck in both the variety and the absolute musical value of his methods.

Again, Mozart had been trained as a virtuoso on both the violin and the clavier. He was quick to perceive the latent capacities of the developing pianoforte. While the number of his larger and abler works for the latter is not large, it is only fair to recognize his kinship in a limited sense with the new school of pianists of which the young Beethoven was already showing himself a leader.

In spite of the pathetic brevity of his life and the still more pathetic failure of suitable opportunity in it, Mozart stands out as one of the most striking instances of the intuitive grasp and abounding inspiration of pure genius. Even from his boyhood, he needed but the call of an occasion to bring before him both the appropriate method of procedure and the musical ideas to be expressed. His marvelous natural gifts were broadly developed by the exacting discipline and the wide chances for travel provided by his wise and energetic father. In spite of the fact that he was cut off in early manhood, he went further than all his contemporaries in indicating the great paths of growth upon which the coming century was to set forth.

Wolfgang Amadeus Mozart (d. 1791) was born in 1756 at Salzburg, the second of the two surviving children of Leopold Mozart, the violinist and composer (see sec. 149). He was five years

younger than Maria Anna Mozart (d. 1829), who was his companion-artist throughout his early life. Both were precocious, Wolfgang beginning to pick out intervals on the clavier at 3, to play little pieces at 4, to compose in form at 5, to read violin-music in trio at sight and perform in public before he was 6, and to play the organ between 6 and 7. Before he was 10 he was said to have been able to play at sight anything for either clavier, organ or violin. At 7 his first sonatas were published, at 8 he wrote his first symphony, at 9 for a test produced two Italian arias, at 10 similarly one act of an oratorio, at 11 a musical comedy, at 12 his first full opera, and at 14 a grand opera at Milan, besides demonstrating power in fugue-writing. This amazing readiness was wholly natural, coëxisting with a perfect boyishness otherwise. It was guided with the utmost care and even some sternness by his father, who early divined his son's true rank and devised the plans for his systematic development which were carried forward with infinite self-sacrifice until after 1780.

Apart from home instruction, Mozart's education was principally effected by a series of journeys planned by his father with the minutest care and carried out (until 1775) under his personal direction. Thus, during the 19 years before he was 25, Mozart was away from Salzburg over ten times for periods varying from a few weeks up to more than three years and aggregating about nine years in all. The chief objective of the first trip (1762) was Munich, of the second (1762-3) Vienna, of the third (1763-6) Munich, Stuttgart, the Rhine from Heidelberg to Cologne, Paris (*via* Brussels), London, the Low Countries, Paris again, Lyons, Switzerland and Munich again, of the fourth (1767-8) Vienna, of the fifth (1769-71) all the chief Italian cities, from Milan to Naples, of the sixth (1771) and seventh (1772-3) Milan, of the eighth (1773) Vienna, of the ninth (1774-5) Munich, of the tenth (1777-9) Munich, Mannheim and Paris, returning in reverse order, and of the eleventh (1780-1) Munich. The father's purpose was to make known his son's genius, to secure money, to acquaint him with musicians of all schools and with all prevalent styles, to attract to him the indispensable attention of wealthy patrons, especially at the courts where music was emphasized, to find opportunities for conspicuous and remunerative composition, and, in the end, to win for him some distinguished post commensurate with his abilities. The youth was presented everywhere as an incipient master, and, though he did receive some lessons and much helpful suggestion, especially on the third and fifth trips, he was generally accepted as a competitor on equal terms with other artists. The number of famous and talented singers, players and composers whom he met, often intimately, was enormous, and the social interest he excited was phenomenal. But the expenses of these experiences were heavy and ultimately forced the father into serious debt. And the son was volatile, fond of bright and witty society, and liable to forget his 'mission' in the pleasures of the moment or to sacrifice large aims to petty impulses.

No full summary is possible of the infinitely varied artistic influences to which Mozart was subjected during these formative years, but a few salient points may be named. In Salzburg there was little stimulating or agreeable, though there were a few good musicians, like Michael Haydn. At London (1764-5) much close intimacy with Christian Bach seems to have given him a decided impetus. At Vienna (1768) he heard Gluck's *Alceste* just as he was writing his own first extended opera, though then he probably had no real sense of Gluck's innovating aim. At Bologna (1770) he roused the enthusiasm of the veteran Martini and learned much from him. During the Italian tour generally he heard representative works of the Neapolitan order, including some by Jommelli and Hasse. At Augsburg (1777) he first saw the possibilities of the pianoforte, as revealed in the instruments of Stein. At Mannheim (1778) he was deeply impressed by the quality of the famous orchestra, found numerous congenial artistic friends, like Cannabich, and heard much to awaken his thought regarding German opera. Here, too, began his romantic attachment to the young soprano, Aloysia Weber, which alarmed his father, delayed and disarranged his tour, and ended only the next year in complete disappointment. In Paris (1778) he stood by during the thick of the Gluck-Piccinni quarrel, but aimed to keep out of it, though he studied attentively the operas of both composers and many by Grétry and other Frenchmen. From the start his strongest bent was toward dramatic music. Hence his eagerness to master the vocal and instrumental methods of the opera everywhere and the abandon with which he threw himself into every commission that offered. Yet his peculiar relation to the Archbishop of Salzburg and the predilections of his father led also to fruitful attention to Catholic church music. And the whole spirit of the time moved him to constant effort in the field of purely instrumental music. Measured by achievements, his early period was almost equally significant in all three fields.

The family fortunes were largely dependent upon the Archbishop, in whose service Leopold Mozart had been since 1743. The earlier prelate, Sigismund, was interested in music, but chiefly on its sacred side. During his régime the father had long leaves of absence and the son some recognition at court, as in 1770, when he was made concertmaster. In 1771, however, Sigismund died and was followed by Hieronymus, a pig-headed, mean-spirited man, detested by his subjects and disliked by his equals. Under him the Mozarts were systematically snubbed and tantalized. In 1778 Wolfgang was reluctantly reinstated as concertmaster, but in 1781, at Vienna, he was dismissed with gross insults. Thenceforward he was thrown on his own resources.

Trusting to his éclat in high society in Vienna, Mozart hoped for work as teacher and composer and especially desired an operatic commission, as the Viennese stage was then probably the best in Europe. In 1782 his second mature opera, *Die Entführung*, had great success. But the Weber family was now living in Vienna and he had become engaged to Constanze, a younger sister of Aloysia. Her circumstances at home led to a hasty marriage, which, though in itself happy, involved innumerable troubles, for the wife had neither health nor skill in managing and the husband lacked steadiness of purpose and loved gayety overmuch. He was drawn hither and thither by random impulses, often suggested by indiscreet or designing friends. He gave lessons considerably, as to young Hummel and the Englishman Attwood, and to many who were only half in earnest. He often appeared as a virtuoso and always with great applause. The sale of compositions was less remunerative, especially in the absence of copyright protection. He had many friends and became infatuated with Freemasonry, but not all his incessant sociality was judicious or beneficial. His aggregate income was not small, as then counted, but he had no wit for economy, indulged in many follies, and fell deeper and deeper into debt. The last ten years were filled with a maze of occupations, great and small, but also with an equal maze of difficulties, under which at last his health gave way. He had a lingering hope for some court honor — a hope only partially met, late in 1787, by his appointment as private musician to the Emperor, virtually succeeding Gluck, though at less than half the latter's salary. In 1789 he visited Dresden, Leipsic and Berlin, where from patriotic motives he declined an oᴉfer to become royal choirmaster. In 1791 a conjunction of serious strains occasioned the brief, fatal illness. The circumstances of his death and burial were pathetic in the extreme, the interment being in the common grave of the city paupers. A romantic feature of his last days was the writing, upon a mysterious commission through an anonymous agent, of a Requiem which he himself believed to be for his own funeral and of which the true history was not known in full till about a century later.

Personally, Mozart was exceedingly vivacious, versatile and fascinating, full of droll humor, fond of all sorts of amusements, but capable, too, of acute mental judgments and of noble sentiments. In spite of his father's fidelity, his character lacked poise and firmness in all practical matters, and to this lack is due the tragic contrast between his transcendent genius and his utter failure to win a place suitable to his powers.

At Mozart's death his widow was left with two sons, the younger only four months old. After serious struggles against want, which involved the sale of her husband's manuscripts and the giving of various concerts, in 1809 she was married to *G. N. von Nissen* (d. 1826), a Danish official. She died in 1842. Of the two sons, **Karl** (d. 1859), though somewhat trained in music, first engaged in business and later was in the Austrian civil service at Milan; while **Wolfgang Amadeus** (d. 1844), after study with Neukomm, Albrechtsberger and others, appeared as a pianist in 1805, from 1814 was conductor at Lemberg, and later worked at Vienna.

157. His Style in General. — Mozart's creative power was first shown in published works in his seventh year (1763), and from 1766 he poured forth an incessant stream of works, of which, however, only a small part were published during his life. These works belong to every class of writing then cultivated, and many of those for orchestra, the stage or the church were extended and elaborate. The total number was over a thousand. Spontaneity and versatility were obvious traits of his musical mind. He composed with rapidity and usually with absolute certainty, and the freshness of his invention continued unimpaired to the end. His intuition as to style and method was phenomenal, and he adapted himself to so many forms that it is not easy to say which supplied the norm of his style. Historically his influence has been greatest in the orchestral and the operatic fields.

> The standard edition of his works (1876–86) includes about 35 songs, 20 vocal canons, over 30 concert-arias, several part-songs, much church music, including 15 masses, many motets and several cantatas, a considerable amount of piano music, including 17 sonatas for two hands, 5 for four hands, etc., 17 organ-sonatas, much chamber music, including 42 violin-sonatas, 26 quartets, 10 quintets, etc., many concertos for piano, violin, flute, horn, bassoon, etc., manifold works for orchestra, including 49 symphonies, about 30 divertimenti, etc., and nearly 20 operas and similar works. His fame as an epoch-making genius rests mainly upon certain of the concertos, the later of the symphonies (see sec. 148), and the chief of the operas, beginning with *Idomeneo* in 1781 (see below).

Mozart was first of all a melodist. He resembled Haydn in the clarity and symmetry of his themes, but his conception and expression tended always toward more expansion of feeling, a much greater flexibility and a more glowing beauty. His idioms, instead of resting upon the artlessness and naïveté of the folk-song, have the fluency and amplitude of the finest examples of Italian art. In this he, much more than Haydn, showed himself the inheritor of the best results of the long period during which the art of song had been studiously advanced by generations of opera-writers.

As a harmonist, Mozart marks a decided advance. He was absolutely expert in all the procedures commonly used, but much more ready than his contemporaries to extend them to new applications. Many passages might be cited to show his prophetic grasp of principles not generally recognized till the early 19th century. It is probably true that much that we usually credit to later workers was really present in germ and essence in him. This is one reason for the persistent charm of many of his maturer works and for the indebtedness to him that many later masters have acknowledged.

Again, while Mozart's style was prevailingly homophonic and harmonic, he was also an accomplished contrapuntist, uniting with the solidity and soundness of the older traditions a striking brilliance and beauty of total impression all his own. Here, as always in matters of form and disposition, his instinct was unerring. On this side he stands as the type of the whole classical ideal of composition.

He had the singular advantage of uniting in his style what had been learned in both the vocal and the instrumental fields, and of fusing together tendencies that had been developing separately. He was himself a skillful singer, violinist, organist and pianist. He was almost equally fascinated by the attractions of the concert-stage, with its opportunities for both vocalist and player, of the operatic arena, with its still greater field for intense and complicated effect, and of the church service, with its appeal to higher feeling by less sensational methods. His eminence is due to his consummate power to appreciate and utilize all these at once. And, though his dominant national spirit was clearly German, his experience in all parts of Europe had been so wide that he was in contact with all the diverse tendencies at work in the South and the West. In a peculiar degree, therefore, his style is typical of the whole musical situation as it stood in his day, and of the very best in it.

Mozart's operas exhibit his genius more fully than his other works. Their general style varies much, according to the successive influences that affected him, at first conforming without much revolt to the conventions of the Neapolitans, then being distinctly influenced by Gluck's later masterpieces, and finally catching a fresh flavor from the newly-revived German singspiel. But in them all, especially after 1781, are features of powerful originality. Of these the most conspicuous is the overflowing wealth of musical charm — lovely melodies, delicious combinations of movement, form and color, and masterly construction, both vocal and instrumental. The opera for Mozart was first of all a musical opportunity of the highest order. Herein he showed his kinship with the strongest of his Italian predecessors, though he far surpassed them in abundance and richness of ideas. But he also resembled Gluck in his keen sense of dramatic values. Yet, while Gluck strove after severely ideal total effects with a seriousness that verged upon austerity, Mozart's mind fastened rather upon the finish and effectiveness of single scenes and passages, and preferred the light and humorous. Gluck's theory centred upon the intellectual importance of plot and text, such as he found in tragedies upon Greek themes, while Mozart was notoriously reckless about his librettos, sometimes using absolutely preposterous conglomerations. But Mozart was singularly felicitous in his characterization of personages, however senseless in themselves, so that several of them stand out as monumental artistic creations. And his capacity for sustaining interest and building it up into fine climaxes by sheer musical skill was unique.

Mozart's operas fall naturally into two distinct periods — those of his youth, beginning with *La finta semplice* (1769, Salzburg) and the German operetta *Bastien und Bastienne* (both written in 1768, Vienna), and ending with *La finta giardiniera* and *Il rè pastore* (both 1775, the one at Munich, the other at Salzburg) ; and those of his maturity, which (including several only sketched) numbered at least ten. Of these last *Idomeneo* (1781, Munich), *Die Entführung aus dem Serail* (1782, Vienna), *Le nozze di Figaro* (1786, Vienna), *Don Giovanni* (1787, Prague) and *Die Zauberflöte* (1791, Vienna) were much the strongest. All the earlier works, with his oratorio *La Betulia liberata* (1772), are clearly shaped upon current Italian patterns, with the exception of *Bastien und Bastienne*, which is a true singspiel. In the later works the underlying type is more or less definitely Italian, but the treatment is increasingly original and free, certainly until the climax reached in *Don Giovanni*. The influence of Gluck first becomes noticeable in *Idomeneo*. Ideas connected with Freemasonry play a part in the striking romanticism of *The Magic Flute*.

Among the celebrated operatic singers of the age, most of them more or less connected with Mozart, were the following : —

The sopranos included from about 1740 **Regina (Valentini) Mingotti** (d. 1807) ; from 1747 the extraordinary coloratura artist **Catterina Gabrielli** (d. 1796) ; from 1764 **Lucrezia Agujari (Colla)** (d. 1783), with a range to *c in altissimo* ; from 1768 the Portuguese **Luiza Rosa de Aguiar Todi** (d. 1833) ; from about 1770 **Gertrud Elisabeth (Schmeling) Mara** (d. 1833), who was probably the greatest of all ; from 1774 **Francesca Gabrielli** (d. 1795) ; from 1777 **Antoinette Cécile (Clavel) 'Saint-Huberty'** (d. 1812), who was more actress than musician ; from 1779 **Brigitta (Giorgi) Banti** (d. 1806), who sang by ear only, but very ably ; from 1782 **Amélie Julie Candeille (Simons)** (d. 1834), who sang only in France ; from 1782–3 **Elizabeth (Weichsel) Billington** (d. 1818), who was famous in England and Italy ; and from 1791 **Margarete (Hamel) Schick** (d. 1809), who was known only in Germany. Mara and Todi gave rise to a great partisan dispute in Paris.

Prominent among the evirati from 1763 was **Giuseppe Aprile** (d. 1814), the composer of songs, duets and solfeggi, and a good teacher ; from about 1769 **Gasparo Pacchiarotti** (d. 1821) ; from 1773 **Luigi Marchesi** (d. 1829) ; and from 1783 **Girolamo Crescentini**, the last celebrated artificial soprano.

Other male singers were from 1762 the tenor **Valentin Adamberger** (d. 1804) ; from 1772 the great bass **Ludwig Fischer** (d. 1825) ; from 1780 the tenor **Matteo Babbini** (d. 1816) ; and from 1783 the tenor **Luigi Bassi** (d. 1825).

158. The Singspiel and the Artistic Song. — In the early 18th century the German singspiel lay almost dormant, but from about 1760 it began to reappear in Germany and Austria as a popular type of much influence. Its cultivation proceeded from two centres, the one in Saxony and Prussia, the other at Vienna. In both cases it was obviously stimulated by the success of analogous forms elsewhere, such as the French comic operetta and the English ballad-opera.

The singspiel is properly a play made up of spoken dialogue with interspersed solos, duets and part-songs in a style not far away from the folk-song or its near relatives. Although in nature not a consistent musical type, it was capable of artistic unity and effectiveness. Its power lay in its simple tunefulness and its ready adaptation to comic characters and scenes. Its topics were nearly always taken from common life and its treatment filled with local color. Its revival was one symptom of the reaction against the artificiality of the Italian opera, and, being taken up by original and resourceful writers, who knew how to appeal to the popular sentiment of northern Europe, it exerted a large and healthy influence, though presently its individuality was lost in the rise of the romantic opera.

Depending for its musical success upon the abundant use of
simple vocal melody, its progress was closely associated with the
recognition and development of the artistic song as a distinct
and beautiful branch of composition. The basal type was the true
folk-song, which was imitated in the form known as the 'volks-
thümliches lied,' and then extended by natural steps of unfolding to the longer and richer forms of the 'kunstlied,' including
the dramatic ballade. In this way it helped to prepare the way
for one of the most significant movements of the early 19th
century (see secs. 174, 222).

In the North German group were the following: —

Johann Adam Hiller (d. 1804) was not only a composer, but a useful organizer, teacher and author. Born in 1728, he was finely educated at Görlitz, Dresden and Leipsic, dividing his attention between law, literature and music, and
settled in Leipsic. In 1763 he was conductor of the revived public concerts,
edited the earliest musical weekly (1766-70), in 1771 founded a singing-school,
with choral concerts after 1775, in 1776 initiated Concerts spirituels (name
copied from Paris), was the first conductor (1781-5) at the afterwards famous
Gewandhaus, and, although in 1786 he moved to Breslau, was named in 1789
deputy cantor at the Thomasschule and in 1797 cantor. His singspiele numbered nearly 15, beginning with additions (11 songs and 2 sinfonie) to Stand-
füss' *Der Teufel ist los* (1765 — original work about 10 years earlier) and his
own *Lisuart und Dariolette* (1766), *Lottchen am Hofe* (1767), *Die Liebe auf
dem Lande* (1769), *Der Dorfbarbier* (1771) and *Die Jagd* (1771) — the last
still given. These owed their popularity to his substantial gifts as a writer of
true songs (lieder), as distinguished from the pretentious aria, though in
applying them dramatically he often discarded the simple strophe-plan and even
used some ensemble numbers. From before 1760, also, he composed detached
songs, secular and sacred, with several secular cantatas, an oratorio, a Passion
cantata, church music and some instrumental pieces. He edited useful collections, historical and pedagogical, republished important sacred works (often
with unjustifiable changes of text), and was a striking author (see sec. 165).

Johann André (d. 1799), brought up in the silk business, turned to music
about 1770. From 1774 he took up music-selling at Offenbach, but in 1777
left it to his brother and became conductor at a Berlin theatre. In 1784 he
returned to Offenbach and built up a music-publishing house that issued about
1200 works before 1800 and is still famous. He was a good pianist and the
facile composer of over 25 singspiele, such as *Der Töpfer* (1773), *Erwin und
Elmire* (1776?, text by Goethe) and *Die Entführung aus dem Serail* (1781,
same subject, but not same text, as Mozart's opera in 1782). His method
was like Hiller's, but more exclusively lyrical. He wrote many songs, a few
still popular, with some chamber music. He was perhaps the first to expand
the song to the 'durchkomponierte' ballade (as *Lenore*, 1775).

Georg Benda (d. 1795), the brother of the violinist Franz Benda, after
playing in a Berlin orchestra, moved to Gotha in 1748, becoming ducal choir-

master. His melodrama or ' duodrama' *Ariadne auf Naxos* (1774) made a sensation, and was followed by nearly 15 other stage-works, including the opera *Romeo und Julia* (1776), the melodrama *Medea* (1777?) and the 'monodrama' *Pygmalion* (1780). The text of these melodramas was not sung, but spoken, while music was supplied by the orchestra. From 1778 Benda moved from place to place, writing many church works, secular cantatas, symphonies, clavier-sonatas and concertos, etc.

Johann Friedrich Reichardt (d. 1814) was early taught the lute, the violin and theory, and had a good general education. At 23 (1775) he became royal choirmaster at Berlin, succeeding Agricola, but was too progessive to be wholly popular and was often away, chiefly in France and England. In 1783 he established Concerts spirituels at Berlin. In 1794 he lost his place because of his radical politics. From 1807 for a time he was choirmaster to Jerome Bonaparte at Cassel. He was interested in new ideas, as in Gluck's innovations, and had decided musical gifts, though not always happy in their use. He wrote over 20 stage-works, including singspiele like *Hänschen und Gretchen* (1773), *Jery und Bätely* (1789, text by Goethe), *Erwin und Elmire* (1793), and several operas, mostly for Berlin, with two for Paris (not given) ; also very many fine songs, including 60 by Goethe, solo cantatas and odes, a Passion (1784), psalms, Te Deums, sacred cantatas, several symphonies, including the *Schlachtsymphonie* (on the battle of Leipsic, 1813), chamber music, concertos for piano and for violin, etc. As a critic he was fertile and keen (see sec. 165).

Johann Abraham Peter Schulz (d. 1800), a pupil and later the assistant of Kirnberger, after travel as tutor, in 1773 settled in Berlin, at first teaching and collaborating upon Sulzer's 'Theorie.' From 1776 he conducted at the French Theatre, from 1780 was director for Prince Heinrich at Rheinsberg, and from 1787 choirmaster at Copenhagen, resigning in 1795 because of ill-health. His first and best reputation came from his beautiful *Lieder im Volkston* (1782–90), but he also wrote about 10 successful singspiele and operas (from 1775), several of them to Danish texts and produced at Copenhagen, such as *Aline* (1789), *Hoest-Gildet* (1790), *Peters Bryllup* (1791), etc. His sacred songs, cantatas, Passions, etc., were many and popular.

Johann Rudolph Zumsteeg (d. 1802), the fellow-student of Schiller at Stuttgart, at first destined to be a sculptor, was formed by the choirmaster Poli into a fine 'cellist and song-writer, succeeding his teacher in 1792. He wrote several singspiele (from about 1784), like *Die Geisterinsel, Das Pfauenfest, Elbondokani* and *Zalaor*, over 20 sacred cantatas, many songs and important ballades, dramatically conceived and often finely set, including Bürger's *Lenore* and *Die Entführung*, Goethe's *Colma*, Schiller's *Ode an die Freude, Maria Stuart* (one scene), *Johannen's Lebewohl*, with *Die Büssende, Des Pfarrers Tochter, Ritter Toggenburg*, etc., by lesser poets. In these he was the precursor of Schubert and Löwe.

Less important were **Franz Andreas Holly** (d. 1783), with about 15 singspiele (from about 1768) ; **Christian Gottlob Neefe** (d. 1798), long associated with Hiller at Leipsic and from 1781 organist at Bonn, with many melodious works, including singspiele (from 1772) ; **Karl David Stegmann** (d. 1826), a singer and playwright, chiefly at Hamburg, with over 10 singspiele (from 1773), songs and instrumental pieces; and **Anton Schweitzer** (d. 1787), Benda's successor at Gotha in 1780, with about a score of singspiele (from 1773). Here may be added **Johann Franz Xaver Sterkel** (d. 1817), from 1778 electoral chaplain and from 1793 choirmaster at Mayence, the composer of a great number of songs and piano-works, besides 10 symphonies, etc. As a pianist he was admired by Beethoven in 1791.

The Vienna group of singspiel-writers was at first more limited in influence, contributing less to the development of the song as such; but, on the other hand, their efforts were ultimately valuable in helping forward the advent of true German opera.

Joseph Haydn (d. 1809) was a pioneer, though not an important one. His *Der neue krumme Teufel* (1751?) and the marionette-plays at Esterház (1762) belonged to the singspiel class (see sec. 145). The relation of the operas of **Mozart** (d. 1791) is elsewhere stated (see sec. 155), especially as regards his *Bastien und Bastienne* (1768) and *Die Entführung* (1782). Similarly, the works of their contemporary **Ditters** (d. 1799) are certainly important in this connection (see sec. 153).

Ignaz Umlauf (d. 1796), at first a viola-player, was from 1778 leader at the National Theatre at Vienna, and from 1789 Salieri's assistant at the Imperial Chapel, besides composing for the German Theatre. His *Die Bergknappen* (1778) opened a popular series of which *Die Apotheke* (1778), *Die schöne Schusterin* (1780), *Das Irrlicht* and others were examples.

Johann Schenk (d. 1836) secured notice by his boy-voice and became a pupil of Wagenseil, who sought to form him as a sacred composer in the strict contrapuntal style. A fine mass (1778) was specially admired and for a time he pressed on in church music. But from 1785, at first anonymously, he took up dramatic writing in folk-style, achieving such success that he forsook his earlier ambition. Several of his dozen singspiele long held the stage, such as *Die Weinlese* (1785), *Die Weihnacht auf dem Lande* (1786), and especially *Der Dorfbarbier* (1796). His later years were embittered by the lack of continued success. In 1793 he acted as Beethoven's secret helper with the latter's exercises in counterpoint for Haydn.

Ferdinand Kauer (d. 1831), born in Moravia, from 1795 was employed in Vienna theatres as leader or 'cellist, always poorly paid, even when his works were drawing large audiences. He was extremely prolific in composition — about 200 singspiele and operas, of which *Das Donauweibchen* was the best, many masses and other church music, and an indefinite number of instrumental works. In 1830 most of his MSS. were lost in an inundation. **Wenzel Müller** (d. 1835), also a Moravian, a pupil of Ditters, had a similar career, and is also said to have written over 200 singspiele and similar works (from 1783), such as *Der Fagottist* (1792), *Das Neusonntagskind* (1793), etc. **Franz Xaver Süssmayr** (d. 1803), came to Vienna about 1790 and studied with Mozart, assisting him on *Titus* and completing the score of the Requiem. From 1792 he was leader at different theatres and produced singspiele, like *Der Spiegel von Arkadien* (1794) and *Soliman II.* (1799), besides other works. **Ignaz Walter** (d. 1822), a Bohemian, trained at Vienna, worked as singer and leader there and at Prague till about 1790, when he went to Germany, writing several singspiele (from about 1793), such as *Dr. Faust* (1797) and *Der Spiegelritter* (1798), besides a coronation-cantata (1790).

Here for convenience may be inserted two composers who were influential upon music in Scandanavia : —

Friedrich Ludwig Aemilius Kunzen (d. 1817), son of K. A. Kunzen of Lübeck, was a cultivated pianist, who, after traveling as a virtuoso and short residences at Berlin (collaborating with Reichardt), Frankfort and Prague, in 1795 succeeded Schulz as choirmaster at Copenhagen. He had already written one Danish opera, *Holger Danske* (1789), and won applause by his *Das Fest der Winzer* (1795, Prague), and now produced a series of Danish operas and much other music, which not only placed him at the head of Danish musicians, but made him noted elsewhere. He issued a collection of Danish songs (1816).

Johann Christian Friedrich Häffner (d. 1833), who studied at Schmalkalden and Leipsic, went to Stockholm in 1780 as organist and assistant at the opera, becoming in 1794 royal choirmaster, but removed in 1808 to Upsala as director and organist at the cathedral. His advancement was due to three operas in the style of Gluck, the first of which was *Electra* (1787), but he later became specially interested in collecting and editing Swedish national songs and chorales (from 1819).

159. Secular Music in England. — After the accession of George III. (1760) there was a notable outburst of secular music in England, taking the form of light 'operas,' part-songs, glees and 'catches,' detached songs or ballads. Comic song-plays or comedies with incidental songs were exceedingly popular in London, having a vogue like that of analogous forms in France and Germany. These plays stimulated the writing of detached songs, but, being mostly undertaken by writers not broadly trained in composition and surrounded by an atmosphere not artistically musical, had little intrinsic value or beneficial influence.

The development of the glee or unaccompanied part-song, however, was characteristic and brilliant, somewhat recalling the madrigal period of a century and a half before. Writing of this sort attracted many church musicians, who brought to it disciplined talent and often delicate and original sentiment. Some of these, also, were producers of admirable solo songs.

Among the able church composers who also undertook song-plays and operas were **Samuel Arnold** (d. 1802), who at 23 (1763) began as composer at Covent Garden, writing in all over 40 works, mostly comic, the first being *The Maid of the Mill* (1765), which was largely a pasticcio, but notable as the first native music-drama since Purcell; **William Jackson** of Exeter (d. 1803), with a few stage-pieces (1767–83), including *The Lord of the Manor* (1780), several odes and many songs; and, much later, **Thomas Attwood** (d. 1838), the eminent organist at St. Paul's, with over 20 operettas (1792–1807) and many fine glees and songs.

Charles Dibdin (d. 1814), a Winchester choirboy, at 15 (1760) went to London and sought dramatic employment. *The Shepherd's Artifice* (1762), in which he figured as author, composer and actor-singer, was so successful that he followed it up with about 70 others (till 1798), besides 30 musical monologues — the latter containing most of his famous sea-songs. He engaged in several speculations, wrote at length on his experiences and on the stage (1788–1803), edited a periodical and published novels.

Michael Arne (d. 1786), the son of T. A. Arne, early showed talent for stage-writing, beginning with *The Fairy Tale* (1763) and *Almena* (1764), the latter jointly with Battishill. The best of his 9 plays was Garrick's *Cymon* (1767).

Thomas Linley, Sr. (d. 1795), at first a singing-teacher at Bath and from 1774 concert-conductor at London, produced over 10 song-plays (1768–88), two of which were adapted from Grétry. He was an accomplished writer of songs and madrigals. His gifted son, **Thomas Linley, Jr.** (d. 1778 at 22), was Mozart's boyhood friend.

James Hook (d. 1827) showed enormous fertility in some 2000 songs, cantatas, catches and the like, including about 25 plays (1771–1809), many odes, an oratorio (1776), etc.; **Thomas Carter** (d. 1804), after becoming noted for his songs at Dublin, produced a number of song-plays at London (1775–92); **Michael Kelly** (d. 1826), first famous as a singer in Italy and at Vienna, produced over 60 song-plays (from 1789); and **William Reeve** (d. 1815), an actor and singer, followed with about 40 (1791–1811), partly in conjunction with **Joseph Mazzinghi** (d. 1844).

William Shield (d. 1829), a viola-player, came to London in 1772, was long connected with prominent theatres, and produced nearly 40 plays of various degree (1778–1807), many songs, some beautiful in simplicity, some full of technical difficulty, and part-songs. From 1817 he had a court position, and at his death was buried at Westminster. His originality as a song-writer is specially noted.

Stephen Storace (d. 1796 at 32) was a precocious violinist and was sent as a boy to Naples for study. At 22–3 (1785–6) he brought out two operas at Vienna, and knew Mozart well. Returning to England, he quickly produced almost 15 stage-works (1788–96), several of them adapted from European singspiele, but including his own *The Haunted Tower* (1789), *The Pirates* (1792) and others. His sister, **Ann Storace** (d. 1817), his companion in study and travel, was a famous soprano, who, after success in Italy and at Vienna, sang in opera in England for many years.

The artistic cultivation of part-songs was much stimulated by the founding in 1761 of the *Catch Club*, still a flourishing institution. Most of the famous glee-writers were enrolled in this, and all at some time won prizes in its annual competitions. A somewhat similar organization was the *Glee Club*, founded in 1787 and disbanded in 1857. In this many members of the Catch Club were also enrolled. [The term 'catch' originally meant a round or canon written out as a single melody, but came to be used for a variety of whimsical and comical forms. 'Glee,' it should be noted, means simply a song, whether gay or serious, but is restricted by usage to a part-song, unaccompanied.] Another club was the *Madrigal Society*, founded in 1741, devoted to a different form of music, but including many of the same members and indirectly conducive to the same purposes.

The list of favorite glee-writers prior to 1800 includes the following: —

Samuel Webbe, Sr. (d. 1816), was the most active of the circle, winning 27 medals in the Catch Club trials (1766–94) and publishing 9 collections (1774–95). His 'Glorious Apollo,' written for the Glee Club, was always sung at the opening of its meetings. He also wrote masses, etc., for the Portuguese Chapel, where from 1776 he was organist, music for the English service, 2 secular cantatas and some solfeggi. His son, **Samuel Webbe, Jr.** (d. 1843), was less notable along the same lines.

Benjamin Cooke (d. 1793), pupil of Pepusch and in 1752 his successor, at 12 (1746) was deputy organist at Westminster Abbey, in 1757 choirmaster and in 1762 organist. He was highly esteemed as a theorist. His church compositions were excellent, but not many, and his glees are famous (2 collections, 1775, '95). His son, **Robert Cooke** (d. 1814), followed in his steps.

John Stafford Smith (d. 1826), pupil of Boyce and Nares, a leading glee-writer from 1773 and Hawkins' helper on his 'History,' entered the Chapel Royal in 1784 and succeeded Arnold as organist in 1802. He published 5 collections of his own and 2 of a valuable historical character (1779, 1812).

William Hayes (d. 1777) and his son **Philip Hayes** (d. 1797), both associated with Oxford, where they were organists and professors, publishing glees of value (1757, by William, and about 1780–89, by Philip); **Jonathan Battishill** (d. 1801), the well-known organist and anthem-writer, with 2 collections of glees; the **Earl of Mornington [G. C. Wellesley]** (d. 1781), a self-trained, but skillful amateur at Dublin, where he was professor (1764–74), whose glees were edited by Bishop (1846); **Luffman Atterbury** (d. 1796) of the Chapel Royal, with more than one collection (from 1775?) and an oratorio (1773); **Stephen Paxton** (d. 1787), with 2 collections and some masses; **John Danby** (d. 1798), organist at the Spanish Chapel, with 4 collections (1785–98) and some Catholic music; **Richard John Samuel Stevens** (d. 1837), from 1786 organist at the Temple Church and from 1801 professor at Gresham College, with 3 collections and a fine edition of old church music; and **Reginald Spofforth** (d. 1827), with one collection, — all these rank high.

John Wall Callcott (d. 1821) was the most fertile of the list, writing glees, canons and catches literally by hundreds, many of them winning medals from the Catch Club (from 1785). In 1791 he had lessons from Haydn. From 1789 he served as organist, mainly at an Orphan Asylum. In 1807, under the strain of ten years' effort to compile a musical dictionary and of an appointment to lecture at the Royal Institution, he became insane. His glees, variously published during his life, were collected by Horsley (1824).

CHAPTER XXII

THE RISE OF PIANISM. SACRED MUSIC

160. The Improved Piano. — The inevitable connection between the improvement of mechanical implements and the advance of artistic styles is finely illustrated by the reaction of the experiments in piano-making from about 1760 upon the entire character of keyboard music. Until that date the piano was not much more than a curiosity. Inventors had not seriously attacked its mechanical problems and players found it less useful than the powerful harpsichords that were common. But the political disorders in central Europe about 1760 sent many workmen to England and these, apparently stimulated by the influence of Christian Bach, began a movement for better devices that had important sequels. Somewhat later came a new interest in piano-making in Austria and Bavaria, soon paralleled also in France. Between 1780 and 1790 competent instruments, with various forms of action, began to become fairly plentiful, and before 1800 the supremacy of the harpsichord ceased.

It is impossible here to give any sufficient account of the gradual process of improvement in the piano, but some notes upon pioneers will be useful.

Christian Ernst Friederici (d. 1779), a Saxon organ-builder, is commonly said to have made the first 'square' pianos, perhaps before 1760, but no example remains. He was taught by Silbermann.

Johann Zumpe, a German workman, became well known in England about 1765 for the excellence of his small pianos. These had a simple and fairly effective action in which the hammer was thrown, without escapement, by a leather-headed wire jack (popularly called 'the old man's head') and the damper lifted by another ('the mopstick').

Americus Backers (d. c. 1781), a Dutchman in Tschudi's employ at London, soon after 1770 developed the Cristofori action by using a jack that engages a shoulder on the hammer-butt and 'escapes' past it, the movement being regulated by a screw, and by supplying the check to catch the recoil of the hammer. This action was the germ of the so-called 'English action,' later developed by the Stodarts and the Broadwoods. In 1786 **John Geib** invented the 'hopper' or 'underhammer' in place of the fixed jack.

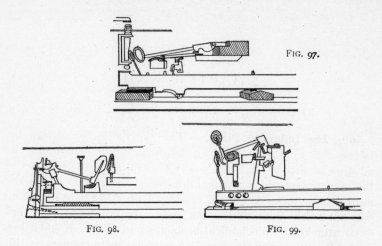

FIG. 97.

FIG. 98.

FIG. 99.

FIG. 97. — Diagram of Perfected Cristofori Action (1720).
FIG. 98. — Diagram of Perfected Viennese Action (c. 1802).
FIG. 99. — Diagram of Perfected English (Broadwood) Action (1880).

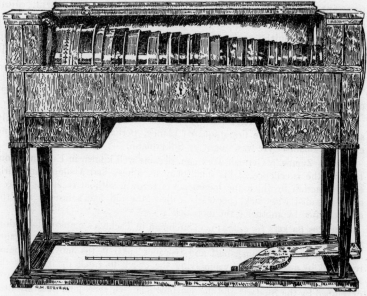

FIG. 100. — Glass Harmonica.

Burkhardt Tschudi (d. 1773), from about 1728 a harpsichord-maker in London, had from 1761 a Scotch employee, John Broadwood (d. 1812), who in 1769 became his son-in-law and in 1770 his partner. The latter succeeded to the business, and the firm, after the admission of two sons in 1795 and 1807, became John Broadwood & Sons, which title still persists. From 1773 Broadwood used Zumpe's method of making square pianos and from 1780 a model of his own, in which for the first time the tuning-pins were placed on the left, besides from 1788 stretching the heavy strings over a separate bridge. He was the first to apply the damper-pedal and the 'soft pedal' substantially as now.

The tendency of the English makers was toward a somewhat stiff, but positive, action, and a firm, sonorous tone. Their standard of effect was the harpsichord, with its adaptation to the concert-stage and to use with the orchestra. Ultimately, with improvements in the stringing, the hammers and the soundboard, their instruments developed a fine capacity for a sustained singing tone. Meanwhile, in Austria another line of progress began, tending toward a lighter action and a sweeter, more delicate tone. The effects here were suggested rather by the clavichord, with its fitness for private use and for the chamber ensemble. This type proved less valuable and influential than the other, but served to differentiate a significant school of pianists.

Andreas Stein (d. 1792) seems to have been the restorer of piano-making in Germany. He was a leading builder of organs and harpsichords, at work at Augsburg before 1777, when Mozart first tried his pianos. His action was novel in that the hammer is reversed, the head toward the front, and is carried bodily by the key-tail, while the hammer-tail 'escapes' from a notch in a fixed hopper behind. The dampers could be raised by a knee-lever and the keys shifted by a pedal for *una corda* effects. The practical success of his instruments led Mozart to turn to the piano.

Nanette Streicher (d. 1833) was Stein's daughter, a precocious player at 8 (1777) and a capable and cultivated woman. She inherited the business, which she moved to Vienna and managed with energy for over 40 years, partly with her brother Matthäus and later with her husband, Johann Andreas Streicher, and their son. She and her brother greatly improved the Stein action and became the founders of the Viennese type of construction. She was an intimate friend of Beethoven.

Sébastien Érard (d. 1831), a young harpsichord-maker from Strassburg, made the first French piano in 1777, following foreign models. He and his brother were opposed for a time by the luthiers' guild, but in 1785 received a royal permit to make pianos independently. From 1786 Érard lived in London, and in 1796, returning to Paris, introduced the English grand action there. His own important improvements in both the piano and the harp belong to the next period (see sec. 183).

In many early pianos mechanical devices were added for modifying the quality of the tones, as by interposed leather strips above the hammers, or for supplementing them by independent attachments of various kinds.

The century was also somewhat prolific of experiments with peculiar keyboard instruments of a different type.

The most prominent of these was the 'harmonica,' the tones of which were produced by friction upon glass bowls. Before 1750, sets of bowls, tuned by placing water in them, were played by means of the moistened finger (as by Gluck at London in 1746), but *Benjamin Franklin* (d. 1790), while in London in 1763, greatly improved the contrivance by fixing the tune wholly by the size of the bowls and mounting them on a rotating axis with the lower edges in water. A keyboard was added in 1785–6 by Hessel and Röllig. Several noted players appeared, a method was issued by J. C. Müller (1788), and considerable special music written (as by Hasse, Mozart, Beethoven, etc.). Somewhat related instruments were Chladni's 'euphon' (1790) and 'clavicylinder' (1799), Leppich's 'panmelodion' (1810) and Buschmann's 'uranion' (1810).

Various efforts were made to perfect a satisfactory keyboard viol, having strings sounded by friction, as by Gleichmann (1709), Le Voirs (1740), Hohlfeld (1754), Garbrecht (1790), Mayer (1795), Kunze (1799) and Röllig (1800), but without significance.

161. The Vienna Pianists. — Associated with the Viennese pianos, with their easy, shallow touch and their rather small, though sensitive, tone, was a school of composers and players of which Mozart was the type. In writing for the piano, as for the clavichord, he selected his thematic material with instinctive care and developed it with exquisite skill. Essential structure was emphasized, and subsidiary or decorative material rigorously held in check. In playing, Mozart sought for an unobtrusive and strictly controlled style, more solicitous about precision, clarity and smoothness than sonority, showy rapidity or complication of effects. Mechanism of execution was simply the means for bringing out structural values in the composition. The piano, he evidently felt, was to be handled with caution and restraint. If combined with other instruments, it was to be merged in the ensemble rather than forced into extreme prominence.

The forms most used were the sonata, the chamber trio, quartet or quintet, and the concerto — all usually developed in three movements. The variation was especially popular at this period, by some writers cultivated to excess. In the hands of composers not gifted in invention the style of Mozart's day tended toward formality and mannerism, and to-day it seems somewhat insipid. But, it is to be remembered, the practice of extemporization was fairly universal and was carried to a pitch of learning and dexterity that is now rare. In performances of this sort every device of development was often utilized, from the set variation to the elaborate polyphonic fantasia or fugue. We may doubt, therefore, whether extant works fully represent the accomplishments of the time.

The traditions of this school of composing and playing, then, were typically those of the classical period generally. As handed on to the 19th century, they blended beneficially with the new tendencies then arising, since they kept in view the need of substantial thematic ideas and of symmetry, order and finish in their elaboration.

No attempt will here be made to enumerate the line of able clavier-players through the middle of the 18th century. Somewhat famous examples, in addition to some already named, were **Johann Gottlieb Goldberg** (d. c. 1760?), about 1740 a pupil of Friedemann Bach and his father, later chamber musician to Count Brühl at Dresden, who was an amazing improvisator and the composer of difficult concertos, sonatas, preludes, fugues, etc. ; and **Johann Friedrich Gottlieb Beckmann** (d. 1792), for many years organist at Celle, who also excelled in extemporization and contrapuntal work, but chose a popular style in his sonatas (from 1769) and single or double concertos (from 1779.)

Mozart (d. 1791) secured his youthful triumphs (from 1762) upon the harpsichord (see secs. 156–157). From 1777 he turned to the piano, which he learned to appreciate at Augsburg. The characteristics of the instruments at hand combined with his predilections to keep his style smooth and objective, though not lacking in geniality and vivacity. In his 25 concertos (mostly from his mature period) he attained one of his highest successes, happily emphasizing the capacity of the piano for melody, and welding it and the orchestra into a beautiful unity. His sonatas were generally less significant.

Franz Duschek (d. 1799), a pupil of Wagenseil, from 1763 was a teacher at Prague, where he and his talented wife became leaders. Besides being a fine player, he wrote (from 1773) several concertos and sonatas (mostly in MS.). The Duscheks were ardent admirers of Mozart (from 1777) and helped to his successes at Prague in 1786–7.

Anton Eberl (d. 1807), a public player from youth and an opera-writer at Vienna at 16 (1782), attracted the notice of Gluck and Mozart, the latter of whom he imitated so well that his works were passed off by publishers as Mozart's. In 1796 he toured with Mozart's widow and then spent some years at St. Petersburg. His works (from 1792) were numerous and elaborate, including many concertos and chamber pieces.

Johann Nepomuk Hummel (d. 1837) as a boy, 7–9 years old (1785–7), was a pupil of Mozart, and, after tours in northwestern Europe, of Albrechtsberger and Salieri (from 1793). He was intimate with Beethoven, about 1807 assisted in the Esterhazy establishment, from 1811 taught in Vienna, from 1816 was court-choirmaster at Stuttgart and from 1819 at Weimar, but with frequent absences. His works numbered about 125, including not only piano-sonatas, concertos and ensemble music (notably the Septet, Op. 74), but also several masses and other church music (still used), 4 operas and other dramatic music, and an elaborate piano-method (1828). Though most active after 1800, his style allied him with the earlier period. His playing was careful and exact in form, but lacked success in slow movements. As a composer, he followed Mozart, though without the latter's richness of material. Yet he was one of the ablest of improvisators, and became the teacher and inspirer of many great players.

Other important members of the Vienna circle, already mentioned, were **Joseph Haydn** (d. 1809), **Wanhal** (d. 1813) and **Pleyel** (d. 1831).

It was into this atmosphere that **Beethoven** (d. 1827) came in 1792, only 22 years old, but already an accomplished virtuoso. It is easy to understand what a sensation his virile, original methods of interpretation and improvisation occasioned. From that time he was wholly identified with Vienna, exerting a profound immediate influence and beginning the first pianistic epoch of the next century (see next sec.).

162. The Clementi School. — Contemporaneous with the foregoing group was another that took its impetus from the Italian Clementi and found its favorite implement in the English type of piano, with its deep and somewhat stiff action, its large and vigorous tone, and its general capacity for brilliant and massive effects. Great emphasis was put upon a 'singing tone,' conceived in a sense more masculine and eminent than with the Viennese, a tone that could even dominate in the orchestral ensemble. Emphasis also fell upon the studied development of octaves and chords, passage-work and varied figuration, and every sort of embellishment peculiar to the keyboard — upon everything by which the individuality and power of the new instrument could be exhibited. In short, this group displayed a strong instinct for executive virtuosity, doubtless often indulged for its own sake, but also evinced a growing sense of how the study of the keyboard might react upon the whole theory of composition, bringing in novel materials and idioms of expression that were peculiarly germane to the piano. Starting from about the same point as the other school, these players went much further in uncovering the latent possibilities of the instrument, in seeking after means for dramatic, intense effect and thus in making their playing more of a self-expression. The forms used were nominally the same, but the treatment was less academic and restrained.   Insensibly, as time went on, the old patterns were transformed into those of the post-classical and romantic schools.

It must be conceded that the general style here in view was open to abuse by foolish or dishonest artists.   But, on the other hand, its early evolution was mainly directed by intelligent and earnest leaders, and the critical demands that it was obliged to meet were usually severe, so that charlatanry was quickly detected.   The custom of extemporization was a wholesome check upon empty pretension.

Upon the minute studies which this school made of every aspect of executive equipment was based the splendid virtuosity of the 19th century.   Indeed, in this direction there was no clear demarcation between the two centuries, and most of the leading early masters worked both before and after 1800.

Muzio Clementi (d. 1832), born in 1752 at Rome, was first trained there by church musicians, early becoming an organist and a composer in the contra-puntal style.   In 1766 his remarkable talent attracted notice from Peter Beckford, an Englishman, who took him to London for further education.   In 1770 he captured the public by his phenomenal playing, in 1773 published important sonatas, and from 1777 was conductor of the Italian opera.   In 1781 he toured as a virtuoso to France and Austria, at Vienna competing brilliantly with Mozart (who criticized his mechanicalness).   From this time, probably owing to his contact with Mozart, his style acquired more feeling and a higher musicianship.   Except for a trip to Paris in 1785, he remained in England for 20 years, engrossed in many activities, among them a connection with instru-ment-making, etc., which in 1798 led to the founding of the firm of Clementi & Co. (later Collard & Collard).   Between 1802 and '10 he made several tours, including two to Russia, and in 1820–1 was in Leipsic.   His activity as teacher, composer and business man continued unabated to the end.   He wrote almost wholly for the piano — about 100 sonatas, nearly half of them for the piano with other instruments, many minor pieces, several pedagogic works, chief of which was the famous *Gradus* (1817) — but also some good symphonies.   His style was strictly classical, resourceful and full of nervous energy.   He made demands upon the executant which are felt to be taxing even yet.   His historic position was strategic, since he lived from the death of Bach till after that of Beethoven, and his power is indicated by the number of distinguished pupils whom he trained, and by the fact that his work was used by Beethoven as a corner-stone for his own.

Ludwig van Beethoven (d. 1827), born and brought up at Bonn, was a phenomenal player from early years, studying under Neefe, the court-organist, whose deputy he was at 11.   In 1787 he visited Vienna, meeting Mozart and giving signs of future power.   In 1791 he made a short tour up the Rhine, especially winning notice as a wonderful improvisator. Late in 1792 he was sent by the Elector to Vienna and the first striking period of his life began (see sec. 168). The points to be here observed are that his youthful reputation and his first impression at Vienna were made as a pianist, that his style was formed largely upon the lines of Clementi's, but that the force of his genius early led to a highly original line of expression, which ultimately began a new epoch.

Johann Ladislaus Dussek (d. 1812), born in Bohemia in 1761, was another youthful prodigy, taking up the piano at 5 and the organ at 9 under Jesuit teachers at Iglau, Kuttenberg and Prague. With an Austrian officer as patron, he was taken to the Low Countries and was organist at several places, with a short, but brilliant career as player, composer and teacher at Amsterdam and The Hague. In 1783 he studied with Emanuel Bach at Hamburg and appeared at Berlin. For a time he was a leading virtuoso upon Hessel's harmonica as well as the piano. After wide tours, he lived at Paris and ten years (1790–1800) at London, where he was intimate with Clementi. Resuming a roving life, he was connected with Prince Louis Ferdinand (1803–6) and then dependent on a series of patrons, the last being Talleyrand. He wrote about 15 concertos, over 50 solo sonatas and 80 with violin, several trios, etc., a large quantity of minor pieces, including rondos and variations, with considerable church music, and prepared a piano-method (about 1800). His *Élégie*, op. 61, after Prince Louis' death (1806), the *Farewell*, op. 44, dedicated to Clementi, and several other works, are still well-known. He was one of the promoters of the true 'singing tone,' had an overflowing gift of melodic invention, and was original in harmony and in form. He is often noted as the first famous Bohemian musician.

August Eberhard Müller (d. 1817), a pupil of the Bückeburg Bach, began touring when 14 (1781), playing either piano, organ or flute. From 1789 he was organist at Magdeburg, from 1794 first flute in the Leipsic concert-orchestra, as well as organist at the Nikolaikirche and Hiller's assistant at the Thomasschule, in 1804 succeeding him as cantor, and from 1810 court-choir-master at Weimar. He wrote concertos, sonatas and smaller works, much music for the flute and for church use, some songs and a singspiel, besides editing a favorite piano-method (1804, revised from Löhlein) and preparing a guide to Mozart's concertos and original cadenzas therefor.

Johann Baptist Cramer (d. 1858), born at Mannheim in 1771, the son of the violinist Wilhelm Cramer, was brought up in London, having two years of lessons with Clementi. He made his début in 1781 and from 1788 toured on the Continent, meeting Haydn and Beethoven. The latter was greatly impressed with his ability always. In 1828 he founded the publishing firm of Cramer & Co. at London. From 1835 to '45 he lived abroad, at Munich and Paris. He wrote 7 fine concertos, over 100 sonatas, many shorter pieces, several sets of studies and a famous method (5 parts, 1846). Though his life reached beyond 1850, bringing him into contact with Liszt, he belonged to the early age of pianism, his style being formed upon the theory and practice of the 18th century. He laid stress upon the equal development of the two hands, excelled in the delivery of slow movements, and was a facile and learned improvisator, but in originality did not match Clementi and Dussek.

Joseph Wölfl (d. 1812) may be inserted here.   In one sense he represents
the Viennese group, since he was born at Salzburg in 1772, was taught there
by Leopold Mozart and Michael Haydn, appearing as a violinist at 7 (1779),
and in 1790 and 1795–8 was at Vienna.   But his developed style connects him
with the other.   Besides becoming a pianist able to compete with Beethoven
and to win his high regard, from 1795 he took up light opera and chamber
music.   In 1798 he began a grand tour to Prague, Leipsic, Hamburg, Berlin
and Paris, where he lived 1801–5, producing two operas and making a sensation as a player.   From 1805 he was in London, recognized as a keyboard
artist of the first rank.   His works varied greatly in quality.   He was
thoroughly equipped technically and had power as contrapuntist and improvisator.   With his enormous hands he could strike an octave and a sixth, so
that he could execute passages for others impossible.   He wrote 7 concertos,
nearly 40 sonatas, many preludes and shorter pieces, some trivial, about 50
études, 2 symphonies and a great quantity of chamber music.   Among his
concertos, the *Militaire* and *The Calm* (1806), and among his sonatas the
Non plus ultra and *Le diable à quatre* were specially successful.   To the
Non plus ultra Dussek's *Le retour à Paris* was set forth by the publishers as
an answer, *Plus ultra*.   His 5 or more operas included *Der Höllenberg*
(1795), *Der Kopf ohne Mann* (1798) and *L'amour romanesque* (1804).

Prince Louis Ferdinand (d. 1806), born in 1772, the most gifted of the
Prussian royal family, pursued music assiduously along with his military life.
His playing aroused Beethoven's enthusiasm.   Late in his short life he was
intimate with Dussek and the young Spohr.   His few works were mostly for
chamber combinations — the quartet for piano and strings, op. 6, being
considered the best.   His promising career was cut off at the battle against
Napoleon at Saalfeld.

Less significant names are Johann Wilhelm Hässler (d. 1822), born at
Erfurt and trained there by his uncle, Kittel, in the Bach traditions, who was
a fine organist and wonderfully facile at the clavier, active at Erfurt from
1780, in 1790 appeared at London, and from 1792 settled in Russia, first at
St. Petersburg in court service, later at Moscow as a teacher, with a number
of works (from 1776), largely for the harpsichord;   Friedrich Heinrich
Himmel (d. 1814), a protégé of King Friedrich Wilhelm and a pupil of
Naumann, who wrote operas for different places (from 1792), toured as a
popular pianist, and left a large amount of excellent music, including much
for the church and many songs;   and Franz Lauska (d. 1825), a pupil of
Albrechtsberger, who was first engaged at Munich, then at Copenhagen and
from 1798 at Berlin, being recognized as a fine virtuoso and teacher, with
about 15 polished sonatas (from 1795) and other works.

Associated with Paris more or less closely were the following: —

Nikolaus Joseph Hüllmandel (d. 1823), born at Strassburg and a pupil of
Emanuel Bach at Hamburg, in 1771 appeared as a player at London and,
after a sojourn in Italy, in 1776 settled at Paris as a teacher, returning to
London in 1790.   He knew how to make piano music popular in high society,
and wrote a number of sonatas (from 1780).

Louis Adam (d. 1848), an Alsatian, in 1775 came to Paris as a teacher and
composer, and in 1797 became professor in the Conservatoire, remaining

active for 45 years.   His taste and ability kept him fully abreast of his age. He wrote several sonatas and a method (1802), and taught many players of high rank, like Kalkbrenner and Hérold.   For a time he was much interested in the harmonica as an instrument.

Daniel Steibelt (d. 1823), born in 1765 at Berlin, a precocious pupil of Kirnberger, about 1780 began extended wanderings as a virtuoso and opera-writer which lasted about 30 years.   He was several times in Paris, where his opera *Roméo et Juliette* (1793) was successful, lived for a time at London in much popularity, competed disastrously with Beethoven at Vienna, and in 1811 became director of the opera at St. Petersburg.   His ways were unbearably vain and rough, and he is often called a charlatan.   Yet he had remarkable technique, though lacking in fine expressiveness, and was not altogether unworthy as a composer, though in later years indulging in cheap show-pieces.   His works were numerous, in all the usual forms, including several operas and operettas.

---

163. Catholic Church Music. — The cultivation of music in its ecclesiastical applications necessarily goes on in every period. So in the later 18th century it proceeded steadily in all the principal countries side by side with the new styles of the period, but usually far in the background of general interest. To it many leading composers contributed, often industriously and ably, but the conditions of popular thought were not favorable to any great enthusiasm over it or even to eminent success in it.   The distinctive qualities of sacred writing were widely obscured by the impulse to treat it after the fashion of the opera or the concert-hall.   Against this general drift there were some conservatives who set themselves to preserve purity and dignity.   But these were not numerous enough to give character to the time.

In the Catholic Church the cleavage became wide between the small circle of enthusiasts who sought either to keep alive *a cappella* traditions or at least to employ solid contrapuntal methods with instrumental support and with the admixture of pure harmonic material, and the many opera-writers whose idea of church music was simply to import into it all the sensuous and florid ways of the stage.   Italy naturally presented this cleavage most conspicuously, but Austria and France illustrated it as well.   From this time proceeded tendencies that have persisted ever since, those against which the authorities of the church have recently put forth protest.

In Italy there were a few special students of Palestrina who were worthy perpetuators of his style. **Pasquale Pisari** (d. 1778), from 1752 a bass singer in the Papal Chapel, was a fertile writer of noble masses and motets, some for 8–16 voices, including a cycle of motets for the whole year, written for Lisbon. His friend, **Giuseppe Jannaconi** (d. 1816), 16 years younger, ultimately succeeded Zingarelli as choirmaster at St. Peter's (1811). He made a superb collection of Palestrina's works (transmitted to his pupil Baini), and left a prodigious amount of fine *a cappella* works, including over 30 masses and many motets, some polychoric, with extraordinary canons, etc. Other Roman composers were **Giovanni Battista Casali** (d. 1792), from 1759 choirmaster at St. John Lateran; and **Zingarelli** (d. 1837), the popular opera-writer (see sec. 151), from 1792 choirmaster at Milan, from 1802 at Loreto, from 1804 at St. Peter's and from 1813 at Naples, who, though not a consistent cultivator of the pure style, wrote prolifically for the church, including a cycle of masses for every day in the year, in some of which he showed his versatility by adopting the old *a cappella* methods.

To the many opera-writers already named (sec. 151), such as **Traetta, Guglielmi, Tritto, Paisiello** and others, the following may be added: —

Ferdinando Giuseppe Bertoni (d. 1813) was from 1752 first organist at St. Mark's, Venice, and after a few years elsewhere (1778–84) returned there as choirmaster, succeeding Galuppi. He wrote many motets (from 1743), several oratorios, as *David pœnitens* (1775) and *Il Giuseppe riconosciuto* (1787), a Te Deum (1803), besides over 40 operas (from 1745). **Bernardino Ottani** (d. 1827), pupil of Martini at Bologna, from 1757 choirmaster there and from 1779 at Turin, mingled the composition of his 12 operas (from 1767) with that of almost 50 masses and other sacred music. **Stanislao Mattei** (d. 1825), another pupil of Martini at Bologna and in 1770 his successor at S. Francesco, besides becoming a favorite teacher, produced a great quantity of church music of every kind, one oratorio and a work on theory (1788 and later editions). **Bernardo Bittoni** (d. 1829), from 1773 choirmaster at Rieti and from 1781 at Fabriano, was a remarkable violinist and organist, writing many motets and organ-pieces, with a few masses. **Giuseppe Sarti** (d. 1802), still another of Martini's pupils, returned to Italy from Denmark in 1775 and was choirmaster at Milan in 1779–84. He composed masses and Misereres, etc., of real contrapuntal excellence. An 8-part fugue is noted as one of the best ever written.

In Austria, chiefly at Vienna, Salzburg and Prague, besides **Haydn** and **Mozart**, were the following, several giving special attention to the organ: —

Joseph Seegr (d. 1782), a Bohemian, pupil of Czernohorsky at Prague, where from about 1750 he was an organist and teacher of wide renown — even likened to Bach himself. Though he wrote much vocal sacred music, he is now chiefly represented by organ-preludes, fugues and toccatas. **Franz Brixi** (d. 1771), also an organist and choirmaster at Prague, though living less than 40 years, achieved a fine reputation through about 75 masses and other sacred music, with several oratorios and fugues.

Michael Haydn (d. 1806), from 1762 choirmaster at Salzburg, was one of the strongest and most abundant church composers of the age, his works numbering almost 400 of every description.   His brother reckoned his church style superior to his own, and he was repeatedly sought as assistant choir-master by Prince Esterhazy.   His excellence was overshadowed by his brother's reputation, though his comparative obscurity was partly due to his reticence and unobtrusiveness.   Among his pupils was **Max Keller** (d. 1855), organist at Altötting and a strong writer of masses, organ-preludes, etc.

Maximilian Stadler (d. 1833), a Jesuit priest and abbot, was an expert organist and composer.   Most of his life was spent at Vienna or near by. He was an admirer of Haydn and Mozart, but not of Beethoven.   His compositions were voluminous, including some masses, at least 80 psalms, many motets and cantatas, besides an oratorio, *Die Befreyung von Jerusalem*, and fugues for organ and piano.

Johann Georg Albrechtsberger (d. 1809), the distinguished theorist and teacher of Vienna, where from 1772 he was court-organist and from 1792 choirmaster at St. Stephen's, was another industrious church composer, his works including over 25 masses, at least 80 motets, 6 oratorios (as *Die Pilgrimme auf Golgotha*, 1781), and many organ-preludes and fugues, besides a great quantity of chamber and orchestral music (see sec. 165).

Franz Bühler (d. 1824), trained at Donauwörth as a Benedictine, from 1794 organist at Bozen (Tyrol) and from 1801 choirmaster at Augsburg, was an-other fertile writer of masses, hymns, etc., some of which are still used.

Antonio Salieri (d. 1825), the powerful opera-writer, from 1788 court-choir-master at Vienna, wrote many oratorios, including a Passion (1778), some masses and other church works (mostly after 1790) ; and **Joseph Preindl** (d. 1823), pupil of Albrechtsberger, from 1780 choirmaster at St. Peter's, Vienna, and from 1809 at St. Stephen's, produced many masses, a Te Deum, fine Lamentations, etc.

In Germany should be added a few names : —

Johann Georg Schürer (d. 1786), from 1748 court-composer for sacred music at Dresden, left some 40 masses, 3 Requiems, 140 psalms, many motets and 2 oratorios, besides 4 Italian operas and a singspiel — in all over 600 works. Associated with him at Dresden were **J. G. Naumann** (d. 1801) and **Schuster** (d. 1812), already noted (secs. 151, 153) ;   and also **Franz Seydelmann** (d. 1806), from 1772 court-composer and from 1787 choirmaster, whose remains include about 35 masses, as many psalms, much other sacred music, 3 oratorios (from 1774), several operas (as the singspiel *Arsene*, 1779, and *Il capriccio corretto*, 1783), songs and piano-sonatas.

Georg Joseph Vogler (d. 1814) was a unique genius.   Born in 1749 at Würzburg, he was educated both in theology and in music at the Jesuit college there, becoming an accomplished organist.   In 1770 he entered the service of the Elector Palatine at Mannheim, and in 1774 was sent to Bologna to study with Martini, but, disliking the latter's emphasis on counterpoint, betook himself to Padua both to continue theology and to study with Vallotti.   He also traveled through Italy as a virtuoso, receiving many honors. Late in 1775 he returned to Mannheim, became assistant choirmaster and started a music-school.   In 1778 he removed with the court to Munich, con-tinuing in honor with his patron, though unpopular with the musicians. From 1780 he visited Paris and London, where his theoretical ideas and his

technical facility attracted attention.   In 1784 he was recalled to Munich and
made choirmaster, but in 1785 set out again for a tour in northwestern Germany, becoming in 1786 court-choirmaster at Stockholm and establishing a
school. Having devised many improvements in organ-building ('simplifications') and a portable 'orchestrion' embodying some of them, in 1788 he
went to Prussia, in 1790 to England and then to various Continental countries,
playing, arguing and seeking orders for his specialties.   From 1807 he was
court-choirmaster at Darmstadt, where he founded still another school.   He
was a singular mixture of ability and charlatanry.   His ideas about theory and
instrument-making were original and ahead of his time.   His arrogance and
oddity turned most musicians against him, but he was adept in cajoling the
favor of princes and astonishing the public.   He had the title of Abbé and
affected extreme piety.   He attracted numerous pupils, who were generally
attached to him, and several of them became famous (as Weber and Meyerbeer).   His listed works number over 300, of which the best are choral and
organ-pieces of every description, including many masses, Te Deums, Misereres,
hymns, etc., with over 10 operas (from 1780) in various styles.   As a critic
and theorist he was fertile and enterprising, and his pedagogical influence
was considerable (see sec. 165).

   Peter von Winter (d. 1825), the opera-writer (see sec. 153), was a pupil of
Vogler and, like him, a protégé of the Elector at Mannheim and Munich,
where he was ultimately choirmaster.   He wrote over 25 masses, a few oratorios, many sacred cantatas and smaller sacred works, some of them for the
Protestant service.   Though not a strong contrapuntist or apt at emotional
expression, he was clever in choral and instrumental ensembles.

   In France the most striking sacred composers were Le Sueur and Cherubini, representing the free and the strict styles respectively; but their work
in this field belongs chiefly to the next period.   Among the famous organists
was Nicolas Séjan (d. 1819), working in various Paris churches from 1760 for
more than 50 years.

   In Spain should be named Francisco Saverio Garcia (d. 1809), from 1756
choirmaster at Saragossa, and Pedro Albeniz (d. 1821), choirmaster at San
Sebastiano.

   164. Protestant Church Music. — Neither the Lutheran nor
the Anglican Church offers anything of decided musical interest at this period.   In Germany, to be sure, as in Austria,
attention to thoughtful organ music continued to some extent,
and the average cantor was expected to be something of a contrapuntist.   But the incentives to originality and genius were
extremely small.   In England interest in the noble organ style
hardly existed, as is evidenced by the lack of well-equipped instruments, and only in the cathedrals was choir music carefully
considered.   In both cases the prevalent secular styles influenced
those of the church, awakening a desire for something less

strenuous than strict polyphony.   Yet the reaction toward
operatic styles was not as great as in Catholic countries, since
in both Germany and England the Italian opera was exotic.
Hence, especially in England, there begins to appear a modern church style which avoids technical elaboration and is yet
not without dignity and solemnity — a compromise that has
often proved valuable as a means of religious expression and
impression.   The popular influence of the more sterling English
services and anthems, for instance, has had more historical importance than their technical quality would seem to warrant,
simply because for many communities they were almost the only
forms of artistic music known.   The parallel development of the
simple motet in Germany was delayed till the next period, when
it was stimulated by the liturgical awakening in the Lutheran
churches under the lead of Schleiermacher.

In Germany a few names may be selected :—

Karl Friedrich Christian Fasch (d. 1800), from 1756 associated with Emanuel Bach in the royal band at Berlin and 1774–6 in charge of the opera-
orchestra, was a good contrapuntist.   In 1790 he began a choral society which
became the famous Singakademie.   Before his death he destroyed many
works as unworthy, but some survive — psalms, motets, a mass for 16 voices,
etc., besides many clavier-pieces.

Johann Christian Kittel (d. 1809), the last pupil of J. S. Bach, from 1756
organist at Erfurt, won wide renown by his masterly playing in the old style
and attracted many scholars.   In 1800–1, however, though almost 70 years old,
he was forced to undertake public concerts at Hamburg and Altona, which were
artistically unsuccessful.   His works were chiefly for the organ, including preludes, chorale-elaborations, fugettas and a collection (1801–8).

Contemporary with these was **Johann Christoph Friedrich Bach** (d. 1795),
J. S. Bach's fourth surviving son, who, after studying law, chose music for his
career and from 1756 was chamber musician at Bückeburg.   He excelled as a
harpsichordist, but also wrote many sacred cantatas, an oratorio (1773), some
motets, an opera, *Die Amerikanerin* (1776) and much chamber and clavier
music.   His ability was only moderate.   **Christian Gotthilf Tag** (d. 1811),
from 1755 for 53 years cantor at Hohenstein (Saxony), is cited as a typical
German church musician of the time, plodding, methodical and prolific.
Georg Michael Telemann (d. 1831), from about 1773 cantor at Riga, was
another.   More conspicuous was **Johann Gottfried Schicht** (d. 1823), who as
a law-student at Leipsic came under Hiller's influence, played the violin and
the piano at the Gewandhaus, and in 1785 succeeded Hiller as conductor there,
from 1798 was organist at the New Church and from 1810 cantor at the
Thomasschule.   He wrote 3 oratorios (from 1785), several masses, many
motets, and edited a noted Choralbuch (1819).   **Justin Heinrich Knecht**
(d. 1817), from 1771 director and later organist at Biberach and in 1807–9

choirmaster at Stuttgart, was a popular teacher and good theorist. He was also a fluent writer of vocal and organ-pieces, besides clavier music and a rather striking ' Nature ' symphony. He edited a Choralbuch (1799–1816), an Orgelschule (1795–98), and many theoretical books. **Johann Gottfried Vierling** (d. 1813), from about 1780 organist at Schmalkalden, was an accomplished player and contrapuntist, publishing sacred cantatas and organ-pieces, a Choralbuch (1789) and a work on preluding (1794).

Examples of the more popular style were **Johann Friedrich Doles** (d. 1797), a pupil of J. S. Bach, but far from adopting his methods, who from 1744 was cantor at Freiberg (Saxony) and from 1756 in the Thomasschule at Leipsic; **Christian Ehregott Weinlig** (d. 1813), from 1767 organist at Leipsic and from 1780 at Dresden, where in 1785 he succeeded his teacher Homilius as cantor of the Kreuzschule; **Cornelius von Königslöw** (d. 1833), from 1773 organist at Lübeck, writing oratorios (from 1781) and imitating his predecessor Buxtehude's *Abendmusiken*.

In England active workers included **Richard Langdon** (d. 1803), from 1753 organist at Exeter, from 1778 at Bristol and from 1782 at Armagh; **William Jackson** (d. 1803), from 1755 a teacher at Exeter and popular for his songs and glees, and from 1777 organist at the cathedral; **Edmund Ayrton** (d. 1808), from 1754 organist at Southwell, from 1764 in the Chapel Royal and from 1780 its choirmaster, succeeding Nares, with 4 services and 10 anthems; **Samuel Arnold** (d. 1802), pupil of Gates and Nares, in 1783 Nares' successor at the Chapel Royal, and in 1793 Cooke's at Westminster, the writer of several oratorios (from 1767), including *The Prodigal Son* (1777), and over 20 anthems, and the editor of a not entirely successful edition of Handel's works (about 40 vols., from 1786) and of a standard collection of *Cathedral Music* (4 vols., 1790); **John [Christmas] Beckwith** (d. 1809), pupil of P. Hayes, from 1780 organist at Norwich, writer of about 15 anthems, some organ-preludes (1780), glees and songs, besides a collection of chants (1808), containing a brief history of chanting; **William Russell** (d. 1813), pupil of Arnold, from 1789 organist at various London churches and from 1801 pianist at Covent Garden, with 2 oratorios, 2 services, a few anthems and preludes, with several odes; and **John Page** (d. 1812), a tenor singer at Windsor and London, who made good collections of anthems (1800), glees (1804), etc.

Several of the stronger writers of the next period began active work before 1800, such as **Attwood, Clarke-Whitfeld, Wesley** and **Crotch** (see sec. 186).

It is in this period that the earliest stirrings of independent musical composition appeared in America, though their fruits, mostly hymn-tunes and anthems, were of the slenderest absolute value.

The pioneers, as has lately been shown, were **Francis Hopkinson** (d. 1791) and **James Lyon**, both composing as early as 1759. From 1770 many collections of sacred music containing more or less original matter appeared in New England, as by **William Billings** (d. 1800), **Andrew Law** (d. 1821), **Daniel Read** (d. 1836), and others.

CHAPTER XXIII

THEORETICAL AND LITERARY PROGRESS

165. Literature about Music. — Nothing better marks the advance in musical intellectuality than the gain in the amount and quality of the writing about musical questions.   In this respect the great productiveness of the 19th century was now clearly foreshadowed.   The changes that were going on in practical methods began to be accompanied in the field of theory by attempts to rationalize the facts and to rearrange the principles of composition from the harmonic rather than the contrapuntal centre ; but on the whole, owing to the influence of certain leading minds, theory remained more conservative than practical composition.   Criticism, however, was freer and more progressive. It now began to be less intensely personal and subjective in character than earlier in the century, and in many quarters reached out after some sort of objective æsthetic system, though it must be said that the usual type of æsthetics was strongly *a priori* rather than inductive.   In the field of pedagogics, the most notable feature was the beginning of a systematic treatment of keyboard technique, stimulated by the rapid advance of the piano and its public use.   It was not yet perceived how great an influence this was to have upon the detail of all composition.

More important than these movements was the awakening of a true sense of historical investigation and presentation, shown both in the publication of histories proper and in the accumulation of historic materials by patient research.   While the historical works actually produced are now as a rule superseded by later ones, the impetus and example of students like Martini, Hawkins, Burney, Gerbert and Forkel are still matters of admiration.

The increasing thoughtfulness of the musical public is evidenced by the quantity and variety of books, periodicals and pamphlets, of which repeated editions were often demanded.

Acoustical questions continued to command attention, especially from those in search of harmonic foundations. As examples we may cite works by **Kirnberger** of Berlin (d. 1783) on temperament (1760); by **Johann Heinrich Lambert** (d. 1777), a Prussian civil official, on implements of research, flute-tones, etc. (1763–75); by **Berlin** of Drontheim (d. c. 1775) on tonometry by logarithms (1767); by **Giordano Riccatti** (d. 1790), an Italian nobleman of Treviso (works from 1767); by **Marpurg** of Berlin (d. 1795) on temperament (1779); by **Vallotti** (d. 1780), the Paduan organist (1779); and by the Englishman **Matthew Young** (d. 1800), a general treatise (1784). To these may be added writings (1800–07) by **Vogler** (d. 1814) and **Türk** of Halle (d. 1813).

Ernst Chladni (d. 1827) led the age in musical physics, surpassing Sauveur in the reach and exactitude of his investigations. Born in 1756 and extraordinarily educated in geography, medicine, law and physics, from 1787 he devoted himself wholly to the phenomena of sound. He traveled widely as a lecturer and was highly honored, as by Napoleon in 1808. His best demonstrations were regarding 'partial-tones' and the vibrations of rods and plates. Besides his classic treatise, *Die Akustik* (1802), he published many lesser works. He wasted energy in perfecting the 'euphon' and 'clavicylinder,' instruments whose tones were produced by friction upon glass rods or tubes.

The number of works on composition was considerable, ranging from elaborate treatises to popular handbooks. The ablest were by Italians or Germans. Many of them were marred by needless polemics.

Giambattista Martini (d. 1784) of Bologna, besides being a strong composer, was the most learned theorist of the old school and a teacher sought after from all quarters. His published works did not begin till 1757, when he was over 50. After two smaller works (1757, '69), came his famous treatise (2 vols., 1774–6), valuable both for copious examples from early masters, mostly of the Roman school, and for profound annotations and discussions. The standpoint, as in the case of Fux, was that of advanced mediæval theory, but held without severity. For years Martini also labored upon a History (3 vols., 1757–81, 4th unfinished), but did not get beyond ancient times. He left much material in MS., including polemical essays against Eximeno, Riccieri and others, a dictionary of terms, some acoustical discussions, and valuable catalogues of musicians and books, made up out of his extraordinary library (17,000 vols.). He was full of kindness for musicians, young and old, as shown in his welcome (1770) to the boy Mozart, and his acquaintance was almost as wide as his fame. **Giuseppe Paolucci** (d. 1777), choirmaster at Venice, Sinigaglia and Assisi, Martini's pupil, anticipated his method by a notable treatise (1765–72). **Giambattista Mancini** (d. 1800), another pupil, long a teacher at the court of Vienna, followed (1774).

Francesco Antonio Vallotti (d. 1780), the great organist of Padua, issued a striking treatise (1779, unfinished) that helped to show that the old contrapuntal theories and the new harmony were not essentially antagonistic. His style was clear and his reasoning generally cogent. **Luigi Antonio Sabbatini** (d. 1809), pupil of Martini and Vallotti, from 1766 choirmaster at Rome and from 1786 at Padua, followed with several important works (1789–1802).

2 D

Antonio Eximeno (d. 1808), born in Spain, after training as a Jesuit, worked at Rome. He strongly advocated (1774) the relaxation of the strictness of the old school, and was criticized by conservatives like Martini.

Nicola Sala (d. c. 1800), the veteran teacher and composer of Naples, when over 90 years old, put forth a treatise (1794) which, however, has been severely attacked (Fétis).

Johann Georg Albrechtsberger (d. 1809) from 1772 became the chief theoretical master in the Viennese circle, his greatest pupil being Beethoven. He put forth a monumental treatise (1790), often translated, besides other works (complete edition by Seyfried, 1826).

Johann Philipp Kirnberger (d. 1783), a pupil of J. S. Bach and the admirer of his sons Friedemann and Emanuel, from 1758 worked at Berlin, disputing with Marpurg and others the leadership of German thought. He was an able theorist, though not always judicious or temperate (chief work, 1771-9, others, 1773-82).

Christoph Gottlieb Schröter of Nordhausen (d. 1782) was the author of a work on harmony (1772). **Georg Joseph Vogler** (d. 1814) was as independent in theory as elsewhere (see sec. 163). In general, he followed his teacher Vallotti, though with views of his own, often in advance of his day (works, 1776-1802, and posthumously on the fugue). **Heinrich Christoph Koch** (d. 1816), a little-known musician at Rudolstadt, wrote ably from the new melodic and harmonic standpoint (1782-93, besides a brochure on enharmonic modulation, 1812).

Pierre Joseph Roussier (d. 1790), a follower of Rameau, wrote many works (from 1755), including studies upon ancient mathematical speculations. **Jean Baptiste Mercadier** (d. 1815) attempted (1776) to replace both Rameau and Tartini by theories of his own.

Among the many handbooks of less significance were those of **Johann Lorenz Albrecht** (d. 1773), organist at Mühlhausen (1761); of **Johann Samuel Petri** (d. 1808), a Silesian cantor (1767, '82); of **Ernst Wilhelm Wolf** (d. 1792), court-choirmaster at Weimar (1788); of **J. H. Knecht** (d. 1817), a useful teacher at Biberach (works, 1785-1803); of the bombastic **Johann Gottlieb Portmann** (d. 1798), from 1766 at Darmstadt (1785-98); of **Daniel Gottlob Türk** (d. 1813), the well-known teacher at Halle (1791-1800); of **Honoré François Marie Langlé** (d. 1807), trained at Naples, but from 1764 at Paris and after 1791 in the Conservatoire (1793-1805); of **August Friedrich Karl Kollmann** (d. 1829), a teacher and organist in London (1796-1806); of **Carlo Gervasoni** (d. 1819), choirmaster at Borgo Taro (1800-12); and of **Callcott** (d. 1821), the English glee-writer (1806).

To these may be added special studies on questions of metrics by **Giovenale Sacchi** (d. 1789), a Barnabite monk at Milan (1770-8); and the remarkable didactic poem, *La musica* (1779), by the Spaniard **Tomas de Yriarte** (d. c. 1791), which treats of a variety of theoretical and critical points.

Connected with the theorists were the critics, though many of them approached music purely from the literary or the speculative side.

In the Gluck controversy at Paris the protagonists against him were **Jean François Marmontel** (d. 1799), **Jean François de Laharpe** (d. 1803), **Claude**

Philibert Coquéau (d. 1794) and Pierre Louis Ginguené (d. 1816), and, in his favor, François Arnaud (d. 1784), Jean Baptiste Antoine Suard (d. 1817) and Gaspar Michel Leblond (d. 1809) — the dates of their writing being 1777-83. Other students of Gluck's music were Friedrich Just Riedel (d. 1785), and Karl Spazier (d. 1805), the one in 1775, the other in 1795.

Among general critiques rather notable are those of Reichardt (d. 1814), the great song-writer, especially his *Briefe* (from 1774) ; and the autobiography of Karl Spazier (d. 1805), professor at Giessen (1792-6), who also wrote on church music. Some of Reichardt's observations were attacked (1789) by Johann Karl Friedrich Rellstab (d. 1813), a Berlin publisher.

Musical æsthetics now begins to take shape as a branch of a general theory of the fine arts. A prominent writer was Johann Georg Sulzer (d. 1779), professor at Berlin (works from 1757), in whose encyclopædic *Theorie der schönen Künste* (1772-4, much extended after 1792 by other editors) the musical articles were mainly supplied by J. A. P. Schulz (d. 1800), at first with the help of Kirnberger. Somewhat similar works were undertaken by Johann August Eberhard (d. 1809), professor at Halle (1783, 1803-5) ; by Christian Friedrich Michaelis (d. 1834), teacher at Leipsic (1795-1800, and later) ; and by the erratic Daniel Schubart (d. 1791) of Stuttgart (1806, edited by his son). The relations of poetry and music were variously discussed by John Brown (d. 1766) in 1763 ; by the Marquis de Chastellux (d. 1788) in 1765 ; and by Michel Paul Gui de Chabanon (d. 1792) in 1779 — all these works being translated more or less. Still further writers were Karl Ludwig Junker (d. 1797) on music in general (1777, '86) ; Johann Jakob Engel (d. 1802) on dramatic depiction in music (1780) ; and the brothers Von Dalberg (d. 1817, 1812) on a variety of subjects (from 1787).

Treatises upon particular instruments or instruction-books were frequent, those pertaining to the organ and the piano being the most conspicuous.

Thus, regarding organ-building, appeared in 1766-78 (3 vols., and a 4th added in German by J. C. Vollbeding, 1793) the notable treatise of François Bedos de Celles (d. 1779), a Benedictine of St. Maur; with others in 1779 by Johann Samuel Halle (d. 1810), a teacher at Berlin ; in 1801 by Georg Christian Friedrich Schlimbach of Berlin (d. after 1806) ; in 1804 by Johann Heinrich Zang of Schweinfurt (d. 1811) ; and in 1806 by Vogler (d. 1814) — the latter proposing simplifications and improvements, not all of which secured acceptance. Among organ instruction-books may be noted those in 1766-1810 by Joachim Hess (d. c. 1810), for over 50 years at Gouda (Holland) ; in 1795-8 by Knecht of Biberach (d. 1817), Vogler's special rival ; and in 1801-8 by Kittel of Erfurt (d. 1809).

Regarding violin-playing there were noted works (1756) by Leopold Mozart (d. 1787), and (1791-6) by Francesco Galeazzi of Rome (d. c. 1819) ; regarding flute-playing several (1786-1800) by Johann Georg Tromlitz (d. 1805) of Leipsic, as well as the autobiography (1807) of Friedrich Ludwig Dulon (d. 1826), a widely-known blind flutist ; and regarding trumpet and drum music (1795) by Johann Ernst Altenburg of Weissenfels and Bitterfeld (d. 1801). John Gunn (d. c. 1824) issued various instruction-books for the piano, 'cello (1793) and flute, besides an important history of Scottish harpers (1807).

Regarding piano-playing now begins the long list of methods and studies upon which modern technique rests. Back of those meant for the piano lay many devised for the clavichord or harpsichord, such as the famous example (1753-87) by **K. P. E. Bach** (d. 1788) and that by **Georg Simon Löhlein** (d. 1781) of Leipsic and Danzig (1765-81, with many later editions, as by J. G. Wetthauer, 1791, and A. E. Müller, 1804). All the great virtuosi of the period contributed, though usually coming to formal publication only after years of teaching. Examples are those by **Clementi** (d. 1832), whose best pedagogical work was his *Gradus* (1817); by **Dussek** (d. 1812); in 1798-1804 by **Louis Adam** (d. 1848) for the Paris Conservatoire; and about 1810 by **J. B. Cramer** (d. 1858), **Wölfl** (d. 1812) and **Pollini** (d. 1846).

This period witnessed the advent of the genuine historical investigator, whose conclusions rest upon documents and personal research. The earliest was **Martini** (d. 1784), whose *Storia* has been mentioned above. Contemporaneous with him were two Englishmen who accomplished much more.

John Hawkins (d. 1789), born in 1719, was trained in mathematics and the law, continuing to practise the latter through his life. He was interested in literary studies and was a special friend of Samuel Johnson. Musical matters attracted him early, and, becoming wealthy through marriage, he retired to Twickenham, collected a superb library and devoted himself to preparing his great *History* (5 vols., 1776, republished 1853 and 1875). He also wrote an account of the Academy of Ancient Music (1770). His *History* came into immediate competition with the first volume of Burney, at first unsuccessfully, because not so brilliantly written, but later with increasing appreciation of its accuracy.

Charles Burney (d. 1814), born in 1726, was brought up as a musician, for a time being a pupil of Arne. He composed much dramatic music (1745-66), with several piano- or violin-sonatas and concertos, etc. From 1749 he was organist in London and from 1751 at Lynn Regis, where the project of his *History* was formed. Returning to London in 1760, while continuing musical production, he began collecting materials. In 1770 and 1772 he made extensive tours on the Continent, enjoying opportunities to visit libraries and consult with musicians. He published accounts of these tours (France and Italy, 1771, Germany, the Netherlands, etc., 1773). His *History* (4 vols., 1776-89) came out slowly, but secured quick popularity for its readableness and freshness. He also wrote accounts of the youthful prodigy Crotch (1770) and of the Handel Commemoration (1785), besides a life of the poet Metastasio (3 vols., 1796). He was an exceedingly affable and cultivated man, and had a prodigious circle of famous friends.

Less important histories were published in 1788 by **Johann Nikolaus Forkel** (d. 1818), reaching only to the middle of the 16th century; in 1792 by **Christian Kalkbrenner** (d. 1806), who was in court service at Berlin, later chorusmaster at the Paris Opéra; and in 1793 by **Richard Eastcott** (d. 1828). More or less useful Almanachs and other annals were prepared in 1778 and 1792-8 by **Christian Gottfried Thomas** (d. 1806), a Leipsic composer and publisher; in 1782-4 by **Karl Ludwig Junker** (d. 1797), who also put forth (1776) studies of some 20 composers, including Emanuel and Christian Bach, Boccherini, Ditters, Grétry and Haydn (poorly done); in 1782-4 and

1789 by **Forkel**; and, concerning the French theatre, with many sidelights upon the opera, from 1750 by **Joseph de Laporte** (d. 1779), a series continued after his death by **N. B. Duchesne** and others (48 vols. to 1815); and by **Louis François Beffara** (d. 1838), a police-commissioner at Paris (35 vols. in MS., destroyed by fire in 1871).

Special studies were made on ancient music in 1770–81 by **Pierre Joseph Roussier** (d. c. 1790), and in 1778 by **Giovenale Sacchi** (d. 1789); and on mediæval music by **Jean Benjamin de Laborde** (d. 1794), a pupil of Rameau and long a favorite at court (5 vols., 1780-1, with a life of Raoul de Coucy, 1781), whose method was confused and untrustworthy.

Martin Gerbert (d. 1793), trained as a Benedictine and from 1764 abbot at St. Blaise, had access there to valuable MSS. (burnt in 1768), from which (and from researches in many other libraries in France, Germany and Italy) he compiled invaluable collections of mediæval writings about music (1774, '84) and of German liturgies (1776-9), which remained unique sources until improved and supplemented by 19th-century investigators.

Stefano Arteaga (d. 1799), a Spanish Jesuit who worked at both Bologna and Paris, a close friend of Martini, prepared a valuable work on Italian opera (1783), which was translated into German by Forkel (1789) and into French (1802).

An attempt was made in 1783 by **Johann Sigmund Gruber** (d. 1805), a Nuremberg lawyer, to draft a comprehensive sketch of the literature about music. In 1792 appeared the better work of **Johann Nikolaus Forkel** (d. 1818), musical director at Göttingen, one of the first diligent students of historical sources, whose book was the basis of the later works of Lichtenthal and Becker.

Edward Jones (d. 1824) made remarkable collections of old Welsh music (1784–1802), of Greek and Oriental airs (1804) and other national music. **George Thomson** (d. 1851) was indefatigable in gathering Scotch, Irish and Welsh melodies (17 vols., 1793–1841), provided with modern accompaniments. Irish music was collected in 1786 by **Joseph Cooper Walker** (d. 1810) and from 1796 by **Edward Bunting** (d. 1843), the latter writing also upon the history of the harp.

Père Amiot (d. c. 1794), a Jesuit missionary, drafted a volume on Chinese music (1780), largely from native sources, though with what accuracy is disputed. **William Jones** (d. 1794), a judge at Calcutta, wrote ably of Hindu music (1784).

Out of the many musical biographies that now began to accumulate a few may be instanced, such as those on Vallotti by **Sabbatini** (1780); on Martini by **Guglielmo della Valle** (1784-5); on various composers and on Metastasio by **J. A. Hiller** (1784-6); on Handel by **Reichardt** (1785); on Marcello by **Sacchi** (1789); on Metastasio by **Burney** (1796); on Piccinni by **Ginguené** (1800); on Fasch by **Zelter** (1801); on Naumann by **A. G. Meissner** (1803-4); and on J. S. Bach by **Forkel** (1803),— the last being a work of decided scholarship. Autobiographies were given out by **Schubart** (1791), **Spazier** (1792), **Ditters** (1799), **Reichardt** (1805) and **Dulon** (1807).

Works of a dictionary character also began to be important, such as those by **Sulzer** on the fine arts generally (1772-99, continued by Blankenburg); by **Johann Georg Meusel** (d. 1820) on living art-workers (1778-1803); by **G. F. Wolf** on terms, etc. (1787); by **Joos Verschuere-Reynvaan** (d. 1809) on the same (1790-5, only to 'M')—a pioneer work in Dutch; by **Ernst Ludwig Gerber** (d. 1819), two invaluable works on musicians (1790-92, 1812-4); besides many articles (from 1794), by **Johann Gottfried Geisler** (d. 1827) on instruments (1792-1800), by **Knecht** on terms (1795), and, most scholarly of all, by **Heinrich Christoph Koch** (d. 1816) on terms (1802) and on musicians (1807). **Johann Wilhelm Hertel** (d. 1789) left in MS. a volume of additions (1752-60) to Walther's *Lexicon*, besides editing a collection of Italian and French works about music (1757-8).

Throughout the half-century, experiments continued with periodicals of different sorts—almost 20 in all. Most of these lived but a short time. The conspicuous exception was the important *Allgemeine musikalische Zeitung*, founded at Leipsic in 1798, probably by Friedrich Rochlitz, and published by Breitkopf & Härtel, which continued till 1848. Several of the others, though not permanent, were interesting expressions of literary enterprise and often contained articles of value.

From this period date several famous publishing houses, such as that of **Schott** at Mayence, founded about 1770; that of **André** at Offenbach, founded in 1774 by Johann André (d. 1799) and greatly advanced by his son Johann Anton André (d. 1842); that of **Artaria** at Vienna, founded in 1778; that of **Leuckart** at Breslau (now Leipsic), founded in 1782; and that of **Simrock** at Bonn and Cologne (now Berlin), founded in 1790.

The process of lithography having been invented in 1798 by Aloys Senefelder of Munich, it was immediately applied to the printing of music, largely through the efforts of **Franz Gleissner** (d. after 1815), whose own first symphony was lithographed in 1798. André and Breitkopf & Härtel were prompt to take up this improvement.

166. Summary of the Half-Century.—The age of Haydn, Gluck and Mozart presents most interesting contrasts with both that which preceded and that which followed. But these contrasts differ in nature and in intensity. At each stage we see ideas coming to consummation that had long been germinating, but the three stages differ in the ideas chosen for expression. In passing out of the Bach-Handel period music went through a sort of revolution, and again in entering upon the 19th century it experienced another revolution, but in a different direction.

Beginning with Haydn's work, a novel type of musical structure presented itself. The attention of composers now swung with emphasis either to explicit melodiousness or to a harmony that was melodically controlled. The organic interdependence of melody and form was more clearly apprehended. And there

was a new insight into the nature of chords and the philosophy of arranging them in sequence. The outlines of these
ideas had long been visible, steadily developing in Italian opera
and in German writing of various kinds, but they hardly became
regnant until the Austrian melodists made them conspicuous.
Hence the profound difference of manner between most music
before 1750 and that afterward. The older composers had
worked with the instinct of true counterpoint or of a half-con-
trapuntal harmony. Now we encounter rather the instinct of
the pure solo song or of a song-like harmony. In short, as the
controlling factor in musical conception, monophony now fully
replaces mediæval polyphony. That this principle, first perceived in part fully two centuries before, now took possession of
the whole range of composition, is a most significant fact.

Closely associated with this was the general acceptance of the
modern notion of tonality, with its classification of chords by
their relation to a definite major or minor key, and its system of
relative keys radiating in several directions, into which modulation can occur by definite processes. The vague and shifting
tonality of the earlier periods was at last given up — with some
loss of peculiar effects, but with an evident gain in unity and
consistency.

We now notice a great advance in the valuation of certain instrumental methods as compared with vocal. The chamber
quartet (or other small group) and the orchestra now for the
first time attain their modern eminence. There was a consequent
emphasis upon every device in the nature of the materials or in
their detailed handling that should make the total result clear, interesting and telling for its own sake, apart from all ideas that
may be conveyed by words. Thus the interests of 'absolute music'
received an attention wholly new, at least in degree and significance. Following close upon this exaltation of the ensemble
of solo instruments, came the rapid rise of the piano as a concerted instrument of unsuspected possibilities. Although some
of these steps had been previously foreshadowed, nothing earlier
had more than a fraction of the importance of what was now
done.

But the vocal field was not neglected. Here there were two
events of capital significance — the reclamation of the opera to
dramatic sanity by Gluck, with the infusion into it of a more

varied and vital musical content, especially by Mozart, and the recognition of the detached song as an object worthy of serious artistic attention. These movements had some connection with those mentioned above, but were still more akin to the new spirit that was to display itself after 1800. In these two quarters we observe the subjective and romantic impulses of the future already bestirring themselves.

In pure theory the period lacked the guidance of any one leader of the first order of constructive genius, except that of the conservative Martini, but in research and criticism it made great gains, though the literary aspect of the art was still far from mature or adequate. But it is noteworthy that among thinkers of a broad philosophic scope the serious consideration of topics relating to music begins to have a more secure and honorable place.

The great defects of the period were those of the age as a whole, namely, the exaltation of conventional regularity over sincere personal conviction or feeling, and the inevitable drift toward formalism in expression. Yet, although this stage in development naturally produced a great mass of works that now seem manneristic and hollow, it served a purpose in fastening attention upon the purely external charm of tonal patterns and qualities, thus providing invaluable ways and means to the period following. The essential importance of the period is shown by the fact that the styles now known as 'classical,' as they were exemplified by the greater masters, like Haydn and Mozart, not only served as the basis or model for all work in the next period, but have held their place to some degree ever since.

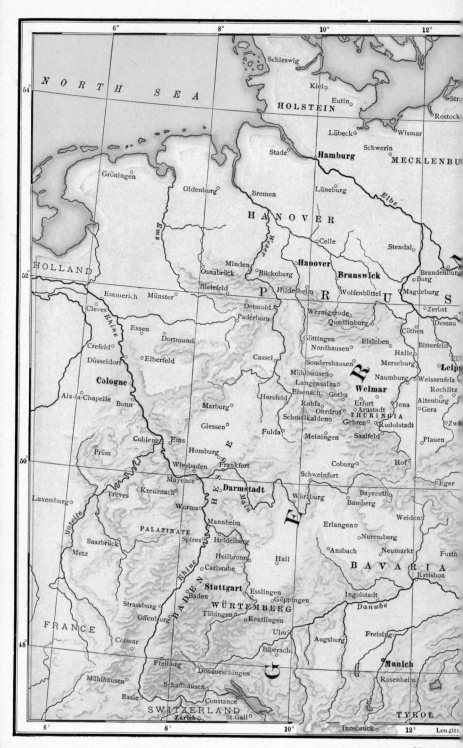

MAP III.—

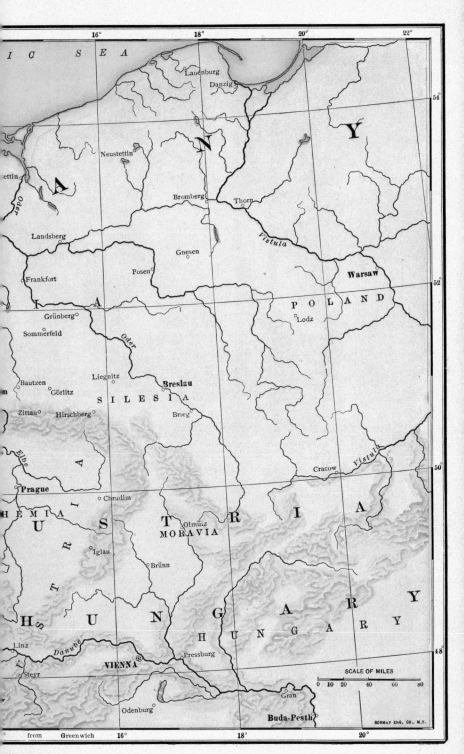

AUSTRIA.

PART VII

THE EARLY NINETEENTH CENTURY

PART VII

THE EARLY NINETEENTH CENTURY

CHAPTER XXIV

THE ADVENT OF BEETHOVEN

167. General Survey. — The treatment of the 19th century in musical history presents many serious difficulties. The mere multitude of items is far more bewildering than in any previous period, since, for example, the number of composers to be considered is at least four times as great as in the 18th century. The division of the material into classes is often exceedingly difficult, not only because the work of individual composers often extends into many different fields of production, but because the methods and spirit of the fields themselves cross and interpenetrate. The essential cosmopolitanism of music becomes more conspicuous, arising both from the frequent transfers of musicians from land to land and from the ready diffusion of their printed works. All lines of development, therefore, become more complicated, so that summary statements require incessant qualifications.

It is convenient to separate the century roughly into three large periods, namely, that of Beethoven, Weber and Schubert (to about 1830), that of Mendelssohn, Schumann and Chopin (to about 1860), and that of Wagner and his contemporaries, with their successors to the present time. The matters to be considered under these three divisions do not necessarily lie within the time-limits named, but often overlap in various ways. Yet for clarity of thought some division must be made.

In political history France occupies the centre of the stage. The 18th century had closed with the gigantic convulsion of the French Revolution, which not only wrought a bloody transformation in France, but shook the whole of Europe. With it began the gradual overthrow of the mediæval notion of society as existing for certain privileged classes, and the setting up of the modern ideas of equality and liberty, with a new valuation of the individual in all relations.

But before the fruits of the Revolution could be gathered came the amazing career of Napoleon (Consul, 1799–1804, Emperor, 1804–15), with his audacious intrigues and campaigns for supremacy in the face of all Europe. His empire was strengthened by the humiliation of Austria (Vienna occupied, 1805, '09), of Prussia (Berlin taken, 1806), of Portugal and Spain, and of the Pope, but reverses set in from the fruitless invasion of Russia (1812), and the end of his dream of dominion came with the battles of Leipsic (1813) and Waterloo (1815). All sorts of collateral struggles grew out of these, such as the War of 1812 between England and America.

When at length Napoleon was displaced, the demand for popular liberty under constitutional guarantees again became insistent, showing itself in repeated revolutionary undertakings in different countries far on into the middle of the century — of which the end is not yet.

The principal rulers of the period were, in France (besides Napoleon), Louis XVIII. (1814–24); in Austria, Francis I. (1792–1835); in Prussia, Frederick William III. (1797–1840); in England, George III. (1760–1820) and George IV. (1820–30); and in Russia, Alexander I. (1801–24). Without trying to summarize the powerful literary influences of the time in any of the leading countries, we may content ourselves with recalling that in Germany now came the first impress of philosophers like Kant (d. 1804), Fichte (d. 1814) and Hegel (d. 1831), and of poets like Herder (d. 1803), Schiller (d. 1805) and Goethe (d. 1832). It was just about this time that the general advance of method began in historical and physical science which became characteristic of the whole century.

In the musical world certain salient points may be noted about the early part of the century. First of these is the dominance of Beethoven as an original, epoch-making genius of the first rank — one who made himself felt immediately and whose power has not since departed, in spite of the great changes in recent years. Next comes the separation under Weber of the German opera as a distinct type, incorporating into itself some of the constructive ideas of Gluck, with much of the best instrumental progress, and beginning to express the deeply romantic imagination of the German peoples. Side by side with this stood a fresh illustration of the inexhaustible vitality of Italian opera under Rossini and others, and the equally fresh renewal of French opera under Boieldieu and Auber. Here falls the memorable work of Schubert, a melodist of endless fertility, especially influential in bringing the art-form of the song to full honor. Pianism and violinism as specialties take on new elaboration, affecting still more the whole current of musical expression. The sensational popular power of the virtuoso is repeatedly demonstrated, while the activity of countless teachers, of many strong music-schools and of choral societies, with the wider scope of business interests in publishing music and making instruments, is creating a vast public of musical amateurs and well-wishers. The study of musical theory in all its parts, and the publication of varied works of history and criticism, continue with steadily augmenting influence.

The conspicuous note of the age was a new individualism, with an irrepressible instinct for personal freedom in thought and feeling as well as in political and social relations. Hence the formalism of the 18th century began to be disrupted by the unconventional ideas of innovators and reconstructors. The emphasis began to be transferred from regularity to originality, from studied restraint or indifference to free, passionate, even lawless feeling, from conformity to academic rule to outspoken self-revelation. This mighty movement toward vital truth, which recalls that of the 16th century, naturally found its immediate expression in music. Indeed, it is from this period that we may date the close association of musical art with the inner spirit of modern society.

> Vienna continues to be on the whole the chief musical centre, with Paris not far behind, especially as regards the opera. But the signs multiply that presently various German capitals are to become more conspicuous, since the leadership in musical progress is now passing emphatically into German hands.

168. Beethoven's Historic Place. — Beethoven is commonly counted one of the three supreme musical geniuses, by many the greatest of the three. To perceive how phenomenal he was one must needs place him against the background of the later 18th century and in the atmosphere of the stirring decades of the opening 19th. We must recall that he was not forty years younger than Haydn and not fifteen years younger than Mozart, so that his early maturity came just when their sway was at its height. We must also recall that in him wrought, even from youth, the progressive instincts of a mighty seer and leader, an idealist and a creator. Only so can we understand with what a shock he shook the whole musical world, or why from him is dated a new era, so that for more than half a century after his death masters in the upper ranks were proud to call themselves his disciples.

Beethoven was emphatically an innovator, the founder of a new order. Of this, however, he himself was probably at first unaware. He set up no revolutionary program in advance. His own thought was doubtless "not to destroy, but to fulfill."

But the quality of his character was such that he could not be true to himself without breaking through all the conventions and rising out of all the platitudes of the age into which he came. Music to him was no entertaining kaleidoscope of tones and rhythms, but the warm word of the heart. To see how true this was, one must know in some detail the story of his life. It must be added, however, that this story should be interpreted always by the message of his music. Life and art are here, probably more than in the case of any previous composer, inseparable. The purely psychological problem in this case has perennial interest. But the fact that this strange personality and this inspired genius came upon the stage just when he did, also gives his career unique historical importance. His advent set forward the whole process of musical development by a startling leap, the momentum of which lasted long afterward.

Beethoven's life may be variously divided. In any case his early years at Bonn (1770–92) stand by themselves. At Vienna his work shows three stages or ' manners,' whose limits may be roughly stated thus : — (a) To the conviction that his deafness was incurable (1802), (b) to his last public appearances as a player and the beginning of his guardianship over his nephew (1814-5), and (c) to his death (1827). This makes four periods in all, but the line between the first and second ' manners ' is indistinct.

Ludwig van Beethoven (d. 1827) was born in 1770 at Bonn on the Rhine. On the father's side he came of Belgian stock, his grandfather (d. 1773), an able musician, having come from Antwerp to the Electoral Chapel at Bonn in 1733 (choirmaster from 1761). His father (d. 1792) was a singer in the Chapel since 1756 — an intemperate, shiftless and harsh man. His mother (d. 1787) came from Ehrenbreitstein — apparently a sweet and gentle character. Of the seven children, three sons survived, Ludwig the eldest, Caspar (d. 1815) and Johann (d. 1848).

Beethoven's boyhood was made painful by poverty and by the eagerness of the father to use the boy's talents to make money. He was silent and sensitive, not fond of play, and received but a slight education except in music. His precocity in the latter led to comparisons with Mozart. He had lessons at 4, played in public at 8, composed a cantata and some variations at 10, assisted his first good teacher, Neefe, the court-organist, at 12, became cembalist or conductor at the theatre at 13, and had his first salary as assistant organist at 14. In 1787 he somehow managed to visit Vienna, there meeting Mozart, who prophesied that he would " make a noise in the world." In 1788 the Elector reorganized his opera-troupe, attracting to it several noted musicians. Beethoven had useful violin-lessons from Ries, and played the viola in the orchestra. From 1789 part of his father's salary was paid to him as conservator. In 1790 and again in 1792 Haydn passed through Bonn. In 1791 the Elector took his establishment up the Rhine to Mergentheim, where

Beethoven heard Sterkel play and won notice by his own extemporizations. By 1792 he had produced some compositions, largely piano-variations, had begun the lifelong habit of keeping 'sketch-books' for recording and elaborating his musical ideas and was recognized as a pianist of extraordinary power. He had also begun to win the friendship of cultivated people, notably Mme. von Breuning and Count Wald-stein, who were of the utmost value to him socially and mentally. In 1792, perhaps at Haydn's suggestion, the Elector gave him leave to remove to Vienna, where apparently his only sup-port at first was his salary of 150 florins, which ceased in 1794.

At Vienna Beethoven for two years had lessons in counterpoint from Haydn (secretly also from Schenk), and for about a year from Albrechtsberger. He was a conscientious pupil, but both teachers regarded his radical im-pulses with distrust. He also consulted Salieri and Förster. He made his way among wealthy and intelligent ama-teurs, like the Lichnowskys, Van Swieten and Lobkowitz, thus securing some teaching, much warm appreciation, and substantial help for the per-formance of compositions. He was always dependent upon such patronage, simply because at that time there was no other way for a musician to subsist. That he not only kept his many powerful friends, but fascinated them, was remarkable in the face of his low origin, uncouth manners, extreme sensi-tiveness and unaccountable moods. That he repaid their forbearance with esteem is shown by the long list of his dedications of important works. He was often violent in judgment and speech, so that he alienated many who were not sensible of his innate worth. He came into immediate competition with the popular pianists of the day, vanquishing those who essayed to meet him openly. The profound expressiveness of his playing, with his com-mand of technique and structure, was seen to be unrivaled.

Amid these stimulating circumstances his creative powers now gradually came into action, though used with a unique caution, every work being developed slowly, often with great alterations, and put forth only in what he felt to be its final shape. The first great productions date from about 1795, including 3 trios, 3 sonatas, a concerto and the scena *Adelaide*; in that year he also began public playing. In 1796 he visited Nuremberg, Prague and Berlin, decidedly enlarging his acquaintance and his renown. Composition became his consuming occupation. By 1800, besides lesser works, the sep-tet, 6 quartets, about 10 sonatas and the First Symphony were completed. What he wrote commanded the enthusiasm of the public and good prices from publishers. He entered the field of the drama with the ballet *Prome-theus* and that of oratorio with *The Mount of Olives* (not given till 1803), while the stream of piano and chamber works went on. But amid all this success he had increasing trouble with his hearing, which by 1802 reached a point where it menaced his mental balance, as is evidenced by the passionate letter, addressed to his brothers, which is commonly called his ' Will' — one of the few intimate revelations in words of his inner life.

Notwithstanding many serious drawbacks to be named, the dozen years before 1815 were indescribably fruitful and brilliant. The flow of inspiration was at its height, and leading publishers were ready to transmit its products to the world. The sequence of only the greater works can be noted here, the dates given being, as far as possible, those of composition rather than of publication. Of the piano-sonatas, Nos. 12–15 were written in 1801, Nos. 16–20 in 1802, Nos. 21 and 23 ('Waldstein' and 'Appassionata') in 1804, No. 22 in 1805, No. 25 in 1808, Nos. 24 and 26 in 1809, and No. 27 in 1814. The 'Kreutzer' sonata for violin belongs to 1803 and the 'cello-sonata in A probably to 1808. The three 'Rasumowsky' quartets date from 1806–7, the sextet in E♭ from 1809, the quartet in F minor from 1810. The triple concerto comes from 1804, the fourth piano-concerto from about 1805 and the fifth from 1809. The Third or 'Heroic' symphony (originally planned in honor of Napoleon) was completed in 1804, the Fourth in 1806, the Fifth and Sixth ('Pastoral') in 1808, the Seventh and Eighth in 1812. The overture to *Coriolanus* belongs to 1807, the music for *Egmont* to 1810, that for *The Ruins of Athens* and for *King Stephen* to 1811. The Mass in C was composed about 1807 and the cantata *Der glorreiche Augenblick* in 1814. The opera *Fidelio* was perhaps begun in 1803, but first given in 1805, just after the French occupied Vienna, and, after successive revisals, in 1806 and 1814. When one considers the magnitude and variety of these many works, and especially the essential novelty of their contents, it is easy to see with what an astonishing decade the century opened.

The turmoil of artistic creation — always extreme in Beethoven's case — was intensified by several complications. The catastrophe of his deafness steadily became more oppressive and disabling, inducing physical and mental irritation, shutting him off from society and friendship, and from 1814 bringing his career as a public virtuoso to a close. He was again and again desperately in love, in two or three cases with women of the upper classes, but was always thwarted by the fact of his low origin, the uncertainty of his fortune or the infelicities of his temperament. The management of practical affairs, from the securing of lodgings to the performance and publication of compositions, occasioned him infinite discomfort and worry. He held no official position and had no fixed income. In 1808 Jerome Bonaparte invited him to be choirmaster at Cassel. This led a trio of noblemen in 1809 to assure him an annual stipend of about $2,000, if he would remain at Vienna, to continue until he should receive, as was hoped, a post at the court. The struggle with France, however, so depreciated the Austrian currency that the net amount soon shrank to $800 and finally to $550, and part of this involved prolonged lawsuits. In spite, therefore, of the extraordinary brilliance of these years, Beethoven was subjected to extreme strain and his health was often far from good. Just before 1815, however, matters improved and it seemed as if a happier period was to follow.

Late in 1815 his brother Caspar died, leaving to him the guardianship of a son, then not nine years old. This charge proved a progressive and culminating disaster. Beethoven believed it necessary to separate the boy from his mother's influence, but to do this required lawsuits which lasted till 1820. He lavished upon the lad the pent-up affection of his nature, but often with such wrong-headed intensity as to alienate his best friends and exhaust himself in all sorts of practical entanglements, besides seriously checking his artistic production. To crown all, the nephew was singularly unworthy, being stupid, lazy, ungrateful and morally at least weak; he failed in study and in business, and in 1826 actually attempted suicide, for which fiasco he was banished from Vienna. (He finally went into the army, and died in 1858.) Beethoven went with him to the farm of the third brother Johann, where he was thoroughly unhappy. Late in 1826 he decided to return to Vienna, took a violent cold on the journey, contracted dropsy, and, after much suffering, died in March, 1827, the end coming amid a terrific thunderstorm. The funeral drew a great concourse and was conducted with the utmost respect and reverence.

The recital of these events is necessary to the understanding of the record of the last period of his artistic life. Upon the perpetual agony of deafness, which became almost absolute, were piled the manifold distresses connected with the scapegrace nephew. The internal struggles of the composer's mind had no adequate vent except through composition, and, while the number of works produced now became relatively small, their size, intricacy and significance were vastly increased. Almost everything was laid out upon a titanic scale, as if to achieve the impossible. Of the piano-sonatas, No. 28 dates from 1815, No. 29 from 1818-9, No. 30 perhaps from 1820, and Nos. 31 and 32 from 1821-2. The final quartets were produced in 1824-6, that in B♭ being his last work. The overture *Die Weihe des Hauses* belongs to 1822. The Ninth or 'Choral' Symphony was begun in 1817 and completed in 1823. The *Missa solennis*, originally intended for the installation of the Archbishop of Olmütz in 1820, was begun in 1818, but not finished till 1823. In his last years Beethoven came to feel that what he had produced was insignificant in comparison with what remained in his mind. Of these projected works we have but slight indications, though we know that they were to include a great Requiem and a Tenth Symphony, of the latter of which some sketches have been identified.

In personal appearance Beethoven was short, stocky and muscular. His movements were angular and absent-minded, and his dress often careless or odd in the extreme. His face was full of strength, but its expression was usually stern and forbidding. But it was a sure index of his mood, and could vary instantly from genial courtesy to boisterous mirth or the flare of anger. His eyes were dark and piercing, and his hair black, thick and coarse.

He was wont to spend his mornings and evenings in labor at the piano or his table, often becoming intensely excited and absorbed in the travail of composition. His afternoons he loved to pass in the open country, where he often conducted himself so wildly as to seem insane. His concentration upon his work was always complete, but the realization of his thoughts cost infinite apparent pain and contest — more than in the case of any other composer of

2 E

the first rank. Hence his habitual mien was restless, perturbed, or passionately eager.

In character he was the soul of truth and honor, but given to freakish misunderstandings and resentments. His temper varied from warm affection for his friends to unreasonable aversion and abuse. He was excessively sensitive to both condescension and fancied slights, and was liable to go off into a rage on imaginary provocations. His manners were often uncouth, his speech uncontrolled and his actions sometimes violent. Yet the force and nobility of his manliness were obvious, so that he fastened to himself not only the respect, but the affection, of numerous intelligent friends. Latent within him was a wealth of love and devotion which he longed to expend, but which never found an object on which to rest. Temperamentally religious in a high degree, he was so uninstructed that his only creed was a curious catena of pantheistic propositions, while his practical action was governed by the simplest elemental instincts of uprightness.

His physical and mental constitution involved him in ceaseless contradiction and struggle. Doubtless he inherited bodily infirmities, which were intensified by irregular living, so that his body and mind reacted unfortunately upon each other. Yet even in his worst conflicts there was something heroic and sublime about him. Of this higher or deeper nature his music was verily the voice, so vital and commanding that to it all the world was forced to listen.

169. Salient Features of his Style. — One of the most striking characteristics of Beethoven's work is the difference between his earlier and his later style. This difference is not simply due to the ordinary growth in mastery on the part of one who starts as a scholar, for even the earliest style is masterly in its way. It is rather the expression of profound psychical changes, which induced him to attempt ever new methods of utterance.

> That which throws greatest light upon this process is the existence of a long line of 'sketch-books,' recording more or less clearly the steps through which he approached almost all of his significant works. Although somewhat analogous cases of artistic growth may be cited, in none of them is the degree of change so extraordinary or the process of it so minutely traceable.

It has long been customary to classify his work under three successive 'manners.' Beethoven himself recognized the transitions between these, and they have been extensively elaborated by historians and critics. The division is useful, if not defined too sharply by mere dates. In external form, the works of the first period closely follow the orderly methods of Mozart, those of the second present increasing impulsive deviations from strict regularity — abrupt shifts, expanded episodes, a marked tendency to let the material dictate new idioms — and those of the third often show the positive overbalancing of all formal factors by the stress of self-expression, so that the result is difficult, abstruse, occasionally almost incoherent. Even in the first ' manner,' we notice the composer's desire to *say* something, to communicate, rather than merely to *make* something impersonally attractive. In the second, this greatly increases, showing itself sometimes in impatient or humorous caprice, sometimes in novel and daring cumulations of energy and animation, sometimes in wistful pathos or ecstatic elevation, but with all elements under perfect artistic control. In the third, the subjective values are not only intensified, but often marked by a different quality. The conceptions are usually gigantic, the strain of emotion constant and even agonized, the sense of struggle more pervasive. By common consent these final works are felt to represent one of the highest efforts of musical art to utter the deepest experiences of the human spirit. But to appreciate them requires a perception made sympathetic both by study and by much acquaintance with life.

The merely technical innovations of Beethoven are relatively few. His prevailing general method is that of the sonata, though he was also fond of variations. Within the sonata outlines he was freer than his predecessors in key-contrasts and modulation, the constituent materials were far better connected and blended, his ' subjects' strikingly fresh and telling, especially in rhythmic structure, his subsidiary matter and episodes often raised into great prominence, and his introductions and codas sometimes surprisingly expanded and enriched. His frequent replacing of the stiff minuet by a piquant or fiery scherzo was a genuine novelty, as was also his building out of some extended works by means of a grand finale, sometimes in variation-form. He was singularly free from dependence upon stock-phrases or conventional passages, as well as from mannerisms of his own. All this illustrates not only his originality, but how radical was his revolt from the habitual commonplaces of the 18th century.

His melodic freshness and richness are conspicuous, surpassing even Mozart's in many ways. The difference lies in extension of phrase, fullness of harmonic substance, power of climacteric and often pathetic suggestion, readiness of development and transformation. Every passage has its own character, individual and unmistakable, and each is fraught with meaning as well as formal beauty.   Much of the vigor of his themes is dynamic and rhythmic.   He was one of the first to realize how fully the vitality and point of musical thought depends upon these elements in design. His directions about shading and other features of expression were imperative and minute.

His harmonic method is an obvious expansion of that of the Haydn-Mozart age, peculiar chiefly in its greater freedom, especially in contrasts and shifts.   Counterpoint, as a rule, he uses more incidentally than with consistent deliberation, except in certain of his later works.   Even then he is very free to modify details so as to heighten emotional effect.

His instinct for instrumentation was acute.   He greatly advanced the range of pianism by his perception of the piano's possibilities.   He elevated music for the violin and other solo instruments by giving it more to say, and by making technique the servant of ideas.   The orchestra he wielded with imperial mastery, bringing to light beauties of combination or alternation, and devices of sonority and grandeur that have never since been forgotten.

His treatment of the voice is on the whole not so sympathetic or successful.   Of songs he wrote many, those of more or less dramatic quality being specially fine.   His union of soloists and chorus with the orchestra in the Ninth Symphony was almost an absolute novelty, but was effected from the orchestral point of view.   His distinctly choral works, such as his masses, are similarly conceived.   His one opera and his one oratorio more or less illustrate the same point.

The core of Beethoven's style is instrumental, but in a very much more advanced sense than in the case of Haydn.   The older master worked along lines of conception and execution that still betrayed their derivation from vocal methods.   With Beethoven there comes to the front a new structural technique, resting frankly upon principles not suggested by either the folk-song or the choral motet.   In this regard, far more than in any innovation as to external form, lies one of the main reasons for his epoch-making influence.   While apparently adopting the established procedures of his time, he came to regard them from a new point of view, so that the inner texture of his greater works was wholly modern.

Another general remark concerns the dramatic spirit that pervades much of his strongest work.   Of explicit drama he wrote little, since he vainly sought for acceptable texts, but it needs no acumen to see dramatic explanations for the way in which, even in purely instrumental works, he arranges and marshals his material.   Ingenious contrasts of character, intricate interplay of opposing forces, absorbing development of situation and climax — all these may again and again be discerned. These qualities escape verbal statement in analyzing given cases, simply because words are too concrete to describe the abstract plot implied, though, of course, the tone-forms by which the plot is enacted are themselves intensely concrete. Beethoven there· fore verged closely upon ' program-music,' but he himself warns us against too definite a visual or verbal interpretation of what is meant. In this dramaticness of conception he is again highly modern.

No one can possibly overlook the tremendous sincerity and seriousness of purpose in Beethoven's art. He came at a time when to make music was chiefly to offer a refined amusement to the privileged and luxurious. He himself, notwithstanding the utter democracy of his nature, was always dependent upon aris- tocratic patronage and was impelled to express himself in terms that only high mental culture could understand. Yet he made no bid for ordinary popularity, offered no concessions to the tastes of patrons, made no displays to catch attention from either the unlearned or the learned. He attempted only what he felt to be worthy in itself, what appealed to his own exalted man- hood, what he believed was inherently true and beautiful. His success, in his own day and since, shows how truly representa- tive he was of the ideal human spirit. We now know, much more than did most of those who were then defining the prin- ciples of æsthetic criticism, that in such sincerity and seriousness, when proceeding from an essentially noble character, lies the finest possibility of art.

For all these reasons — and more that might be given — we do well to exalt Beethoven as the founder of modern musical art.

Beethoven's works may be succinctly classified thus : — (a) For the piano alone, 32 large sonatas for 2 hands and one for 4, with over 100 smaller pieces, including many variations and dances ; (b) for piano with other instruments, 5 concertos, 1 triple concerto, 8 trios, 3 quartets, 1 quintet ; (c) for chamber instruments, 9 violin-sonatas, 1 violin-concerto, 5 'cello-sonatas, 1 horn-sonata, 5 trios, 16 quartets, 2 quintets, 2 sextets, 1 septet, 2 octets, besides some other pieces ; (d) for orchestra, 9 sympho- nies, 12 overtures, with other incidental numbers for dramas, 1 choral fan- tasia, perhaps 10 minor works ; (e) for voices, 1 opera, 1 oratorio, 2 masses, with about 10 cantatas or similar works, several concert-solos, almost 250 songs, including about 160 written to Scotch, Irish and Welsh words at the suggestion of George Thomson of Edinburgh, 18 canons. A stand- ard complete edition is published by Breitkopf & Härtel (1862–1904).

Elaborate publications have been made of his extant exercises in counterpoint and of the numerous 'sketch-books.' Also over 500 letters have
been edited.

170. His Immediate Environment. — A peculiar interest attaches to the circle of persons in which Beethoven's personality developed and exercised itself. Although he had early
discipline in playing the piano and violin, and in composition,
apparently he got little more from teachers than some useful
foundations. That which made him great was his own. But,
especially at Vienna, he was much in contact with a large
number of musicians, many of considerable power, from some
of whom he derived valuable stimulus. Even in his youth at
Bonn he began to know the operas and church music of the
day, and at Vienna he doubtless kept in touch with most of the
dramatic and concert works there popular. It is not clear that
he was much of a student, except in the pianistic and orchestral fields that were his specialties. Very few of the composers
whom he knew aroused his enthusiasm ; for many of them he
had nothing but disdain and scorn. His deafness and his
conscious superiority usually combined to keep him aloof from
ordinary musical society. His isolation would certainly have
been greater than it was had it not been for the earnest and
persistent enthusiasm that he evoked among aristocratic amateurs.

He gave many lessons, but mostly to those who made no
striking application of them in professional activity. He was
too individual and too idealistic to be a successful routine
teacher. He certainly founded no 'school' of followers. His
immense ability and éclat actually overshadowed several composers who were working along somewhat similar lines with
himself, though this result was not of his seeking.

Beethoven's most useful teachers were *C. G. Neefe* (d. 1798), organist
at Bonn from 1781, from whom he parted in 1792 with much respect, and
Franz Ries (d. 1846), violinist at Bonn from 1774, whose son *Ferdinand*
(d. 1838) was 1801–5 one of Beethoven's pupils and helpers at Vienna ;
besides the veterans *Haydn*, *Schenk*, *Albrechtsberger* and *Salieri*. He
was a careful student of the works of Emanuel Bach, Clementi, Mozart
and Cherubini. The style of the latter appealed to him so much that he
said he meant to imitate it in sacred works which he did not live to produce. He derived something from *Emanuel Aloys Förster* (d. 1823), a
worthy writer of piano and chamber works.

At Vienna among his intimates were the violinists *Wenzel Krumpholtz* (d. 1817) and *Schuppanzigh* (d. 1830), the 'cellist *Joseph Linke* (d. 1837), the violinist *Schindler* (d. 1864), the mechanician *Mälzel* (d. 1838) and the publisher *Haslinger* (d. 1842). Other leading violinists of the city from 1800 were *Mayseder* (d. 1863) and *Franz Clement* (d. 1842), with the violist *Franz Weiss* (d. 1830). He knew a long line of pianists, some with admiration, some with unconcealed dislike, such as *Hummel, Wölfl, Prince Louis Ferdinand* (at Berlin), *Himmel, Steibelt, Gelinek, Vogler, Moscheles, Halm* and *Hüttenbrenner*. He gave lessons to *Czerny*, and in 1823 welcomed the boy *Liszt*. During his life the Austrian opera-writers most active at Vienna were *Gyrowetz* (d. 1850), *Weigl* (d. 1846), who was Salieri's colleague and successor at the court, *Seyfried* (d. 1841) and *Konradin Kreutzer* (d. 1849) ; and among those more identified with sacred music were *Eybler* (d. 1846), *Blahagk* (d. 1846), *Gänsbacher* (d. 1844), *Drechsler* (d. 1852) and *Sechter* (d. 1867). No mention can here be made of the many artists who spent but a brief time in Vienna, prominent among whom were *Paër, Weber* and *Spohr. Schubert* lived his whole life there, but made no personal expression of his reverence for the older master till the latter's last days.

Space fails adequately to mention the great circle of patrons and friends to whose appreciation, liberality and forbearance Beethoven owed so much. It is interesting to recount the more than 50 distinguished persons whom he honored by dedications of works. Prominent among these were the Von Breuning family, Count Waldstein, Prince and Princess Lichnowsky, Prince Lobkowitz, Count and Countess Browne, Archduke Rudolph, Count Fries, Prince Galitzin, Princess Kinsky, Countess Keglivics, and the Russian ambassador Count Rasumowsky, besides the Empress Maria Theresa, the King of Prussia and the Emperor and Empress of Russia. As a rule, these dedications signify relations that were much more than formal or ceremonious. The formation of the Lichnowsky quartet (about 1793) and the Rasumowsky quartet (1808), both led by Schuppanzigh, had much to do with the growth of his chamber music. (Lichnowsky and Rasumowsky both married daughters of Countess Thun.)

CHAPTER XXV

THE ROMANTIC OPERA AND THE SONG

171. The Genius of Weber. — Parallel with the latter half of Beethoven's career was that of Weber, who shares with him the honor of unlocking the musical productiveness of Germany. Weber, though also a pianist, stands contrasted in his less thorough discipline as a composer, in his shining gifts for social and practical success, and in the objectivity of his imagination. He was the exponent, not so much of a universal humanity as of the peculiar phase of national awakening through which Germany was passing. He accordingly aroused an instant enthusiasm which had notable fruits.

Weber made his mark as a keyboard virtuoso, ready, original and daring, and made large contributions to piano literature; but his significance lies in his sudden elevation of the German opera into renown, and his expansion of the range of orchestral expression. His general dramatic ideal was like that of Gluck and Mozart, but he had far greater musical facility and intensity than the former, and a more concentrated and serious purpose than the latter. His work was perfectly adapted to the conditions of his time, so that it forthwith started an operatic current which diverged sharply from that of the prevalent Italian school and soon engaged many other powerful geniuses, of whom Wagner became at length chief. Weber's gifts were essentially romantic in quality, especially as regards the exaltation of imaginative warmth and passion over statuesque regularity and elegance. His melodic and structural invention was remarkable and his command of effect, both vocal and instrumental, full of originality. In particular, he was a fascinating colorist in orchestration.

Weber also rendered real service in raising the status of musicianship in the eyes of society. His titled descent and his cultured manners gave him the entrée into exclusive circles and his essential worth inspired respect for his art.

Carl Maria von Weber (d. 1826) belonged to an extensive family in which musical ability was frequent. His father and the father of Mozart's wife were brothers, so that he and Mozart were cousins by marriage, though the latter died while Weber was but a child. His

father (d. 1812) was something of a soldier, a respectable viola and double-bass-player, and able to turn his hand to other things. Twice married, he had many children, the most musical of whom were Fritz and Edmund in the first set, both pupils of Haydn, and Carl, the eldest of the second set. The latter was born in 1786 at Eutin (near Lübeck), where since 1779 the father had been choirmaster or band-leader.

The elder Weber was versatile and restless. His second wife was a good stage-soprano and all the children had talent. So the family moved from place to place, giving concerts and plays in a half-gipsy fashion. During his first 25 years the young Carl was never in one place more than three years, often only a few months. The range of his travels was from Lübeck and Hamburg on the north to Munich and Salzburg on the south, and from Breslau on the east to Stuttgart and Mannheim on the west. Thus he saw a deal of the world, especially on the theatric side.

His first good teaching in music was in 1796 from J. P. Heuschkel (d. 1853), court-oboist and organist at Hildburghausen, who gave him sound training in piano-playing. In 1798 at Salzburg he had careful lessons in composition from Michael Haydn. In 1799 these were continued at Munich under J. N. Kalcher (d. 1826), the court-organist. Here he began concert-playing and wrote several extended works (later burnt). Here, too, he and his father became absorbed over the new process of lithography, and the family moved to Freiberg (Saxony), intending to adopt it as a business. But, encountering a good dramatic company, Weber undertook his first real opera, *Das Waldmädchen* (1800), which later had some success at Vienna and Prague. In 1801-2 at Salzburg he wrote *Peter Schmoll* (1803 ? Augsburg). From 1802 he began independent studies, which in 1803 were stimulated by close relations at Vienna with Vogler. Here, too, he met Haydn and Beethoven and was intimate with Hummel and other players.

On Vogler's nomination in 1804, Weber became conductor at the theatre at Breslau. Here was disclosed his latent ability as leader and manager. Among his admirers were Berner and Klingohr, from whom he derived much on the pianistic side. In 1806, accidentally swallowing some acid, he ruined his voice, at least for singing. In this year he left his post, friction having developed, especially with the previous concertmaster, Schnabel. After an interval at a Silesian castle and some concert-giving, in 1807 he became secretary to Duke Ludwig of Württemberg at Stuttgart — a place of moral risk, as the Duke was

a spendthrift and the court life corrupt.   Weber fell into dissipation and pecuniary difficulties, but also did considerable serious reading, especially of
philosophy, and was led by Danzi, the theatric choirmaster, to write the opera
Silvana (1808–10) and some other works.   In 1810 he incurred the king's dis-
favor, was arrested for an alleged sale of preferments and, though cleared of
guilt, was banished.   He went to Mannheim, where Ritter and Gottfried
Weber welcomed him, and thence to Darmstadt to visit Vogler, who set him
at the quixotic task of revising some of Bach's chorales.   His mind was beginning to teem with ideas, literary as well as musical, and, with G. Weber,
Meyerbeer and others, he formed a circle for the advancement of musical
criticism.   In 1810 *Silvana* was given at Frankfort, Caroline Brandt, his
future wife, in the title-rôle.   Soon after, he completed *Abu Hassan* (1811).
These two years brought much self-examination, resulting in a giving up of
wild habits and a new artistic consecration.

The years 1811–12 were occupied by short sojourns in Munich, Prague,
Leipsic, Gotha, Weimar, Berlin, etc.   His list of compositions for piano and
for orchestra steadily increased, his playing and conducting aroused enthusiasm,
and his original and fascinating personality attracted hosts of friends.   In 1813
he accepted the directorship of the Prague theatre, where the idea of genuine
German opera had long been accepted, though feebly illustrated.   Weber's
zeal and skill in the oversight of details soon produced performances of unexampled excellence.   In 1814 he made a brilliant visit to Berlin, where his
facility, especially in writing patriotic music, fell in happily with the jubilations
over Napoleon's downfall.   As it became evident that Prague did not offer a
field for the full realization of his ideals, in 1816 he resigned.

Soon he was called to the similar post at Dresden which he held for ten
years.   Here for the first time German opera was given the same official honor
as Italian — a fact that roused some hostility.   But Weber set himself to
creating interest by explanatory newspaper-articles, by a careful selection of
works (not confined to those in German), by unheard-of pains in rehearsal,
and by steady improvements in soloists, chorus and orchestra, all tending
toward extreme perfection in the total effect.   He gradually became the sole
active court-musician, Morlacchi being much in Italy.   In 1817, using a
libretto by Kind, he began *Der Freischütz* (completed 1820), and, though he
often digressed into fine piano composition, his passion for dramatic work
attained its climax.   But his health was uncertain, giving signs of the final
breakdown.   In 1820 he visited Leipsic, Halle, Göttingen, many North German cities and Copenhagen, everywhere greeted with amazing enthusiasm.
In 1821 at Berlin came his greatest triumph, the production of *Der Freischütz*, which was the turning-point in the contest between the German and
the Italian schools.   Similar warmth was shown later at other capitals, notably
at Vienna, whither Weber was urged to remove.   For Vienna he soon set to
work upon *Euryanthe*, whose first productions in 1823, however, were not
well received.   This disappointment and the precariousness of his health led
to much depression, from which he was roused by an opportune commission
from England.   Though sinking into consumption, he began *Oberon* early in
1825, and in 1826, by way of Paris, crossed to England and conducted the first
performances at London.   Unable to return, he died there.

Weber's personality had a singular charm. He had social polish and versatility, a fund of humor and gayety, and a magnetic instinct. The very irregularity of his early life gave him social and mental experience, including mastery of dramatic technique and knowledge of the spirit of the German people. Intellectually he was alert in several fields, with a bent toward literary production. He dabbled in novel-writing, besides planning various works about music, such as a dictionary, a history, a periodical and some critical essays. He was sensitive to the rising spirit of Teutonic nationalism, which he fed by stirring patriotic songs. He was the first musical spokesman for the fanciful and romantic strain in German imagination — the taste for the magical and miraculous, for gnomes, fairies and goblins.

Though undoubtedly reckless in his youth, his later years were full of earnestness, and he won the respect of a wide circle. His one important pupil was Benedict (d. 1885), later active in England.

Weber's works include (a) 7 operas (1800–26), with sketches for two others, incidental numbers for several more and many detached dramatic pieces, besides several cantatas (notably *Kampf und Sieg*, 1815); (b) 4 piano-sonatas (1812–22), 8 sets of variations, many polonaises, rondos and dances, with lesser pieces for four hands; (c) 2 piano-concertos (1810–12), the famous *Concertstück* (1821), violin-sonatas, concertos for clarinet, bassoon and horn, and several other concerted works; (d) 2 symphonies (1806–7), 3 detached overtures (besides about 10 with dramas), and a few other orchestral works; (e) over 100 songs of various degree and about 20 noted part-songs for male voices; (f) 2 masses (1818–19).

172. The Romantic Opera. — The word 'romantic' has different shades of meaning according to the connection in which it is used, and, to some extent, according to the prepossessions of the one using it. As applied to literature and kindred fine arts the term implies that the subject chosen is unusual and fanciful, that the treatment is unconventional and exciting, and that the total spirit is freely expressive of the artist's personality and mood. In all these regards 'romantic' stands opposed to 'academic' or 'classical.' Minds differ in their predisposition toward one or the other, and in certain periods one or the other predominates as a norm. The opening decades of the 19th century were strongly marked by extensive movements that are generally recognized as romantic. These were nowhere stronger than in Germany.

The rise of the German romantic opera was a symptom of the age. It had clear relations with the trend of German poetry, fiction and criticism. Its literary type was the romance or the fairy-tale. The materials of this type were explicitly fanciful, often impossibly extraordinary. The indispensable ele-

ment of picturesqueness was secured by employing sources like
oriental tales, the many mediæval legends and myths, or the
treasury of Teutonic folk-lore about the peopling of all nature
with mystic beings, good and evil. But these materials were
handled realistically as facts, not fictions, with a sincerity and
earnestness that shows some sense of their symbolic quality.
There was apt to be much that was fantastic and uncanny,
certainly some air of mystery and wonder. But much was also
made of the imaginative treatment of physical scenery and
phenomena, and of homely, naïve human life — in each case
seizing upon aspects that pique the fancy and stir the heart.
The musical drama at once caught the new literary note, reacting with relief from the hollow ideas, worn-out sentiment and
affected conventionality of the usual Italian opera. As against
the latter, the new German opera came like a refreshing breeze
from the open country, and a voice from a hearty and uncontaminated society. Of this musical movement Weber was not
the founder. It was 'in the air' before his day. Indeed, the
revival of the singspiel and the new recognition of the song
are plain evidences of its existence. Weber's distinction
lay in his eminent success in bringing the tendency to full-
rounded artistic expression.

Without implying that the romantic opera had a fixed or regular
method (which was precisely what it avoided), it is possible to make
some statements about its usual features, which grew out of its untrammeled dramatic nature.

The strict recitative was rare, its place being taken, where necessary, by
spoken dialogue; but declamatory passages might occur anywhere. The
formal aria, though its outlines remain, was so disguised as to seem a free
lyric or dramatic utterance, passing over constantly into the scena. The
simple folk-song type of melody became more frequent — folk-like airs,
not actual popular songs (as in the ballad-opera). Concerted passages,
for soloists or chorus, abounded, not as set numbers by themselves, but as
natural incidents in the action. In all these regards we see the desertion
of the notion that the opera is a concert-form, made up of items devised
for the behoof of star singers. The dramatic plan and ensemble are now
supreme.

But the freshness of the type was nowhere more evident than in the
handling of the instrumentation. The new resources of the orchestra were
freely drawn upon to heighten the realism and impressiveness of the
scenes, to set forth the sequence of emotions, to supply 'atmosphere.'
To this end the overture was made significant, not as a detached set of
movements in conventional form, but as a real prelude to the action,

generally emphasizing some of its characteristic 'motives.' Purely orchestral numbers in the course of the play became rare, simply because not dramatically germane, but, instead, the functions of the 'accompaniment' were freely expanded, bringing it into full coördination with the vocal elements.

In all these regards we see the working of the same ideas for which Gluck contended and which Mozart exemplified, but the application was now in the hands of leaders more enterprising than either, working with technical methods more elaborate and unfettered than had been possible a generation earlier. At every point we note the beginnings of the monumental type of musical drama later to be illustrated by Wagner and his contemporaries.

As a help to appreciating the extensive drift toward the romantic opera, a number of writers should be named who were popular for the time, though several of them dropped out of sight later.

Joseph Weigl (d. 1846), a pupil of Albrechtsberger and Salieri, was from before 1800 theatre-choirmaster at Vienna and from 1825 Salieri's successor. He was a favorite of Maria Theresa, an agreeable man and a smooth melodist. Of his about 30 operas (from 1782, '89) some were in Italian. *La Principessa d'Amalfi* was praised by Haydn. Others were *Gli amori marinari* or *Der Corsair* (1797), *Die Uniform* (1798), *Das Waisenhaus, Die Schweizer-Familie,* his strongest work (1809), *Die Jugend Peters des Grossen* (1815), *Der Bergstürz, Nachtigall und Rabe* (1818), etc. He also wrote a Passion (1804), an Easter oratorio, and, in later life, church music.

Friedrich Heinrich Himmel (d. 1814), the pianist, studied in Italy, in 1795 succeeded Reichardt as choirmaster at Berlin and traveled widely as player and composer. Besides Italian operas, like *Semiramide* (1795, Naples), *Alessandro* (1798, St. Petersburg), *Vasco da Gama* (1801, Berlin), he was prompt to seize the new opening for German romances, as in *Fanchon* (1804), *Die Sylphen* (1806), and *Der Kobold* (1811). In spite of his dissipated habits, he was popular as a player and especially as a song-writer.

Ignaz von Seyfried (d. 1841), trained by Mozart, Haydn, Albrechtsberger and especially Winter, from 1797 was theatre-choirmaster at Vienna, producing over 100 stage-works of unoriginal but pleasing quality, and considerable church music. Among his operas may be named *Der Wundermann am Rheinfall* (1799), *Die Druiden* (1801), *Feodora* (1812), *Ugolino* (1821), etc. After 1828 he devoted himself to literary work.

At about this point in the series **Weber** entered the field with *Das Waldmädchen* (1800), followed at intervals by other operas, of which *Silvana* (1810), *Der Freischütz* (1821), *Euryanthe* (1823) and *Oberon* (1826, London) are historically the chief. Of these, *Euryanthe* was the only one in which there is not some spoken dialogue.

Konradin Kreutzer (d. 1849), a good pianist and clarinettist, about 1804 came to Vienna, studied with Albrechtsberger, in 1812 went to Stuttgart and thence to Donaueschingen, returned in 1822 to Vienna, working at two different theatres, and in 1840-6 was at Cologne. He was a gifted composer and enjoyed great popularity. Besides his 30 operas (from 1800), he wrote well for the piano and for chamber combinations, and also excellent songs and male part-songs. Among his dramatic works were *Jery und Bätely* (1810), *Conradin von Schwaben* (1812), *Cordelia* (1819), *Libussa* (1822), *Der Taucher* (1824), *Der Verschwender* (1833) and *Das Nachtlager von Granada* (1834), of which the last two are still given.

Ernst Theodor Hoffmann (d. 1822) pursued law, music and literature more or less together, the emphasis being upon music between 1805 and 1816. From 1808 he was theatre-director at Bamberg, from 1810 over the signature 'Kreisler' wrote witty essays for a Leipsic journal (collected, 1814), and in 1813–4 conducted opera at Leipsic and Dresden. He was brilliantly versatile. Besides other undertakings, he wrote about 10 stage-works (from 1801), such as *Schärpe und Blume* (1805, libretto also), *Der Trank der Unsterblichkeit* (1808), *Aurora* (1811) and his masterpiece *Undine* (1816). He admired Mozart so ardently that he adopted the name Amadeus. Beethoven and Weber were interested in him, and his affinity with the poet Richter ('Jean Paul') commended him strongly to Schumann. After 1816 he was in the Prussian civil service.

Adalbert Gyrowetz (d. 1850) wrote extraordinarily much and mostly very well, and yet to-day is almost forgotten. His active career extended from the lifetime of Mozart to the period of Mendelssohn. Born in Bohemia and educated at Prague, he came in 1786 to Vienna, finding cordial welcome from Mozart and his circle for his early symphonies. Under a liberal patron he spent two years in Italy, appearing as a violin-virtuoso, writing in 1787 his first quartets, and studying with Sala at Naples. In 1789 he visited Paris (where symphonies of his had been given as Haydn's) and settled in London, receiving much applause as an orchestral writer. In 1797 ill-health caused his return to Vienna, where his legal and linguistic accomplishments got him work as a diplomatic attaché. In 1804 he was given a post at the opera under Weigl, continuing till 1831. His later years were made bitter by poverty. His facility was enormous in every field — 60 symphonies, about 80 chamber works, 40 piano-sonatas, 19 masses, and numerous lesser pieces, vocal and instrumental, besides some 70 stage-works. Of the latter, the first was *Semiramis* (1792, London, the score lost by fire before performance), and the very successful *Agnes Sorel* (1806), *Der Augenarzt* (1811), *Die Prüfung* (1813), *Helene* (1816) and *Felix und Adele* (1831). Beethoven highly commended *Robert* (1813), and *Der Augenarzt* held its popularity for years. His autobiography (1848) has some importance.

Although **Beethoven's** *Fidelio* (1805) can hardly be counted as a typical romantic opera, its spirit and style are not only thoroughly German, but clearly related to more fanciful works. Its moral elevation reflects the character of the composer's personality, and its dramatic intensity illustrates the German recoil from Italian frivolity.

Ludwig Spohr (d. 1859), best known as violinist and instrumental composer (see sec. 181), while concertmaster at Gotha became deeply interested in dramatic work (from 1806). In all, he wrote 10 operas, of which the finest were *Faust* (1818), *Zemire und Azor* (1819), *Jessonda* (1823), which he considered his masterpiece, *Der Berggeist* (1825) and *Der Alchymist* (1830). He had obvious limitations and mannerisms, but also refinement, imaginative

penetration and abundant technical equipment. His handling of the overture
and of accompaniments is masterly, and many scenes and passages are original,
beautiful and impressive. He and Marschner were, next to Weber, the
strongest exponents of the new operatic ideal, though he did not have their
fervor or freedom. His peculiar critical attitude prevented his full sympathy
with either Beethoven or Weber, while at the same time he was powerfully
contributing to the advance of the new German school.

Here may be mentioned a series of ready and popular composers of no permanent influence, namely, **Johann Nepomuk Poissl** (d. 1865), a lifelong court-
musician at Munich, with some 15 operas (from 1806), of which the strongest
was *Der Untersberg* (1829); **Karl Ludwig Blum** (d. 1844), an actor and
many-sided musician, from 1822 stage-manager of the opera at Berlin, with
50 operettas (from before 1810) and adaptations of the French vaudeville,
Das Rosenhütchen (1815) being specially successful; **Franz Volkert** (d. 1845),
director of one of the Vienna theatres, with about 150 taking stage-works
(1810–30); **Peter Joseph von Lindpaintner** (d. 1856), pupil of Winter at
Munich, from 1812 conductor there and from 1819 at Stuttgart, winning fame
by his skill, with over 20 operas (from 1811), notably *Der Vampyr* (1829) and
Lichtenstein (1845), besides instrumental music and songs; and **Friedrich
Kuhlau** (d. 1832), the able flutist, from 1810 at Copenhagen, with a few careful operas there (from 1814). (For **Schubert**, see sec. 174.)

Heinrich Marschner (d. 1861), born in 1795 at Zittau, represents a later
group than most of the foregoing. Musically precocious, he had good teaching at Leipsic, in 1816 began opera-writing at Pressburg, in 1817 visited
Vienna, meeting Beethoven, attracted the notice of Weber, with whom from
1822 he was associated at Dresden, from 1826 was opera-director at Leipsic
and from 1831 at Hanover, with a wide renown. Besides incidental stage-
music to many plays, he produced about 15 operas, of which *Der Vampyr*
(1828), *Der Templer und die Jüdin* (1829, plot from 'Ivanhoe') and *Hans
Heiling* (1833) placed him among the strongest of the early German opera-
writers. He also wrote excellent piano and chamber music, and remarkable
songs and part-songs. His genius resembled Weber's, with a striking power
in depicting weird and outlandish scenes as well as those of homely simplicity.
His command of harmonic and orchestral resources was superb, his melodic
inspiration abundant, and his dramatic sense sure and vigorous.

Karl Gottlieb Reissiger (d. 1859), a fellow-student with Marschner at
Leipsic, in 1821 began opera-writing at Vienna, studied with Winter at
Munich, in 1824 was sent by the Prussian government to Italy to report upon
conservatory methods, taught at Berlin for a time, in 1826 organized the
Hague conservatory, and succeeded Marschner and Weber at Dresden. His
operas numbered about 10, the most popular being the melodrama *Yelva*
(1827), *Die Felsenmühle von Étalières* (1829) and *Turandot* (1835). He was
an industrious composer of chamber music, and of pleasing piano-pieces and
songs. He also wrote much church music, including 10 masses with orchestra
and the oratorio *David*.

Xaver Schnyder von Wartensee (d. 1868), the Frankfort teacher and song-
writer, wrote one fairy opera, *Fortunat* (1829).

173. Schubert's Brief Career. — In one sense there is no more pathetic story in musical annals than that of Schubert. He lived less than thirty-two years, cut off before the world had seen but a mere glimmer of his genius. His lot was full of material misfortune and social isolation, largely due to his peculiar make-up, but none the less sad. Though working for fifteen years in Vienna, then the musical capital of the world, his professional opportunities were pitifully meagre and the recognition of his worth confined to an obscure circle of admirers. Yet from his sixteenth year he poured forth a stream of works, over eleven hundred in all, such as no other composer has equaled. Among these were hundreds of songs that mark him as a prince in this beautiful branch of art, but among them, too, were remarkable instrumental and dramatic works that bring him into relation with Beethoven on the one hand and with Weber on the other. In positive inspiration he was fully as wonderful as Mozart, though his technical learning was much less. In spirit and poetic sensibility he was a shining exponent of the new romanticism, though his favorite idiom of expression was instinctively regular and classical. In the influence that he finally exerted he stands with the great masters just named as a powerful factor in bringing German music to the full consciousness of its mission. He therefore exemplified movements in musical art that were already plainly visible, but the drift and final goal of which were not yet seen, least of all by so unconscious an artist as Schubert himself.

Franz Schubert (d. 1828) was born in 1797, the third surviving son of a schoolmaster at Lichtenthal, a suburb of Vienna. His surroundings were plain and poor, but his father (d. 1830) and his elder brothers, Ignaz (d. 1844) and Ferdinand (d. 1859), were eager for music, which was the household's one luxury. Besides instruction from them, he had lessons from Holzer, the parish choirmaster, at 11 sang in the choir and, having a lovely voice, was soon transferred to the Imperial Chapel and choir-school, where he remained till 1813, having some fair instruction and many physical hardships. His chief delights came from the work of the school orchestra, of which he was first violin and deputy conductor, from rare chances to hear important operas, and from frequent quartet practice at home, finally enlarged to small symphony performances. His objects of admiration were Mozart and Beethoven. His evident genius might have secured him a grant from the Emperor for further study if he had made more effort in non-musical branches. When his voice broke (1813), to avoid military service he taught primary scholars in his father's school, mixing with the daily drudgery as much music as he could and beginning habits of constant composition.

In 1816, failing to obtain appointment as head of a new music-school at Laibach, for a few months he shared the lodgings of Von Schober, a well-to-do university-student, and gradually came into contact with other compan- ions and well-wishers, some of whom might have become powerful patrons had he been less shy and less inclined to Bohemian ways. In 1816 he won the notice of J. M. Vogl (d. 1840), an eminent baritone, who became his firm friend and advocate. In the summer of 1818 he taught at the Hungarian country-place of Count Johann Ester- hazy. From 1819 for two years he lived in poor lodgings with the sombre poet Mayrhofer, varied with a summer trip or two with Vogl or Von Scho- ber. From 1820 he began to have dramatic commissions, but with little public success, and to make more friends through the efforts of the Sonn- leithner family, as well as to see some songs actually published. In 1822 he  met Weber and Beethoven for the first time, though without important result, owing to his timidity and inexperience. He was offered the post of court-organist, but declined it, probably because of his distaste for regularity. In 1824 he taught again at the Esterhazy home, and fell in love with the second daughter — quite hopelessly, of course. In 1825, after a happy season of creation at Vienna, he and Vogl had a fine trip to the Tyrol. These trips did much to counteract the strain of the winters, with their incessant production, excitement and reckless joviality — habits which again and again brought on severe illnesses. In 1826 he sought without success to be made second choirmaster at the court, as well as to serve as con- ductor at the court theatre. In 1827 Beethoven, during his last illness, was astonished to learn something of Schubert's works, which he had not appre- ciated, and the latter saw him twice and was one of the mourners at his funeral. In the summer he had a fine trip to Gratz. In the spring of 1828 occurred the only public concert of his works, which brought him applause and some money — the latter soon gone. His health now gave way. He became depressed and was subject to recurrent mental delusions. Late in 1828 he died of exhaustion. He was buried close to Beethoven, according to his urgent desire, executed with unselfish fidelity by his father and brother. Among his meagre effects, estimated at perhaps $15, was "a pile of old music, valued at 10 florins ". (about $1.50), which doubtless contained many scores through which later his fame was to be established.

In personal appearance he was short, thick-set and round-shouldered — in no sense distinguished. His face was round and chubby, his complexion pasty (owing to poor food), his hair thick and black, his eyes keen and alert, but excessively near-sighted. In manners he was as shy and awkward as a

2 F

child, especially when out of the rough student-circle whose ways he loved. He drew back from high society, though his simplicity, gentleness and sincerity attracted cultivated friends. His temperament was sunny and contented, even amid want and obscurity, though occasionally, especially toward the end, he had periods of depression.

For almost 15 years his daily habit was to compose steadily in the mornings, and to spend the afternoons with friends or in the suburbs, and the evenings in careless camaraderie. He usually lived in miserable quarters, shunning all stated duties. He had an omnivorous craving for poetry, chiefly because it roused instant musical inspiration. His song-texts were drawn from over 100 different poets, including over 70 from Goethe, nearly 50 from Schiller, over 40 from Müller, etc. He was fascinated over the opera, but was uncritical about his librettos, most of them being trashy and extravagant. The interest in orchestral writing steadily grew upon him, and his freedom in it kept pace. Composition was his one object in life. His method of work was almost incredibly rapid and sure, being often guided by a sort of *raptus*. Even extended works presented themselves to him in final form at once, so that writing out was only incidental. He made no preliminary sketches and hated revisions. In all these regards he was the opposite of Beethoven.

His continued poverty was due partly to the lack of stated employment, partly to the small prices derived from his works, and partly to his imprudence or sheer generosity. He was wanting in business tact, finesse and wisdom, and was utterly unconscious of the real worth of his works. He made them for the pleasure of making them. His public success was hindered by unsympathetic managers and publishers, and by hostile press criticism.

His moral instincts were direct and strong, but he seems not to have had any special religious sentiments, though nominally a Catholic. Within his home circle his affections had always a childlike intensity.

174. His Works and Style. — Schubert's entire artistic manner was dominated by the song idea. Pellucid melodies in perfect form welled up within him in endless abundance. Primarily these were conceived for vocal delivery, but works for solo instruments, the piano or ensemble groups were similarly treated. Yet his extraordinary fertility of expression was not only melodic, but harmonic and coloristic as well. His grasp of the resources of tonality was intuitive, his readiness in elaborating characteristic accompaniments astonishing, and his sensitiveness to the varying timbre of both voices and instruments acute and original. His special weaknesses, due to his imperfect early discipline, were in contrapuntal structure, in the organic development of his tone-materials, and in compression and restraint when he sought to arrange them in an extended plan. Many of his works are amazingly long and diffuse, though not dry or empty. He never fails of ideas, but is sometimes feeble in unfolding and disposing them when the scale of presentation is large. His zeal for operatic effort was strong during the middle of his career, but in dramatic technique he was too inexperienced to be often successful.

Schubert's melodic inspiration differed from that of Mozart, for instance, in that it preferred to attach itself to a definite thought or sentiment, usually literary in origin, of which it was the musical embodiment and to which it absolutely conformed. Even in his instrumental works, there seems to be behind the utterance some suggestion or impulse that is not simply tonal. Hence what he says is apparently freighted with meaning as well as clothed in outward charm. But we look in vain for the signs of personal experience in the composer corresponding to the implications of his works. That he caught instantly and perfectly by his imagination all sorts of suggestion from without is evident, but that he actually lived what he wrote, except through imagination, is uncertain. He sought to depict what the eye of his fancy saw rather than to disclose hidden depths within himself. Yet, against this, the repose of his usual style corresponds to the contentment of his normal mood, while in the subtle pathos that often creeps in we may perhaps see the unconscious reflection of his unhappy circumstances.

A rough summary of his works is as follows : — (*a*) about 650 solo songs, ranging in size from brief snatches and ballads up to protracted odes and scenas, covering an indescribable variety of topics and lines of feeling, and including many sets or ' cycles ' of pieces, held together usually by some slight dramatic connection ;   (*b*) perhaps 60 part-songs, chiefly for male voices ;   (*c*) 6 masses, those in A♭ (1822) and E♭ (1828) being the largest, 2 sacred cantatas, notably *Miriams Siegesgesang* (1828), and several motets and hymns, some of the latter elaborate ;   (*d*) 18 dramatic works (from 1814), some only fragments, but including the operas *Alfonso und Estrella* (1822), and *Fierabras* (1823), with incidental music to *Rosamunde* (1823), of which only parts of the last were given during his lifetime ;   (*e*) 24 piano-sonatas (3 for 4 hands) and a vast quantity of lesser pieces, like impromptus, moments musicals, dances, marches, etc. ;   (*f*) 20 string-quartets, besides other chamber pieces ;   (*g*) 10 symphonies, some incomplete, of which the most famous are the ' Unfinished ' (1822) and that in C (1828), and many overtures, the finest of which is that to *Rosamunde*. Remarkably fertile years were 1815, with almost 200 works, 1816, with 125, and 1817, with 70. In later years the number was much smaller, but the size of the works larger. Many works recorded appear to be lost, many have only recently been published, and many are not often heard, usually on account of their length.

As Schubert gradually became known, his success with the song proved a mighty stimulus to other composers, though the perfection along his chosen lines made the opening of new styles almost imperative.   He certainly drew the bonds between music and poetry closer than they had ever been before.   Some of his piano works deserve special note because they antedated many of the same general character that have been more influential.   They were among the earliest examples of the true 'song without words.'   His accompaniments and much of his dramatic and symphonic work mark him as one of the first masters of instrumental effect.   His kinship with Beethoven is obvious, amounting often to direct imitation, as well as with Mozart, though from the latter he differs in the richness and poignancy of his emotional content.   The knowledge of his works in detail was so long delayed that their historic significance was obscured and, even now, is likely to be underrated.

The 'discovery' of Schubert was largely due to the researches of Schumann before 1840 and the cordial interest of Mendelssohn not long afterward.

Among those who at this time were either song-composers of note or useful in furthering the cause of artistic singing, were the following : —

Karl Friedrich Zelter (d. 1832), born in 1758 at Berlin and educated in the trade of a mason, but always eager for music, was a pupil of Fasch and from 1791 his helper in the Singakademie.   In 1800 he succeeded him as conductor.   During his régime the society began regular public concerts in 1801, dedicated a building of its own in 1827, and reached a membership of over 400 singers.   Zelter was a passionate admirer of Goethe (correspondence, 1833-4) and set many of his poems.   In 1809 he started the first 'Liedertafel,' the germ of the great 'Sängerbund,' and was educationally a leader.   He was one of the first to redirect attention to Bach, thus awakening Mendelssohn's enthusiasm.   Besides considerable church music, he wrote many songs and almost 100 cantatas and part-songs for male voices, in some of which he approached the rich style of Schubert and Löwe.   To his circle belonged Luise Reichardt (d. 1826), the gifted daughter of J. F. Reichardt (see sec. 157), who from 1814 was a teacher at Hamburg, with beautiful sacred and secular songs (from 1800) ;   the lawyer Friedrich Wollanck (d. 1831), whose many songs were so much admired by Weber that he urged him to undertake dramatic works (from 1811) ;   Karl Friedrich Rungenhagen (d. 1851), who assisted Zelter from 1815 and succeeded him in 1833 and wrote an enormous number of agreeable songs and part-songs, besides many other works.   (Concerning this entire group, see secs. 218-219.)

Georg Friedrich Bischoff (d. 1841), choirmaster at Frankenhausen (Thuringia), conceived the idea of organizing large music-festivals, and after experiments from 1804, the first important example occurred there in 1810, the conductor being Spohr. Out of this grew many others, of which the most celebrated were the annual Lower Rhine Festivals, instituted at Düsseldorf in 1818.

Besides masters like **Beethoven, Weber** and **Schubert,** whose songs belong to the highest class, though, of course, with decided individual differences, and the many simpler writers, to be named among those busy with popular education, in this period began the fruitfulness of **Marschner** (d. 1861) and of **Löwe** (d. 1869), which reached to the middle of the century (see sec. 222).

The importance of stimulating part-singing as a popular art was beginning to be recognized afresh, and among the helpers in this direction were such writers and teachers as **Friedrich Silcher** (d. 1860), working first at Stuttgart and from 1817 at Tübingen, with many good collections, largely original, and **Xaver Schnyder von Wartensee** (d. 1868), from 1817 active at Frankfort. (See also sec. 218.)

Louis Niedermeyer (d. 1861), a Swiss by birth, in his early life was an important song-writer, working first at Geneva and from 1823 at Paris, and making excellent settings of poems by Lamartine, Hugo and other poets (mostly before 1835). His later activity was in opera and especially sacred music (see secs. 204, 221).

CHAPTER XXVI

ITALIAN AND FRENCH OPERA

175. New Life in the Italian Style. — The underlying principle of the Italian opera has always been the capture of the
favor of audiences, especially by exploiting brilliant soloists
in highly colored or showy melodies and by other devices
essentially sensational. But between the followers of this style
in any given period there has often been much difference, some
being content with imitating the vapid, *ad captandum* ways of
their predecessors, and some reaching out with originality and
genius toward a better dramatic ideal. At the opening of the
19th century these extremes were sharply marked. On the
one hand were the writers who worked principally in Italy
alone, often with Naples as a centre, who went on gratifying
the popular craving for flowing airs, clever effects and conventional comedy or pathos without real advance. On the other,
were those aware of the great movements going on in other
departments of musical creation, generally because they carried
on their work outside of Italy, and who sought to infuse into
Italian writing elements akin to those elsewhere prominent.
Besides several worthy, but not highly inspired, writers of this
second class, the period is notable for the phenomenal career of
Rossini, who certainly had genius and success, however he may
be classified as to principles. His vogue spread throughout
Europe and, with the help of several later writers of the same
class, served to delay until after the middle of the century the
triumph of better ideas.

Among lesser composers the following were especially productive or
popular : —

Vittorio Trento (d. after 1824), born at Venice, was active there from his
youth, producing bright comic operettas (from 1780). In 1797 he was in
London, gaining popularity with *The Triumph of Love* and other works, including *Ifigenia in Aulide* (1804). After 1806 he served for a time as opera-
director at Amsterdam, and later at Lisbon. He was very prolific — his *Climene*
(1811, London) being numbered his 53d. At Venice he had special success
with *Gli assassini* (1801).

Vincenzo Federici (d. 1826), born at Pesaro, after working at London as cembalist and composer, from 1803 was active at Milan and Turin, from 1809 a teacher in the Milan conservatory and ultimately its head. He wrote 15 operas, including *Castore e Polluce* (1803), *La Zaira* (1806) and *La locandiera scaltra* (1812, Paris), in a style of the Cimarosa type.

Giuseppe Mosca (d. 1839), a Neapolitan, trained under Feneroli, began opera-production at Rome (1791). After some years (1803–9) at Paris, he later was director at Palermo and at Messina. His 44 operas were fluent, but unoriginal. In them appears the device of a grand crescendo which Rossini later employed. His brother, **Luigi Mosca** (d. 1824), working at Naples, wrote 14 operas (from 1797), an oratorio and several masses.

Pietro Generali [Mercandetti] (d. 1832), born at Rome, was a pupil of Durante, at first in church music. From 1800 he also produced about 50 operas, mostly comic, of which *I baccanali di Roma* (1815, Venice) was the chief. He is regarded as the forerunner of Rossini. He was finally choirmaster at Novara, writing only sacred music, including the oratorio *Jefte* (1827).

Vincenzo Lavigna (d. 1837) was brought up at Naples and began about 10 rather notable operas at Milan with *La muta per amore* (1802). In 1809 he settled at Milan, where he taught the young Verdi.

Stefano Pavesi (d. 1850), also a Neapolitan scholar, after curious military adventures, brought out an opera at Venice (1803) which led to many commissions till 1830. From 1818 he was choirmaster at Crema, his birthplace. Of his more than 60 operas, *I baccanali* (1807), *Ser Marc' Antonio* (1810) and *La donna bianca* (1830) may be named.

Giovanni Tadolini (d. 1872), born at Bologna and educated there by Mattei, was from 1811 Spontini's assistant at Paris. Beginning with *La fata Alcina* (1815, Venice), he secured decided popular favor by 7 other operas, among them *Il credulo deluso* (1817, Rome). From 1830 he was again at Paris, returning in 1839 to Bologna. He wrote excellent songs and romances.

Although Italian opera-writers were usually unaware of the changes that were setting in elsewhere in the world of composition, or unresponsive to them, yet there were some notable exceptions, chiefly those who lived and worked under German influences. These made various efforts to combine their native melodiousness with stronger harmony and richer instrumentation, sometimes with considerable success. They often carried the public with them, but as a rule failed to make any permanent mark. Yet what they did is worthy of mention as a sign of the times.

As illustrations of this class, most of whom were somewhat direct rivals of the Germans on the one hand and of Rossini and the French school on the other, the following should be named : —

Ferdinando Paër (d. 1839), born at Parma, after slight training, in 1787 began opera-writing there in the ordinary style. He soon acquired reputation and was called to Venice as director. In 1797, with his wife, a good singer, he went to Vienna, where, learning from Mozart's style and consorting somewhat with Beethoven, his methods took on more depth and value.   In 1803 he had so far won a place in Germany that he was made choirmaster at Dresden, but in 1807 Napoleon allured him away to Paris, where in 1812 he succeeded Spontini, remaining at the Opéra under Louis XVIII. and as chamber-musician under Louis Philippe.   His success was not continued at Paris, owing to the popularity of Rossini and his own tendency to intrigue.   Of his over 40 operas, the best-known were *Griselda* (1796, Parma), the famous *Camilla* (1799, Vienna), *Achille* (1801, Vienna), *Sargino* (1803, Dresden), *I fuorusciti* (1804, Vienna), *Eleonora* (1805, Dresden, same subject as Beethoven's *Fidelio*) and *Agnese* (1811, Parma).   He also wrote secular cantatas, 2 Passions, considerable church music, and pieces for orchestra and for piano.   His style was flowing, without learning or decided force.

Simon Mayr (d. 1845), though a Bavarian, was launched as composer at Bergamo and Venice.   He was so successful with oratorios (from 1791) and church music that Piccinni advised his undertaking dramatic music.   His first opera, *Saffo* (1794, Venice), caught the popular taste, and before 1814 over 70 more were called for.   From 1802 he was cathedral-choirmaster at Bergamo and from 1805 also professor in the new conservatory, refusing numerous invitations elsewhere.   From 1816 he wrote only for the church, and in his later years became blind.   His noted works for the stage were *Lodoïska* (two versions, 1795, Venice, 1800, Milan), *Ginevra* (1801, Trieste), *Adelasia ed Aleramo* (1807, Milan), *Medea* (1812, Venice) and *Rosa bianca e rosa rossa* (1814, Rome).   Among his sacred works were elaborate Requiems and other masses, many psalms, etc.   He exerted an important influence, since he blended German and Italian methods and was a thoughtful student.   His chief pupil was Donizetti.   He published the first biography of Haydn (1809) and left theoretical works in MS.

Gasparo Spontini (d. 1851), born near Ancona and educated at Naples under Sala and Tritto, began his remarkable career with *I puntigli delle donne* (1796, Rome), followed by 15 more — all in the fluent Neapolitan style. In 1803 he betook himself to Paris, where he soon entered upon a new period which belongs in another connection (see sec. 178).

Francesco Morlacchi (d. 1841), a pupil of Caruso, Zingarelli and Mattei, at first devoted himself to sacred composition (fine Miserere for 16 voices).   His first operatic venture was in 1807, quickly followed by others, of which the best was *Le Danaïde* (1810, Rome).   From 1810, like Paër, he was choirmaster at Dresden, where he became immensely popular, as he now added much from German sources to his ready Italian manner.   The shifting political situation forced him within two years to write occasional pieces for both sides of the struggle between Napoleon and the Allies, his sympathies being with the former.   In 1817 his position was complicated by the advent of Weber, also as choirmaster.   Their inevitable rivalry was mitigated by Morlacchi's frequently betaking himself to Italy.   He wrote over 20 operas, the most popular, besides *Le Danaïde*, being *Raoul de Créqui* (1811), *Il barbier di Siviglia* (1814), *Gianni di Parigi* (1818) and *Colombo* (1828, Genoa).   At his death he was working on *Francesca di Rimini*. He was a prolific church composer, with 10 solemn masses (1810–39), 3 oratorios, a Requiem for the King of Saxony (1827), etc. His extraordinary reputation was temporary, marking the end of Italian supremacy upon the German stage.

The following two composers stand apart, in that they were more purely Italian in method and worked far on into the next period. But they are here important because brought into immediate relations with Rossini.

Giovanni Pacini (d. 1867) was a Sicilian, educated at Bologna and Venice by Marchesi, Mattei and Furlanetto. He began writing for the stage at 17 (1813) and during his first period of 20 years produced over 40 operas, such as *La sacerdotessa d'Irminsul* (1817, Trieste), *L'ultimo giorno di Pompeia* (1825, Naples), *Niobe* (1826, Naples), and *Gli Arabi nelle Gallie* (1828, Turin). His second period, when his competition with Rossini became more marked, began in 1840 (see sec. 203).

Saverio Mercadante (d. 1870), a pupil of Zingarelli, after serving as first violin at Naples, made his operatic début in 1819, and won renown with *Elisa e Claudio* (1821, Milan), *Didone* (1823, Turin), *Gli amici di Siracusa* (1824, Rome), *Doralice* (1824, Vienna) and *La rappresaglia* (1829, Cadiz). Later examples from his list of about 60 operas were *I briganti* (1836, Paris), *Il giuramento* (1837, Milan), and *Le due illustri rivali* (1839, Venice). In 1827-30 he worked mostly at Madrid and Lisbon, from 1833 succeeded Generali as choirmaster at Novara, and from 1840 followed Zingarelli as head of the Naples conservatory. About this time he lost the sight of one eye, and finally became totally blind. He also wrote much for the church, as well as many orchestral works, including funeral-pieces for Bellini, Donizetti, Pacini and Rossini. He was gifted, but hasty and over-fond of noisy rhythm.

176. Rossini, Donizetti and Bellini. — The stimulating conditions of the new century were now strikingly illustrated by the rise of a group of Italian opera-writers of such varied gifts as to give them a dominance that lasted until the middle of the century and affected the whole progress of musical art. Of this group Rossini was the first to appear and the most spectacular. But he was soon reinforced by Donizetti and Bellini, who shared in the movement he created, although they differed from him in many points of genius.

Although the lives of Rossini and Donizetti extended much beyond the first third of the century and their power still longer, the movement was fully outlined before 1830 and its characteristics plainly belong to that general period. They may therefore be summarily considered at this point.

The whole operatic world was stirred about 1815 by the advent of Rossini, the most forceful Italian genius since Scarlatti. His rapid ascent to fame was astonishing and the influence he exerted, either directly or through the imitators he inspired, was immense. His power lay in his sheer vitality, the witty vivacity of his mind, his keenness in measuring the popular appetite and his energy in keeping that appetite supplied with novel sensations. But he was more than versatile. While not failing to maintain the conditions of telling vocal effort through cantabile melodies, with their capacity for emotional impression, through sparkling coruscations of ornament and through all kinds of concerted numbers, he had early become engaged through the study of German composers upon the problems of instrumentation, and he saw the need in Italian methods of radical improvement on this side. He gradually deserted the bare recitative for a style of accompanied declamation more consistent with a sustained musical work. He gave great attention to the whole factor of accompaniments. · He enriched his scores with novel effects in rhythm, harmony and tone-color, and sought to weld together successive items into irresistible cumulations of effect. With all his instinct for popular éclat and his love of glittering externals, he was much more than a clever trickster. He had positive technical genius. He represented the Italian spirit of his day at its acme of enterprise. Yet, with the exception of one or two of his best works, he wrought without a profound sense of the nature of the musical drama. His standard was fixed by an ambition for immediate success with popular audiences as he found them rather than by any inspired convictions. Technique to him was of greater moment than either structure or imagination. He was unprincipled in his plagiarisms from other composers and from his own works, and he often wrote with reckless and impudent haste. The narrowness of his ambition is shown by his poverty of accomplishment except in opera. The essential lack of elevation in his artistic influence made the movement of which he was the head a positive obstacle in the way of progress long after he had ceased to produce.

Gioachino Rossini (d. 1868) was born in 1792 at Pesaro, his father being a petty civil official. When he was only 4 years old, his father was arrested for republican sympathies and his mother became a singer in comic opera, the boy being left to be brought up by a butcher in Bologna. His slender education included music-lessons, and at 10 his talent had already made him worth something as singer, horn-player and accompanist. At 13 he found good friends in the tenor Babbini and the civil engineer Giusti, who much advanced his general culture. At 15 he entered the conservatory, having lessons in counterpoint under Mattei. He had no patience with strict composition, but progressed rapidly in lighter work. He became absorbed in studies of Haydn's and Mozart's works (being called 'the little German') and acquired facility in orchestration. He was then and always popular for his gay spirits and his ready versatility.

At 18 (1810) he wrote his first stage-work, the farce *La cambiale di matrimonio*, for a Venice theatre, followed in 1811 by an opera buffa (Bologna) and in 1812 by an opera seria (Rome). These were so successful that in the next ten years he was incessantly busy, hurrying from city to city and bringing out no less than 30 stage-works of various kinds, mostly comic — 9 at Venice, 10 at Naples, 5 each at Milan and Rome and 1 at Lisbon. His initial success at Milan was with *La pietra del paragone* (1812), in which he used his afterwards overworked crescendo. The first significant effort was *Tancredi* (1813, Venice), which, though not free from plagiarisms, revealed his extraordinary verve and ingenuity. *Il turco in Italia* (1814, Milan) later came into much favor. In 1815, cast down by a transient set-back, he was about to drop composing when Barbaja, the Naples manager, engaged him to prepare two operas a year on a good salary (partly derived from the public gambling-houses, of which Barbaja was also proprietor). Though opposed by the Neapolitan circle, he made a hit with *Elisabetta* (1815 — plot curiously like that of Scott's 'Kenilworth'), in which he began to discard the *recitativo secco*. In the same year at Rome he produced *Il barbiere di Siviglia* (first called *Almaviva*), which at the outset was resented because on a libretto already famous with Paisiello's music, but which soon captivated the world as the brightest and wittiest of comic operas. In 1816 appeared *Otello*, in which the transition from pure recitative was carried to completion. 1817 was marked by the comic opera *Cenerentola* (Rome), which is counted as the second-best in its class, and by the romantic *Armida* (Naples), which is full of imaginative splendor. In 1818 came the partly noble *Mosè in Egitto* (completed 1827), which later figured as an oratorio, and the florid *Ricciardo e Zoraide* (both at Naples). The violent revolution of 1820 at Naples drove out the king, ruined Barbaja and set Rossini planning a visit to Vienna. On the way, at Bologna, he married Isabella Colbran, a wealthy singer, seven years his senior.

At Vienna he was well received, made friends by his humor and affability, and secured applause for his carefully drafted *Zelmira* (1822). Soon after, Prince Metternich asked him to provide amusement for the royalties gathered at the Congress of Verona, for which he wrote and conducted a series of clever cantatas. In 1823 was produced one of his most ambitious and thoughtful works, *Semiramide* (Venice), which, however, was not at first liked. Late in the year he set out, by way of Paris, for London, where he was lionized by high society, including special favor from George IV.

During 1824–6 he was director of the Théâtre Italien at Paris, where he decidedly improved the technical standard of performance, revised and reproduced some of his earlier works, and brought out *Il viaggio a Reims* (1825), as well as Meyerbeer's *Il crociato*, the first of the latter's works to be heard in Paris. From 1826 he was named Royal Composer and Inspector, with a salary, but no stated duties. He continued to revive and improve old works (notably his *Mosè* in 1827), and began seriously to study Beethoven. In 1829 he reached his highest artistic point in *Guillaume Tell*, in which he successfully discarded mannerisms and achieved genuine dramatic success without losing the brightness and ease of his native style. Entering into a new contract to write only for Paris and to supply a new work every other year for ten years, he retired to Bologna, filled with plans for inaugurating an epoch in French musical drama.

The Revolution of 1830 changed everything. His contract was repudiated by the new government (though later enforced by a lawsuit), and the interest in dramatic music fell ludicrously. Rossini returned to Paris, but wrote nothing except the flamboyant *Stabat Mater* (1832). In 1836 he heard Meyerbeer's *Les Huguenots*, resolved to write no more operas, and settled again at Bologna. In 1843 he had a severe illness, relieved by an operation. In 1847, forced out of Bologna by political causes, he was married a second time (to an adventuress) and removed to Florence, lapsing into much sensuality. In 1855 he came again to Paris, established himself at Passy as a sort of musical divinity, indulged in some new works and revamped some old ones, cultivated the piano with much whimsicality, and in 1868 died, receiving a prodigious public funeral. His large property, after providing for a prize at the Institut for dramatic composition, was mostly given to found a conservatory at his birthplace Pesaro.

In all, his dramatic works numbered about 40, not counting revisions, and his cantatas about 10. His chief sacred works were the *Stabat Mater* (1832–41) and the *Messe solennelle* (1864), with a few other short pieces. He also wrote some miscellaneous music for voice and for piano.

Donizetti and Bellini differed from Rossini, as well as from each other, in the quality of their genius, although with him they constituted a group that long held sway in many quarters. Neither of them had Rossini's abounding vigor and variety or his instrumental originality, and both tended to exalt forms of melody that were more sentimental than pyrotechnic. But Donizetti had some gift for genuine dramatic intensity, though he did not always exert it, and Bellini, though wanting in vivacity and wit, had decided melodic grace of an emotional type and considerable tragic solemnity. Of the two, Donizetti had the broader musical culture, while Bellini was the more consistently poetic. Neither of them sympathized with the rougher and more vulgar sides of Rossini's style, though they were obviously anxious to imitate him as far as they could. Both contented themselves chiefly with supplying works in which flowing and expressive arias occupied the attention, usually with a neglect of the orchestral element. Their influence fell in with that of Rossini to hold Italian opera in its old position and to retard appreciation by the dramatic public of the vigorous new forces that were at work.

Gaetano Donizetti (d. 1848), born in 1797 at Bergamo, a weaver's son, showed artistic aptitudes from the start and received a good education, including training in music from Mayr at Bergamo and Mattei at Bologna. To avoid becoming either a lawyer or a teacher, as his father urged, he tried the army, and while stationed at Venice produced his first three operas (1818–20), with only fair success. But *Zoraide di Granata* (1822, Rome) gained him honor and a release from soldiering. All his early works were plainly in imitation of Rossini. Up to the end of 1830 he brought out 31 operas — 20 at Naples and the rest at Venice, Rome, Palermo, Milan, Mantua and Genoa.

A better period opened with *Anna Bolena* (1830, Milan), and during the next 14 years appeared over 30 more, of which the most noted were, in the lighter vein, *L'elisir d'amore* (1832, Milan), *La fille du régiment* (1840, Paris) and the sparkling *Don Pasquale* (1843, Paris), and, on the serious side, *Lucrezia Borgia* (1833, Milan), *Lucia di Lammermoor* (1835, Naples), *La favorite* (1840, Paris) and *Linda di Chamounix* (1842, Vienna). Though from 1835 holding official posts at the Naples conservatory, Donizetti moved from place to place, living much at Paris. The strain of incessant production brought on serious brain-trouble, culminating in 1845 in the paralysis from which he died.

Beside his 65 operas, he wrote a large number of songs and canzonets, many string-quartets of some value, masses and other sacred works, etc.

Vincenzo Bellini (d. 1835) was born in 1801 at Catania, the son of an organist, who was his first teacher. At 18 a patron sent him to Naples to study with Tritto and Zingarelli, and there he lingered for many years (till 1827), making studies of both German and Italian composers, especially Pergolesi, and writing ambitious trial-works, including a symphony and a first opera (1825). The manager Barbaja noted his talent and called for works at both Naples and Milan, of which *Il pirata* (1827, Milan) was enormously successful, owing largely to the skill of the tenor Rubini. At intervals followed *I Capuletti ed i Montecchi* (1830, Venice), *La sonnambula* (1831, Milan), *Norma* (1831, Milan) and *I Puritani* (1835, Paris), with some less striking works, 10 in all. After 1827 the able librettist of all except the last was *Felice Romani* (d. 1865). A few months after the first giving of *I Puritani* (1835) persistent labor brought on a fatal illness, adding another name to the list of short-lived composers. The funeral was a notable tribute of respect and affection from the composers and singers of Paris.

177. The French Opéra Comique.—At the opening of the century the French taste for dramatic music found its greatest satisfaction in forms like the 'vaudeville' (a song-play with much spoken dialogue) and the 'opéra comique' (derived from the Italian opera buffa and distinguished also by some admixture of dialogue). But the Parisian stage at this epoch was also a favorite arena for the more sustained and ambitious opera seria, though usually by composers of foreign origin or training. In the competition between the lighter and the heavier types the opéra comique tended to adopt the technical ways of its statelier cousin, so that the merely formal distinctions between the two were diminishing. Notable changes were the replacing of spoken dialogue by some sort of accompanied recitative, and the elaboration of ensemble effects at the ends of the acts. These movements resulted on the one hand in giving the opéra comique a stronger individuality and, on the other, in setting up a French type of grand opera with literary characteristics that allied it slightly with the German romantic opera, and musical ones that resembled those of the Italian opera seria, while its spirit and flavor remained essentially French. The influences that combined in the final outcome on both sides were many and complicated, traceable partly to Weber, partly to Rossini, partly to purely French traditions. For purposes of thought, the opéra comique and the grand opera should be discussed separately, but their reactions upon each other were constant and profound.

> The 'opéra comique' is essentially entertaining. Its appeal comes from a dexterous union of a piquant plot, laughable situations, a spicy text, clever acting, varied styles of song and sparkling instrumentation. In melody and movement, in dialogue and ensemble, in the blending of vocalism with orchestration, it must be adapted to instant appreciation. Yet the finish of detail must gratify the cultured taste, and the histrionic and musical elements must be thoroughly amalgamated. From the typical opera buffa it is separated by its higher literary quality, by its wit and satire, by its disdain of long-drawn melodies of a sentimental cast, by the dash and glitter of its instrumentation, by its elastic dramatic structure. From the older vaudeville it differed much as the German romantic opera differed from the singspiel, in musical elaboration and unity. From the grand opera it differed at first in the use of some spoken dialogue, but chiefly in its topics, in avoiding tragic or heroic sentiments, and in requiring little sustained effort from the hearer. Ostensibly the opéra comique declined to aspire to the highest and most serious art, and yet afforded scope for extreme artistic finesse. Thus, without setting before itself any urgent program of achievement, it adjusted itself perfectly to the French temperament, becoming, like the non-musical drama of society, a mirror of manners and social ideas, and often a vehicle of delicious satire.

It should be noted that the Italian opera buffa was originally a genuine 'comic opera,' having a subject, characters and situations that were distinctly ridiculous. In the French opéra comique, and in all the other allied forms of the 19th century, the farcical element was by no means constant. Many works are true 'comedies' or 'comedy-operas,' being distinguished from the serious opera by the lighter quality of their materials and the piquant course of their plots. It was this latter tendency that made it easy for the opéra comique, for instance, to pass over later into the 'drame lyrique,' with its accent upon poetic fancy and elegant construction (see sec. 204).

An institution that has been enormously influential upon the trend of all French musical art was the *Conservatoire de musique*. This was nominally a product of the Revolution epoch, being organized in 1795. But back of it lay two previous enterprises, the *École royale du chant* (1784) and the *École gratuite de musique* or *Institut national* (1792), the latter of which was at first meant to utilize as instructors the members of the Garde Nationale and to supply musicians for the army. The head of the former enterprise was the symphonist *Gossec*, and of the latter the bandmaster *Bernard Sarrette* (d. 1858), a man of remarkable enthusiasm, pertinacity and, as it proved, executive ability. After a brief initial experiment with other managers, in 1796 Sarrette was made director. Although his training had not been comprehensive, under him the new institution at once leaped into a commanding position, especially as regards dramatic music. The liberal annual subsidy from the government (originally about $50,000) enabled him to gather a remarkable array of talent in the teaching force and to lay out instruction on broad lines. He continued until thrown out by the political changes of 1814–5. Since then the governmental support has usually provided well for faculty, library and other equipment, buildings and prizes. The number of pupils has averaged about 600, and that of the instructors is now about 80. There is now an extensive system of related schools in the provinces (at Lille, Nancy, Nantes, Rennes, Dijon, Lyons, Toulouse, etc.). The directors since Sarrette have been *Perne* (from 1816), *Cherubini* (from 1822), *Auber* (from 1842), *Ambroise Thomas* (from 1871), *Dubois* (from 1896) and *Fauré* (from 1906). The later eminence of the institution is due to the artistic breadth and administrative wisdom of Cherubini and Auber.

The relation of the Conservatoire to dramatic music has been close and constant. Indeed, through all its early history the cultivation of this was its one great object — thus differing from some other analogous enterprises. The most coveted of the prizes offered is the *Prix de Rome* (established in 1803), given for excellence in dramatic composition and entitling the holder to four years in Italy.

One of the undertakings of the Conservatoire has been the publication of official text-books in harmony, singing, piano-playing, etc. These have conduced powerfully to unity and thoroughness, though sometimes their continued use has delayed wholesome progress.

Parallel with the Conservatoire, though controlled by different principles, are the subsidized opera-houses of Paris, of which the *Grand Opéra* is the chief (administered under the name of the 'Académie de musique'), devoted to musical drama of the highest class. The opéras comiques at the opening of the 19th century were especially encouraged by two rival enterprises, the more conservative *Théâtre Favart* and the more radical *Théâtre Feydeau*, which, after ruinous competition, were united in the *Opéra-Comique*.

Of the 18th-century opera-writers (see sec. 155) several retained active influence after 1800, especially **Grétry** (d. 1813), **Cherubini** (d. 1842), **Méhul** (d. 1817) and **Le Sueur** (d. 1837). Of these, Cherubini was obviously the most able, though not characteristically French.

François Adrien Boieldieu (d. 1834) was the founder of the new era in the opéra comique. Born at Rouen and indifferently brought up, he there essayed two operas (1793-5) and many songs that gave him experience and a local name. In 1795 he went to Paris and gradually secured recognition, especially by *La famille suisse* (1797) and *Le Calife de Bagdad* (1800). Some graceful piano and chamber pieces won for him in 1800 a place as teacher of piano at the Conservatoire. He profited from contact with Méhul and Cherubini, and kept up diligent study, as was shown by *Ma tante Aurore* (1803). An unfortunate marriage with a ballet-dancer may have been one occasion for his sudden going in 1803 to St. Petersburg, where he became court-choir-master, but where, though nominally obligated to produce three operas a year, he accomplished little.

Returning to Paris in 1811, he made hits with one or two old works and especially with *Jean de Paris* (1812). In 1817 he succeeded Méhul at the Conservatoire, and brought out *Le petit chaperon rouge* (1818). After an interval, and then in direct competition with the overladen style of Rossini, came his masterpiece, *La dame blanche* (1825), which scored a phenomenal triumph and still, after hundreds of representations, holds its freshness. In this were combined with utmost skill and elegance naïve melody, strong character-drawing and fine dramatic grouping. His last work, *Les deux nuits* (1829), was not successful, owing to its libretto, and he gradually succumbed to consumption. In all, he wrote about a dozen operas alone and collaborated with various composers in about as many more. His genius had no great breadth, but his refinement and delicacy of touch were exquisite — a grateful contrast to the noisy showiness of Rossini.

More or less contemporary with Boieldieu and helping forward the movement of which he was finally the leader were the following: —

Henri Montan Berton (d. 1844), the son of P. M. Berton, after slight training, undertook light opera at 17 (1784). From 1795 he was professor of harmony at the Conservatoire and from 1816 of composition. From 1807 he was conductor at the Théâtre Italien. Among his almost 50 operas, many written jointly with others, were *Ponce de Léon* (1797), *Montano et Stéphanie* (1799), *Le délire* (1799), *Aline* (1803), *Françoise de Foix* (1809), etc., besides oratorios, cantatas and songs. He was a ready melodist, but superficial in construction. His literary works were many, but not striking. He was bitterly hostile to Rossini.

Rodolphe Kreutzer (d. 1831), the violinist, though of German descent, was born at Versailles and all his life was identified with Paris. From 1790 he produced over 40 operas of moderate value, but *Paul et Virginie* and *Lodoïska* (both 1791) were popular for a time.

Luc Loiseau de Persuis (d. 1819), finely educated as a violinist, came to Paris in 1787 to produce an oratorio. His gifts as a player secured him good positions, including (from 1810) leadership at the Opéra. He was ambitious and energetic, and, with the aid of his friend Le Sueur, secured a hearing for about 20 operas (from 1791) and ballets, but was chiefly important as manager and conductor.

Nicolò Isouard (d. 1818) was more able. Born at Malta, but trained at Paris for a naval and business life, while acting as a clerk at Palermo and Naples he assiduously studied music, so that at 20 (1795) he began opera-production at Bologna, and later was organist and choirmaster at Malta, diligently exercising himself in composition. From 1799 he was in Paris, a favorite society pianist, in close touch with Kreutzer and with able librettists, and writing about 50 operas, of which the best-received were *Cendrillon* (1810), *Joconde* (1814) and *Jeannot et Colin* (1814). He belongs to the same refined and delightfully clear class as Boieldieu, but was less original and careful. The latter's success embittered him, occasioning the dissipation that cut short his life.

Charles Simon Catel (d. 1830) studied under Gossec and Sacchini at the École royale and early entered its teaching force. From 1790, besides accompanying at the Opéra, he was one of the leaders of the National Guard music, for which he wrote extensively. From 1795 he was prominent at the Conservatoire. He wrote 11 operas (from 1802) in a highly elegant style, but they were not popular, owing to their supposed learning. Examples are *Sémiramis* (1802), *Les Bayadères* (1810) and *Wallace* (1817). He was useful in systemizing music-study, and wrote an excellent text-book on harmony (1802).

Giuseppe Blangini (d. 1841), a choirboy at Turin and a pupil of Ottani, early noted as a tenor and 'cellist, in 1799 came to Paris, where he became the rage as a singing-teacher. From 1806 he held positions under members of the Napoleon family, continuing under Louis XVIII., but being thrown out in 1830. Of his 30 operas (from 1803), many did not come to representation. Yet he was a graceful writer, excelling in romances and vocal notturni.

Giuseppe Catrufo (d. 1851), born at Naples and trained by Sala and Tritto, brought out his first operas at Malta (1792) and in northern Italy, in 1804 settled at Geneva and began a series of about 15 French operettas, from 1813 at Paris. The most notable of these was *Félicie* (1815). From 1835 he worked in London.

Daniel François Esprit Auber (d. 1871) was the successor of Boieldieu, and and in fertility and piquant brilliancy his superior. He was born in 1782 at Caen, the son of an art-dealer who vainly desired him to enter business. At Paris and London he early had musical advantages and began writing songs and pieces for the 'cello and the violin. His first opera (1811) was drafted for a private circle of amateurs. Cherubini, hearing it, offered to guide his further study. As fruits of this came a mass and two more operas (1812-3), the second of which was publicly given. Neither this nor the next (1819) won much notice, but *La bergère châtelaine* (1820) gave him a foremost place

2G

among composers of opéra comique. His quick and sure renown was largely due to his association for forty years with the gifted librettist *Eugène Scribe* (d. 1861). Between them were produced about 40 works, mostly of the comedy class, of which noted instances were *Le maçon* (1825), *Fra Diavolo* (1830), *Le Dieu et la Bayadère* (1830), *Le cheval de bronze* (1835) and *Les diamants de la couronne* (1841). In *La muette de Portici* [*Masaniello*] (1828) he turned aside from his usual path to meet Spontini, Rossini and Meyerbeer on their own ground with a historical drama of remarkable beauty and power (so telling in its portrayal of revolutionary sentiments as to have had a share in evoking the political uprising in Belgium in 1830).

In 1829 he became an Academician. In 1842 he succeeded Cherubini as head of the Conservatoire, remaining in service almost 30 years and evincing great tact and ability, though during the last 10 years he had difficulties with Lassabathie, the government supervisor. From 1857 he was imperial choir-master to Napoleon III. He was singularly modest and retiring, but not wanting in energy or wit. He was devoted to Paris and hardly left it for a full half-century, remaining even during the siege by the Germans in 1870.

In style his music is full of sparkle and spirit, not usually strong in passionate or ensemble effects, but skillful on the side of melody and orchestration. There is about it always a fascinating polish and elegance. He is often spoken of as the last of the masters of the old opéra comique; and was highly respected as a Nestor among opera-writers.

Louis Joseph Ferdinand Hérold (d. 1833) belongs in the same class with Boieldieu and Auber, but his achievements were more limited. Born in 1791, the son of a good pianist, he studied at the Conservatoire under Catel, Adam and Méhul, winning the Prix de Rome in 1812 and then working at Naples to good purpose, especially in orchestral writing. There he gave his first opera (1815). Returning by way of Vienna to Paris, he joined Boieldieu in an ephemeral work (1816), upon which followed his own very successful *Les rosières* and *La clochette* (both 1817). In restless eagerness he now produced several operas upon inferior librettos, with the exception of *Le muletier* (1823), wrote quantities of salon music for the piano, including many sonatas, served in 1820–7 as accompanist and trainer at the Théâtre Italien and from 1827 as chorusmaster at the Opéra, where he produced a series of ballets of such expressive grace that they permanently raised the artistic quality of the form. He then displayed his real ability in three fine works, *Marie* (1826), *Zampa* (1831) and *Le pré aux clercs* (1832), the last two setting him high among his contemporaries, almost side by side with Weber himself. Unfortunately, he then fell a victim to consumption, being but 42 years old. His last work, *Ludovic*, was finished by Halévy (1833) and was well received. He had all the traits of brilliant refinement that belonged to his school, with rather noticeable dramatic and orchestral gifts of his own. But circumstances checked his development and his influence.

It remains to mention **Michele Carafa** [**di Colobrano**] (d. 1872), who had a career somewhat like that of Catrufo. He was born at Naples, studied under Ruggi and Feneroli, began there as an opera-writer (1802) and then entered the French army. From 1814 he wrote nearly 10 Italian operas, mostly for

Naples, and from 1821 about 20 for Paris. The most popular were *Le soli-taire* (1822) and *Masaniello* (1827), the latter competing with Auber's masterpiece. From 1827 he lived at Paris and from 1840 was on the Conservatoire staff. His style was hasty and unoriginal, but not unattractive.

As an exaggerated instance of the operas written in collaboration, which were frequent during this period, may be cited *La Marquise de Brinvilliers* (1831), prepared by no less than nine composers — Auber, Batton, Berton, Blangini, Boieldieu, Carafa, Cherubini, Hérold and Paër.

Here may be inserted a note upon two composers in Portugal and Spain, whose work was loosely connected with the movements here described: —

Marcos Antonio Portogallo (d. 1830) was born in 1762 at Lisbon. After study there and at Madrid, where he was accompanist at the Opéra, he went to Italy, speedily appearing as a composer. *Il molinaro* and *L'astuto* (both 1790) gave him renown and were followed by about 25 others in quick succession, among them *Il Principe di Spazzacamino, Fernando in Messico* (1797) and *Il filosofo seducente* (1798). From 1790 he had been court-choirmaster at Lisbon, which he visited at intervals, and from 1799 he became opera-director there, continuing to write both comic and serious works. In 1810 he followed the royal family to Rio de Janeiro, where he spent most of his later life. His operas numbered about 40, many of them widely known in Europe. He also wrote extensively for the church.

Ramon Carnicer (d. 1855) was a Catalonian, trained at Barcelona, where he produced his first opera (1818). After 1820 he appeared with success at Paris and London. From 1828 he was conductor at Madrid and from 1830 professor in the conservatory. He is called the founder of the 'zarzuela' or Spanish operetta. Of his 9 operas the best was *Colombo* (1831). He also composed freely in other forms.

178. The Historical Opera. — While the romantic opera in Germany and the opéra comique in France were thus winning their way to perfection and acceptance, the old and severer type of opera was not wholly laid aside. It is true that the classical type of Gluck, even as perpetuated and enriched by Cherubini, was losing its hold. But a new style was being evolved which preserved the large lines, the pathetic quality and the stateliness of detail, but applied them to topics that lay close to the deep national enthusiasms now everywhere awakening, and brought into the treatment every new resource of vocal and instrumental effect. This type may be called the 'historical,' if we emphasize the class of subjects in which it found its greatest power. Technically, it is better known as the French 'grand' opera, to distinguish it from all lighter types and locate it in the country that was its favorite habitat.

In France the grand opera was expected to consist of five acts, with elaborate ballets in the second and fourth, and to have neither spoken dialogue nor bare recitative, but to be orchestrally accompanied throughout. In this sense Weber's *Euryanthe* was a grand opera, though it does not belong to the dramatic class here under consideration.

The exact point at which the historical type began cannot be stated, since it became distinct only gradually. The peculiar quality of Spontini's genius had much to do with its definition, and Meyerbeer became ultimately its chief promoter. From about 1825 it proved attractive to many writers, some of whom did not pursue it except in one or two works.

Among the most noted examples by the opera-writers already named are *Masaniello* by both Carafa (1827) and Auber (1828), *Guillaume Tell* by Rossini (1829), *Colombo* by both Morlacchi (1828) and Carnicer (1831), *Anna Bolena* by Donizetti (1830), *Lucrezia Borgia* by Donizetti (1833), *I Puritani* by Bellini (1835), etc. Hérold's *Zampa* (1831) was a striking example of a grand opera upon a fanciful subject.

This type of opera had great significance. For one thing, it was really cosmopolitan, though the historical facts used were apparently national, since its emphasis, even in the midst of any amount of local color, was necessarily upon the broadly human and heroic. It afforded scope for the musical expression of the grander and more passionate dramatic sentiments, with the coöperation of every device of stage-setting, vocal utterance and instrumental depiction. In its appeal to the imagination and the heart it was profoundly serious and valuable, while at the same time it might be universally entertaining. It had all the sincerity of the German romantic opera with more reality in its materials and with a far greater chance for tragic appeal. Its relation with literature was obvious, but with a literature based upon facts rather than pure fancy. Yet its genesis and its popularity arose not from a conscious intention to use the musical drama didactically, but from a growing recognition of the imaginative and symbolic aspect that all history wears.

Gasparo Spontini (d. 1851) is as hard to classify absolutely as Cherubini. Both were Italians (see sec. 175), but attained their artistic eminence under German influence and in France. When Spontini first came to France in 1803 his style was not well received. But he at once made such careful studies of Mozart and Gluck that his *Milton* (1804), though short, was felt to be the precursor of a totally new style, full of beauty and sentiment. This was followed by the nobly conceived and carefully executed *La vestale* (1807), which not only swept all popular hostility before it, but won the special prize offered by Napoleon and adjudicated by Méhul, Gossec and Grétry. This in turn was followed by *Fernand Cortez* (1809, remodeled 1817 and 1823), which belongs to the same grand class. The excellence of these was largely the fruit of the dramatic genius of the librettist *Étienne de Jouy* (d. 1846) who not only supplied fine texts, but influenced the composer in forming his new style. In 1809 Spontini married the daughter of J. B. Érard (brother of the famous piano-maker). In 1810–2 he was conductor of the Théâtre Italien, where he instituted great improvements in the repertory and representations, including the first performance at Paris of Mozart's *Don Giovanni* in its original form, and organized series of concerts at which Haydn's symphonies and other German music were given. From 1814 he was court-composer to Louis XVIII. and wrote several 'occasional' stage-pieces for the new régime and, after prolonged labor, the opera *Olympie* (1819), which he regarded as his masterpiece, though its value was only slowly admitted by the public and chiefly in Germany.

In 1820, as the fruit of negotiations that began in 1814, he was made director of opera to the king of Prussia, with a large salary, extraordinary facilities and ample liberty. The Berlin opera had become the best in Germany, owing to the exertions of Count Brühl, who had been supervisor since 1815. Spontini and Brühl were awkwardly conjoined in the management, and Spontini's idiosyncrasies involved complications. Still, he scored a phenomenal success by the renderings of his three great operas, which he prepared with unheard-of deliberation and pains. But at this juncture Weber's *Der Freischütz* was first given, and immediately public favor began to veer away from Spontini. He struggled to compete with *Nurmahal* (1822) and *Alcidor* (1825), but the librettos were poor and fanciful subjects were unsuited to his mind. He rose once more to his grand style in *Agnes von Hohenstaufen* (1829), and for years kept at work upon sundry extensive projects, never completed. In 1840 came a change of monarchs. His enemies entrapped him into a show of disloyalty for which he was legally convicted, but in 1841 he received a technically honorable dismissal. He never recovered from his disappointment and disgrace, and, except on rare occasions, spent his last years in obscurity.

His character was suspicious, despotic and finical. His technical equipment, especially in harmony, was defective. His genius lacked variety and lightness of touch. Yet he was a most patient worker, a follower of ideals, and a born dramatist. The stern vigor of his personality came out in his terrific discipline at rehearsals, in the prodigious intensity of the effects he sought and in the serious elevation of his best works. His career was tragic, but not without useful consequences.

The instinct for practical success in sustained effort which Spontini lacked was conspicuous in his versatile and ambitious contemporary Meyerbeer, whose life and work belonged both to the present period and to the next, but who may well be considered here because expressive of the tendency toward the grand historical opera.

Giacomo Meyerbeer [properly Jacob Meyer-Beer, the 'Meyer' being adopted at the wish of a rich relative] (d. 1864) was born at Berlin in 1791 of wealthy and cultivated Jewish parents, who gave him every opportunity. He early studied with Lauska and Clementi, becoming a concert-pianist at 6, and with Zelter, B. A. Weber and, in 1810–2, Vogler. While at Darmstadt with the latter and having as fellow-pupils Weber and Gänsbacher, he wrote an oratorio (1811, Berlin) and two contrasted operas, one sacred, the other comic (both 1813, Munich). In 1814, when the latter, *Abimelek* or *Die beiden Kalifen*, was repeated at Vienna, Meyerbeer heard Hummel play and forthwith proceeded to reconstruct his own style to match, with good public success. But dramatic composition was his ambition, and he accepted Salieri's advice to make his style more fresh, elastic and vocal by Italian study.

From 1815 he was in Venice, carried away by Rossini's warmth and fluency and winning a series of local triumphs with some 5 Italian operas, of which *Romilda e Costanze* (1815, Padua) was the first and *Margherita d' Angiù* (1820, Milan) the best. He also wrote a German opera, *Das brandenburger Thor* (not given), in connection with which his German friends, especially Weber, sought to recall him from his path of imitation, the result being in *Il crociato in Egitto* (1824, Venice) a signal triumph, with some indications of his later power. This work was given by Rossini at Paris in 1826, which fact led to Meyerbeer's going thither to live, producing nothing for several years.

Having made exhaustive studies in the literature of French opera and having joined forces with the librettist Scribe, Meyerbeer now advanced by a single stride to his most characteristic style in *Robert le Diable* (1831, Paris), which is both romantic and historical in topic and both Italian and French in detail, with a bold and novel richness of total effect. This was followed by the epoch-making *Les Huguenots* (1836, Paris), and after a time by *Le Prophète* (completed 1843, but not given till 1849), the two strongest illustrations of his genius.

About this time he became court-choirmaster at Berlin, there bringing out *Das Feldlager in Schlesien* (1843), without much success until the advent of the brilliant Swedish soprano Jenny Lind, who for several years was closely connected with his fortunes. He also displayed power in the music for his brother's tragedy *Struensee* (1846), and exerted his commanding influence to revive Weber's *Euryanthe* (1845) and to gain a hearing for Wagner's *Rienzi* (1847).

About 1850, doubtless owing to the unremitting labor and anxiety involved in his habits of work, his health became precarious. But he still continued to produce at intervals, notably *L'étoile du Nord* (1854, Paris) and *Le pardon de Ploërmel* or *Dinorah* (1859, Paris), both attempts to compete with French writers of opéra comique on their own ground. Finally came *L'africaine* (begun 1838, developed during the whole 25 years following, first given 1865), which is dramatically composite, though musically full of interest. He wrote considerable other music, especially many cantatas and small stage-works, some choruses and ballades, and some striking orchestral overtures and marches, besides much piano music (not published).

His personality offers much singularity. His mind was highly trained and well stored. He was a persistent student and experimenter, subjecting some of his works to an exasperating amount of revision. He had intense artistic ambition, supported by a florid and grandiose imagination, and much capacity for flights of beauty and tragic power. Yet he was extraordinarily susceptible to circumstances and suggestions, so that his manner was vacillating, indecisive, inconsistent and at times timid. He was eager for showy effects and unscrupulous about how he secured them. His over-anxiety to capture his audience and his seeming want of assurance about his own convictions kept him from being a genius of the highest order, though his power to grasp grand conceptions, to build up impressive scenes and to handle the orchestra seemed to offer materials for a nobler achievement than he actually won. But the clever use of his talents gave him for a time a commanding place in the musical world, driving Rossini from his eminence and, with him, holding back the transition to Wagner.

179. Opera-Singers and Librettists. — With the changes that now began to come over the operatic world the artistic importance of both vocalists and librettists became perceptibly greater. To be sure, the old tyranny of the singers was broken, so that they no longer dictated to the composer what and how he should write, but, on the other hand, new possibilities of dramatic and musical coöperation with the composer were opened. The score now became something to be really interpreted and portrayed, and, while the chances for vocal display were not lessened, the average amount of genuine stage-ability demanded was decidedly increased. Hence the greater operatic stars now began to show a more varied lustre, involving a fuller participation in the light and warmth of the composers themselves. Every advance in the dramatic intensity of operatic style involved heavier demands upon the performers as many-sided artists.

The work of preparing texts, also, now acquired a fresh distinction, since it was becoming clear that mere hack work, without dramatic insight and poetic tact, did not supply the materials for the strongest operatic effects. Occasionally superior music might triumph over the emptiness or foolishness of its text, but normally the two factors should work together and be fused into a real unity. Hence now a few writers of opera-books began to stand out as efficient agents in the growth of the musical drama upon modern lines.

Of the stage-singers of the period only a few distinguished examples can be cited, such as the following : —

Among the great sopranos were from 1795 **Angelica Catalani** (d. 1849), who, after triumphs in Italy, Portugal and England, in 1814-7 was head of the Théâtre Italien in Paris, then resuming tours and retiring in 1828 ; from 1803 **Pauline Anna Milder (Hauptmann)** (d. 1838), known in Austria and Germany ; from 1804 **Teresa Belloc** (d. 1855), a favorite Rossini interpreter, retiring in 1827 ; from 1815 **Giuditta (Negri) Pasta** (d. 1865), who sang till 1829 mostly in Paris or London ; from 1820 **Henriette Sontag** (d. 1854), known in Germany and at Paris, who retired in 1830, but reappeared in 1848 and died in Mexico while on a great American tour ; from 1821 the gifted artist **Wilhelmine Schröder (Devrient)** (d. 1860), who worked almost wholly at Dresden in all styles from Weber to Wagner, retiring in 1847 ; and from 1822 till 1835 **Nanette Schechner (Waagen)** (d. 1860).

The one great contralto was from 1825 **Maria (Garcia) Malibran** (d. 1836), who made a fabulous fortune in London, America, Paris and Italy, and died suddenly at only 28.

The greater tenors were from about 1790 **Manoel del Popolo Vicente Garcia** (d. 1832), who, after singing and writing operettas in Spain and at Paris, in 1811-6 studied in Italy, oscillated between London and Paris, introduced Italian opera into the United States and Mexico in 1825-9, became a famous teacher and produced in all about 50 operas ; from 1793 till 1829 **Gaetano Crivelli** (d. 1836) ; from 1796 the English **John Braham** (d. 1856), also a composer of songs and stage-pieces ; from about 1795 **Niccolò Tacchinardi** (d. 1859), till 1831 known chiefly at Florence and Paris ; from 1797 **Domenico Ronconi** (d. 1839), who in 1825 settled as a teacher at Milan ; from 1811 **Karl Adam Bader** (d. 1870), a specialist in Spontini's works at Berlin ; from 1814 the enormously successful **Giovanni Battista Rubini** (d. 1854) ; and from 1821 the Parisian **Adolphe Nourrit** (d. 1839, suicide).

The more noted basses were from 1810 **Christian Wilhelm Fischer** (d. 1859), working mostly at Dresden and Leipsic ; from 1812 the remarkable **Luigi Lablache** (d. 1858), a foremost artist for 40 years ; from 1813 **Nicolas Prosper Levasseur** of Paris (d. 1871) ; and from 1818 till 1859 **Antonio Tamburini** (d. 1876), a universal favorite.

The two greatest writers of librettos were **Gaetano Rossi** (d. 1855), who worked long at Venice, writing over 100 opera-texts, including those of Rossini's *Tancredi* and *Semiramide*, of Meyerbeer's *Il crociato*, of Donizetti's *Linda di Chamounix* and of Mercadante's *Il giuramento;* and **Eugène Scribe** (d. 1861), who devoted his talents to the upbuilding of the French opéra comique, also preparing over 100 texts, of which brilliant examples were those of Boieldieu's *La dame blanche,* Auber's *Masaniello, Fra Diavolo, Les diamants de la couronne* and many others, Halévy's *Manon Lescaut* and *La juive,* Meyerbeer's *Robert le Diable, Les Huguenots, Le Prophète, L'étoile du Nord* and *L'africaine,* and Verdi's *Les vêpres siciliennes* — besides writing a number of novels.

CHAPTER XXVII

INSTRUMENTAL VIRTUOSITY

180. Pianism and Pianists. — After the preparatory steps taken in the previous period (see secs. 160–162) and with the eminent keyboard masters then appearing still active, it is not surprising that the 19th century opened with a brilliant advance in pianism. Chief among the older pianists who were still at work were Beethoven, Clementi, Hummel, and Cramer. From the point of view of creation, the greatness of Beethoven eclipsed all other factors, his concertos and sonatas, indeed, fully holding their eminence till the present time. But, on the other hand, other trains of influence, originating with many-sided geniuses like Weber and Schubert, or with specialists in playing the piano or writing for it, like Field, Kalkbrenner, Moscheles, Czerny and many others, deserve to be remembered for their intrinsic value or their historic consequences.

All but the earliest of Beethoven's piano-works clearly belong to the new period, even though a few of them were completed before 1800. His piano style was much affected by his command of the color and the details of orchestration. Yet at the same time it was truly pianistic, with a thorough perception of the capacities and limitations of the instrument. He was fully equipped as a virtuoso and his keyboard writing made large technical demands, but the urgency of his constructive ideas and of his impetuous and glowing sentiment pushed the essential materials always into the foreground. Technique and its triumphs were for him means to an artistic end, not ends in themselves. This earnestness of effort, combined with his originality of conception, placed his works for the piano in a class by themselves. So it is not strange that he can hardly be said to have founded a school of piano music. It is true that Schubert caught something of his ideality and copied some of his expressions, and that pupils like Ries and Czerny sought devotedly to perpetuate his manner. But his influence was general rather than special, setting up a new ideal for all musical art rather than precise models of style.

The historic eminence of Weber and Schubert rests mainly upon other works than those for the piano, though both wrote fruitfully for it. They resembled Beethoven in that they used the piano as but one medium for expressing what they were also putting forth otherwise. Weber had the instinct of a finished executant and the greater dramatic impulse, while Schubert had the higher lyric inspiration and the nicer sense of form. Neither of these became a dominating force in pianistic development. This is still more true of Meyerbeer, the remaining great pianist among the masters already mentioned.

In the rapidly widening circle of specialists the two 'schools' of Mozart and of Clementi can still be traced, though with steadily lessening distinctness. The chief exponent of the former was Hummel, of the latter, Clementi himself. As they drew together, new tendencies declared themselves. One of these, led by the English Field and furthered by the Bohemian Moscheles, pointed toward the elegance of Mendelssohn and, to a less degree, toward the sentimentality of Chopin. Another, fostered by the attention given by teachers and virtuosi to technique, aimed more at astounding brilliance of superficial effect than at solidity of intrinsic contents. To this latter tendency the rising French school of pianists, in which Kalkbrenner was conspicuous, contributed more and more.

In referring to the leading pianistic figures of the time, it is convenient to draw a rough distinction between the virtuosi and the pedagogues, though most of the important artists were both.

To the list of virtuosi already given (secs. 161-162) these may be added :—

Francesco Pollini (d. 1846), born in Illyria, a pupil of Mozart and Zingarelli, became noted before 1790 as a keyboard performer, uniting qualities from both Viennese and English schools, and in brilliance ranking with the best. From 1809 he taught in the new Milan conservatory. He is known by many piano-works, including some (from 1820) in which he used the novel device of three staffs, so as to indicate a cantabile melody with florid accompaniment. He also wrote a method (c. 1810), besides operas (from 1798), a Stabat Mater, cantatas and songs. He was one of the forerunners of the 'brilliant' school.

John Field (d. 1837) was born at Dublin in 1782 of a musical family and was severely drilled in music as a child. At 12, when taken to London, he was employed by Clementi for ten years as an exhibitor of pianos — an uncouth and offish youth, but a marvelous performer, able to impress even Parisian critics (1802) by his treatment of Bach's fugues. In 1804 Clementi took him to Russia, where he remained, first at St. Petersburg and from 1823 at Moscow, enjoying immense success as player and teacher. In 1832-4 he visited London and toured through France and Italy, where his health broke down. Russian admirers came to his help and took him back, by way of Vienna, to Moscow, where he died. His qualities as a player are evinced by his works, which include 7 concertos, several sonatas, 2 fantasias, many airs, rondos, etc., and 18 'nocturnes.' Especially in these last appear his gifts in delicate sentiment and the graceful development of melodic material, foreshadowing the intimate and passionate keyboard lyrics of the Chopinesque order.

Ferdinand Ries (d. 1838) was born at Bonn, the son of Franz Ries the violinist, and studied at Munich with Winter and at Vienna with Beethoven and Albrechtsberger.   After four years of destitution at Paris and Vienna, he won success as a player at Cassel, Stockholm, St. Petersburg and (from 1813) London, where he remained till 1824 in favor as player, composer and teacher. Retiring then to his home near Bonn and from 1830 living at Frankfort, he conducted eight of the Lower Rhine Festivals (from 1825), in 1834–6 was town-musician at Aix-la-Chapelle, and had just succeeded Schelble as head of the Cäcilienverein at Frankfort when he died.   He was noted for a lifelong devotion to Beethoven, bearing with his violent peculiarities, laboring assiduously to make his works known and aiming to imitate his style.   His genius was not powerful enough to make him more than a worthy disciple.   Among his over 200 works are 9 concertos, about 50 able sonatas, many shorter pieces, 6 excellent symphonies, 4 overtures, many chamber works, 3 operas, including *Die Räuberbraut* (1828), and 2 oratorios.   With Wegeler he prepared invaluable reminiscences of Beethoven (1838).

Friedrich Kalkbrenner (d. 1849) was born in 1788, the son of Christian Kalkbrenner (d. 1806), an able Jewish musician, who from 1799 was chorusmaster at the Paris Opéra.   He was taught by Adam and Catel, and at Vienna by Clementi and Albrechtsberger.   In 1805–6 he toured in Germany and France with success, and settled at Paris as a leading teacher, being helpfully influenced by Dussek.   From 1814 he worked with similar success in London, where from 1818 he was much interested in Logier's 'chiroplast.'   After a German tour he returned to Paris in 1824, became one of the firm of Pleyel & Cie. and resumed his place as a teacher.   His technique was exceedingly perfect, including special dexterity with the left hand, with the wrist in octave-playing and with the pedals, and his tone was broad and noble.   His conceit was excessive, both as to his playing and his teaching, as was shown in his offer to instruct Chopin in 1831.   He wrote fluent concertos, sonatas, chamber works and small pieces, including excellent études; also a method (1830) and a work on harmony (1849).

Ignaz Moscheles (d. 1870) was a Bohemian, born in 1794 of Jewish parents. He was early trained at Prague by Dionys Weber, and from 1808 at Vienna by Salieri and Albrechtsberger.   He was intimate with Beethoven and competed with Meyerbeer and Hummel.   From about 1815 his place as a foremost concert-pianist was fully won, and he toured brilliantly in Germany, France and Holland.   From 1822 he was mostly in London, where he had increasing renown.   In 1824 he gave lessons to Mendelssohn at Berlin and later was intimate with him at London.   In 1846 he joined Mendelssohn in the Leipsic conservatory, where he long continued one of the ablest teachers.   His life and influence therefore reached over the whole of the half-century from 1815. As a player he was precise, rhythmically exact, agile and vigorous, with great capacity for varied interpretation and original improvising.   His predilection for strong construction on conservative lines kept him from fully appreciating Chopin.   His many works, all for the piano solo or with other instruments, including 7 concertos, several sonatas and fine studies, have nobility and graceful sentiment, united with sound scholarship.   Altogether, he occupies a larger historic place than is sometimes realized.

Other famous players were **Ludwig Berger** (d. 1839), pupil of Gürrlich and Clementi and an admirer of Field, who from 1812 gave concerts at Stockholm and London and from 1815 lived at Berlin, where he trained many able pupils, was active in founding a second Liedertafel and wrote admirable piano and vocal works, of which his études and others are still valued ; the Russian **Maria (Wolowska) Szymanowska** (d. 1832), a pupil of Field, who from 1815 lived at Warsaw, touring throughout Europe, elicited fulsome admiration from Goethe, and left some studies, mazurkas, etc. ; **Franz Schoberlechner** (d. 1843), trained by Hummel and Förster, who made his début at 10 (1807), toured in Italy in 1814, becoming choirmaster at Lucca and taking up opera and church music, from 1823 lived mostly at St. Petersburg, where he married a celebrated soprano, and finally retired to Florence — compositions brilliant, but shallow ; **Henri Bertini** (d. 1876), who was taught in the Clementi tradition, began touring at 12 (1810), lived for a time in England, from 1821 worked at Paris as teacher and composer, exerting a wholesome influence against the showy style, and left some 200 works for piano and chamber ensembles, including classical études ; and **Charles Mayer** (d. 1862), trained by Field, whose style he copied, and living from 1814 at Paris, from 1819 at St. Petersburg and from 1846 at Dresden — a refined and effective player, an industrious teacher and a valuable contributor to piano literature.

Among those whose significance was greatest as teachers the following may be emphasized : —

Louis Barthélemy Pradher [Pradère] (d. 1834), a pupil of Gobert and Berton, at 21 (1802) became professor in the Conservatoire, continuing till 1827, when he removed to Toulouse and became head of a school there. He was helpful in lifting the French school into prominence, and many of his pupils were later famous, especially Herz. He wrote a concerto, several sonatas and other piano works, 7 light operas (1804–23) and many songs.

Pierre Joseph Guillaume Zimmerman (d. 1853), a pupil of Boieldieu, Rey, Catel and Cherubini at the same time as Pradher and Kalkbrenner, at 26 (1811) began to teach at the Conservatoire and from 1816 was the head of the piano department. Although an accomplished player and composer, he devoted himself to the faithful teaching of an enormous list of pupils. He wrote 2 concertos, 24 études, many dances and smaller pieces, 2 operas, many songs and an elaborate *Encyclopédie du pianiste* (3 parts).

Friedrich Wieck (d. 1873), though showing musical talent as a boy, was first educated for the Lutheran ministry at Wittenberg, became a private tutor near Querfurt, was musically intimate with A. A. Bargiel, a Berlin teacher, set up at Leipsic a piano-factory and a circulating library, and finally, when nearly 35 years old, adopted piano-teaching as a life-work, at first upon Logier's system, but soon according to his own ideas, from about 1820 at Leipsic and after 1840 at Dresden, where he also taught singing. He developed a remarkable pedagogical system and trained many great pupils, among whom were his noted daughters Clara (Mme. Schumann) and Marie. Mendelssohn vainly sought him for the Leipsic conservatory in 1846. His house at Dresden was a great resort for musicians. He composed little, principally piano-studies.

Aloys Schmitt (d. 1866) was a virtuoso at 14 (1802) and then a pupil of André. From 1816 he worked at Frankfort, except for sojourns at Berlin and Hanover (1825-9). He was most successful as teacher and composer, writing 4 concertos, many sonatas, rhapsodies, variations, studies, chamber and orchestral music, besides 4 operas, 2 oratorios and church music. His style was dry, but solid.

Karl Czerny (d. 1857), born at Vienna in 1791, was trained by his father and by Beethoven (in 1800-3), besides closely studying the styles of Hummel and Clementi. From before 1810 he won renown as a teacher at Vienna, where he remained throughout his life, exerting a valuable and lasting influence. He was astonishingly productive, writing about 1000 works in literally every class except opera. The most valued are those for teaching purposes, especially *Die Schule der Geläufigkeit, Die Schule des Legato und Staccato*, etc., which together form a vast instructive apparatus. He was fertile in 'arrangements' of orchestral works, operas and oratorios, being encouraged to such work by Beethoven's comments on his piano version of *Fidelio* (1805). He also published a brief history (1851) and an autobiography.

Lesser names include **Anton Halm** (d. 1872), from 1811 working at Vienna, where he was one of Beethoven's circle, with excellent studies, sonatas, pianotrios, other chamber music and a mass; **Heinrich Birnbach** (d. 1879), from 1814 at Breslau and from 1821 at Berlin, with piano and orchestral works and a manual on composition (1845); and **Joseph Christoph Kessler [Kötzler]** (d. 1872), from 1820 mostly at Lemberg and Vienna, with many difficult, but useful, studies, etc.

Johann Wenzel Tomaschek (d. 1850) occupies a unique position, though not as well known as he merits. He was born in 1774 at Skuč (40 m. east of Prague), was a choirboy at Chrudim and Iglau, from 1790 studied law at Prague, but with diligent pursuit of music as well, and in 1799 entered the service of Count Bouquoy as composer. He soon became the leading musician of Prague, recognized as a superior player, training many fine pupils and developing extraordinary power as a composer. In 1798 he received a memorable impetus from hearing Beethoven, and was later favored by the latter's intimacy. His over 100 published works include a concerto, 5 sonatas, 36 eclogues, 6 rhapsodies, 3 ditirambi, 6 allegri capricciosi, some orchestral and chamber works, masses and church works, many songs, cantatas and ballads in Bohemian and German, and 3 operas, as *Seraphine* (1811). His style was remarkably elaborate, finished and able, placing him close to Beethoven himself. Schumann is said to have been considerably influenced by it. His autobiography (1845) appeared in the periodical *Libussa*.

181. Violinism and Violinists. — Music for the violin and its relatives at this period shows the same interesting interplay between technical and artistic impulses as music for the piano. On the one hand, we have the specialist's eagerness to extract novel effects from his intrument and make a popular sensation with it. On the other, is the query of the broader musician as to how through it the range, intensity and warmth of expression may be augmented, especially in applying the general ideas of

large construction elsewhere accepted.   But in the violin family
there was no such advance in the instruments themselves as in
the case of the piano.   The one decided mechanical gain was
the perfecting of the bow by Tourte (see sec. 149).   The field
for violin music, however, was constantly broadened by the rise
of interest in the orchestral and chamber concert as a social
institution.

The significant link between the older and newer violinism
was the veteran Viotti (see sec. 149), whose style rested upon
the Corelli tradition, and whose long artistic life brought him
into touch with both the Mozart and the Beethoven periods.
He not only clung to the broad style of playing, but is notable
as the one to apply to the violin-concerto the full system of
sonata-form and the new resources of orchestration.   Through
his pupils and his leadership of the Paris Opéra he exerted a
large influence upon the brilliant and energetic French group of
players.   Valuable progress was still more stimulated by the
genius of Spohr, who held the purest technical traditions with a
greater general musicianship, and who fully maintained the
excellence of the Mannheim and other German groups.   Another line of development was strikingly illustrated by Paganini,
the whimsical, but immensely gifted 'wizard of the bow.'   He
represented a growing class of players whose supreme aim was
to astonish and emotionalize audiences.   This aim is always
liable to descend into charlatanism, but often has value in advancing the standards of dexterity and the apparatus of effect.

Among the older violinists still at work about 1800 and afterward, besides
Viotti (d. 1824), Kreutzer (d. 1831) and others already mentioned, were
Isidore Berthaume (d. 1802), a Parisian who when a boy (1761) appeared at
the Concerts spirituels, later (1783) became their conductor and went to
Russia in 1791 ;   Pierre Lahoussaye (d. 1818), from 1779 also active at Paris,
finally professor in the Conservatoire ;   the brothers Johann Friedrich Eck (d.
1809?) and Franz Eck (d. 1804), both associated chiefly with Munich ;   and
Alessandro Rolla (d. 1841), from 1782 at Parma and from 1802 a well-known
conductor and teacher at Milan.

Andreas Romberg (d. 1821), though not specially influential, deserves mention for his industrious activity.   Born in 1767, at 7 he was heard in public
and joined his cousin Bernhard (see below) in varied travel until after 1800.
From 1795 he knew Haydn and Beethoven at Vienna.   From 1801 he taught
at Hamburg and in 1815 succeeded Spohr at Gotha.   Besides stage-works
(from 1790), excellent secular choral pieces, like *Das Lied von der Glocke* and
other poems by Schiller, and much sacred music, he wrote 10 symphonies, over

20 violin-concertos, over 30 quartets and many other solo and chamber works —all in a style reminiscent of Mozart.

Pierre Rode (d. 1830), born at Bordeaux in 1774, was there a pupil of Fauvel and from 1788 at Paris of Viotti, appearing as a player in 1790. From 1794 he toured in Holland, Germany, England and Spain (where he met Boccherini), from 1800 was employed by Napoleon and from 1803 (with Boieldieu) by Alexander I. at St. Petersburg, from 1808 was again at Paris, from 1811 toured in Germany and Austria (Beethoven writing a sonata for him in 1812), and, after a sojourn at Berlin, retired to Bordeaux. From 1795 he was on the staff of the Conservatoire. His early playing was of the finest quality, broad, sympathetic and full of energy (so that Spohr, for instance, regarded it as ideal), but from about 1810 he gradually lost his certainty and power, and in 1828 his life was shortened by a fiasco at Paris. His writing was for the violin exclusively — 13 concertos, over 20 quartets, about 25 duos, many variations, 24 famous caprices, 12 études and a method (with Baillot and Kreutzer). He trained a few good pupils.

François Baillot (d. 1842) was born near Paris in 1771, studied from 1780 with Sainte-Marie and from 1783 at Rome with Pollani, in 1791 returned to Paris and in 1795 adopted music as a career. His full powers immediately awoke, so that he became professor at the Conservatoire, undertaking hard theoretical studies as well. In 1805–8 he toured in Russia, in 1815–6 in the Low Countries and England, and in 1833 in Switzerland and Italy. In 1802–5 he was in Napoleon's orchestra, from 1814 organized concerts for chamber music, in 1821–31 was concertmaster at the Opéra and from 1825 was also in the court-orchestra. He was remarkable both as a soloist and in ensemble, retaining his mastery to the end. He and Rode, though rivals, were close friends, being the strongest representatives of the classical style in France. Like Rode, he wrote only for the violin — 9 concertos, 3 quartets, 15 trios, 6 duos, about 30 variations, nearly 40 études, etc., besides a method (with Rode and Kreutzer), an excellent manual, *L'art du violon* (1834), and essays on Grétry (1814) and Viotti (1825). He had many fine pupils.

Charles Philippe Lafont (d. 1839) was first trained by Berthaume and at 11 (1792) toured in Germany. After further study with Kreutzer and Rode, from 1801 he toured through northern Europe, in 1808 succeeded Rode at St. Petersburg, from 1815 was court-violinist at Paris, and from 1831 toured with the pianist Herz. He was noted for precision and finish, but lacked sentiment and breadth of interest. He wrote 7 concertos, many fantasias, variations and lesser pieces, with about 200 songs and 2 operettas.

Niccolò Paganini (d. 1840) stands alone, representing no particular school. He was born in 1782 at Genoa of poor parents, who, however, gave him all possible opportunity. At Genoa he was taught by Servetto and Costa, at Parma by Rolla and Ghiretti. In 1795 he began public playing, for which he practised inordinately. At 16 he ran away, toured through northern Italy and indulged in much dissipation, especially gambling, to which he was a lifelong devotee. From 1801 he spent much time upon the guitar, but in 1804 returned to Genoa and resumed prodigious violin-study, with some composing. In 1805 began his triumph as an unparalleled virtuoso, which grew in Italy till 1828, when he extended it to Vienna, Berlin, Paris and London

(1831-3), with other cities on the way. The results of these thirty years amply fed his passion for applause and money. His remaining years were spent mostly at Paris or at Parma. In 1836 he engaged in a disastrous speculation at Paris. His death was hastened by years of wild excitement and sensual indulgence. His personal appearance was bizarre, his habits eccentric, his temperament hot and erratic, his character ignoble or unbalanced. Popular rumor made him the child of the Evil One, so uncanny were his ways and so marvelous his performances. He mystified his hearers by using strange tunings, was eager to invent unheard-of effects and made himself absolute master of detailed technique. But he was more than clever. He had warmth and pathos in slow playing and matchless brilliance in rapid work, with a wonderful beauty of tone. He probably has not been surpassed in double-stopping, harmonics, left-hand *pizzicati*, and the use of the G-string alone. But he was not always a sympathetic interpreter outside his own field nor successful in ensemble. His lack of general musicianship and of artistic purpose is shown in his limited work as composer. He published only 24 capriccios, 12 sonatas and 3 quartets; later were added 2 concertos, a sonata, several sets of variations and the *Moto perpetuo*. His enormous éclat roused a host of imitators and turned the whole current of violin style toward brilliance of effect, without the genius that in his case gave distinction.

Giovanni Battista Polledro (d. 1853), born near Turin, at 15 (1796) studied there with Pugnani, advancing at once into notice. During the next fifteen years he toured throughout Europe, with considerable residences at various cities (as five years at Moscow). From 1814 he was concertmaster at Dresden, and from 1824 royal conductor at Turin. In 1812 he met Beethoven at Carlsbad. His style was a fine example of the large and solid method of the older schools, uniting dexterity with feeling. He wrote 2 concertos, many duos, trios, studies and smaller works, a symphony, a mass, etc.

Ludwig Spohr (d. 1859) holds a high place for his long and useful career as violinist and composer. He was born in 1784 at Brunswick, both parents being musical. Among his early teachers were the organist Hartung, from whom came his only formal training in composition, and Maucourt, the court-violinist. He was a methodical student, and at 14 won some notice by a concerto. Soon he secured the favor of the Duke and was given a place in the court-orchestra. His patron in 1802 entrusted him to Franz Eck, with whom he traveled *via* Hamburg and Strelitz to St. Petersburg, studying assiduously and composing. In 1803 he heard Rode, whom he took as a model, and in 1804 he toured with great success to Berlin (where he played with the young Meyerbeer), Leipsic and Dresden. From 1805 he was concertmaster at Gotha, where he married the harpist *Dorette Scheidler* (d. 1834), with whom he made tours. In 1810 he conducted the first German festival at Frankenhausen. From 1812 he was opera-conductor at Vienna, where he knew Beethoven, though without full appreciation. In 1816 he visited Italy, meeting Rossini and playing with Paganini at Venice. From 1817 he was opera-director at Frankfort. In 1820 he paid his first visit to England and also to Paris. After a brief residence at Dresden, where he was intimate with Weber, in 1822, on Weber's nomination, he became court-choirmaster at Cassel, where he remained active for 35 years, achieving his final reputation and exerting valuable influence. He was a friend of Mendelssohn and, rather curiously, an early appreciator of Wagner. He repeatedly visited England, where he was greatly admired, and often conducted German festivals. His last appearance was as conductor at Prague in 1858.

His high rank as a violinist is generally acknowledged. He cast his weight on the side of solid technique and sterling artistic value, usefully offsetting the sensational drift of the day. He was a fine quartet-player as well as soloist, and a superior conductor. His ability as a teacher was attested by numerous pupils. His work as composer was many-sided, evincing broad culture, but with some limitations. His style was formed on strictly classical lines, Mozart being his early enthusiasm. But he was intellectually romantic, and is akin to Schubert and Mendelssohn in the fusion of formal refinement with imagination. He was somewhat strong as a contrapuntist and an original student of orchestration. Yet all through his work ran certain mannerisms, the most conspicuous being an excessive use of chromatic melody and harmony.

His compositions number about 200, including (*a*) 9 symphonies, 8 overtures, 15 standard violin-concertos, a quartet-concerto and other complex works, a great number of chamber works, such as over 30 quartets, quintets, etc., and 3 sonatas for harp and violin; (*b*) 10 operas (see sec. 172); (*c*) 4 oratorios, of which *Die letzten Dinge* (1826) and *Des Heilands letzte Stunden* (1835) [known in English as *The Last Judgment* and *Calvary*] are the best, a patriotic cantata, a mass and other sacred music; (*d*) a famous *Violinschule* (1831, 3 parts). His autobiography (1860-1) is a notable treasury of reminiscences, as well as a revelation of his upright and earnest character.

Joseph Mayseder (d. 1863), a Viennese, pupil of Wranitzky, at 11 (1800) gave his first concert, joined Schuppanzigh's quartet, from 1816 was in the court-band, from 1820 soloist at the court-theatre and from 1835 imperial violinist, receiving many unusual honors. Be'ween 1815 and '37 he was heard in concert at Vienna, but made no public tours. He was intimate with Beethoven and admired by Paganini. The beauty of his tone was noted and as a teacher he had much repute. He wrote over 60 able works, including 3 concertos, 2 concertinos, 3 quintets, 7 quartets, etc.

Joseph Böhm (d. 1876), born at Pesth, trained by his father and later by Rode, at 8 (1803) toured in Poland and Russia, in 1815 came to Vienna and, after a sojourn in Italy, from 1819 for 30 years taught at the Vienna conservatory with distinguished success. He played in the court-orchestra in 1821-68. He excelled his contemporary Mayseder in tone and general style, but his works were few and slight.

Karl Joseph Lipinski (d. 1861), born in Poland, was mostly self-trained. From 1810 he was conductor at Lemberg, from 1814 studied at Vienna, and in 1817-8 was intimate with Paganini at Milan. For 20 years he traveled hither and thither, encountering Paganini (as a rival) at Warsaw in 1829 and knowing Schumann at Leipsic in 1835. From 1839 he was concertmaster at Dresden, where he raised the band to great excellence. He had a specially noble tone and much skill in double-stopping, and his conception was notably poetic. He wrote 4 concertos and many lesser pieces, besides editing Galician folk-songs (2 vols., 1833, with Zalewski).

2 H

Charles Auguste de Bériot (d. 1870) was the founder of a Belgian school of players, an offshoot from the French. He was born at Louvain in 1802, had foundation training there, and at 9 played in public. In 1821 he appeared at Paris and later in England. From 1821 he was royal violinist at Paris and from 1826 at Brussels. From 1830 he toured extensively, partly with Mme. Malibran, whom he married in 1836 (she died the same year). In 1842 he declined a place in the Paris Conservatoire, but in 1843 accepted one in the Brussels conservatory. In 1852 ill-health caused his retirement and in 1858 he became blind. His style allied him with Paganini as an executant and with the French opera-writers as a composer. He wrote with fluent elegance 10 concertos, 4 trios, many variations and études, and a good, but prolix, method (1858).

Johann Wenzeslaus Kalliwoda (d. 1866) was born at Prague in 1800, studied there with Dionys Weber and Pixis, and from 1816 played in the theatre-orchestra. From 1823 he was conductor to Prince Fürstenberg at Donaueschingen (So. Baden), retiring in 1853 to Carlsruhe. Though a refined and pleasing player, he was more notable as a popular composer of no special strength. His works included 7 symphonies, 14 overtures, 13 orchestral fantasias, 2 concertos, 7 concertinos, many chamber and solo works, and much effective vocal music, with 2 operas. The worth of some of these attracted the interest of Schumann.

Wilhelm Bernhard Molique (d. 1869) was born at Nuremberg, and studied under his father and Rovelli, succeeding the latter as leader at Munich in 1822. He also had lessons from Spohr. From 1826 he was leader at Stuttgart under Lindpaintner, and in 1849 removed to London. From 1822 he made many long tours. As a player he followed the solid school of Spohr, and as composer ranked high for both invention and construction. His works included a symphony, 6 excellent concertos, 8 quartets, several concertanti for various combinations, numerous lesser pieces, etc., besides the oratorio *Abraham* (1860, Norwich) and 2 masses.

Among scores of other players and composers the following names may be cited : —

From the French group — **Alexandre Jean Boucher** (d. 1861), active for more than 60 years, with more cleverness than musicianship; **François Antoine Habeneck** (d. 1849), the best-known of three brothers, a public player at 10 (1791), then a pupil of Baillot, long professor at the Conservatoire (1806–15, '25–48), Kreutzer's successor as Opéra-conductor in 1826 and the founder of the Conservatoire concerts in 1828, where he made Beethoven's symphonies known in Paris, the composer of 2 concertos and some other works; **Jacques Féréol Mazas** (d. 1849), also a pupil of Baillot, who, after orchestral work from 1805, in 1811–29 toured all Europe, was then teacher at Paris, Orleans and (from 1837) Cambrai, and left works still highly regarded, including 2 concertos, much chamber music, many fantasias, excellent studies, methods for both violin and viola, and 3 operas; **Chrétien Urhan** (d. 1845), a pupil of Le Sueur and an assistant of Baillot in quartet work, from 1816 in the Opéra-orchestra, prominent at the Conservatoire concerts in the use of Woldemar's 5-string violin, and the composer of interesting chamber pieces; **Jean Henri Simon** (d. 1861), pupil of Lahoussaye and Rode, a prominent teacher at Antwerp, writing 7 concertos, etc.; and **Charles François Jupin** (d. 1839), pupil of Baillot, from 1826 teacher and conductor at Strassburg, with several violin-works and an opera (1834). These last illustrate how the influence of Parisian masters radiated to other cities.

From the Austrian group — **Ignaz Schuppanzigh** (d. 1830), a masterly ensemble-player, much associated with Beethoven, especially as teacher of the viola (1794), leader of the Lichnowsky quartet (1794-5), conductor at the Augarten (1798-9), leader of the Rasumowsky quartet (1808-16 and again later); **Franz Clement** (d. 1842), who was heard as a prodigy in England soon after 1790, at 18 (1802) became conductor at Vienna, about 1816 was associated with Weber at Prague, in 1818 returned to Vienna and after 1821 toured with the singer Catalani, winning a high place by extreme dexterity, graceful sentiment and a phenomenal memory, and writing 6 concertos and 25 concertinos, studies and many lesser pieces, besides other works (for him Beethoven wrote his concerto in D, 1806); and **Leopold Jansa** (d. 1875), a Bohemian who from 1824 was in the Vienna court-orchestra, from 1834 was conductor and teacher at the university, and from 1849 taught in London, writing in all 4 concertos, nearly 40 duos, 8 quartets, etc.

From the various German groups — **Friedrich Witt** (d. 1837), from about 1790 leader at Oettingen and, after tours, from 1802 court-choirmaster at Würzburg, writing 9 symphonies, some chamber works, 2 operas (1804, '06), 2 oratorios and church music; the five brothers **Moralt**, four of whom, **Joseph** (d. 1828), **Johann Baptist** (d. 1825), **Philipp** (d. 1829) and **Georg** (d. 1818), formed a quartet that was famous at Munich from before 1800 and was one of the first to make extended tours for the rendering of chamber music; **Ludwig Wilhelm Maurer** (d. 1878), pupil of Haack at Potsdam, who from 1801 was in the royal orchestra, from 1806 in Russia, meeting Rode and Baillot and becoming choirmaster to a Moscow noble, from 1818, after touring in Germany and France, choirmaster at Hanover, from 1832 again at Moscow and from 1845 at Dresden, writing 8 concertos, a double concerto, a concertante for 4 violins, a symphony, 2 quartets, etc., besides 6 operas; **Friedrich Ernst Fesca** (d. 1826), appearing first at Magdeburg, then a pupil of A. E. Müller at Leipsic, in the orchestra there, from 1806 at Oldenburg, from 1808 at Cassel and from 1815 at Carlsruhe, producing in a graceful and effective style 20 quartets, 5 quintets, 3 symphonies and 4 overtures, besides 2 operas (1819, '23) and excellent church music; **Johann Nikolaus Konrad Götze** (d. 1861), a representative pupil of Spohr, A. E. Müller and Kreutzer, who, after successful German and Austrian tours, from 1826 was court-director at Gotha, retiring in 1848, and the composer of some chamber music and several operas (from 1814); **Thomas Täglichsbeck** (d. 1867), pupil of Rovelli at Munich, who traveled widely as a virtuoso and in 1827-48 was court-choirmaster at Hechingen, producing many violin-pieces, 2 symphonies, an opera (1823) and some vocal music; **Johann Hermann Kufferath** (d. 1864), pupil of Spohr and Hauptmann, from 1823 director at Bielefeld and from 1830 at Utrecht, where he became influential as a vocal teacher, producing good overtures, cantatas, sacred works and a vocal method (1836); and **Jakob Zeugheer** (d. 1865), born at Zurich, pupil of Wassermann and Fränzl, who in 1824-30 led a noted quartet ('Die Gebrüder Herrmann') which imitated the Schuppanzigh and Moralt quartets in touring through Germany, France, Belgium and England with much acceptance, and who from 1831 was conductor and teacher in Manchester and from 1838 at Liverpool, writing considerable instrumental music and an opera.

A notable Swedish violinist was **Johann Friedrich Berwald** (d. 1861), pupil of Vogler, whose extraordinary precocity in playing and composing made him known throughout northern Europe before he was 10 (1798), and who settled in 1816 at Stockholm, where from 1834 he was royal choirmaster, composing concertos, quartets, symphonies, etc.

From the Italian group — **Giuseppe Maria Festa** (d. 1839), born in 1771 near Naples and first trained there, developing into an able player and a remarkable conductor, working first throughout Italy, from 1802 at the Paris Opéra and from 1805 at Naples, and writing quartets, duos, etc.; **Pietro Rovelli** (d. 1838), pupil of his grandfather and of Kreutzer, who became famous from about 1810 at Paris, Weimar, Munich and Vienna, and from 1819 was choirmaster and concertmaster at Bergamo, worthily upholding the Viotti traditions and training good pupils; and **Carlo Bignami** (d. 1848), eminent from about 1825 as soloist and conductor, from 1837 bringing the Cremona orchestra to striking perfection and winning the highest commendation from Paganini.

Here should be named some virtuosi on other stringed instruments, such as the viola-player **Franz Weiss** (d. 1830), in the Rasumowsky and Schuppanzigh quartets at Vienna; many 'cello-players, like **Bernhard Romberg** (d. 1841), considered the first of the German 'cellists of the day, who made important extensions in technique and wrote striking concertos (see sec. 149); **Friedrich Dotzauer** (d. 1860), in the Dresden orchestra in 1811-52 and a noted teacher; **Nicolas Joseph Platel** (d. 1835), from 1813 at Antwerp and from 1824 at Brussels; **Charles Nicolas Baudiot** (d. 1849), from 1802 professor in the Paris Conservatoire and in the court-orchestra, the author of two methods; **George Onslow** (d. 1852), a wealthy nobleman, trained first as a pianist, but later enthusiastic over chamber music, of which he wrote an enormous amount with skill and elegance; the brothers **Wilhorski** (d. 1863, '56), prominent in Russia; **Joseph Merk** (d. 1852), from 1818 active at Vienna; and the contrabassist **Wenzel Hause**, teacher at Prague and the author of fine studies and a method (1828).

182. Other Instrumental Music. — The opening period of the century was marked by an immense interest, particularly at Paris, in the whole range of instrumental music. This is illustrated not only by the attention to the piano and the violin as the chief artistic implements, but by parallel attention to several of the wind instruments of the orchestra, and to the harp and the guitar as modern successors of the lyre and the lute. In every case efforts were made to better the mechanism of the instrument itself, so as to improve its quality or extend its possi-

bilities — sometimes with notable results.   In all cases, too, the
number of virtuosi multiplied, bringing the several instruments
into widespread popularity as sources of concert effectiveness,
and endeavoring to utilize upon them the leading forms of composition, like the concerto, the fantasia or divertissement, the
variation, the étude, etc.   Furthermore, the field of chamber
music was extended by ingenious experiments with unusual combinations, in which sometimes the less-known instruments were
made prominent.   The chief centre for all this enterprising activity was Paris, where both concertizing and teaching along
novel lines received support from the Conservatoire and the
public.

From the multitude of able workers in this field we can select only some
bare lists of the best-known players, composers and teachers, many of whom
continued active through the next period.

Famous flutists were Étienne François Gebauer (d. 1823), from 1801 in the
orchestra of the Opéra-Comique; Benoît Tranquille Berbiguier (d. 1838),
pupil of Wunderlich at Paris, where from 1815 he wrought as a remarkable
virtuoso and fertile composer; Friedrich Kuhlau (d. 1832), already mentioned
as an opera-writer at Copenhagen (see sec. 172), who wrote fluently for flute,
violin, piano and voice; Jean Louis Tulou (d. 1865), Wunderlich's best pupil
and in 1813 his successor at the Opéra, as well as from 1827 professor at the
Conservatoire — a strong objector to the Böhm improvements; Louis Drouet
(d. 1873), Tulou's chief competitor at Paris, and in 1836–54 choirmaster at
Coburg; Kaspar Kummer (d. 1870), from 1813 also at Coburg; Johann
Wilhelm Gabrielski (d. 1846), from 1816 court-player at Berlin; Anton
Bernhard Fürstenau (d. 1852), from 1820 in a similar position at Dresden, writing abundantly and well; and Christian Gottlieb Belcke (d. 1875),
from 1819 at Leipsic and from 1834 at Altenburg.

Among the oboists were Karl Bochsa (d. 1821), a Bohemian who finally
became a music-seller at Paris; Gustave Vogt (d. 1870), from about 1800
eminent at the Opéra-Comique and the Conservatoire; Friedrich Eugen
Thurner (d. 1827), for some years touring from Cassel and Brunswick as centres,
and dying insane at Amsterdam; and Joseph Sellner (d. 1843), from 1811
with Weber at Prague and from 1817 a famous teacher and conductor at
Vienna, the author of a classic method.   Distinguished bassoonists were Karl
Almenräder (d. 1843), from 1812 at Frankfort and from 1820 at Nassau (near
Coblentz), introducing useful improvements in his instrument and writing
about it (1824);   and Karl Bärmann of Munich (d. 1842).

In the line of clarinettists were Johann Simon Hermstedt (d. 1846), from
1800 choirmaster at Sondershausen, where he invented improvements in the
instrument; Heinrich Joseph Bärmann (d. 1847), court-player at Munich, intimate with both Weber and Mendelssohn, and a prolific composer; Friedrich Müller (d. 1871), from 1803 in the court-band at Rudolstadt, retiring in

1854; Franz Thaddäus Blatt (d. after 1830), from 1818 teacher in the Prague conservatory; and Friedrich Beer (d. 1838), prominent in French army music, from 1831 professor at the Conservatoire, writing a fine method (1836) — also an able bassoonist.

There were numerous horn-players of renown, like Karl Jakob Wagner (d. 1822), from 1790 active at Darmstadt, where, besides much orchestral music, he produced 5 operas (1810–21); Louis François Dauprat (d. 1868), in youth a band-player in the army, from 1808 at the Paris Opéra, in court service and teacher at the Conservatoire; Martin Joseph Mengal (d. 1851), from 1825, after a somewhat similar career, conductor at Ghent, Antwerp and The Hague, and from 1835 head of the Ghent conservatory; Joseph Émile Meifred (d. 1867), pupil of Dauprat and from 1833 on the Conservatoire staff, with several methods (from 1829); Jacques François Gallay (d. 1864), also a pupil of Dauprat, a court-player and in 1842 Dauprat's successor at the Conservatoire; Wouter Hutschenruijter (d. 1878), a Dutchman, working at Rotterdam, Schiedam and Delft, producing a variety of both instrumental and vocal works, including an opera, sacred music and songs; together with Thomas Harper (d. 1853), a popular trumpeter at London; and Friedrich August Belcke (d. 1874), the pioneer virtuoso on the trombone.

The harp continued to attract artistic notice, among the good players and composers being Marcel de Marin of Toulouse (d. c. 1861); Martin Pierre Dalvimare (d. 1839), in 1800–12 prominent at Paris; François Joseph Nadermann (d. 1835), pupil of Krumpholz, also well-known at Paris, being active, with his brother, in his father's harp-factory and from 1815 in opposing Érard's improvements in mechanism; François Dizi (d. 1847), a protégé of Érard at London and from 1830 at Paris, with a method (1827); Robert Nicolas Charles Bochsa (d. 1856), son of Karl Bochsa the oboist, a precocious player and composer in many forms, pupil of Méhul, Catel, Marin and Nadermann, from about 1806 in court service, from 1817 in London, where he conducted concerts and opera, from 1839 (when he ran away with Bishop's wife) on extended tours, including America and Australia, with 8 operas (from 1813), etc., besides much for the harp and a method; and Antoine Prumier (d. 1868), Nadermann's successor in 1835.

Among the guitar-players were Ferdinando Carulli (d. 1841), a Neapolitan who in 1808 came to Paris and became the founder of the artistic style for his instrument, writing elaborately for it, with a method and a theory (1825); Fernando Sors (d. 1839), a Spanish refugee at Paris, with many orchestral works and 2 operas, besides his guitar-pieces and a method; Dionisio Aguado y Garcia (d. 1849), another Spaniard, working at Madrid, with a method (1825); and Marco Aurelio Zani de Ferranti (d. 1878), born at Bologna, but known throughout Europe, settling in 1827–46 at Brussels and in 1855 returning to Italy.

183. Problems in Instrument-Making.

— The whole first half of the 19th century was marked by energetic efforts to improve the construction of instruments. Undoubtedly most of these efforts were inspired mainly by economic motives, being designed to make profit out of the rapidly widening popular interest in music. But most of them were also guided by truly artistic ambitions and were put forth under the lead of experienced musicians, so that their total value to artistic progress was immense, even though some experiments were failures and the utility of others was but slowly perceived.

Naturally, the interest in piano-making much outstripped all others of these business interests, since the piano was seen to be on the whole the most widely available of musical implements. Upon its construction was brought to bear so much inventive genius, in both Europe and America, that in sonority, tone-graduation and durability the instrument was actually revolutionized. Improvements in orchestral instruments, also, like the flute, the oboe, the clarinet, several brass instruments, the harp, etc., now came in rapidly, bringing notable gains in beauty of tone, variety of effects and ease of manipulation. Such improvements made solo-playing far more impressive, and greatly enriched orchestral and chamber ensembles. In the general development of musical mechanisms the intricate problems of the organ were not forgotten, though the conquest of some of them was still delayed. The invention of the reed-organ was really a notable event, in spite of its small value as a concert instrument, since its simplicity and cheapness speedily made it a useful agent in the popularization of music.

Altogether, then, it is important to remember that side by side with the splendid advance made in composition and in technique went a purely mechanical advance in implements that was indispensable for attaining the total artistic results.

In piano-making the chief centres continued to be London, Paris and Vienna. But it is notable that several of the signal improvements in structure were first conceived by workers in America. When we consider how far behind America was in musical culture as compared with any European country, its ingenuity and enterprise in this regard from about 1800 is astonishing. Before 1840, American pianos had begun to rank among the best.

During the 18th century the special problem in piano-making was that of the action. Of this two main types were prominent, the English and the Viennese, differing in the position and articulation of the hammer (see sec. 160). In 1809 a notable gain was made by Érard's invention of a double escapement, enabling the hammer-stroke to be repeated without releasing the key. But before 1800 it was seen that the next great

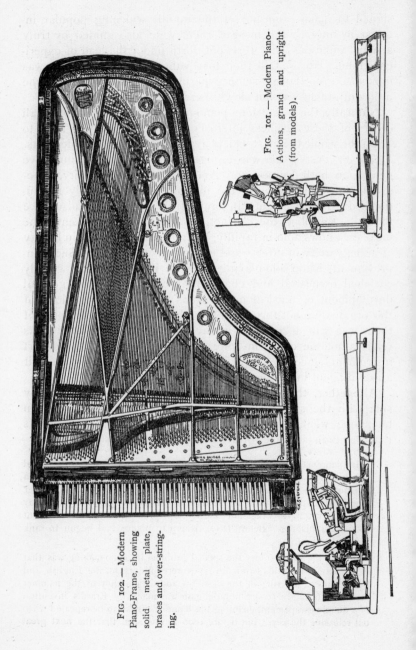

FIG. 101.— Modern Piano-Actions, grand and upright (from models).

FIG. 102. — Modern Piano-Frame, showing solid metal plate, braces and over-stringing.

problem was to secure a fuller tone, with more sustained or 'singing' quality, and more variety. For this longer, heavier and tenser strings were demanded. At the same time the compass of the keyboard was being stretched from 4–5 octaves in the earlier patterns to 5½ and 6 before 1795, and to 7 by about 1825, with two or three strings to most of the keys. Hence the strain upon the frame was mounting up prodigiously. Hitherto the frame had been made wholly of wood, most ingeniously built up. In 1799 a London patent was taken out for longitudinal metal braces, and by 1808 Broadwood began to use steel tension-bars ; but the union of wood and metal was not altogether successful. In 1825, however, the first full iron frame in one piece was introduced by Babcock of Boston, Mass., and in 1831 a similar feature appeared in London. Metal frames, either of combined sections or cast solid, soon generally displaced the old wooden ones, except for small instruments. For a time the union of different materials necessitated ' compensating ' devices to meet variations in temperature. The important safeguard of 'agraffes' to keep the strings from being displaced by the hammer-blows was first used in 1808. 'Overstringing' came in about 1835, allowing for a decided consolidation of the frame.

In the search for sonority the character of the string-wire was a critical point. In the 18th century only brass or iron was used, but of so poor a quality that no great tension was possible. In the early 19th, brass was gradually given up and the iron was much improved. In 1834, if not earlier, the introduction of steel wire changed the whole problem, making possible the enormous tensions now common (amounting in present concert grands to 20–30 tons !). Still another most important factor was seen to be the material, form and fitting of the soundboard — a matter that was mainly settled empirically, as in the shaping of the body of the violin.

In the 18th century the two standard forms of piano were the ' grand ' (shaped like the harpsichord) and the 'square' (like the clavichord). In 1800 Hawkins of Philadelphia patented the first true 'upright,' which involved radical modifications of both frame and action. This type was soon developed in Europe and became a favorite, as it still remains.

In the long line of distinguished piano-makers, following pioneers like Broadwood and Stein (see sec. 160), the following may be named as specially enterprising at this period in invention or the establishing of factories : —

Sébastien Érard (d. 1831), after returning from London to Paris in 1796 (see sec. 160), made his first grand, in 1809 introduced agraffes and worked out the principle of the ' repeating ' action (patented by his nephew in 1821), and contributed to the betterment of the harp and the reed-organ. Pierre Érard (d. 1855), his nephew, worked first as his uncle's representative at London, but later became the head of the establishment at Paris. The latter published a treatise on the Érard system in general (1834).

In Germany the great firm of Schiedmayer was founded at Erlangen in 1781 by Johann David Schiedmayer (d. 1806), transferred in 1809 to Stuttgart by his son Lorenz Schiedmayer (d. 1860), and greatly developed by four grandsons, becoming equally noted for pianos and reed-organs ; and other houses were started in 1794 at Barmen by **Johann Adolph Ibach** (d. 1848), with whom various descendants were later associated, in 1814 at Breslau by **Michael Schnabel** (d. 1842), and in 1828 at Vienna by Ignaz **Bösendorfer** (d. 1859).

Wilhelm Leberecht Petzold, who was trained at Dresden in 1806 with J. Pfeiffer, opened a noted factory at Paris, winning a reputation for unusual solidity of workmanship, and devising peculiar varieties of uprights, etc.

The celebrated house of Pleyel & Cie. was started at Paris in 1807 by the pianist **Ignaz Joseph Pleyel** (d. 1831), who was joined in 1811 by Pape, in 1821 by his son **Camille Pleyel** (d. 1855) and in 1824 by the virtuoso Kalkbrenner. The fame of the Pleyel pianos was aided from 1831 by Chopin's interest in them.

Johann Heinrich Pape (d. 1875), a Hanoverian, for a time with Pleyel, from about 1815 for nearly fifty years not only pursued established lines of manufacture, but originated countless new forms, usually more ingenious than commercially available. He was the first to perfect the felting of the hammer-heads, and he contests with Böhm the honor of introducing overstringing.

Robert Wornum (d. 1852) had a factory in London from 1810, and from 1811 was specially successful in perfecting the action of uprights, particularly in the form known as the 'cottage piano.'

American piano-making began soon after 1800, the chief pioneers being **Alpheus Babcock** and **John Osborne** of Boston. The latter trained **Jonas Chickering** (d. 1853), who in 1823 founded the Boston firm which under him and his sons immediately became celebrated for original inventions and fin workmanship.

Heinrich Engelhard Steinweg (d. 1871), from about 1820 an organ-builder at Seesen (Brunswick), before 1830 turned to piano-making, soon developing a successful factory. In 1848, with four of his sons, he removed to New York, leaving his eldest son, **Theodor** (d. 1889), to continue the business at Seesen In 1853 the famous firm of Steinway & Sons was established in New York. (The German house since 1859 has been at Brunswick.)

American organ-building began before 1750, but the first extensive manufacturer was **William M. Goodrich,** who worked at Boston in 1805–33. The important Boston firm of **E. & G. G. Hook** was founded in 1827.

In violin-making specially noted was **Jean Baptiste Vuillaume** (d. 1875), who inherited his expertness from his father and from 1817 worked at Paris, at first with Chanot and Lété, from 1828 independently. He had great success in counterfeiting old Italian instruments, but was an original investigator and inventor as well, perfecting powerful violas and double-basses, and improving strings and bows.

The standard type of flute at the opening of the century was one in which the lower part of the tube was slightly conical. In 1832 **Theobald Böhm** (d. 1881), a Munich player of eminence, greatly improved the orchestral value of the instrument by making the bore cylindrical and radically altering the system of keys and fingering. Similar improvements were perhaps earlier achieved by **William Gordon** (d. after 1839), a Swiss army officer. The Böhm system was later extended to oboes, bassoons and clarinets. Its value lies in the equalization of quality and in ease of manipulation.

During the 18th century clarinet-making gradually advanced, but without producing entirely competent instruments. In 1814 **Ivan Müller** (d. 1854), a Russian player, then working in Paris, perfected the form with 13 keys which for the first time made playing possible in all scales. Though not at first approved by academic judges, this form was soon widely advertised by Müller's brilliant tours and by his method (1825). He also invented an alto clarinet, which, however, did not dislodge the already accepted basset-horn. Both the clarinet and the basset-horn were ably handled by the leading orchestral writers of the period, so that much incentive was given to their makers.

The bass clarinet was little used until after 1830. Its perfecting was largely due to **Charles Joseph Sax** (d. 1865) and his son **Adolphe Sax** (d. 1894).

The father founded a factory at Brussels in 1815, in which the son was trained. The latter went to Paris in 1842 and was followed by his father in 1853. There they developed an immense business, especially in brass instruments. In 1842 the son exhibited the 'saxophone,' a novel union of a clarinet mouthpiece with a metal conical tube. In 1845 he devised the 'saxhorn,' a developed bugle, and the 'saxotromba.' All these were made in sets or 'families' of differing pitch, and are specially valuable in military bands. A large number of less useful inventions followed.

Wilhelm Friedrich Wieprecht (d. 1872), from 1824 in royal service at Berlin and from 1838 chief of the Prussian military bands, in 1835, with the help of others, perfected the 'bass tuba' and in 1849 the less useful 'bathyphon' (somewhat resembling the bass clarinet), besides other novelties. He contested with Sax the invention of the saxhorn, but without success in the courts.

In harp-making the main problem, aside from details of strength and sonority, was to provide for chromatic tones and especially for complete shifts of key

FIG. 103. — Saxophones.

without multiplying strings. Early in the 18th century experiments began with little 'crooks' (adjustable metal angles inserted by the hand or controlled by a pedal) by which the strings could be raised a semitone. From about 1780 **Pierre Joseph Cousineau** (d. 1824) produced two or three ingenious devices of the same class, including a complete double action (securing a rise of either one or two semitones). Various drawbacks in all these were finally overcome by **Sébastien Érard**, the piano-maker (see above), who began improving the harp before 1790. By 1810 he had perfected a double action with studded disks revolved by pedals so as to grip the strings

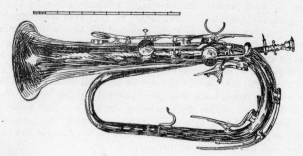

FIG. 104.

FIG. 105.   FIG. 106.

FIG. 104. — Keyed or Kent Bugle.
FIG. 105. — Tenor Ophicleide.
FIG. 106. — Bass and Alto Saxhorns — the former also called Euphonium.

and raise the pitch. Thus the harp became a complete transposing instrument without adding strings or disturbing the fingering. His work was continued by **Pierre Érard** (see above), who published an account of the improvements made (1821).

The guitar was extensively studied from about 1800, several varieties being used, such as the 'English' (really the Italian 'cetera,' see fig. 68) and the Spanish, the former showing its kinship with the lute by its wire strings (partly in unison pairs) and its pear-shaped body, and the latter having gut and silk (overspun) strings and a body shaped like an '8.' The Spanish gradually became the general favorite. In 1828 **M. Salomon** (d. 1821), a French guitarist, invented the 'harpo-lyre,' having 21 strings in three sets, the middle six susceptible of 'stopping' against a fretted neck (as in the guitar), the rest giving only 'open' tones.

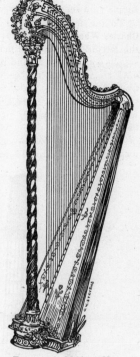

FIG. 107. — Modern Harp.

The essential principle of the 'orgue expressif,' 'harmonium' or 'reed-organ' is that of the Chinese cheng (see sec. 11), the tones being produced from small metal tongues ('reeds') that play freely in openings which they do not quite cover. This principle of the 'free reed' seems to have reached Europe by way of St. Petersburg, where experiments were made with it about 1780. In 1788 these efforts became known to the organist Vogler, who in 1790 induced one of the Russian mechanicians, Rackwitz, to join him in Holland and develop free-reed stops for the pipe-organ (see secs. 149, 163). Though this plan had some result, the more important historic fact is that soon free reeds were utilized for many much smaller instruments. They were specially useful because their tones could be made loud or soft without change of pitch.

Just before 1800, free reeds were carefully studied by the piano-maker **Érard** (see above) and by **Gabriel Joseph Grenié** (d. 1837). The former introduced them in various combinations with the piano and the pipe-organ. In 1810 the latter brought out his 'orgue expressif,' in which the tone-intensity was governed by valves. This Érard in turn greatly improved. Meanwhile analogous inventions were appearing in Germany and England. From about 1820, instruments multiplied under an amusing variety of names. Not only was the wind-supply regulated, but much ingenuity was put upon improving the tone-quality by modifying the reeds or the 'channels' in which they were set. The ablest summary of these experiments was made by **Alexandre François Debain** (d. 1877), whose 'harmonium' was patented in 1840. The 'percussion' (little hammers to put the reeds into quick action) was first applied by **Pierre Alexandre Martin** (d. 1879).   Devices for strengthening the melody-notes began to be added about 1860.   Before 1850, American makers entered the field, introducing several novelties, among them the twisting of the reeds to improve their speech and tone, and the reversion of the wind-supply (drawing the air *inward* through the reeds).

To the free-reed group belongs the 'concertina,' invented in 1829 by **Charles Wheatstone** (d. 1875), the eminent English physicist.   In 1829, also, the 'accordion' was first made in Vienna by **Damian.**   In these the wind-supply comes from a hand-bellows, to which the reeds are attached, and the keys are small finger-levers or studs.   In England the name 'seraphine' was from 1833 applied to a kindred instrument played from a keyboard.

Johann Christian Dietz of Emmerich (d. c. 1845) added to the experiments with friction instruments by his 'melodeon' (1805) and 'trochléon' (1812), besides producing a keyboard harp (1814).   In 1810 **Friedrich Kaufmann** of Dresden (d. 1866) brought out the 'harmonichord,' in which Weber was for a time interested.   These are but specimens of many efforts.

FIG. 108. — Guitars.

CHAPTER XXVIII

CHURCH AND ORGAN MUSIC

184. Confused Tendencies in Catholic Music. — The drift toward demoralization in sacred music which was notable before 1800 became more conspicuous later. The general musical world was but slightly concerned with church music in any form, except as a necessity in liturgical routine, and there was no controlling standard of taste regarding it. In different localities it was treated in diverse and even capricious ways. At Rome and occasionally elsewhere in Italy there were some who sought to hold to the lofty purism of the old 16th-century style, though usually with concessions on the side of accompaniments. But generally in Italy and also in France came a marked increase of the theatric style, bringing over into the church whatever of sensuous charm and sumptuous splendor had proved popular in the opera. Apart from the Italians the most striking group of writers was that of Vienna, who tended to apply to sacred music the energetic form and brilliant instrumentation of the Viennese school of concert music. In this group, as in that of the Italians, the degree of independence and warm sincerity varied greatly, many composers having only a superficial sense of the sacred music problem, while a few entered into it with real sympathy. Here and there single composers made significant attempts to utilize all the resources of modern methods in a spirit fully analogous to that of the best early contrapuntists. Of these the most notable was the cosmopolitan and many-sided Cherubini, whose dignified nobility of expression went far toward offsetting the tawdry sensationalism of Rossini and his imitators.

Luigi Cherubini (d. 1842), already mentioned as an opera-writer (see sec. 154), had his early training at Milan under Sarti wholly in the strictest sort of church music. But from 1780 for 30 years he then gave himself up to opera-writing. Not till 1809 and still more after 1816, when he became royal choirmaster and head of the Conservatoire, did he resume the serious

479

contrapuntal style. This latest period of his career reached to about 1830, only one important work coming later. He wrote in all the forms required by the Catholic service, including many shorter pieces, but his renown rests mainly upon his 11 masses and 2 Requiems. Of the former, those in F (1809, 3 voices), D minor (1811), C (1816), G (1819, coronation of Louis XVIII.) and A (1825, coronation of Charles X.) are counted the strongest. The Requiem in C minor (1816) is his most famous work, though that in D minor (1836) is fully as noble — the maturest expression of his genius. His ultimate style was so comprehensive that it cannot be classified with any school. He could write almost in the purest manner of the Palestrina period, but had also perfect command of the resources of modern vocalism and instrumentation. These he knew how to use with imagination and earnestness. He therefore illustrates a consummate blending of the old and the new.

Marco Santucci (d. 1843), another learned contrapuntist, was almost exactly Cherubini's contemporary. A pupil of Feneroli at Naples, from 1797 he was choirmaster at the Lateran in Rome, succeeding Anfossi, and from 1808 was connected with the cathedral of Lucca. Though somewhat productive, few of his works remain — a Requiem, 2 Magnificats, a Te Deum, some soprano cantatas, several psalms, many organ-versets and a set of suonate in fugued style for the piano. An early motet for 16 voices (1806) was curiously commended by a Neapolitan jury as 'new,' simply because they did not know the Palestrina style.

Giuseppe Baini (d. 1844), born at Rome in 1775 and trained by his uncle and by Jannaconi, entered the choir at St. Peter's in 1802 as a bass and in 1817 succeeded his teacher as choirmaster. He thus had over 40 years' intimate contact with music of the severe order and access to the papal archives. Though writing somewhat freely in the regular forms, he is chiefly known as a composer by his Miserere (1821). His lifelong enthusiasm for Palestrina was shown by a famous monograph (1828) and by a projected complete edition of Palestrina's works.

Giuseppe Pilotti (d. 1838) exemplifies a parallel development under the austere impress of Martini. Brought up in poverty as an organ-maker, he was finally enabled to study with Mattei (Martini's pupil), and at once showed unusual talent. After serving as choirmaster at Pistoia, in 1826 he followed Mattei at Bologna and from 1829 was also professor of counterpoint at the Lyceum. Excepting two operatic ventures (1810, '16), his works were all for the church.

Pietro Raimondi (d. 1853) presents the amazing anomaly of success at once in popular opera and in stupendous church counterpoint. Born at Rome in 1786, he had long training at Naples from Tritto, and, after some hardships, settled in Genoa, where his first opera was produced (1807). To this succeeded not less than 80 other operas and ballets for various stages (notably *Il ventaglio*, 1831, Naples), the vogue of which was often considerable, though checked by the rage for Rossini. From 1824 he was theatre-director at Naples, from 1832 professor of counterpoint at the conservatory of Palermo, and in 1852 for a few months choirmaster at St. Peter's in Rome. His operatic work continued till about 1845. But along with this ran a stream of sacred works, including 8 oratorios, masses, Requiems, the whole of the Psalms, innumerable motets, etc., mostly in an extremely learned *a cappella* style, many also with orchestral accompaniment.   His specialty was devising fugues for various numbers of voices which could be rendered by separate choirs or combined polychorically (as 6 choirs of 4 voices that could be united into one of 24, 16 of 4 that could be made one of 64, etc.).   To crown all, he completed (1852, Rome) a set of three oratorios, *Potifar, Giuseppe* and *Giacobbe*, which were first given separately and then combined into a composite rendering. The mental power evinced in all this was phenomenal and in all his works are passages of beauty and originality; but he spent himself in achieving *tours de force*.

In addition to **Generali** (d. 1832), **Paër** (d. 1839), **Mayr** (d. 1845) and **Morlacchi** (d. 1841), who were prominent in sacred music as well as in opera (see sec. 175), the less important names may be given of **Giuseppe Niccolini** (d. 1842), the writer of about 60 operas (from 1793) in the Neapolitan vein, who from 1819 was choirmaster at Piacenza and thenceforth composed prolifically for the church; and **Melchiore Balbi** (d. 1879), from 1818 opera-director at Padua and from 1854 cathedral-choirmaster, who, after a few operas (1820–5), turned to church works and theoretical studies.

What may be called the Viennese type of Catholic music was a part of the 'classical' style as a whole of which Vienna was the original centre.   It began with Haydn and Mozart, and was sustained by a host of lesser writers.   It tended to differ from Italian types, as a rule, in having less mere sentimentality of melody and conventional theatric passion, and, on the side of scholarship, in adhering more to the German style of instrumental counterpoint than to the more archaic vocal counterpoint of the South.   Its whole structure was usually much affected by the forms of instrumental concert music which all the great Viennese masters pushed into the foreground.   Hence came a compactness and clarity, a certain nervous vigor, a general air of intellectuality that were less frequent in the common Italian work.   The voices were perhaps treated less 'vocally,' but the instrumental side had much elegance and force.   Of course, behind these external characteristics played the personality of the individual composer, varying widely in religious earnestness and profundity of spiritual imagination.   Yet even strong individuality could not far outstep the limitations of the general style, which was more concerned with outward finish and brilliance than with depth of conviction.   That the style, however, stands in somewhat close relation with the feeling of Catholic musicians is shown by the fact that it has continued in fairly general use ever since.

21

The more striking names in the long Vienna list are as follows : —

Joseph von Eybler (d. 1846), born in 1765, grew up in contact with Haydn and Mozart and was a pupil of Albrechtsberger, who placed his genius "next to Mozart." For 30 years from 1794 he was choirmaster at the great Benedictine monastery and from 1804 also Salieri's assistant in the Imperial Chapel, succeeding him there in 1824. Though from 1794 he wrote much chamber music, piano-sonatas and dances, 2 symphonies and a few operas, he is almost wholly known as a church composer of decided strength and nobility. Among his over 30 masses, 7 Te Deums, many motets and 2 oratorios (including *Die vier letzten Dinge*, 1810), his Requiem in C minor is counted the best. Eybler attended Mozart in his last sickness and was the one who first endeavored to complete the latter's Requiem.

Less important names of the same period were **Weigl** (d. 1846), who after about 1825 (see sec. 172) wrote 10 masses, several motets and cantatas and 2 oratorios (including a Passion, 1804) ; **Joseph Ignaz Schnabel** (d. 1831), plainly of the Vienna group, though identified with Breslau, where from 1805 he was cathedral-choirmaster and from 1812 also efficient in stimulating music at the university, the Catholic schools and among the general public, writing a large amount of meritorious church music ; and **Seyfried** (d. 1841), equally abundant and popular in opera (see sec. 172) and in sacred works, including several sacred operas, like *Abraham, Saul* (1823), etc.

Beethoven (d. 1827) was in no way fitted for practical success in church music. His two masses, that in C (1807, for the Esterhazy Chapel) and the *Missa solennis* (1818-23), stand quite by themselves. The latter is a unique concert-work, ranking in individuality and sublimity with Bach's B minor mass, though in a wholly different style. The oratorio *Christus am Oelberge* [*The Mount of Olives*] (1803) is burdened by a hasty and melodramatic libretto. All these works have importance as self-expressions on Beethoven's part and as passionate efforts to find adequate embodiments for religious feeling, but have no close relation with general progress.

Johann Gänsbacher (d. 1844), a Tyrolese, educated first at Innsbruck and from 1801 under Vogler and Albrechtsberger at Vienna, had an uneasy career, partly in the army, until 1823, when he followed Preindl as choirmaster at St. Stephen's, Vienna. Over 200 works of his are listed, but very few have been published. His style was too good to be popular, but not original enough to endure.

Sigismund von Neukomm (d. 1858), born in 1778, belongs to the Vienna group because brought up under Michael Haydn at Salzburg and from 1798 a special protégé of the aged Joseph Haydn at Vienna. After the latter's death in 1809 he made the grand tour of northern Europe and settled at Paris, where he succeeded Dussek as the favorite of Talleyrand. In 1816 he became royal choirmaster in Brazil, returning in 1821 to his Paris connections. From 1826 he traveled often and widely, being specially popular in London until displaced by Mendelssohn. Throughout his long career he was extolled as virtuoso (upon several instruments) and composer, receiving countless honors. His works number over 1000, including many piano- and organ-pieces and about 200 songs, besides some chamber music, a symphony, orchestral fantasias and an opera. For the Catholic service he wrote 15 masses, 5 cantatas and many psalms, and for the English Church a Morning and Evening Service complete. He also produced several oratorios, including a trilogy on the Entombment, the Resurrection and the Ascension (c. 1826), *Das Gesetz des alten Bundes* [*Mount Sinai*] (c. 1810), *David*, and cantatas for Easter and Whitsunday. He was an enthusiast over Palestrina, but in his superficial facility was quite unable to follow in that master's steps.

Joseph Drechsler (d. 1852), a Bohemian, worked from 1807 in Vienna, first as teacher and opera-director, later as organist and choirmaster, in 1844 following Gänsbacher at St. Stephen's. An indefatigable worker of no small ability, he stands credited with 17 masses, 3 cantatas and many motets for the church, 5 operas and many lesser stage-works, instrumental pieces and songs, an organ-method, a harmony and other instruction-books.

To these may be added several whose work likewise extended into the next period, such as Joseph Blahagk (d. 1846), from 1802 an operatic tenor and from 1824 Preindl's successor at St. Peter's, with numerous works ; Ignaz Aszmayer (d. 1862), a pupil of Michael Haydn and at first organist at Salzburg, from 1815 pupil of Eybler and in 1824 his successor at the Schottenstift, from 1825 court-organist, and from 1838 Weigl's assistant and in 1846 his successor as court-choirmaster, with about 60 works, including 15 masses and 3 oratorios ; and Franz Schubert (d. 1828), whose sacred works form but a small section of his total production, but are marked by the same charm (see secs. 173-4). Schubert's masses were all written for the parish church of Lichtenthal ; the largest of them is that in E♭ (1828). His brother, Ferdinand Schubert (d. 1859), was also a considerable sacred composer.

Among the church musicians associated with Dresden, mention has already been made of Morlacchi (d. 1841), choirmaster from 1810 (see sec. 175), and Reissiger (d. 1859), opera-director from 1827 (see sec. 172). With these may be named the eminent contrapuntist August Alexander Klengel (d. 1852), a pupil of Clementi, who was court-organist from 1816. He was a diligent student of Bach and among his works (wholly for the piano) was a set of 48 canons and fugues intended to rival the *Wohltemperirtes Clavier*.

To this period also belong the Portuguese pianist João Domingos Bomtempo (d. 1842), who, after several years at Paris and London, about 1823 returned to Lisbon, becoming in 1833 court-choirmaster and head of the conservatory, the composer of several masses and a Requiem (1819), besides piano-pieces and a method (1816) ; and the Spaniards Juan Bros (d. 1852), choirmaster at Malaga, Leon and Oviedo, with many church works of renown in Spain ; Francisco Xavier Gibert [Gisbert] (d. 1848), a Madrid priest, said to have had a notable genius for *a cappella* writing ; and Francesco Andrevi (d. 1853), choirmaster at Valencia, Seville and Barcelona (also in 1832-42 at Bordeaux), another strong church writer.

185. The Revival of Protestant Organ Music. — In the circle of German Protestantism the special feature of the period was a notable reawakening of interest in the organ as a vehicle of musical expression. It had seemed as if the early enthusiasm for this instrument in Germany, having reached its culmination in the

18th century in Bach, was exhausted. It is true that no second Bach appeared to carry the development to new heights. But the lapse in interest that occurred after Bach's death was now succeeded by a revival that merits attention, if for no other reason because of its service in recalling the works and style of Bach himself to popular memory and appreciation. It seems strange that he should ever have been forgotten or ignored, but, since he was, a positive movement was needed to restore him to his rightful place. The most useful single agent in bringing to light the Bach traditions as preserved by his pupils was the eminent organist Rinck, but the Englishman Wesley and later the youthful Mendelssohn were powerful coadjutors. In consequence, the number of strong players and composers in this noble branch of musical art suddenly advanced, introducing a new strain of serious expression that had value in shaping later progress. In both the Lutheran and the Anglican Churches this was somewhat coincident with a renewed attention to the enrichment of public worship in other ways.

Christian Rinck (d. 1846) was born in Thuringia in 1770 and was brought up in contact with much organ music. From 1786 he studied with Kittel of Erfurt, the last survivor among Bach's best pupils, in 1790 became town-organist at Giessen and in 1805 took a similar post at Darmstadt, where from 1819 he was court-organist, besides teaching in the gymnasium. His tours as a virtuoso, with his numerous and varied works, gave him an immense reputation and attracted a host of pupils. His genius as a composer was not of the highest class, but his style had solidity and vigor, so that its influence was wholesome. He published almost countless preludes, postludes, chorale-elaborations, variations, etc., and a famous *Orgelschule* (1818), besides a large number of sacred vocal works, including a mass, a Vater Unser, cantatas, duets, solos, a Choralbuch for Hesse (1814) and other collections, not to speak of some piano works.

Michael Gotthard Fischer (d. 1829) was trained by Kittel at Erfurt, and worked all his life there as organist in the two leading Protestant churches and as teacher. He was well known as a player and as a fertile composer, not only of large numbers of organ-pieces, including some fugues, but of 2 symphonies, some choral works and a chorale-collection (1821).

Johann Christian Bartel (d. 1831), educated at Leipsic, was from 1792 teacher near Chemnitz, from 1797 cantor at Greiz, then toured as a virtuoso, and from 1804 was Krebs' successor as court-organist at Altenburg. He produced many organ works, cantatas, psalms and some piano-pieces, of which only a few have been published.

Christian Gottlob August Bergt (d. 1837), at first educated at Dresden and Leipsic for the church, from 1802 was organist at Bautzen, where he led a choral society. He was a fruitful and admired composer in many forms, including 3 Passions, several cantatas, hymns, motets, chorales and over 60 organ-pieces, besides operettas (from 1801), many part-songs, trios and songs, several symphonies and some piano-sonatas.

Johann August Günther Heinroth (d. 1846), son of a veteran organist at Nordhausen, after study at Leipsic and Halle, taught at various places (including a Jewish school at Seesen) and in 1818 followed Forkel at Göttingen. He greatly improved the musical service of the Jewish synagogues, and wrote some vocal music and many pedagogical works (from 1821).

Friedrich Schneider (d. 1853), born in 1786 near Zittau, studied there with Unger and developed precociously. From 1807 he was organist at the university church at Leipsic and in 1813 was transferred to the Thomaskirche. From 1810 he also began service as opera-conductor. From 1821 he was court-choirmaster at Dessau, where he greatly bettered the orchestra, founded fine choral societies and a noted music-school (1829), and conducted many festivals at various places (1819-47). He had a long line of eminent pupils, and was altogether a figure of influence and worth. His most successful works were some of his 16 oratorios, such as *Das Weltgericht* (1819) and *Die Sünd-fluth* (1823). He also wrote 14 masses, 25 cantatas, some motets and an organ-method (1829-30), besides other instruction-books, 7 operas, 400 male choruses, 200 songs, a great number of symphonies and overtures, 60 piano-sonatas, etc.

Johann Schneider (d. 1864), his brother, born in 1789, was far more distinguished as an organist, being counted before 1820 as the finest player in Germany. He too was a pupil of Unger, in 1811 followed his brother at Leipsic, from 1812 was at Görlitz, from whence he made many brilliant tours, and in 1825 became court-organist at Dresden, a post that he made famous through the musical world. He was a specialist in the music of Bach, an expert in technique and registration, and the trainer of a large number of great pupils. His published works, all for the organ, were few and not specially significant.

To these might be added many more, such as Johann Gottlob Werner (d. 1822), whose active career began at Freiberg (Saxony) in 1798 and who from 1819 was cathedral-organist at Merseburg, writing many organ-pieces, instruction-books for organ (1805, '23), piano (1806) and in theory (1818-9), and two Choralbücher; Johann Andreas Dröbs (d. 1825), a self-taught Er-furter who from 1810 was organist of the Petrikirche at Leipsic — a worthy teacher and composer; Friedrich Wilhelm Riem (d. 1857), precocious as a pianist, pupil of Hiller at Leipsic, from about 1807 organist and singing-teacher there, and from 1814 cathedral-organist at Bremen and founder of a school; Karl Heinrich Zöllner (d. 1836), well known from before 1820 as a facile virtuoso and composer in many forms, gifted, but inconstant; Bern-hard Klein (d. 1832), who studied at Paris under Cherubini, and, after some service at the Cologne cathedral, was from 1818 at Berlin as teacher and conductor, a strong sacred composer of oratorios and motets, besides 3 operas and some piano works; and August Wilhelm Bach (d. 1869), a fine player who was Klein's colleague as teacher at Berlin from 1822, succeeding Zelter in 1832, and training many excellent pupils, besides writing organ and vocal music, and editing a popular Choralbuch (1830).

Among the Germans who cultivated Catholic music with success may be named **August Ferdinand Häser** (d. 1844), one of a large musical family, who from 1797 was cantor at Lemgo, in 1806–13 on concert-tours with his sister, and from 1817 teacher and conductor at Weimar, composing much choir music, an oratorio (1817), 3 operas, songs, 2 instruction-books in singing, etc. ; **Michael Henkel** (d. 1851), a pupil of Vierling, who was all his life associated with Fulda as cantor and court-musician, a prolific writer; **Georg Vincent Röder** (d. 1848), from 1805 court-choirmaster at Würzburg, from 1830 conductor at Augsburg and from 1839 royal choirmaster at Munich, producing choir music in abundance; and **Kaspar Ett** (d. 1847), from 1816 court-organist at Munich, a diligent student of the strict contrapuntal styles of the older masters.

To this period belongs the impulse in the music of the Russian Church which led to its modern artistic importance. Historically, the musical liturgy of Russia was derived from mediæval sources in a way analogous to that of the Catholic Church, but its development was meagre and insignificant until vivified by the enthusiam and technical skill of Bortnianski, who brought into it something of the nobility of western styles.

Dimitri Bortnianski (d. 1825) was born in 1751. At St. Petersburg and Venice he studied with Galuppi and became infatuated with Italian music, producing 2 operas (1776–8). About 1782 he returned to Russia, becoming imperial music-director and ultimately completely reforming the style of the Imperial Choir. His compositions, in a manner analogous to that of the old Italian school, included a mass, many fine psalms, etc., mostly *a cappella*.

186. Music in England.—Although during the opening decades of the century the interchange of music and musicians between England and the Continent noticeably increased in volume and frequency, English musical production was still almost without influence upon the great currents of progress. The three main lines of activity were the drafting of numerous ballad-operas and operettas, often 'adapted' freely from larger Continental works so as to feed the popular appetite for dramatic amusement, the production of many glees and songs, and the supply of music for the Anglican church service. The last two classes enlisted the best musicianship, but these were exactly the classes least likely to be elsewhere appreciated or reproduced, even when they were so much as known. Yet, though comparatively isolated, English musical interest was considerable in amount, often discriminating and alert in quality and, in some few cases, marked by original power.

The connection of England with the rise of pianism and its literature has already been noted. It also shared promptly in the Bach revival on its organ side. It contributed some excellent instrumentalists and singers. And it stood ready to extend enthusiastic greeting to such geniuses as Weber and Mendelssohn. The first visit of the latter in 1829 marked the beginning of a new era in the growth of musical life in England.

Among the notable institutions founded in this period the following may be mentioned: —

The *Birmingham Festivals*, after five experimental gatherings (1768–90), from 1796 were held triennially, continuing with but one exception to the present time. With their firm establishment they steadily broadened from their original exclusive devotion to Handel's choral works, becoming one of the factors in the stimulation of general musical taste.

The *Concentores Sodales* was a society founded by Horsley in 1798 to promote practice and production along lines like those of the earlier Glee and Catch Clubs. It continued until 1847.

The *Philharmonic Society* began in 1813 and became at once the centre of instrumental music of the highest order for the Kingdom. For a long period its rehearsals and concerts were conducted by the principal members in turn. Occasionally visiting conductors appeared, as Cherubini (1815), Spohr (1820, '43), Weber (1826), Mendelssohn (1829, '42, '44, '47), etc.

The *Royal Academy of Music* was organized in 1822 through the exertions of Lord Burghersh (later Earl of Westmoreland). This school, after many vicissitudes, has now become a large and highly influential institution. Its principals have been *Crotch* (from 1822), *Potter* (from 1832), *Charles Lucas* (from 1859), *W. S. Bennett* (from 1866), *Macfarren* (from 1875) and *Mackenzie* (from 1888). It is partially supported by a subvention from the government.

Samuel Wesley (d. 1837), born in 1766, the son of Charles Wesley the poet and hymnist, was musically gifted, like all the Wesley family. Before he was 10 he had become an expert organist and violinist, and had written parts of an oratorio; at 11 he published a set of lessons for the harpsichord. At 21 he suffered a serious accident which affected his brain, disabling him for seven years then and twice afterwards for a like period. In the intervals between these attacks he made himself famous as an exceptional organist, as the first Bach enthusiast in England, and as an abundant and strong composer. His works included services, about 10 anthems, 3 masses and many antiphons (indicating his early interest in the Roman Catholic service), innumerable hymn-tunes, many glees and songs, 5 symphonies, 3 overtures, some chamber music, about 10 organ-concertos, many preludes, fugues, etc., and much piano music. In 1808–9 he wrote a series of important letters to his friend Jacob regarding the works of Bach. His brother **Charles Wesley** (d. 1834) was also a good organist.

William Crotch (d. 1847), born in 1775, was equally precocious, playing in public before he was 4, at 11 becoming an organist at Cambridge, and at 14 writing an oratorio. From 1790 he was organist at Oxford, where in 1797 he succeeded Philip Hayes. From 1800 he lectured much at Oxford and London, and in 1822–32 was the first principal of the Royal Academy. He was a fine organist and a successful teacher. Besides text-books, he wrote some 20 anthems, 3 oratorios, including *Palestine* (1812), 3 organ-concertos, fugues, etc., and several cantatas and glees.

Thomas Attwood (d. 1838), born in 1765, studied first under Nares and Ayrton, then at Naples and with Mozart at Vienna. From 1787 he worked in London, from 1796 as organist at St. Paul's and as composer to the Chapel Royal. For about 20 years he was much engaged upon dramatic music, but afterward devoted himself to church writing. He was a close friend of Mendelssohn. His works, in a tasteful and solid style, include over 20 operas and operettas (1792–1807), many songs, glees and piano-pieces, 5 services and about 20 anthems, including those for the coronations of George IV. and William IV.

John Clarke [-**Whitfeld**] (d. 1836), a pupil of Philip Hayes, from 1789 was organist at Ludlow, from 1793 choirmaster at Dublin, from 1799 organist at Cambridge and from 1820 at Hereford, besides being from 1821 professor at Cambridge. He published services and anthems (4 vols. from 1805), many songs and glees, an edition of Handel's works (17 vols., 1809) and an anthem-collection. His church music is still somewhat used, and his settings of poems by Walter Scott were long popular.

George Smart (d. 1867), pupil of Ayrton and Arnold, was from 1791 an organist, violinist and teacher in London, from about 1801 in constant request as a conductor, especially for the Philharmonic Society (1813–44) and of numerous festivals (from 1823), and from 1822 organist to the Chapel Royal. He was an authority upon the traditional renderings of Handel, and was intimate with Weber and Mendelssohn. He edited Gibbons' madrigals (1841) and wrote some anthems, glees and canons (collections, 1863).

Lesser names of those working mainly in sacred music are **Thomas Greatorex** (d. 1831), from 1788 a popular teacher and conductor in London and at festivals, and from 1819 organist at Westminster, writing some church music and a few glees; **Benjamin Jacob** (d. 1829), from 1794 organist at Surrey Chapel (Rowland Hill's) and famous, with Wesley and Crotch, as a superior organist; **Matthew Camidge** (d. 1844), son of John Camidge and in 1803 his successor as organist at York, publishing tunes (1789), a collection of *Cathedral Music* (about 1800), including 6 anthems of his own, and a small musical catechism; and **Thomas Adams** (d. 1858), from 1802 noted as a phenomenal organ-player, excelling in extemporization, with many organ works — fugues, preludes, interludes, variations — also some anthems, tunes and songs. Adams was much concerned in making effective the public concerts given from 1817 upon the 'apollonicon,' a large and ingenious mechanical organ.

William Horsley (d. 1858), from 1794 a London organist and soon active in reviving glee music and promoting vocal concerts, was a prolific writer of excellent glees (5 collections, 1801–7), many songs, 3 symphonies, besides tunes (1820, '28) and elementary handbooks (1825, '47). He edited Call-cott's glees, with a biography (1824), miscellaneous glees (1832) and one volume of Byrd's *Cantiones* (1842). He was one of Mendelssohn's friends.

Henry Rowley Bishop (d. 1855) early displayed lyric and dramatic ability. From 1804 he wrote fluent stage-pieces, from 1810 was conductor at various theatres, from 1841 was professor at Edinburgh and from 1848 at Oxford, receiving knighthood in 1842. Besides many fine songs and glees, he wrote an enormous number (about 80) of operettas and adaptations of European operas (1804–41), such as *The Circassian Bride* (1809), *Guy Mannering* (1816), *Maid Marian* (1822), *Cortez* (1823), etc., and edited collections of national songs, etc.

William Hawes (d. 1846), for nearly 30 years connected with the Chapel Royal, was from 1824 a successful opera-director, bringing out adapted works and several of his own (1829–35). He was also a good composer and editor of glees and madrigals, besides being interested in music-publishing.

Among many other secular composers were **Jonathan Blewitt** (d. 1853), from 1811 prominent at Dublin, returning to London in 1826, with about 10 stage-pieces and many popular Irish ballads; **John Davy** (d. 1824), from before 1800 a violinist and teacher in London, with many favorite songs and about 15 plays (from 1800); **Thomas Simpson Cooke** (d. 1848), born at Dublin and early active in theatre music, from 1813 a tenor in London, a good singing-teacher and from 1828 manager and conductor, with about 15 operettas (1814–35), partly adapted, and numerous glees and songs; **Thomas Forbes Walmisley** (d. 1866), pupil of Attwood, from 1810 organist in London, a good glee-writer (from 1814); **Charles Edward Horn** (d. 1849), a stage-singer and composer, with about 25 operettas (1810–30), who also lived in the United States in 1833–43 and from 1847 (finally as conductor of the Handel and Haydn Society) — the writer of many songs and glees, and 2 oratorios; **John Parry** (d. 1851), a Welsh player upon the clarinet and flageolet, from 1807 teaching in London, long the conductor of Welsh festivals, where he was called 'Bardd Alaw' (Master of Song), in later life a musical critic and writer upon Welsh music, with incidental music to several plays (1814–29); **William Beale** (d. 1854), a choirboy under Arnold and R. Cooke, from 1816 in the Chapel Royal, from 1820 organist at Cambridge and from 1821 in London, with successful madrigals and glees (from 1813); and the **Earl of Westmoreland** [till 1844 **Lord Burghersh**] (d. 1859), active as a soldier and diplomat, but also a diligent musician, with 7 Italian operas at Florence and London (1821–45), 3 symphonies, chamber and piano-pieces, songs, glees and some church music — besides being the promoter of the Royal Academy in 1822.

CHAPTER XXIX

GROWTH OF MUSICAL LITERATURE

187. Musical Publications. — Along with all other lines of intellectual development in the first decades of the century, the
scientific, philosophical and historical discussion of music grew
steadily in dimensions and importance. On the side of science,
acoustical problems were still further investigated, many interesting questions about rhythmic and metric structure brought
into view, the modern doctrines of chord-building and harmonic
progression reduced to more satisfactory form, and the systematic presentation of all the technical divisions of composition, now
including to some extent instrumentation, made more logical and
complete. The leading theorists were almost all teachers at the
Paris Conservatoire. On the side of æsthetics, continued
interest was shown, though without any notable contribution
except from the psychological point of view represented by
Herbart. The practical spirit of the period was illustrated by
the many energetic efforts to diffuse musical knowledge and
enlarge popular education in it by various pedagogical plans,
like those of Logier and Galin, aiming sometimes at the improvement of teaching in music-schools, sometimes at a promotion of
song as a part of general education. The number of pedagogical books for the voice and for various instruments becomes bewildering, implying not only a widespread conviction of the
value of discipline and system, but a progressing popular demand
for instruction. Though no striking general work on musical
history was put forth, a goodly number of special studies in
various directions, particularly biography, attest the advance of
the historical spirit. Criticism for the time being was but
slightly represented. In Germany an awakening of interest in
the management of church services evoked many articles and
small brochures upon the treatment of sacred music. The founding of musical periodicals and of publishing houses went on
more or less everywhere.

In the following summaries only such names are included as fall more or less completely within the period 1800–30. Many writers who continued active later are elsewhere mentioned (see secs. 227–228).

The discussion of acoustical questions naturally connected itself with musical theory and æsthetics, though also pursued as a part of pure physics. The chief acousticians of the time were **Chladni** (d. 1827), already mentioned (see sec. 165), and **Savart**.

Félix Savart (d. 1841), trained as a mechanician and surgeon, about 1815 began careful studies in sound, and about 1820 was made professor of acoustics at the Collége de France. The brilliance of his researches in every branch of the subject was made known through many technical papers in the *Annales de physique et de chimie*. They decidedly influenced the scientific construction of instruments, especially those of the wind class. His demonstrations, appliances and ascertained laws are still everywhere used. In 1819, just after Savart began his work, **Charles Cagniard de la Tour** (d. 1859) perfected the improved 'sirène,' which is used in determining the vibration-numbers of tones.

Other acoustical publications were made by **Georges Marie Raymond** (d. 1839) upon the physical basis of music (1813); by **Gottfried Weber** (d. 1839), the eminent theorist, on wind and stringed instruments (from 1816); by **Ernst Heinrich Weber** (d. 1878), professor at Leipsic, on physiological acoustics (from 1820); by **Ernst Gottfried Fischer** (d. 1831), professor at Berlin, on the vibrations of strings, etc. (from 1825); and, most notably, by **Johann Heinrich Scheibler** (d. 1838), in the silk business at Crefeld, who from 1834 made important studies in tuning, invented a remarkably accurate series of standard forks, and advocated the so-called 'Stuttgart pitch' (a = 440, c = 528), as against Sauveur's pitch (c = $512 = 2^9$).

Among the writers upon æsthetics were the critic **Rochlitz** of Leipsic (d. 1842), in some early essays (1796); the oriental scholar **Guillaume André Villoteau** (d. 1839), in comparisons of music with other arts (1807); **Johann Gottlieb Wendt** (d. 1836), professor at Göttingen, with several essays (from 1808); **Ignaz Franz Mosel** of Vienna (d. 1844), in a work on dramatic style (1813); the celebrated professor at Göttingen, **Johann Friedrich Herbart** (d. 1841), who approached the subject from both the psychological and philosophical sides (1811, '24–5, '31); **Friedrich Konrad Griepenkerl** of Brunswick (d. 1849), a follower of Herbart (1827); **Wilhelm Christian Müller** (d. 1831) of Bremen (1830); the bibliographer **Lichtenthal** (d. 1853) of Milan (1831); and **Karl Christian Friedrich Krause** (d. 1832) of Munich (posthumous).

From the multitude of writers on theory only a selection can be made, including those who either displayed real mastery or acquired popular influence.

The only striking Italian theorist (except Cherubini) was **Bonifazio Asioli** (d. 1832), who from before 1780 was famous as a precocious sacred composer, as a remarkable piano-virtuoso and (from 1785) as a popular opera-writer, and who, having come to Milan in 1799 as court-choirmaster, from 1808 was professor of composition at the new conservatory, retiring in 1814 to Correggio.

He was very prolific in works for the church, and in other vocal and instrumental pieces, and produced 7 operas, an oratorio and many cantatas ; but
he is best known for lucid and able text-books (from 1809), treating not only
of harmony and composition, but of singing, the piano, the clarinet, the double-
bass, etc.

The French line of theorists includes these : —

Charles Simon Catel (d. 1830), already referred to as an opera-writer (see
sec. 177), who was the first professor of harmony in the Conservatoire (from
1795). His text-book (1802) was used there until about 1820. He was the
first French authority to give up the imperfect theory of Rameau and to regard chords as built up normally in thirds, the type-forms being derived from
the harmonics of the dominant. **Jérome Joseph Momigny** (d. 1838), from
1800 a music-publisher in Paris, advocated a system like Catel's, though justi-
fied by different reasoning and put forward with needless conceit (several books,
1806-34). He made the first clear statement of the doctrine of measure,
phrase and period.

Anton Reicha (d. 1836) was born at Prague in 1770 and was brought up
by an uncle there and at Bonn. From 1788 he was a flutist in the Bonn
orchestra (with Beethoven) and undertook orchestral composition. From
1794 he taught at Hamburg and in 1799 went to Paris with operatic aspirations.
From 1802 he was in Vienna, on familiar terms with Beethoven and other
leading musicians. In 1808 he returned to Paris and now had some success
with operas. But he won his place chiefly as a teacher and a writer of orchestral and chamber works. In 1818 he followed Méhul as professor of counterpoint at the Conservatoire. He published an extended treatise (1824-6) and
several other theoretical works (from 1814). He had the faculty of clear presentation, and his writings long commanded respect. His principal power as a
composer lay in chamber music (over 100 works), much of which is highly
esteemed. He was also a fine pianist and the ambitious writer of sonatas,
fugues, études and variations.

Luigi Cherubini (d. 1842), the many-sided composer (see secs. 154, 163,
184), professor at the Conservatoire from 1816, was recognized as the most
powerful contrapuntist of his day. He transmitted his learning to many pupils,
and late in life (1835), assisted by Halévy, published a famous treatise on
counterpoint that is a classic. He had rare gifts in combining richness of
structure with clarity and beauty, and his varied experience gave him a remarkable breadth of style and sympathy.

Gottfried Weber (d. 1839), a prominent lawyer, from 1802 at Mannheim,
from 1814 at Mayence and from 1818 at Darmstadt, was an enthusiastic musical
student and organizer. Through a diligent use of authorities, like Kirnberger
and Knecht, he elaborated a compendium of composition (3 vols., 1817-21),
which was the most important German text-book of the period and remained
useful long after. It contained the first use of certain symbols (letters and
numerals) for designating chords which are still common. He published
other theoretical manuals (1822, '33) and wrote much for periodicals, especially
for *Cäcilia*, a magazine which he edited at Mayence from 1824 till his death.
He composed considerable vocal music, sacred and secular.

Works of less importance were issued in 1801 by **Pietro Gianelli** of Venice (d. 1822?); in 1802-29 by **Antonio Calegari** of Padua (d. 1828), whose early ideas were extremely mechanical; from 1812 by **William Crotch** of Oxford (d. 1847); from 1815-6 by **Johann Heinrich Göroldt** of Quedlinburg (d. after 1835); in 1818-9 by **J. G. Werner** of Merseburg (d. 1822); in 1820 by **Friedrich Schneider** of Leipsic and Dessau (d. 1853); in 1820-4 by the Portuguese **Rodrigo Ferreira da Costa** (d. 1825); from 1826 by **August Swoboda** of Vienna; in 1827 (ed. by Seyfried) by **Joseph Preindl** of Vienna (d. 1823); from 1828 by **Dionys Weber** of Prague (d. 1842); about 1830 on instrumentation by **Giuseppe Pilotti** of Bologna (d. 1838); in 1830 by **Daniel Jelensperger** of Paris (d. 1831); in 1830-2 by **Domenico Quadri** of Milan and Naples (d. 1843); and in 1834 by **Victor Dourlen** of Paris (d. 1864), a follower of Catel.

On rhythm and metre there were several notable discussions, as from 1796 by the Leipsic professor **Johann Gottfried Jakob Hermann** (d. 1848); from 1807 by **Johann August Apel** (d. 1816), also of Leipsic, who strongly opposed Hermann's views; and in 1821 by **August Böckh** of Berlin (d. 1867).

In the field of history, the only apparently comprehensive work was one in 1819 (2 vols.) by the London organist **Thomas Busby** (d. 1838), which was neither original nor well-ordered. More important were monographs on special topics, as in 1799 on music in Bremen by **W. C. Müller** (d. 1831); in 1804-7 on ancient and modern music in the Orient by **G. A. Villoteau** (d. 1839), who went with Napoleon's Egyptian expedition in 1798; in 1810 on contrasts between ancient and modern styles by **Joubert de La Salette** (d. 1832), who also wrote on notation; in 1817 on the Thomasschule in Leipsic by **Friedrich Wilhelm Ehrenfried Rost** (d. 1835); in 1818 on the half-century of music in Vienna and in 1835 on the Royal Library there by **J. F. Mosel** (d. 1844); in 1821 on the mediæval modes by the Moravian **Peter Mortimer** (d. 1828); in 1824 on notation systems by **G. M. Raymond** (d. 1839); in 1827-32 an able series of articles on topics in ancient and mediæval music by **François Louis Perne** (d. 1832), who in 1818 succeeded Catel at the Paris Conservatoire; in 1829 on the rise of the chorale by **Johann Friedrich Naue** (d. 1858), organist at Halle; in 1829-32 on Gregorian music and on the organ by **Franz Joseph Antony** (d. 1837), organist at Münster; and in 1831-2 some notes by **Georg Christoph Grosheim** (d. 1847).

Contemporaneous Italian music was discussed in 1811 by the Venetian **Giovanni Agostino Perotti** (d. 1855); in 1822 (2 vols.) by the Russian **Gregor Wladimir Orlow** (d. 1826); and again in 1836 by the Viennese **Franz Sales Kandler** (d. 1831). The problem of Mozart's *Requiem* was opened soon after 1820 by **Gottfried Weber** (d. 1839), to whom replies were made in 1826-7 by **Stadler** (d. 1833) and **Mosel**.

Criticism mingled with history was represented by various keen articles (from 1810), by **E. T. A. Hoffmann** (d. 1822); by the valuable miscellanies *Für Freunde der Tonkunst* (4 vols., 1824-32) of the Leipsic editor **Johann Friedrich Rochlitz** (d. 1842), which are specially strong upon vocal music; and by the famous essays *Ueber Reinheit der Tonkunst* (1825) of the Heidelberg professor **Anton Friedrich Justus Thibaut** (d. 1840), which latter were attacked (1826) by the Swiss publisher **Hans Georg Nägeli** (d. 1836).

In the field of biography, the more important monographs were those on Guido (1811) by Luigi Angeloni (d. 1842); on Salieri (1827) by I. F. Mosel (d. 1844); on Mozart (1828) by Georg Nicolaus von Nissen (d. 1826) and his wife (Mozart's widow); on Palestrina (1828) by Giuseppe Baini (d. 1844), which was revised in German (1834) by F. S. Kandler (d. 1831), who had previously (1820) written on Hasse; and on Beethoven (1838) by Ferdinand Ries (d. 1838).

Sketches and studies of varying value included many on Haydn (from 1810), as by Georg August Griesinger (d. 1828), Albert Dies (d. 1822) and Giuseppe Carpani (d. 1825); a series (1803-10) on various composers before and after 1800 by Ignaz Ferdinand Arnold (d. 1812); two books (1810, '30) on sundry violinists from Corelli to Paganini by François Fayolle (d. 1852); accounts of Grétry (1814) and Viotti (1825) by the violinist Baillot (d. 1842); eulogies on Paisiello, Monsigny and Méhul (1817-9, collected with others, 1834-7) by Antoine Chrysostome Quatremère de Quincy (d. 1849); and a long line of critiques of Rossini (from 1818) by Carpani (d. 1825), Joseph Louis d'Ortigue (d. 1866), Johann Gottlieb Wendt (d. 1836) and others, including the celebrated plagiarist 'Stendhal' (d. 1842). The singer Mara was treated (1823) by Grosheim (d. 1847); and Malibran (1836) by Isaac Nathan (d. 1864).

Autobiographies appeared in 1830 (2 vols.) by the singing-master Jacopo Gotifredo Ferrari (d. 1842), in 1833 by the organist Rinck (d. 1846), and in 1834 by the singer Blangini (d. 1841).

General works of the dictionary class were published in 1786 (much enlarged after 1800) by Thomas Busby (d. 1838); in 1801 (3 vols., much enlarged, 1820) by Pietro Gianelli (d. 1822?); in 1810-11 (2 vols.) by Fayolle and Choron; in 1814-15 (4 vols.) by Giuseppe Bertini (d. after 1847); and in 1812 (incomplete) by Franz Xaver Glöggl (d. 1839).

More significant were a Bohemian *Künstlerlexikon* (3 vols., 1815-8) by Gottfried Johann Dlabacz (d. 1820), embodying materials collected since about 1785; the scholarly encyclopædia and bibliography (4 vols., 1826) by Peter Lichtenthal (d. 1853); and a trade-list of books, etc. (from 1817) by Carl Friedrich Whistling, which was later extended by others.

Among the collections of folk-song material may be named for Wales those of the clarinettist and critic John Parry (d. 1851) in 1810 and after; for Sweden that of Erik Gustaf Geijer (d. 1847) and Arvid August Afzelius (d. 1871) in 1814-6 (3 vols.); and for Galicia that of the violinist Lipinski (d. 1861) in 1834.

Persistent efforts were made for ten years from 1812 to establish a strong musical periodical at Vienna, but without permanent result. In 1824 Gottfried Weber (d. 1839) founded his *Cäcilia* at Mayence and carried it on with incredible industry for fifteen years; in 1842-8 it was continued by Dehn. Valuable influence was exerted during 1824-30 by the *Berliner allgemeine musikalische Zeitung*, edited by Marx (d. 1866). The *Eutonia* of Breslau and Berlin, devoted to music in schools, lasted nine years, 1828-37. In France the *Revue musicale* of Fétis (d. 1871) began in 1827; in 1834 it was merged with another venture into the *Revue et gazette musicale*, which was continued ably until 1880.

In England the initial periodical was the *Quarterly Musical Magazine*, founded in 1818 by Richard Mackenzie Bacon (d. 1844), which appeared until 1829. In 1823 William Ayrton (d. 1858), a London teacher and critic, founded the *Harmonicon*, which also persisted for about a decade.

Fortunato Santini (d. 1862), a Roman abbé and organist, about 1800 became famous as a collector and copyist of rare and valuable scores, accumulating by indefatigable research at least 1000 works representing every period, of which he issued a catalogue (1820). Many of his copies were unique, because scored from detached parts found at different places. He himself composed worthily in strict style, and was also active in making German music and musicians known in Italy.

In Germany important libraries were collected by **Georg Pölchau** of Berlin (d. 1836), which became the nucleus of the music section of the Royal Library, and by **A. F. J. Thibaut** of Heidelberg (d. 1840), the latter being peculiarly rich in folk-music.

A sure evidence of the increasing popular interest in music was the growth of the business of publishing and selling music. The early decades of the century saw the founding of many houses that have since acquired international fame. Thus at Berlin the house of **Schlesinger** was started in 1795, and that of **Trautwein** in 1820. In Leipsic the firm of **Peters** was developed in 1814 out of an earlier enterprise. In Hamburg the house of **Cranz** was founded in 1813, and that of **Schuberth** in 1826, with a Leipsic branch from 1832. In Vienna **Antonio Diabelli** (d. 1858), a pupil of Michael Haydn, in 1824 formed the firm known by his name; similarly **Tobias Haslinger** (d. 1842), a pupil of Glöggl, after many years as a subordinate, in 1826 was advanced to proprietorship. At Milan the now famous house of **Ricordi** began in 1808 very modestly under Giovanni Ricordi (d. 1853), who had studied engraving at Leipsic. At Paris the firm of **Richault** was established in 1805, and that of **Schlesinger** in 1823 by the eldest son of the Berlin publisher. In London the great business of **Novello** had its start in 1811 under Vincent Novello (d. 1861), a good composer and editor of sacred music, with which in 1867 was united that of **Ewer**, founded in 1820; that of **Chappell** in 1812; that of **Boosey** in 1816; and that of **Cocks** in 1823.

188. Summary of the Period. — The first third of the 19th century had close connections with both the period before and the period following. It witnessed the crowning achievements of the Viennese school which began under Haydn, and was therefore the time when the 'classical' movement attained its strongest expression. But it was also the birth-time of the 'romantic' movement, the most characteristic embodiments of which were to start from other centres than Vienna. In some sense the former movement was expressive of the general spirit of the 18th century, while the latter was equally expressive of that of the 19th. But it may also be said that the 'classical' attention to form and method was a necessary stage in artistic development, a stage that was indispensable before the 'romantic' exaltation of personal mood and fancy could proceed with freedom. The earlier emphasis was not so much the result of an age of formalism and externality as an instinctive attempt to master the mechanism of artistic embodiment, without which free creation cannot be confident and sure.

Broadly judged, the period seems most notable for its fruitfulness in instrumental writing, being in this respect the direct consequent of the Haydn-Mozart age. For both the piano and the orchestral ensemble, large and small, Beethoven stands out as altogether the most powerful and prophetic genius, his greatness being so impressive that it dominates the picture of the whole period. The vocal productions of the time have proved less enduring save only in the case of Schubert's songs and Löwe's earlier ballades, but these represented an artistic movement as yet not widespread. There were, of course, several lines of operatic enterprise in vigorous operation, but none of these, not even the brilliant innovations of Weber, can be said to have acquired definite directive influence before 1830. The various types of opera, however, were plainly struggling toward new ideals, so that the way was being prepared for fresh constructive advance. Sacred music was probably less important than in any previous age, even the limited revival of German organ music lacking in creative vigor.

The musical world at this juncture was somewhat full of startling contrasts. At precisely the same time, and sometimes side by side in the same place, diverse types of art and artists competed for attention and applause. It is hard to conceive, for example, of a more glaring antithesis than that between the gigantic and passionately serious spirit of Beethoven and the heartless sensationalism of Rossini. Various other pairs of contemporaries are almost equally impossible to classify together — such as Rinck and Paganini, to take a somewhat bizarre instance. The coincident vogue of styles so divergent as the French opéra comique, the new German romantic opera and the more flamboyant of Italian works commands a degree of wonder. The local juxtaposition of Beethoven and Schubert at Vienna, almost without personal contact, or of Weber and Morlacchi at Dresden, or of Cherubini and Spontini at Paris, stimulates inquiry and surprise. The truth seems to be that the musical world was awaking to a new breadth of activity, was putting forth energy in many directions at once, and was passing through a time when no one influence was generally recognized as dominant enough to serve as a unifying centre.

Yet it is clear that in this period certain lines of effort were pushing into significant importance. One of these was the development of piano technique, especially under the influence of Clementi and his followers. Here preparation was being made for the epochal achievements of a series of pianistic masters in the next period. Another was the discovery of how to make free application of the orchestra to the portrayal of emotion and passion in dramatic connections, especially exemplified by the gifted Weber. This plainly foreshadowed not only the interesting later growth of the historical opera, but also the extraordinary innovations of Wagner. Still another was the uncovering of the hidden resources of the song as a medium of intimate self-expression, accomplished chiefly through the unconscious and unostentatious impulse of Schubert. Out of this grew immediately an efflorescence of song-writing that gave fragrance and beauty to the whole field of musical art, reacting upon instrumental style as well as vocal.

In the matter of tools, the practical completion of the piano was an event of capital importance, providing an instrument remarkably efficient for both private and public use. The steps in the process of improvement were taken so gradually that their full value was not at once seen. Certainly the perfected piano, with its iron frame, its steel strings and its extremely powerful and responsive action, supplied to the next period an implement of performance of which the 18th century could hardly have more than dreamed.

On the sides of theory, research and pedagogy this period should not be treated apart from that which followed (see secs. 225–228). We may simply note that here began the shaping of the modern doctrine of harmony, the scholarly investigation of many questions of æsthetic, critical or historical importance, the organization of several of the many influential conservatories, the better systemization of instruction in technical

2 K

branches, and the first definite experiments with music as a topic of public school instruction.

Throughout the 18th century the profession of music acquired social status most often through the favor of courts and of wealthy or titled patrons. From the opening of the 19th, this dependent and somewhat servile relation gradually became less typical. Music was working toward independence, so that it might appeal to public respect not simply as an appendage of a luxurious or privileged class, but as one of the aspects of general popular culture.

PART VIII

THE MIDDLE NINETEENTH CENTURY

PART VIII

THE MIDDLE NINETEENTH CENTURY

CHAPTER XXX

SCHUMANN AND ROMANTICISM

189. General Survey. — The middle third of the 19th century is often designated as the 'romantic' period, since in it worked several of the strongest exponents of the romantic movement as applied to music, and since the trend of all composition was consciously or unconsciously away from studied adherence to 'classical' practice. That romanticism should take hold upon musical art was inevitable in an age when individuality was for the first time claiming its rights on the largest scale, but it is also true that music could not further advance without becoming much more romantic than it had been. Its very nature as an art forbade its being always confined within the limitations of academic æsthetics. Romanticism in music was no new discovery with the period here considered. Certainly much of the best work of the preceding period had been emphatically romantic in spirit and style, and truly romantic qualities may be traced more or less in still earlier periods. Yet in the mental attitude of an original critic and leader like Schumann and in a type of genius like Chopin's, for example, we encounter an intensity of romantic warmth that is new. Beginning about 1830, there were so many musicians that were moved by this spirit that they gave to their time a peculiar quality that may well be distinguished from that of any preceding time.

In the fine arts generally, 'classical' and 'romantic' are terms whose meaning is largely relative to each other. But they also have a certain amount of absolute meaning. Both may refer either to the spirit or purpose with which the artist approaches his work or to the formal qualities of the work itself.

The aim in classical art is to realize an ideal beauty which is not necessarily attached to the artist's personality and has significance somewhat as a universal type. Works in the classical spirit are objectively beautiful, commending themselves even when the percipient regards them as if they were simply impersonal *things*. The production of classical art is apt to be largely governed by rules or formulæ, the observance of which constitutes a sort of artistic ritual, so that it not seldom becomes academic and even mechanical. Its products are generally marked by qualities like clarity, symmetry, restraint, repose, and a finish of detail that is as nearly as possible final.

The aim of romantic art, on the other hand, is to present some product of imagination or depiction of mood or other embodiment of personality, which is unusual in character or intensity, and the beauty of which largely inheres in the emotion felt over it by the artist and by the sympathetic observer. Works in the romantic spirit, therefore, are subjectively beautiful, impressive more or less in proportion as they are consciously felt to be personal and intimate, involving a high degree of imaginative or sensitive sympathy. The production of romantic art is distinctly impatient of rules and models, since in it individuality is always exalted. Hence its products escape all simple classification, and sometimes run to extremes of obscurity, irregularity, whimsicality, passion, and to a choice of topic or treatment that is a surprise or a challenge.

The rise of romanticism in music was undoubtedly stimulated by literary romanticism, a movement which affected leading countries of Europe in different ways and not exactly at the same time, but which was at its height in Germany and France about 1830 and after. But literary romanticism made much of a choice of topics distant from common experience — a feature inapplicable to music except in the opera. A broader statement is that all romanticism is an attempt to get away from the typical to the peculiar, from the conventional to the picturesque, and is really a phase of the modern desire to exalt the individual in his tastes, fancies, moods and experiences. This at least is true of musical romanticism. The movement toward a fuller recognition of individual rights had long been gathering strength, and, beginning with the French Revolution of 1792, it forced the progressive reconstruction of European politics and society. The process was most conspicuous in the manifold and severe upheavals in government that filled the middle of the century with ferment, disorder and war. But it declared itself as well in a novel independence and enterprise in every domain of thought and science.

In the political world France still held the centre of the stage, though, in the delicate balance of European affairs, more as an occasion or initiative of disturbance than as an arbiter. The French Revolutions of 1830, which brought in Louis Philippe as ' citizen-king,' and of 1848, which drove him out, were signals for complicated outbreaks elsewhere, all tending to assert the rights of the people at large, or of subject states, to self-government. Thus, after 1830, Poland made a fierce, but unsuccessful, effort to throw off the tyranny of Russia, while in England a series of

drastic reforms were enacted by legislation.   After 1848, a fever of revolution spread through central Europe.   In self-defense the ruling powers
drew together in coalitions, but in so doing were obliged to grant popular guarantees, such as the Prussian Constitution of 1850.   Every royal
house felt in danger and strove to repress republican and socialistic
demands.   Among the greater states, Prussia pushed steadily to the
front, while Austria tightened her grip on Hungary and Italy in spite of
fiery patriotic revolts.   In 1851, by the famous 'Coup d'État,' the new
French Empire was set up under Napoleon III.   In 1853-6 occurred the
exhausting Crimean War, fought by England and France in defense of
Turkey against Russia.   In 1859 France and Austria clashed over Italy.
In 1866 Prussia made the triumphant display of strength against Austria
which began the consolidation of Germany.   Upon the heels of this
came the Franco-Prussian War of 1870-1, which united all Germany into
an Empire.   These last two wars indirectly led to the freedom and union
of Italy in 1871.   Meanwhile the British Empire was steadily advancing
in power, especially because of its great colonial possessions in India,
Canada and Australia.   And the United States was gradually acquiring
its present vast territory, being finally consolidated by the bloody Civil
War of 1861-5.

The principal rulers of the period were, in France, Louis Philippe
(1830-48) and Napoleon III. (1852-70) ; in Prussia, Frederick William
IV. (1840-61) and William I. (1861-88, Emperor from 1871); in
Austria, Ferdinand I. (1835-48) and Francis Joseph (1848-   );
in England, William IV. (1830-7) and Victoria (1837-1901) ; and in
Russia, Nicholas I. (1825-55) and Alexander II. (1855-81).

The period in music was not dominated by a single composer
as the preceding period had been by Beethoven.   Yet several
leaders appeared whose closeness of practical touch was even
greater than Beethoven's.   Among these was Meyerbeer, who
for a time continued to be the central figure in the operatic field.
Outside of this field, but potent in every other, was the indefatigable and versatile Mendelssohn, especially notable for his services to the cause of musical education.   In the domain of
criticism and especially as the spokesman of the romantic spirit
in the best sense, Schumann held a unique position, besides
being an original composer of marked power.   From about
1840 the immense vigor and genial magnetism of Liszt advanced
him into a sort of imperial leadership, which, however, he was
magnanimous enough gradually to transfer to Wagner, the time
of whose greatest public power did not arrive until after 1860.
Still more than in any previous period, the eminence of Germany
declared itself, though as the period closed it was evident that
other countries were awaking to new musical life.

190. The Career of Schumann. — Although at the outset of the period Schumann was an unknown quantity, the rapidity of his development and his work both as critic and as composer revealed him as a significant romantic force.   Hence, though with some distortion of chronological truth, he may well be cited at once as an exponent of the spirit of the time.

In him, as in his close contemporary Mendelssohn, came out, as never before, the value of general culture in union with musical genius.   His mind was broadly educated and his outlook upon music was not simply that of the executive artist.   He had gifts as an original thinker and a forcible writer.   His location at Leipsic put him in touch with the intellectual movements of the age.   Though his work as composer was late in maturing, was imperfect in detail, and was not at once appreciated, he yet represented his time in important regards.   He now seems to have been greater than his contemporaries knew.   At all events, he merits careful consideration as a noble illustration of what was happening in the musical world.

Robert Schumann (d. 1856) was born in 1810 at Zwickau, a Saxon manufacturing town, the son of a bookseller, author and translator, his mother being a doctor's daughter, hardly her husband's equal in culture.   From his father he derived a strong taste for reading, skill in writing and a useful knowledge of the book-trade.   From his mother came a marked sensibility and sentimentality, which showed itself in all the five children, of whom he was the youngest, and developed in them all into some degree of mental unbalance.   His early education was desultory.   He was extremely vivacious, a universal favorite and a leader among his fellows.   At 7 he had already shown musical aptitude, liberally fostered by his father.   Before he was 12 he had read much music, had organized a school-boy orchestra, had essayed composition, and was locally noted as a pianist, though he had had no good instruction. About 14 his character suddenly changed to decided dreaminess and reticence. He became a devotee of the mystic writer Richter ('Jean Paul') and indulged in much imaginative fantasy.   At 16 he lost his father, and his mother determined to make him a lawyer.   She sent him to Leipsic to study, but there he became so much engaged in music, with lessons from the sterling teacher Wieck, with eager enthusiasm for Schubert's works, and with some social vogue as an improviser, that at 20 he was transferred to Heidelberg and then sent on a trip to Italy.   At length, however, what he humorously called 'the twenty-years' war' ended in his mother's consent that he should take music as a life-work.

In 1830 he returned to Leipsic, and sought under Wieck and other teachers to repair the defects of his early training.   His initial ambition was to become a piano-virtuoso, and he began such strenuous practice, aided by a device to

free the fourth finger, that presently he permanently crippled his right hand.
He then turned to composition, at first wholly for the piano, and plunged into
arduous technical discipline under Dorn. He also soon appeared as a critic,
writing a florid article in 1831 about
Chopin, then just becoming known at
Paris. He drew about him a group of
enthusiasts whose purpose was to oppose 'Philistinism' in music (whatever
they felt was commonplace, academic,
dry), and whom he hence dubbed the
'Davidsbund.' So urgent was his activity that in 1834, in company with
two or three others, he founded the
Neue Zeitschrift für Musik as the
organ of advanced ideas, continuing
as its editor till 1844 and as a contributor still longer. Through this journal his vigorous, fearless and broad-
minded attitude became manifest and
influential. In 1835 Mendelssohn came
to Leipsic, and he and Schumann were
intimate, Schumann, at least, with the

most cordial appreciation. In 1836 began his romantic courtship of Clara
Wieck, then 17 years old, whom he knew intimately because living in the
Wieck household. She was already a pianist of the first rank, and was coming into a beautiful and noble womanhood. Her father opposed the match
because uncertain of Schumann's prospects, and only in 1840 was compelled
by legal pressure to give his consent. Meanwhile, in 1838–9, Schumann
spent most of a year at Vienna, hoping to find there a better opening for his
Zeitschrift, and incidentally unearthing many of Schubert's neglected scores.
During these years his creative faculty became more evident and his piano-
works grew in variety and power. From 1840, the year of his marriage, for
several years he put forth his full energy as a composer. In that year he was
chiefly occupied upon some 150 songs, in 1841 upon orchestral composition,
in 1842 upon chamber works, and in 1843 upon the first of his larger vocal
works. In 1843, when Mendelssohn organized the Leipsic conservatory,
Schumann was one of the original faculty, teaching piano and composition,
though greatly hampered by his extreme reticence. Until 1844 his life was so
absorbed in study as to be almost devoid of public incident. He was seldom
away from Leipsic, but early in 1844 he and his wife made a brilliant tour to
Russia.

The mental strain of ten years of intense application now brought on a
nervous breakdown, and in the fall of 1844 Schumann moved to Dresden, where
he gradually recovered. Here he was thrown into intimacy with Hiller and
somewhat with Wagner. He was able by degrees to resume even extended
composition, including in 1848 the opera *Genoveva* (not given till 1850) and
his *Faust* music (given in 1849 on the centenary of Goethe's birth). Especially from 1849 for a period his ability to work returned in full. From 1847

he succeeded Hiller as conductor of a male chorus and later of a small mixed chorus, writing somewhat for both. In 1850 he was made director at Düsseldorf, again in succession to Hiller. Though he and his wife were received with enthusiasm and he began his work with high hope, his strength was unequal to the task and his methods were so ineffective that late in 1853 he was virtually displaced. He continued active, however, in composition in various forms, and made some artistic trips with his wife. Thus, for example, they were twice welcomed with acclaim in Holland, and in March, 1852, a cycle of his works was given in Leipsic. But from about 1852 he was increasingly subject to attacks of extreme mental depression, combined with startling vagaries of fancy and auditory illusions. Early in 1854, at Düsseldorf, he one day stole away from his home and threw himself into the Rhine, but was rescued by some boatmen. It was now clear that his mind had permanently given way, and he was cared for in a private asylum at Endenich (near Bonn) until his death in 1856. He was buried at Bonn, where in 1880 a statue was erected in his honor.

His sincere and kindly nature revealed itself in his frank and noble face. Though usually extremely silent, especially with strangers, he was keenly observant and almost clairvoyant in his estimation of character. At home and among his few intimates he was often bright and witty. Every one felt the guileless exaltation of his personality and the vigorous independence of his intellect. He was respected even where he was but partially understood. In writing he expressed himself with wonderful freedom and force, as his many letters and critical works show. This literary gift, joined with his fertility as a composer, made him known far better than he could ever be through speech. He was greatly drawn to young people, especially if they had aspirations, and he detected the promise of artistic achievement with amazing accuracy and sympathy. He was entirely free from jealousy or envy, but had a proper sense of his own dignity and power. His family life with his devoted wife and his five children was in every way ideal.

191. His Work as Composer. — Schumann began his active musical career somewhat late and without thorough discipline. Hence, as his life was short and at the end broken by physical disability, his creative period was hardly more than fifteen years (1832–51, with breaks after 1844). Hence, too, he was obliged to make up defects in training by the most concentrated study. Only a mind of great endowments could have accomplished so much in this short time.

From the outset his style showed rare originality and fullness. He was often careless about exact form, seemed to be trying experiments with patterns, harmonies and styles, and was not always perfectly at home in the idioms of expression. Some of his works are over-crowded with matter and over-strenuous in treatment. His marked tempi and his other indications of expression often seem extreme. Yet in spite of all drawbacks, the affluence of ideas, the impetuosity of sentiment, the variety of imaginative suggestion, and the positive beauty of conception are on the whole most impressive, especially when considered in relation to the time in which they appeared. Into the circle of precisians and pedants Schumann came as a thorough revolutionist, but his purpose was not destructive or unsympathetic with the past. He simply sought to widen the range of musical utterance in the direction of vivid personal revelation. In this he resembled Beethoven, though he lacked Beethoven's instinct for style, depth of pathetic experience and ecstatic ideality. Schumann's strenuousness was not that born of pain, but the voice of restless mental energy. It is not strange that the full sense of his greatness came slowly and has not been universal among music-lovers. Yet he is a foremost illustration of the connection of modern music with the spirit of modern life — versatile, eager and full of vitality.

Schumann's compositions belong to almost every principal class except church music. It is impossible to classify them briefly, since many of the most characteristic are extremely varied and novel in form. For the piano alone may be cited the *Papillons* (1831), a toccata (1833), the *Études symphoniques* (1834), the *Carnaval* (1835), 3 sonatas (1835–8), the *Novelletten* (1838), a concerto (1841–5), considerable 4-hand work, including the *Bilder aus Osten* (1848), and a multitude of characteristic pieces of every kind; for the piano with strings, the *Fantasiestücke* (1842), a quartet and quintet (1842), 3 trios (1847–51), many pieces for a solo instrument with piano (1849), 2 violin-sonatas (1851), and some other chamber works; for orchestra, 4 symphonies, from the 'Spring' (1841) to the 'Rhenish' (1850), one other symphonic work, and 4 concert-overtures (1850–3); the opera *Genoveva* (1848), and many scenes for *Faust* (1844–50) and for *Manfred* (1848); the cantatas *Das Paradies und die Peri* (1843), *Adventlied* (1848), *Nachtlied* (1849), *Neujahrslied* (1850), *Der Rose Pilgerfahrt* (1851), and several choral ballades; many part-songs and choruses; almost 250 songs, many of them arranged in cycles of extreme interest (from 1840). He wrote several series of pieces for children or about them, many that concern nature, many full of the excitement and intrigue of society, many instinct with the warmth of German patriotism, many charged with poetic mysticism — indeed, the circle of sentiments represented is much too large to be described.

In many of the earlier works for the piano there are fictitious names or cabalistic signs attached which are the same that were more freely used in the literary works (see sec. 192).

Schumann's style marks an epoch because in it for the first time, at least on a broad scale, the details of form are not so much derived from established rules or formulæ as freshly generated from the necessities of the idea or sentiment. Form, in short, is made distinctly the servant of imagination, rather than a mould to which imagination must conform. Hence in every direction Schumann enlarged the scope of technical procedure, presenting novel melodic figures and phrase-plans, stretching the processes of harmonic sequence and modulation, devising intricate time-figures (carrying syncopation, for example, to excess), and searching for new colors and contrasts of quality and effect. All this was not the token of technical restlessness, but simply the fruit of exuberant imagination. Schumann's mind was phenomenally sensitive to impressions from persons, scenes and fancies, and for every vivid impression he strove to find a genuine musical expression. The topics that attracted him were amazingly varied, but always of an elevated and noble class. There is a marked absence of the abnormal and morbid. The marks of culture and spiritual distinction are everywhere to be seen. He clearly discerned the possibilities of music as an embodiment of the human spirit in its freest play of fancy, and his own endowments were so ample that he was able to open many new paths into inexhaustible fields of beauty.

On the formal side Schumann's style is strikingly unconnected with that of the Haydn-Mozart period. It presents many points of kinship with both Beethoven and Bach, for both of whom Schumann had the deepest reverence. His relation to them, however, was not imitative, for temperamentally he was diverse from both. He resembled Weber probably more than any preceding master, though his genius was not dramatically, but lyrically, centred.

Among his works those for the piano are the most spontaneous, especially the briefer ones. The interest of compressed, vivid sketches in tone had already been perceived by Field, and the keyboard song and the etherealized dance were being beautifully treated by several, but in emotional picturesqueness Schumann stands alone. In his longer piano-works, however, he belongs with those who were beginning to develop the orchestral capacity of the instrument. All his instrumental writing, though often full of technical difficulty, proceeds less from the technical than the ideal point of view. He does not seek to display the genius of the instrument for its own sake, but to load its tones with general musical significance. The same is true of his handling of vocal effects. In many cases his compression of style is almost extreme.

By common consent the best of his songs, certain of his chamber works and a few for the orchestra are regarded as the strongest utterances in their respective classes in the period following Beethoven and Schubert. In the terse form of tne song, including some works for chorus, his genius was thoroughly at home. Here and in writing for the chamber ensemble, he loved to fill every detail with meaning, so that the entire structure is vital and animated. In consequence, his practice prefigured the most modern type of polyphony — far removed from the old strictness, but for its purposes fully as legitimate. His mastery of orchestral technique and of the conditions of dramatic effect was not complete, yet the wealth of idea, the richness of total conception and the splendor of .color in many movements cannot be denied.

Schumann left hardly any who can be called direct disciples except, perhaps, his wife, though there were several young artists who were closely attached to him and derived much from him. As critic and to some extent as composer he commanded respect, but his peculiarities prevented his moulding pupils after himself, and many of his works acquired standing only gradually. Hence the full impress of his art was not immediate. In bringing to light his real significance no one was more efficient than Madame Schumann, who, as one of the foremost pianists of the period, was able to force public attention to him.

Clara (Wieck) Schumann (d. 1896) was almost ten years her husband's junior, being born at Leipsic in 1819. From her father she received such able training that at 9 she made her début, at 11 appeared at the Gewandhaus, at 13 began touring and at 17 received court-honors at Vienna, soon after also winning great applause at Paris. At 21 (1840) she became Schumann's wife, and during the following years was his devoted companion and inspirer. After 1856 she lived for a time at Berlin and from 1863 at Wiesbaden, finally, t⁀ support herself and her children, resuming public work and in 1878–92 teaching at the Hoch conservatory in Frankfort. Besides her gifts as executant and interpreter, which were widely known in Germany and England, she was talented as a piano-composer and made a deep impression as a noble and forceful artist.

Prominent names usually associated with Schumann are the following : —

Robert Volkmann (d. 1893), born in Saxony in 1815, came to Leipsic in 1836 and learned much from K. F. Becker and Schumann. From 1839 he taught at Prague, and from 1842, except for a sojourn in 1854–8 at Vienna, lived at Pesth, becoming professor of theory at the National Academy and acquiring a considerable Hungarian flavor in his style. His many works, illustrating a strong romanticism, include 2 symphonies, 2 overtures, 3 string-serenades, abundant chamber music, many piano-pieces in various forms, including transcriptions, 2 masses for male voices, considerable other church music, dramatic scenas, songs, etc.

Theodor Kirchner (d. 1903), also a Saxon, born in 1824, was one of the young men in whom Schumann took a lively interest. From 1838 he studied at Leipsic, from 1843 was organist at Winterthur, from 1862 taught in the Zurich conservatory, in 1873–5 was head of the Würzburg conservatory, and from 1875 lived successively at Leipsic, Dresden and Hamburg. He was chiefly a writer for the piano, excelling in brief, imaginative works after Schumann's best pattern, besides some chamber-music and songs.

Woldemar Bargiel (d. 1897), born at Berlin in 1828, had less personal contact with Schumann than the foregoing, but belonged to his group. From about 1850 he taught at Berlin, then in the Cologne conservatory, from 1865 was director of the Music-School at Rotterdam, and from 1874 returned to Berlin, first in the Hochschule and from 1882 as head of the School for Advanced Composition. His powerful works include a symphony, 3 overtures, notable chamber, piano and vocal pieces.

Still other names in the Schumann succession are Julius Otto Grimm (d. 1903), who, after teaching at Göttingen, was from 1860 head of the Cäcilienverein at Münster, writing a symphony, 2 fine string-suites in canon-form, piano-pieces and songs; Albert Dietrich, from 1855 conductor at Bonn and from 1861 court-choirmaster at Oldenburg, writing the opera *Robin Hood* (1879), music to *Imogen* (1891), a striking symphony, several cantatas, chamber and piano music, and songs; and the younger Brahms (d. 1897) and Jensen (d. 1879), who are elsewhere discussed (see secs. 214, 222).

192. His Work as Critic. — Schumann's mental power was nowhere better shown than in his estimates of music and musicians. His spirit was genial and kind, eager to acknowledge merit and to bestow praise. His knowledge and taste had been assiduously developed by study and reflection, so that he was broadly responsive. He made it his business to know the works of many periods and schools. Severe habits of self-discipline gave him fine powers of analysis and a keen sense of perspective. He was ready to weigh the opinions of other critics, if intelligent, but his conclusions were absolutely his own, and, once made, were tenaciously held. As we now look back to them, we marvel that as a rule they were so just and right. He was, of course, eager to welcome every touch of romantic fervor, but was catholic enough to recognize worthy effort in any style. His chief limitation lay in a certain aversion to the operatic styles of his day, which led him not only to condemn the meretricious and vulgar, but to regard with doubt much that might well have roused his interest.

Fully as remarkable as his wisdom in framing critical judgments was his felicity in putting them into words. He knew

how to speak his thought clearly, forcibly, with elegance, often
with brilliant wit, but also with unfailing graciousness, even
when finding fault. His literary impulse led him to an easy
amplitude of style, often full of apt discussion or illustration,
yet nothing is said that is not worth saying. Though he
abounds in quotable apothegms, there is none of the journalist's
eagerness to seem clever. The thrill of imaginative ideality is
seldom absent, and many pages are made charming by the
play of quiet humor.

> In his earlier works the extravagant dialect of Jean Paul and his
> school is much in evidence, but this gradually disappears. For several
> years (from about 1833) he often used the device of introducing imagi-
> nary personages, giving voice to varying views. Some of these, like
> 'Florestan,' 'Eusebius' and 'Meister Raro,' refer to aspects of himself —
> the first standing for his impulsive and fanciful eagerness, the second for
> his quieter and more contemplative thoughtfulness, and the third for his
> cool judgment as between opposing impulses. A variety of other names
> refer to various friends, especially to his colleagues in the *Zeitschrift*
> enterprise and to Clara Wieck. Many of these fictitious names were
> freely used with his shorter piano-works as well as in his literary writings.
>
> Prominent among the composers to whom he gives careful attention
> were the following: — Bach, Beethoven, Schubert, Weber, Field, Berlioz,
> Mendelssohn, Chopin, Liszt, Wagner, Henselt, Heller, Franz, Bennett,
> Gade, Clara Wieck, and (in 1853) Brahms. When one considers how
> rich the period was in the outpouring of musical inspiration, it is easy to
> see what a magnificent field it offered for a truly great critic.

But Schumann's influence extended beyond what is often considered to be the domain of criticism. He recognized the value
of genuine music-history and perceived its large structural outlines. Although not himself a historian by formal publication,
he was thoroughly historical in habit of thought. He had a
fine sense of the large movements of musical art, and of the
relation of composers and styles to them. He had the scholar's
desire for accuracy and willingness to spend time in research.
He did valuable service in bringing to light forgotten works of
Schubert, and he set a pattern in the important task of puri-
fying scores from errors and glosses. He was also pedagogi-
cally wise, and his many aphorisms about the spirit, methods
and objects of music-study have permanent validity and co-
gency. Hence it is safe to call him the first shining example
of truly modern musical scholarship, one whose influence has
been enduring and altogether beneficial.

In founding the *Neue Zeitschrift* in 1834 Schumann's special coad-
jutors were his teacher *Friedrich Wieck* (d. 1873) ; *Julius Knorr* (d.
1861), a Leipsic piano-virtuoso and a teacher of renown ; and *Karl
Banck* (d. 1889), who from 1840 was a singing-teacher at Dresden and a
well-known critic. During the first year Knorr was nominally editor.
In 1835–44, when Schumann was in charge, he was specially assisted by
Konstantin Julius Becker (d. 1859), who from 1843 also taught in
Dresden ; *Ferdinand Präger* (d. 1891), a leading piano-teacher in
London ; *Friedrich Hieronymus Truhn* (d. 1886), then theatre-direc-
tor at Danzig ; and *Ernst Wenzel* (d. 1880), one of the early staff at
the Leipsic conservatory.

In 1844 the editorship passed to *Franz Brendel* (d. 1868), another of
Wieck's pupils, who carried it on for over 20 years in conjunction with
his historical writing. In 1856–60 he was assisted by *Richard Pohl* (d.
1896), then at Weimar, later a powerful writer on behalf of Wagner and
Berlioz ; in 1863–7 by *Heinrich Porges* (d. 1900), later of Munich ;
and from about 1865 by *Hermann Zopff* (d. 1883). Among the contributors during this period, when the Wagner question had become
acute, were the Lutheran pastor *Karl Adolf Tschirch* (d. 1875) ; *A. J.
Rühlmann* (d. 1877), professor in the Dresden conservatory ; the
young opera-writer *Cornelius* (d. 1874), then at Weimar ; *Karl
Emanuel Klitzsch* (d. 1889), cantor at Zwickau ; *Karl Kossmaly* of
Stettin (d. 1893) ; the poet *Peter Lohmann* of Leipsic ; and *Paul
Fischer* (d. 1894), cantor at Zittau. All these, except Kossmaly, were
strong advocates of Wagner and the new school generally.

After 1868, under the régime of *Christian Friedrich Kahnt* (d. 1897),
who had been publisher since 1857, *Zopff* was promoted to be editor,
continuing till his death (1883), assisted for a time by the impulsive *Otto
Reinsdorf* (d. 1890), later of Vienna and Berlin, with contributors like
Jean Schucht (d. 1894), *Friedrich Stade* and *Bernhard Vogel* (d. 1898).

The *Zeitschrift* is the organ of the *Allgemeiner deutscher Musikverein*,
founded in 1859 to promote the newer tendencies in composition.

193. Leipsic as a Literary Centre. — There was good reason
why an intellectual leader like Schumann should have chosen
Leipsic as his fulcrum of influence, for Leipsic throughout the
early and middle 19th century was the chief headquarters both
for the publication of music itself and for the prosecution of
scholarly work about music. Doubtless this musical eminence
arose from the leadership which it had long before secured in
all kinds of literary activity, but it was now accentuated by
several circumstances. Among these may be named the broad
and enterprising policy of the publishers Breitkopf & Härtel,
the location here of the *Allgemeine musikalische Zeitung*, and
the striking conjunction of artistic efforts in the Thomasschule
(with its intimate relation to the city churches), the University,

the Gewandhaus orchestra and finally the brilliant Conservatory
— these together making the city a Mecca for musicians for
many decades.   That Schumann should settle here and found
his new magazine was almost inevitable.   After the mid-point
of the century other cities in Germany became rivals of Leipsic
in influence, but before that time it was plainly the musical
centre for the whole of northern Europe.

The constructive work of *Breitkopf & Härtel* in publishing, often on
an extremely liberal scale, complete, critical editions of the works of great
composers became most striking during the later decades of the century
(not here under review), but the same spirit has always marked their
policy.   The 19th-century development of the firm was due to the energy
of *Gottfried Christoph Härtel* (d. 1827) and his sons and grandsons.
About 1800 the process of printing from soft-metal plates was introduced,
and in 1805 the new process of lithography.   Early examples of extensive
editions issued were the works of Mozart (1798–1816), Haydn (1800–6),
Clementi (1800–18) and Dussek (1814–8).   Foremost among the monumental publications of later years were the works of Bach (1851–96),
followed by those of Handel (vols. 1–18, 1859–64), Mendelssohn, Chopin,
Schumann, Schubert, Palestrina, Schütz, Grétry, Lassus, Sweelinck, Victoria, Gluck, Berlioz, etc.   Besides these, from about 1850 the firm has
been active, with others, in issuing cheap editions of classical works.
As illustrating the importance of Leipsic as a publishing centre, the
following list may be given of the leading houses established there during
the century: — in 1800 the Bureau de Musique of *Hofmeister*, from which
in 1814 branched off the extensive business of *C. F. Peters;* in 1831 the
house of *Kistner* (succeeding to that of *Probst*) ; in 1832 the branch of
Schuberth's Hamburg house; in 1846 those of *Siegel* and *Röder;* in
1850 that of *Senff;* in 1851 that of *Kahnt;* in 1862 those of *Forberg* and
Garbrecht; and in 1866 those of *Fritzsch* and *Seitz.*
The *Allgemeine musikalische Zeitung* (quarterly since 1811) was founded
in 1798 by *Breitkopf & Härtel* and *Johann Friedrich Rochlitz* (d. 1842),
who was editor till 1818 and contributor till 1835.   In 1826–42 the editor
was *Gottfried Wilhelm Fink* (d. 1846); in 1843–4 *Hauptmann* (d.
1868), the cantor at the Thomasschule and professor in the new conservatory; in 1846–8 *Johann Christian Lobe* (d. 1881), a diligent
teacher and composer; in 1868–71 and 1875–82 the indefatigable
Friedrich Chrysander (d. 1901).   Though always more conservative
than the *Neue Zeitschrift*, the *Zeitung* has been a power in musical
scholarship and criticism.
Among many other periodicals, mention may be made of the *Signale
für die musikalische Welt* (weekly), founded in 1843 by *Bartholf Senff*
(d. 1900) and edited by him till his death; the two weeklies, *Die
Sängerhalle* and *Die neue Sängerhalle*, founded in 1861 and 1862 in
connection with the fresh interest in male choruses that led in 1862 to
the organization of the Deutsche Sängerbund out of the previously dis-

connected Liedertafeln — the editor of the former being *Heinrich Pfeil*
(d. 1899), and of the latter for about 10 years the poet *Konrad Müller*
[*von der Werra*] (d. 1881), who was the projector of the Sängerbund;
and the *Musikalisches Wochenblatt*, founded in 1870 by *Oscar Paul* and
Ernst Wilhelm Fritzsch, and conducted by the latter in the interest of
the newest ideas and workers.

The cantorate of the Thomasschule, involving the control of the music
in the four city-churches, was filled by a dignified series of scholars : —
from 1800 by the organist and composer *A. E. Müller* (d. 1817) ; from
1810 by the composer *J. G. Schicht* (d. 1823) ; from 1823 by the excellent theorist *Theodor Weinlig* (d. 1842) ; from 1842 by the greater
theorist *Hauptmann* (d. 1868) ; from 1868 by Hauptmann's colleague
at the conservatory, *E. F. Richter* (d. 1879) ; from 1879 by the conductor, composer and scholar *Wilhelm Rust* (d. 1892) ; and from 1892
by the composer *Gustav Schreck*.

At the University prominent musical directors were from 1842 *Gottfried
Wilhelm Fink* (d. 1846) ; from 1843 (at first as organist) *Hermann
Langer* (d. 1889) ; from 1887 the noted organist, composer and critic
Hermann Kretzschmar ; from 1898 the eminent conductor and composer
Heinrich Zöllner ; and from 1907 *Max Reger*. Among the university
professors who have investigated and published in musical fields
are *C. F. Michaelis* (d. 1834), who wrote on æsthetics and pedagogy from 1795 ; *Johann Gottfried Jakob Hermann* (d. 1848), the
author of important works on metrics from 1796 ; the physiologist
Ernst Heinrich Weber (d. 1878), with works on acoustics from 1820 ;
the medical professor *Karl Ludwig Merkel*, who discussed the apparatus of the voice from 1856 ; the physicist *Gustav Theodor Fechner*
(d. 1887), with works on psycho-physics and æsthetics from 1860 ;
and the prolific and learned *Hugo Riemann*, with discussions of history
and theory from 1878.

In addition, may be mentioned several literary workers not holding
institutional positions, such as from 1825 the organist, historian and
book-collector *Karl Ferdinand Becker* (d. 1877), who left his library to
the city, with his successor in the care of the music section of the City
Library, the critic and editor *Alfred Dörffel* ; for a few years (1847–51)
the great archæologist and biographer *Otto Jahn* (d. 1869), later of
Bonn ; the critic and lexicographer *Eduard Bernsdorf* (d. 1901) ;
from 1866 the historian, theorist and piano-expert *Oscar Paul* (d. 1898) ;
the teacher, lecturer and essayist *Albert Karl Tottmann*, author of a fine
summary of violin and viola music (1873) ; the intelligent editor of
essays *Paul von Waldersee* (d. 1906) ; and from 1880 for some years
the industrious historian, lexicographer and composer *August Reissmann*
(d. 1903), who here completed his lives of Bach, Handel, Gluck and
Weber, and his account of the Opera.

In estimating the importance of Leipsic as a centre, the activity of
the purely artistic workers mentioned later (secs. 195-7) must also be
considered.

CHAPTER XXXI

MENDELSSOHN AND THE LEIPSIC CIRCLE

194. Mendelssohn's Usefulness. — Beginning some years earlier than Schumann, and then continuing side by side with him, ran the picturesque and influential career of Mendelssohn. The vivacity of his genius, his eminent intellectual equipment, and his gifts for social leadership and organization early gave him a commanding position, which he used with zestful earnestness for the advance of artistic culture until cut off in the midst of his years. Like Schumann, he was drawn to Leipsic, and there, as a conductor and teacher, he found ample scope for his irrepressible vitality. His extensive travels had given him a wide reputation. The stream of compositions from his pen was constant and full of charm. Pupils and inquirers came to him from far and wide. His style and his ideas were for a time standard in many circles. Thus he had an opportunity in many respects unique, and he met it with superb élan.

But the quality of his musical impulse was distinctly different from Schumann's. He was poetic and romantic without doubt, but with no such depth of conviction. He was too well poised for strange intensities or daring flights. He had an exquisite sense of form and balance, analogous to Mozart's, and a stronger craving for objective beauty than for subjective expression. Hence he was more inclined than Schumann to cling to the classical patterns of style and to the unpassionate classical spirit. With him commenced a new stage in the classical development, one that was warmed and enriched by a new fullness of feeling, and that sometimes pushed out toward new paths, but which, after all, was more the natural sequel of the past than a starting-point for the future.

For this very reason he performed a real service in his day. Without seeming to oppose the ultra-romantic outreaching after self-declaration and unfettered imagination, he yet compelled attention to the just claims of symmetry, technical finish and outward grace, and of a style that is true to general or ideal humanity as well as to the individual. He unconsciou. ly avoided in his own practice the expression of abnormal and morbid moods, and even drew back from the embodiment of poignant pathos. In his own nature there was a marvelous buoyancy united with hearty religious earnestness, and the fields of composition in which he succeeded best were those in which these were reflected. His technical expertness and flow of creative inspiration were happily adequate to make the expression of these qualities efficient in offsetting tendencies in which they were lacking. And to his personal influence Mendelssohn added the massive and continued power of the several organizations and institutions with which he was identified, so that the effectiveness of his ideas was larger and more lasting than through his work as an individual.

Mendelssohn is also to be remembered, like Handel, for his strong impress upon the progress of music in England. From the first of his eleven trips thither (1829) he was idolized by musicians and public, and became the model upon which for half a century almost all English musicians sought to shape themselves. Although perhaps this fact resulted in a one-sidedness of English style and taste during this period, the sterling value of the influence thus exerted cannot be gainsaid.

Felix Mendelssohn-Bartholdy (d. 1847) came of a wealthy and intellectual Jewish family, which finally adopted Christianity. His grandfather was the famous Moses Mendelssohn (d. 1786), the philosopher, Jewish historian and Biblical student. Both his father and his cultivated mother were identified with Berlin, though at his birth in 1809, the father was a banker at Hamburg. All the circumstances of his youth were extremely stimulating. The parents were deeply interested in training their four children, gave them fine tutors in varied subjects, surrounded them with choice social, literary and artistic influences, and led them early into a symmetrical and ample culture. The eldest child was Fanny (d. 1847), and between her and Felix there was always a peculiar comradeship. They were both precocious musicians, excelling as pianists and composers, besides becoming accomplished in other ways. Felix studied at Berlin under Berger, Zelter and Henning, and was twice taken to Paris for lessons (under Mme. Bigot) or advice (from Cherubini). Before he was 10 he had played in public in a trio, and at 12 was already a methodical and fertile composer for the voice, the piano and other instruments. His father provided expert performers to interpret his larger pieces, but not till he was 16 consented to his taking music as a career. By this time he was already acquainted with many of the ablest musicians of his time. He was a diligent, accurate and versatile student, a finished master of the technique of composition and performance while yet but a boy, and on fire with ambition and inspiration. The analogy often drawn between him and Mozart is close and just, for they both developed with phenomenal rapidity and were strongly akin in stylistic gifts. His training gave him command of a wide range of musical literature, and his prompt enthusiasm for Bach and Beethoven indicated the vigor of his tastes. At 12 he fell under the fascination of Weber, and at 15 received lasting benefit from lessons from Moscheles. The variety of influences that touched him was indescribable, yet without affecting his spontaneity. In 1825 the Mendelssohn family first occupied the extensive mansion and park which became the rendezvous of musical and literary people for many years.

In 1825, when 17, Mendelssohn revealed the charm and strength of his style by the quartet in B minor, the short opera *Die Hochzeit des Camacho* (performed in 1827 under Spontini), and the octet for strings, followed (1826) by the extraordinary *Midsummer Night's Dream* overture — these and many other works of this first period being exquisitely romantic. Though the opera was greeted with applause, it was immediately withdrawn by Spontini, his jealous opposition being the first of many checks to Mendelssohn's ambition that made him strongly dislike Berlin. In 1828, with a few select singers, he began the study of Bach's St. Matthew Passion which led to its triumphant revival by the Singakademie under his leadership exactly a century after its first performance at Leipsic. This achievement, notable as a factor in the general Bach revival, increased the jealousy of many Berlin musicians. Partly because of this, Mendelssohn gave up study at the university and set out upon a long tour, visiting in 1829 London and Scotland, in 1830 Munich, Vienna and all the chief Italian cities, especially Rome, and in 1831 Switzerland, Paris and London again. His activity was incessant and varied, including brilliant appearances as pianist or conductor, constant composition in many forms, from songs to symphonies, much serious study and thoughtful sight-seeing, and abundant social gayety. He thus widened his circle of friends, and enriched his imagination and spirit. As he was returning in 1832, Zelter died and he was pushed forward as a candidate for the leadership of the Singakademie, but was not elected — another source of bitterness toward Berlin. In 1833, however, he conducted the Lower Rhine Festival at Düsseldorf with such éclat that he was forthwith appointed town-musician there. After another trip to England he took up his varied duties with eagerness, though he soon withdrew from the opera-direction. In 1835 he conducted the Lower Rhine Festival at Cologne. Just before this he accepted an invitation to become conductor of the Gewandhaus orchestra at Leipsic.

At Leipsic he found conditions most congenial. The orchestra was already famous, and was now strengthened by the addition of David as concertmaster. There was no professional friction, and the public was enthusiastic. The relief from the coolness of Berlin and the complications at Düsseldorf was most welcome. He plunged ardently into rehearsals and concerts, besides pushing on always with composition. His versatility and endurance were constantly taxed, but his fidelity and zest responded to every call. In 1836, after memorable concerts at Leipsic, he conducted the festival at Düsseldorf, producing the oratorio *St. Paul* (begun in 1832). He also led the Cäcilienverein at Frankfort, where he met Cécile Jeanrenaud, daughter of a Swiss clergyman, to whom in 1837 he was happily married. In 1837 he visited England, conducting *St. Paul* at Birmingham and repeatedly displaying his mastery as an organist, particularly in Bach's works. In spite of labors as organizer and leader, he was constantly adding to his list of great works — the 42d Psalm (1837) and the violin-concerto (1838), for example. In 1839 he gave Schubert's Symphony in C, which Schumann had recovered at Vienna. In 1838 and 1839 he conducted festivals at Cologne and Düsseldorf. In 1840 came the unique *Lobgesang* ('Symphonie-Cantata') and other music at the 400th anniversary of the invention of printing. This he repeated at Birmingham.

In 1829 the University of Berlin had tried in vain to induce him to become professor. In 1840 came an offer from the new king Friedrich Wilhelm IV. to take charge of the music section in a projected Academy of Arts. This he accepted, though with misgiving, and removed to Berlin in 1841. He now received the title of Kapellmeister from both Saxony and Prussia. The resumption of life at Berlin was disagreeable, and the new enterprise vague and beset by difficulty, so that he often visited Leipsic for relief. In 1842 he conducted the Düsseldorf festival once more, again went to England, and made a trip to Switzerland. Before that year was over it was clear that the proposed music-school was infeasible, and he was eager to leave. But the king ordered the formation of the since famous Domchor and named Mendelssohn as director, an appointment that he could hold without being in constant residence.

Returning to Leipsic, he secured a grant from the king of Saxony for the foundation of a conservatory, opened early in 1843. The success of this long-cherished scheme, though full of satisfaction, brought infinite labor and care. From now till the end his life was desperately crowded. The king of Prussia had imposed large tasks upon him in composition. He was often in request for special duties here and there. His friends and correspondents multiplied steadily, and his advice and assistance were lavishly given. As his mother had recently died (and his father some years before), in 1843 he moved once more to Berlin, becoming master of the Mendelssohn mansion. In 1844 he made a long and strenuous English trip. Duties at Berlin were pressed upon him, but fulfilling them was made exasperating by stupid officials, selfish musicians and an apathetic public. At the end of 1844 he withdrew to Frankfort, chiefly to secure rest from excessive strain.

In the fall of 1845 he took up work again at Leipsic, teaching, conducting and composing. In 1846 he led a chain of festivals at Aix-la-Chapelle, Düsseldorf, Liège and Cologne, and in August conducted at Birmingham the first performance of *Elijah* (first planned in 1837). This was his greatest triumph and one of the most thrilling of historic musical occasions. At once he set about an elaborate rewriting of the work, not completed for some months. Though Gade had been from 1843 conductor at the Gewandhaus, Mendelssohn often took his place. Commissions from Berlin continued to arrive. He was at work on a third oratorio, *Christus*, was always seeking a suitable opera-libretto, was occasionally on duty at Dresden, kept up teaching and correspondence, and was ceaselessly active otherwise. In the spring of 1847 he went once more to England, acting repeatedly as conductor and as soloist. Hardly had he returned when he heard of the sudden death of his sister. The shock broke him down. Periods of depression and suffering became frequent, and after a few months he died. The funeral at Leipsic was an extraordinary tribute of respect and affection, and the burial was at Berlin. Commemorative concerts were given throughout Europe, with notable tokens of sorrow.

Mendelssohn was full of charm and magnetism. He was vivacious and social, fond of gayety and fun, kind and tactful, many-sided in his interests, eager to spend himself for friends or any good cause, punctilious in performing duties, high-minded in every instinct and impulse. He was so approachable that he was overwhelmed with drafts upon thought and energy. He doubtless was too prodigal of his powers, but the breadth and intensity of his personal influence were momentous for musical progress. His every effort went toward elevating the standard of musical art, and his example helped musicianship to its rightful place in the world's thought. The reality of his religious convictions gave his character and work a fervor of high quality.

The Mendelssohns had five children. The widow died in 1853 at Frankfort.

195. His Works and Style. — In spite of the distractions of his career, Mendelssohn produced an extraordinary body of compositions, ranging over almost the entire circle of large forms. His technique as composer was masterly, sure and solid in its learning, and often finely original in invention. As has been suggested, his style shows an intimate blending of classical and romantic features. This mixture was historically useful, though it has stood in the way of his just appraisement by some critics. Probably his power is best shown in certain of his chamber works, in his orchestral overtures, and in his oratorios. These are rich in idea, finished in execution and eloquent in spirit. Yet it is true that he had his mannerisms, that his studies and tastes led him often to follow models from the past, and that his freshness of inspiration was not so constant in his

later years as in the earlier.   It is a question whether his persistent joyousness of sentiment militates against his artistic
greatness.   Here he presents a striking contrast to many composers who are thought to embody the spirit of modern life.
The absence of morbidness need not be regretted, but, since
his art is seldom or never the voice of sorrow, darkness or struggle, it is in so far not a full rescript of life.   But he should not
be compared with others without remembering that the converse
of this is also true.

A fairly complete summary of Mendelssohn's works is as follows: —
(*a*) 4 symphonies, including the 'Reformation' (1830), the 'Italian'
(1833), the 'Scotch' (1842), 7 concert-overtures, including the *Midsummer Night's Dream* (1826), the 'Hebrides' (1830-2), the *Meeres-
stille und glückliche Fahrt* (1832), a famous violin-concerto (1844) and
2 piano-concertos, besides some other ensemble pieces; (*b*) 7 quartets,
2 quintets and an octet for strings, 2 trios, 3 quartets and a sextet for
piano and strings, and a few violin- and 'cello-sonatas; (*c*) 3 piano-
sonatas, a capriccio, rondo capriccioso, several fantasias, caprices, variations, fugues, 8 books of *Lieder ohne Worte* (1830-45), characteristic
pieces, etc., and several pieces for four hands; (*d*) 6 organ-sonatas
(1844-5), and several preludes and fugues; (*e*) the comic opera *Die
Hochzeit des Camacho* (1825), fragments of *Lorelei*, the singspiel *Die
Heimkehr aus der Fremde*, 2 *Festgesänge*, music for Goethe's *Die erste
Walpurgisnacht* (1831-2), Sophokles' *Antigone* (1841), Shakespeare's
Midsummer Night's Dream (1842), Racine's *Athalie* (1843-4), Sophokles' *Œdipus at Colonus* (1845), with a great number of quartets
for male or mixed voices, over 80 songs and some duets; (*f*) the oratorios *St. Paul* (1836) and *Elijah* (1846), portions of *Christus*, the
Lobgesang (1840), 8 Psalms, including the 42d (1837), the 95th (1838),
and the 114th (1840), the cantata *Lauda Sion* (1846), and many motets
and anthems, some *a cappella*.   In addition, there are many early works
not published in popular form.   A standard edition of his works is issued
by Breitkopf & Härtel (1874-7).

Of his innumerable letters a large number have been published (from
1861).

Mendelssohn differed widely from Schumann in that he added
little to the formal resources of music.   For the most part he
used patterns and methods already known.   The same is true
of technique and orchestration.   Yet certain styles he handled
with such special grace that they became fresh under his hand.
Familiar instances are his nimble scherzos, his gay caprices, his
elegant piano-songs, some of his oratorio arias and choruses, and
the development-sections of his ensemble works.   His instinct

for instrumentation was sound and vivid, and his mastery of vocal effect unquestioned.

He was a pianist and organist of the first order, and a good viola-player. Although his keyboard technique was ample, with some peculiar excellencies in crispness and clarity, he disdained the use of it for its own sake. His strength lay in the absolute rendering of the musical idea as he conceived it. As an interpreter he was therefore exceptionally able, especially as regards the works of Bach, Mozart and Beethoven. His powers of improvisation were superb, and he had an extraordinary musical memory. As a conductor he was strict and conservative, but so tactful and full of enthusiasm as to command unbounded devotion from players and singers.

He had the gift of free self-expression in speech and deed, and the desire to impress himself upon others. His mind was clear and orderly, his sympathies warm, and his spirit contagious. Hence he was a brilliant and powerful teacher, especially with advanced students. Here he was the opposite of Schumann. Hence, while the latter left almost no disciples and was not generally understood till long after 1850, Mendelssohn inspired a host of pupils and admirers in many lands, so that his immediate influence for a generation was immense. These followers, some of them close imitators, are sometimes called 'the Mendelssohnian school,' though they were not closely affiliated, except, perhaps, in England. To this class are often referred several masters of the second rank, especially Hiller, Bennett, Gade and Reinecke, with other leaders at Leipsic, although in most cases these had strong characteristics of their own which widely distinguished them from Mendelssohn, particularly as their work continued for decades after his death, when they were subject to altogether different influences.

Ferdinand Hiller (d. 1885), born in 1811 at Frankfort, came of a wealthy Jewish family. There and at Weimar he studied with Aloys Schmitt, Hummel and others, developing precociously as pianist and composer. After visiting Vienna, from 1828 he lived at Paris, playing much in public, especially works of Bach and Beethoven, and associating with leading musicians. From 1836 he was in Frankfort, conducting the Cäcilienverein. In 1839 Rossini paved the way for his first opera at Milan, and in 1840 Mendelssohn took up at Leipsic his effective oratorio *Die Zerstörung Jerusalems*. After a year in Rome with Baini, in 1843-4 he conducted the Gewandhaus concerts, and later produced two operas at Dresden. From 1847 he was

town-musician at Düsseldorf, and from 1850 at Cologne, where he founded
the successful conservatory. For over 30 years he remained active as a
teacher and favorite conductor throughout the Lower Rhine district. His
works include 6 operas, 2 oratorios, several cantatas, many motets, part-songs
and songs, 3 piano-concertos, many sonatas, suites, études and lesser pieces,
an abundance of excellent chamber music, 4 overtures and 3 symphonies —
all marked by romantic feeling and technical vigor. He also wrote important
essays and reminiscences.

William Sterndale Bennett (d. 1875), born at Sheffield in 1816, was trained
as a choirboy at Cambridge and then at the Royal Academy in London, where
in 1833 he became known as composer and pianist. In 1837 (aided by the
Broadwoods) and again in 1842 he lived at Leipsic, being intimate with
Mendelssohn and Schumann, and producing works at the Gewandhaus. He
then made his home in London, giving chamber concerts, founding the Bach
Society (1844), conducting the Philharmonic (1856-66), from 1856 serving
as professor at Cambridge, and from 1866 being head of the Royal Academy.
His published works are few and chiefly confined to the piano, including 4
concertos, 2 sonatas, 2 rondeaux, a toccata, 2 capriccios, etc., a sextet for
piano and strings, 4 striking overtures, a symphony, the pastoral *The May
Queen* (1858), an oratorio, *The Woman of Samaria* (1867), festival odes,
songs, part-songs and anthems. His style has individuality, being marked
by extreme clarity, strength and even daring, but is wanting in warmth, so
that it lacks popular appeal. He presents interesting analogies and contrasts
to both Mendelssohn and Chopin.

Niels Wilhelm Gade (d. 1890) was born in 1817 at Copenhagen, the son of
a joiner and instrument-maker, who intended him to follow the trade. From
this at 15 he rebelled, was taken up by the violinist Wexschall and the organist Berggreen, entered the court-orchestra and blossomed at once into a
virtuoso. His powers as composer quickly matured, and in 1840 his overture
Nachklänge aus Ossian made a sensation, winning in 1841 a prize and a royal
scholarship. In 1842 came his first symphony, which Mendelssohn reproduced at Leipsic. Thither Gade went in 1843, remaining five years, in close
contact with Schumann and especially Mendelssohn. He was the latter's
substitute from 1843 and his formal successor in 1847. In 1848 he returned
to Copenhagen, where he became the most efficient promoter of Danish music,
universally respected and admired. He was conductor of the Musical Society
and in 1861–83 court-choirmaster. His works consist chiefly of highly poetic
cantatas, such as *Comala* (1846), *Frühlingsbotschaft, Zion, Die Kreuzfahrer*
(1876), *Psyche*, etc., 8 strong symphonies, 5 concert-overtures, 4 violin-
sonatas, a violin-concerto, some chamber music, many graceful piano-pieces
and a sonata, many songs and part-songs. His style has similarities to that
of Mendelssohn, but with a strong Scandinavian flavor and a more poetic
romanticism. He was gifted in orchestration and was a superior conductor.
His adherence to Mendelssohnian models decreased in his later years, when
he veered toward the style of Schumann.

On **Reinecke** see sec. 197. No attempt is made here to enumerate the
many English composers who pursued the paths opened by Mendelssohn
(see sec. 223).

196. The Gewandhaus Orchestra and the Leipsic Conservatory.
The artistic influence of the two institutions at Leipsic with
which Mendelssohn was specially associated has been notably
pervasive and beneficial.   The Gewandhaus orchestra has had
a striking career of almost a century and a half, numbering
among its conductors, members and visiting artists a host of
great names.   Especially from Mendelssohn's advent in 1835,
it has ranked as a model for the musical world, though its eminence is no longer unique.   Educationally, the conservatory,
which from the start has been linked with the orchestra in the
closest affiliation, has been even more influential, since it has
counted its pupils by hundreds and thousands, drawn from all
Europe and from America.   Its able faculty has included many
who have continued long in service, so that its policy has been
stable and its impression cumulative.   Thanks to the impulse
at its foundation, it has been at once conservative and progressive, though usually not as ready for novelties as some enthusiasts have desired.   Unlike the Paris Conservatoire, its connection with operatic music has been comparatively slight; but in
the training of instrumental and vocal composers and of general
teachers it has served a noble purpose.   It has been the pattern
upon which a long list of other schools have been formed.

The Gewandhaus Concerts properly date from 1763, when regular performances began under J. A. Hiller, though not given in the building
known as the Gewandhaus until 1781.   At that time the present system
of government by a board of directors began.   The conductors during
the first 70 years were from 1763 *J. A. Hiller* (d. 1804);   from 1785
J. G. Schicht (d. 1823);   from 1810 *Christian Schulz* (d. 1827); and from
1827 *Christian August Pohlenz* (d. 1843).   The standard of excellence
was already famous.   But in 1835 Mendelssohn brought new éclat and
enterprise, especially as he soon had the invaluable help of the violinist
David.   The list of conductors has been from 1835 *Mendelssohn* (d.
1847);   from 1843 *Ferdinand Hiller* (d. 1885);   from 1844 *Gade* (d.
1890);   from 1848 *Julius Rietz* (d. 1877);   from 1860 *Reinecke;*   and
from 1895 *Arthur Nikisch.*   In the list of concertmasters are to be
named the following: — from 1797 *Bartolomeo Campagnoli* (d. 1827);
from 1817 *Heinrich August Matthäi* (d. 1835);   from 1836 *Ferdinand
David* (d. 1873), with whom from 1850 was associated *Raimund Dreyschock* (d. 1869);   from 1873 *Engelbert Röntgen* (d. 1897), who was
assisted in 1874–82 by *Henry Schradieck;* from 1882 *Henri Petri,*
assisted in 1883–91 by *Adolf Brodsky,* in 1888 by *Arno Hilf* and in 1897
by *Felix Berber* (till 1903).   Among the other great violinists closely

associated with David just before 1850 were *Wasielewski*, later of Bonn, and the young *Joachim*, later of Hanover and Berlin. In the line of leading 'cellists have been in 1849-60 *Friedrich Grützmacher*; in 1859-62 *Karl Davidow* (d. 1889); in 1866-74 *Emil Hegar*; in 1874-81 *Karl Schröder*; in 1881-6 his brother *Alwin Schröder*; and later *Julius Klengel*. Long terms of service have been notable in many other cases, as for 56 years from 1777 of the double-bassist *Karl Gottfried Wilhelm Wach* (d. 1833); for 36 years from 1835 of the timpanist *E. G. B. Pfundt* (d. 1871); for 45 years from 1840 of the clarinettist *Bernhardt Landgraf* (d. 1885); for 29 years from 1846 of the violist *Friedrich Hermann*; for over 40 years from 1864 of the hornist *Friedrich Adolf Gumpert* (d. 1906); for about 25 years from 1867 of the oboist *Gustav Adolf Hinke* (d. 1893); for 28 years from 1867 of the flutist *Wilhelm Barge*, whom in 1895 *Maximilian Schwedler* followed, the latter having been second flute since 1881. Almost all of these made their mark as virtuosi and composers. Many other names might be given. No summary can be offered of the many virtuosi, instrumental and vocal, who have appeared at the concerts during the last hundred years, or of the innumerable works performed. In 1884 the old building, with its fascinating associations, was replaced by a splendid modern hall.

The Leipsic Conservatory is indissolubly connected with the Gewandhaus orchestra, since from its foundation in 1843 it was housed in the same complex of civic buildings and has been directed usually by the same officers. *Mendelssohn* was the originator of the whole plan, the one who secured the assignment of 20,000 thalers from the king of Saxony which was the first pecuniary basis, and the inspirer of the first teachers and students. But his leadership was brief. The directors since his time have been from 1847 *Konrad Schleinitz* (d. 1881); from 1881 *Otto Günther* (d. 1897); and from 1897 *Karl Reinecke*. The distinguished theory-teachers have been from 1843 *Hauptmann* (d. 1868); from 1843 also *E. F. Richter* (d. 1879); in 1848-60 *Julius Rietz* (d. 1877); from 1851 *Robert Papperitz* (d. 1903); from 1860 *Reinecke*; from 1869 *Oscar Paul* (d. 1898); from 1871 *Jadassohn* (d. 1902); and in 1872-83 and from 1897 *Alfred Richter*. Among the piano-teachers have been in 1843-65 *Louis Plaidy* (d. 1874); from 1843 *Ernst Wenzel* (d. 1880); from 1846 *Ignaz Moscheles* (d. 1870); from 1860 *Reinecke*; from 1864 *Theodor Coccius* (d. 1897); from 1873 *Johannes Weidenbach* (d. 1902); in 1875-98 *Bruno Zwintscher*; from 1877 *Alois Reckendorf*; and from 1886, *Adolf Ruthardt*. The violin-teachers include from the Gewandhaus leaders *David, Dreyschock, Röntgen*, and *Brodsky*, with the violist *Friedrich Hermann* and, since 1883, *Hans Sitt*. The 'cellists *Grützmacher, Davidow, Hegar*, the *Schröders*, and *Klengel* have likewise shared their energies. Among the vocal teachers have been in 1853-67 *Franz Götze* (d. 1888); and from 1877 *Friedrich Rebling* (d. 1900). The first teacher of music-history was *Brendel* (d. 1868); and the first organ-teacher (till 1856) *K. F. Becker* (d. 1877). No account is possible of the multitude of talented and famous pupils that have been sent out. In 1887 the conservatory was housed in a fine new building of its own.

Among the many musical societies of the city the oldest and most noted is the *Euterpe*, whose concerts have been led by many able conductors, and in whose programs have been famous renderings of many new and 'advanced' works. Among the conductors are these names: — about 1840 *Jean Verhulst* (d. 1891); in the '50's, *August Ferdinand Riccius* (d. 1886), *Hermann Langer* (d. 1889) and *Julius von Bernuth* (d. 1902); in the '60's, *Hans von Bronsart*, *Adolf Blassmann* (d. 1891) and *Robert Heckmann* (d. 1891), with *Jadassohn* as assistant; in the '70's, *Alfred Volkland*, *Johann Svendsen* and *Wilhelm Treiber* (d. 1899); and in 1881-6 *Paul Klengel*.

The *Riedel-Verein* was founded in 1854 by *Karl Riedel* (d. 1888), who remained the conductor till his death, being succeeded by *Hermann Kretzschmar* (till 1897), and he in turn by *Jean Louis Nicodé* and then by *Karl Georg Göhler*.

In the long line of conductors at the theatre or the opera may be mentioned in 1800-10 *Christian Schulz* (d. 1827); in 1810-21 *Friedrich Schneider* (d. 1853); in 1826-31 *Marschner* (d. 1861); in 1844-5 *Lortzing* (d. 1851) and *Joseph Netzer* (d. 1864); in 1847-54 *Julius Rietz* (d. 1877); in 1854-64 *A. F. Riccius* (d. 1886); etc.

Among the Leipsic organists to achieve reputation were, at the Thomaskirche, from 1801 *Johann Georg Hermann Voigt* (d. 1811), from 1812 *Friedrich Schneider* (d. 1853), in 1814-22 *F. W. Riem* (d. 1857), from 1827 *C. A. Pohlenz* (d. 1843), [from 1843 apparently *Hauptmann* (d. 1868),] from 1869 *Louis Papier* (d. 1878), from 1878 *Wilhelm Rust* (d. 1892); at the Petrikirche and Nikolaikirche, in 1825-56 *K. F. Becker* (d. 1877), from 1851 *E. F. Richter* (d. 1879); at the latter alone, in 1868-99 *Robert Papperitz* (d. 1903); and at the Johanniskirche, from 1878 *Robert Schaab* (d. 1887) — besides the virtuoso *Christian Fink*, living here in 1853-60. Among the pianists and piano-teachers the more distinguished were until 1840 *Friedrich Wieck* (d. 1873); until 1844 his daughter *Clara Schumann* (d. 1896); from 1831 *Julius Knorr* (d. 1861); from about 1835 *Heinrich Encke* (d. 1859); from 1846 *J. C. Lobe* (d. 1881); from 1852 *Jadassohn* (after 1871 in the conservatory); from 1867 *Heinrich Wohlfahrt* (d. 1883); from about 1870 *Moritz Vogel*; in 1872-85 *Heinrich von Herzogenberg* (d. 1900); and from 1872 *Alexander Winterberger*. A noted vocal teacher and organizer of choral societies from 1820 was *Karl Zöllner* (d. 1860), who in 1833 started the *Zöllner-Verein*, which after his death grew into the extensive *Zöllnerbund*.

Of those best known as composers, besides many in the above lists, it may be added that here in 1827-33 *Wagner* came to the first consciousness of his mission; that here in 1833-44 *Lortzing* made his first operatic ventures, though with but slight success; that here from 1842 worked the original *Hermann Hirschbach* (d. 1888), from about 1850 the gifted Englishman *Pierson* (d. 1873), from 1859 the opera-writer *Franz von Holstein* (d. 1878), from about 1865 the popular writer of dramatic works *Victor Nessler* (d. 1890), and in 1875-83 the piano-composer *Kirchner* (d. 1903), a student under Mendelssohn and Schumann over 30 years before.

197. Certain Other Leipsic Masters. — The disability of Schumann and the early death of Mendelssohn removed them from the Leipsic circle before 1850. But the vigor of the Leipsic influence was maintained by other leaders, individually less original, but of collective significance. Since Mendelssohn himself had been deeply interested in the structural side of composition and had busied himself almost wholly upon instrumental and choral forms, and since he naturally gathered about him those whose interests were similar, the distinctive drift of his circle was emphatically conservative. The elaboration of harmony and counterpoint in symmetrical and logical forms was exalted, with only such expansions of the older classical procedure as could be readily deduced. Hence, on the whole, Leipsic influence was against the free expression of peculiar individuality, of intense or whimsical moods, and of picturesquely novel ideas. In all this it was not in harmony with many of Schumann's impulses nor with the cravings of many younger radicals. The departments of composition which it specially favored were orchestral and chamber writing, piano works of careful workmanship, and dignified choral music. To the opera in all its varieties it paid comparatively little attention. Its ambition was to foster solid and serious creation for its own sake without caring whether or not the results were popularly sensational or spectacular. Here it stood in opposition to several other tendencies of the time. Naturally enough, those who were deeply moved by these tendencies found the Leipsic circle staid and even reactionary.

The two older members of the group were Hauptmann and Moscheles, both leaders in the conservatory staff.

Moritz Hauptmann (d. 1868) lived during exactly the same years as Rossini, being born at Dresden in 1792. He was an architect's son and was first trained for that profession. Incidental musical study brought out his latent gifts and led to his seeking Spohr's instruction at Gotha in 1811. From 1812 he was a violinist in the Dresden court-orchestra, besides teaching in the household of Prince Repnin, who in 1813–4 was the Russian governor of the city. From 1815 he was with the Prince in Italy and then at St. Petersburg, Moscow and Pultowa, employed in many noble families. He also kept up mathematical studies, with special attention to acoustics. In 1820 he returned to Dresden, and from 1822 was violinist in the court-orchestra at Cassel under Spohr, now evincing power as a theorist, training many fine pupils and putting forth violin and chamber music, choral works, songs and the opera *Mathilde* (1826), written with careful finish. From 1842, at the urgency of Mendelssohn and Spohr, he was made cantor of the

Thomasschule at Leipsic and in 1843 professor of counterpoint and composition in the new conservatory. He became one of the chief factors in the
school's success, impressing himself upon hosts of pupils for 25 years and
winning many official honors. His theory and practice placed the highest
value upon clear, vigorous construction and perfection of detail, but his spirit
was so broad that he held the respect of many who were less conservative.
His writings included *Die Natur der Harmonik und Metrik* (1853), *Die
Lehre von der Harmonik* (1868), an exposition of Bach's *Art of Fugue*,
some essays (collected 1874), and many letters (collected 1871–6). In these
he made a powerful contribution to modern theory, and also exhibited a
masterly conception of musical art. His theoretic system, resting upon an
analysis of tonality in its major and minor dualism, has been further developed by **Arthur von Oettingen** of Dorpat (in 1866), by **Otto Tiersch** of Berlin
(from 1868), by **Adolf Thürlings** of Bonn (in 1877), by **Ottokar Hostinský** of
Prague (from 1877) and by **Hugo Riemann** (from 1880).

Ignaz Moscheles (d. 1870) has already been treated (see sec. 180). His
influence was more conservative than that of Hauptmann.

Close contemporaries of Mendelssohn and Schumann were the following : —

Ernst Friedrich Richter (d. 1879), born in Saxony in 1808, educated at
Zittau and Leipsic (pupil of Weinlig), became Hauptmann's assistant at the
Conservatory in 1843 and in 1868, after leading the Singakademie in 1843–7
and serving from 1851 as organist at three of the city churches, his successor
as cantor at the Thomasschule. He was an excellent teacher and published
valuable text-books on harmony, counterpoint and fugue (1853–72). He was
also a sound and effective composer of both instrumental and choral music,
including the oratorio *Christus der Erlöser* (1849).

Ferdinand David (d. 1873) was the third in the great triumvirate with
Hauptmann and Moscheles. Born in 1810 at Hamburg, he early had instruction from Spohr and Hauptmann at Cassel, at 15 appeared as violinist at the
Gewandhaus, from 1827 played in a theatre-orchestra at Berlin, from 1829 was
leader in the private quartet of a noble at Dorpat (whose daughter became
his wife), and was well known as a concert-player throughout Russia till 1835.
In 1836 Mendelssohn secured him as concertmaster for the Gewandhaus and
in 1843 engaged him in the conservatory. In both positions he won world-
wide renown as virtuoso, trainer and inspirer, so that to him much of the
Leipsic prestige must be attributed. He was not only a great interpreter in
the noble style of Spohr, but a strong composer for his instrument and for
chamber and orchestral combinations, besides one opera (1852), and the
author of a foremost method and numerous standard editions of violin-classics.

Julius Rietz (d. 1877), born in 1812, was brought up at Berlin in the same
general circle with Mendelssohn, and was trained as a 'cellist, playing in a
theatre-orchestra from 1828. In 1834 he became Mendelssohn's assistant at
Düsseldorf and in 1835 his successor, first as opera-conductor, later as town-
musician, besides touring as a virtuoso. In 1847–54 he was conductor at the
Leipsic theatre and the Singakademie, and from 1848 also conductor at the
Gewandhaus and professor of composition in the conservatory. In 1860 he
removed to Dresden to be court-choirmaster and later also the artistic head

of the conservatory there.   He was an accomplished conductor and a worthy conservative composer. His works included 3 symphonies, notably that in E♭, several good overtures, such as the *Lustspielouvertüre*, 'cello, violin, clarinet and piano-concertos, violin, flute and piano-sonatas, a great amount of church and other choral music, and songs, besides 4 operas (1833–59). He did important work as the editor of standard editions of classical masters, including Mendelssohn. He was uncompromising in his opposition to radical tendencies, making many enemies in consequence.

Considerably younger than the above are two more —

Karl Reinecke (d. 1910), a specially interesting figure in the group, was born of musical parentage at Altona in 1824, and developed into a piano-virtuoso, appearing in Denmark and Sweden in 1843. After study with Mendelssohn and Schumann at Leipsic and further tours, in 1846–8 he was court-pianist at Copenhagen. Thence he went to Paris, in 1851–4 taught in the Cologne conservatory, in 1854–9 was town-musician at Barmen, and in 1859–60 conductor at Breslau. In 1860 he came to the Gewandhaus and the conservatory at Leipsic, where he has filled out almost a half-century of fruitful teaching and composing, with frequent tours as a favorite classical pianist. In 1895 he gave up his post as conductor, and in 1897 became head of the conservatory. His régime as conductor was marked by a somewhat rigid adherence to the standards of Mendelssohn. His over 250 works cover a wide range — 3 symphonies, 9 concert-overtures, incidental music to Schiller's 'William Tell,' a string-serenade, concertos for violin, 'cello, harp and piano (4), a quintet and a quartet with piano, 4 string-quartets and 7 trios, 4 violin-sonatas, 3 'cello-sonatas, many piano-sonatas and sonatinas, characteristic pieces, studies, etc., 6 operas and operettas (from 1867), the oratorio *Belsazar*, many cantatas, 2 masses, and very many part-songs and songs. His style is marked by sound learning and fresh versatility, and furnishes an interesting continuation into the later period of Mendelssohn's type of romanticism.

Salomon Jadassohn (d. 1902), born in 1831 and first trained at Breslau, studied from 1848 at Leipsic under Hauptmann and one year at Weimar under Liszt, and taught at Leipsic from 1852. After short terms as conductor of the Psalterion chorus and the Euterpe concerts, from 1871 he was professor of composition and instrumentation in the conservatory, where he became renowned as teacher and composer. Besides able text-books (1883–95), he wrote some 130 strong and often brilliant works, including 4 symphonies, 4 serenades, 2 overtures, a piano-concerto, much chamber music, a psalm and several choral ballades, motets, duets, songs and piano-pieces, some of which evince extraordinary contrapuntal facility.

CHAPTER XXXII

NEW LIGHTS UPON PIANISM

198. Chopin as a Tone-Poet. — During almost precisely the same years as Mendelssohn lived the Polish pianist and composer Chopin, contributing to musical art an influence that has been singularly potent and persistent. Representing a different racial stock and moved by a peculiar national spirit, Chopin gave voice to an intense and poignant strain of poetic romanticism that was eminently original and fresh. His genius was matured before the world at large knew much about it, but, when he stepped forth into publicity, his captivating qualities as a virtuoso made his style instantly famous. His choice of Paris as a residence introduced him to a society specially sensitive to his artistic type. But the sentiments and the forms that he loved lay so close to the modern spirit generally that he stands out as an artist, not merely of a nation or a social class, but at least of a period, if not of a constant aspect of experience. Accordingly, his works, though relatively few and almost wholly confined to a single field, have become standard everywhere in both public and private use.

Emotionally, Chopin presents many contradictions, from languorous dreaminess and voluptuousness to fiery and heroic ardor, from a sentimentality that verges upon the morbid to noble virility. But this mixture of qualities is not unusual, and in his case the directness with which they were revealed and the consummate art with which they were embodied give his works an extraordinary appeal. His passionateness and pathos may well be traced to the tragic national history into which he was born, but his symmetry of form, his exquisite feeling for tonal beauty, his delicacy of detail, his finesse in planning his effects — all these recall rather the Gallic element in his blood. In the perfect unity and balance between conception and form, his style resembles Mendelssohn's, but the difference in materials and impulses was extreme.

Technically, Chopin was almost wholly a lyric artist, usually choosing forms that are song-like in essence. Within this field he followed methods that were not radically different from classical practice, except that his melodies were more flexible, more expanded, much fuller of sensuous warmth. But he drew his song-patterns from new sources, having often singular pathos or picturesqueness. And he treated his materials in detail without being governed by the ordinary conventions of harmony or counterpoint. He had but slight impulse to true thematic development and but small power in the architectonic handling of complex tonal processes. But, on the other hand, he had extreme facility in melodic invention, an absolutely fresh insight into the capacities of the piano, and a marvelous gift for decoration and color. Some intimations of progress in these directions had already appeared, but the advance that he achieved was superbly rapid and sure. The art of pianism as an independent specialty took on a new importance under his hand.

Frédéric Chopin (d. 1849) was born in 1810 at a village not far from Warsaw. As a young man his father had come to Poland in 1787 from Nancy (E. France) and, after business and military experience, was from about 1805 a private tutor, from 1810 teacher in the new Lyceum and later in a school of his own. His mother was of a good Polish family. Of the four children, two older sisters lived to become talented writers. Chopin's early years fell amidst dark times for his country. The infamous partitions of Poland (1772–95) had given most of it to Russia and were still bitterly resented — the constant unrest culminating in 1830 in the first of several fruitless insurrections. Probably the Chopin family suffered from the situation, since their livelihood depended upon people in high society.

Chopin received a fair education, the best of it being in music. His first master was the Bohemian Zywny, a worthy teacher of the old school. At 9 he played a piano-concerto in public, and soon after began some composition. At 14 he entered the Lyceum, where he was noted for his spirits and his dramatic talent, and began lessons with Elsner, the head of the young conservatory and a wise, intelligent teacher. At 15 (1825) he put forth his first published work, though he had previously written several dances. Leaving the Lyceum in 1827, he concentrated upon music to such purpose that many other works were produced, and in 1829, when he was induced to play at Vienna, he scored a real success. In 1830 he gave three memorable farewell concerts at Warsaw and then set out for Breslau, Dresden, Prague, Vienna, Munich and Stuttgart, whence in the fall of 1831 he passed on to Paris. At Stuttgart he heard of the capture of Warsaw by the Russians and the collapse of the insurrection.

His nationality, his high-bred, aristocratic ways, and the charm of his art speedily brought him into notice. His virtuosity was not unrivaled, but his lack of sonority and his comparative feebleness as an interpreter of others' works were made up by the beauty of his own ideas and the perfection with which he set them forth. He at once became intimate with leading musicians, including such varied types as the aged Cherubini, the ambitious Rossini, the facile Auber, the poetic young Bellini, the caustic and eccentric Berlioz, the laborious Meyerbeer, the egotistic Kalkbrenner (from whom he had some quasi-lessons), the ardent Liszt, the buoyant Mendelssohn (then on his grand tour), and many others. His genius was effusively acclaimed by Schumann in Leipsic. From 1832 he began concert-giving and teaching, besides publishing from time to time. Though much courted by 'society,' and aspiring "to create a new art-era," he had not the physical or mental verve to be a leader or to command a steady income. (He is said even to have meditated coming to America!) His public appearances as a player ceased with 1835, when the weakness of his constitution began to be seen. In 1834 he attended the festival at Aix-la-Chapelle, and in 1835 and '36 visited Dresden and Leipsic, coming into close contact with the Mendelssohn circle and with Schumann. In 1837 he made a trip to England, partly for his health.

Late in 1836 began his strange and regrettable intimacy with 'George Sand' (Mme. Dudevant), the restless, sophistical and coarse novelist. With her in 1838-9 he went to Majorca, where he fell seriously ill — the beginning of the fatal consumption. Afterwards they lived in Paris or Nohant. During this period he issued many of his finest works, and occasionally played at concerts for his friends and admirers. In 1847 he and George Sand parted; probably she was tired of him. Late in that year came out his last work, and early in 1848 he played once more in a private concert. The approach of the Revolution drove him to England, where, in spite of his failing health, he made some private appearances at London, Manchester, Glasgow and Edinburgh. Returning to Paris, he died there in 1849, and was accorded a stately funeral at the Madeleine.

The most salient of his personal characteristics were his sentimental sensitiveness and his instinctive refinement. He had great fascination for many persons, was considerate and often impulsively generous, at times displayed ardent enthusiasms, but was prone also to periods of extreme dejection. Intellectually, he was acute and appreciative, occasionally indulging in keen criticism. He lacked vigor of purpose and loftiness of aim — a typical poet of the introspective order. His life moved wholly within the ways and the feelings of aristocratic society, which was his world.

His works are almost wholly for the piano and in dance-forms or song-forms. They include (*a*) over 50 mazurkas, 15 waltzes, nearly as many polo-naises (one with 'cello), 4 scherzos, the *Marche funèbre*, a bolero, a tarentelle; (*b*) 19 nocturnes, 25 preludes, 27 études, 4 ballades, 5 rondos (one with orchestra and one for two pianos), 3 impromptus, a berceuse, a barcarolle, 3 fantasias (two with orchestra), 3 variations; (*c*) 4 sonatas (one for 'cello), 2 piano-concertos, a trio for piano and strings. He also left a small group of Polish songs.

To pianism proper Chopin contributed a wealth of delicate embellishments and refinements, including original melodic and accompaniment figures, with important dynamic and rhythmic devices (such as a fresh use of the 'tempo rubato'), which much increased the resources of expressive effect. He discarded the rigidity or quiescence of the hand and arm in favor of absolute elasticity. Beauty of tone and shading he exalted above dexterity, though his filigree-passages call for extreme fluency. The ingenious use of the pedals now becomes an important factor in artistic impression.

Here may well be mentioned the names of a number of pianists who either were Poles or worked long at Warsaw, viz: — the Bohemian **Wilhelm Würfel** (d. 1852), in 1815-26 teacher in Elsner's school and later at Vienna; **Maria** (**Wolowska**) **Szymanowska** (d. 1832), one of Field's pupils who, while living at Warsaw, was court-pianist at St. Petersburg and well known in Germany; **Albert Sowinsky** (d. 1880), trained at Vienna and from 1830 a teacher and player at Paris; **Jozef Nowakowski** (d. 1865), Chopin's fellow-student and finally, after tours, a teacher at Warsaw, with about 60 piano and orchestral works; **Ignacy Félix Dobrzynski** (d. 1867), another comrade of Chopin's both in Warsaw and in Paris, who also returned to Warsaw as an opera-conductor, with many strongly national piano-pieces and songs, some cham-ber music, a symphony, 2 operas, etc.; **Édouard Wolff** (d. 1880), still a third close friend and imitator of Chopin, settled from 1835 at Paris, with numerous piano works, many of them valuable, nearly 40 striking duos for piano and violin (written with De Bériot and Vieuxtemps), a concerto — about 350 in all; **Antoine de Kontski** (d. 1899), an effective and indefatigable virtuoso, whose headquarters were successively Paris, Berlin, St. Petersburg, London and Buffalo, N.Y. — the brother of the violinist **Apollinaire de Kontski** (d. 1879), who, after tours and service at St. Petersburg, founded a school at Warsaw; **Aloys Tausig** (d. 1885), a pupil of Thalberg, from about 1840 a favorite teacher at Warsaw (where his son Karl was born in 1841), later going to Dresden; not to speak of many later teachers at the conservatory, like **Ferdinand Quentin Dulcken** (d. 1902), the brilliant **Alexander Zarzycki** (d. 1895), head of the conservatory from 1879, the able **Joseph Wieniawski**, working here about 1870, and the now famous **Ignace Jan Paderewski**, first a pupil and in 1878-83 a teacher. With these should be grouped **Karl Mikuli**

(d. 1897), a pupil of Chopin in 1844–8, who, after touring in Russia and other Slavic countries, was from 1858 head of the Lemberg conservatory and from 1888 of a school of his own, and whose edition of Chopin's works is critically important.   He also composed in Chopin's style.

Akin to Chopin and for a time associated with him at Paris was **Stephen Heller** (d. 1888), who was born in Hungary in 1815 and trained by Halm at Vienna.   From 1827 he became known as a concert-player there, in Hungary and Poland, and later in Germany.   After spending some years quietly at Augsburg, in 1838 he went to Paris, where, except for a few tours, he lived for 50 years.   His temperament was too sensitive to make him a thoroughly successful virtuoso, but under congenial conditions his playing was full of grace and vivacity.   He wrote several hundred short piano works — characteristic pieces, ballades, études, nocturnes, songs without words, dances, etc. — full of healthy poetry, with great daintiness of rhythm and figure.   In genuine invention they compare well with Mendelssohn's, in structure are stronger than Chopin's, and in imagination recall Schumann.

199. Salon Music. — In conjunction with the spread of the romantic spirit, the general adoption of pianism as a specialty from about 1825 led to a striking multiplication of small piano works in forms not previously conspicuous.   The vogue of these has always been due to their intimate or personal character, and their adaptation to domestic use or the smaller functions of polite society.   This type received a powerful impetus from composers like Schubert, Schumann, Mendelssohn and Chopin.   For them this was an inevitable result of their search for tone-forms to express relatively transient moods and fancies — an irrepressible outbreak of lyricism.   But the expansion of the style into immense proportions was due to workers of much lower degree, whose call to action was often the mere popular demand for graceful and 'pretty' bagatelles, and whose method had more cleverness than inspiration.   The term 'salon music' has acquired a more or less disparaging sense in consequence.   Yet all writing in this style is not necessarily sentimentally vapid or structurally mechanical.   When the small piano-form has been touched by the hand of genius it has had the same real and concentrated beauty as that of a fine miniature or a delicate aquarelle.   And, even in its shallower illustrations, parlor music is a large social force, bringing myriads of persons into touch with tonal art and serving at least as an introduction to larger things.   As a type, it is dangerous only when known in its poorer examples alone and when cultivated wholly out of relation to other types.

The forms most used are naturally either songs or dances, both of which are essentially lyrical. The many song-patterns have been described by a great variety of names, not always used consistently, such as ' song without words,' ' romance,' ' nocturne,' ' reverie,' ' ballade,' ' fantasie,' ' caprice,' ' étude,' etc. More indefinite terms are ' impromptu,' ' prelude,' ' albumblatt,' ' charakterstück,' etc. Often a picturesque suggestion is given by titles like ' kinderscenen,' ' flower-song,' and the like. The dance-patterns most used are the waltz, the mazurka, the polonaise, the galop and many others of the large class of modern round dances, most of them in triple rhythm.

The two centres from which salon music in its lighter forms was specially propagated before or near the middle of the century were Paris and Vienna, and they have continued to be prominent. But players and publishers carried it everywhere, calling out production in all countries. Furthermore, at both these centres and in Germany and northern Europe generally the making of brief, characteristic piano-pieces of decided artistic quality soon became a specialty, supplying a charming and useful element in musical literature.

Reserving for longer mention the most distinguished composers and players, it may here be noted that the French group, including Belgians, Spaniards and some others, contains names like these : — **Franz Hünten** of Coblentz (d.1878); **Pedro Albeniz** (d. 1855), from 1830 active at Madrid; **Camille Marie Stamaty** (d. 1870), who from 1835 pushed his way into the front rank of Parisian teachers, producing important études, etc. ; **Henri Rosellen** (d. 1876) ; **Charles Henri Valentin Alkan** (d. 1888) ; the accomplished **Antoine François Marmontel** (d. 1898), from 1832 a player of mark and from 1848 one of the best teachers at the Conservatoire, with numerous didactic works ; **Jacques Mathieu Joseph Gregoir** (d. 1876), from 1848 teacher at Brussels ; **Ignace Leybach** (d. 1891), from 1844 organist at Toulouse ; **Jean Henri Ravina**, in 1834-7 a teacher at the Conservatoire and later a virtuoso and composer ; **Henry Charles Litolff** (d. 1891), from 1851 the well-known publisher ; **Wilhelm Krüger** (d. 1883), who, driven from Paris by the war of 1870, was then court-pianist at Stuttgart ; **Charles Samuel Bovy** [' Lysberg '] (d. 1873), long a teacher at the Geneva conservatory ; **Georges Mathias**, from 1862 on the Conservatoire staff ; **Jacob Blumenthal**, from 1848 pianist to Queen Victoria ; the Belgian **Désiré Magnus** (d. 1884) ; **Auguste Dupont** (d. 1890), from 1852 in the Brussels conservatory ; the popular American **Louis Moreau Gottschalk** (d. 1869) ; **Joseph Ascher** (d. 1869), pianist to the Empress Eugénie ; **Renaud de Vilbac** (d. 1884), from 1856 organist at one of the Paris churches ; **Martin Lazare** (d. 1897), who, after wide tours, worked at Brussels ; **Charles Delioux**, prominent from about 1850 ; **Eugène Ketterer** (d. 1870) ; **Damaso Zabalza y Olaso** (d. 1894), from 1858 at Madrid, later professor of theory at the conservatory ; and **Louis Gobbaerts** of Brussels (d. 1886).

With Vienna may be associated many minor Bohemians and Hungarians, as well as a few others. To this general group belong **Karl Maria von Bocklet** (d. 1881), from about 1830 a successful teacher; **Joseph Fischhof** (d. 1857), from 1833 in the conservatory; **Leopold von Meyer** (d. 1883), a rather eccentric player who toured extensively; **Ignaz Amadeus Tedesco** (d. 1882), a Bohemian, best known in Russia, chiefly at Odessa; the Bavarian **Rudolf Schachner** (d. 1896); **Imre Székely** (d. 1887), noted for his Hungarian fantasias, from 1852 living at Pesth; **Albert Jungmann** (d. 1892), who, after teaching at Rome, was from 1853 a publisher at Vienna; **Julius Schulhoff** (d. 1898), a Bohemian whom Chopin befriended at Paris, and who, after tours, was popular there as a teacher, removing in 1870 to Dresden, where also he was honored; **Vincent Adler** (d. 1871), a Hungarian, long at Paris and from 1865 in the Geneva conservatory; the refined player and composer **Alfred Jaell** (d. 1882), from 1843 almost constantly on tours throughout Europe; **Joseph Löw** (d. 1886), a prolific composer at Prague. Here may be added the Russian **Alexander Villoing** (d. 1878), the teacher at Moscow of the Rubinstein brothers.

In passing, a few Italian pianists may be mentioned, such as **Theodor Döhler** (d. 1856), who began at Naples, was long in court-service at Lucca and lived finally at Florence, besides touring throughout Europe; **Stefano Golinelli** (d. 1891), for many years (till 1870) active at Bologna, part of his many works being in large forms; and the four brothers **Fumagalli**, all more or less associated with Milan.

In Germany, even more than in France, the impulse to supply salon music blended with pedagogical efforts, it being clearly seen that through the use of entertaining pieces of graded difficulty the young student might be introduced to the art of piano-playing and thus to some acquaintance with musical art in general. Although it is true that the emphasis upon piano music has thus been sometimes made so exclusive as to engender the notion that it is central or supreme, yet such cases merely illustrate how efforts that are not essentially harmful may be misused.

Without attempting to distinguish between the mere writer of salon pieces, the virtuoso of second or third rank and the pedagogue who uses popular styles, the following names are given as illustrating the immense expansion of piano study and practice in Germany:— **Jakob Schmitt** (d. 1853), an excellent teacher at Hamburg, with many didactic pieces; the Bohemian **Franz Xaver Chwatal** of Magdeburg (d. 1879); **Louis Kufferath** (d. 1882), in 1836–50 director of the Leeuwarden conservatory; **Charles Voss** (d. 1882), from 1848 well known in Paris, writing also some striking concertos; **Fritz Spindler** (d. 1905), the celebrated Dresden teacher, whose works likewise extend to large forms, including 3 symphonies; **Theodor Kullak** (d. 1882), the still more celebrated teacher at Berlin, where in 1850 he founded a famous Akademie; **Albert**

Löschhorn (d. 1905), another strong Berlin teacher, with varied works in a fine style; **Louis Köhler** (d. 1886), who, after a short operatic career, from 1847 was so prominent a piano-teacher at Königsberg that he was called a second Czerny; the able general composer **Raff** (d. 1882), whose reputation was first made as a piano composer and who produced much in the salon style, besides greater things (see sec. 210); **Siegmund Lebert** (d. 1884), best known as the promoter in 1856-7 of the Stuttgart conservatory; **Johann Vogt** (d. 1888), successively teacher at St. Petersburg, Dresden and Berlin; **Karl Wehle** (d. 1883), a Bohemian, trained at Leipsic and Berlin, who toured the world and then settled at Paris; the Dane **August Winding** (d. 1899), later head of the Copenhagen conservatory; **Wilhelm Speidel** (d. 1899), in 1848-54 at Munich and from 1857 associated with Lebert at Stuttgart, a composer for chorus and orchestra as well as piano; **Louis Schottmann**, since about 1855 a prominent Berlin teacher; the Hamburg conductor and teacher **Ludwig Deppe** (d. 1890); **Gustav Lange** of Berlin (d. 1889); **Ludwig Stark** (d. 1884), Lebert's strongest coadjutor at Stuttgart and an able choral composer; **Karl Kölling** of Hamburg; **Friedrich Damm** of Dresden; **Robert Pflughaupt** (d. 1871), from 1862 at Aix-la-Chapelle; **Franz Bendel** (d. 1874), a teacher with Kullak at Berlin, with some large works; **Albert Biehl**, noted for his advanced technical studies; **Alexander Dorn** (d. 1901), son and pupil of Heinrich Dorn, who worked in 1855-65 in Egypt and from 1868 at the Berlin Hochschule; **Dionys Pruckner** (d. 1896), from 1859 a distinguished member of the Stuttgart circle; **Alexander Winterberger**, successively at Vienna, St. Petersburg and Leipsic; the Russian **Nicolai von Wilm**, in 1858-75 a leading teacher and composer at St. Petersburg; **Heinrich Döring**, since 1858 prominent at Dresden, writing not only good piano-studies, but male choruses, chamber suites and sacred music; **Anton Krause** (d. 1907), in 1859-97 conductor and excellent teacher at Barmen; the Bohemian **Hans Schmitt**, since 1862 a successful teacher in the Vienna conservatory; **Friedrich Baumfelder** of Dresden; **Emil Breslaur** of Berlin, not only a specialist in piano-teaching, but a leading spirit in the organization of piano-teachers into societies; **Anton Deprosse** (d. 1878), who lived chiefly at Munich; **Isidor Seiss**, since 1871 a teacher in the Cologne conservatory; **Louis Brassin** (d. 1884), teacher at Berlin and St. Petersburg; and scores of others.

To this list might also be added the names of many composers whose eminence was chiefly won in other fields.

200. The Bravura Pianists. — The increasing valuation of the piano and its music was further evidenced about 1825 by the advent of many virtuosi who were more notable as technical experts than as musicians in the large sense. As a rule, they sought to feed the popular appetite for sensation, though not without some degree of artistic skill in method. Under their influence the resources of pianistic dexterity were developed to the utmost, the public interest in piano music stimulated, and to some extent the literature of the instrument enriched. To this class

Liszt himself undoubtedly belonged and in it he became a prince. But in his case the basis of general musicianship was broader and deeper than in that of his contemporaries Herz and Thalberg. As time went on, the separation between the more mechanical and the more artistic groups became wider — the one contenting itself with showy effects such as the perfected piano made peculiarly possible, the other seeking to use the piano as a medium for important musical expression, and yet keeping in touch with other fields of creation and performance. In the end, of course, the second group drove the first out of the larger musical centres; but for two or three decades the spectacular school was in high favor and renown.

It should be noted that there is no real dividing-line between salon music and concert music of the bravura order. The latter is cast often in larger forms and necessarily abounds in technical difficulties, but the difference is more one of degree than of kind. And much of the success of virtuosi was secured by their specially effective renderings of small pieces that were entirely suitable for salon use. Among the compositions of the bravura artists there was usually a marked absence of elaborate forms like the sonata and the concerto.

Henri Herz (d. 1888), born at Vienna in 1806, studied first with his father and with Hünten at Coblentz, but at 10 was taken to Paris, soon winning success at the Conservatoire. In 1821 he derived benefit from observing Moscheles. His playing and his brilliant, but shallow compositions became the fashion, and he was much sought as a teacher. In 1831 he toured Germany with the violinist Lafont, and in 1833 appeared at London with Moscheles and Cramer. From 1842 he was professor at the Conservatoire, but also entered upon a piano-making enterprise which was so unfortunate that in 1845–51 he made a comprehensive American tour to recoup himself. He then started a piano-factory of his own, this time with striking success. In 1874 he gave up his professorship. His 200 works include 8 concertos, some sonatas and rondos, a large number of variations on operatic airs, etc. Of them only his études and his method are now much regarded. His letters from America were collected and published (1866).

Sigismund Thalberg (d. 1871), born at Geneva in 1812, was brought up at Vienna, studying with Sechter, Hummel and the bassoonist Mittag, though originally destined for a diplomatic career. At 14 he was privately famous, at 17 (1829) played in public and published some works, and in 1830 toured in southern Germany with success. From 1834 he was court-pianist, but from 1835 for over 20 years lived mostly at Paris, though with many long tours through northern Europe and to America. After 1858 his home was at Posilippo (near Naples), where he died. He had somewhat unusual hands and was an indefatigable technical student, so that he was unsurpassed in the execution of both cantabile and bravura passages. He was a better artist than Herz, but won his popularity, not by a broad interpretation of masterpieces or by serious creation of his own, but by the faultless treatment of salon music on a concert scale. His published works include showy fantasias and transcriptions, nocturnes, caprices, dances, a concerto, a sonata, etc., and he also produced 2 unsuccessful operas (1851–5).

Marie Félicité Denise (Moke) Pleyel (d. 1875), pupil of Herz, Moscheles and Kalkbrenner, may be named here, though she was more than a bravura player, winning praise from critics as diverse as Mendelssohn, Liszt, and Auber, and ranking with the best virtuosi of the period. In 1848–72 she taught with distinction at the Brussels conservatory.

Ernst Haberbier (d. 1869), born in 1813 at Königsberg, had great success from 1832 at St. Petersburg, becoming court-pianist in 1847. For years afterward he toured in England, Denmark, Sweden, northern Germany and to Paris, displaying special brilliance in rapid passages divided between the hands. His last years were spent as a teacher at Bergen. He left some effective concert-pieces.

Jakob Rosenhain (d. 1894), born in 1813 and trained at Mannheim and Frankfort, was from 1825 a prominent touring virtuoso, from 1849 making his home at Paris, where he was intimate with Cramer, and later at Baden-Baden. He was an ambitious and enterprising composer, writing not only substantial concert-pieces, études, etc., for the piano, but a piano-concerto, chamber music, 3 symphonies and 4 operas (1834–63).

Émile Prudent (d. 1863), born in 1817, stepped into prominence in 1833 and was counted in the same class with Thalberg, like whom he toured abundantly and had a large following as a teacher. His composition lay chiefly in the same field, but evinced more sentiment. He might have advanced to higher work had not his career been cut short.

Alexander Dreyschock (d. 1869), a Bohemian, born in 1818, was a precocious player, soundly trained at Prague by Tomaschek. From 1838 for about 20 years he was constantly occupied with tours. In 1862 he was called by Rubinstein to the new St. Petersburg conservatory, being also director of the operatic school and court-pianist; but failing health occasioned his retirement in 1868. He excelled in difficult feats with octaves, sixths and thirds, and for the left hand alone. He chose mostly to play his own pieces, but undertook some wider interpretation, though without sympathy. His writing was in the usual display-forms, with a few concerted works and an opera.

Heinrich Rudolf Willmers (d. 1878, insane), born at Berlin in 1821, after touring in 1838–53, lived at Vienna except during 1864–6, when he taught at the Stern conservatory at Berlin. He was famous for his execution of trills, especially in complicated ' chains,' and of staccato passages.

Joseph Wieniawski, the brother of the eminent Polish violinist, was trained first at Paris and later by Liszt at Weimar. After a few years at Paris, from 1866 he taught in the conservatories of St. Petersburg, Warsaw and Brussels, besides touring freely. His works include many études and dances, with several orchestral compositions.

Somewhat apart from the rest of this group stands **Adolf Henselt** (d. 1889), born in Bavaria in 1814, who was first trained at Munich by Frau von Fladt, but studied also with Hummel at Weimar and Sechter at Vienna. He became known as a phenomenal player in 1837, and from 1838 was in court service at St. Petersburg and in high repute as virtuoso, teacher and composer. He seldom traveled, and for 50 years was famous only by report outside of Russia. He gave excessive attention to abnormal stretches in legato, for which he devised peculiar studies. Although he adhered generally to the old-fashioned securing of tone by finger-action only, his style was much more emotional and poetic than others of his group, and also approached the massiveness of Liszt. He is best known by a concerto, many fine études and some beautiful short works.

Among noted women pianists were **Louise (Dumont) Farrenc** (d. 1875), from 1821 the wife of the flutist and historical student J. H. A. Farrenc and from 1842 professor at the Paris Conservatoire, producing a great variety of orchestral, chamber and piano music; **Luise (David) Dulcken** (d. 1850), sister of the great violinist and wife of F. Q. Dulcken, who from 1828 became conspicuous at London, being the teacher of Queen Victoria; **Marie Léopoldine Blahetka** (d. 1887), a member of the Viennese group, who from 1840 lived at Boulogne; and **Louise Japha (Langhans)**, a pupil of the Schumanns at Düsseldorf, who, after concertizing with her husband, was from 1863 prominent at Paris and from 1874 at Wiesbaden. The last two were gifted in composition.

201. Liszt and the Orchestral Style. — Side by side with Chopin's comparatively short and pathetic career ran the first half of Liszt's long and showy one. Like Chopin, he brought into music a decidedly new national flavor, also eastern, but from untamed Hungary instead of humiliated Poland. Like him, he developed precociously into a masterly virtuoso and early sought Paris as headquarters. But, unlike him, he stood forth, even in youth, as a consummate swayer of audiences and master of men, as an interpreter of the whole range of piano literature, and ultimately as a versatile composer and an imperial force in musical progress. Before 1850 his work was closely linked with Chopin's, but later was still more intimately interwoven with Wagner's. His eminence is partly due to his readiness to appreciate great art wherever found and to throw himself generously into its furtherance. His power of absolute creation and the message that he brought were not so significant as his breadth of sympathy and his power of leadership. As a player he speedily reached a place of incontestable supremacy, and then as a teacher he stamped a deep impression upon the whole texture of musical thought.

Liszt, when a boy, came into the Vienna atmosphere, with its strong interest in instrumental styles of composition. Beethoven was at the acme of his power, and the city had long been the home of leading players, both pianists and others. Ensemble music was everywhere exalted. To these stimuli his ardent spirit responded, so that later, when he became known as a virtuoso throughout northern Europe, his style tended more and more toward fullness of color and splendor of effect such as the orchestra has, but which had been attempted upon the piano only rarely. Liszt's technical accomplishments were so extraordinary that he promptly expanded the range of pianism in several directions, almost stepping beyond the verge of what is germane to it, at least establishing a new standard of dexterity and eloquence for it. Happily, hand in hand with this capacity for dazzling mechanism went a fine culture of mind which opened to his sympathetic use the whole range of keyboard music from Bach to Chopin, and from the daintiest bagatelle to the most massive concerto.

Liszt's service to piano music went much beyond the enrichment of technique. It included manifold illustrations of how the piano can reproduce by suggestion the effect of much that was not originally written for it or conceived from its point of view. 'Arrangements' of vocal, organ and orchestral works had not been unknown, of course, but in Liszt's hands they took on a new importance, since in him was united consummate command of the instrument and profound sympathy with the aim and structure of concerted composition. In his own playing of the piano works of others he knew how not only to render them in accordance with the conventions of the period or school to which they belonged, but also, while preserving their individuality, to clothe them with something of the freshness and breadth of modern orchestral style. And in his many 'transcriptions' he did the same thing with freedom and authority.

Liszt was also notable as one of the first to make a deliberate and powerful use of 'program music'—music in which the imagination is directed in advance by some literary motto or plan in accordance with which the development proceeds. The legitimacy of this method has been somewhat hotly debated (see sec. 211). Doubtless much depends on the degree of emphasis upon it, on the particular series of ideas or sentiments chosen, and espe-

cially on the creative originality displayed.   Liszt's own efforts
in this field — which were not confined to his earlier period or
to his piano works — often have a vigor and beauty hard to
deny.   Hence here again he effected a considerable expansion
of the range of artistic style (see sec. 210).

Franz Liszt (d. 1886) was born in 1811 at Raiding, a small town in western Hungary (35 m. southeast of Vienna).   His father was employed as
manager on one of the Esterhazy estates — a musical amateur who played the
piano and other instruments.   At 9 the son was so far advanced that his
playing before a company of noblemen led them to proffer an annual scholarship of about $1000 for six years to ensure his education.   This the father
accepted, gave up his position and took the boy at once to Vienna.   There
he studied under Czerny, Salieri and Randhartinger with such rapid growth
that when, at the opening of 1823, he appeared in public his playing made a
sensation, moving even Beethoven to an unusual display of emotion.   He was
now taken to Paris, but as a foreigner was declined at the Conservatoire by
Cherubini, and began private study under Reicha and Paër.   His ambition at
first lay in the field of opera, and in 1825 his operetta *Don Sanche* was successfully produced.   He also made some tours as a pianist in England and
Switzerland.

His annual stipend ceased in 1826 and his father died the next year.   This
forced him to choose a pianistic career, teaching and touring.   He had the
entrée into society through high-born Hungarian friends, and he came to
know the foremost literary and musical lights of Paris, including Victor Hugo,
Lamartine, 'George Sand,' Paganini, Berlioz and Chopin.   For a time he was
much interested in the socialistic program of Saint-Simon, and was deeply
stirred by the excitement of the Revolution of 1830.   Already he showed the
peculiar mixture of aristocratic tastes with revolutionary propensities which
marked him later.   In 1834 began his connection with the Countess d'Agoult,
known in literature as 'Daniel Stern,' with whom he lived about ten years,
mostly at Geneva, and by whom he had three children.   In 1835 Thalberg
appeared in Paris, and in 1836 he and Liszt contested for supremacy, the
latter being plainly the stronger.

From 1839 Liszt's time was largely occupied by far-reaching concert-tours
throughout Europe.   Everywhere his amazing technique, his masterly inter-
pretations and improvisations, and his unique magnetism placed him at the
head of the increasing circle of pianists.   His ambition, to be the Paganini of
the piano, was fully realized, and his pecuniary profits were so large that his
independence was secure.   In this connection came out his fine generosity.
In 1837 he sent a large gift for the sufferers by an inundation at Pesth, in
1839 established a fund for the poor in his native town, and in 1839, also,
when the subscriptions to the proposed Beethoven monument at Bonn lagged,
made up the needed balance of about $10,000.   These are but instances of a
life-long habit.   After 1847 it is said that he gave no concerts for his own benefit.

As early as 1842 he had become a favorite at Weimar, where he appeared
year after year.   In 1849 he became court-choirmaster, a position that he

made illustrious for several years, there beginning the second division of his life (see sec. 210).

Liszt's piano works — only partly belonging to the period before 1850 — include (*a*) a long list of transcriptions and arrangements from the most varied sources, as from Bach's organ-fugues, Beethoven's symphonies, overtures and other orchestral works by Weber, Mendelssohn, Meyerbeer, Rossini, Berlioz, Wagner, Raff, Glinka, etc., vocal works by Arcadelt, Mozart, Beethoven, Schubert and innumerable opera-writers ; (*b*) 14 *Rhapsodies* on Hungarian themes, besides many other national works ; (*c*) a quantity of original works, from brief and often very beautiful characteristic pieces up to extended con- cert-fantasias, études of extreme difficulty, 2 concertos and several other works with orchestra.

As a composer, Liszt seldom showed creative power of a high order, except in smaller lyric forms, and many of his themes are pretentious, but hollow. He was thoroughly impatient of the limits and regularities of accepted form and style, and struck off into vagaries of structure that seemed to his contem- poraries lawless. But he had gifts of sensational effect, of grandiose sentiment, of coruscating decoration, and, while these hardly constituted him a constructive artist of the first rank, his application of them certainly broadened the scope of composi- tion and prepared the way for other composers of the most modern type. His affiliation with Berlioz in this regard was notable, and he may even be likened somewhat to Schumann, though much inferior to him in positive imagination.

202. Rubinstein and Bülow. — Liszt gave a powerful impetus to interpretation as one of the functions of concert pianism. In this field were later conspicuous two other great players, whose careers were exactly parallel in years, but who were temperamentally and otherwise widely contrasted. One of them, Rubinstein, was not only a supereminent pianist, but an ambitious and abundant composer in the largest concerted forms, besides being the effective link in advanced musical culture between Germany and Russia — in one sense the pro- genitor of the modern Russian school. The other, Bülow, was likewise not only a pianist of the highest rank, but a most thorough and masterly orchestral and operatic conductor, a critical editor of musical scores, and one of the early promoters of Wagner's ideas. Both utilized their hold upon the public to restore to attention the whole range of keyboard composition, often through carefully planned series of historical programs — Rubinstein, with his Slavic warmth, having on the whole the greater sympathy with romantic tendencies, while Bülow, with his acute intellectuality, inclined to magnify classical precision, symmetry and structural energy.

> It is curious that Rubinstein, probably because disappointed in his own operatic ambitions, was unable to appreciate the rich promise of the Wagnerian movement into which the cooler Bülow threw his splendid energy with enthusiasm.

Both artists were more or less associated with Liszt, Bülow being his pupil and intimate friend. Both, like him, became everywhere known by means of prodigious concert-tours, extending in their cases to America as well as Europe. Thus, and as teachers, both were profoundly influential in molding popular taste upon larger lines than the bravura players had followed. Rubinstein naturally exerted special power in his native Russia, though his sympathies allied him closely with Germany as well, while Bülow was most active at Berlin, Munich, Meiningen, Frankfort and other German centres. On the side of execution, Rubinstein resembled Liszt in his liking for intense sensuous beauties and for grandiose orchestral effects, while Bülow, though not lacking in impetuosity and abandon, was far more of a precisian, polishing his performances to an extreme of nicety. Both had marvelous memories, but Bülow's mind retained even the most elaborate orchestral scores.

Anton Rubinstein (d. 1894) was born in 1830 in Bessarabia (SW. Russia), but was brought up at Moscow, where his father was a maker of pencils. His parents were of Jewish stock, though nominally members of the Orthodox Greek Church. His mother was cultivated and a good pianist, being his first teacher. At 7 began lessons with Villoing, who in 1839–40 took him to Paris. Here he won notice from Chopin and Liszt, but was declined admission to the Conservatoire. Before returning home he toured as a youthful prodigy. At 14 (1844) he and his brother were taken to Berlin, Anton studying under Dehn and in 1846–8, his father having died, touring in Austria. From 1848 he was at St. Petersburg, a favorite with the Grand Duchess Helen and beginning to write operas. He had long been composing freely, and in 1854–8 made a grand tour in Germany, France and England to bring his works to public notice. His success was followed in 1858 by his appointment as court-musician to the Czar and in 1859 as leader of the Musical Society. In 1862 he started the conservatory and was its director till 1867 (again in 1887–90). In 1867–70 came his most brilliant tour in Europe, followed in 1872–3 by another in America.

Meanwhile he was assiduously adding to his compositions, especially in the dramatic field. His last years were spent mostly in Berlin and Dresden, where he continued to give important recitals. The success of Wagner embittered him, so that he professed despair about the whole future of music. With the so-called 'neo-Russian' school he had little sympathy, though for it he had laid foundations.

His works for the piano include 5 concertos, fantasias with orchestra, 4 sonatas, a suite, preludes, études, barcarolles, tone-pictures and many salon-pieces, besides works for four hands or two pianos. The same qualities appear in them as in his larger works (see secs. 205, 214)—considerable melodic richness, fluent and often grandiose plans, a striving after extreme distinction, and yet a lack of inspiration, compacted structure and sustained power. As an author, he is known from *Memoirs* (1889) and sarcastic critiques (1892-7).

His brother **Nicolai Rubinstein** (d. 1881), five years younger, was in 1844-6 his fellow-student at Berlin, thence returning to Moscow. There in 1859 he founded the Musical Society and in 1854 the conservatory, of which he was the head almost 20 years, besides giving concerts regularly at St. Petersburg. He, too, was a remarkable player, an able conductor and an excellent composer of salon and concert music.

With Anton Rubinstein at St. Petersburg was associated from 1852 the talented Austrian **Theodor Leschetizki**, who had been trained by Czerny and Sechter, and had begun concert-giving at 12 (1842). After more than 25 years there as teacher, conductor and composer, from 1878 he toured extensively and in 1880, marrying his pupil Annette Essipoff, established himself at Vienna, becoming one of the best-known of teachers. His works include many striking concert-pieces and an opera (1867).

Hans von Bülow (d. 1894), born at Dresden in 1830, was first trained there by Wieck and Eberwein. In 1848-9, while beginning law-study at Leipsic and Berlin, he kept up his musical work, finally choosing it for his career. Amid the revolutionary ferment of the times he became so much interested in Wagner that in 1850-1 he followed him to Zurich, receiving from him a strong impulse to orchestral conducting. After brief service as conductor in Switzerland and study with Liszt at Weimar, in 1853-5 he gradually won his way as a virtuoso, in 1857 succeeding Kullak as teacher in the Stern conservatory at Berlin and in 1858 becoming court-pianist there. In 1857 he married Cosima Liszt, from whom in 1869 he was divorced (she becoming Wagner's wife in 1870). From 1864, at Wagner's urgency, he was court-pianist at Munich and from 1867 royal choirmaster and head of the conservatory, but in 1869 removed to Florence, where he was active on behalf of German music. Resuming tours in 1872 and visiting America in 1875-6, in 1878-80 he was court-conductor at Hanover, and in 1880-5 in a similar position at Meiningen, where he developed an orchestra of extraordinary brilliance. In 1885-8, after another American tour, he taught much at Frankfort and Berlin, besides conducting concerts at St. Petersburg. From 1888 he led a successful concert series at Hamburg until his health failed.

In his case the educational instinct was always prominent. From 1849 he wrote many articles in advocacy of Wagner and new ideas. At Munich he devoted great pains to the production of Wagner's *Tristan* and *Die Meister-*

singer. Wherever he went, his programs showed a desire to improve popular knowledge and taste. He prepared invaluable critical editions of Beethoven's sonatas, works by older writers like Bach and Handel, Cramer's études, etc His early *Briefe* (collected 1895) show how varied and active were his mental interests. Of his compositions but few are published — fine transcriptions from Wagner and Berlioz, some concert-pieces and songs, with several works for orchestra.

With Bülow may be grouped his coadjutor **Karl Klindworth**, born at Hanover in 1830. He was mostly self-taught until 1852, when he secured means for a year's study with Liszt. Rapidly developed into a fine player, from 1854 he taught in London, also giving or conducting some concerts. From 1868 he was professor at the Moscow conservatory. In 1882–93 he worked with Bülow at Berlin, conducting the Wagner-Verein and the Philharmonic, founding and directing a school for pianists, and continuing fine work, begun at Moscow, as arranger and editor of Wagner's *Ring*, Chopin's works (1878), Beethoven's sonatas, various elaborate orchestral works, etc. He himself wrote notable études, a difficult Polonaise-Fantasie, etc.

Other distinguished players and teachers, doing good work for the establishment of a large view of piano literature, were the Russian **Eduard Mertke** (d. 1895), in 1853-9 a violinist at the Gewandhaus and from 1869 piano-teacher at the Cologne conservatory, publishing arrangements of works by Hummel, Weber and Mendelssohn, an edition of Chopin, original studies and a suite, besides 2 operas and 2 cantatas ; and the Austrian **Anton Door**, a pupil of Czerny and Sechter, who, after traveling as a virtuoso, from 1859 taught at Moscow and since 1869 in the Vienna conservatory, making a name as a superior teacher and an enterprising editor of the classics and introducer of novelties.

To these should be added **Karl Tausig** (d. 1871), born at Warsaw in 1841, studying there with his father and from 1855 with Liszt. He rose at once to an astonishing mastery of technique and interpretation, actually outshining his master at many points. At 17 (1858) he appeared publicly at Berlin under Bülow's auspices, and then lived first at Dresden and later at Berlin, founding a school for advanced pianists and giving concerts constantly throughout Germany and Russia. At 30 his dazzling career was cut short. He left some important arrangements and transcriptions, invaluable studies, etc.

> The enormous demand for pianos led to constant accessions to the ranks of piano-makers. Among the businesses founded after 1830 may be mentioned those of *Debain* at Paris (1834), *Brinsmead* at London (1835), *Biber* at Munich (c. 1835), *Knabe* at Baltimore (1839), *Feurich* at Leipsic (1851), *Blüthner* at Leipsic (1853), *Bechstein* at Berlin (1856) and *Kaps* at Dresden (1859).

2 N

CHAPTER XXXIII

THE OPERA ASIDE FROM WAGNER

203. Verdi and the Italians. — Throughout the middle of the century native opera in Italy had little significant to offer except the striking career of Verdi. In general, her fertile opera-writers were quite content tó supply what the annual seasons everywhere demanded in the old, familiar style, aiming simply at luscious or humorous vocal effects and theatrically thrilling episodes with the minimum of choral or orchestral richness, and without thoughtful dramatic treatment of either characters or plot. The literary quality of librettos remained neglected. Popular impression depended upon captivation by star-singers, and was liable to be upset by trivial and unreasonable causes. What was called 'learning' was resented, with any energetic deviation from traditions. Italy had but slight knowledge of the splendid movements in musical art elsewhere in progress. For piano salon music and for songs there was a constant demand, but not for any serious form of orchestral or chamber music. Church music, of course, was indispensable, but it was largely controlled by operatic standards, and, except in a few places, had lost all memory of the old polyphonic ideality. Furthermore, all Italy was stirring with eagerness for release from foreign dominion, especially that of Austria, and was groping toward the national unity that has now come to pass.

Into this situation was projected before 1840 the sturdy figure of the young Verdi, a man of the people, Italian to the core, a dramatic enthusiast and a great melodist, yet a student, susceptible to suggestions from all sources, a real master of the voice and ultimately of orchestration, in artistic endeavor endowed with an elastic endurance seldom equaled. His long life made him a link between the age of Rossini and that of fully developed Wagnerism, and his genius was so resourceful and plastic that in his works is illustrated much of the tremendous transition between these two extremes. He not only brought lustre to the departing glory of the old Italian opera, but clearly led the way toward the new era of to-day in which fresh creators are finding their place.

Giuseppe Verdi (d. 1901) was born in 1813 (a few months after Wagner) near Busseto (Parma) in an innkeeper's family. At 7 his musical tendencies became marked, at 10 he acted as village-organist, at 12 had lessons from

Provesi, the leader of the musical society at Busseto, at 16 was enabled by the merchant Barezzi (later his father-in-law) to begin serious study at Milan, though not accepted at the conservatory, and at 20 succeeded Provesi at Busseto, where he married. He was composing in various forms, especially church music and piano-pieces. In 1838, with his first opera, *Oberto*, complete, he moved to Milan, where the work was given at La Scala with such success that three more operas were contracted for by the manager Merelli. While working on the first of these, the comic *Un giorno di regno* (1840), his wife and two children suddenly died, a bitter bereavement which, with the failure of the opera, utterly discouraged him.

Merelli, however, finally induced him to undertake *Nabucco* (1842) and *I Lombardi* (1843), which were decided successes. The second had so strong a patriotic flavor that the Austrian police forced a change in the plot of the fine *Ernani* (1844, Venice), lest it should provoke an insurrection. These works established his Italian reputation, and were followed (till 1850) by 10 other works at various theatres. All were written in the prevalent style, though with many evidences of independent force, especially in *Attila* (1846, Venice) and *Luisa Miller* (1849, Naples). During this period he spent a brief time at London and Paris, producing one work in each city and receiving invaluable impressions from other styles.

The results of these stimuli came out in *Rigoletto* (1851, Venice), *Il trovatore* (1853, Rome) and *La traviata* (1853, Venice), which soon brought him international fame. To these succeeded at intervals 7–8 works which for sundry reasons did not win great applause, except *Un ballo in maschera* (1859, Rome) and *Don Carlos* (1867, Paris). In general, they continued to exemplify the usual Italian type, but they were executed by one who had at command a limitless fund of spirit, technical ingenuity, and sense of form and color. From about 1860 there were signs of a new desire to emphasize richness of instrumentation and weld details into a powerful unity of effect.

Verdi's third manner is often called an imitation of Wagner, but it was rather the organic growth in an Italian artist induced by the study of a far richer style than his own. Though nearly 60 years old, Verdi now began a

final series far overtopping all his earlier works, including *Aïda* (1871, Cairo),
Otello (1887, Milan) and *Falstaff* (1893, Milan) — the last, though finished
in his 80th year, being one of the strong works of to-day.   In the last two he
had the benefit of fine librettos from the poet-composer *Arrigo Boito*, one of
the brightest lights of the 'neo-Italian' group.   Verdi also made a deep
impression by his Requiem (1874) in honor of the national patriot Mazzini.

In all, his operas number over 30, most of them serious.   Even those
which were not counted successful contain important passages.   Besides
operas he wrote little.

Personally, his was a character of rugged independence and noble purpose.
His simplicity of life, warm-heartedness, generosity, fervid love of country,
with his brilliant genius, made him the idol of Italy.   And he held the esteem
of musicians everywhere by his versatile industry and his sincere excellence.

Of the opera-writers already mentioned (secs. 175–176) **Rossini** produced
nothing after 1830; but there were still active **Pacini** (d. 1867), with 40
operas after 1840, including his best, *Saffo* (1840, Naples), and several others,
like *Medea* (1843, Palermo) and *La Regina di Cipro* (1846, Turin) ;   **Donizetti** (d. 1848), with all his best-known works between 1830 and '43 ;   and
Mercadante (d. 1870), with his masterpiece, *Il giuramento* (1837, Milan), and
some others about the same time.

Others who had already appeared before 1830 were **Pier Antonio Coppola**
(d. 1877), from 1816 a mediocre rival of Rossini, who made a hit with *Nina
pazza per amore* (1835, Rome), followed by *Gl'Illinesi* (1837, Turin), etc.,
leading to his appointment about 1839 as conductor at Lisbon ;   the fine
Neapolitan contrapuntist **Carlo Conti** (d. 1868), who had success with *L' Olimpiade* (1829, Naples) ;   and **Luigi Ricci** (d. 1859), also of Naples, among
whose 30 works were *Amina* (1829, Rome), *Chiara di Rosemberg* (1831,
Milan), and *Un'avventura di Scaramuccia* (1835, Milan), which were
admired outside of Italy.

From 1829 to '43, when Verdi first became a power, many composers
began to be heard, among whom were the following : — **Lauro Rossi** (d.
1885), trained at Naples, from 1832 conductor at Rome, in 1835–44 on an
operatic tour to Mexico, Havana and New Orleans, from 1850 head of the
Milan conservatory, and in 1871–8 Mercadante's successor at Naples,
producing almost 30 operas, of which the chief were *I falsi monetari*
(1835, Milan), *Il domino nero* (1849, Milan) and *La contessa di Mons* (1874,
Turin), besides an oratorio (1833), church music, etc.;   **Errico Petrella** (d.
1877), another Neapolitan pupil, born the same year as Verdi and for a
time his rival in Italy, with over 20 operas (none between 1839 and '51), such
as *Le miniere di Freibergh* (1839, Naples), *Le precauzioni* (1851, Naples),
Marco Visconti (1854, Naples), *Elnava* (1855, Milan), *Ione* (1858, Milan),
La contessa d'Amalfi (1864, Turin), *I promessi sposi* (1866, Lecco) and
Giovanna II (1869, Naples) ;   **Alberto Mazzucato** (d. 1877), whose 7 operas
(1834–44) were outclassed by Verdi's, but who from 1839 was an able teacher
at the Milan conservatory and from 1872 its director, besides being concertmaster at La Scala in 1859–69 and an industrious literary worker ;   **Federico
Ricci** (d. 1877), with about 20 operas (at first with his brother Luigi), among
them *La prigione d'Edimburgo* (1837, Trieste), *Corrado d'Altamura* (1841,

Milan) and the brilliant *Crispino e la comare* (1850, Venice); **Teodul Mabellini** (d. 1897), a well-trained pupil of Pilotti and Mercadante, whose special successes were with *Rolla* (1840, Turin), *Il conte di Savagna* (1843, Florence) and *Baldassare* (1852, Florence), and who from 1843 was identified with Florence as conductor and from 1859 as professor of composition at the conservatory, writing also an oratorio, much sacred music, cantatas, songs and piano-pieces; **Alessandro Nini** (d. 1880), who, after teaching singing at St. Petersburg in 1830–7, was from 1843 choirmaster at Bergamo, with several operas, chief of which was *La marescialla d'Ancre* (1839, Padua), and excellent church music, including a notable Miserere; the genial tenor **Jozef Poniatowski** (d. 1873), who in 1848–70 was a Tuscan diplomat at Paris, and who wrote 12 tuneful operas (from 1838) in Italy or at Paris; **Achille Peri** (d. 1880), conductor at Reggio, somewhat an imitator of Verdi, with about 10 operas, the first of popularity being *Dirce* (1843, Reggio), and an oratorio (1860, Milan); and **Carlo Pedrotti** (d. 1893), who in 1840–5 was conductor at Amsterdam, lived long at Verona, from 1868 was director of the Turin conservatory and from 1882 of the Rossini school at Pesaro, with about 15 buffo operas, including *Romea di Montfort* (1845, Verona), *Gelmina* (1853, Milan), *Tutti in maschera* (1856, Verona), and *Il favorito* (1870, Turin).

Among the numerous writers entering the field from 1843 onward the following may be selected as for some reason notable: — **Francesco Chiaromonte** (d. 1886), pupil of Raimondi and Donizetti, who, after a career as a tenor, undertook composition, was expelled from Naples as a revolutionist in 1850, went to Genoa, from 1855 was chorusmaster at Paris and London, and from 1862 taught at Brussels, producing 9 operas (1844–55), especially *Caterina di Cleves* (1850, Naples), an oratorio (1884) and a method for singers; **Antonio Cagnoni** (d. 1896), from 1852 choirmaster at Vigevano, from 1873 at Novara and from 1887 at Bergamo, with over 20 operas (from 1845), chief of which was the farce *Don Bucefalo* (1847, Milan), besides good church music and an unproduced grand opera, *Re Lear* (1893); the famous double-bassist **Bottesini** (d. 1889), with 8 well-written operas (1847–80), including *L' assedio di Firenze* (1856, Paris), *Ali Baba* (1871, London), etc., an oratorio (1887, Norwich), orchestral and chamber music and songs; **Francesco Schira** (d. 1883), from 1842 a favorite singing-master at London, whose 3 early operas (1832–7) at Milan and Lisbon, were outranked by 5 later ones (from 1849), such as *Theresa* (1850, London), *Nicolò de' Lapi* (1863, London) and *La selvaggia* (1865, Venice), besides some other works; **Pietro Platania** (d. 1907), from 1863 director of the Palermo conservatory and from 1888 of that at Naples, with 5 operas (from 1852), including *Spartaco* (1893, Milan), orchestral music and a treatise on fugue; **Giorgio Miceli** (d. 1895), long a teacher at Naples and in 1887–94 Platania's successor at Palermo, with 6 operas at Naples (from 1852), including *Il conte di Rossiglione* (1854), 2 sacred operas (1885–6), and church and chamber music; **Filippo Marchetti** (d. 1902), from 1881 the head of the Rome conservatory, with 8 ambitious operas, notably *Gentile da Varano* (1856, Turin), *Giulietta e Romeo* (1865, Trieste), *Ruy Blas* (1869, Milan) and other vocal and instrumental works; and **Carlotta Ferrari**, a pupil of Mazzucato at Milan, with 3 successful works (1857–71), church music and songs, besides librettos and poems.

Measured by the Italian standard, the one composer in the period now under consideration to be counted with Verdi was **Amilcare Ponchielli** (d. 1886), who was trained at Milan. While a student he wrote an operetta (1851) and while organist at Cremona undertook opera (1856). His general fame, however, did not come till later, with *I promessi sposi* (revised, 1872, Milan), *I Lituani* (1874), *La gioconda* (1876), *Il figliuol prodigo* (1880) and *Marion Delorme* (1885), besides other music. In originality he did not rank high.

Here may well be added the Brazilian **Antonio Carlos Gomez** (d. 1896), a pupil of Rossi at Milan, who produced in Italy or at Rio de Janeiro several works (from 1861), including *Il Guarany* (1870, Milan), *Salvator Rosa* (1874, Venice), *Maria Tudor* (1877, Milan) and *Lo schiavo* (1889, Rio).

204. Development of the Opéra Comique. — The form of opera for which French composers have shown a spontaneous and unwearied capacity is the opéra comique, the nature of which, however, has not been constant. At its outset, it was in part an adaptation of the not over-refined Italian opera buffa to the gay and witty taste of France, in part an evolution from the only half-musical vaudeville, and in part, too, a light application of some technical methods found in non-Italian forms of serious opera. In the hands of Boieldieu and Auber the type became distinct and so satisfactory that it not only led onward to the modern French opera, but more or less influenced all but the most strenuous tragic opera everywhere (see sec. 177).

Largely because of its adaptable nature, it was open to the influence of somewhat delicate poetic tendencies and even of vigorous imagination. Hence, as time went on and the usual range of social topics became somewhat exhausted, the opéra comique often acquired a sentiment and fancy that were not its original characteristics. Out of it grew the modern French romantic opera. From about 1860 its distinctness as a type steadily diminished, for in technical methods it approximated the grand opera, and in substance and structure it was more romantic than merely diverting. Meanwhile, however, the old craving for amusement pure and simple was satisfied by the rise of the brief, captivating operetta of the Offenbach type.

The progress of the opéra comique through the middle of the century was not dominated by any one composer, though Auber continued to be one of its leading exemplars. Neither did it call out any composer of first-rate genius. But in their respective ways there were several able contributors, like Halévy,

Adam, Grisar and Thomas in the older group and Gounod, Reyer, Delibes and Bizet in the later. With these latter the drift toward romanticism became evident.

A special word should be added about the influence of this French type upon opera elsewhere. The fact that Paris maintained itself as on the whole the leading operatic centre of Europe made whatever was done there notable. Although the true opéra comique could not well be transported bodily to other social conditions, except in selected instances, yet the styles it favored were diligently studied by composers, and its vivacity, sparkle and verve became objects of fruitful emulation everywhere. As a counterpoise to Italian sentimentality and exaggerated passion, and to German excess of seriousness or learning, it certainly had value.

Of the composers already named (sec. 177), **Auber** alone continued to produce long after 1830 (till 1869), being represented by works like *Fra Diavolo* (1830), *Le bal masqué* (1833), *Le domino noir* (1837), *Les diamants de la couronne* (1841), *Haydée* (1847) and *Manon Lescaut* (1856) — some 30 in all. His suavity and elegance of style were widely acknowledged, and his freshness of invention continued almost unabated. Into the field of opéra comique the restless **Meyerbeer** essayed to enter with his *L'étoile du Nord* (1854) and *Dinorah* (1859). His influence served to help forward the transformation of the type into something more pretentious and less individually French.

Fromental Halévy (d. 1862) was of Jewish descent, born at Paris in 1799. In 1809–19 he studied at the Conservatoire, especially with Berton and Cherubini, finally winning the Prix de Rome. Before returning to Paris in 1822 he had written 3 operas, considerable church music and a few piano works. From 1827 he was teacher of harmony at the Conservatoire, from 1833 of counterpoint and from 1840 of composition, being closely associated with Cherubini in his last years and collaborating on his theoretical treatise (1835). From 1827, also, he was accompanist at the Théâtre Italien and in 1830–56 chef de chant at the Opéra. In 1836 he succeeded Reicha as member of the Academy, being from 1854 its secretary. His first efforts to gain recognition were disappointing, but success began to come with *Clari* and *Le dilettante d'Avignon* (both 1829) and the ballet *Manon Lescaut* (1830). But his fame was made in 1835 by the almost simultaneous production of the grand opera *La juive* and the opéra comique *L'éclair*, each a masterpiece in its field. During the next 23 years he wrote almost an opera per year, sometimes in the lighter vein, as *Les mousquetaires* (1846), *La dame de pique* (1850) and *Le Nadab* (1853), often, too, in grand opera form, as *La reine de Chypre* (1841), *Charles VI* (1843) and *La tempesta* (Italian, based on Shakespeare, 1850, London). He had genuine poetic susceptibility, with positive musical and dramatic gifts, and was learned in the technique of composition, but sought to be too versatile, produced too much, often with poor librettos, distorted his natural style in the desire to emulate Meyerbeer, was often obscure and generally unequal. For all these reasons he failed of a decided hold upon the public. He is also known by music for *Prometheus Unbound* (1849), 2 cantatas, songs, male part-songs, a text-book in elementary singing, and two collections of reminiscences and eulogies (1861–3). Two unfinished operas were completed by his son-in-law Bizet.

Adolphe Adam (d. 1856), slightly younger than Halévy and less well educated, sprang into popularity with him in 1829. A favorite pupil of Boieldieu, he followed him in producing over 50 comparatively light, but tuneful works, often intensely humorous, but much more 'taking' than original. Among them were *Le chalet* (1834), *Le postillon de Longjumeau* (1836), which at once became famous throughout Europe, *Le brasseur de Preston* (1838), *Le roi d'Yvetot* (1842), *Cagliostro* (1844), etc., besides many brilliant ballets, like *Giselle* (1841). His few efforts in grand opera were wholly unsuccessful. In 1847, having quarreled with the Opéra-Comique, he started an independent operatic enterprise, which in the Revolution of 1848 failed disastrously. Five years of hard work were needed to recover himself. From 1849 he was his father's successor at the Conservatoire. He continued to compose and also became known as a genial newspaper critic. Some of his articles and reminiscences were published posthumously (1857–9).

Albert Grisar (d. 1869), though Belgian by birth, was identified with Paris from 1830, where he first studied and in 1836–40 produced 8 pleasing comedies. From 1840 he spent several years in careful study with Mercadante at Naples. From 1848, again in Paris, he wrote about 25 more works, of which only half were actually performed, besides some scenas and over 50 songs. Among the later operas were *Gilles ravisseur* (1848), *Les porcherons* (1850), *Le chien du jardinier* (1855), and 4 after 1860. His talent was poetic and graceful, but slender and unoriginal.

Ambroise Thomas (d. 1896) stands on a higher level than the foregoing. Born at Metz in 1811, he had four brilliant years at the Conservatoire under Zimmerman, Kalkbrenner, Dourlen and the veteran Le Sueur, taking the Prix de Rome in 1832. He immediately began writing chamber, church and piano music to good purpose. After visiting the the chief Italian cities and Vienna, he began at Paris the series of nearly 25 operas and ballets by which gradually his fame was secured. In 1851 he became an Academician, and in 1871 took Auber's place as head of the Conservatoire. His last 25 years were largely occupied by fruitful administrative and educational effort. His work as a composer exhibited interesting stages of growth, which at once illustrated and directed the progress of French opera. His first 10 works, from *La double échelle* (1837) to *Mina* (1843) and the ballet *Betty* (1846), were opéras comiques, written with graceful and careful finish, but not essentially different from the best of Auber or Hérold. The second series of 8 included *Le Caïd* (1849), *Le songe d'une nuit d'été* (1850), *Raymond* (1851), *Psyché* (1857), etc., which, though not strikingly successful with the public, marked the transition to romantic poetry through which the old opéra comique was to acquire new vitality. Finally came larger and finer works, including the famous *Mignon* (1866) and the grand operas *Hamlet* (1868) and *Françoise de Rimini* (1882), which belong to the modern period. His style is characterized by great dramatic truth, by striking versatility in handling characters and situations and by a thorough mastery of orchestration. Had his gift of real musical invention been greater, he would have ranked among the best opera-writers. Besides his operas, he also wrote fine male choruses, some religious works, including 2 masses, 2 cantatas and considerable chamber music.

Among the many lesser writers who appeared before about 1850 may be named **Antoine Louis Clapisson** (d. 1866), a violinist and collector of instruments (his collection becoming in 1861 the nucleus of the Conservatoire museum), with over 20 clever operas (1838–61) and about 200 songs ; **Prince de la Moskowa [Joseph Napoléon Ney]** (d. 1857), the distinguished son of Marshal Ney, who in 1843 organized and conducted a society for the study of vocal works from the 16–17th centuries, published a remarkable collection for it (11 vols.), was known as a critic, and wrote 2 successful operettas (1840,'55) ; **Paul Mériel** (d. 1897), a leading musician at Toulouse, finally in charge of the conservatory, with 6 stage-works (c. 1840–86), including the grand opera *L'armorique,* a symphony, an oratorio and chamber music ; the violinist and critic **Georges Bousquet** (d. 1854), with 3 operas (1844–52) and considerable other music ; **Jean François Eugène Gautier** (d. 1878), from 1848 assistant conductor at the Théâtre Lyrique, and from 1864 chef de chant at the Théâtre Italien and professor at the Conservatoire, with 14 operas (1845–64), an oratorio, etc. ; **François Bazin** (d. 1878), winner of the Prix de Rome in 1840 and from 1844 professor at the Conservatoire, first of singing, then of harmony and from 1871 of composition, with 9 operas (1846–70), including *La nuit de la St.-Sylvestre* (1849) and *Madelon* (1852), besides a manual on theory ; **Louis [or Aimé] Maillart** (d. 1871), who won the Prix de Rome in 1841 and wrote 6 operas, including *Gastibelza* (1847), *La croix de Marie* (1852) and *Les dragons de Villars* (1856) ; **Napoléon Henri Reber** (d. 1880), from 1851 professor of harmony at the Conservatoire, from 1862 of composition and from 1871 inspector of branch institutions, distinguished as a general composer and theorist, with a few stage-works (1848–57) and an unperformed grand opera (see sec. 212) ; **Félix Marie [or Victor] Massé** (d. 1884), the Prix-winner in 1843, from 1860 chorusmaster at the Opéra, from 1866 professor of counterpoint at the Conservatoire and from 1872 an Academician, gaining popular applause by his early songs and about 20 operas, from *La chambre gothique* (1849), *Galathée* (1852) and *Les noces de Jeannette* (1853) to *Paul et Virginie* (1876) and *Une nuit de Cléopâtre* (1877) ; **Aristide Hignard** (d. 1898), an ambitious worker, with about 10 operas (from 1851), including the grand opera *Hamlet* (1888), besides vocal and piano-pieces ; and **Jean Alexandre Ferdinand Poise** (d. 1892), pupil and imitator of Adam, with 14 operas, from the successful *Bonsoir, voisin* (1853) to *Le médecin malgré lui* (1887).

Friedrich von Flotow (d. 1883), though German by birth, was a Parisian by training and in style. In 1835–48 and 1863–8 he worked at Paris and often visited it later. In 1856–63 he was court-intendant at Schwerin, and after 1868 lived chiefly near Vienna. Of his over 25 stage-works, mostly light, the most successful were *Le naufrage de la Méduse* (1853, Paris), *Stradella* (1844, Hamburg), the popular *Martha* (1847, Vienna), *Indra* (1853, Berlin) and *L'ombre* (1870, Paris). His easy melodiousness was not supported by much structural skill.

In the works of the next group of composers, especially when produced after 1870, the distinctly romantic tendency is more manifest, so that in many instances the type is no longer called 'opéra comique,' but 'drame lyrique.'

Among those early in this field were the eminent orchestral composer ot oriental predilections **Félicien David** (d. 1876), who wrote a few striking operatic works, especially *La Perle du Brésil* (1851), *Herculanum* (1859) and *Lalla Rookh* (1862); **Léon Gastinel**, with about 10 operas (from 1853), extending to recent years, besides oratorios, masses, works for orchestra, etc.; **Louis Étienne Ernest Reyer**, David's successor in the Academy (and, like him, at first fond of oriental color), librarian at the Opéra and a brilliant critic, with 7 operas (from 1854), including the important *La statue* (1861), and the more elaborate *Sigurd* (1884) and *Salammbô* (1890), besides choral works — in his later writing frankly adopting Wagner's ideas; **Louis Pierre Deffès** (d. 1900), pupil of Halévy, Prix-winner in 1847 and long in charge of the Toulouse conservatory, with 15 operas (1855–98), often very successful, and many choral and orchestral works; **Léo Delibes** (d. 1891), pupil of Adam, from 1853 accompanist at the Théâtre Lyrique, in 1865–72 assistant chorus-master at the Opéra and from 1881 professor of composition at the Conservatoire, still more successful with a long list of works of varying dimensions, especially the ballets *La source* (1866), *Coppélia* (1870) and *Sylvia* (1876), and the operas *Jean de Nivelle* (1880) and *Lakmé* (1883), besides choruses and songs.

Especially characteristic in this connection was **Charles François Gounod** (d. 1893), born in 1818 and at first devoted to sacred music. He entered the dramatic field with the grand operas *Sapho* (1851) and *La nonne sanglante* (1854), and only later with the comic *Le médecin malgré lui* — none with much favor. But his brilliant *Faust* (1859) was an instant and general success, and was soon followed by 5 others, of which the more notable were *Mireille* (1864) and *Roméo et Juliette* (1867). Later he added 3 more (1877–81) of less value. He excelled in suave melody and harmony, and in handling the orchestra in accompaniments and entr'actes. But his vivacity was not sustained in comic writing, and his lack of vigor kept him from full success in serious drama. In the poetic domain between he was more at home.

Outside the limits here set lie most of the works of several other composers who first appeared about 1860, like **Georges Bizet** (d. 1875), whose efforts before *Carmen* (1875) had little influence, partly because of their Wagnerian flavor; **Samuel David** (d. 1895), writer of many comedies; and **Ernest Guiraud** (d. 1892), an American by birth, from 1876 professor of harmony at the Conservatoire.

One reason why the opéra comique began to approximate to the grand opera was the appearance from 1855 of the extremely light opéra bouffe or farcical operetta, especially as devised by Offenbach. The popularity of this small and trivial form was so great that the opéra comique in self-defense sought to retain its hold upon artistic taste by becoming poetically and musically richer, leaving the field of broad humor to the newcomer.

The pioneers in establishing these ephemeral, but often clever operettas were Florimond Ronger ['Hervé'] (d. 1892), a singer who started the Folies Concertantes in 1855, but was soon outranked and betook himself to other cities, with about 50 works (from 1855); Jacques Offenbach (d. 1880), a Jewish 'cellist, in the orchestra of the Opéra-Comique since 1835, who founded the Bouffes Parisiens in 1855 and had enormous success for many years, with about 100 works (from 1853); Émile Jonas, also of Jewish birth, in 1847-66 professor of solfeggio at the Conservatoire, with about 20 works (from 1855); and the more gifted Alexandre Charles Lecocq, with nearly 50 works (from 1857), the special vogue of which did not begin until 1868.

Another reason for the change in the opéra comique was the curious fact that grand opera, though nominally the highest form of French musical drama, was seldom actually written by Frenchmen. The repertory at the Opéra was made up either of repetitions of older works, or of those produced by foreigners. Until about 1850 the field was strongly dominated by Meyerbeer and the Italians.

Among the more or less isolated works of this class should be mentioned 4 operas (1828-55) of moderate success by the Swiss Niedermeyer (d. 1861); Benvenuto Cellini (1838) and Les Troyens (1863) by Berlioz (d. 1869); François Villon (1857) and L'esclave (1875) by Edmond Membrée (d. 1882); and Le jugement de Dieu (1860) by Auguste François Morel (d. 1881).

Intimately connected with French styles were the operas and operettas of Belgian and Dutch composers, most of whom either studied or worked more or less at Paris. The Spanish school of dramatic music received its early impetus from Italy, but its most characteristic development since about 1830 has been in the making of 'zarzuelas' or comic operettas, which are obviously analogous to French forms.

The Belgian list includes 2 operas at Antwerp by the young Jean François Joseph Janssens (d. 1835); 5 at Brussels (1845-52) by Adolphe Samuel (d. 1898), who was also a good symphonist and theorist (see secs. 213, 225); nearly 20 (from 1847) by Karel Miry (d. 1889), assistant director at Ghent; 8 (1848-60) by Édouard Gregoir (d. 1890), the historical student of Antwerp, over 10 (1848-64, mostly at Paris) by the historian Gevaert (d. 1908), then of Ghent and from 1871 director of the Brussels conservatory; and several (from 1856) by Benoît (d. 1901), from 1867 director of the Antwerp conservatory and a fertile author.

Although Holland received its strongest musical impulse from Germany, many of its early operas were French, as, for example, *Guillaume de Nassau* (1832, Hague) by **Costard de Mézeray** (d. 1887), then court-conductor; *Le Bandit* (1840, Hague) by the energetic **Jean Bernard van Bree** (d. 1857); many operas and ballets (from 1840) at Amsterdam by **Anton Berlijn** (d. 1870); and *La siège de Leyde* (1847, Hague) by the Parisian **Adolphe Vogel** (d. 1892).

Among Spanish composers may be named **Miguel Hilario Eslava** (d. 1878), choirmaster from 1832 at Seville and from 1844 at Madrid (see sec. 221), with 3 Italian operas (1841–3); **Pascual Arrieta y Corera** (d. 1894), from 1857 professor at the Madrid conservatory and from 1877 its director, with about 50 works (from 1845), including the ambitious *Isabel la Católica* (1850); **Rafael José Maria Hernando**, with about 15 works (from 1848); **Joaquin Gaztambide** (d. 1870), with 40 popular comedies (from 1850); **Francisco Asenjo Barbieri** (d. 1894), from 1868 professor at Madrid, with over 60 (from 1850), also very successful; **Cristobal Oudrid** (d. 1877), with over 30 (from 1850); **Manuel Fernandez Caballero**; and many others.

205. Austrian and German Opera. — The development of opera in German during this period wholly lacked the concentration so conspicuous in that of French opera. Austria stood slightly apart from Germany in that its operatic styles were more closely related to those of Italy or France, especially the latter, though opera in German, often romantic in spirit, was becoming more frequent. Germany was still split up into numerous states, no one of which had absolute precedence, and between them there was much jealousy. Musically, the foremost countries were Saxony (including the many Saxon duchies), Bavaria and Prussia, with Leipsic, Weimar and Dresden in the first, Munich in the second and Berlin in the third as leading operatic centres. But there were many others — Stuttgart and Darmstadt in the southwest, Hamburg and Hanover in the northwest, for example — and German influence was strong in Holland, the Scandinavian countries, Poland and Russia. Although the popular vogue of Italian opera continued in many quarters, enthusiasm for the romantic treatment of German themes or for a national comedy parallel to the French opéra comique was increasing, and in every capital and large city native composers were pushing into view. Many of these doubtless represented the 'capellmeister' type of composer — well-trained, but uninspired. The ablest successors of Weber were Marschner and Lortzing, but even Marschner was not powerful enough to create a type of style. Soon after 1840 'the new school' began to make itself felt under Wagner at Dresden and Liszt at Weimar, but until after 1860 its ambitious program was strenuously opposed by most of the leading critics and not understood by the general public.

Among Austrian opera-writers may be named **Ludwig Wilhelm Reuling** (d. 1879), in 1830–54 conductor at Vienna, with over 35 works (from about 1825), chiefly comic and light, but including the romantic *Die Feuerbraut* (1829, Trieste) and the historical *Alfred der Grosse* (1840, Vienna) ; **Anton Emil Titl** (d. 1882), working first at Prague and from 1850 at Vienna, with 5 romantic works, including *Die Burgfrau* (1832, Brünn) and *Das Wolkenkind* (1845, Vienna), with other music ; **Johann Vesque von Püttlingen** [' J. Hoven '] (d. 1883), a lawyer and civil official, with 6 well-received operas, including *Turandot* (1838), *Johanna d'Arc* (1840) and *Liebeszauber* (1845) ; the Tyrolese **Joseph Netzer** (d. 1864), with 5 operas (from 1839), including *Mara* (1841) and *Die seltene Hochzeit* (1846), besides many songs and orchestral works ; and the exceedingly popular writer of operettas **Franz von Suppé** (d. 1895), conductor at various Vienna theatres, with about 65 works (from 1834), which from 1860 followed in quick succession. With the latter may be grouped **Richard Genée** (d. 1895), with some 15 operettas (from 1857).

The Bohemian or Czech group includes **Franz Škraup** (d. 1862), in 1827–57 conductor of the Bohemian theatre at Prague, where he was prompt to produce Wagner's early works, with about 10 operas (from 1826), including *Oldřich a Božena* (1828) and *Libušin sňatek* (1835) ; the song-writer **Joseph Dessauer** (d. 1876), with 5 works, beginning with *Lidwinna* (1836, Prague) ; **Johann Friedrich Kittl** (d. 1868), in 1843–65 director of the Prague conservatory, with 4 German operas (1848–54) ; **Franz Skuhersky** (d. 1892), pupil of Kittl, from 1854 conductor at Innsbruck, from 1866 head of the Prague Organ-School and from 1869 court-choirmaster, with 5 operas (from 1861), including *Vladimir*, *Lora* and *Der General*, besides 20 masses, etc., and important theoretical works (from 1879) ; the distinguished **Friedrich Smetana** (d. 1884), in 1848–56 a teacher at Prague and in 1866–74, after some years in Sweden and Germany, opera-conductor there, with 8 operas, beginning with *Braniboři v Čechách* (1865), *Prodaná nevěsta* (1866) and *Dalibor* (1868) ; **Johann Nepomuk Škraup** (d. 1892), from about 1835 active as choirmaster and teacher at Prague, with *Švédove v Praže* (1867) and *Vineta* (1870) ; **Wilhelm Blodek** (d. 1874), from 1860 in the Prague conservatory, with the comic *V studni* (1867) ; and **Karl Bendl** (d. 1897), from 1865 conductor at Prague, with 5 operas, beginning with *Lejla* (1868) and *Bretislav* (1869).

The small Hungarian or Magyar group includes **Andreas Bartay** (d. 1856), with 3 early works, including *Esel* (1839) ; **Franz Erkel** (d. 1893), the first conductor of the National theatre at Pesth, founder of the Philharmonic concerts, and the first professor of the piano and instrumentation at the conservatory, with 9 operas (1840–74), especially *Hunyády László* (1844) and *Bank Bán* (1861) ; the flutists **Franz Doppler** (d. 1883), in the Pesth orchestra till

1858, and his brother **Karl Doppler** (d. 1900), conductor there till 1865, each with a few operas (from 1847 and 1852) ;   the violinist **Karl Hubay** (d. 1885), with *Szekler Mädchen* (1858) and 2 others ;   and **Mosonyi [Michael Brandt]** (d. 1870), with *Szép Ilonka* (1861).

Of the German romanticists already named (see sec. 172), a few continued active after 1830, especially **K. Kreutzer** of Vienna (d. 1849), with more than a dozen works, including his best, *Das Nachtlager von Granada* (1834) and *Der Verschwender* (1836) ;   **Lindpaintner** of Stuttgart (d. 1856), with about 10, among them *Die Genueserin* (1838, Vienna) and *Lichtenstein* (1845, Stuttgart) ;   **Marschner** of Hanover (d. 1861), with 7, including *Des Falkners Braut* (1832, Leipsic), *Hans Heiling* (1833, Berlin), and *Adolf von Nassau* (1843, Hanover) ;   and **Reissiger** of Dresden (d. 1859), with 3 (1835–46).

Gustav Albert Lortzing (d. 1851), born of theatrical parents in 1801, had an unsettled youth somewhat like Weber's, becoming a ready actor and stage-singer, and picking up some musical knowledge.   His first works (1824–32) were short and light.   From 1833 he was tenor at the Leipsic theatre, where he produced 7 operas, including the popular *Die beiden Schützen* (1837), *Czar und Zimmermann* (1839), *Hans Sachs* (1840) and his masterpiece *Der Wildschütz* (1842).   His success led to his becoming conductor in 1844 and again in 1848, in each case speedily quarreling with the management.   From 1844 he went hither and thither, producing 4 more operas, including *Undine* (1845, Hamburg) and *Der Waffenschmied* (1846, Vienna), and some operettas at Berlin, where for a year he conducted small stage-pieces.   He died in poverty, leaving 2 further operas, of which *Regina* has lately (1899) been given with success.   His melodic gifts were exceptional, and his works have a singular freshness of humor and style, so that several of them are still popular.

Heinrich Dorn (d. 1892), born in 1804, was thoroughly trained at Königsberg and Berlin.   After residence at Frankfort, Königsberg and Leipsic (where he taught Schumann), from 1832 he was cathedral-choirmaster and finally theatre-conductor at Riga, from 1843 town-musician at Cologne, where in 1845 he started the school that later became the conservatory, and in 1849–69 court-opera-conductor at Berlin, thereafter teaching and writing critiques. Of his 13 operas and operettas (1826–65), *Die Nibelungen* (1854, Weimar) had the best success.   He also wrote church music, including a Requiem (1851), orchestral works and many popular songs.   He was an able conductor and a solid musician of the old school.   In criticism he was strongly anti-Wagner — perhaps because of early contacts with him at Leipsic and Riga. Side by side with him at Berlin was the piano-virtuoso **Wilhelm Taubert** (d. 1891), from 1831 court-accompanist and in 1842–70 also court-conductor and choirmaster, with 6 operas (from 1832), including *Macbeth* (1857) and *Cesario* (1874), incidental music to many plays, symphonies, chamber music, songs, etc., in a style sound, but not vigorous or inspired.   (Regarding the whole Berlin circle, see sec. 213.)

Of less significance are many others, like **Franz Gläser** (d. 1861), from 1817 conductor at Vienna, from 1830 at Berlin and from 1842 at Copenhagen, with 13 operas (from 1824), especially *Des Adlers Horst* (1833, Berlin) ;   the Frenchman **Hippolyte André Chelard** (d. 1861), trained in Italy, whose failure with 2 operas at Paris (1827–8) was made up by successes at Munich, where he produced 4 operas, including *Die Hermannsschlacht* (1835), followed by 2 comedies at Weimar (1842–4); the eminent symphonist **Franz Lachner** (d. 1890), most of whose 4 operas (1828–49) were brought out at Munich, including *Caterina Cornaro* (1841) and *Benvenuto Cellini* (1849); the violinist and critic **Louis Schlösser** (d. 1886), long in court service at Darmstadt, with 6 operas (from about 1835) and much instrumental music; the talented, but short-lived **Otto Nicolai** (d. 1849, aged 39), trained at Berlin and Rome, whose 4 early works (1838–42) were Italian in text and style, though reproduced in German at Vienna, where in 1841–7 he was court-choirmaster, but whose famous comedy *Die lustigen Weiber von Windsor* (1849) was brought out at Berlin, where from 1847 he was opera- and cathedral-conductor; **Franz Xaver Pentenrieder** (d. 1867), court-choirmaster at Munich, with the popular *Die Nacht auf Paluzzi* and one other (1846); **Karl Mangold** (d. 1889), violinist, chorus-master and in 1848–69 court-conductor at Darmstadt, with 4 operas, including *Tannhäuser* (1846), several concert-dramas and successful chorus music and songs; **Gustav Schmidt** (d. 1882), conductor at Frankfort, with 4 operas, beginning with the favorite *Prinz Eugen* (1845); the cultivated **Franz von Holstein** (d. 1878), brought up as a soldier, but in 1853–9 thoroughly trained as a musician, partly by Hauptmann, with 6 operas (from 1845), including the successful *Der Heideschacht* (1868, Dresden) and others later, fine overtures, chamber music and songs; **Ernst II.** (d. 1893), Duke of Saxe-Coburg-Gotha, with 7 stage-works (1846–73), including *Santa Chiara* (1853), *Casilda* (1855) and *Diana von Solange* (1858), besides other works; **Heinrich Frankenberger** (d. 1885), from 1847 in the Sondershausen orchestra, with 3 works (1847–63); the Munich conductor and intendant **Karl von Perfall** (d. 1907), with 4 operas (1853–86), favorite cantatas and melodramas, including *Dornröschen*, and excellent songs and part-songs; **Wilhelm Karl Mühldorfer**, from 1855 conductor at Ulm, from 1867 at Leipsic and since 1881 at Cologne, with 5 romantic works, beginning with *Im Kyffhäuser* (1855); **Wilhelm Westmeyer** (d. 1880), with *Amanda* (1856, Coburg) and *Der Wald bei Hermannstadt* (1859, Leipsic) and good chamber music; **Theodor Hentschel** (d. 1892), in 1860–90 conductor at Bremen, with 5 works, beginning with *Matrose und Sänger* (1857, Leipsic); the Bohemian **Theodor Bradský** d. (1881), with *Roswitha* (1860, Dessau) and several others; and **August Langert**, from 1860 conductor at various places and from 1873 at Gotha, with a series from *Die Jungfrau von Orleans* (1861, Coburg) and *Die Sängers Fluch* (1863, Coburg). Several of these last belong rather to the next period.

The Weimar circle and Wagner are considered elsewhere (see secs. 206–210).

In Denmark mention should be made of the distinguished **Emil Hartmann** (d. 1900), from 1840 director of the Copenhagen conservatory and from 1849 court-conductor, whose 4 operas (1832–46) were among his earliest works; **Siegfried Saloman** (d. 1899), whose first 3 operas (1844–7) were written at Copenhagen, including *Das Diamantkreuz* (1847); and **Henrik Rung** (d. 1871), with 8 works, beginning with *Die Erstürmung von Kopenhagen* (1847) and *Federigo* (1848).

The Polish group includes **Karl Kasimir Kurpinski** (d. 1857), in 1810–41 conductor at Warsaw, with nearly 25 facile operas (1811–26), besides ballets; **Victor Kazynski**, with 3 fairly successful works (1840–8) at Wilna, Warsaw and St. Petersburg; and **Stanislaw Moniuszko** (d. 1872), who was trained at Warsaw and Berlin, from 1840 worked at Wilna and from 1858 was conductor at Warsaw, with 15 tuneful operas (from before 1845), much church music and many songs.

In Russia musicians from foreign countries had long been made welcome, so that the public was familiar with many different styles. A conspicuous early instance in the operatic field was that of the Venetian **Catterino Cavos** (d. 1840), the first (1799) of his 13 Russian operas being so successful as to lead to his becoming court-conductor.

Alexis Werstowski (d. 1862), a prominent Moscow official, wrote 7 operas, of which *Askold's Grave* (1835) had signal success, being the pioneer work of truly Russian quality.

Michail Glinka (d. 1857), born of noble family in 1804, is, however, usually counted as the founder of Russian opera. Trained at St. Petersburg and Moscow, and in Italy and Germany, he early became a fine pianist, but made his reputation by the operas *Life for the Czar* (1836) and *Russlan and Liudmilla* (1842), which were not only thoroughly Russian, but eminently modern in dramatic and musical workmanship. After 1844 Glinka made long visits to France, Spain, Italy and Germany, partly to introduce his works. He also wrote brilliant instrumental and vocal music.

The violinist **Alexis Lwoff** (d. 1871), a high army officer, in 1836–55 conductor of the imperial choir, wrote three operas (1840–6), besides a youthful work. The noted pianist **Alexander Dargomyzski** (d. 1869), who at first followed Italian and French styles, won his place as an opera-writer by *Esmeralda* (1847, but written in 1839) and still more by *Russalka* (1856), leaving also a third opera (1872), written upon modern lines.

Anton Rubinstein (d. 1894), already referred to as a pianist (see sec. 202), was specially ambitious in dramatic composition, producing not only 13 operas (from 1852), about half of them in German, but also 5 sacred concert-operas (from 1870), all in German. In his style the mixture of native and acquired elements seems to have been unfortunate, his romanticism lacking delicacy, his Slavic intensity leading to gigantic efforts that are more grandiose that sublime, and his invention being unequal to the strain he put upon it. His best dramatic works all belong to the recent period, and have suffered from inevitable comparison with those of other composers.

Belonging to a very different group was **Alexander Serow** (d. 1871), an enthusiastic Wagnerite, who led the way toward the 'New-Russian' school with 3 powerful works, *Judith* (1863), *Rogneda* (1865) and *Wrazyia siela* (1871).

From the long list of famous operatic singers of the period only a selection can be made of some whose international renown was striking : —

The sopranos included from 1819 the French **Cinthie** (**Montalant**) **Damoreau** (d. 1863) ; from 1828 the Italians **Guilia Grisi** (d. 1869), and, from 1832, **Fanny** (**Tacchinardi**) **Persiani** (d. 1867) ; from 1834 the Spanish **Maria Dolores Nau**;

from 1837 the French **Pauline Viardot-Garcia**; from 1838 the Swedish **Jenny Lind** (d. 1887); and, from 1843, **Henriette Nissen** (d. 1879); from 1846 the Italian **Adelaide Borghi-Mamo** (d. 1901); from 1849 the German **Therese Tietjens** (d. 1877) and the French **Caroline (Miolan) Carvalho** (d. 1895); from 1852 the English **Euphrosyne Parepa-Rosa** (d. 1874); from 1857 the Belgian **Désirée Artôt**; from 1859 the French **Zelia Trebelli [Gillebert]** (d. 1892), the Austrian **Pauline Lucca** and the Italian **Adelina Patti**.

Among the altos were from 1811 the Italian **Benedetta Rosamunda Pisaroni** (d. 1872); from 1839 the Italian **Marietta Alboni** (d. 1894); from 1841 the English **Charlotte Sainton-Dolby** (d. 1885); from 1843 the Russian **Daria Leonowa** (d. 1896); from 1853 the German **Amalie (Weiss) Joachim** (d. 1899); and from 1854 the English **Adelaide Phillipps** (d. 1882).

Important tenors were from 1825 the French **Gilbert Louis Duprez** (d. 1896); from 1837 the Bohemian **Joseph Aloys Tichatschek** (d. 1886); from 1838 the French **Gustave Hippolyte Roger** (d. 1879), and the Sardinian **Giuseppe Mario** (d. 1883); from 1839 the English **John Sims Reeves** (d. 1900); from 1840 the Italian **Enrico Tamberlik** (d. 1889); and from about 1845 and later the Germans **Theodor Wachtel** (d. 1893), **Franz Nachbaur** (d. 1902), **Albert Niemann** and **Ludwig Schnorr von Carolsfeld** (d. 1865).

Conspicuous basses were from about 1835 the Tyrolese **Anton Mitterwurzer** (d. 1872); from 1847 the Italian **Leone Giraldoni** (d. 1897), and the Belgian **Camille François Everard**; from about 1850 the Hungarian **Johann Nepomuk Beck** (d. 1904); and from 1852 the French **Jean Baptiste Faure**; from 1854 the German **Albert Eilers** (d. 1896); from 1857 the English **Charles Santley**; from 1859 the German **Franz Betz** (d. 1900); and from 1860 the Styrian **Emil Scaria** (d. 1886).

In the field of professional librettists no one attained the level of **Eugène Scribe** (d. 1861), who has already been named (see sec. 179). Among lesser workers were **Antonio Ghislanzoni** (d. 1893), long editor of the Milan *Gazzetta musicale*, **Angelo Zanardini** (d. 1893), the Parisians **Michel Carré** (d. 1872) and **Jules Barbier** (d. 1901), who wrought jointly, and the German operetta-writers **Richard Genée** (d. 1895) and **Camillo Wälzel** ['F. Zell'] (d. 1895), who also were colaborers. Under this general head, however should be mentioned the remarkable work of **Wagner** (d. 1883) in supplying the poetic texts which are an integral part of his music (see secs. 207-208).

CHAPTER XXXIV

WAGNER AND THE RECONSTRUCTED OPERA

206. The Situation Confronting Wagner. — The time at which Wagner appeared was one favorable to a great musical dramatist. Under the lead originally of the Viennese composers, orchestral music had become highly significant, disclosing in a new way the capacity of pure music (without words) through forms essentially its own to depict and symbolize complicated emotional experiences, and bringing an advanced type of art into intimate relation with the mental life of the age. To this orchestral evolution romanticism was adding a corresponding expansion of piano music, and notable enrichments in both solo and choral song. But the great field of dramatic music was as yet but imperfectly affected. It is true that Gluck a half-century before had opened the contention for dramatic sincerity, that Weber had lived long enough to start a fresh movement toward imaginative intensity, and that several composers were endeavoring to make the tragic opera what its common name implied — a really 'grand' or capital artistic type. But Gluck's efforts came before the forms of composition were fully ready to bear the strain demanded, and he was also entangled in the old academic notion about the subjects to be taken for operatic treatment. Weber's genius, real and fresh as it was, was exercised upon subjects without much moral grandeur, if, indeed, it was capable of attaining to them, and hence missed the greater inspirations, being animated more by fancy over the picturesque than by profound imagination. And Meyerbeer and other writers of grand opera, with perhaps a partial exception in Marschner, had not enough original force to construct more than a pretentious variant among the types of concert-opera that had long been prevalent. The technical resources of the opera had plainly been enriched, and the range of topic and plot broadened — on this side the French opéra comique having a useful influence. But the main current of opera-writing had not turned far from the old channels. From 1830 to 1850 European society was in turmoil politically and intellectually. The time was ripe for a new voice in the musical drama. When just at this juncture Wagner began to utter the seething thoughts within him, it was at least evident that his was a new voice. Whether or not it was the voice of a master was for a long time not clear to the musical world. His advent and the discussions which it aroused at least forced a profound readjustment of musical values and judgments. Finally they effected a genuine reconstruction of the opera.

Richard Wagner (d. 1883) was born at Leipsic in 1813, the youngest of nine children. His grandfather and father were petty civil officers, much interested in the theatre. The father soon died, the mother speedily married again, and the boy was then brought up at Dresden by his step-father, Ludwig Geyer (d. 1821), an actor, poet and portrait-painter. He had good schooling at the Kreuzschule, being eager for Greek, German poetry and the tragic drama, but not caring much for music, though he did not escape the impress of Weber. In 1827 the family moved back to Leipsic, where his education continued at the gymnasium and from 1831 at the university. Contact here with orchestral music, especially that of Beethoven, awakened ardent musical ambition. Besides private study, he had lessons from C. G. Müller (d. 1863), in 1829–38 conductor of the Euterpe concerts, later of Altenburg, and also from Theodor Weinlig (d. 1842), the cantor of the Thomasschule. He plunged into minute studies of Beethoven's symphonies, and wrote a sonata, a polonaise and a symphony in classical style — the latter given under Pohlenz at the Gewandhaus in 1833. He knew Dorn, but not Schumann. In 1832 he visited Vienna and Prague, hoping to gain a hearing for his symphony, and at Prague was courteously treated by Dionys Weber, director of the conservatory. Only in his nineteenth year did he draft his first dramatic libretto and write some fragments of the music. All his early enthusiasm was for instrumental composition.

In 1833 Wagner was at Würzburg, becoming chorusmaster at the theatre where his brother was tenor. Here he wrote the opera Die Feen, an extravagantly romantic work, with which he returned to Leipsic. In 1834 he became conductor for a theatric troupe having headquarters at Magdeburg. He now sketched a second symphony and completed the tragic opera Das Liebesverbot, given with small success (1836). The troupe ended in bankruptcy. To the pretty actress Minna Planer, whom he followed to Königsberg, he was married late in 1836. The season 1836–7 was spent at Königsberg, entangled again with a failing troupe, but with negotiations for a vacancy at Riga. The only significant friendship here was with the Polish pianist Eduard Sobolewski (d. 1872). After some months at Dresden, he was named director at Riga, with a fair salary and a prospect of good support. Beginning there in 1837, he soon set to work upon the historical opera Rienzi and began sketches for Der fliegende Holländer. His duties included some orchestral concerts, at which the Norwegian violinist Ole Bull played. In 1839, his contract having expired, he impulsively left his debts behind him and set out for Paris, going by sailing vessel through the Baltic to London and stopping a month at Boulogne to ingratiate himself with Meyerbeer. The latter's introduction gave him access to the Opéra management, but led to no commission. The projected production of the *Liebesverbot* at a lesser house was upset by the latter's failure. Wagner was kept from starvation only by all sorts of hack work for the publisher Schlesinger and casual essay-writing, in which his critical ability and his constructive theories began to appear. He formed a few useful friendships, especially with Berlioz, one or two artists and some literary people, besides doing careful study upon German myths. When he sought to get *Der fliegende Holländer* accepted at the Opéra, the only result was an offer for the libretto (given in 1842 with music by the Frenchman Dietsch). Two of his overtures were heard at concerts, but without success. In 1840 *Rienzi* was finished and was sent to Dresden for examination, and in 1841 *Der fliegende Holländer* was similarly submitted at Berlin. His restless imagination was also at work upon other plans. In the spring of 1842 he left Paris for Dresden.

The successful production at Dresden first of *Rienzi* (1842) and soon after of *Der fliegende Holländer* (1843) led to Wagner's being made court-choir-master in place of Morlacchi (d. 1841). For a brief time the two operas were in request at other cities, bringing Wagner some much-needed income. Though beset by opposition active and passive, he pushed on energetically to raise the level of the Dresden opera by giving works of high class, to establish significant orchestral concerts, and to consolidate the choral interests of the city (being leader of the Liedertafel for a time). He was also full of original projects for librettos and operas. *Tannhäuser* was soon finished and given (1845), but was violently attacked by the critics. *Lohengrin* was finished in 1847 (first given by Liszt at Weimar, 1850). His position grew increasingly difficult. His personality was passionate and uncompromising, his ambition and ideality ardent, his musical dialect unconventional. The conservatives and sticklers for usage found him incomprehensible or obnoxious. Schumann (in Dresden in 1844-50) and Hiller (there in 1845-7) only partially understood him. His local friends were few, such as the conductors Fischer and Röckel, the singers Tichatschek and Schröder-Devrient, and the violinist Uhlig. At Berlin he was supported by the editor Gaillard, at Cassel by Spohr and at Weimar by Liszt. But he was bitterly assailed by the critics Schladebach and Banck, and was viewed with jealousy by Meyerbeer. In 1848 he made two or three untactful moves, especially a project for a National Theatre, and presently became seriously involved in the heated political discussions and uprisings that succeeded the Revolution at Paris. In 1849 he was forced to flee as a suspect to Liszt at Weimar, whence he was smuggled off to Paris, and soon settled at Zurich.

The fifteen years that followed were mainly occupied by literary work and composition. His essays and books, with the productions of his earlier operas at various places, brought him some money, but he was partly supported by Liszt and other friends. His inquisitive mind prompted him to extensive researches in the history of the drama and in the stores of legend from which drama may be fed. His eagerness for expression found relief in copious literary production, both polemic or philosophic prose and highly original poetry. And soon began to come forth the titanic operatic cycle in which he embodied his ultimate theory of the opera and by which his fame was later to be established. From 1854 he became deeply interested in the writings of Schopenhauer (d. 1860), whose pessimistic philosophy plainly affected all his subsequent thought and art. The spell of his personality drew some friends around him, like the revolutionary poet Herwegh (d. 1875), the Berlin merchant Wesendonck (d. 1896) and his poetic wife (d. 1902), the musician Baumgartner (d. 1867), and others. The young Bülow followed him as a special pupil. Through him and Abt (till 1852 director at the Zurich theatre) he had some contact with dramatic music, and from time to time he undertook subscription-concerts, at which extracts from his operas were given. In 1855 *Tannhäuser* was produced at Zurich. In 1855, also, he served as conductor for the London Philharmonic, there again meeting Berlioz. The prose drama ' Wieland der Schmiedt ' (intended as the basis for a French opera) and the poems of the Nibelungen Tetralogy were completed before 1853. The music for *Das Rheingold* was drafted in 1853–4, that for *Die Walküre* in 1854–6, and that for *Siegfried* begun in 1857. In 1857–9 he turned aside to complete *Tristan und Isolde*, for which he hoped soon to get a hearing at Carlsruhe. In 1858 began the difficulties with his wife that ended in their separation in 1861 (she died in 1866 at Dresden). He moved to Venice and Lucerne, whence in 1859 he went to Paris. In 1860 he hazarded concerts there and at Brussels which involved him in debt and roused much hostile criticism. Some partisans on his side were won, however, and in 1861, by direction of Napoleon III., *Tannhäuser* was produced at the Paris Opéra, but was soon driven from the stage by riotous opposition. Happily, just here his banishment from Germany was revoked, and he was called to Vienna to assist in the giving of *Lohengrin* (which he had never heard) and the laborious, but fruitless rehearsals of *Tristan*. On his way back, Liszt and the Weimar circle gave him a memorable reception, and at Mannheim he found an opening for a new work, *Die Meistersinger*, to which he now devoted himself at Paris (not finished till 1867). In 1862–4 he gave concerts at Leipsic, Vienna, Prague, St. Petersburg, Moscow, Pesth and other cities, being received with special enthusiasm in Russia. But he was in despair over his finances and the impossibility of completing the immense works on hand. At this juncture, while at Stuttgart, he received a summons from the young Ludwig II. of Bavaria, who had just come to the throne, to settle in Munich and there work out with ample support his dramatic ambitions. (Curiously, the day that this invitation came, Meyerbeer died at Paris.)

The story of the triumphal period after 1864 can be only summarized here. A cardinal factor in it was the unwavering support of the eccentric, but art-loving king. But there came gradually a marvelous change in the attitude of the public and the critics toward Wagner's ideas. He had been pursued for twenty years by every sort of enmity and derision, until his music had become a literary by-word. But now his importance began to be seen and finally his mastership to be accepted with enthusiasm. The king's original plan was to found at Munich a special Wagnerian theatre, but local hostility was so intense that at the end of 1865 Wagner withdrew to Triebschen (Lucerne), where he completed *Die Meistersinger* (1867) and *Siegfried* (1869). There he met Cosima Liszt, the divorced wife of Bülow, and in 1871 moved to Bay-reuth, where it was proposed to build an opera-house upon a new plan for the production of his works. This difficult project, with liberal help from the king and from admirers in all parts of the world, was consummated in 1876, when complete performances of the Nibelungen cycle (*Götterdämmerung* having been finished in 1874) were given on a scale of notable elaboration. The enormous debts incurred were gradually lifted by the proceeds of concerts and operas elsewhere. His last opera, *Parsifal*, was written in 1877–82. Failing health caused him to spend the following winter at Venice, where, in 1883, he suddenly died. The burial was at Bayreuth.

Wagner was not above medium height, but his erect, alert carriage and his striking and expressive face made him distinguished. He was active and ardent, rather unconventional in manner, though instinctively refined and genial, and a ready and eloquent talker. He was a constant and varied reader, and full of intellectual interest. He loved luxury and was keenly sensitive to beauty in every form. Like strong characters generally, he exerted fascination upon those who stood close to him in friendship, but he was uncompromising in his attitude toward opponents.

207. Growth of his Artistic Ideal. — The evolution of Wagner's artistic attitude presents highly interesting points, psychological and philosophical, of which only a few can here be stated. His first and always central artistic impulse was dramatic. For it he sought expression variously, but chiefly through poetry and music. His musical awakening came only after his propension toward poetry and the literary drama was clearly manifest. Yet, when at length he threw himself with ardor into music, his early ambition seems to have been to emulate Beethoven in the symphonic sphere. It appeared, however, that his creative faculty was not fully at home in 'absolute music.' The ways of such music were too formal in procedure and at the same time too indefinite in mental intention and suggestion. They may also have seemed too difficult of intense application in stirring the public. Wagner could never remain satisfied with any artistic means that did not give scope for vivid and powerful popular effect. Accordingly, from his twentieth year he settled upon the opera as his favorite and almost only form.

It would seem that in the opera his individuality found itself only by progressive experiments. His successive works exhibit a steady and remarkable development. Yet the adoption in some form of most of the technical methods by which he is distinguished, considering how novel and radical they were, was astonishingly speedy. At first he was strongly inclined to take up the ideals of the German romantic opera. But these did not meet his craving for realism in his materials or for ideal sublimity in general topic. Hence in *Rienzi* he turned frankly to the historical opera, acknowledging, however, that in musical treatment he was making a concession to current styles in order to gain a hearing. But this again did not meet his desire, except that it was popularly successful. He longed for subjects of extreme magnitude, in which there was room for rich imagination and symbolism. The purely romantic type lacked sublimity and tragic pathos. The purely historical opera lacked scope for pure imagination and ease of symbolic application. Hence he gradually evolved a new type, carrying to culmination tendencies that had been somewhat discernible for more than half a century, but handled in detail in a way wholly his own. The final success of this climacteric effort came from the fact that in Wagner as an artist of the first rank there was an organic combination of the power fully to assimilate the best in previous styles and the power to create for himself an original method of expression.

Wagner's theory of the opera rested on the view that it was properly a drama in music, as the Florentines and the earliest Venetians had conceived it, not a musical work dramatically arranged and presented. Its genesis must be from subject, plot and characters through text, action and setting to the detailed musical embodiment. Here he was fully at one with Gluck and Weber at their best, and in radical opposition to the Neapolitan concert-opera. But he outran all predecessors in his insistence upon heroic and ideal topics, drawn from sources so removed from common life as to rouse the imagination to full activity, and, like all great artists, he instinctively sought subjects that were rich in moral symbolism or implication. He found the sublimity that he needed mainly in the vast treasures of Teutonic mythology, thus securing a field of ideality analogous to that constantly employed by the Greek dramatists, but a field close to the traditions and genius of the whole Germanic race. And he further distanced all forerunners in the vigor with which he proceeded for himself — not through a librettist — to work his materials into plots, to select, individualize and combine his personages, and to construct the text in full.   In all this his work was that of a true dramatic poet.   His final method — the persistent use of a rugged, archaic diction in strongly alliterative verse — was part of his general effort to remove the hearer's mind from ordinary associations and stimulate the imagination to the utmost.   But this handling of the text also followed from his doctrine that in the final embodiment the three expressional elements, language, action and music, must be so blended as to be inseparable — a trinity with the effect of organic unity.   As he proceeded, the composite conception of these three took shape in a text ready for stage presentation, a plan of actors, costumes, settings and detailed action, and a musical score that should give complete tonal utterance to the sentiments thus made to deploy before the audience.   Concerning his literary and histrionic method this is not the place to speak.   But the strictly musical features are remarkable.

The heart of the Wagnerian opera as a musical work is the orchestra, which is treated not as an accessory, but as the central exposition of the whole drama   Here we see the function of the Greek 'chorus' raised to its highest power, except for the absence of words.   The drama moves on amid a continuous depiction by the instruments of the emotional process involved.   The text and the action supply the images of fact and the intellectual conceptions generally which are to be associated with this emotional process, and which justify it.   At many points the momentum of thought may be enough to enable the orchestra to proceed almost or quite unaided.   No preceding composer had ventured thus to transfer the emphasis to what had been considered a mere apparatus of accompaniment. Furthermore, into the instrumentation was poured a wealth of technical invention for which earlier writers offer but meagre suggestion.   The make-up of the orchestra was enlarged by adding new instruments to the standard classical nucleus.   New effects were devised, such as the use of extended passages for divided violins playing in harmonics.   A system of 'leitmotive' was gradually developed — characteristic themes regularly attached to particular emotional or personal elements in the plot, recurring in some form whenever these special elements appear in fact or even in thought.   All the received methods of composition — harmony, counterpoint and form — were stretched to their limits with an imperial originality and independence, so as to increase their emotional expressiveness to the utmost.   This making the orchestra the dramatic protagonist was the most daring feature of his work.   Its substantial validity is attested by its profound effect not only upon all later opera-writers, but also upon most later writers of purely orchestral music.   It was a consummation of the great orchestral development that began with the classical Viennese composers, but it was executed in terms wholly different from theirs. Many of the details correspond to those in the orchestral innovations of Berlioz.

The vocal elements — soloists and chorus — are treated chiefly as mere parts of the tonal ensemble. They are prominent only so far as dramatic exigencies require, especially where fact or thought is emphasized, or where the traits and passions of the individual personage are in the foreground. The traditional division of acts into scenes is almost wholly discarded. Neither recitatives nor arias in set form are found, though the technical methods of both are freely used. The favorite solo style is a sort of arioso, in which the dramatic and the lyric are blended — a type of melody lyrically far richer than the recitative and dramatically more flexible and revelatory than the aria proper.

The Wagnerian melody was so novel as to challenge general criticism. Technically, it differed widely from classical melody — in 'form' or lay-out, in its framework of chords and modulations, in its extreme flexibility, in its wealth of pictorial or passional suggestion. Its basis was not the naïve and symmetrical folk-song, but the ecstatic or epic declamation. His operas were at first said to be unmelodic because of their lack of 'tunes,' but they were really packed with melody of the most varied and vivid import. The projection of this is mostly orchestral and polyphonic, but in the ensemble the soloist singer is often highly conspicuous.

In consequence of his theory of absolutely ductile melody, Wagner was an apparent innovator in harmonic procedure, in counterpoint, in 'form,' and in vocalization, as well as in instrumentation. He was seemingly impatient with all the old rules, formulæ and traditions. His demands upon singers were thought by some to be preposterous. Yet, when closely analyzed, his innovations in harmonic and contrapuntal procedure and in the art of vocal delivery appear to be more or less plain extensions of antecedent practice — a sort of liberation for dramatic effect of implicit and latent energies. Hence under his influence, as it became better understood, began a reconstruction of artistic methods that is one of the salient features of all recent composition, instrumentation and vocalization.

208. Influence of his Views. — Compared with other composers, Wagner was unique in the amount and substance of his literary production. His mind was studious and reflective, acute in analysis, and prone to express itself in words. Circumstances forced him to philosophize, and copious writing was a relief for his pent-up energy. The body of his writings is altogether too large to be summarized here, except to note that they belong to several distinct classes, including much that is strictly philosophical in aim and method, much of a critico-historical character, much upon the art of conducting and of large musical exposition in general, besides abundant autobiographical material and the librettos of his eleven operas from *Rienzi* to *Parsifal*. The most of these writings date from the Zurich period, so that in date they lie close to the mid-point of the century.   Their appearance then was the signal for heated debates that lasted twenty years, if not longer.   The extreme partizanship developed prevented a cool estimate of Wagner's views.   But the logic of events tended to substantiate his main contentions, and in the recent period Wagnerism, at least as applied to the opera, has been a dominant force.   Yet it is also clear that his doctrine about the opera cannot be regarded as absolutely final or complete, since it provides only for opera in its highest and most strenuous forms. The central thesis, however, regarding the control of the music-drama by dramatic considerations, is plainly sound and capable of universal application.

> Wagner's collected writings fill ten volumes (1871–85).   With the autobiographies may be classed many notices of particular works and events, and reminiscences of Spontini, Rossini, Auber, etc.   The more noted philosophical essays or treatises are *Die Kunst und die Revolution* (1849), *Das Kunstwerk der Zukunft* (1850), *Oper und Drama* (3 parts, 1851), *Das Judenthum in der Musik* (1852), '*Zukunftsmusik*' (1864), *Ueber das Dirigieren* (1869), many essays on the Bayreuth enterprise, *Religion und Kunst* (1880), etc., with striking studies of Liszt's symphonic poems and of Beethoven (1870).

Many who do not accept Wagner's theory of the opera in all its details, and who perhaps are but slightly informed as to his philosophy of music in general, have yet been quick to follow some of his technical methods.   Two or three of his characteristic traits of style may well be emphasized here, since they have exerted a wide influence, far beyond the limits of the opera.

> Wagner threw his whole weight with those who were breaking away from classical strictness and regularity.   Classical practice had made much of the structural plan of composition and of the perfection of its elements or units taken separately.   The smaller elements of 'form,' for instance, must be clear-cut, the themes brief and symmetrical, the part-writing guided by careful rules derived from the old vocal counterpoint, the melodic figures and passages selected as far as possible from certain conventional lists, the chords not distorted by extraordinary tones, the modulations managed according to established usage.   This stage in practice was necessary to fix the elementary logic of musical construction. But it made composition too much like architecture.   Tonal units were treated too much like lifeless bricks or stones.   Against this relatively dry and mechanical artistry the romanticists rebelled.   But at first they did not know how to break away from it.   Wagner had the courage and the creative inspiration to attempt a radically new procedure.   His desire

was to restore all the time- and tune-elements of music to what he held to be their native plasticity and vital expressiveness. Hence the enormous variety of his phrase-schemes, of his metric patterns, of his melodic and harmonic formulæ. Hence the untrammeled flow of his counterpoint and the exhaustless evolution of his themes. The old stiff formality, as of a military drill, is replaced by the free interplay of social intercourse. When the involved and novel effects of his scores were first heard, it is not strange that they were voted chaotic, incomprehensible, iconoclastic. But, as we now see, this reaching after liberty and vitality was simply the next logical step for musical art. Wagner's importance consists not in his absolute invention of processes hitherto unknown, but in the vigor with which he extended them to legitimate conclusions and in the absolute value of the ideas and feelings which he expressed through them. His powerful influence speedily affected every important type of composition, simply because the musical world was ripe for an advance.

Wagner's elaborate use of the 'leitmotiv' in dramatic effect was evidently important for his purposes. As a technical device it was not new. But his use of it was unexampled in extent and power. It simply illustrates his sense of the living quality in his tonal materials. A thought, a sentiment, a person, a thing, if we are to employ it artistically, must be so embodied as to declare its individuality. If it is active in a dramatic process, it must reappear in its own recognizable form. If circumstances require, its tonal shape may change, though without sacrificing its identity. Just as the original concept plays in and out through the plot and the action, so its tonal counterpoint may be woven into the tonal fabric by which the drama is illuminated and enriched. Here we have a special application of the old notion of thematic development, but the motif is now not a tone-formula, but a plastic organism, not a bit of glass in a musical kaleidoscope, but a living actor in society.

Wagner's characteristic tendency to push to conclusions the methods that current practice employed is finely illustrated in his free treatment of the orchestra as an implement. He insists that all instruments shall be fully developed in compass and timbre, and that their technique shall be adequate for extreme demands. He often writes for more instruments of a kind than had been customary, and for some unusual representatives of the wind groups. The various strings must be numerous enough to be divided, if need be, without loss of dignity and sonority. His scores call often for piccolos, an additional flute, oboe, clarinet and bassoon, for doubled or tripled horns, extra trumpets, trombones and timpani, for the cor anglais, the bass clarinet, the bass trumpet, the bass and even the tenor tuba, etc. His primary object was to get full harmony on occasions without mixing qualities, but he also secures wonderfully expressive effects by complex novel combinations. Most of his technical innovations were paralleled or transcended by Berlioz (from whom he doubtless received much impetus), but as an orchestral colorist and strategist he was thoroughly original. The artistic occasion for even his most exceptional effects is always a dramatic necessity, rather than the virtuoso's desire for the novel or surprising for its own sake.

These are but illustrations. Throughout the whole range of
musical procedure Wagner was emphatically an expander and
fulfiller, if not an absolute pioneer. The influence of his technical work became fully manifest only in the latter part of the
century.

209. The Dresden Circle. — Since Wagner's earliest years were
spent at Dresden and his first successes were won there, this is
the natural place for some notes upon the personnel of its
musical circle. The Saxon court for fully two centuries had been
notable for its attention to music. In church music it had long
maintained two establishments, one Catholic, the other Protestant. In opera Dresden had been one of the strongholds of Italian influence in Germany, though with the advent of Weber in
1816 it was gradually carried over to the support of German
ideas. The court kapelle had some repute among the orchestras
of central Europe. The musical forces usually included distinguished vocalists and instrumentalists. But the policy of
administration did not secure chiefs of commanding enterprise
except at intervals, as in the cases of Weber and Wagner. Outside of the court circle the only musical institutions of special
significance have been the Kreuzschule, an ancient foundation
like the Thomasschule at Leipsic (though never so eminent),
and the conservatory, founded in 1856.

For convenience of reference, a summary follows of the leading musical
personalities at Dresden during the century: —

The list of court-choirmasters contains several overlapping terms, due
to the fact that various functions in church music, the opera and the
orchestra have sometimes been distributed. In 1800 three choirmasters
were in titular service — *J. G. Naumann* (d. 1801), *Franz Seydelmann*
(d. 1806) and *Joseph Schuster* (d. 1812), with the last two of whom in
1802–6 *Ferdinando Paër* (d. 1839) was associated as operatic leader.
From 1810 the Italian *Morlacchi* (d. 1841) was in charge, but during his
incumbency came in from 1816 *Weber* (d. 1826), in 1824–26 *Marschner*
(d. 1861), from 1826 *K. G. Reissiger* (d. 1859) and from 1829 *Joseph
Rastrelli* (d. 1842). Reissiger was still in office when in 1843–9
Wagner (d. 1883) was given place as opera-director. He was succeeded
in 1850–72 by *Karl Krebs* (d. 1880), and in 1860 Reissiger was followed
by the accomplished *Julius Rietz* (d. 1877), previously of Leipsic, and
Krebs in 1873 by *Ernst Schuch*. Rietz was succeeded in 1877 by *Franz
Wüllner* (d. 1902), and he in turn from 1883 by *Adolf Hagen*.

In the court-orchestra the post of concertmaster was held in 1814–24
by the Italian *Polledro* (d. 1853) ; in 1839–59 by the Pole *Lipinski* (d.

1861); in 1861–73 by the Dresden *Franz Schubert* (d. 1878), who had been in the orchestra since 1823; in 1873?–89 by *Johann Christoph Lauterbach*, with *Henri Petri* and *Eduard Rappoldi* (d. 1903) as later incumbents. Other violinists were from 1841 Wagner's friend *Theodor Uhlig* (d. 1853); in 1844–86 *Ferdinand Hüllweck* (d. 1887); and from 1847 *Karl August Gustav Riccius* (d. 1893). A number of 'cellists were important players and composers, as in 1811–52 *Friedrich Dotzauer* (d. 1860); in 1817–64 *F. A. Kummer* (d. 1879); from 1860 *Friedrich Grützmacher* (d. 1903), previously at Leipsic; and from 1864 the Pole *Karasowski* (d. 1892). *Anton Schubert* (d. 1853), the uncle of the violinist, was double-bassist in 1790–1844. Valued flutists were from 1820 *A. B. Fürstenau* (d. 1852), and from 1842 his scholarly son *Moritz Fürstenau* (d. 1889).

The double series of court-organists included from 1816 *A. A. Klengel* (d. 1852); from 1825 *Johann Schneider* (d. 1864); from 1854 *Edmund Kretschmer* (d. 1908); and from 1864 *Theodor Berthold* (d. 1882) and *Gustav Merkel* (d. 1885).

The cantors at the Kreuzschule were from 1785 *Christian Weinlig* (d. 1813); from 1814 his nephew *Theodor Weinlig* (d. 1842); from 1817 *Hermann Uber* (d. 1822); from 1822 *Friedrich Wilhelm Agthe* (d. 1830); from 1830 the celebrated *Julius Otto* (d. 1877); and from 1876 *Friedrich Oscar Wermann* (d. 1906).

Other important church musicians were in 1842–56 and from 1861 *Volkmar Schurig* (d. 1899); from about 1852 *Friedrich Baumfelder*; from 1855 *K. A. Fischer* (d. 1892); and from 1858 *Merkel* (d. 1885).

The conservatory was started in 1856 by the chamber-musician Tröstler, but in 1859 was acquired by *Friedrich Pudor* (d. 1887), to whom succeeded in 1887 his son *Heinrich Pudor*, and he sold it in 1890 to *Eugen Krantz* (d. 1898). The artistic directors have been from 1860 *Julius Rietz* (d. 1877); and in 1877–84 *Franz Wüllner* (d. 1902). Prominent teachers, including several from the court forces, have been from 1856 the pianist and historian *Adolf Julius Rühlmann* (d. 1877); the 'cellist *Kummer* (d. 1879); in 1857–67 the theorist *Adolf Reichel* (d. 1896); the flutist *Moritz Fürstenau* (d. 1889); since 1858 the eminent pianist *Heinrich Döring*; from 1859 the pianist *Emil Leonhard* (d. 1883); in 1861–77 the violinist *Lauterbach*; from 1861 the organist *Merkel* (d. 1885); in 1862–1900 the theorist *Wilhelm Albert Rischbieter*; in 1865–74 *Ludwig Meinardus* (d. 1896); from 1869 the later proprietor *Krantz* (d. 1898); from about 1875 the historian *Emil Naumann* (d. 1888); from 1874 the baritone *Gustav Scharfe* (d. 1892); in 1877–93 the violinist *Rappoldi* (d. 1903); since 1884 the able theorist and composer *Draeseke*, etc.

Among the more noted piano-teachers of the city have been since 1841 *Fritz Spindler* (d. 1905); from 1850 *Charles Mayer* (d. 1862); from about 1855 *Aloys Tausig* (d. 1885); in 1860–78 *Magnus Böhme* (d. 1898); from about 1860 *Heinrich Germer*. Among the singing-teachers have been in 1848–54 *Ferdinand Sieber* (d. 1895), and from 1862 *Louis Schubert* (d. 1884).

Among the greater opera-singers may be named in 1823–47 the soprano *Wilhelmine Schröder-Devrient* (d. 1860); from 1832 the bass *C. W. Fischer* (d. 1862); in 1835–60 the soprano *Maschinka (Schneider) Schubert* (d. 1882); in 1838–72 the tenor *Tichatschek* (d. 1886); in 1839–70 the baritone *Mitterwurzer* (d. 1872); from 1842 the bass *Wilhelm Dettmer* (d. 1876); from 1860 the tenor *Schnorr von Carolsfeld* (d. 1865), etc.

Prominent writers and critics were from 1839 the civil official *Friedrich Wilhelm Opelt* (d. 1863); from 1840 Schumann's friend *Banck* (d. 1889); the physician *Julius Schladebach* (d. 1872); in 1848–60 *Otto Kade* (d. 1900), later of Schwerin; from 1857 *Ludwig Hartmann;* and from 1859 *K. E. Schneider* (d. 1893). It is to be remembered, also, that in 1844–50 *Schumann* made his home in or near Dresden. Of these, Banck and Schladebach were outspoken in their opposition to Wagner.

210. Liszt and the Weimar Circle.

Along artistic lines the strongest influence in Wagner's favor came from the cordial and faithful enthusiasm of Liszt and the circle of which he was the centre. Liszt had won his leadership as a piano-virtuoso, but after settling at Weimar in 1848, though he still wielded immense power as the teacher of many piano-pupils, he turned his energies more and more to conducting and composition. He became the apostle of musical progress, transformation, even revolution. Around him gathered many who were tired of the formality and pedantry of conventional styles, and who were seeking for something which their opponents derisively termed 'the music of the future.' For a full ten years he used his place at Weimar to bring out neglected or novel operas and orchestral works with loving care. His own composition passed over almost wholly into symphonic and choral forms, often of marked originality and importance.

It was natural that Liszt should have been drawn to Wagner, since in artistic aims they were akin. His warm admiration was invaluable to the latter in the dark days of unpopularity and exile, and his practical wisdom helped to check the extremes of thought and action to which Wagner was liable, and to bridge the chasm between him and his detractors. Liszt had no such imperial gifts of creation as Wagner, nor so profound a mind; and he had the good sense and the unselfishness to merge his light in the blaze of the greater master — to his own final glory as well as Wagner's. Yet his own creative achievements were not small. Into orchestral writing he introduced a change of method analogous to that which Wagner made in the opera. The two composers were actuated by similar impulses at about the same time without explicitly deriving direction from each other. We may doubt, however, whether Liszt would have made the significant advance he did if he had not felt the stimulus of Wagner's style and caught the spirit of his revolution.

While other prominent groups in Germany were conservative in tendency, the Weimar circle became noted for its radicalism. Here began several lines of progress which ultimately gave character to the succeeding period, with its tendency to reconstruct the whole fabric of musical style.

The early, pianistic career of **Franz Liszt** (d. 1886) has already been sketched (see sec. 201). It is supposed that one of the influences that diverted him into other paths was his passionate attachment to the Princess von Sayn-Wittgenstein of Russia, whom he met in 1846–7, and who exerted herself to turn him to larger efforts than those of a popular virtuoso. He had been connected with the Weimar court as a visiting artist since 1843. From 1849 he was court-choirmaster in residence, with every facility. The most striking feature of his incumbency was the series of operatic and orchestral performances under his direction. These included, among others, Wagner's *Tannhäuser* in 1849, his *Lohengrin* in 1850, Raff's *König Alfred* and Rubinstein's *Das verlorene Paradies* in 1851, Berlioz' *Benvenuto Cellini* in 1852, Wagner's *Der fliegende Holländer* in 1853, Schubert's *Alfonso ed Estrella* and Rubinstein's *Die sibirischen Jäger* in 1854, Schumann's

Genoveva, Lassen's *Landgraf Ludwigs Brautfahrt* in 1857, Cornelius' *Der Barbier von Bagdad* in 1858, besides large orchestral works by Berlioz, Schumann, Raff and others. His fame as a conductor led to his directing many festivals in 1852–9, as at Ballenstedt, Carlsruhe, Vienna, Magdeburg, Aix and Leipsic. His advocacy of Wagner and Berlioz aroused widespread discussion, with a ranging of critics and composers into parties throughout Germany. In the war of ideas the *Neue Zeitschrift* at Leipsic became the leading organ of the 'New-German' spirit. Of special importance in this movement were Liszt's own 'symphonic poems,' including *Tasso* (1849), *Prometheus* (1850), *Orpheus*, *Les Préludes* and *Mazeppa* (all 1854), *Die Ideale*, the

Faustsymphonie and *Die Hunnenschlacht* (all 1857), etc., his cantatas *Die Macht der Musik* (1850) and *An die Künstler* (1853), and his piano-concertos (1855–7) — all works cast in large moulds, full of poetic inspiration and tending to break away from traditional conventions of form.   To this period, also, belong many of his literary writings, such as the essays on *Lohengrin* and *Tannhäuser* (1851), on Chopin (1852), on Field's Nocturnes (1859) and on Hungarian Gipsy-Music (1861).

In 1859 he left Weimar in irritation over the hostility shown to Cornelius' *Barbier*, and in 1861 his official place was filled by Lassen.   He settled now in Rome.   His complex nature included a strong vein of religious mysticism, which here became conspicuous.   At Weimar he had written several masses, the most celebrated being the *Graner Festmesse* (1855, for the dedication of the cathedral at Gran), and 3 psalms.   His union with the Princess, after long negotiations, was disapproved by the Church and was renounced.   He pursued theological studies far enough to receive the title of Abbé from the Pope (1866), and his works now came to include the oratorios *St. Elizabeth* (1862), *Christus* (1866) and *Stanislaus* (unfinished), the Hungarian *Coronation Mass* (1867) and the *Requiem* (1868), besides short works for voices, orchestra or piano.

The Weimar court often indicated its good-will, and from 1869 Liszt resumed life there each spring and summer.   In 1870 he there conducted the Beethoven Centenary, and in 1884 the Jubilee of the Allgemeiner deutscher Musikverein.   From 1873 he was busy over plans for a National Academy of Music at Pesth, of which he became honorary president.   Thenceforward he divided each year between Pesth, Weimar and Rome.   Pupils continued to flock to him.   His influence as a leader did not abate, nor his zeal for Wagner and all fresh enterprises.   To his long roll of compositions were added the cantatas *Die Glocken* (1874), *St. Cecilia* (1874), *Die Kreuzesstationen* (1876), the organ-mass (1879), the symphonic poem *Von der Wiege bis zum Grabe* (1881), the last Hungarian Rhapsodies, many songs and choral pieces, etc.   Among his later writings was the essay on Franz (1872).   In 1886, full of honors, he died at Bayreuth while attending a Wagner festival.

It would be quite impossible to name or trace all the lines of personal development that diverged from Weimar during its brilliant period under Liszt's direction.   It became for a time an artistic centre to which came pupils and aspirants of every degree.   But several composers and writers deserve emphasis because of their talent and later influence.   Of these Raff was chief, but there were many others.

Joseph Joachim Raff (d. 1882), a Württemberger, born in 1822, after some training became a school-teacher, but with much private study of music.   At 21, securing Mendelssohn's attention, he was enabled to publish a few piano-pieces, and then devoted himself to composing.   At 23 Liszt took him along on a tour, but from 1846 he settled at Cologne as composer and critic.   His hope to study with Mendelssohn, to get commissions from a Vienna publisher, and to have his opera, *König Alfred*, given at Stuttgart, were all disappointed. Bülow, however, helped to introduce his works to the public. From 1850 he was Liszt's assistant at Weimar, where his opera was given (1851) with other works, and where he championed Wagner and the new ideas with his pen. In 1856 he moved to Wiesbaden, married the daughter of the actor Genast, and became a favorite piano-teacher. In 1863 his first symphony won in a competition at Vienna, and in 1870 his opera *Dame Kobold* was given at Weimar. From 1877 he was head of the new Frankfort conservatory founded by Dr. Hoch. Raff was a prolific composer (over 230 works), often in a hasty and superficial vein, but in larger forms sometimes showing much power. The list includes 11 symphonies, such as *Im Walde* (1869) and *Lenore* (1872), 4 orchestral suites, 9 overtures, a striking piano-concerto, a large amount of chamber music, a host of piano works, several choral cantatas, church music, an oratorio (1882), many attractive songs and part-songs, besides 4 operas not given, etc. In spite of his sympathy with the new styles, much of his writing follows old lines, though with decided novelty in melodic invention. He used contrapuntal devices with extreme freedom and grace.

Peter Cornelius (d. 1874), born at Mayence in 1824, aimed first to be an actor, but at 23, under the care of his uncle, the distinguished painter, turned to music, studying with Dehn at Berlin and in 1852 joining Liszt at Weimar. Like Raff, he served Liszt as a sort of secretary and entered the field as a literary worker. In 1858 his opera *Der Barbier von Bagdad* failed because of mean attacks, and he followed Wagner to Vienna. In 1865 the latter got him a place in the Munich Music-School. The same year his opera *Der Cid* was given at Weimar. His *Gunlöd* was left incomplete, but was finished by Hoffbauer and Lassen (1892, Strassburg). For these works he wrote the texts with poetic skill, and published poems besides (1861). He is also known by original songs, duets and part-songs. His style has kinship with Wagner's, though somewhat extreme in details.

Hans von Bronsart, born at Berlin in 1830, also came from Dehn to Liszt in 1852. His early success was as a touring pianist. In 1860–2 he led the Euterpe concerts at Leipsic, in 1865 followed Bülow as conductor at Berlin, from 1867 was intendant and choirmaster at Hanover, and from 1887 in the same posts at Weimar, retiring in 1895. His best-known works are a trio, a piano-concerto, an orchestral Phantasie and the choral symphony *In den Alpen* (1896), besides another symphony, a cantata, piano-pieces and an unperformed opera. His wife, Ingeborg (Starck) von Bronsart, also a pupil of Liszt, is a fine pianist and the gifted writer of several operas and many piano works.

Eduard Lassen (d. 1904), born at Copenhagen in 1830, was finely trained at the Brussels conservatory, winning many prizes, and from 1851 traveled widely in Germany and Italy. His opera *Landgraf Ludwigs Brautfahrt* was given at Weimar in 1857. In 1858, at Liszt's suggestion, he was made conductor there, and in 1861 succeeded as choirmaster, retiring in 1895. He wrote 2 other operas, *Frauenlob* (1860, Weimar) and *Le captif* (1865, Brussels), incidental music to 'Oedipos in Colonos' (1874), 'Faust' (1876), 'Pandora' (1886), Hebbel's 'Nibelungen' and 'Circe,' 2 symphonies, several overtures,

2 P

cantatas, *Biblische Bilder*, and highly successful songs. Under him Wagner's *Tristan* was produced in 1874 for the first time away from Munich.

Leopold Damrosch (d. 1885), born at Posen in 1832, first studied medicine at Berlin, winning his degree at 22, but also pursued music to such purpose that he soon became a violin-virtuoso and in 1855 was engaged at Weimar as soloist in the court-orchestra. There he married the soprano Helene von Heimburg. From 1859 he worked at Breslau, first as conductor of the Philharmonic concerts, later, after tours with Bülow and Tausig, as founder of an orchestral society, chamber concerts and a choral society, besides being for a time conductor at the theatre. Called to New York in 1871 as conductor of the Arion, he there started the Oratorio Society in 1873 and the Symphony Society in 1878, organized a large festival in 1881 and conducted German opera in 1884-5. He was a versatile and finished composer — a symphony, 3 violin-concertos, 7 cantatas, many songs, etc. But he was most noted as an organizer and as a zealous apostle of modern styles.

Alexander Ritter (d. 1896) was a German, though born in Russia in 1833. As a boy he was Bülow's comrade at Dresden, where he studied with the violinist Schubert. After two years at the Leipsic conservatory, he married a niece of Wagner and in 1854 joined the Weimar group. From 1856 he lived mostly at Stettin or Dresden, and in 1863 settled at Würzburg, where in 1875 he established a music-store. From 1882 he was in Bülow's orchestra at Meiningen, and from 1886 lived at Munich. Though not specially forceful, he was favorably known for his symphonic poems, 2 comic operas (1885-90) and good songs.

Felix Draeseke, born at Coburg in 1835 and first trained at Leipsic, though younger than the foregoing, was prominent with them at Weimar, from 1857 being an energetic champion in print of the new ideas. From 1864 he taught at the Lausanne conservatory, with one year (1868-9) at Munich, and in 1876 moved to Dresden, where since 1884 he has been a leading professor in the conservatory. His compositions, in modern vein, include 3 symphonies, 3 overtures, concertos for piano and for violin, much chamber music, several cantatas, striking church music, an oratorio, 4 operas (from 1867), etc., besides theoretical works (from 1879).

Among literary workers more or less connected with the Weimar group were the court-official **Franz Müller** (d. 1876), an early supporter of Wagner in many essays (1853-69) ; the abundant historical writer **Reissmann** (d. 1903), whose talent for authorship was awakened here in 1850-2 ; and the influential editors of the *Neue Zeitschrift*, **Franz Brendel** (d. 1868) and **Richard Pohl** (d. 1896).

Among the greater pianists who went forth from Liszt imbued with modern enthusiasms were **Rudolf Viole** of Berlin (d. 1867), **Bülow** (d. 1894), **Klindworth** of London, Moscow and Berlin, **Pflughaupt** of Aix (d. 1871), **Julius Reubke** (d. 1858), **Pruckner** of Stuttgart (d. 1896), **Winterberger** of Vienna, St. Petersburg and Leipsic, **Theodor Ratzenberger** of Düsseldorf (d. 1879), the brilliant **Karl Tausig** (d. 1871), and many others later.

Here may well be added some details about the personnel of the Weimar kapelle. The court-choirmasters during the century included from 1810 *A. E. Müller* (d. 1817); from 1819 the pianist *Hummel* (d. 1837); in 1836–50 the French opera-writer *Chelard* (d. 1861); in 1849–61 *Liszt* (d. 1886); from 1857 for a short time *Karl Stör* (d. 1889), who had been in court employ since 1827; in 1861–95 the Dane-Belgian *Lassen* (d. 1904); in 1889–94 also *Richard Strauss*; in 1895 *Eugen d'Albert*; and in 1895–8 *Bernhard Stavenhagen.* Among the concert-masters were in 1849–52 the great *Joachim* (d. 1907), who did not agree with Liszt's radicalism; in 1853–5 *Laub* (d. 1875); in 1854–61 *Edmund Singer*, later of Stuttgart; in 1863–84 *August Kömpel* (d. 1891); besides the soloists in 1855–8 *Leopold Damrosch* (d. 1885) and in 1862–72 *Isidor Lotto*, later of Strassburg. Other violinists of note were from 1803 *Karl Eberwein* (d. 1868); in 1826–48 *Johann Nikolaus Konrad Götze* (d. 1861); and in 1853–67 *Ludwig Abel* (d. 1895). In 1812–42 the theorist *J. C. Lobe* (d. 1881) was flutist and later violist. Among the 'cellists were in 1850–66 *Bernhard Cossmann*, later of Frankfort; from 1870 for a time *Ernest Demunck*, later of London; in c. 1871–85 *Eduard Jacobs*, later of Brussels; and from 1876 *Leopold Grützmacher* (d. 1900).

From 1830 the town-organist was the learned expert *Johann Gottlob Töpfer* (d. 1870), who was followed in 1870 by *Alexander Wilhelm Gottschalg.*

In Liszt's time there was a close connection between Weimar and Sondershausen (35 m. northwest). The orchestra there, developed under previous choirmasters, as from 1800 *Johann Simon Hermstedt* (d. 1846) and in 1844–52 *Gottfried Herrmann* (d. 1878), from 1853 advanced to great perfection under *Eduard Stein* (d. 1864), one of Liszt's intimates — an eminence fully maintained later, in 1867–70 by *Max Bruch*, in 1871–80 by *Max Erdmannsdörfer*, and in 1881–86 by *Karl Schröder.* (It was here that the noted Schröder quartet was formed in 1871.)

CHAPTER XXXV

SYMPHONISTS AND INSTRUMENTALISTS

211. Competing Orchestral Ideals. — The middle of the century was a time of transition in every department of composition. The divergences of ideal were specially conspicuous in orchestral music, partly because of the close interrelation of such music with dramatic music.

A considerable number of composers adhered in general to the forms and the ways of the classical style, with its emphasis upon tonal design and formal development. The romantic craving for picturesqueness or for the warmly personal touch led constantly toward modifications of the strict classical patterns of structure, but with no deliberate intention in this group to set them aside. Spohr is one typical illustration here. Mendelssohn is another, with greater flexibility and animation. And there were numerous lesser writers who may be counted as essentially classicists.

The more positive romanticist Schumann theoretically went further than any of the foregoing group in the effort to find outlet for subjectivity and a new range of imagination. But Schumann himself was hampered by his imperfect knowledge of the technique of instrumentation. And the full influence of his style was delayed until a later point.

Over against all these stood the class of deliberate innovators in technical method. Wagner and the many who came to be affiliated with him aimed to reconstruct style on the basis of a new view of the nature and function of melody. The classical type of melody came from folk-music, and from such music came also a tendency to adopt compact and highly symmetrical forms of development. The new type, so far as it had any vocal prototype, came from far more sentimentalized and impassioned song-patterns or from free dramatic declamation. And the treatment of materials departed widely from the conventional etiquette of the classical period, in some respects recalling

the imperial freedom of Bach. Division into distinct movements was less obligatory, and within movements the old rigidity
of plan was more and more thrown aside. Development was
determined by impulse or some dramatic plan rather than by
the fixed regimen of sonata-form. Although Wagner was
probably the most original thinker in this new movement,
Liszt became its most conspicuous leader. It was on the basis
of the latter's work that the ' New-German' school rested.

But closely connected with the whole work of Wagner and
Liszt was another tendency, essentially radical in nature, though
unable to proceed alone. This was the movement of the
so-called ' colorists' or impressionists. Here the Frenchman
Berlioz was an energetic leader. His style was evolved from
a novel regard for the expressive capacity of tone-qualities or
timbres as compared with that of tone-patterns. Berlioz himself was not eminent in melodic or harmonic invention, but he
had a remarkable instinct in perceiving and utilizing the powers
of orchestral instruments. He was emphatically an orchestral
virtuoso, with the virtuoso's desire to exploit effects. His experiments naturally reacted upon general style. But in music,
as in pictorial art, color-effects can never be divorced from
effects of outline and plan. Hence the orchestral colorists
and the dramatists drew together, each group deriving something from the other.

The term 'program-music' is constantly applied to most of Berlioz'
work and much of Liszt's, since they often directed the hearer's mind by
verbal titles, mottoes or 'arguments,' and even strove to depict the
sequence of physical facts by tonal means. This entire line of effort has
been the topic of endless debate — perhaps unnecessarily. Music, being
a progressive or discursive art, must pursue some plan or program of
procedure. This plan may be one of tonal patterns and dispositions, as
in the older polyphony and in all classical writing; or of dramatic
characters and events, as in the opera and the oratorio; or of personal
sentiments, however occasioned, as in the song or ballade; or of anything else where there is a distinct process or flux of thought and feeling.
That this process or flux may be associated with concrete images, such as
may also be embodied to some extent in words, action or pictures, is
abundantly shown by all music with a continuous verbal text. The only
question is whether textless music for instruments is essentially hampered
or distorted by having the definite direction of a verbal title or other
intellectual annotation. It is certainly true that any attempt to restrict
music to those processes of thought that can be thus definitely described

in words must break down utterly. Artistic music must always have
interest and value over and above that which inheres in any text, title or
argument — the hearer, however, being free to supply some imaginary interpretation of the tonal formulation of feeling which he hears. But
there would seem to be no essential impropriety in the composer's having
in his work some definite mental impulse or in his communicating this to
the hearer. Hence the use of the 'program' idea seems to be legitimate.
It is the abuse of it by the selection of unsuitable topics or by making
some extreme statement of it normative of all musical art that is to be
resisted.

The one special form of composition that arose in this transitional
period was the 'symphonic poem,' the invention of which is usually
ascribed to Liszt. This form cannot be precisely defined as can the
forms of classical style. It was not governed by what may be called
architectonic rules. In essence it was dramatic, and hence its building
up was analogous, not to the processes of physical manufacture or formal
logic, but to those of free social activity. Its materials were themes
symbolizing personages, situations or ideas. These themes, with their
pictorial or emotional suggestiveness, were, so to speak, put into action
and made to deploy as actors on a stage. The interest, as in a drama,
depended on the interplay of contrasted elements, on the transformation of the factors under changing conditions, on the on-go of events
toward a dénouement. Of course, the way in which this dramatic unfolding was wrought out varied indefinitely with the nature of the topic
chosen and the angle of feeling whence it was approached. Liszt's success with this form was due to his ready absorption of artistic ideas from
Berlioz on the one hand and Wagner on the other. Since his day the
symphonic poem or something akin to it has been a recognized form of
orchestral composition, and its acceptance has enriched the whole field
of instrumental art.

Under the influence of these new tendencies the strict regularity of the
classical symphony tended to vanish. The number, order and character
of movements became somewhat variable, and their internal structure
began to show wide freedom. All this was the natural result of the new
ideas about form in relation to expression which began with Beethoven.

212. The Work of Berlioz. — The duration of Berlioz' artistic
career falls almost exactly into the period here being discussed.
Its beginning was coincident with the early work of Mendelssohn,
Schumann, Chopin, Liszt and Wagner. But it started amid the
peculiarly academic conditions of Paris, and it proceeded at first
without close connection with the strong German development.
Berlioz was instinctively revolutionary in impulse. His independence and the severity with which he expressed himself
prevented his holding intimate relations with other musicians.
He was intensely ambitious for recognition and sought eagerly

to make his works known.   He turned restlessly from one form
of composition to another, tending always to adopt bizarre and
extravagant projects, usually involving an unwieldy apparatus
of performance.   Amid his audacities there were times when he
came close to sublimity and also when he displayed extreme
lyric beauty, but on the whole his creative powers were unequal
to the tasks he put upon them.   Nevertheless, the vigor of his
artistic ambition could not be overlooked, and his special studies
in all details of instrumentation made him an authority.   His
historical importance, then, lies not so much in his philosophy
of musical art, or in his absolute contributions to musical literature, as in the stimulus he gave to the study of musical ways
and means.   The fact that he came just when he did was of
importance in furthering the movements of which Wagner and
Liszt were the leaders.   And the circumstance of the war between France and Germany just after his death favored the
consideration of his works by his countrymen when anything
bearing the German stamp would have been distasteful.

Hector Berlioz (d. 1869), born in 1803 not far from Lyons, was the son of
an able doctor who finally sent him to Paris as a medical student.   In youth
he learned the flute and guitar, but at Paris from 1822 he embarked upon
general musical study, though involving a break with his father.   At the
Conservatoire he had courses with Reicha and Le Sueur, supporting himself
by singing in a theatre-chorus until at length his father's favor was regained.
As early as 1825 he essayed work in the largest forms — a *Messe solennelle*
with orchestra (given at St. Roch and in 1827 at St. Eustache), an oratorio,
an opera, etc.   Two overtures followed, including that to *Waverley*, which,
with a *Scène héroïque grecque*, were given at the Conservatoire (1826) — the
first of five attempts to win the Prix de Rome.   In spite of Cherubini's opposition, success came in 1830 with the cantata *Sardanapale*.   Before this he
had written most of the 'symphonie fantastique,' *Épisode de la vie d'un
artiste* (1829), and some fragments later used in other works.   Unhappy at
Rome and Naples, he secured leave to return after only a year and a half,
bringing the monodrama *Lélio*, the overtures to *King Lear* and *Rob Roy*, the
scena *La captive* and sketches of the overture *Le corsaire*.   In 1833 he
married the Irish actress Henrietta Smithson (they separated in 1840).
Already well known as a ready writer, from 1834 he was on the staff of the
new *Revue et gazette musicale* and for many years remained noted as one of
the most brilliant of Parisian critics (essays collected 1853–63).   His greater
compositions during these years were the symphony *Harold en Italie* (1834),
the *Messe des morts* (1837), the grand opera *Benvenuto Cellini* (1838), which
was not popularly successful, the dramatic symphony *Roméo et Juliette* (1839)
and the *Symphonie funèbre et triomphale* (1840), besides several cantatas and

songs. From 1839 he came into the Conservatoire circle as librarian, but was never professor.

The attention of German critics had long been arrested by the novelty of Berlioz' efforts, and his overtures had begun to be heard. So in 1842-3, when he made a grand tour through Germany as far as Berlin and Hamburg, he was a much-heralded personage. By Liszt and the Weimar circle he was specially honored, and his general reception was flattering. The result was a marked change in his standing at Paris. In 1845 he gave concerts at Marseilles, Lyons and Lille, and also made a tour to Vienna, Pesth, Prague and Breslau. In 1847 he visited Russia with success. He was mentioned as a possible associate with Girard as conductor of the Opéra. In 1852 he conducted the New Philharmonic concerts in London, from 1853 often led the Baden-Baden orchestra, and in 1866-7 made trips to Vienna and St. Petersburg. From 1851 he was several times on the juries of Expositions at Paris or London, and in 1856 became an Academician. His later compositions included the dramatic legend *La damnation de Faust* (1846), a Te Deum for three choirs (1849), the trilogy *L'enfance du Christ* (1852-4), the opéra comique *Béatrice et Bénédict* (1862), and the grand opera *Les Troyens* (two parts, 1858-63). Of his first German tour he wrote a long account (1844). His monumental work on instrumentation was issued in 1843 (later augmented). He left an autobiography (1870) of exceptional interest. Many of his letters have been published (by Bernard, 1879, and by Gounod, 1882). Among his writings were the poetic texts for *L'enfance du Christ* and his last two operas.

Berlioz made exhaustive studies of the technical capacities of all classes of orchestral instruments. He was able to suggest many extensions in the range of their ordinary use. He had a marvelous perception of the emotional and pictorial effects most germane to each. He was ingenious in making unheard-of combinations for special purposes. In his larger works he delighted in massing together enormous groups of a single kind (as, for example, 14 timpani in the Requiem), or combining prodigious complexes of instruments and voices (his ideal orchestra would have included over 400 players, assisted by a vast chorus and the largest organ). These sensational means were desired not merely for overwhelming effects of loudness, but for indescribable richness of tone-color even in delicate passages.

So far as direct influence went, Berlioz' ideas were most immediately effective as they were incorporated into the styles of Liszt and Wagner. In France his precepts and example became in time profoundly stimulating, but their effect was not widely felt until after his death. The modern French interest in orchestral writing, apart from the opera, developed slowly. It has always had a dramatic cast. Berlioz' influence upon it has mainly affected the technique of orchestration rather than the elements of construction. His successors have abundantly supplied the elements in which he was deficient.

Johann Georg Kastner (d. 1867) worked side by side with Berlioz in minute
study of the technique of instrumentation.   Born at Strassburg in 1810, he
was a precocious organist, and, after studying theology for a time, brought
out 4 German operas (1832–5).   Going then to Paris for further study, besides
writing 4 French operas, including the noteworthy *Le dernier roi de Juda*
(1844), he prepared a long and careful series of didactic methods, mostly for
instruments, beginning with a general treatise (1837).   He was much interested in developing the military band and in building up choral societies.
His zeal for enlarging popular knowledge was shown in 6 elaborate symphony-
cantatas with long historical and explanatory introductions (1852–62).   His
instrumental works included 3 symphonies, 5 overtures, 10 serenades for wind
instruments, a saxophone-sextet, etc., but his style, unlike that of Berlioz, was
not at all radical.

Among the few French composers at work upon purely orchestral writing
were the opera-writer and theorist N. H. Reber (d. 1880), with 4 symphonies,
an overture, a suite, the scènes lyriques *Roland* and many refined chamber
works;   the poetic orientalist Félicien David (d. 1876), whose first symphony
(1838) was followed by the notable orchestral ode *Le désert* (1844), a second
ode *Christophe Colomb* (1847) and the 'mystery' *L'Eden* (1848) — all partly
vocal;   the able pianist Louis Lacombe (d. 1884), with 2 dramatic symphonies,
Manfred (1847) and *Arva* (1850), besides many piano works;   and Camille
Saint-Saëns, who, though entering the field as early as 1851, belongs among
the host of younger men, like Théodore Dubois and Jules Massenet, with the
older César Franck (d. 1890), who led onward toward the modern school of
French writing (see sec. 231).

Here we may recall that the founder of the Conservatoire concerts in 1806,
with their obvious influence upon instrumental music, was François Antoine
Habeneck (d. 1849), who from 1826 was also conductor at the Opéra.   In
succession after him, usually in both offices, were from 1846 Narcisse Girard
(d. 1860);   in 1860–3 Théophile Tilmant (d. 1878);   from 1863 François
Georges Hainl (d. 1873);   and in 1873–85 Édouard Marie Ernest Deldevez
(d. 1897).   None of these, except the last, was specially known as a composer.   Another influential conductor was Jules Étienne Pasdeloup (d. 1887),
who started important symphony concerts in 1851.

213. Some Conservative Leaders. — Against what they felt to
be the technically demoralizing tendencies of the Liszt-Wagner
movement in instrumentalism, stood several conservative groups.
They were not closely united, and had no single centre around
which they could rally.   A few, like Lachner, derived prepossessions direct from the Viennese classicists at the opening
of the century.   Many, like Taubert and Kiel, were drawn into
the peculiarly reactionary atmosphere of Berlin, with its neglect
of instrumental work and its prejudice against even the mild
romanticism of the Saxon circle.   Many more, not only in Germany, but beyond, in Scandinavia, Holland and England, were

guided by the powerful influence of the Leipsic conservatory, with its exaltation of elegance, symmetry and dignity, sometimes to the discouragement of warmth and spontaneity. Only a few, like Volkmann and Brahms, came early into the more strenuous and progressive succession to Schumann and were thus ready to make some combination of intricate classical texture with the expression of a wider range of feeling and ideas. It is slightly noticeable that in this last group valuable impetus was received from the source that was fruitful in the case of masters as dissimilar as Haydn and Liszt, namely, the national music of Hungary. Somewhat analogous interminglings of older technical methods with fresh national or racial materials and sentiments were to be seen in still other cases, Russian and Scandinavian.

Without attempting the difficult task of a full classification, several prominent composers are here grouped together who on the whole opposed the transformations of style advocated by the ‘ New-German ’ enthusiasts.

Franz Lachner (d. 1890), a Bavarian, born in 1803, had training from Ett at Munich and from Stadler and Sechter at Vienna, where he was one of Beethoven’s later friends and also prominent among the ‘ Schubertiaden.’ There in 1826 he became conductor at the Kärnthnerthor Theatre, and started the Philharmonic concerts. After two years at Mannheim, in 1836 he was made court-conductor at Munich, where for over 30 years he was a distinguished force. From 1865 he gradually withdrew from activity because of his distaste for the Wagnerian movement. His works include 8 strong symphonies, 8 brilliant orchestral suites, several overtures and much chamber music, besides organ and vocal works, church music, 2 oratorios and 4 operas (1828–49). His style is full of solid learning and contrapuntal ingenuity. Personally he was greatly esteemed throughout southern Germany. His brother **Ignaz Lachner** (d. 1895) was likewise industrious and worthy, serving as conductor at Vienna, Stuttgart, Munich, Hamburg, Stockholm and Frankfort till 1875.

The musical eminence of Munich in the modern period dates almost wholly from the accession of Ludwig II. in 1864. Early in the century the choirmasters were the opera-writer *Winter* (d. 1825) and *Ferdinand Fränzl* (d. 1833). Winter was followed by his pupil *Joseph Hartmann Stuntz* (d. 1859), but his influence was slight. After Lachner came in 1864–5 *Wagner* (d. 1883); in 1867–9 *Bülow* (d. 1894); in 1870–7 *Franz Wüllner* (d. 1902); in 1872–94 *Hermann Levi* (d. 1900); from 1877 *Joseph Rheinberger* (d. 1901); in 1894–7 *Richard Strauss;* in 1897–8 *Max Erdmannsdörfer;* in 1898–1900 *Bernhard Stavenhagen,* and from 1900 *Hermann Zumpe* (d. 1903). The Royal Music School, founded in 1846 by *Franz Hauser* (d. 1870) and directed by him till 1864, was radically reorganized in 1867 under *Bülow.*

Wilhelm Taubert (d. 1891) was born at Berlin in 1811 and spent his whole life there, first as pianist and teacher, from 1831 as court-accompanist, in 1842–69 as court-conductor (choirmaster from 1845), and after that as head of the musical division of the Akademie.　He was intimate with Mendelssohn and belonged to the same general group, emphasizing as conductor a strict conservatism.　His works include 4 symphonies (1831–55), 3 overtures, chamber music, 6 operas (1832–74) and successful incidental music to plays (till 1891).　(See also sec. 205.)

Karl Grädener (d. 1883), born in 1812 at Rostock, beginning as a 'cellist at Helsingfors, was in 1841–51 musical director at Kiel University, and then, except for 3 years (1862–5) at the Vienna conservatory, prominent at Hamburg.　Best known by his able choral works and by piano-pieces after the manner of Schumann, he also wrote 2 symphonies, a piano-concerto and much chamber music, including fine violin- and 'cello-sonatas, with a keen sense of form and harmonic richness.

Théodore Gouvy (d. 1898), though of French descent and from 1846 living much at Paris, belonged with the milder romanticists and his works received special attention in Germany.　They include 7 symphonies, 2 overtures, a variety of chamber pieces, 2 masses, 6 effective dramatic scenas and the opera *Der Cid* (1863, accepted at Dresden, but not given), besides lesser works for the piano or the voice.

Friedrich Kiel (d. 1885), born in Rhenish Prussia in 1821, was at first self-taught, but later studied with Kummer and Dehn.　His coming to Berlin in 1844 distinctly furthered the cause of instrumental music, though his eminence was not fully recognized until after 1860.　From 1866 he taught at the Stern conservatory, later at the Hochschule.　His many chamber works, with his better-known choral ones, display a dignified command of the technique of construction in a style akin to that of the Leipsic masters and not without warmth.

The direct impress of the Leipsic circle upon that of Berlin was strengthened by **Richard Wüerst** (d. 1881), from 1846 a teacher in Kullak's Academy and later a prominent critic, with 2 symphonies, overtures, a violin-concerto, quartets, 6 operas, including *A-ing-fo-hi* (1875);　and still more by **Bargiel** (d. 1897), the step-brother of Mme. Schumann, who began teaching at Berlin, thence went to Cologne and Amsterdam, and in 1874 returned to Berlin, where, as a striking exemplar of the Schumann traditions, he became highly regarded (see sec. 191).　The subsequently famous **Albert Becker** (d. 1899), born in 1834 and trained by Dehn, began teaching at Berlin in 1856, entering the field of composition about 1860, most notably in sacred music.　The Silesian **Eduard Franck** (d. 1893), trained at Breslau and for many years at Cologne and Berne, came to Berlin in 1867, first in the Stern conservatory, then at Breslaur's.　The older **Ludwig Meinardus** (d. 1896), a pupil at Leipsic and for a time of Liszt, as well as of Marx, after serving as chorus-leader at Glogau from 1853, as teacher at the Dresden conservatory from 1865 and as critic at Hamburg from 1874, spent his last years at Bielefeld.　He is notable as one of the few pupils of Liszt who remained a strong conservative. Though best known for his choral works and his critical writings, he also wrote 2 symphonies and much chamber music.

Among the Dutch and Belgian leaders of this period, many of them trained at Leipsic, may be emphasized **Jean Verhulst** (d. 1891), a pupil of Mendelssohn, from 1842 royal conductor at The Hague, from 1848 also at Rotterdam, and the organizer of many popular festivals, with a symphony, 3 overtures and 3 quartets, besides sacred works; **Anton Berlijn** (d. 1870), long conductor at Amsterdam, with many orchestral and chamber works; **Hubert Ferdinand Kufferath** (d. 1896), from 1844 for a half-century influential at Brussels as conductor and pianist, with some symphonies; the Belgian **Adolphe Samuel** (d. 1898), in 1865 the projector of popular concerts at Brussels, and from 1871 head of the Ghent conservatory, with 7 symphonies, many overtures and quartets, and 5 operas (1845–52); and the many-sided **Richard Hol** (d. 1904), from about 1850 at work at Amsterdam and from 1862 town-musician at Utrecht, besides serving as conductor at The Hague, with varied strongly romantic instrumental and vocal works.

In Denmark the Nestor among musicians was **Emil Hartmann** (d. 1900), born in 1805, the son and pupil of a Copenhagen organist, whose musical productiveness began about 1825 and lasted a full 70 years. From 1849 he was court-conductor. Gade married his eldest daughter and the two composers were always associated. He was an admirer of Spohr and in his younger days wrote symphonies, overtures and chamber music in regular form, though his mature genius was better shown in 4 operas (1832–46) and smaller works for the piano or the voice. **Niels Wilhelm Gade** (d. 1890), born in 1817, became the noted link between Leipsic and Copenhagen, where he worked from 1848. His style reflected that of Mendelssohn at first, later that of Schumann, but with original Scandinavian freshness of his own (see secs. 195–196). Another link with Leipsic was **Erik Siboni** (d. 1892), at work in Copenhagen from 1853 and teacher at Sorö from 1864, with 2 symphonies, an overture and some chamber pieces, besides choral works and an opera (1862). The new Scandinavian movement in instrumental music began with the Norwegian **Edvard Hagerup Grieg** (d. 1907), born in 1843, whose work belongs wholly to the recent period (see sec. 232).

214. Liberal Tendencies in Austria and Russia. — While the whole of northern Germany was largely controlled by deliberate conservatism, either of the moderate Leipsic type or of the more severe Berlin variety, in Austria, Bohemia and Hungary, also in Russia, there was a far greater readiness not only to throw instrumental music into the foreground, but to handle its forms and styles with freedom. Within the general circle of which Vienna is the centre orchestral music had been cultivated with fine constructive instinct for nearly a century. Proximity to the folk-music of the Czechs and the Magyars seemed to yield a persistent stimulus. At all events, in this quarter appeared some of the promptest illustrations of how the sterling constructive vigor of classical and post-classical composers could be combined with fresh thematic materials, elastically disposed for emotional or dramatic effect, and with sympathetic use of the modern studies in instrumentation. A few of the leading writers took their impetus from the intellectualism of Schumann, but more were susceptible to the sensational style of Liszt and Berlioz. In Russia a pronounced national type of composition began to take shape, deriving some outlines from German sources, but more and more tending to devise its own path in accord with the Slavic temperament and traditions. This Russian movement almost from the start had a clear analogy with the efforts of Wagner and the ' New-Germans.'

As in the preceding section, no attempt is made to classify the names selected beyond arranging them approximately in the order of appearance.

Two early Bohemian composers on classical lines were **Wenzel Heinrich Veit** (d. 1864), a civil official at Leitmeritz, self-taught, but expert, with a symphony, an overture, and many quintets and quartets; and **J. F. Kittl** (d. 1868), trained at Prague, where in 1843 he followed Dionys Weber as head of the conservatory, with 3 symphonies (one given by Mendelssohn at Leipsic in 1840) and several chamber works, besides 4 operas (1825-54) and church music. The Tyrolese **Johann Rufinatscha** (d. 1893), long prominent at Vienna as a teacher, wrote 5 symphonies, 4 overtures, a piano-concerto, etc. The Hungarian **Mosonyi [Michael Brandt]** (d. 1870), though classically trained, after living from 1842 at Pesth and being intimate with Liszt, became eager, especially about 1860, to emphasize national qualities. In this vein he wrote a memorial symphony, a symphonic poem, an overture, besides 3 operas (from 1857).

Robert Volkmann (d. 1883), born in Saxony in 1813, studied chiefly with K. F. Becker at Leipsic, receiving help from Schumann's kindly interest. From 1839 he taught at Prague, but in 1842 removed to Pesth, where he worked for over 40 years (except 1854-8 at Vienna), and where he was professor of harmony and counterpoint at the National Academy. Among his numerous works are 2 able symphonies, a *Festouvertüre* and one to *Richard III.*, 3 famous serenades, 6 quartets, 2 trios, a 'cello-concerto, etc., besides piano and vocal works. He united old and new features with a notable clarity and euphony of style. Occasionally he chose Hungarian themes. Properly, he is to be classed as a transplanted German composer, somewhat connected with Schumann.

Friedrich Smetana (d. 1884), on the other hand, was not only deeply imbued with the most advanced ideas of the new school, but devoted to the exploitation with vigorous originality of the national music of Bohemia. He was born in 1824 and was trained as a pianist by Proksch at Prague and by Liszt. His life was largely associated with Prague, where he taught in 1848-56 and where in 1866-74 he was conductor at the National Theatre, retiring because of increasing deafness. He wrote 9 symphonic poems, beginning with the cycle 'My Country,' a symphony, 2 quartets, a trio, etc., besides 8 Bohemian operas (from 1865), piano works and songs.

Anton Bruckner (d. 1896) was born in Upper Austria, also in 1824. His early studies were mostly alone and on the organ. In 1855 he became cathedral-organist at Linz, later studying with Kitzler and Sechter. From 1867 he followed the latter as court-organist at Vienna, being also professor at the conservatory and from 1875 lecturer at the university. He twice toured in western Europe as a virtuoso organist of the first rank. His learning as a contrapuntist and his sympathy with the most advanced ideas of style are shown in 9 symphonies, and abundant chamber and choral music. On the whole, however, he is more abstruse than inspired.

Karl Goldmark, born in Hungary in 1830, received his formal education, as far as it went, in Vienna and has always worked there. From 1858 he became prominent as a pianist and composer, among his early works being chamber pieces, the overture *Sakuntala* and a cyclic orchestral work. In 1875 came his brilliant opera *Die Königin von Saba*, to which 4 more have succeeded. His orchestral list includes 2 symphonies, 5 overtures and a symphonic poem, written in a style full of spirit and warmth, but not profound.

A Bohemian, trained at Prague, but working elsewhere, is **Joseph Abert**. Entering the Stuttgart orchestra as a double-bassist, his talent for composition led to his promotion in 1867 to be conductor at the court-theatre, whence he retired in 1888. His works include 6 symphonies (from 1852), overtures, quartets, the symphonic poem *Kolumbus* (1864), 5 operas (1858–90), songs, etc.

The so-called 'New-Russian' movement came into view before the close of the middle period of the century, though its full development as a national school belongs to the recent period. In the field of opera the young Slavic enthusiasts were quick to parallel Wagner's theories by a program of their own aiming at the same dramatic results, but naturally through somewhat different technical means. In the field of orchestral music they turned into paths like those of Berlioz and Liszt, particularly as the Slavic artistic drift is toward sensuous richness, passionate extravagance, and a certain recklessness and whimsicality of procedure. Against this New-Russian movement, however, stood Rubinstein — a genuine Slav whose style had been shaped largely upon German lines. The result of his attitude was an unfortunate alienation between him and his urgent compatriots, an exaggerated desire on his part to belittle the achievements of Wagner, and finally a morbid pessimism regarding the future of musical art. But these critical opinions did not prevent him from expressing his individuality through a variety of important works, orchestral and vocal, some of which have considerable significance.

The pioneers were **Michail Glinka** (d. 1857), whose orchestral pieces, including 2 unfinished symphonies and some chamber works, began before 1845, and who, though a pupil of Dehn, had the audacity of style to win Berlioz' cordial interest; **Alexander Dargomyzski** (d. 1869), whose orchestral efforts consisted only of fantasias on popular dances and songs; and Prince **Yourij Galitzin** (d. 1872), notable not as a composer, but for the orchestra that he organized about 1860 for the performance through Europe and America of Russian works.

Mily Balakirew (d. 1910), born in 1836 and known as pianist from 1855 and as conductor at Prague and St. Petersburg from 1866 (retiring, however, in 1872), produced 3 overtures (Russian 1862, Czech, Spanish), the symphonic poem *Tamara* and a symphony (1897). He supplied much of the trained information that guided the projectors of the New-Russian movement about 1855 —**Alexander Borodin** (d. 1887), **Modest Mussorgski** (d. 1881), **César Cui** and **Nicolai Rimski-Korsakow** — and his house was their original rendezvous (see sec. 232). The very influential opera-writer and critic **Serow** (d. 1871), though personally in close contact with the above, was not marked as an orchestral writer (see sec. 205).

Anton Rubinstein (d. 1894), most famous as a pianist (see secs. 202, 205), wrote in all 6 symphonies, beginning in 1854, of which the most famous are the 'Ocean' (1857) and the 'Dramatic' (1875), 3 overtures, a symphonic poem, 3 character-pictures and a suite, besides 5 piano-concertos and a large amount of chamber music. In spite of his critical predilections, his style links him closely with the Liszt movement, but with an instinctive adherence to methods in technical procedure recalling the German romanticists. His use of orchestral resources was lavish and rich, and the exuberance of his imagination often results in passages of beauty and power.

The modern master of Russian orchestral production, **Peter Tschaikowski** (d. 1893), with his 6 symphonies, 7 symphonic poems, 4 suites, exquisite chamber works, etc., lies outside the period here under consideration.

Brahms became known before 1850. This fact alone would make reference to him here necessary, though his most effective work was in the last period of the century. His maturity was reached early, but the affiliations of his style were not at once clear. Schumann believed him the opener of 'new paths' — meaning, however, paths fresh in romantic imagination. At the same moment Liszt counted him an accession to the ranks of the New-Germans. And a little later Hanslick and others cited his works as antidotes to Wagnerian heresies. It was amid incessant and excited controversy in critical circles that he went his way, calmly working out his impulses, sturdily holding his independence, and finally taking his place as one of the foremost geniuses of the century. His adherence in the main to the older forms and methods, his love for rhythmic and metric

intricacy, his prodigious contrapuntal technique, his avoidance
of dramatic forms and even of the dramatic point of view, his
disdain of sensuous beauties of effect for their own sake — all
these characteristics allied him with those called conservatives.
But in his evident intellectuality and technical learning there
worked a varied and profound imagination, creative gifts extremely individual and original, sympathies that were far from
narrow, and a power of self-expression full of dignity and commanding force.   In the midst of the prevalent tendencies of the
day he stood in the unique position of one who retained vital
kinship with such dissimilar earlier masters as Bach, Beethoven
and Schumann, while fully alive to the new sources of artistic
material (such as the Hungarian) and to the new emotional drift
of the 19th century.   In some respects his style showed an organic blending of old and new elements which have been counted
incompatible.   For all these reasons his work has singular interest and value.

   Johannes Brahms (d. 1897) was born in 1833 at Hamburg, the son of a
player in the theatre-orchestra.   Under Eduard Marxsen of Altona (d. 1887)
he developed first as a pianist, but with sound training, also, in the technique
of composition.   In 1848-9 he was heard in concerts, and in 1853, when on a

tour with Remenyi, he encountered Joachim, through whom he was introduced
to Liszt and Schumann.   The latter's
heralding of him in the *Neue Zeitschrift*
as the awaited musical Messiah created
a sensation, opening the way for his first
publications, but also provoking animated discussion.   In 1854-8 he was court-
conductor at Detmold, with much
leisure for composition.   In 1859 his first
piano-concerto (at Leipsic) occasioned
criticism, actually because so rich in content and so bare of display.   After short
sojourns at Hamburg and Winterthur
(with Kirchner), in 1862 he settled in
Vienna.   From 1860 his style seemed to
undergo a change, intricacy and learning
being now less obtrusive.   His only
official posts were as conductor of the
Singakademie in 1863-4 and of the Gesellschaft der Musikfreunde in 1871-4.
In 1864-9 and again in 1874-8 he was absent from Vienna for various purposes, including concert-giving.   He took pains to retain connection with
Mme. Schumann, who was a sympathetic friend and interpreter.   For the

most part, his life was without external incident, being spent in the quiet and secluded pursuit of artistic ideals. He died of a painful disease and was buried close to Beethoven and Schubert.

His works were not extraordinarily numerous, but they were elaborated with the minutest care and earnestness. At first they were chiefly for the piano, the solo voice or the chamber ensemble. In 1860 came the earliest of his serenades for orchestra. Several choral works followed, notably the *Deutsches Requiem* (1867–8, Vienna and Bremen), the *Triumphlied* (1872–3, Vienna and Cologne, celebrating the German victories) and the *Schicksalslied* — all displaying marvelous technical and emotional power. At intervals came many important piano works, including 2 concertos, manifold songs of extreme beauty and a succession of chamber works. The 4 symphonies (1876–86) were notably different from each other, displaying the complex structure, rhythmical and melodic fertility, sustained energy and disdain of merely superficial effect that mark his whole style. With these appeared the *Akademische Festouvertüre* (1881) and the *Tragische Ouvertüre* (1881) in contrasted tones of sentiment.

In the fields of the song, the choral cantata, the classical quartet and the symphony, Brahms certainly ranks as the chief master in the period just after 1850.

215. Famous Violinists and 'Cellists. — It is interesting to note about the middle of the century a gradual change in the critical estimate of virtuosity as a profession. Touring for the purpose of appealing to a variety of audiences continues common, of course, but the number of great players who thus become known is less in proportion to those whose powers are concentrated upon stated work in some local circle where they are associated with a fixed orchestra or similar organization. In other words, the virtuoso begins to lose the marks, once considered necessary, which remind us of the strolling mountebank of the Middle Ages, and finds his higher place in connection with some institution maintained as a stated means of local education. In consequence, virtuosity of the highest rank now usually involves readiness in ensemble playing, in conducting, in solid composition, in broad musicianship, as well as the power to sway casual audiences to enthusiasm or to execute difficult feats. Furthermore, the work of teaching on the part of solo instrumentalists becomes more orderly and thoughtful, so that they compete more equally with teachers in other branches. The trend of progress is everywhere toward greater dignity and breadth in the virtuoso's conception of himself and toward higher respect for him on the part of the musical public.

Space fails to present the cumulative evidence for these statements.   But a few selected masters of stringed instruments require special mention.   Of the violinists already in full career when the period opens the chief was certainly **Spohr** (d. 1859), since 1822 fruitfully at work at Cassel (see sec. 181, where others are also named).

Ferdinand David (d. 1873) is a typical example of the best class.   Born at Hamburg in 1810 and hence the close contemporary of Mendelssohn and Schumann, after study with Spohr and Hauptmann, and a brief experience in a theatre-orchestra in Berlin, from 1829 he led the private quartet of a Russian noble at Dorpat (whose daughter he married), and played often in Russian cities.   From 1836 he was concertmaster of the Gewandhaus orchestra as reorganized by Mendelssohn.   Here he exercised phenomenal influence as trainer, interpreter, teacher and composer.   He was Mendelssohn's devoted coadjutor, and naturally entered the new conservatory as one of its ablest professors, attracting strong pupils from all quarters.   His compositions included 2 symphonies, 5 concertos, much chamber music, etc., and he edited violin classics and a famous method.

Delphin Alard (d. 1888), though younger, came into view about the same time.   Trained by Habeneck at Paris, he at once found place at the Opéra and later in the court-orchestra, of which he became concertmaster.   From 1843 he was professor at the Conservatoire.   His style combined the brilliance of Paganini with the breadth of the best German masters.   He prepared a fine method, good editions of violin music and many original works.

Famous examples of touring players were the superficial, but clever **Ole Bull** (d. 1880), the Norwegian player who began his career in 1832, often visiting America and doing much for the cause of music in his native land; **Camillo Sivori** (d. 1894), a Genoese in the Paganini line who began his travels as a boy about 1827; and **Heinrich Wilhelm Ernst** (d. 1865), a Moravian, trained by De Bériot and on tour extensively from 1834, after 1850 living in London.

Henri Vieuxtemps (d. 1881), born in Belgium in 1820, was developed by De Bériot, Sechter and Reicha into broad musicianship, appearing in concert about 1830.   From 1837 he was known in several countries as both player and composer, becoming court-musician and conservatory professor at St. Petersburg in 1846-52, and in 1871-3 at the Brussels conservatory, ceasing work because of paralysis.   His numerous works included 6 concertos, many fantasias, some studies, a suite, etc., which are standard favorites.

Other representatives of the French school were **Prosper Sainton** (d. 1890), who, after experience at Paris and Toulouse, with some tours, from 1845 lived in London as a leading teacher and concertmaster, with 2 concertos and some other works; **Charles Dancla**, professor at the Conservatoire since 1857, a noted ensemble player, and a prolific composer of elaborate concert and pedagogic works; and **Hubert Léonard** (d. 1890), from 1852 De Bériot's successor at the Brussels conservatory, with 5 concertos, many teaching-pieces, etc.   Contemporary with these was **Antonio Bazzini** (d. 1897), brought up at Brescia, but broadened by tours in Germany, who from 1873 was at the Milan conservatory, from 1882 its director, with a variety of works, vocal and instrumental, in which he united Italian and German styles.

Joseph Joachim (d. 1907), born at Pressburg (Hungary) in 1831, was on the whole the greatest name in the period and since. After study at Vienna, he came to Leipsic in 1843 and immediately rose to eminence, finally being David's assistant. In 1849–54 he was leader under Liszt at Weimar, was then conductor and soloist at Hanover, and in 1868 was called to take charge of the new Hochschule at Berlin, where he was extremely influential. As an interpreter he was unrivaled, and as a composer productive, in a style having usually a pathetic intensity, though following classical models of form.

From the east came also the Hungarian Eduard Remenyi (d. 1898), from 1848 for a half-century known round the world as a concert-player of extraordinary brilliance; the Bohemian Ferdinand Laub (d. 1875), from 1853 Joachim's successor at Weimar, from 1855 a foremost master at Berlin, and later at Moscow and Carlsbad; and the Pole Henri Wieniawski (d. 1880), a widely-traveled virtuoso, in 1860–72 at St. Petersburg and in 1874–7 Vieuxtemps' successor at Brussels. The last two were composers to a limited extent.

Of the same period was the Spaniard Gesù Monasterio (d. 1903), trained at Paris, who from 1861 was the centre of classical violinism at the Madrid court and conservatory. The Belgian François Jéhin (d. 1899), born in 1839, developed early as a virtuoso, known through Europe and America, and from 1893 settled at Montreal and from 1896 at Brussels.

Among famous teachers should be mentioned Georg Hellmesberger [Sr.] of Vienna (d. 1873); Lambert Meerts of Brussels (d. 1863); and Lambert Joseph Massart of Paris (d. 1892).

Noted quartets were formed by Joseph Hellmesberger [Sr.] of Vienna (d. 1893), in 1855 by Karl Müller of Meiningen, and later by Joachim, Laub, Jean Becker (d. 1884) and others.

As illustrations of the many 'cellists of substantial musicianship may be named Friedrich August Kummer of Dresden (d. 1879); Adrien François Servais (d. 1866), from 1836 touring and from 1848 at the Brussels conservatory; Karl Schuberth (d. 1863), from 1835 honored at St. Petersburg; Alfredo Piatti (d. 1901), working from 1849 at London; Georg Goltermann (d. 1898), from 1853 prominent at Frankfort; Friedrich Grützmacher (d. 1903), from 1849 at Leipsic and from 1860 at Dresden; his brother Leopold Grützmacher (d. 1900), successively at Leipsic, Schwerin, Prague, Meiningen and Weimar; and Joseph Diem (d. 1894), from 1866 at the Moscow conservatory.

Mention should also be made of the famous double-bassist Giovanni Bottesini (d. 1889), a great concert-player and a prolific composer of operas (1847–80), orchestral and chamber music, and songs.

216. Other Instrumentalists. — The rapidly increasing interest in orchestration tended to direct attention afresh to the possibilities of every solo instrument, encouraging the invention of improvements and of altogether new forms, stimulating extreme virtuosity and the exact methods of teaching by which it is attained, and drawing out special compositions of various kinds. In particular, the enterprising efforts of Berlioz, Kastner, Wagner and Liszt expanded the whole range of orchestral art, bringing into view many novelties in construction, execution and expressive application. The gains in color, variety, tonal breadth and emotional impressiveness were in many cases of the utmost value. Practically all the resources of the most modern orchestra were developed before 1865, and their use in dramatic, symphonic, chamber and solo works made clear.

Reference has already been made (sec. 183) to the improvements and novelties introduced from about 1830 by **Böhm** of Munich (d. 1881), **Sax** of Brussels and Paris (d. 1894) and **Wieprecht** of Berlin (d. 1872). Another important creator of instruments was the Bohemian **Václav František Červený** of Königgrätz (d. 1896), who for 30 years from 1844 not only invented a long series of notable brass wind-instruments, but greatly improved the mechanism and shape of several forms already in use (including the timpani). His favorite invention was the waldhorn group. He set up a factory which has furnished instruments to leading military bands everywhere. In 1863 the French bandmaster **Sarrus** matched the saxophone with the 'sarrusophone'—a brass instrument with an oboe mouthpiece— which has been made in a variety of sizes. These newer brass instruments have not as yet been specially useful in the concert-orchestra, but they have increased the resources of the military band. The composite instrument now known as the 'orchestrion' was developed out of earlier experiments in 1851 by **Friedrich Theodor Kaufmann** of Dresden (d. 1872).

FIG. 109. — Sarrusophones.

Celebrated flutists of the period were **Jean Rémusat** of London and Paris (d. 1880); **Giulio Briccialdi** of London (d. 1881); **Franz Doppler** (d. 1883), chiefly of Vienna, who also wrote several operas (from 1847); his brother **Karl Doppler** of Pesth and Stuttgart (d. 1900); **Joseph Henri Altès** of Paris (d. 1899); **Ernst Wilhelm Heinemeyer** of Hanover and St. Petersburg (d. 1869); and **Wilhelm Barge** of Detmold and Leipsic.

Among the oboists were **Apollon Barret** of Paris (d. 1879); **Antoine Joseph Lavigne** of London (d. 1886); and **Franz Xaver Jelinek** of Salzburg (d.

1880). Noted bassoonists were **Jean Baptiste Joseph Willent** of Brussels and Paris (d. 1852); and the distinguished Dutch composer and conductor **Johannes Meinardus Coenen** of Amsterdam (d. 1899).

The clarinettists included **Hyacinthe Eléonore Klosé** of Paris (d. 1880); **Arnold Joseph Blaes** of Brussels (d. 1892); **Henry Lazarus** of London (d. 1895); **Bernhardt Landgraf** of Leipsic (d. 1885); and **Karl Bärmann** [Sr.] of Munich (d. 1885).

Among the hornists were **Johann Gottfried Rode** of Berlin (d. 1857), and **Désiré Artôt** of Paris and Brussels (d. 1887). Important cornettists were **Joseph Arban** of Paris (d. 1889), and **Julius Kosleck** of Berlin. In the Leipsic orchestra from 1835 was the timpanist **Ernst Gotthold Benjamin Pfundt** (d. 1871), the inventor of the 'machine-head.'

The harp continued to be carefully studied, prominent virtuosi being **Théodore Labarre** of Paris (d. 1870); **Elias Parish-Alvars** of Vienna (d. 1849); **Félix Godefroid** of Paris (d. 1897); **Karl Oberthür** of London (d. 1895); **Ange Conrad Prumier** of Paris (d. 1884); and **John Thomas** [Aptommas] of London.

Music for the zither advanced into considerable artistic importance. The instrument was specially improved and cultivated by **Max Albert** of Berlin (d. 1882).

Besides the eminent conductors already named, mention should be made of **Karl Liebig** (d. 1872), in 1843–67 head of an orchestra at Berlin; **Benjamin Bilse** (d. 1902), from 1843 town-musician at Liegnitz, developing an exceptional band, and in 1868–84 leader of famous concerts at Berlin; **Karl Müller** (d. 1894), from 1846 at Münster and from 1860 at Frankfort; **Johann Herbeck** (d. 1877), from 1853 influential at Vienna; **Julius von Bernuth** (d. 1902), from 1857 at Leipsic and from 1867 at Hamburg; and many others later.

217. Waltz Music. — Among the many dances that have become standard objects of artistic treatment none has been so popular as the waltz, which was evolved from the simple Austrian ländler about 1780. Originating probably in Bohemia and proceeding from Vienna as a centre, by 1800 it had become fashionable in all European cities. The purely musical waltz-form was promptly utilized by the Viennese composers generally, beginning with Mozart and Beethoven. It was finally expanded by Schubert, while Weber lifted it into an orchestral type. Later the romantic and the bravura pianists used it constantly for salon and concert pieces, often with extreme beauty of sentiment and effect, though usually without reference to actual dancing. But meantime, at Vienna and to some extent elsewhere, waltzes for dancing became notable in the hands of clever composers and conductors who made the form a specialty.

A variety of other dances later came into similar musical importance, such as the galop, the polka, the polonaise, the redowa, the mazurka, etc.

The first of the Vienna waltz-makers was **Joseph Lanner** (d. 1843), who organized a popular quartet and orchestra soon after 1820. His pupil **Johann Strauss [Sr.]** (d. 1849) formed another orchestra in 1826, with which in 1833-8 he toured through Europe. One of his three sons, **Johann Strauss [Jr.]** (d. 1899), was the most celebrated of the whole series, beginning competition with his father in 1844, and from 1871, after winning international renown, writing many bright operettas. Among the numerous other workers in the field were from 1834 **Joseph Labitzky** (d. 1881); from 1836 the Frenchman **Louis Antoine Jullien** (d. 1860); from about the same time the Viennese **Philipp Fahrbach [Sr.]** (d. 1885); from 1841 the Dane **Hans Christian Lumbye** (d. 1874); from 1843 the Hungarian **Joseph Gungl** (d. 1889) and his nephew **Johann Gungl** (d. 1883); and from about 1847 the Hungarian **Kéler-Béla** (d. 1882). In Paris the two most famous dance-makers were from about 1820 **Jean Baptiste Joseph Tolbecque** (d. 1869) and from about 1835 **Philippe Musard** (d. 1859).

CHAPTER XXXVI

CHORAL MUSIC. THE SONG. THE ENGLISH SCHOOL

218. The Revival of Choral Music. — The keen attention to instrumental music which began in the later 18th century was so absorbing that for a long time choral music was relatively neglected. Various kinds of church services, to be sure, demanded fresh material, and this was continually supplied, though usually without much originality or depth. The only branch of vocal music (aside from the opera) that made distinct advance during the opening years of the 19th century was the song, but even this was wrought upon only by some scattered composers.

With the definite access of romantic feeling, however, it was inevitable that choral music should receive new consideration. The conservative party emphasized it because it was to them the normal medium for the application of the older counterpoint which they admired, and because it was opposed to the prevalent instrumentalism which they disliked. Workers like Mendelssohn and Schumann found in it the means for embodying poetic conceptions too varied or exalted for merely solo treatment. And the most radical experimenters with orchestral color, like Berlioz and Liszt, fully recognized the tonal splendor of large vocal combinations and were quick to utilize such impressive effects in building up their complex ensembles. So it came to pass that from about 1820 onward the volume of dignified choral music for concert purposes rapidly increased, and also the variety of its forms.

In the competition for popular effectiveness and artistic achievement choral music is noticeably handicapped. Orchestral music is supported and purveyed by salaried bands of professional players under constant discipline and giving frequent concerts in extended series, often in more than one place. But choral music, with comparatively few exceptions, is set forth by volunteer organizations largely made up of amateurs, having much less rehearsal and giving concerts at much longer intervals. The consequence of all this is that the resources of choral music are popularly not as well understood as those of orchestral music, its repertory is rela-

tively unfamiliar, and in some cases the fine success of particular composers with it is comparatively unknown. Even if we allow for the
obvious fact that choral effects cannot vie with orchestral in variety and
in certain kinds of intensity, it is only fair to remember also that choral
music has not even yet attained the artistic eminence that is possible,
simply because in most places it has not been given similar opportunity.

One element in this development was the multiplication in all
the leading musical countries of singing clubs and societies.
Whether this was a cause or an effect may be debated, but
the fact is impressive in any case. One reason for it was the
desire to do justice to some of the older composers, especially
Handel and Haydn. But in part it was a spontaneous expression of the new sense of music as a popular fine art, having
exceptional educational and social applications, especially as it
was seen that in choral music large numbers of amateurs can
personally engage in the production of extremely artistic results.
The choral concert and festival, accordingly, became common,
constituting a new opportunity for the composer and a new
means of contact between musical art and the public. To meet
the demand thus presented there was a marked increase not
only in oratorios, psalms and sacred cantatas, but also in similar
works upon secular texts, including manifold settings of brief
lyrics and odes. Many of these latter, of course, were written
in part-song style, paralleling the simpler solo songs, but the
tendency increased to build them out into complex works with
orchestral accompaniment and with some solo passages. In
all this we see an effort to strike a fresh balance between vocal
and instrumental music of an elaborate sort.

The Berlin *Singakademie*, founded by Fasch in 1790–2, was the prototype of a long series of choral societies, the earliest of which followed
in this order : — Leipsic and Stettin in 1800, Münster in 1804, Dresden in
1807, Zurich in 1808, Vienna in 1812–4, Potsdam in 1814, Bremen in
1815, Chemnitz and Hall (Swabia) in 1817, Innsbruck in 1818, Frankfort in 1818–21, Hamburg and Güstrow in 1819, Jever in 1820, Oldenburg
in 1821, Cassel in 1823, etc.

The German institution known as the *Liedertafel* or male choral club
began in 1808 under Zelter as an offshoot from the Berlin Singakademie.
Similar clubs soon followed elsewhere, as at Frankfurt-an-der-Oder and
Leipsic in 1815, at Magdeburg and Weida in 1818, at Berlin ('Junior')
in 1819, at Dessau in 1821, at Hamburg and Danzig in 1823, at Königsberg and Leipsic (University) in 1824, etc. At first the aim was to
gather small, exclusive groups of experts — a modern analogue to the

mediæval Meistersinger guilds. But presently the popular and social idea became dominant, membership being open to all with fair singing ability, and the objects being quite as much convivial or patriotic as strictly musical. Pioneer efforts in this latter direction began in 1810 at Zurich under Nägeli and soon spread through South Germany generally. In Austria similar movements began with the founding of the Vienna Männergesangverein in 1843. Gradually in each country and province federations of singing-clubs were perfected, chiefly for the holding of large festivals, and out of these about 1860 under Müller von der Werra was evolved the comprehensive *Deutscher Sängerbund,* uniting more than 70 federations and over 80,000 singers.

The somewhat parallel French institution of the *Orphéon* had a different genesis, being the outgrowth from 1835 of the singing-classes in the public schools. But in practical working this has led in both France and Belgium to similar results on a larger scale. Before the Franco-Prussian War the Orphéonistes counted about 3250 local clubs and nearly 150,000 members. The organizer of the movement was Wilhem [Bocquillon] (d. 1842), but its later success was due to Gounod, who was its general director in 1852–60, and to François Bazin (d. 1878), the opera-writer (see sec. 204).

Among the best-known writers of male choruses and part-songs were **Karl Zöllner** (d. 1860), who taught at Leipsic from 1820 and in 1833 started the noted Zöllner-Verein ; **Julius Otto** (d. 1877), from 1825 an equally prominent conductor at Dresden ; **Franz Weber** of Cologne (d. 1876) ; the indefatigable **Ludwig Erk** of Berlin (d. 1883) ; **Vincenz Lachner** (d. 1893), from 1836 at Mannheim and from 1873 at Carlsruhe; **Karl Mangold** of Darmstadt (d. 1889) ; **Heinrich Esser** of Vienna (d. 1872) ; **Wilhelm Tschirch** (d. 1892), from 1843 at Liegnitz and from 1852 at Gera ; **Friedrich Lux** (d. 1895), from 1841 at Dessau and from 1851 at Mayence; **Karl Reinthaler** of Cologne and Bremen (d. 1896); the Swiss **Karl Attenhofer,** from 1867 at Zurich; and **Eduard Kremser** of Vienna. After 1860 many other writers became influential, such as **Reyer** in France and **Bruch** in Germany.

219. The Berlin Circle. — The modern importance of Berlin as the capital of Germany began to develop only after Napoleon's career was checked in 1813–5. In the outburst of patriotic aspiration following the War of Liberation, intellectual and artistic interests, including music, received much attention. But those who happened to be leaders in musical matters chose to apply themselves almost exclusively to choral music of a somewhat antique type. Hence arose a Berlin group or school which long stood aloof from the exuberant instrumentalism of the Viennese group and from the several phases of romanticism represented by Mendelssohn, Schumann and Chopin, as well as from the radicalism of Wagner, Liszt and Berlioz. The

Berlin Akademie became the stronghold of an extreme conservatism, and it was not until toward the end of the period now under
review that the liberal spirit came in which has since made
Berlin one of the progressive musical capitals of the world.

It may be that the attitude of certain Berlin masters, like
Grell, Dehn and Kiel, served a useful purpose as a counterpoise
to the impulsive swing of style away from the traditions of the
old vocal counterpoint. They certainly helped to keep musical
education from forgetting solid structure in composition amid its
desires to exploit impressionistic and sensational devices. Probably this reactionary influence did good in the end, though its
intolerant narrowness exasperated the many who were eagerly
searching out new paths. It at least resulted in making Berlin
a centre for choral music of a severe type, for able teachers of
the art of singing, for musical theorists and for scholarly investigators of music-history.

One of the most influential organizations was the *Singakademie*, led
from 1800 by *Zelter* (d. 1832); from 1833 by *Rungenhagen* (d. 1851),
who was chosen in competition with Mendelssohn; in 1851–76 by *Grell*
(d. 1886); in 1876–1900 by *Martin Blumner* (d. 1901); and since
1900 by *Georg Schumann*.

The now famous *Domchor* began to receive special attention about
1830. In 1842 it was reorganized under Mendelssohn's advice, but its
eminence from 1843 was chiefly due to the training of *August Heinrich
Neithardt* (d. 1861), who was succeeded in 1861–89 by *Rudolph von
Hertzberg* (d. 1893), assisted in 1862–81 by *Heinrich Kotzolt* (d. 1881),
who was a specialist in *a cappella* music.

Among many choral societies the most celebrated was the *Gesangverein*,
founded in 1847 and till 1874 conducted by *Julius Stern* (d. 1883).

The earliest of the music-schools was the *Institut für Kirchenmusik*,
projected in 1819 by *Zelter* and directed till 1832 by him and *Bernhard
Klein* (d. 1832). Later directors were from 1832 *A. W. Bach* (d. 1869);
from 1869 the organist *Haupt* (d. 1891); and since 1892 *Robert
Radecke*. The *Akademie der Künste* was formed in 1833, not simply
as an educational institution, but as an honorable society of specialists.
Mendelssohn's brief and unhappy relation with it occurred in 1841–2.
The Institut, the Akademie (Abtheilung für musikalische Composition)
and the much later Abtheilung für ausübende Tonkunst (founded
in 1869 under Joachim) were in 1875 merged into the significant
Hochschule für Musik.

Two other schools were of importance. The *Conservatorium* was
founded in 1850 by *Marx, Kullak* and *Stern*, and from 1857 was directed
by the latter alone, his successors being in 1883–8 *Radecke*, from 1888
the singer *Jenny Meyer* (d. 1894), and since 1895 *Gustav Holländer*.

The *Neue Akademie der Tonkunst* was established in 1855 by *Theodor Kullak* (d. 1882), followed in 1882 by his son *Franz Kullak*, who disbanded it in 1890. Both institutions attracted hundreds of pupils.

In the list of royal choirmasters during the period were in 1830–42 *Franz Gläser* (d. 1861), in 1842–69 *Wilhelm Taubert* (d. 1891), and in 1849–69 *Heinrich Dorn* (d. 1892). In 1842–51 *Meyerbeer* was the dominant operatic power.

Those who gave character to the circle included various kinds of workers — choral composers or conductors, organists, theorists and literary students. Almost all of them were strong teachers.

Eduard August Grell (d. 1886), born in 1800, came to be the chief representative of the Berlin ideas. Beginning in 1817 as an organist, in 1839 he followed Hellwig at the cathedral. From 1832 he assisted Rungenhagen in leading the Singakademie and in 1851 succeeded him both there and as teacher of composition in the Akademie. He held tenaciously to the superiority of choral music over instrumental, and his contrapuntal genius was exemplified in a series of fine sacred works, including a mass for 16 voices, an oratorio, a Te Deum, many psalms, motets and songs. His official positions and his undoubted learning gave him great influence.

Neither **Karl Friedrich Rungenhagen** (d. 1851) nor **August Wilhelm Bach** (d. 1869), though prominent officially and as teachers, attained high rank as composers, though the former was an industrious producer.

Siegfried Dehn (d. 1858) was at first a law-student at Leipsic, but from 1829 developed rapidly at Berlin as a musical theorist. From 1842 he was musical librarian at the Royal Library and also for some years editor of the *Cäcilia*. His teaching and his books (from 1837) made him influential.

Adolf Bernhard Marx (d. 1866), born at Halle in 1795, was one of Zelter's pupils. From 1824 for several years he edited the *Berliner allgemeine musikalische Zeitung*, contending manfully for German composers, including Beethoven. From 1830 he was professor at the university, becoming distinguished as a theorist, historian and pedagogical reformer (works from 1828). He was intimate with the young Mendelssohn. As a composer he was not significant, though he essayed many forms.

Karl August Haupt (d. 1891), born in Silesia in 1810 and trained at Berlin, from about 1830 held various positions there as organist, becoming a virtuoso and teacher of international reputation. He was prominent in the Institut and the Akademie. His published works include an *Orgelschule*, a Choralbuch (1869) and some songs.

Friedrich Kiel (d. 1885), born in Rhenish Prussia in 1821, was trained as a violinist at Berleburg and Coburg, and from 1842 in composition by Dehn at Berlin, where he settled. From 1866 he was teacher of composition at the conservatory and from 1870 at the Hochschule. His works include 2 noble Requiems, the first of which (1859–60) established his reputation, a Missa solemnis (1865), a Te Deum (1866), a Stabat Mater (1869), the oratorio *Christus* (1871–2), much other church music, many chamber works, pianopieces and songs. In style he illustrated the pursuit of classical ideals under modern conditions, somewhat after the fashion of Mendelssohn.

From the long list of other noted workers appearing before 1860 may be selected *Franz Commer* (d. 1887), the first librarian of the Institut and an intellectual leader, *Ludwig Erk* (d. 1883), *Ferdinand Schulz* (d. 1897), *Gustav Engel* (d. 1895), *Georg Vierling* (d. 1901), founder of the Bach-Verein about 1855, and *Ferdinand Sieber* (d. 1895) ; the organists *Julius Schneider* (d. 1885), *Ludwig Thiele* (d. 1848), *Ernst David Wagner* (d. 1883), and *Hermann Küster* (d. 1878), Grell's successor at the cathedral in 1857 ; and the theorists or scholars *Von Winterfeld* (d. 1852), *Flodoard Geyer* (d. 1872), *Karl Friedrich Weitzmann* (d. 1880), *Friedrich Bellermann* (d. 1874), his son *Heinrich Bellermann* (d. 1903), *Robert Eitner* (d. 1905), *Hermann Mendel* (d. 1876), *Emil Naumann* (d. 1888), and *August Reissmann* (d. 1903).

Although until toward the end of the period there was no general instrumental composer of eminence associated with Berlin, the court-orchestra contained several specialists who wrote worthily, such as the brothers *Moritz* and *Leopold Ganz* (d. 1868, '69), *Karl Böhmer* (d. 1884), *Hubert Ries* (d. 1886), *Karl Hering* (d. 1889), *Eduard Wendt* (d. 1890), and *Ferdinand Laub* (d. 1875).

The earlier Berlin pianists were *Theodor Oesten* (d. 1870), *Rudolf Viole* (d. 1867), *Albert Löschhorn, Theodor Kullak* (d. 1882), who from 1846 was court-pianist, and *Louis Schlottmann*.

220. Organ Music. — The form of church music which showed decided vitality was the one connecting it with the prevailing instrumentalism — music for the organ. The Bach revival continued to bear fruit in various ways, sometimes in the diligent cultivation of the strict style in which he was eminent, sometimes in modifications looking toward a more modern expressiveness and sensuous brilliance. Catholic organists were naturally less influenced by the Bach traditions than others. The German players and composers generally clung to the older methods, but the romanticism that has now become characteristic of the French school was beginning to manifest itself. The steady improvement of organ-mechanism was providing varied tone-colors to simulate orchestral effects, and ingenious devices for handling the keyboards and the stops. Before the period closed, the capacity of the organ as a concert-instrument began to be appreciated, so that it was more used in recitals of a varied character and in combination with the orchestra. In thus enrolling the organ among the resources of concerted music, Berlioz and Liszt were active. Whether these developments promoted the best interests of the organ style may be doubted, but they constituted a noticeable feature in musical progress.

The more noted organists of the German school were **Töpfer** of Weimar, (d. 1870), who was also an expert on construction (books from 1833); **Ernst Köhler** of Breslau (d. 1847); **Julius Schneider** of Berlin (d. 1885); **A. F. Hesse** of Breslau (d. 1863); **Haupt** of Berlin (d. 1891); **August Gottfried Ritter** of Erfurt and Magdeburg (d. 1885); **J. G. Bastiaans** of Amsterdam (d. 1875); **Wilhelm Volckmar** of Homburg (d. 1887); **Ludwig Thiele** of Berlin (d. 1848); **Gustav Rebling** of Magdeburg (d. 1902); the Bohemian **Josef Krejči** of Prague (d. 1881); **Johann Georg Herzog** of Munich and Erlangen; **Jan Albert van Eijken [Eyken]** of Elberfeld (d. 1868); **Merkel** (d. 1885) and **K. A. Fischer** (d. 1892), both of Dresden. Almost all of these were composers in many other forms besides those suited to the organ.

Among those belonging to the French school were **Louis James Alfred Lefébure-Wély** (d. 1869); **Antoine Édouard Batiste** (d. 1876); **Félix Alexandre Guilmant**; and the Belgians **Nicolas Jacques Lemmens** (d. 1881) and **Alphonse Mailly** of Brussels. Mention may also be made of the organ-expert **M. P. Hamel** of Beauvais (d. after 1870).

For convenience, a few other church musicians who were influential in non-Catholic circles may be here inserted, such as **Salomon Sulzer** (d. 1890), who, as cantor from 1825 at the chief synagogue of Vienna, became a noted reformer of Jewish music; **Gabriel Lomakin** (d. 1885), who from 1830 worked fruitfully to promote choral music at St. Petersburg, rearranging and augmenting the treasures of Russian liturgical song; **Johann Friedrich Schwencke** (d. 1852) and his son **Friedrich Gottlieb Schwencke** (d. 1896), whose successive terms as organists of the Nikolaikirche at Hamburg, and as composers and editors for the Lutheran service, covered almost 70 years from 1829; and the able teacher **Immanuel Faiszt** (d. 1894), from 1846 known as an organist and chorus-leader at Stuttgart, from 1859 director of the conservatory there and a conservative composer of vocal and organ works.

Concerning church music in England see sec. 223.

221. Catholic Music. — In a measure analogous to the reactions in other quarters, was the increasing desire among many Catholic church musicians to throw aside the theatric or at least concertistic forms of liturgical music which the 18th century had made prominent. The reaction had two aims — to restore Gregorian song in its historical purity for the detail of the ritual, and to emphasize *a cappella* polyphony after the Palestrina manner wherever more elaborate music was possible. The centre of this movement was Ratisbon, but sympathizers appeared elsewhere. The full results of the effort were delayed until the next period, when investigation became more searching, and when finally the authorities at Rome took mandatory action to enforce uniformity of practice throughout the Catholic world. Naturally, the reaction encountered opposition from those who had become wonted to unlimited freedom or who seriously believed that some compromises with modern styles of musical expression were desirable in sincere church music. Hence at the centres of Catholic music — in Austria, Bavaria, Italy and France — we find representatives of many different styles working side by side.

The Ratisbon circle received its character from **Karl Proske** (d. 1861). Born in 1794, he was first a physician, but in 1823 took up theology at Ratisbon, specializing in church music, gathering a fine library, raising the cathedral-choir to high efficiency, and from 1850 editing invaluable collections of contrapuntal masterpieces, especially *Musica divina* (from 1853). With him were associated the choir-regent **Johann Georg Mettenleiter** (d. 1858), who was both composer and author; his brother **Dominicus Mettenleiter** (d. 1868), whose interest lay in historical studies; **Joseph Schrems** (d. 1872), cathedral-choirmaster from 1839 and Proske's successor as editor of *Musica divina*; and **Joseph Hanisch** (d. 1892), cathedral-organist from 1839, a fine player and sound composer. Later came **Franz Witt** (d. 1888), a priest who in 1867 founded the influential Cäcilienverein and was a strong advocate of ancient styles; **Johann Georg Wesselack** (d. 1866), and **Michael Haller**, choir-regents after Mettenleiter; **Josef Renner** (d. 1895), from 1858 a teacher of singing and choral conductor; and **Franz Xaver Haberl** (d. 1910), in 1871-82 cathedral-choirmaster and the most celebrated writer and editor of the group (works from 1864). (See also sec. 227 for the evolution of the Solesmes group.)

Others who were interested in the *a cappella* revival were **Michael Töpler** (d. 1874), trained at Breslau and Berlin, from 1825 at Brühl and a pioneer in antique music in western Germany; **Eduard Rottmanner** of Speyer (d. 1843); **Raimund Schlecht** (d. 1891), a learned scholar at Eichstädt; **Karl Kempter** of Augsburg (d. 1871); **Bernhard Kothe** (d. 1897), from 1851 at Oppeln and from 1869 at Breslau; **Heinrich Oberhoffer** of Luxemburg (d. 1885), founder in 1862 of the periodica *Cäcilia*; **Joseph Förster**, since 1852 a leading organist at Prague; and **Michael Hermesdorff** (d. 1885), cathedral-organist at Trèves.

At Vienna the great contrapuntist of the period, though not in antique styles only, was **Simon Sechter** (d. 1867), from 1824 court-organist and from 1851 professor in the conservatory, who was a very influential teacher as well as a prolific composer. Other church musicians, mostly of the rather showy Viennese school, were **Joseph Drechsler** (d. 1852); **Benedict Randhartinger** (d. 1893), who was prominent in the Imperial Chapel from 1832; **Gottfried Preyer** (d. 1901), from 1838 in the conservatory and for a time its director, and from 1853 choirmaster at St. Stephen's; **Ludwig Rotter** (d. 1895), who succeeded Sechter in 1867; and **Franz Krenn** (d. 1897).

With these may be grouped other industrious workers, such as **Wenzel Emanuel Horák** (d. 1871) and **Robert Führer** (d. 1861), both of Prague; **Johann Kaspar Aiblinger** (d. 1867) and **Franz Lachner** (d. 1890), both of

Munich; **Peter Singer** of Salzburg (d. 1882); **Karl Ludwig Drobisch** of Augsburg (d. 1854); **Moritz Brosig** (d. 1887) and **Adolf Greulich** (d. 1890), both of Breslau; and the Hungarians **Franz Seraph Hölzl** of Fünfkirchen (d. 1884), and **Paul Křizkowzky** of Brünn (d. 1885).

In Italy the extreme advocate of the Palestrina style was **Baini** of Rome (d. 1844). Most Italian composers usually preferred more modern manners, sometimes verging upon the merely theatric. Representative names are those of the opera-writer **Mercadante** (d. 1870), from 1833 at Novara and from 1840 head of the Naples conservatory; **Alessandro Nini** of Bergamo (d. 1880); the two distinguished Roman contrapuntists **Gaetano Capocci** (d. 1898) and **Salvatore Meluzzi** (d. 1897); **Stefano Ronchetti-Monteviti** of Milan (d. 1882); **Antonio Buzzola** of Venice (d. 1871); **Teodulo Mabellini** of Florence (d. 1897); **Cesare Aria** of Bologna (d. 1894); and **Nicolò Coccon** of Venice (d. 1903). (Concerning *Raimondi* and also *Baini*, see sec. 184.)

In France and Belgium there was a large amount of notable investigation of the problems of Gregorian music (see sec. 227). An influential practical worker was **Louis Niedermeyer** (d. 1861), who in 1853 resuscitated Choron's Church Music School (lapsed since 1830), obtaining for it a government subsidy, and started the church music periodical *La Maîtrise*. Among many opera-writers who also worked in sacred music, **Gounod** (d. 1893) was conspicuous (see sec. 204).

The most famous Spanish church musician was **Miguel Hilario Eslava** (d. 1878), from 1832 choirmaster at Seville and from 1844 in the chapel of Queen Isabella (see sec. 204).

FIG. 110. — German Cabinet Organ (17th century).

222. The Song and Ballade. — Just at the epoch when the most gigantic types of dramatic and choral writing were being undertaken, the smallest of the important vocal forms, the song, at length secured its destined maturity and eminence. The most original path-breaker was undoubtedly Schubert, though his full greatness was not seen until years after his death. Soon after came Mendelssohn, who also kept closely to classical models of form. Later, Schumann treated the problem of the song in a manner much less regular and popular, but richer in personal expression and in imaginative suggestion. By about 1850 we find that important composers rarely failed to cultivate song-writing to some degree, and by this time several eminent specialists in the song field, like Löwe and Franz, were already in evidence. The sudden expansion of song literature about the middle of the century, like that of piano literature, is bewildering to analyze or summarize.

A few salient types should be emphasized in thought, though they are not always actually distinct. One of the simplest is the 'folk-like' song (*volkthümliches Lied*), which emulates the naïveté of the genuine folk-song, with its balanced lines, recurrent stanzas, obvious metric and harmonic patterns, and unobtrusive accompaniment. In such a song the sentiment resides in the total effect rather than in the details, and success often depends much upon the indefinable magnetism of the singer. From this type branch off innumerable varieties of more deliberately 'artistic' songs (*Kunstlieder*), in which either the tonal structure is studiously elaborated for its own sake, or homely symmetry and transparency are replaced by a reasoned effort to render fully the contrasts, evolutions and depths of feeling implied in the text. In such songs the details assume great expressional importance, successive stanzas are often handled differently and the functions of the accompaniment are highly elaborated. Nothing is more distinctive of the romantic period than the manifold discoveries then made of ways to compress exquisite beauty and thrilling passion into brief phrases and passages, where words, vocal melody and instrumental setting are so blended as to reflect the deepest emotions of the heart. Still a third type is that of the 'ballade,' which is not so much lyric as epic or dramatic. This has an essential kinship with the operatic aria, but its treatment is more condensed and nervous, and it is wholly independent of theatric action and accessories, even when in intensity it attains tragic sublimity.

The simpler types of song are specially apt for private or domestic use, while the more complex ones are obviously adapted to the salon and the concert-hall. At every point the evolution of song music presents analogies with the evolution of the smaller forms of piano music. From the study of the song as an artistic type came a fruitful stimulus for writing of other kinds, directing artistic attention to the infinite expressiveness possible in narrow limits through the dexterous manipulation of detail.

Reference has already been made to **Schubert** (secs. 173–174), **Mendelssohn** (secs. 194–195) and **Schumann** (secs. 190–191), as well as to earlier composers (sec. 158).

Karl Löwe (d. 1869), born near Halle in 1796, was a trifle older than Schubert, and his artistic production began almost as early (in 1818); but his eminence came later. He was a noted boy-singer, receiving aid in his schooling from Jerome Bonaparte, and having careful instruction from Türk and Naue, besides knowing the famous Reichardt. Though entered at Halle University as a student in theology, before 1820 his passion for music had determined his career. From 1821, on nomination of Zelter, he was town-musician at Stettin, whence he resisted calls to remove, though he made many tours as singer and composer. Disabled by a stroke of apoplexy, he spent his final years at Kiel. He was an industrious composer of oratorios, 5 operas, piano, chamber and orchestral works, but his fame rests on his almost 40 ballades (chiefly 1818–47), of which *Edward, Der Erlkönig, Heinrich der Vogler, Der Nöck, Harald, Tom der Reimer, Oluf, Prinz Eugen* and *Odins Meeresritt* are the most noted. His style has a general kinship with that of Schumann, and the latter doubtless derived something from it. But his union of lyric and dramatic elements and his mastery of compressed tonal expression were highly individual. His style gave a powerful stimulus to the whole range of writing for the solo voice with piano accompaniment.

More closely connected with Schumann was his slightly younger contemporary **Volkmann** (d. 1883), already emphasized as an instrumental writer (see sec. 214), whose many songs and choral works of varied character are important.

Robert Franz (d. 1892) was born in 1815 at Halle. His musical aspirations were at first checked, but finally found development under Schneider of Dessau. From 1837 he pursued private studies of Bach, Handel and the earlier 19th-century masters to such purpose that in 1843 he stepped forth as one of the finest song-writers of the romantic school, being welcomed by critics as diverse as Mendelssohn, Schumann and Liszt. He now became organist at one of the Halle churches and was later conductor of the Sing-akademie and director at the university, but increasing deafness and nervous disorders, beginning about 1849, forced his retirement in 1868. By this time his renown had spread so widely that musicians in different countries united in raising a large fund for his support. His songs altogether number about 350, ranging through many subjects and styles, but marked always by extreme beauty of melody, refinement of conception and fullness of detailed finish, uniting in a remarkable degree the older strength of structure with modern expressiveness. He also wrote choral music, sacred and secular, but no instrumental music. He was an expert in the styles of Bach and Handel, and from 1860 prepared remarkably fine revised editions of a long list of their choral works. His musicianship was therefore much broader than his original works would indicate.

2 R

Of a different class from the foregoing was **Franz Abt** (d. 1885). Born in 1819 and trained at Leipsic, from 1841 he was theatre- and chorus-conductor at Zurich, where later he was slightly connected with Wagner. From 1852 for 30 years he was court-conductor at Brunswick. He wrote over 3000 songs and part-songs, mostly simple and popular, but with a naïve grace that has made them generally admired.

Adolf Jensen (d. 1879) belongs to a later generation, being born at Königsberg in 1837. He was precocious as a composer. In 1856 he taught in Russia, hoping later to study with Schumann. After serving as conductor at Posen, in 1858-60 he studied with Gade, and in 1866-8 taught at Berlin. But his health was feeble and he was forced to try different residences, finally dying of consumption. His works include about 160 solo songs, many concerted vocal works, some orchestral pieces and many beautiful piano works. His style belongs to the Schumann order, with a peculiar strain of rich feeling and tonal warmth.

To these greater names may be added some others out of the multitude of those who were fertile in songs of various kinds : —

Among the Germans and Austrians were **Joseph Dessauer** (d. 1876), living mostly at Vienna ; **Ernst Friedrich Kauffmann** of Ludwigsburg (d. 1856), writing while in prison for political radicalism ; the Bavarian **Karl Krebs** (d. 1880), from 1827 opera-conductor at Hamburg and in 1850-72 at Dresden ; **Karl Friedrich Curschmann** of Berlin (d. 1841) ; **Friedrich Wilhelm Kücken** (d. 1882), in 1851-61 at Stuttgart and later at Schwerin ; **Wilhelm Heiser** of Berlin (d. 1897) ; **Karl Eckert** (d. 1879), from 1853 at Vienna, from 1861 at Stuttgart and from 1869 at Berlin ; **Justus Wilhelm Lyra** (d. 1882), a clergyman famous for his student-songs ; and the Weimar masters **Liszt** (d. 1886) and **Lassen** (d. 1904).

Among Italians who cultivated the popular song were the Neapolitans **Guglielmo Luigi Cottrau** (d. 1847), **Luigi Bordese** (d. 1886), and **Nicola de Giosa** (d. 1885) ; the Tuscan **Luigi Gordigiani** (d. 1860) ; the Florentine **Ciro Pinsuti** (d. 1888) ; the Roman teacher **Leopoldo Mililotti** ; and many others.

Other national strains of expression were represented by the Frenchmen **Auguste Mathieu Panseron** (d. 1859), and **Gustave Nadaud** (d. 1893) ; the Russians **Alexander Alabjew** (d. 1851), **Alexis Werstowski** (d. 1862), and **Nicolai Titow** (d. 1875) ; the Pole **Stanislaw Moniuszko** (d. 1872) ; the Swede **Adolf Fredrik Lindblad** (d. 1878), and the Norwegian **Halfdan Kjerulf** (d.1868) ; the Hungarian **Franz Erkel** (d. 1893) ; the Bohemians **Joseph Nesvadba** (d. 1876), and **Ludwig Prochazka** (d. 1888) ; and the Greek **Spiridion Xyndas** (d. 1896).

223. Music in England. — The great feature within the English circle during this middle period was the impress of Mendelssohn, exerted through repeated visits between 1830 and 1846. His magnetic influence did much to bring the English public into touch with some phases of the musical life of Europe and to

enforce a high standard of technical correctness in both composition and performance. Contact with Continental music
was steadily increased through the English students who now
began to frequent Leipsic for training. The Mendelssohnian influence inevitably produced a general tendency merely to imitate
his style, accepting it as representing all that was good in musical art. Not until the next period did English musicians really
shake themselves free from the bondage of this tradition and
begin to bring to light original powers of their own, so as to
take their place among the constructive forces of the large musical world. It is only fair to say, however, that amid this dor-
mancy of creative power of a high order, there were worthy
efforts to diffuse sound musical notions in popular thought, so
that when the new life manifested itself there had been provided
a basis of popular interest and knowledge for it to rest upon.

The three styles of music most cultivated were the same that
had been favorites in previous epochs, namely, a sober and
reverent type of cathedral music, now broadened by the efforts
of a large number of competent workers, wholesome and graceful songs and part-songs, and operettas that usually approached
the style of the ballad-opera or the singspiel rather than that
of the Continental opera. Instrumental music was freshly handled only by a few writers, most of them late in the period.
London absorbed most of the best musical life of the Kingdom, but here and there, especially in connection with the great
choral festivals, provincial centres of importance were being
established.

In the field of cathedral music, of course wholly designed to meet the
needs of the Anglican service, the more productive workers were **John Goss**
(d. 1880), trained in the Chapel Royal and known as an organist from 1821,
who in 1838–72 was Attwood's successor at St. Paul's, being also composer
to the Chapel; **James Turle** (d. 1882), in 1831–75 the successor of Greatorex
at Westminster Abbey; **Henry John Gauntlett** (d. 1876), specially useful
for his interest in the improvement of the organ; **Samuel Sebastian Wesley**
(d. 1876), like his father a great organist, located from 1835 at Exeter, from
1842 at Leeds, from 1849 at Winchester, and from 1865 at Gloucester;
Henry Smart (d. 1879), another excellent player and a skillful writer not only
of church music, but of an opera (1855) and several graceful cantatas (from
1864); **G. A. Macfarren** (see below); **George Job Elvey** (d. 1893), in
1835–82 organist at Windsor Castle; **Edward John Hopkins** (d. 1901),
whose activity began in 1834 and who from 1843 for 55 years was the honored

organist at the Temple; **Edwin George Monk** (d. 1900), pupil of Macfarren and in 1859–83 organist of York Cathedral; **George Cooper** (d. 1876), from 1856 the admired organist of the Chapel Royal; **John Matthew Wilson Young** (d. 1897), in 1850–95 organist of Lincoln Cathedral; **Samuel Reay** of Newcastle and Newark; **John Bacchus Dykes** (d. 1876), a clergyman distinguished for his gift as a writer of hymn-tunes; **William Henry Monk** (d. 1889), from 1847 connected with King's College, London; **William Spark** (d. 1897), in 1850–80 organist at Leeds and editor of much organ music; **F. A. G. Ouseley** (see below); **Robert Prescott Stewart** (d. 1894), all his life a fruitful worker at Dublin; **William Thomas Best** (d. 1897), with an international reputation as an organist, working from about 1845 at Liverpool, especially in 1855–94 at St. George's Hall; **Charles Steggall**, professor at the Royal Academy from 1851 and organist at Lincoln's Inn; **Henry Hiles** (d. 1904), whose varied activity as composer and theorist belongs mostly to the recent period; **John Baptiste Calkin** (d. 1905), long known in London churches; **H. S. Oakeley** (see below); **William Joseph Westbrook** (d. 1894), a specially fruitful organist; **George Mursell Garrett** (d. 1897), organist first at Winchester, then at Madras, and from 1857 at Cambridge; **Edward Henry Thorne**, from 1853 organist at Henley, Chichester, Brighton and several London churches; **Edmund Hart Turpin**, another conspicuous London organist; **Joseph Barnby** (d. 1896), trained at York, from about 1855 active at London, especially as a choral conductor and the writer of part-songs and the graceful cantata *Rebekah* (1870); **John Naylor** (d. 1897), in 1856–83 at Scarborough and then at York Cathedral; the Netherlander **Berthold Tours** (d. 1897), violinist and editor; **Scotson Clark** (d. 1883), a clergyman who attained wide repute as a concert-organist; and **John Stainer** (d. 1901), beginning his career as organist in 1854, in 1872–88 Goss' successor at St. Paul's and finally professor at Oxford, and a powerful influence upon musical education and scholarship. All these contributed freely to the immense literature of anthems, services and hymn-tunes which has had so wide an influence throughout the English-speaking world. Several of them produced extended choral works in the later period.

Many of the foregoing were able writers of songs and part-songs, especially Smart, Macfarren, Reay, Hiles, Garrett and Barnby. The old line of real glee-makers was successfully prolonged by **Robert Lucas Pearsall** (d. 1856), living mostly in Switzerland, with many madrigals (from 1840); by **James Coward** (d. 1880), from 1857 organist at the Crystal Palace; and by **Henry David Leslie** (d. 1896), who from 1855 was the indefatigable leader of a famous chorus for *a cappella* singing. Still more inevitably were those named below more or less active in the song field. Among many favorite ballad-writers of unambitious rank was **Joseph Philip Knight** (d. 1887).

English stage-music in this period still ran mostly to light operettas, though with some striking efforts to establish an English operatic type of a higher class.

Two foreigners were early conspicuous as conductors. One was the Neapolitan **Michael Costa** (d. 1884), who came to London in 1830, and after 1846 had charge of the Italian Opera, the Philharmonic and Sacred Harmonic Concerts, and the Birmingham festivals — the composer of 4 Italian operas at

Naples (1826-9) and of 3 ballets, the opera *Don Carlos* (1844) and 2 oratorios in England.   The other was **Julius Benedict** (d. 1885), born at Stuttgart, a pupil of Hummel and especially of Weber, who, after operatic experience at Vienna, Naples and Paris, came to England in 1835 and fully identified himself with English music.   Besides being constantly employed as conductor in London and at the Norwich festivals, he brought out 6 English operas (1838-64), several choral works, piano-pieces and 2 symphonies.   The best of his operas was *The Lily of Killarney* (1862).

Michael William Balfe (d. 1870), born at Dublin in 1808, was the most fertile of the opera-writers.   Coming to London in 1823, he worked first as violinist and singer, with study under good teachers.   In 1825-33 he was in Italy or at Paris, becoming an able dramatic baritone, and writing 3 operas (1829-30).   On his return to London, he made a hit with *The Siege of Rochelle* (1835), followed soon by several other popular works, 2 of them in Italian, besides often appearing as a singer.   In 1841 he went to Paris and scored success with 2 opéras comiques (1843-4), besides producing at London his most popular work, *The Bohemian Girl* (1843), soon reproduced in other countries.   A long line of works in English, French and Italian followed (till 1863), and he was much abroad, visiting Vienna, Berlin, St. Petersburg and Trieste, and receiving extraordinary honors.   In 1864 he retired.   His stage-works numbered about 30.   They are over-facile and shallow, but abound with taking melodies and are often scored with some skill.

William Vincent Wallace (d. 1865), like Balfe, was an Irishman, and also a ready melodist and clever playwright.   Among his 6 operas were the popular *Maritana* (1845) and *Lurline* (1860).   He also wrote much salon music for the piano.   He lived an adventurous life in different parts of the world.

Other writers for the stage were **John Barnett** (d. 1890), whose *Mountain Sylph* (1834) was the first English opera since Arne's *Artaxerxes* (1762), and who wrote several others, with innumerable songs ;   **Edward James Loder** (d. 1865), the chief of whose few works was *The Night Dancers* (1846) ;   **John Hullah** (d. 1884), whose three early plays (1836-8) were later completely forgotten in his activity as promoter of popular song and as lecturer ;   **G. A. Mac-farren** (d. 1887), among whose prolific productions were over 10 operas, including *The Devil's Opera* (1838), *Don Quixote* (1846), *Robin Hood* (1860) and *Helvellyn* (1864), besides many choral works ;   **John Liptrot Hatton** (d. 1886), with a few operas (from 1842), incidental music to various plays, and many songs ;   the famous Italian singing-master **Alberto Randegger**, who settled in London in 1854, producing the comedy *The Rival Beauties* (1864) and several shorter works, besides 2 early Italian operas (1852-4) and many songs ;   and **Frédéric Clay** (d. 1889), the composer of a long line of operettas (from 1859), 2 cantatas and numerous songs.

The list of those who essayed instrumental composition in the larger forms with some degree of power is worthy of more attention than it received in the crowded and eager progress of affairs upon the Continent.   Only some representative names can here be mentioned : —

Cipriani Potter (d. 1871), trained both at London and at Vienna (where he met Beethoven), was from 1822 piano-teacher at the Royal Academy and in

1832–59 its principal. He published only piano and chamber works, but wrote a number of symphonies and overtures besides.

George Alexander Macfarren (d. 1887) was one of the best-trained and most competent composers in the group. From 1834 he taught in the Royal Academy and from 1876 was its principal. His works included 8 symphonies, 7 overtures, several concertos, good chamber music, piano-sonatas, operas and other stage-works, 4 oratorios (1873–83), 6 cantatas, part-songs, duets and songs, besides several theoretical treatises and edited collections.

William Sterndale Bennett (d. 1875), who was Macfarren's close contemporary, has already been mentioned (see sec. 195).

Frederick Arthur Gore Ouseley (d. 1889), born in 1825, the son of a diplomat, was educated for the church, but found opportunity for the large exercise of his musical talents. From 1855 he was professor at Oxford, but threw his strength into the development of a school at Tenbury, which he founded in 1856 and enriched by generous gifts. He is best known from his many services and nearly 90 anthems, his organ-preludes and fugues, his 2 oratorios (1855–73), and several collections of church music, but he also wrote considerable chamber music, and sonatas and pieces for piano. His theoretical knowledge was displayed in a series of fine treatises (from 1868). His great library was left to the college at Tenbury.

Other names in this middle period that might be mentioned are the prolific John Lodge Ellerton (d. 1873); the Irish pianist George Alexander Osborne (d. 1893); Thomas Molleson Mudie (d. 1876), long a teacher at Edinburgh; the gifted Henry Hugo Pierson (d. 1873), who worked mostly in Germany; the pianist and organist Charles Edward Stephens (d. 1892); Walter Cecil Macfarren (d. 1905), from 1846 piano-teacher at the Royal Academy and a varied writer for piano and orchestra; the original and versatile Dutch pianist Eduard Silas, who came to England in 1850 and gradually made his way in the face of the opposition aroused by his extreme radicalism; the eminent pianist and conductor Otto Goldschmidt (d. 1907), from 1852 the husband of Jenny Lind; Herbert Stanley Oakeley (d. 1903), from 1865 professor at Edinburgh University, and strong both as composer and as educator; Henry Charles Banister (d. 1897), professor at the Royal Academy from 1851 and the author of valuable books (from 1872); besides the large and distinguished line of younger composers whose work mainly belongs in the recent period (see sec. 231).

Special mention should also be made of Charles Kensington Salaman (d. 1901), who from 1835 was active in the organization of important concert-series and societies; the German Charles Hallé (d. 1895), from 1836 conspicuous at Paris as a pianist, and from 1848 a teacher in England, becoming famous from 1853 as conductor at Manchester, London and elsewhere; August Manns (d. 1907), also a German, from 1855 conductor at the Crystal Palace and of innumerable other concerts and festivals; William Cusins (d. 1893), from 1867 conductor of the Philharmonic concerts; and the distinguished violinist John Tiplady Carrodus (d. 1895), prominent in leading orchestras from 1853. A strong educational influence from 1851 was exerted by the Austrian Ernst Pauer (d. 1905), widely known as teacher, lecturer, author and composer.

Besides the important *Philharmonic Society*, founded in 1813, and the educational centre in the *Royal Academy of Music*, founded in 1822, both of which have been previously mentioned (see sec. 186), the middle period saw the establishment of the significant *Sacred Harmonic Society*, founded in 1832, and led till 1848 by Joseph Surman (d. 1871) and later by Costa, and of the *Society of British Musicians*, founded in 1834 to encourage composition by Englishmen, which disbanded in 1865. The now influential *Musical Association*, founded in 1874, and the *Incorporated Society of Musicians*, founded in 1882, belong to the next period.

224. Music in America. — The cultivation of musical art in the United States along lines connected with what was being done in Europe made but slight progress before 1840, though performances of opera and oratorio music were not uncommon in a few leading cities. An educational influence of value was exerted by the many leaders in the improvement of New England psalmody, of whom Lowell Mason was the chief. Gradually immigration brought in many trained musicians from across the ocean, especially under the stress of the political disturbances that culminated in the revolutions of 1848. More and more students sought instruction in England or Germany. Standards of artistic judgment and action steadily rose in a few metropolitan centres, and some gifted artists began to appear. Thus the way was prepared for the immense advances that followed in the period after the Civil War. Though nearly all that is significant as a part of the general history of music belongs to that later period, yet the worthy efforts of many pioneers deserve recognition, even though what they actually did is not absolutely remarkable (see sec. 233).

Conspicuous instances of those whose work centred chiefly in the old-fashioned psalmody were **Thomas Hastings** (d. 1872), living at Utica from 1823 and at New York from 1832; **Lowell Mason** (d. 1872), who was immensely influential at Boston from 1827; the Englishman **George James Webb** (d. 1887), from 1830 in Boston; **George Frederick Root** (d. 1895), from 1844 in New York and from 1859 in Chicago; besides many more, mostly associated with Boston.

Pioneers of broader interests were **Ureli C. Hill** (d. 1875), a pupil of Spohr and in 1842 the founder of the New York Philharmonic Society; **John Sullivan Dwight** (d. 1893), in 1852 the founder of the first important American musical periodical and a careful critic; **George Frederick Bristow** (d. 1898), violinist, organist, conductor and fertile composer in New York; **William Henry Walter**, from 1842 a leading organist in New York; **John Henry Cornell** (d. 1894), from 1848 an able organist and theorist in New York; **James Cutler Dunn Parker**, since 1854 similarly known in Boston;

Michael Henry Cross (d. 1897), from 1848 active as organist and conductor in Philadelphia; with many others. The ballad-writer **Stephen Collins Foster** (d. 1864) displayed from 1842 a remarkable gift of naïve expression.

Of international reputation later were the pianist **William Mason**, who was highly trained in Germany and since 1855 has been conspicuous in New York as a Nestor among teachers; **Benjamin Johnson Lang**, since 1852 the eminent conductor and composer in Boston; and especially **John Knowles Paine** (d. 1906), from 1861 settled in Boston and from 1876 professor at Harvard University — a composer of rich capacity in all the greater forms.

Out of some scores of foreign musicians who came to the United States before 1860, important examples were from 1799 the Italian **Filippo Traetta** (d. 1854), a vocal teacher and composer in New York and Philadelphia; from 1838 in New Orleans **Eugène Prosper Prévost** (d. 1872), and in New York the organist **Henry Christian Timm** (d. 1892), and Hummel's pupil **William Scharfenberg** (d. 1895); from 1844 the Irishman **Thomas Ryan** (d. 1903), and from 1847 the Holsteiner **Wulf Fries** (d. 1902), who were long identified with the Mendelssohn Quintet Club of Boston, organized in 1849; from 1845 in New York the Leipsic pianist **Hermann Adolf Wollenhaupt** (d. 1865), and the fine violinist and great conductor **Theodore Thomas** (d. 1905), brought as a boy from Hanover and soon widely known as a masterly educator of public taste; from 1847 the strong English pianist **Richard Hoffman**; from 1848 the violinist **Theodor Eisfeld** (d. 1882), the opera-composer and manager **Max Maretzek** (d. 1897), the famous Boston conductor **Carl Zerrahn** (d. 1906), the pianist **Otto Dresel** (d. 1890), **Hermann Kotzschmar**, long prominent in Portland, and **Hans Balatka** (d. 1899), from 1851 conductor at Milwaukee and Chicago; from 1849 the Austrian pianist **Frederic Brandeis** (d. 1899); from 1850 the Saxon conductor **Karl Bergmann** (d. 1876), and the Russian **Karl Klauser** (d. 1905); from 1852 the singing-master **Julius Eduard Meyer** (d. 1899); from 1853 the violinists **Eduard Mollenhauer** and **Joseph Mosenthal** (d. 1896), both pupils of Spohr; from 1854 **Carl Christian Müller**; from 1856 the violinist **Julius Eichberg** (d. 1893), and the English organist **Frederick Herbert Torrington**, prominent in Canada; from 1857 the conductor **Karl Anschütz** (d. 1870) and the pianist **Robert Goldbeck** of New York, Chicago and St. Louis; and from 1859 the eminent pianist **Sebastian Bach Mills** (d. 1898). Many of these were composers of ability, especially Hoffman, Brandeis, Müller, Goldbeck and Mills. These are but samples of the influential current of musical immigration.

The only strong orchestra organized during this period was the *New York Philharmonic*, founded in 1842. Chamber music was systematically presented by several organizations from about 1850. Important entrances into the field of publishing were the Boston house of *Ditson* in 1832, and the New York house of *Schirmer* in 1848 (Kerksieg & Breusing).

Besides the attention to piano-making that has already been noted (see sec. 183), reference should be made to the violin-makers *August* and *Georg Gemünder*, pupils of Vuillaume, who came to America in 1846–7 and became known as among the best workmen in the world.

CHAPTER XXXVII

MUSICAL EDUCATION AND LITERATURE

225. The Conservatories. — The middle of the 19th century was the time when music-teaching became a notable profession for a multitude of musicians, sometimes working independently, sometimes banded together in institutions, sometimes holding official positions at courts or in theatres, opera-houses, churches, etc. To be a musician has almost always been to be a music-teacher, but musical pedagogy now became a well-recognized vocation, with methods reduced to some system and with constantly improving apparatus.

It is not always remembered how peculiarly dependent music is for propagation upon the mediation of the living teacher or illustrator, impressing himself either privately, in the class-room, or in public performance. The products of musical art cannot be displayed as objects in a museum. It is true that they can be circulated in printed form. But this latter approach is effective only when the user's mind has been prepared by special study under teachers. It is true, also, that a knowledge of music is diffused through concerts, the opera, church services and the like, reaching people somewhat *en masse*; but such renditions involve the action of living exponents, and their full impression is dependent upon some amount of personal study. It is for reasons like these that there has arisen such a prodigious demand for instructors in every branch of music — a demand which must increase in geometrical ratio as it is successfully met.

The success of the Paris Conservatoire (from 1795), combined with the growth of interest in organized education, led throughout the early and middle 19th century to the foundation of many other institutions, larger or smaller, designed as technical music-schools. The main object of the Paris institution was to supply dramatic composers and singers. The object of some other schools was like that of the earliest Italian conservatories — to study Plain-Song and the vocal polyphony required in church services. The object of the Leipsic conservatory (from 1843) was to further instrumental composition and performance.

In almost all cases, the departments most accented were piano-playing, violin-playing, solo and choral singing, harmony and the higher branches of composition. Only gradually was specific recognition given to the need for genuine musicianship and of a comprehensive knowledge of musical history, literature and criticism. It must be confessed that in its earlier stages the conservatory idea was more analogous to that of the trade-school than to that of institutions of general culture.

> The lowest type of conservatory is the mere coöperative union of several teachers, each with his own methods, purposes and clientage, who seek to profit by the practical advantages of consolidated effort. In such a school each teacher goes his own way and pupils are not required to pursue a curriculum. The latter, however, gain from the mere fact of association and from whatever recitals, lectures and the like can be attended by many auditors at once. The ideal conservatory is one in which under competent direction a balanced and progressive curriculum is provided and thoughtfully adjusted to personal needs, so that after a reasonable period the student comes forth not only equipped for his specialty, but with some determinable amount of general musicianship. The difficulty of approaching the ideal is threefold — the economic question of funds or income, the lack of an encyclopædic grasp of musical art as a whole by musicians, and the natural popular demand for little more than a money-winning musical training.
>
> Measured by an ideal standard, the story of European music-schools before 1865 or thereabouts is honorable, but seldom brilliant. The problem of funds was met in almost every instance by a governmental subvention, often on a liberal scale. The problem of curriculum was dependent upon the wisdom of directors, but competition tended to force constant advance. The problem of popular demand was steadily simplified by the rapid increase in the number of educated musicians and the remarkable development of general interest in music of the highest class.

Since about 1860 the increase in the number of conservatories has been more than twice as rapid as before and there has been a marked improvement in their pedagogical system. They have in some cases begun to establish important affiliations with institutions of general culture, such as universities.

> The oldest conservatories are those of Naples (see sec. 91), which were consolidated in 1808; those of Venice, which were not reconstructed on modern lines until recently; and that of Palermo, which became a state institution in 1863.
>
> By 1830, besides that at Paris (see sec. 177), conservatories had been started in 1804 at Bologna, in 1807 at Milan, in 1811 at Prague, in 1813

at Brussels, in 1817 at Vienna and Paris (Choron's Church Music School), in 1819–22 at Berlin (Institute for Church Music), in 1822 at London (Royal Academy), in 1826 at The Hague, in 1827 at Liège, in 1829 at Genoa and in 1830 at Madrid.   That at Bologna was not significant till reorganized in 1881 under *Luigi Mancinelli,* followed in 1886 by *Giuseppe Martucci* and in 1902 by *Enrico Bossi.*   At Milan the director till 1814 was *Asioli* (d. 1832), but the institution was not prominent till restored in 1850 by *Lauro Rossi* (d. 1885), succeeded in 1872 by *Alberto Mazzucato* (d. 1877), *Ronchetti-Monteviti* (d. 1882), *Antonio Bazzini* (d. 1897) and *G. Gallignani.*   At Naples the best-known directors have been from 1837 *Zingarelli* (d. 1837) and from 1840 *Mercadante* (d. 1870), who was followed in 1871–8 by *Lauro Rossi* (d. 1885).   At Prague the directors have been from 1811 *Dionys Weber* (d. 1842), in 1843–65 *J. F. Kittl* (d. 1868), from 1865 *Josef Krejči* (d. 1881), in 1882–1901 *Anton Bennewitz* and from 1901 *Karl Knittl,* assisted by *Anton Dvořák* (d. 1904).   At Brussels since the reorganization in 1832 there have been two directors, *Fétis* (d. 1871) and *Gevaert.*   At Vienna the direction was by committee till the appointment in 1844–8 of *Gottfried Preyer* (d. 1901), followed from 1851 by *Joseph Hellmesberger* (d. 1893), *Johann Fuchs* (d. 1899) and *Richard von Perger.*   (On the Berlin Institut see sec. 219, and on the London Royal Academy see sec. 186.)   At The Hague the list includes *Johann Heinrich Lübeck* (d. 1865), *Willem Nicolai* (d. 1896) and *Henri Viotta.* At Liège the standard was set by *Louis Joseph Daussoigne-Méhul* (d. 1875), followed in 1862 by *Étienne Joseph Soubre* (d. 1871) and in 1872 by *Jean Théodore Radoux.*   At Genoa the director since 1898 is *Giovanni Battista Polleri.*   At Madrid recent directors have been from 1877 *Arrieta y Corera* (d. 1894) and *Monasterio* (d. 1903).

Before 1870 this list was increased by the founding of conservatories in 1833 at Ghent and Lisbon, in 1843 at Leipsic, in 1845 at Rotterdam, in 1846 at Munich, in 1850 at Berlin (Stern), in 1855 at Strassburg and Berlin (Kullak), in 1856 at Dresden and Stuttgart, in 1860 at Florence, in 1861 at Warsaw, in 1862 at Amsterdam and St. Petersburg, in 1865 at Turin and Christiania, in 1866 at Moscow and Copenhagen, and in 1867 at Antwerp.   At Ghent the directors have been *Martin Joseph Mengal* (d. 1851), *Jean Andries* (d. 1872), *Adolphe Samuel* (d. 1898), and *Émile Mathieu.*   (On the Leipsic conservatory see sec. 196.)   Recent directors at Rotterdam have been in 1865–74 *Woldemar Bargiel* (d. 1897), in 1874–90 *Friedrich Gernsheim,* in 1890–5 *Richard von Perger,* and later *Sikemeyer.*   At Munich the list includes till 1865 *Franz Hauser* (d. 1870), in 1867–9 *Bülow* (d. 1894), from 1869 *Joseph Rheinberger* (d. 1901) and in 1901–4 *Bernhard Stavenhagen.*   (On the Stern and Kullak schools at Berlin see sec. 219.)   At Strassburg special success has been won since 1871 by *Franz Stockhausen.*   (On Dresden see sec. 209.)   At Stuttgart the first director was *Faiszt* (d. 1894), followed by *Samuel de Lange.*   At Florence the first director was *Baldassare Gamucci* (d. 1892), and at present is *Guido Tacchinardi.*   At Warsaw worked *Apollinaire de Kontski* (d. 1879) and *Alexander Zarzycki* (d. 1895).   At Amsterdam we find till 1895 *Franz Coenen* (d. 1904), followed by *Daniel de Lange.*

At St. Petersburg the series consists of *Anton Rubinstein* (d. 1894), who served in 1862–7 and again in 1887–91, in 1867–71 *Nicolai Zaremba* (d. 1879), in 1871–6 *Michael Asanchewski* (d. 1881), in 1876–87 *Karl Davidow* (d. 1889), in 1892–7 *Julius Johannsen* (d. 1904), and since 1898 *August Bernhardt*. At Turin in 1868–82 *Carlo Pedrotti* (d. 1893) was an energetic organizer, followed now by *Giovanni Bolzoni*. At Moscow the names are *Nicolai Rubinstein* (d. 1881), in 1881–3 *Nicolai Hubert* (d. 1888), in 1883–5 *Konstantin Karl Albrecht* (d. 1893), in 1885–9 *Sergei Tanéjew* and since 1889 *Wassili Safonow*. At Antwerp the first director was *Peter Benoît* (d. 1901), followed by *Jan Blockx*.

226. Certain Pedagogical Specialties. — Both within and without the conservatories much enterprise was shown in improving or extending pedagogical organization and method. Into the detail of most of this we cannot here enter. But certain movements deserve mention because of their wide effects.

From 1800 onward, extensive public school systems steadily developed in all the principal countries, and in many cases, especially in Germany and France, urgent advocates appeared for the practice of singing as a part of the ordinary curriculum. The end in view was simply to give enough elementary facility in musical facts and action so that children should grow up with some readiness to use song in common life with ease and delight, but it was also clearly seen that the psychological and moral effects of singing upon the child-mind were valuable. This general movement was not so much directed by musical enthusiasts for the special furtherance of their art as made a part of the new zeal for systematic and well-rounded popular education. But in its gradual development, with the special methods, text-books and literature which it called forth, it came to have decided importance in several countries as a foundation upon which artistic progress could rest.

> In Germany this movement was interlocked with that which aimed at the improvement of popular song in church services. From about 1810 there was a marked revival of interest in liturgics in the Lutheran church, and hence congregational singing naturally attracted attention. The parallel interest in such singing in America from about 1820 was slightly connected with this German movement.

Plans for class-instruction in singing raised questions about simplifying musical notation. The close association of the staff-notation with the keyboard had made its development more adapted to the needs of playing than of singing. It was felt

that the facts of scale-relationship could be more simply presented to the singer's mind, so that essentially the same relations should always be shown by the same signs. Hence came
the invention of systems in which either numerals or letters
were used to indicate where in the scale the tones desired were
situated. The pictorial element in the staff-notation was sacrificed to gain precision of tonal thought. Out of many experiments two systems of notation were evolved — that of Galin or
Chevé and that known as the 'Tonic Sol-Fa' — which have demonstrated their utility in France and England respectively, not
as complete substitutes for the staff-notation, but as helps to the
right use of that notation or as means for rudimentary teaching.
Both systems were gradually improved until they were capable
of showing all sorts of time-relations and all ordinary intricacies
of modulation. Both gained power through the minute study
of methods of teaching and the preparation of systematic text-
books. The practical success of the Tonic Sol-Fa movement in
England has been prodigious, exercising a large influence upon
the whole musical culture of the nation.

Reference to these matters calls up the fact that during this
period there was a constant multiplication of special 'methods'
for teaching particular musical branches, especially on the part
of leading teachers in the conservatories. All these testified to
the care with which pedagogical processes were being scrutinized
and the system that was becoming characteristic of technical
training. Hence the rate of advance among pupils was greatly
accelerated and at the same time the results made better. This
was specially conspicuous in the acquisition of keyboard and
vocal technique. The number of expert trainers in piano-playing and singing increased everywhere, constituting two groups
of specialists who were constantly bringing out well-equipped
performers. The only untoward result of this activity was the
confusion often introduced into the minds of students and the
public between technical proficiency in execution and genuinely
broad musicianship.

Among the pioneers in promoting popular singing were the following : —

Hans Georg Nägeli (d. 1836), a music-publisher of repute near Zurich, was
one of the first to agitate for school music. He was the head of a Swiss
society for promoting popular song, a strong advocate of the methods of
Pestalozzi, a practical teacher and author of several manuals (from 1812).

About the same time worked **Bernhard Christian Ludwig Natorp** (d. 1846), a Lutheran clergyman and pedagogue, from 1808 at Potsdam and from 1819 at Münster (books from 1813) ; and **Johann Friedrich Naue** (d. 1858), musical director at Halle University (books from 1818). Other names in Germany are from 1815 **Johann Heinrich Göroldt** of Quedlinburg (d. after 1835) and **Friedrich Silcher** (d. 1860) of Tübingen University ; from about 1820 **Johann August Günther Heinroth** (d. 1846), Forkel's successor at Göttingen University, **Gottfried Emil Fischer** of Berlin (d. 1841) and **Xaver Schnyder von Wartensee** of Frankfort (d. 1868) ; from 1823 **Christian Urban** of Danzig ; from 1828 **Karl Schade** of Quedlinburg (d. after 1835) ; and later **Ludwig Erk** (d. 1883), long famous at Berlin. To the efforts of these and others was due the extensive pursuit of music in schools and churches as a specialty.

In France **Alexandre Choron** (d. 1834), a highly educated scholar, was active from about 1810 in improving choir-schools and from 1817 through his notable Church Music School. In the conduct of this enterprise, till checked by the Revolution of 1830, he laid the foundation for all the later French projects for popularizing musical knowledge, preparing many excellent text-books (from 1811). Another leader, of even greater practical importance, was **Guillaume Louis Wilhem [Bocquillon]** (d. 1842), who from 1810 taught in the Lycée Napoléon with such success that from 1819 he was made supervisor in the Paris primary schools. Out of his numerous classes grew in 1833 the Orphéon movement (see sec. 218).

It was in connection with Wilhem's work that the ' méloplaste ' system, invented before 1818 by **Pierre Galin** of Bordeaux (d. 1821), came into notice. This was the first practical application of numerals for notes. The system was advanced by **Joseph François Snel** (d. 1861), **Édouard Jue** (works from 1823), and especially by **Aimé Paris** (d. 1866), who added a method for teaching time-patterns, and later by **Émile Chevé** (d. 1864), who brought the whole to a complete statement (1850).

In England popular instruction by classes was urged as early as 1810 by **Joseph Kemp** (d. 1824), previously organist at Bristol. But their first large application was in 1841 under **John Hullah** (d. 1884), a very successful imitator of Wilhem, whose activity as teacher and author continued till 1880. From his system was derived the present organization of English schoolteaching in singing. Another active teacher was **Joseph Mainzer** (d. 1851), vocal instructor in schools, from 1841 at Manchester.

The Tonic Sol-Fa system was first outlined about 1840 by **Sarah Ann Glover** (d. 1867), a teacher at Norwich ; but its development was due to **John Curwen** (d. 1880), a clergyman of Plaistow. The latter carefully perfected details of notation, teacher-training and publication, and from about 1855 the propagation of the method through classes and associations was rapid.

It is extraordinary with what bitterness almost every one of these efforts to popularize music was opposed by musicians. Teaching by classes doubtless involved difficulties, and each particular movement used novel methods that were somewhat debatable ; but these facts do not excuse the hostility often displayed.

Soon after 1810 **Johann Bernhard Logier** (d. 1846), then organist at West-port, Ireland, invented the 'chiroplast,' a mechanical aid in securing a good hand-position in piano-playing. This device was for a time extensively popular, not only in England, but in Germany and France. Logier also advocated teaching piano-playing through simultaneous class-practice. Both parts of his system were strongly criticized and neither of them has persisted in use as proposed. **Friedrich Kalkbrenner** (d. 1849) and **Franz Stöpel** (d. 1836) were leading representatives of Logier's ideas at Berlin and Paris.

As prominent illustrations of the many vocal specialists may be enumerated **Johann Aloys Miksch** of Dresden (d. 1845); **Marco Bordogni** of Paris (d. 1856); **Niccolò Vaccai** (d. 1848), successively at Venice, Trieste, Vienna, Paris, London and Milan; **Franz Hauser** of Vienna and Munich (d. 1870); **Panseron** of Paris (d. 1859); **Gaetano Nava** of Milan (d. 1875); **Manuel Garcia** of Paris (d. 1906), the inventor of the laryngoscope; **Duprez** of Paris (d. 1896); **Heinrich Panofka** of London, Paris and Florence (d. 1887); **Baltasar Saldoni** of Madrid (d. 1890); **Giuseppe Concone** of Paris (d. 1861); **Francesco Lamperti** of Milan (d. 1892); **Bordese** of Paris (d. 1886); **Sieber** of Dresden and Berlin (d. 1895); **Salvatore Marchesi** and his wife **Mathilde (Graumann) Marchesi** of Vienna and Paris; **Julius Stockhausen** (d. 1906), latterly of Frankfort; **Enrico Delle Sedie** of Paris; **Pinsuti** of London (d. 1888); and **Julius Hey** (d. 1909), of Munich and Berlin, the foremost exponent of Wagnerian vocalism (see sec. 222).

227. Historical Studies. — In this period the modern spirit of scholarship became engaged in earnest upon the problems of music-history. At various places original research was prosecuted, usually by those in close contact with large libraries. Manuscript music and other data were here and there collected, collated and sometimes published. Civil and ecclesiastical records began to be systematically searched for statistical facts, and the musical annals of localities, institutions and branches of effort to be compiled. Investigation of the sources thus provided the materials for sound history. Out of this study emerged a much more just and ample conception of the successive stages in musical progress and of the factors at work in it. Fresh and valuable classifications, generalizations and appraisements began to accumulate. It was not until after 1850 that the results began to show in many comprehensive manuals, but before that time the work of research was actively undertaken. Each decade since has witnessed the rapid enlargement of musical scholarship, until now its magnitude baffles description or easy comprehension by any single mind.

The fields of investigation were found throughout the whole historic sequence — especially Greek music, Plain-Song, the

epoch of the Netherlanders, the 16th century, the evolution of
the opera, advances in theory, the development of instruments,
etc. It was too early for students to frame accurate notions of
the drifts of the 19th century. These were still mostly under
the review of criticism rather than of history. But the historians followed hard upon the critics.

François Joseph Fétis (d. 1871) was the most important of the scholars in
the early part of the century, and the first of the illustrious Belgian line of
investigators. Born at Mons in 1784, he showed precocious talent in playing
and composing, and had excellent instruction at Paris and Vienna. Before
he was 20 he had published ambitious compositions, and had begun to study
early mediæval theory and notation. From 1806 he took up the systematic
criticism of Gregorian music with a view to its thorough reform. From 1811
he was deeply engaged upon the modern system of harmony as distinct from
that of Rameau and his followers. From 1813 he was organist and teacher at
Douai, but in 1818 went to Paris, working partly as a composer (7 operas,
1820-32), and from 1821 being on the Conservatoire staff. His manual of
counterpoint (1824), his notable magazine, *La revue musicale* (1827-35), a
significant essay on the Netherlanders (1828), and his courses of historical
lectures (1832), made him a leader. From 1833 for nearly 40 years he was
director of the reorganized Brussels conservatory, court-choirmaster and concert-conductor. His greatest literary work was the *Biographie universelle*
(1835-44), later revised (1860-5) with the help of *Aristide Farrenc* (d. 1865)
and again augmented (1878-80) by *Arthur Pougin* — the first of the great
biographical dictionaries. He began a comprehensive *Histoire* (5 vols., to
the 15th century, 1869-76), wrote monographs on Paganini (1851), on
Stradivari (1856) and on the instruments in the Expositions of 1855 and 1867,
and prepared an extensive list of text-books for singers, pianists, choirmasters,
conductors and composers. From time to time he continued to compose for
the church and the orchestra. His accuracy has proved defective and his
judgment was not always unbiased, but the general value of his works and
the vigorous stimulus they gave are beyond question.

Among those who specialized upon Greek music were from 1818 **Friedrich
von Drieberg** (d. 1856), Prussian court-chamberlain, whose conclusions have
won small acceptance ; in 1840-7 **Friedrich Bellermann** (d. 1874), from 1847
director of one of the Berlin gymnasia ; in 1846 **Karl Fortlage** of Jena (d.
1881) ; from 1854 **Rudolf Westphal** (d. 1892), an authority on rhythmics and
metrics, who taught at Tübingen, Breslau, Jena, etc. ; and from 1866 **Oscar
Paul** of Leipsic (d. 1898).

Gregorian music attracted extensive study, leading to a full reconstruction
of the practical system on a historical basis. Among the many writers may
be named from 1829 **Théodore Joseph de Vroye** (d. 1873) of the Liège
Cathedral ; from 1836 the Paris choirmaster **Adrien Lenoir de Lafage** (d.
1862), who also began a general history (1844), wrote many biographical
sketches, and started a Plain-Song periodical (1859) ; from 1840 ‘ **Théodore
Nisard** ’ [**T. E. X. Normand**], another industrious Parisian student ; from

1841 Joseph Louis d' Ortigue (d. 1866), also of Paris; from 1840 Pietro Alfieri (d. 1863) of the English College at Rome; in 1844-9 the Paris organist Félix Danjou (d. 1866), who discovered the Montpellier antiphonary; in 1848-54 Edmond Duval of Mechlin, whose views were hotly contested; the Jesuit Louis Lambillotte (d. 1855), the interpreter of the St. Gall antiphonary (1851), but not generally accepted as a practical reformer; in 1852-5 J. G. Mettenleiter of Ratisbon (d. 1858); in 1852-9 the Parisian composer and patron Marie Désiré Beaulieu (d. 1863); in 1852-62 the Abbé F. Raillard (d. ?), teacher at Nîmes and Juilly; in 1854-61 Félix Clément (d. 1885); in 1856 François Auguste Gevaert (d. 1908), of Ghent, who reëntered the field later with epoch-making treatises (1890-5); in 1858 Anslem Schubiger of Einsiedeln (d. 1888); and from 1865 F. X. Haberl (d. 1910), of Ratisbon. The founder of the famous Solesmes group of Gregorian specialists was Prosper Guéranger (d. 1875), Benedictine abbot there (works from 1835), from whom Joseph Pothier and André Mocquereau derived the impulse and method of their recent remarkable studies (from 1880).

Karl von Winterfeld (d. 1852), born in 1784, from 1816 judge at Breslau and from 1832 supreme-court judge at Berlin, was one of the earliest of the erudite students of the older church music. His works include monographs on Palestrina (1832), on Giovanni Gabrieli (1834), and on evangelical church music (1840-62), all of masterly scope and method. Valuable publications in the choral field were made from 1830 by Emmanuel Christian Gottlieb Langbecker of Berlin (d. 1843); in 1832 by Heinrich August Hoffmann of Breslau (d. 1874); from 1847 by Eduard Emil Koch of Heilbronn (d. 1871); and in 1852 by Gottfried Döring of Elbing (d. 1869).

Edmond Henri de Coussemaker (d. 1876), born in 1805 in northern France and by profession a judge there, was led by Fétis' writings to adopt historical work. He published invaluable monographs on Hucbald (1841), mediæval instruments (1845), the rise of polyphony (from 1852), the mediæval drama (1861), and Adam de la Hâle (1872), besides superb collections of mediæval documents (1864-76). With him may be grouped many others in the Belgian (and Dutch) series, such as from 1840 Florent Corneille Kist of The Hague (d. 1863); from 1846 Joseph Karel Boers of Nymwegen and Delft (d. 1896); Edmond Vanderstraeten (d. 1895), at first of Ghent and from 1857 in the Brussels library, whose works (from 1851) on music in the Netherlands are of extreme value, especially the collection of historic masterpieces (1867-85); from 1860 Xavier Victor van Elewyck (d. 1888), cathedral-choirmaster at Louvain; from 1860, also, Édouard Gregoir of Antwerp (d. 1890); from 1862 the Chevalier Burbure de Wessembeek (d. 1889), a specialist on Antwerp history; and the composer François Auguste Gevaert, from 1857 at Ghent and from 1871 head of the Brussels conservatory (chief historical works since 1875).

Various mediæval topics were treated from 1821 by Gottfried Wilhelm Fink of Leipsic (d. 1846); from 1826 by Raphael Georg Kiesewetter (d. 1850), who wrote on the Netherlanders, the origin of European music, Guido, the beginnings of secular music, Arabic music, etc.; in 1836-8 by Auguste Bottée de Toulmon (d. 1850), librarian of the Paris Conservatoire; from 1841 by Pietro Alfieri of Rome (d. 1863), with fine collections of Palestrina and many scattered articles; from 1846 by **Edward Francis Rimbault** of London (d. 1876), an indefatigable student of every phase of old music in England; in 1854–5 by **Francesco Caffi** (d. 1874), the historian of St. Mark's in Venice; in 1858 by **Heinrich Bellermann** of Berlin (d. 1903), writing on time-notation.

The development of French music was followed from 1820 by **François Blaze** ['Castil-Blaze'] (d. 1857), and by **Joseph Louis d'Ortigue** (d. 1866). After 1860 came the voluminous studies of **Arthur Pougin, Antoine Ernest Roquet** ['Erneste Thoinan'] (d. 1894), **Adolphe Gustave Chouquet** (d. 1886), and **Félix Clément** (d. 1885).

Various topics in dramatic and operatic progress were discussed in 1849–62 by **Moritz Fürstenau** (d. 1889), writing on Dresden; in 1852–72 by **Ernst Pasqué** (d. 1892), on Darmstadt and Frankfort; on Berlin in 1852 by **Louis Schneider** (d. 1878); on early German opera in 1855 by **Otto Lindner** of Berlin (d. 1867); on both German and French topics from 1863 by **Michel Schletterer** of Augsburg (d. 1893); and on Munich in 1867 by **Karl von Perfall** (d. 1907). Here may be added studies from 1867 on music in Bologna by **Gaetano Gaspari** (d. 1881), and in 1868 on the Imperial Chapel at Vienna by **Ludwig von Köchel** (d. 1877). On the growth of music in particular countries may be noted works in 1852 on Prussia by **Gottfried Döring** of Elbing (d. 1869); in 1853–67 on Spain by **Mariano Soriano-Fuertes** of Barcelona (d. 1880); and in 1859 on Polish opera by **Moritz Karasowski** (d. 1892).

Concerning special forms there were works in 1841 on the mediæval lais, sequences, etc., by **Ferdinand Wolf** of the Vienna Library (d. 1866); in 1846, on the keyboard-sonata by **Faiszt** of Stuttgart (d. 1894); in 1840 on German Hausmusik by **K. F. Becker** of Leipsic (d. 1877); in 1853 on the oratorio by **Chrysander** of Berlin (d. 1901); in 1859 on Russian church music by **Alexis Lwoff** (d. 1871); in 1861 on Gipsy music by **Liszt** (d. 1886); from 1861 on the German Lied by **Reissmann** of Berlin (d. 1903) and by **K. E. Schneider** of Dresden (d. 1893); and in 1863 on piano music by **K. F. Weitzmann** of Berlin (d. 1880).

Organ-building was handled from 1833 by **Töpfer** of Weimar (d. 1870); from 1839 by **Christian Friedrich Gottlieb Wilke** (d. 1848); in 1843 by **Johann Julius Seidel** of Breslau (d. 1856); in 1849 by **Marie Pierre Hamel** of Beauvais (d. after 1870); in 1855 by **David Hermann Engel** of Merseburg (d. 1877); in 1855 by **E. J. Hopkins** (d. 1901) and **E. F. Rimbault** (d. 1876); and in 1859 by **Jean Bertrand** of Paris (d. 1880). Piano-making was similarly discussed in 1853 by **Joseph Fischhof** of Vienna (d. 1857); in 1860 by **Rimbault**; in 1868 by **Edgar Brinsmead**; and in 1869 by **Oscar Paul** of Leipsic (d. 1898). Somewhat comprehensive studies of instrument-making were put forth from 1857 by the **Marquis de Pontécoulant** of Paris (d. 1882); by **Edmund Schebek** of Prague (d. 1895); by **Jules Gallay** of Paris (d. 1897); and by **Karl Engel** of London (d. 1882) — all these being drawn out by the Expositions of 1855 and later.

From the work of these many specialists grew undertakings of a more comprehensive character. Here belong works from 1848 by **Franz Brendel** of Leipsic (d. 1868). But to **August Wilhelm Ambros** of Vienna (d. 1876) belongs the honor of beginning from 1861 a monumental general history, which has since been continued by other hands. Other useful scholars in this field were from 1856 **Emil Naumann** (d. 1888) and from 1861 **August Reissmann** (d. 1903), both of Berlin.

From the multitude of biographical sketches and monographs issued between 1830 and 1870 the following examples may be selected as illustrating the manifold lines of investigation : — **Angelo Catelani** of Modena (d. 1866) made studies of A. and N. Vicentino (1851), Petrucci (1856), Orazio Vecchi (1858), Merulo (1860) and Stradella (1866). Petrucci was also treated in 1845 by **Anton Schmid** of Vienna (d. 1857) ; and Stradella in 1866 by **Paulin Richard** of Paris. Palestrina and Giovanni Gabrieli were discussed by **Von Winterfeld** (see above) ; and Lassus in 1836 by **Henri Florent Delmotte** of Mons (d. 1836), in 1838 by **Auguste Mathieu** of Brussels, and in 1841 by **Kist** of Utrecht ; and Sweelinck in 1859–60 by **Richard Hol** of Amsterdam (d. 1904). Concerning Bach, appeared works in 1850 by **Karl Hermann Bitter** of Berlin (d. 1885), who also wrote on Bach's sons, and from 1873 by **Philipp Spitta** of Berlin (d. 1894) — the standard work ; and concerning Handel in 1857 by **Victor Schölcher** (d. 1893), and from 1858 by **Friedrich Chrysander** of Berlin (d. 1901) — another standard work. Haydn was treated at Vienna in 1861 by **Theodor Georg von Karajan** (d. 1873), in 1861 by **Konstantin Würzbach** (d. 1893), and especially from 1867 by **Karl Ferdinand Pohl** (d. 1887). Mozart was studied in 1844 by the Russian **Alexander Ulibischew** (d. 1858), in 1845 by **Edward Holmes** of London (d. 1859), in 1856–9 with greatest fullness by **Otto Jahn** of Bonn (d. 1869), in 1862–4 by **Ludwig von Köchel** of Vienna (d. 1877), in 1865 by **Ludwig Nohl** of Heidelberg (d. 1885), in 1868 by **Moritz Karasowski** of Dresden (d. 1892), and in 1869 by **Würzbach**. Gluck was treated in 1854 by **Anton Schmid** of Vienna (d. 1857) and in 1863 by **Marx** of Berlin (d. 1866). Beethoven literature was developed in 1838 by **Franz Gerhard Wegeler** of Coblentz (d. 1848) and **Ferdinand Ries** of Frankfort (d. 1838), in 1840–2 by **Anton Schindler** of Vienna (d. 1864), from 1852 by **Wilhelm von Lenz** of St. Petersburg (d. 1883), in 1858 by **Marx** of Berlin, in 1862 by **Édouard Gregoir** of Antwerp (d. 1890), and especially from 1864 by **Nohl** of Heidelberg, **Martin Gustav Nottebohm** of Vienna (d. 1882), and the American **Alexander Wheelock Thayer** (d. 1897). Weber was described in 1862 by **Hippolyte Barbedette** (d. 1901), and especially in 1864–8 by his son **Max Maria von Weber**. Schubert was considered from 1861 by **Heinrich Kreissle von Hellborn** of Vienna (d. 1869) and others ; Mendelssohn in 1848 by **Wilhelm Adolf Lampadius** of Leipsic (d. 1892), in 1850 by **Julius Benedict** of London (d. 1885), in 1866 by **Julius Schubring** and in 1869 by **Eduard Devrient** ; and Schumann in 1858 by **Joseph von Wasielewski** of Dresden (d. 1896).

To these might be added very numerous works of varying merit on many opera-writers and virtuosi, especially those associated with Paris. In the field of special biography **Pougin** of Paris and **Reissmann** of Berlin had already become conspicuous before 1870.

Autobiographies or reminiscences appeared in 1833 from the organist **Rinck** ; in 1847 from the opera-writer **Konradin Kreutzer** ; about 1857 from the pedagogue **Czerny**: in 1859 from the theorist **Lobe**; in 1860–1 from the violinist **Spohr**; in 1865 from the theorist **Marx**; and in 1870 from both **Löwe** and **Berlioz**.

Dictionaries of varying size and value were put forth in 1835 by **August Gathy** of Hamburg (d. 1858); in 1835–8 by **Gustav Schilling** of Stuttgart (d. 1881); in 1844 by **Marie** and **Léon Escudier** of Paris (d. 1880, '81); in 1849 by **Ferdinand Simon Gassner** of Darmstadt (d. 1851); in 1856–61 by **Eduard Bernsdorf** of Leipsic (d. 1901); and in 1865 by **Arrey von Dommer** of Hamburg (d. 1905). Much more important than any of these was the great work of **Fétis** in 1835–44 (2d ed., 1860–5).

Here may be added some of the many periodicals founded during the period, such as in 1824–48 Gottfried Weber's *Cäcilia*, from 1827 Fétis' *Revue musicale*, later merged in the *Revue et gazette musicale*, from 1834 Schumann's epoch-making *Neue Zeitschrift für Musik*, from 1835 the Paris *Ménestrel* and the London *Musical World*, from 1843 the important *Signale für die musika-lische Welt*, from 1844 the London *Musical Times*, from 1845 the Milan *Gazzetta musicale*, from 1847 the *Neue Berliner Musikzeitung*, from 1851 the Berlin *Echo* and the Vienna *Monatsschrift für Theater und Musik*, from 1860 *L'art musicale*, from 1862 the London *Musical Standard*, and from 1869 Eitner's *Monatshefte fur Musikgeschichte*.

228. Theorists and Critics. —The distinctively modern views of harmony and counterpoint began to take shape only from about 1840. They arose from two sources. The more specu-lative theorists felt that current definitions, classifications and rules should be simplified and to some extent restated. And the more radical composers, like Wagner and many others, were instinctively expanding procedure in all directions so vigor-ously that they were making the accepted authorities obsolete. In harmony, the most striking advance was represented by the Leipsic master Hauptmann, whose analysis of chords in rela-tion to tonality and to the antithesis between major and minor marked an epoch. In counterpoint, there was no marked change in formal theory until the next period, though practice was departing widely from the usual standards. Naturally, the vast increase of institutions for formal musical education brought into notice many thoughtful teachers of musical science and structure, who embodied their methods in various text-books, often of considerable magnitude. Toward the end of the period attempts were made to reconstruct harmonic thought upon a chromatic basis, but these were principally useful in calling attention to infelicities of detail in the usual doctrines of chromatic tones and the transformation of chords.

The interrelations of music with physics, physiology and æsthetics continued to be studied more or less, usually by those not otherwise engaged in musical work.   In all these fields substantial progress was made in adjusting thought about music to modern views of natural science and of psychology.

In the domain of criticism, a veritable revolution set in with the work of Schumann on the one side (see sec. 192) and that of Wagner, Berlioz and Liszt on the other.   Late in the period appeared the powerful Viennese critic Hanslick, taking his stand against what seemed to him the dangerous radicalism of the latter group.   Two notable features of publication were, first, the frequency of rational analyses of masterpieces as to structure and content, and, second, the violent combat over Wagnerism and the 'new' schools generally.   The former was intimately connected with historical and theoretical advances.   The latter was the inevitable concomitant of a revolutionary transition in artistic method, and gradually died out as musical thought adjusted itself to new ideas.

The earlier theorists of the period were from 1832 **Anton André** of Offenbach (d. 1842) ; from 1836 **Fink** of Leipsic (d. 1846) ; from 1837 **Marx** of Berlin (d. 1866) ; and from 1840 **Dehn** of Berlin (d. 1858).

From 1844 appeared **Fétis** of Brussels (d. 1871) ; in 1845 **Alfred Day** of London (d. 1849) ; from 1846 **Lobe** of Leipsic (d. 1881) ; in 1853–4 **Sechter** of Vienna (d. 1867) ; from 1853 **E. F. Richter** of Leipsic (d. 1879) ; from 1853 **Weitzmann** of Berlin (d. 1880) ; from 1854 **Hauptmann** of Leipsic (d. 1868) ; from 1860 **G. A. Macfarren** of London (d. 1887) ; from 1860, representing the chromatic school, **Heinrich Joseph Vincent** of Vienna (d. 1901) ; from 1862 **N. H. Reber** of Paris (d. 1880) ; from 1866 **Arthur von Oettingen** of Dorpat ; from 1867 **Ludwig Bussler** of Berlin (d. 1901) ; from 1868 **Ouseley** of Hereford (d. 1889) ; and from 1868 **Otto Tiersch** of Berlin (d. 1892).

In acoustics, contributions were made from 1827 by **Charles Édouard Joseph Delezenne** of Lille (d. 1866) ; from 1834 by **Karl Franz Emil Schafhäutl** of Munich (d. 1890) ; from 1846 by **Moritz Wilhelm Drobisch** of Leipsic (d. 1896) ; from 1853 by **Heinrich Welcker von Gontershausen** (d. 1873) ; in 1855 by **Friedrich Zamminer** of Giessen (d. 1856) ; from 1859 by **Charles Meerens** of Bruges ; from 1863 conspicuously by **Hermann Helmholtz** of Heidelberg and Berlin (d. 1894) ; and from 1864 by **Alexander John Ellis** of London (d. 1890).

Vocal physiology was scientifically treated from 1833 by **Johannes Müller** of Berlin (d. 1858) ; in 1839 by **Heinrich Häser** of Jena (d. 1885) ; from 1846 by **L. A. Segond** of Paris ; and from 1856 by **Karl Ludwig Merkel** of Leipsic.

Musical æstheticians included from 1832 **G. T. Fechner** of Leipsic (d. 1887); from 1837 **Ferdinand Gotthelf Hand** of Jena (d. 1851); from 1838 **Gustav Schilling** of Stuttgart (d. 1881); in 1854 the Vienna critic **Eduard Hanslick** (d. 1904); from 1858 **Adolf Kullak** of Berlin (d. 1862); from 1863 **Karl Köstlin** of Tübingen (d. 1894); and from 1868 **Rudolf Hermann Lotze** (d. 1881), then of Leipsic.

As illustrations of the growing attention to detailed analysis may be cited numerous studies (from 1840) by **Wagner**; many (from 1843) by **Berlioz**; pamphlets (1845-52) on Bach's cantatas and Matthew Passion by **Johann Theodor Mosewius** of Breslau (d. 1858); on Bach's *Kunst der Fuge* by **Hauptmann**; on various Wagner works (from 1851) and on Field's nocturnes by **Liszt**; various works (1852-65) on Beethoven's three styles, etc., by **Wilhelm von Lenz** (d. 1883); on several Wagner works (1853-69) by **Franz Müller** of Weimar (d. 1876); on Handel's *Israel in Egypt* (1854) by **Hermann Küster** (d. 1878); on Beethoven's sonatas and symphonies (1857-8) by '**Ernst von Elterlein**' [**Ernst Gottschald**]; on Schumann's *Faust* music (1860) by **Peter Lohmann** of Leipsic (d. 1907); on Mozart's *Magic Flute* (1862) by **Nohl** (d. 1885); on Beethoven's piano works (1863) by **Marx** (d. 1866); on works by Pergolesi, Gluck, etc. (1863-8) by **François de Villars** (d. 1879); on Beethoven's dramatic writing (1865) by **Hermann Deiters** (d. 1907), then of Bonn; etc.

Among German critics, besides **Schumann** and various historians and theorists already named, may be added from 1823 **Ludwig Rellstab** of Berlin (d. 1860); from 1836 **Rudolf Hirsch** of Vienna (d. 1872); from about 1850 **Ferdinand Hiller** of Cologne (d. 1885), and **Karl Kossmaly** of Stettin (d. 1893); and, chief of all, from 1854 **Eduard Hanslick** (d. 1904), who became one of the most influential champions of ' absolute music' as against Wagner, Berlioz and Liszt, besides being a valuable historian.

Naturally, a period so replete with artistic and literary production was one in which music-publishing was greatly extended. Among the houses established were in 1838 that of *Bote & Bock* at Berlin; about 1840 that of *Heugel* at Paris; in 1846 that of *Röder* at Leipsic; in 1849 that of *Rieter-Biedermann* at Winterthur; in 1851 that of *Litolff* at Brunswick; in 1851 that of *Kahnt* at Leipsic; and in 1853 that of *Augener* at London.

229. Summary of the Period. — The development of Germany before the middle of the century was accompanied by an unprecedented dominance of German influences in the musical world. It was in Germany almost alone that really constructive and directive advance took place in composition, technique, theory and scholarship. The apparent exceptions of Chopin and Berlioz are not sufficient to set this statement aside, since the work of both was at once absorbed into the general current of German thought. A recapitulation of the movements of the time, therefore, must chiefly concern those in progress in Germany.

The novelty and energy of effort made the period one of notable transitions and revolutions, and hence one of debate and conflict. First came the overflow of the romantic tide, strong in sentiment and phantasy, impatient of set patterns and rules, eager to test instrumental means of expression, yet quick to seize upon the neglected capacity of the solo song, and provocative of new intellectual attitudes toward all musical art. Against this stood both the reactive conservatism of adherents to the old vocal polyphony or the stern and condensed style of Bach, and the compromising party made up of Mendelssohn and his many followers, who sought to utter a romantic message in classical phraseology. This general antithesis broke up into various smaller ones, as between romantic freedom and classical regularity, or between intensely subjective expression and the pursuit of tonal beauty of an objective sort, or between styles generated by the peculiarities of instruments and those that were distinctively vocal, or between lyric melody and polyphonic solidity. In all these directions the new and the old were contesting for supremacy, too often without seeing that they were not utterly at variance.

While all this was going on, came the advent of Wagner with his original, radical and powerful conception of the opera, expressed at first mildly and then with gigantic audacity. Here was a challenge to nearly the whole body of operatic conventions, Italian, French and even German. This throwing down of the gauntlet precipitated a war of words more extensive and bitter than any other in music-history, one which outlasted the period before us and which ran out into all sorts of ramifications. In particular, the Wagner question seemed to be entangled with the whole debate about ' program ' *versus* ' absolute ' music, both because Wagner was championed by Liszt and because the Wagnerian theory of the opera had evident analogies with the use of ' program ' in instrumental writing. But the Wagner revolution had much more profound characteristics. Wagner's technical procedures involved great apparent departures from accepted standards and put a severe strain upon tastes educated in simpler methods. And the grandiose scale and fervid profusion of his mature creations staggered conservative comprehension. Had not the essential logic of most of his innovations and the genuine value of his musical ideas gradually become clear, his later works would certainly not have been more than a passing marvel. But the solution of the Wagner problem belongs to the later period (see sec. 230).

The influence of the great triumvirate, Berlioz, Liszt and Wagner, stimulated, if it did not occasion, the advance of several groups who explicitly aimed at setting up 'new' styles of composition, first the 'new-German,' then the 'new-Russian,' and the 'new-French,' followed by others, each desiring to express . its national individuality in terms other than those of past academic formulæ. In perhaps all of these there was something of a feverish reaction against tradition, an over-exaltation of temperament and mood, a curious search for impressionistic effects, even an untamed recklessness and wildness. Yet the revolt from mere authority and the craving for vitality, and even for 'realism,' were inevitable expressions of the spirit of the age. They helped to advance imperfect processes to completion and to open gateways into unoccupied domains (see secs. 231–232).

It may be said, however, that from this period came the now conspicuous tendency to exalt forms and styles of music that appeal only to a limited class of connoisseurs. At the very moment that music was reaching more people than ever before, at least in its more elaborate expressions, it was also becoming more specialized and even esoteric. It is true that music-history has repeatedly shown that sensitiveness to musical art is capable of extraordinarily rapid development, so that what is abstruse to one generation becomes commonplace to the next. But, even with this qualification, some tendencies bequeathed by this middle period to the later one have aroused a degree of question.

However this may be, the period was extraordinarily rich in those enterprises of education and literature that are always the connecting links between rudimentary and advanced art, between popular thought and artistic specialization. These mediating factors included not only the schools of music, the army of detached teachers, the musical periodicals, and the books about music in its many aspects, but also every organized project for presenting the larger musical works to the public, especially the opera and both vocal and instrumental concerts. Through all these avenues of education, as never before, musical art was now beginning to attain its place as a conspicuous and valuable force in the personal and communal culture of modern society.

CONCLUSION

BRIEF SKETCH OF THE LATER NINETEENTH CENTURY

CONCLUSION

BRIEF SKETCH OF THE LATER NINETEENTH CENTURY

230. The Wagnerian Triumph.
231. The National Groups (a).
232. The National Groups (b).
233. Music in the United States.
234. Some Final Words.

CONCLUSION

230. The Wagnerian Triumph. — In the last third of the century the supreme single event was the achievement of Wagner's lifelong ambition. The Bayreuth performances from 1876 onward made an epoch in musical art. They brought out Wagner's later dramas in accordance with all his ideas of apparatus and effect. They demonstrated his power to command popular enthusiasm and critical respect. They led at once to productions elsewhere on a somewhat parallel scale, at least with exceptional attention to the detail of representation. They forced the operatic world to adjust its thought to new ideals of technique on every side. They stimulated a profound remodeling of style on the part of dramatic and orchestral composers in all countries, tending more or less toward an imitation of the Wagnerian procedures, often extremely clever, but, as a rule, without creative energy to be compared with his. They thus introduced into the musical world a ferment whose working is still widely conspicuous.

The first consequence of all this was naturally a fresh attention to the opera as a consummate art-form, viewed now not from the restricted and manneristic angle of the earlier Italian writers, but as a genuine drama in music. Of course, the traditions of each country and school continued to make themselves felt, so that new types were never without evident connection with the past — as, for example, in the case of Verdi. But everywhere the details of treatment began to undergo extensive readjustments to fit them to compete before the critics and the public with the gigantic Wagnerian constructions. The two most striking instances of this process were the evolution of the French drame lyrique out of the opéra comique under a series of composers, and the setting up of a new type of Italian opera under the lead of Verdi. Equally important was the unfolding of the modern German opera, but in this case no such reconstruction was demanded, since the Wagnerian movement was itself characteristically German, an organic extension of drifts that had been strong since Weber's time.

But quite as significant was the reaction of the Wagnerian style upon orchestral music. With Wagner himself the orchestra was a means to an end, but his use of it was so extraordinary that it generated a new style. Here he was in line with several other masters who, consciously or unconsciously, had been breaking away from the strict notions of form and disposition that had been pushed into the foreground by the founders of modern orchestral music. Wagner was attacked by Hanslick and others as the enemy of 'absolute music,' and the effort was made to show that his tendency was so to mingle musical expression with other elements, especially those of literature, that his style was actually subversive of the purity and individuality of music as an art. But the fact proved to be that in his use of orchestral resources — as, indeed, of vocal resources — he disclosed important new possibilities of expression, which could be applied fruitfully without being entangled in dramatic or other literary alliances. Whether or not this was deliberately a part of the program of his ambition, the result showed that his influence upon orchestral music was as rapid and thoroughgoing as upon the opera. Here again the consequences in different countries varied greatly according to the quality of the national genius, but were conspicuous everywhere except in Italy (which has never shown national power in orchestral writing). Inasmuch as the apparatus for orchestral performances of the finest character is generally more available than that of the opera in its most advanced form, the practical effect of this orchestral influence has been more widely felt than that of the operatic influence above mentioned.

The success of Wagner was a crowning triumph for German music. His style and theories were legitimate results of movements in artistic thought that had been progressing in central Europe for more than a century, and that had made German musicians in most respects the lawgivers and prophets of the musical world. Wagner's own spirit was intensely and passionately German. His whole mental training had been in the atmosphere of German science, literature and philosophy. He drew his artistic inspiration mainly from the store of myths accumulated among Teutonic peoples and expressive of their racial consciousness. And his victory was coincident in time with the unification of the German Empire and its advance into a controlling position in European politics. Hence the Wagnerian style at its climax illustrated and declared the German genius for music in an eminent degree. In consequence, the pursuit of advanced composition in German countries was still further stimulated. At the same time the ambition of other nations was powerfully quickened to achieve something parallel for themselves. The potency of Wagner's influence is attested not only by the direct imitations in its own field, but by some of the efforts to match his success through efforts in other fields that are only distantly analogous.

Among those who have been most stimulated by Wagner and Liszt the tendency has been strong to magnify some sort of literary topic or intellectual train of ideas as a guide in laying out musical processes. This is a natural result of the dramatism of the one master and the 'program' style of the other, though some recent works do not belong exactly to either category. A form of composition that has been specially favored is the choral ballade, usually more or less frankly dramatic — a form susceptible of indefinite orchestral expansion and enrichment, and utilizing the varied capacities of both soloists and chorus as well. The endless production of songs of every description goes steadily on, each centring about a specific text, with its theme, its poetic imagery, its chain of sentiments. But purely instrumental writing, also, shows a striking tendency to follow lines of thought somehow supplied to the hearer by a title, motto or argument. The 'program' method in some form is conspicuous in every variety of composition. By some critics this is attributed to Wagner's influence. By others it is held to be a general modern tendency, of which Wagner and Liszt were merely illustrations. However this may be, it is a question whether the essential limits of musical art have not been stretched in this direction about as far as is wise. Certainly nothing extraneous can take the place of genuine freshness of tonal inspiration. The lack of such inspiration among some recent composers has been evidenced on the one hand by a straining after prodigious intricacy of construction or after startling melodic or harmonic extremes, and, on the other, by a misguided choice of morbid and even degenerate themes. Opulence on the side of procedure and technique have no enduring value unless directed and vitalized by genuine artistic initiative and invention.

From the many German and Austrian composers who have worked in the operatic field the following may be selected as illustrating varied tendencies : —

Bernhard Scholz of Frankfort, born in 1835, with 8 operas (from 1858), the latest of which are *Ingo* (1898, Frankfort) and *Anno 1757* (1903, Berlin), and much instrumental music; **Max Zenger** of Munich, born in 1837, with 4 operas (from 1863), notably *Wieland der Schmied* (1880, Munich), the striking oratorio *Kain* (1867), many cantatas, 2 symphonies, etc.; **Victor Nessler** of Strassburg (d. 1890), with 11 operas and operettas (from 1864), especially *Der Rattenfänger von Hameln* (1879) and *Der Trompeter von Säkkingen* (1884), and many choral ballades; **Ignaz Brüll** of Vienna (d. 1907), born in 1846, an able pianist, with 10 operas (from 1864), of which *Das goldene Kreuz* (1875, Berlin) and the comic *Der Husar* (1898, Vienna) have had decided success, besides many other works; **Joseph Rheinberger** of Munich (d. 1901), a prolific composer in all forms, especially those for organ, piano or chorus that admit of great contrapuntal skill, with 3 operas (from 1869), an oratorio, many cantatas, extensive sacred works, a variety of other vocal and instrumental music, etc.; **Heinrich Hofmann** of Berlin (d. 1902), with 7 operas, beginning with *Cartouche* (1869), important orchestral works, chamber music, an oratorio (1896), many choral cantatas, elegant piano-pieces, etc.; **August Klughardt** of Dessau (d. 1902), an admirer of Liszt, with 4 operas (from 1871), 3 oratorios, 5 symphonies, several overtures, symphonic poems, chamber music and many songs; **Hermann Goetz** of Zurich (d. 1876, 36 years old), with 2 operas, especially *Die Zähmung der Widerspenstigen* (1874, Mannheim), a symphony, some cantatas and chamber pieces; **Karl Grammann** of Dresden (d. 1897), with 6 operas (from 1875), 2 symphonies and various other works in Wagnerian style; **Albert Thierfelder** of Rostock, born in 1846, with 5 operas (from 1877), 2 symphonies, several cantatas and chamber works; **August Bungert** of Berlin, born in 1846, with a comic opera (1884) and two extended opera-cycles, *Die Ilias* (2 works) and *Die Odyssee* (4 works), begun in 1871, a symphonic poem, a cantata and other works; **Cyrill Kistler** of Kissingen, born in 1848, with 4 operas (from 1884); **Richard Heuberger** of Vienna, born in 1850, with 8 operas and operettas (from 1886), especially *Mirjam* (1889–94), many works for orchestra and chorus, etc; **Wilhelm Kienzl** of Gratz, born in 1857, with 4 operas (from 1886), especially *Heilmar* (1892, Munich) and *Der Evangelimann* (1895, Berlin), besides much original criticism; **Felix von Woyrsch** of Altona, born in 1860, with 4 operas (from 1886), among them *Wikingerfahrt* (1896, Nuremberg), several chorus works, a symphony, etc.; **Robert Fuchs** of Vienna, born in 1847, with 2 operas (1889, '92), and striking orchestral and chamber music; the distinguished conductor and critic **Felix Weingartner** of Munich, born in 1863, with 3 operas (from 1884), including *Genesius* (1892) and the dramatic trilogy *Orestes* (1902, Leipsic), 2 symphonies, symphonic poems, etc.; **Engelbert Humperdinck** of Berlin, born in 1854, famous for his *Hänsel und Gretel* (1893, Weimar) and 4 other operas; **Max Schillings** of Munich, born in 1868, with 2 operas (from 1894); and **Eugène d'Albert**, born in 1864 (Glasgow), first famous as a pianist, with 7 operas (from 1893), including *Gernot* (1897, Mannheim), *Kain* (1900, Berlin) and *Im Tiefland* (1903, Prague), 2 piano-concertos, a symphony, etc.

Richard Strauss of Berlin, born in 1864, is at present the most conspicuous figure in both the orchestral and the operatic fields. His command of every technical resource is phenomenal, his ambition and energy impressive, and his originality and artistic daring unquestioned.　His first renown came from symphonic poems, like *Don Juan* (1889), *Tod und Verklärung* (1890), *Till Eulenspiegels lustige Streiche* (1895), *Also sprach Zarathustra* (1896) and *Ein Heldenleben* (1899).　His operas include *Guntram* (1894, Weimar), *Feuersnot* (1901, Dresden) and the much-debated *Salome* (1905, Dresden).　He has also written 2 symphonies, much chamber music and many songs.

To these may be added a few more, not so specially distinguished in opera, but otherwise important : —

Joseph Brambach of Bonn (d. 1902), the writer of a number of fine choral cantatas ;　**Felix Draeseke** of Dresden, born in 1835, who for a time was associated with Wagner and Liszt, but later reverted to more conservative styles, with many orchestral and vocal works, besides 4 operas (from 1867), notably *Herrat* (1892, Dresden) ;　**Max Bruch** of Berlin, born in 1838, an eminent composer in the choral field, with also 3 symphonies, striking violin-concertos and other chamber music, etc. ;　**Heinrich von Herzogenberg** of Berlin (d. 1900), with similar works, besides piano-pieces ;　**Jean Louis Nicodé** of Dresden, born in 1853, a master of orchestral style, and a writer for the piano and the voice ;　**Anton Rückauf** (d. 1903), an eminent song-composer ; and **Hugo Wolf** of Vienna (d. 1903), still more famous for his songs.

231. The National Groups (a). — Nationalism in musical art

is no new thing.　Every race, every distinct country, and often limited districts within a single country, have always had idioms of expression, peculiarities of temperament, tendencies of feeling and a range of ideas which the keen observer and critic learns to know as individual and distinctive.　Every composer and player usually betrays in all that he does what was his origin and education in a particular people and land.　Even in the earlier periods, when music was held to be far more homogeneous than now in contrapuntal, dramatic or instrumental method, these national traits made themselves felt.　The whole course of music-history illustrates the principle that, as evolution proceeds, musical art tends to become heterogeneous along lines of race, country and local predilection.

But in these latter days this age-long tendency has received impetus from several directions.　One cause is political — the steady rise of ambition for national freedom and autonomy, with the social and intellectual life appropriate to each racial division.　Another cause is the discovery by scientific criticism of the suggestiveness, for a full knowledge of humanity and society, of traits induced by descent and habitat, what had been merely odd or picturesque becoming significant.　Still another is the advance in musical theory, resulting in a more searching classification of details of procedure and a juster appreciation of the technical value of neglected points. Thus, just at the time when the general qualities of races and regions have been eager to find for themselves ampler expression, the study of peculiar rhythms, melodic and harmonic formulæ, specific dance- or song-types, predilections as to choral or instrumental styles, and the like, has become somewhat common and enterprising. The phrase 'national music,' which was once used mainly to describe types of unconscious folk-music, has now been extended to apply to a number of extremely complicated artistic efforts that seek to create for each principal country a somewhat complete musical style and literature of its own. In the nature of things, since music is a universal art, with a large body of technical processes that are common to all styles, and with a literature that is in cosmopolitan circulation, the amount of local variation that is possible is not extensive ; but the local types are nevertheless full of interest.

Here is an appropriate place to refer to the formation at Leipsic in 1899 of the Internationale Musik-Gesellschaft, intended to bind together musical scholars in all lands. This association has drawn into its ranks a large number of musicians, and has active national branches or 'sections' in nearly twenty countries. It publishes a monthly *Zeitschrift* and quarterly *Sammelbände*, representing the highest quality of scholarship as applied to music.

In this connection it should also be said that historical data of the first importance are constantly being supplied by several great serial publications, like the *Denkmäler der Tonkunst in Oesterreich* (from 1894), the *Denkmäler deutscher Tonkunst* (from 1892), and several other similar undertakings, each aiming to gather the most significant works of olden time in particular countries and to annotate them so that they may be fruitful objects of study.

The French is one of the most individual of recent groups, though in the details of expression not specially marked by the use of purely racial or local peculiarities. Its character inheres rather in certain large qualities of style — in general elegance and brilliance of effect, in extremely dexterous harmony and counterpoint, in ingenious and captivating disposition of both instrumental and vocal materials, and in great definiteness and clarity of conception, usually combined with poetic delicacy and genuine imagination. French musicians have been rigorous and profound students of composition as an art, and are notable for utilizing the results of progress everywhere without losing originality and freedom.   In all the larger branches of composition they have fully held their own with others, and in organ music have become leaders.   Their contributions to the science of musical structure are probably the most important of recent years.

Prominent representatives of the large French group are these: —
Camille Saint-Saëns, born in 1835, is not only the oldest, but one of the most versatile and powerful, having been fruitful in every style, with 5 symphonies, 4 symphonic poems, 5 piano-concertos, much chamber music, about 10 operas (from 1872), including *Samson et Dalila* (1877, Weimar), *Henri VIII* (1883) and the Biblical drama, *Le Déluge*, several cantatas, masses and much church music; **Félix Alexandre Guilmant** (d. 1911), born in 1837, a great organist, with 7 organ-sonatas, many other organ-pieces, 3 masses, motets, and choir music; **Thèodore Dubois**, born in 1837, also a fine organist, with 3 oratorios, as *Les sept paroles du Christ* (1867), many cantatas and choral works, 5 operas (from 1873), and a variety of orchestral pieces, etc.; **Georges Bizet** (d. 1875), whose brilliant promise, especially revealed in *Carmen* (1875), besides earlier operas (from 1857) and in many piano works, was cut short when he was not 37 years old; **Victorin de Joncières** (d. 1903), with 6 operas (from 1867), including *Dimitri* (1876) and *Le chevalier Jean* (1885), music for 'Hamlet' (1862) and considerable orchestral and chamber music; **Jules Massenet**, born in 1842, an exuberantly prolific writer, with about 20 dramas (from 1867), such as *Le Roi de Lahore* (1877), *Hérodiade* (1884), *Manon* (1884) and *Werther* (1892), brilliant orchestral suites and fantasias, etc.; **Alexis Emanuel Chabrier** (d. 1894), with 5 operas (from 1877), mostly comedies; **Émile Paladilhe**, born in 1844, with 6 operas (from 1872), a symphony, 2 masses, etc.; **Charles Widor**, born in 1845, a noted organist, with 10 organ-symphonies, 6 dramatic works (from 1880), choral and chamber works, etc.; **Gaston Salvayre**, born in 1847, with 5 operas (from 1877), a symphony and choral works; **Benjamin Godard** (d. 1895), an expert violinist, with several symphonies and chamber works of distinction, and 8 operas (from 1878), including *La vivandière* (1895); **Vincent d'Indy**, born in 1851, a master of orchestral style, with many symphonies, overtures and other pieces, a few operas (from 1882), especially *Fervaal* (1895-7), etc.; **Alfred Bruneau**, born in 1857, with 5 operas (from 1887), including *L'attaque du moulin* (1893), overtures and symphonic poems, songs, etc.; **Gustave Charpentier**, born in 1860, with the concert-drama *La vie du poète* (1892), several operas, including *Le couronnement de la Muse* or *Louise* (1898, Lille), and impressionistic orchestral works; and, most poetic and original of the present school, **Claude Debussy**, born in 1862, with striking cantatas and symphonic poems, and a few operas, including *Pelléas et Mélisande* (1902), besides smaller works.

To these may be added the Belgian **Edgar Tinel** of Brussels, born in 1854, composer of the oratorio *Franciscus* (1888), striking church music, some cantatas, etc.

2 T

The recent Italian group has shown great zeal in pushing itself forward. The old disdain of foreign styles has given way to a general effort to imitate the Wagnerian technique in orchestration and to achieve intense dramatic success. The warm abundance of melody is usually conspicuous, but few writers evince ability for sustained or intricate construction. Instead, there has been a notable prominence of short, rapidly-moving works, often explicitly 'veristic' in plot and treatment. The opera is still the goal of musical ambition for most musicians, but attention to orchestral and chamber music is becoming steadily greater and more fruitful.

The number of Italian composers who have won international recognition for many works is small; among those who are most prominent are the following : —

Arrigo Boito of Milan, born in 1842, with 4 operas, the best of which is *Mefistofele* (1868–75), some cantatas and many fine librettos; the pianist **Giovanni Sgambati**, born in 1843, with 3 symphonies, a piano-concerto, chamber music and piano-pieces; **Antonio Smareglia**, born in 1854, with 8 operas (from 1879), including *Il vassallo di Szigeth* (1889), a symphonic poem and songs; **Giuseppe Martucci** of Bologna (d. 1909), born in 1856, a student of German methods, with a symphony, a piano-concerto and chamber music; **Giacomo Puccini** of Milan, born in 1858, with 6 strong operas (from 1884), including *La Bohème* (1896, Turin), *Tosca* (1900, Rome) and *Madama Butterfly* (1904, Milan), a mass and chamber works; **Ruggiero Leoncavallo**, born in 1858, a good pianist, with 8 operas (from 1889), especially *Pagliacci* (1892, Milan), *Tommaso Chatterton* (1896, Rome) and *Der Roland von Berlin* (1904, Berlin); **Pietro Floridia** of Milan, born in 1860, also a pianist, with 3 operas (from 1882), such as *Maruzza* (1894, Venice), a symphony and other orchestral and piano works; **Alberto Franchetti**, born in 1860, with 5 operas, beginning with *Asraële* (1888, Brescia), a symphony and chamber pieces; **Spiro Samara**, born in 1861, with 6 operas, the first of which was *Flora mirabilis* (1886, Milan); the conspicuous organist **Enrico Bossi** of Bologna, born in 1861, with strong chamber works, cantatas, church music and symphonic poems, besides 3 operas; **Pietro Mascagni**, born in 1863, whose phenomenally successful *Cavalleria rusticana* (1890, Rome) has been followed by several more; **Crescenzo Buongiorno** (d. 1903), with about 15 operas and operettas (from 1887), the last three in Germany; **Umberto Giordano**, born in 1867, with 5 operas (from 1892), including *Andrea Chenier* (1896, Milan); and, standing apart from all these, **Lorenzo Perosi**, born in 1872, who has made a name by writing many masses and several oratorios of some power (from 1897).

The recent English group has contained several strikingly able writers, whose work has pushed out into every field of composition. Their activity has been the more notable because since the days of Purcell at the end of the 17th century the display of general creative power has been rare among English musicians, in spite of a constant interest in things musical in several English circles.   But the recent group of composers has thus far shown no special homogeneity of style — certainly nothing to compare with the national quality in German, French or Italian writing.   It is simply the fruit of diffused cosmopolitan influences, undominated by a distinct nationalism.   Hence one can hardly speak of an ' English school ' in an exact sense. Yet particular composers have great individuality, and, in several cases, unquestionable genius.

The acknowledged leaders of the group include the following : —

Arthur Sullivan (d. 1900), popularly best known for a series of almost 20 sparkling operettas (from 1867), but also with the opera *Ivanhoe* (1891), 6 oratorios, such as *The Light of the World* (1873) and *The Golden Legend* (1886), incidental music to many plays, overtures, a symphony, songs, etc.; **Alexander Campbell Mackenzie**, a Scotsman, born in 1847, with 4 operas (from 1883), 2 oratorios, including *The Rose of Sharon* (1884), many fine cantatas, sacred and secular, especially *Veni, Creator Spiritus* (1891), several overtures, violin music, etc.;   **Charles Hubert Hastings Parry**, born in 1848, with a portentous list of works of every description, including 4 symphonies, 3 oratorios, beginning with *Judith* (1888), a variety of other choral music, chamber and piano-pieces, church music, etc.;   **Frederic Hymen Cowen**, born in 1852 in the West Indies, also a prolific writer, with 4 operas (from 1876), 4 oratorios, many graceful cantatas, 6 symphonies, 4 orchestral suites, chamber music and songs;   **Charles Villiers Stanford**, born in 1852, with 4 operas (from 1881), especially *Shamus O'Brien* (1896), 2 oratorios, fine choral cantatas, 5 symphonies, chamber music, etc.;   and **Edward Elgar**, born in 1857, with 3 oratorios, especially *The Dream of Gerontius* (1900) and *The Apostles* (1903), choral pieces, overtures, songs, etc.   To these may well be added **Arthur Goring Thomas** (d. 1892), with 3 operas (from 1883), cantatas and choral music;   **Edward German**, born in 1862, with 2 symphonies, incidental music to plays, several symphonic poems, chamber music, 3 operas and songs;   the Scotsman **Hamish MacCunn**, born in 1868, with 2 operas, many original cantatas, as *The Lay of the Last Minstrel* (1888), and overtures; and the part-negro **Samuel Coleridge-Taylor**, born in 1875, with striking orchestral and choral works, especially *Scenes from Hiawatha*.

232. The National Groups (b). — As compared with the German, French, Italian and English groups, those which follow as a rule present much that is technically more fresh and individual.   The reason is simply that the historic evolution of music has been so far dominated by the four peoples named above that the standard features of style are those most natural to them. But during the last century, and especially since about 1850, representatives of other nations and races have become increasingly prominent in composition, introducing turns of expression, peculiarities of temperament, and currents of thought and feeling that are different. This infusion of new forms and materials into current style has been full of picturesque interest and often of essential importance.

> None of these modern groups is really homogeneous, all of them consisting of more or less distinct subgroups or sections, each with its native traditions and modes of expression; but in a brief summary they may be treated roughly as units.

The Scandinavian group (Denmark, Sweden and Norway) is the oldest of these modern groups in point of organized artistic life. It attained its first development early in the 19th century under masters who were in close touch with German music, and was for a time only an offshoot of the latter. But from about 1860, especially under the lead of Grieg, it has been diligently cultivating its own peculiar field with enthusiasm. Scandinavian writing has usually shown a tendency to utilize the minor tonality, the abrupt and whimsical rhythms, and the somewhat pathetic, or at least dreamy, emotion of the national folk-songs and dances. Through it all runs a strain of seriousness which may be a reflection of the colder and darker climate of the North, but also the refreshing vigor and sturdiness that belong to a region where mountains and sea are the salient physical features. Conjoined with these pervading racial qualities has been the eminent poetic delicacy and insight of several individual composers, who have found means of touching the heart of the whole musical world by a striking intimacy and depth of imagination, displayed especially in the smaller forms of composition.

In Denmark are to be noted **Emil Hartmann** [Jr.] (d. 1898), son of a distinguished father (see secs. 205, 213), with 5 operas (from 1867), 3 symphonies, string-concertos and other chamber works, and national songs and dances; **August Winding** (d. 1899), a fine pianist, with much piano music, including a concerto, 2 symphonies, etc.; **Asger Hamerik**, born in 1843, since 1871 head of the Peabody Conservatory in Baltimore, with 4 operas, as *Hjalmar und Ingeborg* (1868), 5 symphonies, 5 *Nordische Suiten*, many other orchestral and choral works of large dimensions, etc.; **Otto Malling**, born in 1848, with a symphony, an overture, national choruses with orchestra, songs and piano-pieces; **Ludvig Schytte** of Vienna (d. 1909), born in 1850, in piano-virtuoso, with characteristic piano music and 2 short operas; **Victor Bendix,** born in 1851, with 3 symphonies, an overture, a piano-concerto and many piano-pieces; and **August Enna,** born in 1860, a self-taught genius, with at least 13 operas, especially *Die Hexe* (1892) and *Aucassin und Nicolette* (1896), besides a violin-concerto, songs, etc.

In Sweden may be named **August Johan Söderman** (d. 1876), with an operetta, incidental music to Schiller's 'Jungfrau von Orleans,' a fine mass, choral works and part-songs; **Anders Hallén,** born in 1846, with 4 operas (from 1881), especially *Hexfallen* (1896), 2 Swedish Rhapsodies, 2 symphonic poems, striking choral ballades and songs; and **Emil Sjögren,** born in 1853, with 2 violin-sonatas, piano works and songs.

In Norway the great name is that of **Edvard Hagerup Grieg** (d. 1907), the most prominent master of the northern group, with 3 notable violin-sonatas, 3 orchestral suites, an overture, piano- and violin-concertos, other chamber works, dramatic ballades, many piano-pieces and songs; with **Johan Svendsen,** born in 1840, with 2 symphonies and other orchestral works, much chamber music, orchestral arrangements of piano works, many songs, etc.; **Johan Selmer,** born in 1844, a writer for orchestra, chorus and the solo voice in an extreme modern style; **Ole Olsen,** born in 1850, of similar tendencies, with an opera, an oratorio (1897), a symphony, 2 symphonic poems, piano-pieces, etc; and **Christian Sinding,** born in 1856, with a symphony, 2 violin-sonatas, important chamber works, many pieces for the piano, songs, etc.

The three musical centres are Copenhagen, Stockholm and Christiania.

The Czech and Magyar group (Bohemia and Hungary) presents striking differences from all the foregoing in the quality and special forms of its melodic, rhythmic and dynamic dialect of expression. In these regards the national music of the Austrian Empire supplies one of the best illustrations of a type that has relatively little connection with established musical language, except so far as traces of its influence entered musical literature through the Viennese writers of the classical and post-classical periods. But, in addition, it is worth noting that on the whole Bohemian and Hungarian music shows a fondness for noisy and hilarious forms whose origin is in ardent social merrymaking, or for somewhat grandiose and sumptuous effects, such as imply a half-barbaric notion of splendor. In these respects this eastern music stands in contrast with the much more personal and subjective musical poesy to which northern composers have tended. While the latter have shown a marked readiness to adopt the introspective and romantic attitude which Schumann so finely illustrated, the music of Austria tends rather to the ostentation or the luxurious sensuousness exemplified by Liszt. Specially successful are its effects of vigorous, dashing rhythm and accent, and of brilliant color in instrumentation.

In the Bohemian list are **Josef Rozkošný** of Prague, born in 1833, with 10 operas (from 1870), overtures, masses and other vocal music; **Eduard Náprawnik** of St. Petersburg, born in 1839, a fine pianist and conductor, with 5 operas, including *Dubrowski* (1895), 4 symphonies, symphonic poems, overtures, chamber music, choral and solo works with orchestra, songs, etc.; **Josef Nešwere** of Olmütz, born in 1842, specially noted for his church music, but also with 3 operas, a symphony, a violin-concerto, piano-pieces, etc.; **Antonin Dvořák** (d. 1904), the best-known and most talented of the group, with 9 operas (from 1874), such as *Selm a sedlák* (1877), the oratorio *St. Ludmila* (1886, Leeds), many choral works, largely sacred, especially a Stabat Mater (1883, London), 5 symphonies, the last being *From the New World* (1894, New York), several orchestral ballades and overtures, 8 string-quartets and much other chamber music, a variety of piano music, songs, etc.; and **Zdenko Fibich** of Prague (d. 1900), with 7 operas (from 1874), including *Sarka* (1898), the trilogy *Hippodamia* (1890–1), many symphonic poems and overtures, 2 choral ballades, 3 symphonies, an orchestral suite, chamber music and many piano-pieces.

Among Hungarians are to be named **Edmund von Mihalowich**, born in 1842, with 4 operas (from 1882), of which *Wieland der Schmied* was on a text by Wagner, a symphony, several orchestral ballades, etc.; **Géza Zichy**, born in 1849, a remarkable one-hand piano-player, with 2 operas, especially *Meister Roland* (1899), a cantata and choral works, piano-studies for the left hand, etc., besides original poems; and the important violinist **Jenö Hubay**, born in 1858, with 4 operas, especially *Der Geigenmacher von Cremona* (1893), a symphony, a violin-concerto and other works for the violin.

The Russian group (Russia and Poland) has been for several decades full of energy and productiveness. Its ambition after world-wide recognition has not only stimulated study and composition at home, but led to organized efforts to propagate itself abroad. The energy and versatility displayed are impressive, supported in the case of Tschaikowski and a few others by unmistakable powers of creation. In all characteristically Russian music there is a strong racial flavor, derived from the extremely varied and fertile folk-music of the several divisions of the empire. This folk-music is one of the most interesting types found in Europe, having instinctive melodic beauty, latent harmonic richness and restless rhythmic individuality. In it are usually to be discerned two rather contradictory strains of feeling — the one sombre and even melancholic, the other

gay, reckless and wild — which have undoubted relations to the
Slavic temperament and the social condition of the country as
a whole. This emotional paradox supplies materials of extreme
artistic value. In point of technical style, Russian art, except
in certain cases, seems not yet to have attained maturity, lacking æsthetic balance and finish. But its vigor and enterprise
have made striking contributions to recent musical literature.

Polish music, though akin to the Russian, has had a separate
history, having been profoundly influenced by both German and
French styles. The national misfortunes are reflected in tones
of deep sadness, as is the national character in passages of
proud dignity and refinement. But the Polish circle is comparatively small.

Prominent Russian names are **Alexander Borodin** (d. 1887), with 3 symphonies, the symphonic poem *Dans les steppes*, string-quartets, piano-pieces,
and the opera *Prince Igor* (1891, finished by Rimski-Korsakow); **César
Cui**, born in 1835, with 8 operas (from 1859), as *William Ratcliff* (1868)
and *Angelo* (1876), 4 orchestral suites, chamber and choral works, many piano-
pieces and songs; **Modest Mussorgski** (d. 1881), with 3 operas, beginning
with *Boris Godunow* (1874), several choral works, piano-pieces and striking
songs; **Peter Tschaikowski** (d. 1893), one of the most gifted orchestral
writers of recent times, with 6 symphonies, 7 symphonic poems, 4 orchestral
suites, several overtures, much chamber music, 11 operas (from 1869), especially *Eugen Onegin* (1879) and *Pique-Dame* (1890), 3 ballets, numerous piano-
pieces and songs; **Alexander Faminzin** (d. 1896), with 2 operas, chamber
pieces, songs, and important critical and historical writings; **Nicolai Rimski-
Korsakow**, born in 1844, with about a dozen operas (from 1873), especially
Snegorotchka (1882), *Sadko* (1897) and *Der unsterbliche Koschtschrei* (1902),
3 symphonies, many other orchestral works, choral cantatas and many songs;
Nicolai Solowiew, born in 1846, with 3 operas, including *Cordelia* (1885), with
interesting piano-pieces and some orchestral works; **Anton Arenski**, born in
1861, with 3 operas (from 1892), 2 symphonies, 4 orchestral suites, chamber
works, original piano-pieces, church music; **Alexander Glasunow**, born in
1865, an exceedingly fertile orchestral writer, with 7 symphonies, 4 suites, 4
overtures, 2 serenades, several symphonic poems, 5 string-quartets and other
chamber music, some piano and choral works, and 2 ballets; **Alexander
Scriabine**, born in 1872, a noted pianist, with many works for piano, besides 2
symphonies, a piano-concerto, etc.; and **Sergei Rachmaninow**, born in
1873, with the opera *Aleko* (1893), a symphony, piano works and songs.

To the Polish group belong **Ladislaus Zelenski** of Cracow, born in 1837,
with 3 operas (from 1885), chamber works, church music, pieces for piano and
organ, etc.; **Sigismund Noszkowski** of Warsaw (d. 1909), born in 1846, with 2
symphonies, cantatas and ballades, the opera *Livia* (1898), piano-pieces and
songs; **Philipp Scharwenka** of Berlin, born in 1847, with choral works, 2

symphonies, piano music and songs; his brother **Xaver Scharwenka**, also of Berlin, born in 1850, a fine pianist, with 3 important piano-concertos and many other piano works, church music and many songs; **Moritz Moszkowski** of Berlin, born in 1854, another able pianist, with numerous popular orchestral and piano works, songs, the opera *Boabdil* (1892), a violin-concerto, etc; and **Ignace Jan Paderewski**, born in 1859, still more famous as a virtuoso on the piano, with works for his instrument, the opera *Manru* (1901), etc.

Here may be added the name of **Jean Sibelius** of Helsingfors, born in 1865, a pioneer in developing Finnish music, with 2 symphonies, several symphonic poems, choral cantatas, part-songs and many songs.

233. Music in the United States.—The development of advanced musical interest in America seems anomalous when compared with contemporaneous European experience, though, if one were to go back far enough, some analogies might be found. In rapidity and variety, however, it is phenomenal. In the brief space of a half-century a strong new aspirant has come into the circle of musical countries, claiming its share in the finest attainments and achievements of the world, and increasingly ambitious to be known as a producer as well as a recipient. The American situation is far too complex to lend itself to brief statement, but it has several points of interest.

As has been noted (see sec. 224), a change began to be seen about 1850. Before that time operatic singers and instrumental virtuosi had found welcome, but music of importance was exotic and sporadic. The influx of well-trained foreign musicians, the influence of native-born students who went abroad for culture, and the general rise of interest in literature and art—all these prepared the way for a healthy expansion. Soon after the Civil War came the epochal activity of the great conductor *Theodore Thomas* (d. 1905), whose extensive tours spread a knowledge of orchestral music. He was speedily followed by many other cultivated and progressive leaders and organizers. Hence, as regards the public performance of important musical works of all kinds, both the appliances and the popular interest to sustain them have advanced with signal rapidity. Now, New York, at least, is one of the most brilliant operatic centres in the world. A considerable number of more or less permanent orchestras are statedly at work, of which the *New York Philharmonic* is the oldest (see sec. 224) and the *Boston Symphony* (sustained by the liberality of a wealthy connoisseur) the most famous. Chamber music is receiving careful attention from several noted quartets in the East and the Middle West. Choral societies of size and proficiency are not infrequent, the oldest of importance being the *Handel and Haydn Society* of Boston (founded 1815). In all the larger cities expert instrumental and vocal performers are numerous. In a number of cases American sopranos have won distinction throughout the world. Most of the principal cities are supplied with a notable array of dignified concerts, often arranged in annual series. In general, the amount of this public musical life is greatest in the East, the two chief foci being New York and Boston, but the area of activity has rapidly extended westward, radiating especially from Chicago and Cincinnati, and is now reaching the South and the Far West as well.

Coincident with this energetic concertistic life are other efforts. Some kind of church music is a practical necessity everywhere, though the absence of any dominant type of service precludes uniformity. For a long period, except in Catholic and Episcopal churches, small choirs (usually quartets) have been common, bringing into prominence a type of sacred music somewhat diverse from any form elsewhere. The use of choral music, however, is steadily increasing. Private teachers, especially of piano-playing and singing, are scattered everywhere, constituting a profession more and more held in honor. Yet, since no system of examination and certification is possible, many pass for musicians without much breadth of training. Musical clubs of amateurs are frequent and often exert useful influence.

Music-schools of various grade have multiplied in the chief cities and towns. Most of these are independent business ventures, but some exist as parts of the educational system of colleges and universities. Ever since the time of *Lowell Mason* (d. 1872), working in Boston from 1828, elementary music has found place in some of the public schools. Of late years, owing to the able efforts of several advocates in different sections, this line of effort has been greatly extended, so that now it affects the schools in hundreds of places. Energetic work is in progress to standardize school instruction and to bring it into relation with the courses offered in higher institutions. Several colleges accept musical attainments as qualifications for admission and many give credit for musical courses as for other subjects. Musical pedagogy along routine lines seems likely to be increasingly affected by this institutional work.

Among national societies one of the most efficient is the *American Guild of Organists* (incorporated in 1896), which confers certificates on examination, holds musical services in several cities and encourages composition by prize contests. The aim of the *Manuscript Society* (formed in 1888) is to foster original composition in all styles. The *Music Teachers' National Association* (founded in 1876) was designed to band together private teachers for mutual benefit. At times it has succeeded in exerting useful influence, though its original function has been chiefly transferred to the ten or more state associations, most of which were formed at its instigation. At present the Association is serving as a useful clearing-house for the discussion of practical questions regarding system in musical pedagogy. With it is loosely affiliated the small circle of members of the Internationale Musik-Gesellschaft, who look forward to establishing an active American branch of that society.

Several of the great libraries, notably the Library of Congress in Washington, the Public Libraries of New York, Boston, Chicago and many other cities, and those of several universities, have given attention to the gathering of scholarly musical literature of several classes. The collection of instruments at the Metropolitan Museum in New York is famous as one of the largest and best-arranged in the world; others of importance are at the University of Michigan, Ann Arbor, and at the National Museum in Washington.

In touching upon the status of composition in America it is necessary to bear in mind one or two factors that have greatly affected its development. One of these is the comparative recency of interest in the more advanced forms of music. Musical culture, like other culture, has always been propagated from land to land, and has always had to pass through a sort of acclimatization in each new country occupied. In spite of the advancement of certain central cities, this is its stage in the United States as a whole.

But there are other elements in the case. Among these is the extremely heterogeneous character of American population. In the pioneer days all the cultured inhabitants were immigrants, coming from diverse points of origin. In the middle period, before the War, homogeneity was being established, but upon different lines in different sections. As these sections have since been drawing together, a new flood of immigration has set in, so extensive and varied as to show that the complexity of races and mental aptitudes is to be far greater than ever before. Because of all this American music has never had a native or national basis like that found in practically all European countries. There is no unconscious folk-music that embodies the national temperament and life. Furthermore, American taste in music has been made extraordinarily eclectic, because all along subjected to the impact of all kinds of influences, some excellent, some inferior, coming from every principal European country. Hitherto, perhaps, this fact has told against the normal unfolding of a national style. As knowledge increases, however, it is possible that this very cosmopolitanism of experience may bring forth a better blending of existing styles into one expressive of the most modern feeling than could be reached in any other country. Yet against the hope of unification, it must be confessed, stands the fact of the enormous extent of the country, the great distances between the large cities, which are natural centres for music, the diverse interests of the different sections, and the consequent

difficulty of interchanging ideas and products.   Such consolidation of musical life as exists in Germany or England, for
example, is at present utterly out of the question here.

From the long list of native-born American composers the selection of
names for mention is not easy.   The following are well-known representatives : —

John Knowles Paine (d. 1906), from 1862 teacher and from 1876 professor
at Harvard University, was not only an expert organist, but an abundant and
striking composer, with 2 symphonies, 2 symphonic poems, chamber music,
the oratorio *St. Peter*, incidental music to Sophokles' ' Œdipus Tyrannus,'
a mass, several choral cantatas, and many shorter works.   In the same year
with him (1839) was born Dudley Buck, in recent years a prominent church
musician in Brooklyn, with many effective choral works, including the oratorio
The Light of Asia (1885), many choir-pieces, organ music, overtures and a
comic opera (1880).   To the next generation belong William Wallace Gil-
christ, born in 1846, since 1873 a prominent organist and conductor in Philadelphia, with a symphony, an orchestral suite, much chamber music, several
prize works for chorus, etc.; Frederick Grant Gleason (d. 1903), from 1877
working at Chicago, with 2 operas, symphonic poems, cantatas, a piano-
concerto, chamber music, etc.; Arthur Foote, born in 1853, since 1878
an organist in Boston, with many chamber works, overtures, suites for
orchestra and for piano, cantatas, part-songs and songs; George Whitfield
Chadwick, born in 1854, since 1897 at the head of the New England Conservatory at Boston, with 3 symphonies, several overtures and symphonic sketches,
string-quartets, choral cantatas, songs, etc.; Edward MacDowell (d. 1908),
born in 1861, thus far the most gifted of the American group, a fine pianist
and fertile composer, with 4 symphonic poems, 2 orchestral suites, important
piano-sonatas, 2 piano-concertos, many lesser pieces, numerous songs, etc.;
and Horatio Parker, born in 1863, since 1894 professor at Yale University,
with the oratorios *Hora novissima* (1893) and *St. Christopher* (1896), many
choral cantatas, a symphony and overtures, organ-pieces and songs.   Prominent among the many younger writers are Henry K. Hadley, organist at Garden
City, N.Y., and Frederick Shepherd Converse of Harvard University, both
born in 1871, and both successful with orchestral writing.

Without attempting any comprehensive statement regarding musicians of
foreign birth, Charles Martin Loeffler, born in Alsace in 1861, may be cited as
a single example of one who has secured special attention for his original
orchestral and chamber works.

Among the heads of musical departments in universities, besides those
noted above, are Hugh Archibald Clarke, born in 1839, at the University of
Pennsylvania, Philadelphia, Albert Augustus Stanley, born in 1851, at the
University of Michigan, Ann Arbor, George Albert Parker, born in 1856, at
Syracuse (N.Y.) University, Peter Christian Lutkin, born in 1858, at Northwestern University, Evanston, Ill., and Rossetter Gleason Cole, born in 1866,
at the University of Wisconsin, Madison.   Many other able musical educators
are in service at various colleges, not to speak of the efficient heads of large
conservatories in many cities.

Conspicuous among those who have written upon historical or critical top-
ics are **William Foster Apthorp** and **Louis Charles Elson**, both of Boston and
both born in 1848, **Edward Dickinson** of Oberlin, born in 1853, **Henry Edward
Krehbiel** and **Henry Theophilus Finck** of New York, with **Philip Hale** of Boston, all born in 1854, **William James Henderson** of New York, born in 1855,
James Gibbons Huneker of New York, born in 1860, **Richard Aldrich** of
New York, born in 1863, **Oscar George Sonneck** of the Library of Congress,
Washington, and **Daniel Gregory Mason** of New York, both born in 1873.   An
acute and original theorist is **Percy Goetschius** of New York, born in 1853.

234. Some Final Words. — As one reviews the path through
the centuries by which music has attained its present expansion
and power, various reflections are suggested.

Some of these pertain to the magnitude and multiformity of
musical efforts and interests.   An individual musician or music-
lover, being naturally engaged with but a few phases of musical
art, is apt not to realize what lies beyond his own immediate
sphere.   Very few can expect to be personally familiar with all
the details of even any large division of the total field, since in
each of the important branches of the art the workers are
counted by hundreds and the works by thousands or myriads.
The important point to be borne in mind is that it is possible,
even without first-hand knowledge of all the data in detail, to
secure a vivid and useful knowledge of the large outlines of
musical evolution, with a practical scheme of thought regarding
epochs and movements, into which whatever detailed knowledge
is obtainable may be fitted.   The first great utility of music-
history is to supply the perspectives whereby persons and things
may be seen in their relations as to time, quality and potency.
The art of music has become what it is, not by the miraculous
intervention of a score or so of 'great composers,' but by the
irresistible momentum of large intellectual and emotional forces
that take hold of nations, periods and classes of mind.   It is
emphatically the function of history to help in discerning what
these forces are and how they have operated.   Furthermore,
the many aspects of music as a large social fact are not disconnected, but organically associated.   They interweave and inter-
act, often in subtle and unexpected ways.   The humbler are
not always insignificant, nor the relatively peculiar and restricted always without influence.   No just view of music or
musicianship can afford to disdain or ignore any side of the

subject, however distant from the standpoint of the observer himself. The instrumentalist cannot say to the vocalist, "I have no need of you," nor the operatic singer to the critic, nor the theorist to the maker of instruments, nor the genius in composition to the promoter of interest among amateurs. The world of music is a cosmos, or, to change the figure, a living organism. Its magnitude and multiformity are appalling, but, happily, historical thought may learn so to regard it all that it shall seem to have vital unity and coherence.

Again, all thoughtful study of music involves endless questions about the worth of styles and works, especially those now current. In the process of the ages certain artistic convictions have been reached and the most ambitious artistic effort is now put forth in some accord with them, while formal criticism stands by to utter opinions for or against these 'tendencies of the age.' Now, criticism and history are not interchangeable terms. They certainly are mental products arising from distinct operations, even when concerned about the same objects of thought. But they cannot be dissociated with safety. This is plainly true of formal criticism, which expresses itself authoritatively in writing. It is also true of the infinitely more abundant exercise of private judgment and taste, which is apt to be unreflective and irresponsible. The critical attitude, however adopted, should not be the slave of history in that it should seek to impose upon to-day the rules and standards of some bygone age. But, on the other hand, in judging the present it should be fully aware of the process by which what now exists has been reached, so as to appreciate it not simply as it seems, but as it is historically. Sudden judgments from momentary impression are valueless, and so-called culture which is merely based upon such judgments is at least shallow, if not false. The vast majority of musicians and amateurs are incessantly viewing music from some critical standpoint. It could be desired that more of them had gained enough historical sense and perspective to know that some 'novelties' are not new, some 'triumphs' not unprecedented, that specialties — even the greater ones — are not the whole of musical art, and that musicianship is not only many-sided, but deep. What is thus true of the social and public judgments that go to make up 'popular interest in music,' is still more true of the judgments and aspirations that shape every form of musical education. Intelligent peda-gogy in every subject needs not simply to provide somewhere for specific historic discipline, but to be shaped and balanced by the encyclopædic view that only historic culture can supply.

History does not deal with the future, though it gives grounds for hopeful optimism. From its point of view, the musical world seems to have been incessantly forced to har-monize two great interests, which are certainly now before us and which are to continue in constant interaction in the future. One of these is the interest of 'high art,' with its technical learning and skill, its delicately sharpened taste, its aspiration to stretch the boundaries of achievement to the utmost. The other is the interest of 'the common people' — always sensitive to music of some sort, yet often seemingly devoid of breadth, depth and intensity of artistic life, and sometimes expressly scornful of the eagerness of an artistic class which it regards as detached and extreme. The chasm between these two inter-ests is certainly obvious to-day. Yet it is surely a lesson of history that it is nothing new and that ways of bridging it have always been possible. Otherwise, music would never have come to the world-wide significance it has. Reconciliation must always be effected by efforts from both sides. The artis-tic instinct may be trusted sooner or later to forsake the pursuit of the merely curious and esoteric for that which is intelligible and impressive to the typical or average human mind. And the infinite work of education has always been to keep raising the level of intelligence and feeling so that the unmusical may become musical and the musical may become more finely artis-tic. The 19th century showed a prodigious expansion of the range of advanced musical art, the pendulum of effort swinging at the end toward what seems like an extreme; but, if this be extreme, it will swing back again. It also showed a wonderful awakening of enthusiasm in various lines of musical education, technical and popular. It is safe to say that this side of music will be still further developed, giving to the art in its highest forms atmosphere in which to live and environment in which to work, and making more real what all earnest believers in music desire — that music shall be the delight, the inspiration and the spiritual purifier of all peoples and classes.

INDEXES

INDEX OF SUBJECTS AND PLACES

INDEX OF PERSONS

Divitis (see Riche)
Dizi, F., 470
Dlabacz, G. J., 494
Dobnek (see Cochlæus)
Dobrzynski, I. F., 532
Döhler, T., 535
Doles, J. F., 399
Domart, P. de, 98
Dommer, A. von, 20, 628
Donati, I., 200
Donato, B., 117, 119
Doni, A. F., 157
—— G. B., 243
Donizetti, G., 441, 444–5, 452
Door, A., 545
Doppler, F., 557, 596
—— K., 558, 596
Dörffel, A., 514
Dorico, V., 114
Döring, G., 625, 626
—— H., 536, 573
Dorn, A., 536
—— H., 558, 603
Dotzauer, F., 468, 573
Dourlen, V., 493
Dowland, J., 149, 157
Draeseke, F., 573, 578, 639
Draghi, A., 179, 186
Dragonetti, D., 353
Dragoni, G. A., 127
Draud, G., 244
Drechsler, J., 423, 483, 606
Dresel, O., 616
Dreyschock, A., 538
—— R., 523, 524
Drieberg, F. von, 624
Drobisch, K. L., 607
—— M. W., 629
Dröbs, J. A., 485
Drouet, L., 469
Dubois, T., 447, 585, 641
Ducange, Sieur, 21, 244
Duchesne, N. B., 405
Ducis, B., 141
Dufay, G., 94–5, 97–8, 123
Dufresne (see Ducange)
Duke, R., 238
Dulcken, F. Q., 532
—— L., 539
Dulon, F. L., 403, 405
Duni, E. R., 284, 356
Dunstable, J., 94, 97–8
Dupont, A., 534
Duport, L., 352
—— P., 352
Duprez, G. L., 561, 623
Durante, F., 270, 280

Duschek, F., 389
Dussek, J. L., 392, 404
Duval, E., 625
Dvořák, A., 619, 646
Dwight, J. S., 615
Dykes, J. B., 612

Eastcott, R., 404
Eberhard von Freising, 82
—— J. A., 403
Eberl, A., 389
Eberlin, J. E., 268
Eberwein, K., 579
Eccard, J., 131, 136
Eccles, J., 189
Eck, F., 462
—— J. F., 462
Eckert, K., 610
Edwards, R., 145, 149
Egenolff, C., 115
Eichberg, J., 616
Eichner, E., 349
Eijken, J. A. van, 605
Eilers, A., 561
Eisfeld, T., 616
Eitner, R., 8, 21, 350, 604, 628
Eleanor, Queen, 86
Elers, F., 131
Elewyck, X. V. van, 625
Elgar, E., 643
Ellerton, J. L., 614
Ellis, A. J., 629
Eloy, 96, 98
Elson, L. C., 652
Elterlein (see Gottschald)
Elvey, G. J., 611
Encke, H., 525
Engel, D. H., 626
—— G., 604
—— J. J., 403
—— K., 626
Engelbert, 83
Enna, A., 645
Érard, P., 473, 477
——S., 387, 471, 473, 475–7
Eratosthenes, 59
Erbach, C., 136
Erdmannsdörfer, M., 579, 586
Erhardi, L., 243
Erk, L., 601, 604, 622
Erkel, F., 557, 610
Ernst II., 559
Ernst, H. W., 594
Escudier brothers, 628
Eslava, M. H., 556, 607
Esser, H., 601

Essipoff, A., 544
Este family, 121
—— M., 149, 212
—— T., 115
Ett, K., 486
Euclid, 59
Eugenius, T., 100
Euler, L., 325
Everard, C. F., 561
Ewer (firm), 495
Eximeno, A., 402
Eybler, J. von, 423, 482
Eycken (see Eijken)

Faber, H., 157
—— N., 220
—— Stapulensis (see Le-Febvre)
Fabricius, J. A., 329
—— W., 227
Fago, N., 270, 279
Fahrbach, P., 598
Faignient, N., 142
Faiszt, I., 605, 619, 626
Faminzin, A., 647
Farabi, al-, 85
Farina, C., 239
Farinelli, 294
—— G., 360
Farrant, R., 146
Farrenc, A., 624
—— L., 539
Fasch, J. F., 263
—— K. F. C., 398, 600
Fasolo, G. B., 223
Faugues, V., 98
Faure, J. B., 561
Fauré, G. U., 447
Fayolle, F., 494
Fayrfax, R., 143
Fechner, G. T., 514, 630
Federici, V., 439
Felstein, S. von, 156
Fendt family, 238
Feo, F., 270, 280
Ferdinand III., 186
Ferrabosco, A., 189
Ferrari, B., 176
—— C., 549
—— J. G., 494
Ferreira da Costa, R., 493
Ferretti, G., 120
Fesca, F. E., 467
Festa, C., 123, 148, 196
—— G. M., 468
Fétis, F. J., 20, 21, 494, 619, 624, 628, 629
Feurich (firm), 545

SUPPLEMENTARY LIST OF DEATH-DATES

HARMONY IN PIANOFORTE-STUDY
ERNEST FOWLES

Harmony as studied in these pages, in connection with the pianist's own instrument, will give him a clear grasp of essential harmonic principles as well as lead him to sure control of the musical expression of his thought and mood in extempore playing.

EXERCISES IN MELODY-WRITING
PERCY GOETSCHIUS, Mus. Doc.

A systematic course of melodic composition, designed for the use of young music students, chiefly as a course of exercises collateral with the study of Harmony.

The presentiment that some change in the study of musical theory will be found necessary, and that it will consist in shifting the objective center from Harmony to Melody, has induced the author to prepare this work. It is not to take the place of Harmony, but is to precede, or to be conducted side by side with it.

HOW TO THINK MUSIC
HARRIET AYER SEYMOUR
—New Edition, Revised and Augmented—

The title of this little book expresses its purpose precisely. The author draws a very sharp line between "playing music" and "thinking music," and shows how the first may be a purely mechanical process, while the second, by its very nature, must develop the melodic and harmonic sense through the medium of what may be called the "mind's ear." In other words it teaches one how to make mentally audible the printed score without the aid of piano or other musical instrument.

A 593

New York : G. SCHIRMER : Boston

Recent Musical Literature

ACTING IN OPERA. Its A-B-C, with descriptive examples, practical hints and numerous illustrations. By GEORGE E. SHEA. Cloth, 8vo, XVI+90 pp.

Opera lovers will enjoy this side-light on the singing-actor's art. Students and teachers of Opera will find it a valuable hand-book.

A NEGLECTED SENSE IN PIANO PLAYING. By DANIEL GREGORY MASON. Cloth, 12mo, 53 pp.

The attainment of ease, fluency and precision in playing, through the cultivation of a sensitive contact between key and finger-tip, is shown to be easily possible in Mr. Mason's Study.

HOW TO THINK MUSIC. By HARRIET AYER SEYMOUR. New edition revised and augmented. Cloth, 12mo, 59 pp.

Teaches one how to make mentally audible the printed score without the aid of piano or other musical instrument.

CHOPIN THE COMPOSER. By EDGAR STILLMAN KELLEY. Cloth, 8vo, VII+190 pp.

The author deals, not with the interpretation of specific works but rather with their structure in an easy style which makes delightful reading of a technical subject.

SKETCH OF A NEW ESTHETIC OF MUSIC. By FERRUCCIO BUSONI. Translated from the German by Dr. Th. Baker. Cloth, 12mo, IV+45 pp.

Among the subjects treated are characterizations of the arts, absolute music, fetish of form, nature and the reformer, and the infinite harmony.

EARLY OPERA IN AMERICA. By O. G. SONNECK. Cloth, 8vo, VIII+230 pp.

Eighteenth-Century Opera in America. The topic sounds illusory but the author has not merely recorded a mass of remote data—he has imparted to it an atmosphere of reality.

G. SCHIRMER

3 EAST 43d STREET   **NEW YORK**

A 592